# MAGILL'S LITERARY ANNUAL
## 1993

# MAGILL'S
# LITERARY ANNUAL
# 1993

*Essay-Reviews of 200 Outstanding Books*
*Published in the United States during 1992*

---

*With an Annotated Categories List*

Volume One
A-Lin

*Edited by*
FRANK N. MAGILL

**SALEM PRESS**
**Pasadena, California     Englewood Cliffs, New Jersey**

LIBRARY OF CONGRESS CATALOG CARD NO. 77-99209
ISBN 0-89356-293-9

FIRST PRINTING

PRINTED IN THE UNITED STATES OF AMERICA

# PUBLISHER'S NOTE

*Magill's Literary Annual*, 1993, is the thirty-eighth publication in a series that began in 1954. The philosophy behind the annual has been to evaluate critically each year a given number of major examples of serious literature published during the previous year. Our continuous effort is to provide coverage for works that are likely to be of more than passing general interest and that will stand up to the test of time. Individual critical articles for the first twenty-two years were collected and published in *Survey of Contemporary Literature* in 1977.

For the reader new to the Magill reference format, the following brief explanation should serve to facilitate the research process. The two hundred works represented in this year's annual are drawn from the following categories: fiction; poetry; literary criticism, literary history, and literary theory; essays; literary biography; autobiography, memoirs, diaries, and letters; biography; history; current affairs; science, history of science, and technology; travel; anthropology and sociology; ethics and law; film; fine arts; philosophy and religion; and women's issues. The articles are arranged alphabetically by book title in the two-volume set; a complete list of the titles included can be found at the beginning of volume 1. Following a list of titles are the titles arranged by category in an annotated listing. This list provides the reader with the title, author, page number, and a brief one-sentence description of the particular work. The names of all contributing reviewers for the literary annual are listed alphabetically in the front of the book as well as at the end of their reviews. At the end of volume 2, there are two indexes: an index of Biographical Works by Subject and the Cumulative Author Index. The index of biographical works covers the years 1977 to 1993, and it is arranged by subject rather than by author or title. Thus, readers will be able to locate easily a review of any biographical work published in the Magill annuals since 1977 (including memoirs, diaries, and letters—as well as biographies and autobiographies) by looking up the name of the person. Following the index of Biographical Works by Subject is the Cumulative Author Index. Beneath each author's name appear the titles of all of his or her works reviewed in the Magill annuals since 1977. Next to each title, in parentheses, is the year of the annual in which the review appeared, followed by the page number.

Each article begins with a block of top matter that indicates the title, author, publisher, and price of the work. When possible, the year of the author's birth is also provided. The top matter also includes the number of pages of the book, the type of work, and, when appropriate, the time period and locale represented in the text. Next, there is the same capsulized description of the work that appears in the annotated list of titles. When pertinent, a list of principal characters or of personages introduces the review.

The articles themselves are approximately two thousand words in length. They are original essay-reviews that analyze and present the focus, intent, and relative success of the author, as well as the makeup and point of view of the work under discussion. To assist the reader further, the articles are supplemented by a list of additional reviews for further study in a bibliographic format.

# LIST OF TITLES

LIST OF TITLES

# TITLES BY CATEGORY

## ANNOTATED

## TITLES BY CATEGORY

# TITLES BY CATEGORY

# TITLES BY CATEGORY

# TITLES BY CATEGORY

## POETRY

page

# TITLES BY CATEGORY

page

## LITERARY BIOGRAPHY

# TITLES BY CATEGORY

# TITLES BY CATEGORY

page

# TITLES BY CATEGORY

page

## SCIENCE
## HISTORY OF SCIENCE
## TECHNOLOGY

page

ETHICS
LAW

# CONTRIBUTING REVIEWERS FOR 1993 ANNUAL

Michael Adams
*Fairleigh Dickinson University*

Terry L. Andrews
*Independent Scholar*

Andrew J. Angyal
*Elon College*

Stanley Archer
*Texas A&M University*

Edwin T. Arnold
*Appalachian State University*

Jean Ashton
*New-York Historical Society*

Dean Baldwin
*Pennsylvania State University,
Erie
Behrend College*

Dan Barnett
*California State University,
Chico
Butte College*

Robert A. Bascom
*United Bible Societies*

Mary G. Berg
*Wheaton College*

Gordon N. Bergquist
*Creighton University*

Harold Branam
*Independent Scholar*

Gerhard Brand
*California State University,
Los Angeles*

Peter Brier
*California State University,
Los Angeles*

Charles Cameron
*Independent Scholar*

Thomas J. Campbell
*Pacific Lutheran University*

John Carpenter
*University of Michigan*

Ethan Casey
*Independent Scholar*

Thomas J. Cassidy
*South Carolina State College*

Patricia Clark
*Grand Valley State University*

Jeff Cupp
*Troy State University*

Frank Day
*Clemson University*

Bill Delaney
*Independent Scholar*

Michael Duncan
*Independent Scholar*

William U. Eiland
*University of Georgia*

Robert P. Ellis
*Worcester State College*

Thomas L. Erskine
*Salisbury State University*

Robert Faggen
*Claremont McKenna College*

Bruce E. Fleming
*United States Naval Academy*

Robert J. Forman
*St. John's University, New York*

Leslie E. Gerber
*Appalachian State University*

Linda Silverstein Gordon
*Worcester State College*

Daniel L. Guillory
*Millikin University*

Donald E. Hall
*California State University,
Northridge*

Terry Heller
*Coe College*

Edward J. Hughes
*California State University,
Long Beach*

Philip K. Jason
*United States Naval Academy*

Paul Jefferson
*Haverford College*

Jonathan Johnson
*Western Michigan University*

Carola M. Kaplan
*California State Polytechnic
University, Pomona*

Steven G. Kellman
*University of Texas at San
Antonio*

Karen A. Kildahl
*South Dakota State University*

Jonathan D. Klein
*Hebrew Union College,
California Branch*

James B. Lane
*Indiana University Northwest*

Eugene S. Larson
*Los Angeles Pierce College*

Leon Lewis
*Appalachian State University*

R. C. Lutz
*University of the Pacific*

Judith N. McArthur
*University of Houston, Victoria*

Janet McCann
*Texas A&M University*

Mark McCloskey
*Portland Community College*

Philip McDermott
*Independent Scholar*

Richard D. McGhee
*Arkansas State University*

Paul D. Mageli
*Independent Scholar*

Peter Markus
*Western Michigan University*

Joss Lutz Marsh
*Stanford University*

Charles E. May
*California State University,*
*Long Beach*

Laurence W. Mazzeno
*Ursuline College*

Kenneth W. Meadwell
*University of Winnipeg,*
*Manitoba, Canada*

Leslie B. Mittleman
*California State University,*
*Long Beach*

Robert A. Morace
*Daemen College*

Gregory L. Morris
*Pennsylvania State University,*
*Erie*
*Behrend College*

Robert E. Morsberger
*California State Polytechnic*
*University, Pomona*

Edwin Moses
*Bloomsburg University*

Daniel P. Murphy
*Hanover College*

John M. Muste
*Ohio State University*

Stella Nesanovich
*McNeese State University*

George O'Brien
*Georgetown University*

Robert J. Paradowski
*Rochester Institute of*
*Technology*

Thomas R. Peake
*King College*

David Peck
*California State University,*
*Long Beach*

John Powell
*Pennsylvania State University,*
*Erie*
*Behrend College*

Ronald Burns Querry
*Independent Scholar*

Edna B. Quinn
*Salisbury State University*

John D. Raymer
*Holy Cross Junior College*

Rosemary M. Canfield
Reisman
*Troy State University*

Bernard F. Rodgers, Jr.
*Simon's Rock of Bard College*

Mary Rohrberger
*University of Northern Iowa*

Carl Rollyson
*Baruch College of the City*
*University of New York*

Joseph Rosenblum
*University of North Carolina at*
*Greensboro*

Robert L. Ross
*University of Texas at Dallas*

John K. Roth
*Claremont McKenna College*

Marc Rothenberg
*Smithsonian Institution*

Barbara Elman Schiffman
*Independent Scholar*

T. A. Shippey
*University of Leeds*

R. Baird Shuman
*University of Illinois at*
*Urbana-Champaign*

Thomas J. Sienkewicz
*Monmouth College*

Harold L. Smith
*University of Houston, Victoria*

Ira Smolensky
*Monmouth College*

Katherine R. Sopka
*Four Corners Analytic Sciences*

Ann Struthers
*Coe College*

James Sullivan
*California State University,*
*Los Angeles*

William L. Urban
*Monmouth College*

James M. Welsh
*Salisbury State University*

Bruce Wiebe
*Independent Scholar*

John Wilson
*Independent Scholar*

James A. Winders
*Appalachian State University*

Michael Witkoski
*Independent Scholar*

Laura Weiss Zlogar
*University of Wisconsin, River*
*Falls*

# AFTER HENRY

*Author:* Joan Didion (1934-     )
*Publisher:* Simon & Schuster (New York). 319 pp. $22.00
*Type of work:* Essays

*Twelve essays on the way we live now, written with the author's characteristic irony and intelligence*

*After Henry* is Joan Didion's ninth book overall and her fifth of journalism—a word that does not begin to do justice either to her style or to her intelligence. The fact that she writes equally well as a novelist and as a journalist/essayist seems, strangely enough, to have worked to her disadvantage in terms of her reputation and critical reception. It is as if, according to the conventional wisdom, a writer can be one or the other but not truly both. There are, of course, novelists who also write essays and reviews (and poetry): John Updike, for example, who is, however, still a novelist first and foremost, an essayist, reviewer, and poet second. There are also journalists who write novels: Robert MacNeil and Nora Ephron, for example, but they are novelists only incidentally. Thus the special problem that Didion poses, especially when Didion-the-stalled-novelist meets Didion-the-frequently-anthologized-journalist in Didion's fourth novel, *Democracy* (1984):

> A poignant (to me) assignment I came across recently in a textbook for students of composition: "Didion begins with a rather ironic reference to her immediate reason to write this piece. Try using this ploy as the opening of an essay; you may want to copy the ironic-but-earnest tone of Didion, or you might try making your essay witty. Consider the broader question of the effect of setting: how does Didion use the scene as a rhetorical base? She returns again and again to different details of the scene: where and how and to what effect? Consider, too, Didion's own involvement in the setting: an atmosphere results. How?"

The essay in question might well have been "In the Islands" from The White Album (1979), which begins, "1969: I had better tell you where I am, and why" and whose second paragraph ends, "We are here on this island in the middle of the Pacific in lieu of filing for divorce." The writing here, even in these two sentences, as everywhere in Didion's work, is, as Roland Barthes has said of Albert Camus' writing, at the "zero degree," a paradoxically styleless style. It is writing that seems not merely bleak, but brittle, not so much at the edge as just over it, the verbal equivalent of the author herself in *Salvador* (1983) looking over the precipice at Puerta del Diablo, one of the execution sites preferred by that country's death squads. As the textbook writer would say, an atmosphere results.

This is the reason that the relatively short essay entitled "Fire Season" seems so representative of Didion's larger concerns in *After Henry* and throughout her work. Even before visiting the Los Angeles County Fire Department Headquarters in June of 1989, Didion, who grew up in Sacramento and has lived most of her life in and around Los Angeles, knew about the twelve years needed before the brush in the hills behind Malibu that had been destroyed in the last big fire would have grown enough to fuel the next one. She also knew about the Santa Ana winds (which, as she reported in an earlier essay, increase not only the chances of fire but the number of homicides in Southern California as well). She did not, however, know about "flame length," "fuel sticks," and "burn index" (a complex formula based on temperature, humidity, wind speed, and the measurable moisture in the brush—the "fuel stick"). "If the fuel stick's up around twelve," one forester explains, "it's pretty hard to get it to burn. . . . Anything under six and it's ready to burn very well." Didion's prose is under six, well under. It deals with the social, political, and psychological equivalents of those "extreme conditions" that, as another forester tells her, cause fires that cannot be controlled, only contained. For those who live in the hills around Los Angeles, the question is never if there will be a fire; it is when. Reading Didion, one feels something similar, existing at or over the edge that is somehow also the very heart, the eye of the storm, feeling a Roderick Usher-like foreboding of the impending struggle with the grim phantasm fear, minus the gothic trappings of Edgar Allan Poe's overripe prose.

And that is why the title piece provides, despite significant differences between it and the eleven other essays, a perfect introduction to this collection. (The rest of *After Henry* is, incidentally, organized by locale: three essays on Washington, D.C., less as a place than as a metonym for the national political life, all first published in *The New York Review of Books*; seven shorter ones on Los Angeles and Hawaii that first appeared in the *New Yorker*; and a long essay on New York originally published in the *New York Review of Books*; "After Henry" first appeared in *New West* magazine.) "After Henry" is "about" Henry Robbins, who was for many years Didion's editor. It is about meeting him in 1966, when Didion had a husband, a baby, little reputation, and even less cash; it is about the kind of editor he was—willing to fly to Los Angeles to read the first 110 pages of *Play It As It Lays* (because Didion did not want to send them to him) and "turning up" at Berkeley to help her get through the lecture she was scheduled to give; it is about his not playing the power game that had publishers at the top, editors just below, and writers at the very bottom, and it is about following him from Farrar, Straus to Simon & Schuster in 1973 but not to Dutton three years later. It is also about his death in 1979 and, more especially, about what he said to her two months earlier, that "I could do it without him," which, she writes, she did not believe then—perhaps still does not even now. As she notes in another of the essays reprinted here, "At nineteen I had wanted to write. At forty I still wanted to write, and nothing that had happened in the years between made me any more certain that I could." That line and the self-doubt it suggests become even more interesting in the context of *Democracy*, the only one of her four novels written "after Henry." It is not so much about its main character, Inez Christian Victor, as it is about Didion's inability to write Inez's story.

Even when her essays are less personal—personal in subject, that is; Didion's tone is always detached, even, perhaps especially, when she is writing about herself—Didion is always present as stylist and as ironically bemused spectator. Hers is not a detachment born of the scientific objectivity associated with late nineteenth century realism. It is a detachment born of estrangement, the detachment of someone for whom disillusionment rather than delusion is the operant mode. That is not to say that Didion cannot be sympathetic, especially when it comes to understanding the insecurity of others, but this sympathy is never sentimental. She understands, as she explains in *The White Album*, that "We tell ourselves stories in order to live," but this need for narrative, Didion believes, must be coupled with a rigorous examination of those stories in terms of their origins and their consequences. In "In the Realm of the Fisher King," for example, an essay-review of books about the Reagan White House, she shows speech writer Peggy Noonan, denied access to "the actual president," inventing "an ideal one." She shows Nancy Reagan as so entirely a product of Hollywood's studio system that she cannot even begin to imagine not being cared for and shows her too as a person whose limited social experience bred "untold social anxiety." Ronald Reagan, on the other hand, appears not to suffer any anxiety at all, so fully is he a creation of his handlers (whether White House or Hollywood). These are the makers of the illusions that others take for reality, but illusions that even the makers delude themselves are real. Didion, whose second novel, *Play It As It Lays* (1970), deals (cinematically) with the film industry and whose fourth, *Democracy*, treats modern American politics as a series of sound bites and photo opportunities, learned the lesson at first hand during the 1988 presidential campaign while covering the California primary and the Democratic and Republican conventions. What she learned, more specifically, was that the "political process," as the candidates and their staffers and attendant journalists liked to call it, was in fact something created of, by, and for insiders only (this in a piece nicely entitled "Insider Baseball"): the politicians, their staffers, pollsters, spin doctors, advisers, and lamentably the press too—all those who "tend to prefer the theoretical to the observable, and to dismiss that which might be learned empirically as 'anecdotal.'"

In a world as self-contained and as protected by a *cordon sanitaire* as the convention sites were—the Omni in Atlanta, the Superdome in New Orleans—"remoteness from the actual life of the country" is endemic and the real outsider is "the increasingly hypothetical voter." "Process" here entails a carefully scripted and choreographed media performance. While some journalists get the story by going for the jugular, Didion gets it by going for the quote, especially when it comes to the press's willingness to repeat uncritically the tale it has been told in press conferences and briefings. Whatever her subject—the Reagan White House, the 1988 presidential campaign, the Patty Hearst case (as California opera, "Girl of the Golden West"), the Writers Guild strike, Los Angeles as "a city not only largely conceived as a series of real estate deals but largely supported by a series of confidence games," a city virtually willed into existence by the *Times Mirror*'s early editor and publisher Harrison Gray Otis and his son-in-law, Harry Chandler, who used the paper to make their self-interest a matter of civic well-being—Didion marshals an imposing and often brilliantly eclectic array of "observable" facts in order to expose delusion in its various forms. Didion is more than an empiricist, however; she is a stylist as well. Her prose is more than simply informative. It is mannered, densely packed, as syntactically labyrinthine as her larger investigative structure:

> That evening, Jeffrey Katzenberg and the other executives of the major studios met with Kenneth Ziffren, a prominent local lawyer who represented several Guild members who, because they had television production companies, had a particular interest in ending the strike; the marginally different formulas suggested by Kenneth Ziffren seemed to many the bone they had been looking for: a way of solving the "presentation problem," of making the strike look, now that the writers understood that it had run out of gas, "like something approaching win-win."

The effect is cumulative, circuitous, complex, impacted, and convincing. The sentence itself is typical in all but one respect, the absence of the parenthetical additions and asides that Didion frequently employs to disrupt and qualify her "narrative." Following a similar logic, a Didion essay does not develop linearly, any more than a Didion novel does: the short takes of *Play It As It Lays*, the doubling of stories in *A Book of Common Prayer* (1977), the assemblage of raw materials (drafts, news items, photographs, film footage) and the resistance to narrative in *Democracy*. It secretes, astounds, and finally overwhelms.

Nowhere does Didion put her highly individual method and extraordinary intelligence to better use than in the collection's last, longest, and most controversial piece, dealing, ostensibly, with the Central Park jogger case. Her title, "Sentimental Journeys," echoes that of Gustave Flaubert's novel, *A Sentimental Education* (1869), as well as her own essay on Patty Hearst. Prepared for by the eleven other essays on other, perhaps more agreeable forms of delusion, "Sentimental Journeys" seems more persuasive and less abrasive than it did when it first appeared in *The New York Review of Books*. What Didion investigates is not so much the jogger case per se as the uses to which it and its principal players were put, the way the "story" was narrated, made familiar, infected by "a pernicious nostalgia." Her essay concerns the ways the players were more or less allegorized and the way the allegorical meanings—never stated outright, only implied—served to disguise and deflect attention away from "observable" reality. Didion covers all the familiar ground: the victim, the accused, the trial, the cast of characters, the newspaper coverage, and of course the side issue of whether the name of this or any rape victim should be made public. Yet she quickly moves beyond the realm of the comfortably familiar, citing *The Autobiography of Malcolm X* (1965), and W. J. Cash's *The Mind of the South* (1961), writing at considerable length of the city official whose adulterous affair ended with his lover's (apparent) suicide, his wrapping the body in a blanket and putting it out with the building's trash, his subsequent conviction for disposing of a human body in an illegal manner, and his being sentenced to seventy-five days of community service. Didion expertly teases out the subtext of this less well known New York story (relegated to twenty-three lines on page twenty-nine of New York *Newsday*); she goes on to discuss and make relevant Frederick Law Olmstead's original plans for Central Park and his reaction to doing business with the city of New York. (As Didion points out, Central Park was always a tale of two stories: Olmstead's pastoral vision of quasi-social harmony and city officials' vision of a vast pork barrel of kickbacks and patronage.) The actual focus of this essay, as distinct from the apparent one, is, as in all the essays in *After Henry*, on "The insistent sentimentalization of experience. . . . A preference for broad strokes, for the distortion and flattening of character and the reduction of events to narrative." As Didion goes on to point out, "The imposition of a sentimental, or false, narrative on the disparate and often random experience that constitutes the life of a city or a country means, necessarily, that much of what happens in that city or country will be rendered merely illustrative, a series of set pieces, or performance opportunities." The mention of "set pieces" and "performance opportunities" takes the reader back, by a curious and certainly circuitous route, to those earlier essays in which "the play's the thing," the postmodern equivalent of all the world's an all-too-literal stage for the histrionics of actor-presidents and others. Exposing their delusions, Didion's novels and essays tell us, as Anthony Trollope once put it, about "the way we live now," more perhaps than most readers want to know, and more certainly than the politicians, the pollsters, the press, and other insiders are willing—maybe even able—to tell.

*Robert A. Morace*

## Sources for Further Study

*Belles Lettres*. VIII, Fall, 1992, p. 14.
*Chicago Tribune*. May 10, 1992, XIV, p. 3.
*The Christian Science Monitor*. June 1, 1992, p. 13.
*Commonweal*. CXIX, October 23, 1992, p. 24.
*Los Angeles Times*. May 5, 1992, p. E5.
*National Review*. XLIV, June 22, 1992, p. 53.
*The New York Times Book Review*. XCVII, May 17, 1992, p. 3.
*Publishers Weekly*. CCXXXIX, March 23, 1992, p. 51.
*Time*. CXXXIX, June 29, 1992, p. 81.
*The Washington Post Book World*. XXII, May 10, 1992, p. 3.

# ALADDIN'S PROBLEM

*Author:* Ernst Jünger (1895-     )
*First published: Aladins Problem,* 1983
Translated from the German by Joachim Neugroschel
Afterword by Martin Meyer
*Publisher:* Marsilio Publishers (New York). 144 pp. $19.00
*Type of work:* Novel
*Time:* The 1950's and the 1960's
*Locale:* East Germany, West Germany, and Poland

*Like Aladdin, Ernst Jünger's protagonist Friedrich Baroh has to decide how to deal with
immense and sudden wealth; his story also reflects the problems of postwar Germany*

*Principal characters:*
> FRIEDRICH BAROH, a sophisticated descendant of Prussian nobles who
> defects to the West, where he becomes wealthy in the funeral business
> BERTHA BAROH, Friedrich's wife, a student of classical languages
> FRIDOLIN GÄDKE, Friedrich's uncle and owner of a funeral parlor
> JAGELLO MÜLLER, a Polish army captain and Friedrich's friend in the East
> SIGI JERSSON, a Jew with a Bohemian life-style and Friedrich's best friend
> in West Berlin
> SERGEANT STELLMANN, Friedrich's tormentor in boot camp
> GRANDFATHER FRIEDRICH BAROH, Friedrich's namesake, the first of his
> family to renounce his aristocratic title
> ALADDIN, the Arabic folk hero whom wealth makes happy
> PHARES, Jünger's favorite character, who appears here to save Friedrich

At the peak of his career, Friedrich Baroh, the thirty-seven-year-old protagonist and
first-person narrator of Ernst Jünger's well-told tale *Aladdin's Problem,* likens himself
to the Arabic folk hero whose life changed instantly when he found the genie-bearing
magic lamp. Having struck it rich with an esoteric scheme for a modern-day necropolis, Baroh, like Aladdin, must confront his new power to realize his material dreams.

Unlike Aladdin, Baroh is deeply disturbed by this. Instead of enjoying his wealth
with his wife Bertha, as did Aladdin with his princess bride, he starts drinking. His
daydreams begin to take up most of his waking life. It is at this point that the
mysterious Phares, a favorite character of the author who appears in many of his
writings, contacts Baroh.

Jünger, a German writer well known in Europe, offers a fascinating, well-written,
and quick-moving reflection on the problems of material success. By making his
protagonist a displaced East German, Jünger weds his philosophical examination to a
deep-cutting scrutiny of the complicated legacy that World War II bequeathed to the
Germans. Through his protagonist's tragicomic struggles, Jünger brings these two
themes together as his novel asks the central question: Are love, friendship, and a
meaningful life still possible in a world full of money but utterly devoid of an overall
moral, spiritual, or ethical guidance system?

In answering, Jünger proceeds deliberately but sure-footedly. His narrative, spiked with on-target aphorisms, never rushes to a conclusion, even though Baroh must make some hard decisions very quickly. In accordance with Jünger's narrative strategy of coupling incremental gains in insight with rapid plot movements, Baroh confesses only to having a problem at the opening of *Aladdin's Problem*. Until the last part of the four-part novel, he mentions neither the exact nature of his life-arresting troubles nor the name of Aladdin.

The novel begins with Baroh's recollection of his family background and his military service in the East German People's Army. The descendant of a long line of East Prussian nobles, in the early 1950's Baroh becomes one of the hundreds of thousands of German refugees who lose their homes, located in the portion of Germany given to Poland after World War II. Too young to have fought in Adolf Hitler's war, Baroh lost his father in Russia and now goes to school in the eastern part of the divided city of Berlin.

By making his protagonist an aristocratic East Prussian German, Jünger combines the ideas of proud heritage and devastating loss, of rich tradition and utter extinction by history. Prussia was devastated by the two world wars of the twentieth century. At the time of the novel's original publication in 1983, even the western part of Prussia was in the hands of a Communist regime.

In Baroh, Jünger skillfully personifies this national loss. *Aladdin's Problem* also addresses the painful question of how a German can come to terms with the consequences of two lost wars, the last one a war of aggression that ended in a general catastrophe for the attackers. Baroh carries Jünger's answer in his mental response to a difficult conversation with his Polish friend Captain Jagello Müller:

> When we [Germans] travel today . . . in faraway countries, we feel that a brother lies under the ground. He calls to us, and we have to restrain ourselves like the sons of Korah in Psalm 88: "Prayer in great tribulation and imminent mortal danger."

The losses incurred by following an evil leader must be accepted and mourned privately.

In this spirit of both accepting the past and remaining conscious of his heritage, after completing school in East Berlin, Baroh goes back of his "own free will" to his family town of Liegnitz, now a Polish city. There, he serves in a rifle regiment of the East German army, which is garrisoned in barracks now belonging to a fellow Warsaw Pact nation. Here, the magic of the past has been reduced to faint archaeological evidence. Looking up at the entrance, Baroh can still discern "the outline of our coat-of-arms appearing under the crumbling plaster." Before the war, he thinks, these military installations had "borne the name of one of my ancestors."

Baroh also encounters the hostility of the sadistic Sergeant Stellmann, who hates the recruit for all that his now obsolete class had stood for. An accident sends Baroh to the military academy. When he returns as a lieutenant, he has the sergeant report to him, enacting a subtle and gratifying revenge. Assigned to the Polish embassy in East Berlin as adjutant to his Polish friend Captain Müller, Baroh defects to the West, a relatively easy task before the building of the Berlin Wall in 1961.

Upon his arrival in West Berlin, Baroh discovers once again that his heritage, even enriched by his military education, cannot translate into material success and a position in society. The genie refuses to leave the bottle. In lines which render vivid the strange atmosphere of Germany's postwar years, Jünger has his protagonist enroll at the Free University of Berlin. The place depresses him: The sciences have become ossified; the humanities politicized. Deliberately tackling the new age head-on, Baroh decides to study media sociology and statistics.

During his studies, Baroh meets his future wife Bertha, whom he loves because she is "not only a good lover . . . but also a reliable companion." Jünger further concretizes his protagonist's past, as Baroh remembers his grandfather and namesake, the first to renounce his title after World War I. "What should I do with it when I call on a client?" grandfather Baroh, working as an insurance agent, once asked. "It would embarrass both of us and interfere with business." He settles on Baroh—a name which sounds similar enough to "Baron" without spelling out the now awkward word.

Unemployed after graduation, Baroh is rescued by his uncle Fridolin Gädke, a commoner who had married into the family and built a prosperous funeral business. As Baroh begins to rise within his uncle's company, he gradually accumulates wealth, the source of his eventual mental distress. Jünger brilliantly uses the fact of his material success to reinforce both his protagonist's standing as an allegorical figure for postwar West Germany (and its "economic miracle") and his ties to Aladdin.

As was the situation in postwar Germany, economic ascendancy for Baroh comes at a price. Totally immersed in his business, and often unable to leave his properly "funereal" business attitude at work, Baroh neglects his wife, Bertha. The two grow apart and eventually separate.

Baroh and a Jewish friend, Sigi Jersson, a survivor of the Holocaust, talk about the impermanency of burial sites in industrial countries. The two friends come up with the idea for an international, all-faith necropolis. Its selling point is the guarantee of graves reserved for eternity, rather than the increasingly common thirty-year lease.

During the worldwide search for a proper site, cynically likened by the author to prospecting for oil, it is Bertha who picks the winning location. Like Aladdin, Jünger has Baroh find his source of unlimited wealth in a cave, in his case the caves formed by a curious geological formation in central Turkey known as the Rock Churches of Cappadocia. Once work commences, Baroh's company's technology successfully transforms this natural wonder into a state-of-the-art burial site. Acknowledging the money-making connection between dead languages and social status, the venture is given the Latinized name Terrestra.

His newfound wealth fails to satisfy Baroh. In the East, as a young lieutenant, he at least had an opportunity to make a moral stand through his defection. By leaving Communism behind, Jünger's protagonist came up with a practical answer to the problem he had confided to his friend Captain Müller:

I was plagued by the question of why we were serving—indeed zealously—a system that we both found repulsive.

This, of course, is the same question Jünger posed to himself while serving in the German Wehrmacht during World War II. Jünger's personal answer was to write—and miraculously to slip past the censors, his allegorical novel *Auf den Marmorklippen* (1939; *On the Marble Cliffs*, 1947), in which barbarian raiders devastate a peaceful country. Later, he was indirectly associated with officers who plotted to kill Hitler.

Incredibly wealthy from the success of Terrestra, Baroh suffers from his inner emptiness. He casts a critical eye on Aladdin's choice. Its problem, Baroh states, "was power with its delights and dangers." "Aladdin preferred the life of a minor despot"; Baroh sneers and rejects it.

At the end of *Aladdin's Problem*, when despair has reduced Baroh to a self-pitying, daydreaming alcoholic separated from his wife, Jünger produces a savior. Contact with Phares changes Baroh. He loses his existential fears and feels "a new affection that both surprised and delighted Bertha and me." The two get together again, and "it was as if we had never known one another before." Even his work "appeared . . . in a new light, as a worthwhile task" instead of money-generating drudgery.

Baroh's salvation through Phares has two aspects and is not necessarily dependent on otherworldly magic. First, Phares is special since he "knows the primal text," or the key to understanding the wonderful substance of the universe. Second, the key to Phares' knowledge is not a private secret. Pointing out that it is within the powers of every willing human being to become like Phares, Jünger takes his novel a final step further. Asked to define his nationality on the job application that Phares initially submits to Baroh, Phares declares himself a "Cosmopolitan." In the European context, this clearly identifies him as a Jew: "Cosmopolitan" was the Soviet code word for its Jewish citizens. Thus, like Baroh's Bohemian friend Sigi Jersson, Phares becomes a powerful symbol for Jünger's hope for reconciliation among the peoples of the post-Holocaust world community.

Its protagonist and his lover saved, *Aladdin's Problem* ends on a high note of tempered optimism. The contemporary world might be threatened by the deaths of spirituality, religion, and hope; however, as long as people are willing to look inward at what truly unites all human beings and the world they live in, there is no end to human joy and fulfillment.

*R. C. Lutz*

## Sources for Further Study

*Library Journal.* CXVII, October 15, 1992, p. 99.
*Los Angeles Times Book Review.* October 11, 1992, p. 6.
*The New York Times Book Review.* XCVII, November 22, 1992, p. 24.
*Publishers Weekly.* CCXXXIX, September 7, 1992, p. 80.

# ALL THE PRETTY HORSES
## Volume One: The Border Trilogy

*Author:* Cormac McCarthy (1933-     )
*Publisher:* Alfred A. Knopf (New York). 302 pp. $21.00
*Type of work:* Novel
*Time:* 1949
*Locale:* Northern Mexico and Southwest Texas

*His connection to the family ranch suddenly severed, John Grady Cole, a young cowboy, finds adventure, love, violence, and manhood in old Mexico*

> *Principal characters:*
> JOHN GRADY COLE, a teenage cowboy, already a man, with tests of that manhood to face
> LACEY RAWLINS, Cole's sidekick and partner in independence from home and family
> JIMMY BLEVINS, a callow, thirteen-year-old tagalong
> ALEJANDRA ROCHA Y VILLAREAL, the daughter of a Mexican rancher, for whose love Cole seems willing to die

Cormac McCarthy's novels are about wanderers, boys and men cut adrift from moorings, whether geographical, emotional, or moral. Black destiny hovers. And McCarthy serves it up in a prose style unashamed of being, now and again, purple. A persuasion of the depths around and in the characters requires a proper rhetorical ballast. Sometimes it sounds Faulknerian, sentences with no ending, swirling contextually and rhythmically. Sometimes it is Hemingway, pronouns repeated, conjunctions holding off periods. The matter borne by this artfulness is darkness, curse, and the simultaneous panorama of fallen nature and fallen humanity. *Suttree* (1979) opens with the main character, son of wealth, living as a bum on the river in Knoxville trotlining for catfish in water three parts sewer. Conventional civilization is unsupportable by the like of Suttree, and vice versa. In *Blood Meridian* (1985), the bloodiness involved in civilizing the wastes of northern Mexico, land of the Apache, removes the humanity of a boy who, typical of McCarthy's stories, wanders onto the scene.

*All the Pretty Horses*, which received the 1992 National Book Award for fiction, takes up the homeless dirge again, but with a tenderness and wistfulness and comedy not so typical of McCarthy. Horses, at least, are tameable and beautiful, capable of driving the pastoral dream of sixteen-year-old John Grady Cole, who heads south to Mexico on horseback with his friend, Lacey Rawlins, in 1949. Life in Texas has ignored Cole. His mother and father are divorced. The mother owns the ranch and will sell. Cole's grandfather, the last real rancher, has just been buried. Cole's girlfriend has found another. Cole, meanwhile, is temperamentally suited for nineteenth century ranch life. His teenage diversion is not tooling around the small Texas town but riding out on the family range and listening to the ghosts of Indian war parties.

> When the wind was in the north you could hear them, the horses and the breath of the horses and the horses' hooves that were shod in rawhide and the rattle of lances and the constant drag of the travois poles in the sand like the passing of some enormous serpent and the young boys naked on wild horses jaunty as circus riders and hazing wild horses before them and the dogs trotting with their tongues aloll and footslaves following half naked and sorely burdened and above all the low chant of their traveling song which the riders sang as they rode. . . .

The ghost Indians Cole hears "bear lost to all history and all remembrance like a grail the sum of their secular and transitory and violent lives." This is surely a novelist "hearing with" the teenage boy, but it establishes Cole's passionate openness to the nonmodern verities which the ensuing forty-five years of history, McCarthy implies, have eliminated from the suburban teenage perspective. McCarthy is making no naïve youth in fashioning John Grady Cole, whose bloodline includes forebears intent on inhabiting wilderness. He loves animals like a young Neanderthal and is not much separated from those Indian boys "jaunty as circus riders."

As Cole and Rawlins light out for the Mexican territory they are pursued and joined by another runaway, Jimmy Blevins. Jimmy rides a beautiful horse and carries a gun, but is a nervous wreck, fearful of thunder, and Cole and Rawlins want no part of him.

> You want to flip to see who gets to shoot him?
> Yeah. Go ahead.
> Call it, said Rawlins.
> Heads.
> The coin spun in the air. Rawlins caught it and slapped it down on top of his wrist and held his wrist where they could see it and lifted his hand away.
> Heads, he said.
> Let me have your rifle.
> It aint fair, said Rawlins. You shot the last three.
> Well go on then. You can owe me.
> Well hold his horse. He might not be gunbroke.
> You all are just funnin, said the boy.

Funnin, as is McCarthy. It is artistic fun to eschew the grammatical manners of printed English to shape a stripped dialogue to enhance the laconic voice of all McCarthy dialogue. It is also fun to escape America, to be sixteen again, to ride horses, to see country, and to meet poor Mexicans, some of whom treat the characters to that embracing hospitality so missing in their own families. And the cause of trouble to come is not malevolent destiny so much as hapless Jimmy Blevins, who loses his mount in that feared thunder, steals his horse back from the small towner who assumed possession, and ignorantly shoots a man. McCarthy says, look at the probable genesis of our mythical Billy the Kid and Jesse James. A boy just into puberty with a horse and gun riding round will sooner or later get in trouble which no juvenile services can prevent. This is where McCarthy wants his characters, as far as possible from institutions, riding over uninhabited country, until they find the dream ranch where they can work as horse tamers.

The ranch is "The Hacienda de Nuestra Senora de la Purisima Concepcion," sitting alongside a nine-thousand-foot mountain range owned by the wealthy hacendado, who has a beautiful daughter with whom John Grady Cole falls in love. But before the love scenes, McCarthy is intent on his book's subject, horses, and the rich interaction between men and horses and the equally savorable interaction between horsemen about horses. Taming horses puts a person closer to elemental life than he will come outside sex.

> They smelled like what they were, wild animals. He held the horse's face against his chest and he could feel along his inner thighs the blood pumping through the arteries and he could smell the fear and he cupped his hand over the horse's eyes and stroked them and he did not stop talking to the horse at all, speaking in a low steady voice and telling it all that he intended to do and cupping the animal's eyes and stroking the terror out.

This is John Grady Cole—at sixteen, recall—doing something in the real world to which the closest anyone living will come is by reading a book or watching a film. Cole is heroic, larger than life, and however doomed McCarthy's trilogy might show him to be, he is someone to be jealous of, unlike McCarthy's earlier personae. Poor Jimmy is a contrast, and Rawlins is an admiring observer.

For McCarthy there are more or less genuine human beings, just as there is genuine cowhide. And a reader will have to admit that there is genuine writing in this novel. By McCarthy's code, if a novelist writes of horses he must know horses, and the knowledge will show in the words he chooses, down to the details of the ropes available for controlling the wild energy they embody: "Stacked on the ground outside the gate were coils of every kind of rope, cotton and manilla and plaited rawhide and maguey and ixtle down to lengths of old woven hair mecates and handplaited piecings of bindertwine." Reading McCarthy is not following the fusions of a fictional dreamer. "Ixtle" is a plant ur-Aztecs knew, and "mecate" is summoned from a lacuna in Webster between "meaty" and "Mecca." This is not cliché Western writing. We are in a Spanish context of cowboyhood. There are things you don't know, McCarthy implies, factual things about the Mexican world, visceral and muscular things about the powerful animals Spaniards brought to this place. Pages later Rawlins says, "Them old hot maggie ropes have eat my hands about up," and the reader beholds a coalescence of McCarthy's gifts, maguey ropes turned idiomatic and familiar in genuine Texas dialect. So full of "the real" is this writing that few readers can be imagined to absorb it fully.

Cole is heroic, McCarthy's attention to his world is heroic, and the woman the protagonist will love is worthy of a hero's ardor, appearing to the accompaniment of her Arabian's clip-clop.

> She passed five feet away and turned her fineboned face and looked full at him. She had blue eyes and she nodded or perhaps she only lowered her head slightly to better see what sort of horse he rode, just the slightest tilt of the broad black hat set level on her head, the slightest lifting of the long black hair. She passed and the horse changed gaits again and she sat the horse more than well, riding erect with her broad shoulders and trotting the horse up the road.

Those eyes alter John Grady Cole's world "forever in the space of a heartbeat." Alejandra is part of the pretty horses world, accessible, soon responsive to Cole's caresses, but not one to be settled down with in years of married life. Their love gets Cole exiled to a Mexican prison, where he will face the old malignity at the heart of life. He is man enough for his world, killing a would-be assassin in a knife fight but losing enough blood to lie near death for days until reprieved obscurely by Alejandra's aunt who had futilely warned him against his involvement with Alejandra. Arabians do not breed with mustangs, and Cole accepts this, though sorrowfully, and heads back to Texas.

To make the return trip more than a bus ride, Cole decides to recapture the horse of the now-dead Jimmy Blevins, a feat requiring Rambo-esque bravado and stubborn persistence in the world of black fate. This is Fredric Henry turning from the dead Catherine in *A Farewell to Arms* (1929), but with a vengeance. It is less satisfying to read. There is nothing more that can happen to the hero, nothing more he can do. He will try to find the horse's owner. He will go back to Texas and ride down highways with cars and pickups and look for Blevins' relations. He finds only a radio preacher named Blevins, no kin, who snores loudly after a big meal.

As Cole rides in the "bloodred sunset" on the last page of *All the Pretty Horses*, the reader wonders what awaits him in the remaining two installments of the projected Border Trilogy. Will he be background for a son living in the final American decadence? Or does "border" promise a continuation of struggle with the old world of horses and the new of gasoline. Nearly every line of *All the Pretty Horses* pledges allegiance to the old world. This is the archaic world, lit by no electric bulbs: "The candleflame caught in the pierglass twisted and righted when he entered the hall and again when he shut the door." Archaic rooms are not flooded with artificial light. People are not right without animals in their hearts. "What he loved in horses was what he loved in men, the blood and the heat of the blood that ran in them." This book is a flight into that world—male companionship based on respect for how you handle a horse, selection of a mate which is no selection or rational choice but a sudden overwhelming alteration based on eye contact. If McCarthy's ardor for this ideal risks the charge of romanticism, he seems willing to take the risk. But it is consciousness of light, tangibilities of all kinds, and only a few escapes into assertions of metaphysical darkness that the book gives a reader. McCarthy fans can reasonably guess that the presence of light in the darkness is this author's real perplexity. He is the artist after all, dispensing light. Anyone who attentively reads this book will testify to the miracle of a creative brain dispensing such light.

*Bruce Wiebe*

## Sources for Further Study

*Booklist*. LXXXIX, April 1, 1992, p. 1412.
*Chicago Tribune*. May 10, 1992, XIV, p. 5.

*The Christian Science Monitor.* June 11, 1992, p. 13.
*Commonweal.* CXIX, September 25, 1992, p. 29.
*Library Journal.* CXVII, May 15, 1992, p. 120.
*Los Angeles Times Book Review.* May 17, 1992, p. 3.
*The New York Times Book Review.* XCVII, May 17, 1992, p. 9.
*Newsweek.* CXIX, May 18, 1992, p. 68.
*Publishers Weekly.* March 16, 1992, p. 64.
*The Washington Post Book World.* XXII, May 3, 1992, p. 1.

# ALMA

*Author:* Gordon Burn (1948-     )
*First published:* 1991, in Great Britain
*Publisher:* Houghton Mifflin (Boston). 210 pp. $19.95
*Type of work:* Novel
*Time:* Primarily 1954-1986
*Locale:* England

*Drawing on the life of Alma Cogan, a popular English singer of the 1950's, Gordon Burn has written a postmodern thriller about the nature of fame*

> *Principal characters:*
> ALMA COGAN, the novel's narrator, formerly a celebrated singer
> FAY COGAN, her mother
> PETER BLAKE, a painter
> MYRA HINDLEY and
> IAN BRADY, serial killers
> LESLEY ANN DOWNEY, one of their victims
> FRANCIS MCLAREN, Alma's most devoted fan

*Alma,* winner of the 1991 Whitbread Award for best first novel, is an astonishing, deeply disquieting work. In subject it bears a certain similarity to *Somebody's Husband, Somebody's Son: The Story of Peter Sutcliffe* (1984), Gordon Burn's account of the Yorkshire Ripper, written from the perspective of Sutcliffe's family and friends. In style and atmosphere, however, *Alma* calls to mind the phrase Donald Greiner has used to describe the fiction of John Hawkes: comic terror. This is not to suggest that Burn in any direct way imitates Hawkes, even at Hawkes's most parodically English in *The Lime Twig* (1961). In fact, Burn makes no use at all of the surreal effects on which Hawkes's fiction relies. *Alma* might well have been less disturbing had it been more surreal, less matter of fact.

For all of its power to disturb, *Alma* is also quite funny. "I always found having my picture taken with members of the public a frankly grim and, in the end, even a distressing experience," narrator Alma Cogan says at the outset. She finds the "terrible conviviality and the unwelcome physical intimacy with total strangers" particularly distressing at a time (1954) when, thanks to continuing postwar shortages, "personal hygiene wasn't high on everybody's list of priorities." Alma's Swiftian description of women smelling of dandruff and cheap perfume and men giving off "stomach-heaving waves of dog and diesel" soon take a darker turn, thus foreshadowing the novel's larger trajectory, a sign that worse and worst are yet to come. The unpleasantness is pervasive, but the "moor grime" casting its "smutty light" and the night sky "lit up with tea-scum" serve merely as backdrop for a violence that is rarely depicted but always lurking just below the novel's oddly placid surface, like the "scenes of domestic mayhem" that she associates with the smells of "total strangers" who are also her fans: "children scalded, wives abused, small dogs dropped from high windows."

The star of this celebrity novel in which real and imaginary people and events are freely mixed is its narrator and title character. Born in 1932, the real Alma Cogan was a popular English singer of the 1950's. With the arrival of the Beatles, her career quickly declined. She died in 1966. Burn's rendering of Alma's background (East End Jewish) and career is vivid and convincing, in part because Alma tells her own story. Authentic in tone and perhaps in fact (though only an Alma Cogan aficionado will know for certain), *Alma* is also a brilliantly conceived and expertly realized fabrication. In a bold "Elvis lives!" move, Burn extends her life by twenty years. She lives on, first in prolonged professional decline and then, this time by choice, in nearly complete obscurity after moving from London to a small English village. Burn's imitation, or appropriation, of Alma Cogan for his own novelistic purposes is in a very real sense warranted by the real Alma's own character. Alma Cogan was, after all, herself an imitation whose string of twenty hits appropriated the songs and styles of American singers Doris Day, Teresa Brewer, Patti Page, Vaughn Monroe, and the Maguire Sisters.

Alma lives alone with the latest of her miniature Pinschers, all named Psyche, at Kiln Cottage, borrowed from a friend. The cottage is in a village that defeats her pastoral expectations and that is "really two villages, Cleeve and Coombe," separated by water and joined only at low tide by a concrete causeway. Alma distances herself from her past in more than just a geographical sense. Realizing what she is—a has-been—and what she was—at best an icon, at worst a cliché—Alma proves to be a keen observer of her world, past and present, and of her own life, even though she acknowledges that she cannot be sure that what she remembers are events as they occurred or only as she read about them in newspapers and magazines or saw them on television. Alma's narration is unsparing, unsentimental, and blackly humorous, especially when she discusses fame's aftermath. An example is her description of the Dorothy Ward House, a retirement home for variety performers where her mother now resides, even though she had never been a performer. She was convinced that it was herself, rather than her daughter, Alma, who had had the career.

"The Old Pro's Paradise," as it used to be referred to (unironically) in the profession, is a bizarre and unnerving place to visit. Very few of its three-dozen inhabitants believe they were anything less than the toast of the town in their day. The difficulty lies in deciding which Hollywood lovely or Broadway legend, which king of comedy or matinee idol they see themselves being this week.

Occasionally, Alma's prose becomes as extravagant as her former stage self. Sammy Davis, Jr., for example, "looked imagineered, cuboid, like a Picasso painting or an Easter Island sculpture." To speak of Alma's style is somewhat misleading, for distinctive as that style may be, it is not a single style at all; rather, it is a succession of voices and interpolated forms. Alma is self-revealing one moment, gossipy the next, speaking directly, then quoting from Noel Coward's or Alan Bennett's diaries, F. Scott Fitzgerald's "The Crack Up," or the memoirs of "one of the old-time movie queens." Her narrative includes song lyrics, newspaper stories, "scripts" of dialogue heard while waiting on queues or visiting the Dorothy Ward House, Jenny Holtzer message art, a Louis MacNeice poem, a stranger's letter, the Tate Gallery's *Acquisitions Catalogue*, and, shortest but perhaps strangest, a bibliographical citation for *The Great Ziegfeld*, "dir. Robert Z. Leonard, Prod. Hunt Stromberg, MGM, 1936; b&w," occasioned by Alma's noting the "striking facial resemblance" between her mother and "Fanny Brice as played by herself."

Hardly a conventional novel, *Alma* is a detailed rendering of the collective unconscious of its time. It depicts a "Reality digitised and broken down into megabits or bongobytes, then replayed as a kind of endless fidgeting or fluttering on the periphery of experience, at the edge of vision. Motes dancing on the air. That's what I see. That's what I seem to be constantly seeing." The fragmented, multivoiced style does more, however, than reflect the times and character of its narrator, a woman who claims to lack application and, except for "the American pulps, the paperback shockers," has "always been a dipper and browser." Like the meaningless snatches of sentences "recited in a disembodied, almost incantatory way" that she hears in her dressing room while awaiting her turn on stage, Alma's megabits and bongobytes take on a mysterious power.

*Alma* problematizes the power of the voice to mystify and fascinate in two direct ways. One is by referring to the dog, Nipper, that appears on every HMV (His Master's Voice) label and therefore on every one of Alma's recordings. The picture was "adapted, so it was said, from a painting showing Nipper the fox-terrier listening to the voice of his dead owner." The other is by mentioning a performance attended by Alma in which a man, Ricci Howe, formerly her "cleaning woman," impersonates Alma, wearing one of her gowns and "moving his lips to the sound of my voice." Ricci's performance leaves Alma feeling "confused" and "disembodied." Burn's performance has a similar effect on a reader made to play the part of Nipper listening to the voice of the male author Gordon Burn impersonating the dead Alma Cogan.

*Alma* is a novel very much about voice: its power, its point of origin, its aura and authenticity. It is also a novel about image: about public image (especially celebrity), about ways of imaging (photographs, film, television, paintings, and words), and about ways of imagining. Photographs, for example, record and recall but also mislead and estrange. Alma, quoting Vladimir Nabokov, sees herself as "A stranger caught in a snapshot of myself." Photos can enliven and, at least metaphorically, even kill. A photograph in a fan magazine serves as the model for Peter Blake's painting of Alma Cogan that figures so prominently and ambiguously in the novel. Painted just as Alma's star was beginning to fall and the Beatles'—another of Blake's subjects—was beginning to rise, "Alma Cogan" eerily combines (in the words of the Gallery's *Acquisitions Catalogue*) nostalgia "with extreme mass-circulation-linked contemporaneity." The painting's strangeness also derives in part from its immediate effect on Alma: "the picture seemed to have aged with me," a postmodern variation on Oscar Wilde's *Picture of Dorian Gray* (1891).

Only after seeing the painting does Alma begin searching out the evidence of her past life, of which she had previously carefully rid herself. Looking for "a photographic reminder of the life locked into the underlayers of the painting," she goes first to the London flat she still owns but only rarely uses, then to the "Crypt" in the Theatre Museum in Covent Garden, and finally to "F.McL.—my taxonomist, my taxidermist, *sammler*, embalmer, stasher and storer, considerer of trifles, tireless tender of the flame. Francis McLaren. Biografiend. Fetishiser. Jealous hoarder of my life." His home in Manchester is less a residence than a shrine where McLaren, who first met Alma when he was eleven years old, lives, and loves, "by proxy." "You don't choose your fans," Alma explains after meeting him. "You have no way of knowing what sparks them off." If the origin of McLaren's disease is uncertain, its symptoms and the prognosis are not. They have been flashed at the Tate Gallery for all, including Alma, to see, parts of Jenny Holtzer's message art: "NOSTALGIA IS A PRODUCT OF DISSATISFACTION AND RAGE" and, in a work of proliferating Mark Chapmans, "LACK OF CHARISMA CAN BE FATAL."

Alma, "more interested in how far McLaren has gone with this than in taking a trip down memory lane," learns the lengths to which what he calls his love has taken him. Alone in "Alma's Room" (the words on the sign he has carefully removed from the door and hidden, but which she finds, takes, and later buries on the moors), she discovers that, in addition to the usual photographs, records, costumes, magazines, and the like, McLaren's collection includes crank tapes sent by male fans and something worse, something to which Alma is curiously, even perversely drawn. This is the tape of Alma's Radio Luxembourg broadcast of December 26, 1964, the day that mass murderers Ian Brady and Myra Hindley first abducted, then sexually abused, and finally murdered Lesley Ann Downey. In fact, it is a copy of the tape that Brady and Hindley made of the murder as Alma sang "The Little Drummer Boy," like Myra playing (however unwittingly) her accomplice's part, providing background, adding accompaniment. Caught in the act, McLaren offers this defense: "My only interest was you." He returns the cassette to its *Ray Conniff: For Sentimental Reasons* box. He explains that the unavailability of the tracks elsewhere gives the tape rarity value.

Design, not derangement, drives Burn to resurrect Alma Cogan and set her story in late 1986, twenty years after the "real" Alma died and the all-too-real Myra Hindley emerged from twenty years of silence, imprisonment, and obscurity to confess to additional murders of victims whose bodies had never been found. To all of its other images, *Alma* adds those of Myra Hindley on front pages and on television screens, including "the figure under the prison blanket with the hand hovering over its head to protect it (the cranial bones and meninges; the cerebro-spinal fluid, the vagus nerve) from the door arch all instinct is to smash it against." *Alma* resembles this extraordinary sentence in the way it treads a fine line between restraint and violence. The novel also resembles the "photohoroscopes" Alma happens to see in a discarded newspaper: images of Brady and Hindley's victims as they might have looked had they not been murdered twenty years before. Resurrected from the dead, the victims, Myra, and, thanks to Burn, Alma too get another chance, get to enjoy another moment of fame.

The English edition of the novel emphasizes the link between pop entertainer and mass murderer by juxtaposing Alma's and Myra's images on the dust jacket. The

American edition substitutes a picture that proves differently but equally disturbing. Disembodied facial features done in bright pastels and black appear in photo-negative style against a garishly bright yellow background. The effect is purposely cheap, grotesque, and macabre: features without a face, image without identity. The endpapers of both the English and American editions are no less unsettling. They reproduce Peter Blake's "Alma Cogan," rendered as if a postcard from the Tate Gallery gift shop. The painting/endpapers enter into dialogue with Blake's original painting and more especially with Burn's brilliant but disturbing novel that is less about Alma Cogan than it is about the nature of fame, the power of the image, the relation between illusion and reality, fiction and history, and frustration, resentment, and violence.

Mannish in appearance and living, in the novel, beyond her time, Alma recalls and combines two figures from T. S. Eliot's *The Waste Land* (1922): the Sibyl, who has been granted her request for eternal life but who has forgotten to ask for eternal youth, and the poem's androgynous narrator, Tiresias, who sees and suffers all. Eliot shows the reader "fear in a handful of dust" as he shores the fragments against his ruin. Burn's approach is similar, but his materials are more accessible and his effect is far more disconcerting. Precisely because *Alma* does not end in a scene of apocalyptic fury, as does one of this extraordinary novel's many precursors, Nathanael West's *The Day of the Locust* (1939), Alma's look "behind the scenes" and Burn's acts of narrative disinterment and disembodied ventriloquism make the potential for violence seem more personal and more pervasive. It also makes the terror, both for Alma and for the reader, more acute, more real. It does so because, like McLaren's tape, *Alma* is "laboriously reconstituted . . . yet for all that, a fluctuating, almost subliminal undercurrent of discords and weird microtones persists."

*Robert A. Morace*


## Sources for Further Study

*Booklist.* LXXXIX, September 15, 1992, p. 120.
*Chicago Tribune.* August 23, 1992, XIV, p. 5.
*Library Journal.* CXVII, August, 1992, p. 144.
*London Review of Books.* XIII, August 29, 1991, p. 19.
*Los Angeles Times.* September 10, 1992, p. E7.
*New Statesman and Society.* IV, August 23, 1991, p. 38.
*The New York Review of Books.* XXXIX, September 24, 1992, p. 25.
*The New York Times Book Review.* XCVII, August 30, 1992, p. 9.
*Publishers Weekly.* CCXXXIX, June 29, 1992, p. 51.
*The Times Literary Supplement.* August 23, 1991, p. 20.
*The Washington Post.* September 9, 1992, p. C2.

# ANAHULU
## The Anthropology of History in the Kingdom of Hawaii

*Authors:* Patrick V. Kirch and Marshall Sahlins (1930-    )
*Publisher:* University of Chicago Press (Chicago). Illustrated. 2 volumes. Volume I: 243 pp.
    $45.00; Volume II: 201 pp. $45.00
*Type of work:* Anthropology, archaeology, and history
*Time:* Prehistory to the mid-nineteenth century
*Locale:* The Anahulu Valley in O'ahu, Hawaii

> *The product of many years of collaboration between an anthropologist and an archaeologist, this pioneering work of historical anthropology seeks to reconstruct "Hawaii's entrance into world history" as that process unfolded in a single representative region*

*Anahulu: The Anthropology of History in the Kingdom of Hawaii* is a monument of interdisciplinary scholarship. The work is divided into two volumes: Volume 1, *Historical Ethnography*, was written by Marshall Sahlins with the assistance of Dorothy Barrère; volume 2, *The Archaeology of History*, was written by Patrick Kirch with the assistance of Sahlins, Marshall Weisler, and Matthew Spriggs. Introducing their respective volumes, however, Sahlins and Kirch both emphasize the thoroughly collaborative nature of their enterprise.

Sahlins is an anthropologist who has been influential both as a specialist in Polynesian culture and as an anthropological theorist; among his many books are *Culture and Practical Reason* (1976), *The Use and Abuse of Biology: An Anthropological Critique of Sociobiology* (1976), and *Islands of History* (1985). Kirch is an archaeologist who has published widely on the archaeology of the Pacific; his previous books include *The Evolution of the Polynesian Chiefdoms* (1984) and *Feathered Gods and Fishhooks: An Introduction to Hawaiian Archaeology and Prehistory* (1985). Both Sahlins and Kirch are members of the National Academy of Sciences.

In some respects, *Anahulu* resembles the five-volume, French-based project, *A History of Private Life*, published in English translation by Harvard University Press (see *Magill's Literary Annual*, 1988-1992). Like that series, *Anahulu* has two principal claims on our attention: the interest of its specific subject, clearly, but also its claim to exemplify an innovative interdisciplinary method.

In another respect, however, *Anahulu* differs markedly from *A History of Private Life*. While the scholars who contributed to the latter project sometimes drew on their own archival research, their essays were largely works of synthesis. In contrast, *Anahulu* is primary scholarship. From facsimiles of mid-nineteenth century land documents to the intricacies of carbon dating, these two volumes demonstrate the nearly surreal mastery of detail of which late-twentieth century scholarship is capable. Kirch's volume in particular will be studied primarily by specialists.

Precisely because Sahlins and Kirch's investigation ramifies into such fine detail, it is important to keep in mind the contexts that give their work meaning: both the explicit context which they provide and the larger, implicit contexts. Sahlins and Kirch summarize their intention with admirable clarity. As Sahlins explains in the introduction to volume 1, they want to trace the impact of the capitalist "World System" on Hawaii following the "discovery" of the islands by Captain James Cook in 1778:

> From London and Boston, Canton and Kamchatka, the political and economic forces of the World System converged on the Islands, principally the ports of Honolulu and Lahaina, whence the effects were carried to remote places such as Anahulu. The modest aim of the present volume, then, is to bring the history of the world into the Anahulu River valley. What we would show is how Hawaii's entrance into this world history, through a series of local mediations, was realized in the cultural forms of Anahulu history.

*Anahulu* thus reflects several of the dominant trends in current scholarship in the social sciences and the humanities. First and most obvious is the vogue for microhistory. The Anahulu Valley takes its name from the Anahulu River, the longest river in O'ahu. In focusing his "historical ethnography" on this region, Sahlins never loses sight of the themes that might be treated on a large scale in a more conventional history. For example, in reproducing records of church membership between 1834 and 1863 in Waialua (the territorial division encompassing the Anahulu Valley), Sahlins graphically documents the impact of the evangelical "Great Awakening" of 1837 among Hawaiian Christians and the "backsliding" that followed, in the context of a larger discussion of the missionaries' limited success and the interaction between Christianity and the rapidly collapsing traditional Hawaiian order.

Another fundamental aspect of *Anahulu* that reflects dominant trends in the humanities and the social sciences is the moral cast of the work. The epigraph to Sahlins' first chapter is from Saint Augustine: "Thou didst at first desire a farm; then thou wouldst possess an estate; thou wouldst shut out thy neighbours; having shut them out, thou didst set thy heart on the possessions of other neighbours; and didst extend thy covetous desires till thou had reached the shore: arriving at the shore, thou covetest the islands . . . " (ellipses Sahlins'). Here, just as much as in any collection of saints' lives, history is seen in moral terms, the object being to document and analyze the malign influence of capitalism, imperialism, colonialism, particularly as those forces have impinged on the lives of indigenous peoples around the world.

Certainly the entry of the World System was devastating for Hawaiians, as it had been for Native Americans, contributing to a severe decline in population and massive cultural dislocation. At the same time, Sahlins and Kirch do not portray their subjects as helpless pawns: "Hawaiians too were authors of their fate and not merely its victims. While capitalism (in all its cultural manifold) was imposing itself on them, and precisely as it could not be denied, Hawaiians synthesized the experience in their own cultural terms." If the long-term effects of European contact were more severe in Hawaii than in other Pacific societies, that was in part attributable to Hawaiian distinctives that "culturally amplified the impact of capitalism." Sahlins shows at length, for example, how the destabilizing effect of European contact encouraged the *ali'i* or chiefs to indulge in "unrestrained competition among themselves in conspicuous accumulation and consumption." This "consuming frenzy" was inspired not only by quotidian greed but also by Hawaiian cosmology.

That is one instance of a problem that has long preoccupied Sahlins: the relationship between history and culture. Here is another way in which *Anahulu* takes its place in a larger context of cultural studies. Current work in cultural studies is full of references to various forces or historical processes which are said to shape social life. Crudely applied, as in classic Marxism, such theories offer what Sahlins ironically refers to as "a physics of the world-historical forces." To clarify his more complex sense of the relation between historical forces—such as those associated with capitalism—and the particular cultures in which they are played out, Sahlins has coined the term "structure of the conjuncture," which he defines in *Islands in History* as "the practical realization of the cultural categories in a specific historical context, as expressed in the interested action of the historical agents."

Sahlins' definition sounds frightfully abstract, but in fact the concept of the "structure of the conjuncture"—which figures prominently in *Anahulu*—is intended to undercut facile abstractions. As Sahlins observes, "the culture of imperialism in Hawaii (as elsewhere) is not reducible to an abstract calculus of greed and gain." He goes on to list some of the conflicts among the diverse agents of imperialism: conflicts between missionaries and merchants, between Protestant missionaries and Catholics, between American interests and those of Britain and France. In turn, members of these diverse groups formed shifting alliances with different factions among the Hawaiians, creating "complex, interethnic 'structures of the conjuncture.'"

Such nuanced analysis is welcome. Even so, Sahlins does not manage to escape the demons of abstraction. When he writes of "personages . . . who synthesized the historical forces as biographical dispositions," he lays himself open to the charge of having a defective sense of what constitutes an individual human being.

In January, 1993, amid the ongoing stories reporting bloodshed and near anarchy in the aftermath of the breakup of the Soviet Union, there was a small flurry of stories from the corner of another empire. That date marked the one hundredth anniversary of the overthrow of the Hawaiian monarchy in 1893, which paved the way for the annexation of Hawaii by the United States in 1898.

Reflecting on the centennial, John Waihe'e, the governor of Hawaii and the first native Hawaiian to hold that office, wrote that "The overthrow of the Hawaiian . . . was a hostile act, an armed takeover of a legitimate government that was an established member of the community of nations." Among native Hawaiians there are increasing calls for some degree of sovereignty, with demands ranging from a "nation-within-a-nation" status comparable to that of Native Americans to complete independence. That is another context in which *Anahulu* is meaningful.

*John Wilson*

## Sources for Further Study

*Library Journal.* CXVII, August, 1992, p. 126.
*The Times Literary Supplement.* February 5, 1993, p. 25.

# ANNIE BESANT
## A Biography

*Author:* Anne Taylor (1933-    )
*Publisher:* Oxford University Press (New York). Illustrated. 383 pp. $59.00
*Type of work:* Biography
*Time:* 1847-1933
*Locale:* England and India

*An atheist lecturer, socialist agitator, Theosophical leader, and mover in Indian affairs, Annie Besant lived several great lives—all of them typically barred to Victorian womanhood*

> Principal personages:
> ANNIE BESANT, an ambitious woman with a gift for public speaking, in quest of human brotherhood
> ELLEN MARRYAT, the childhood teacher who shaped her
> FRANK BESANT, the clergyman husband who stifled her
> CHARLES BRADLAUGH, the "chief" of the National Secular Society, a member of Parliament
> MADAME HELENE PETROVNA BLAVATSKY, the founder of Theosophy

The course Annie Besant's extraordinary life would take, Anne Taylor suggests, was determined on the day her father died, in London, in 1852. Her mother moved the family to genteel Harrow, where boys from the famous school lodged in the house. Here, a desire for the male world of learning they could enter rubbed off on Annie. At the age of eight, her education was entrusted to a stranger, Ellen Marryat, a brilliant woman of independent means attracted by Annie's potential.

Taylor rightly stresses the importance of Marryat in shaping Annie's life. She developed in Annie considerable powers of observation, but also, through "finishing" touches such as foreign travel, kept alive in her a streak of idealistic romanticism, inherited from her Irish mother. Visiting Catholic countries also brought home to her the power of images and symbols, an interest fostered, when she returned at the age of fifteen to her mother's house, by reading in the Fathers of the Church in Harrow School Library—learning meant for scholarly clerics.

Annie brushed aside the doubts it bred. Unquestioningly, she accepted the attentions of a "serious" young clergyman, Frank Besant, whom her mother encouraged. They were married on December 21, 1867. Annie was twenty, soft-eyed, shapely, brilliant, and ignorant; she had powers and ambitions that she could not admit even to herself. "She could not be the Bride of Heaven, and therefore became the bride of Mr. Frank Besant," wrote her journalist friend W. T. Stead years later. "He was hardly an adequate substitute." A son, Digby, was born a year later.

Soon Frank began to show Annie exactly what a clergyman husband expected in a dutiful wife. It was with a sinking heart that she realized that even the thirty shillings she earned for a flimsy short story belonged to him, as her "owner." She felt "degraded by an intolerable sense of bondage." Resistance to his efforts, as she put it, to break her in merged with an eruption of doubt in God when illness nearly killed their daughter Mabel.

Annie appealed for spiritual help to one of the most scandalous figures of the Victorian church—the Reverend Charles Voysey, who had lost his position and founded a "Theistic Church" in London. Through him she met Thomas Scott, publisher of a series of liberal theological pamphlets. She returned to Sibsey ready to challenge authority. A whim seized her one day to enter the pulpit and preach a sermon to the empty church: This was what it was like to enjoy her husband's power. Next came writing: Her pamphlet *On the Deity of Jesus of Nazareth* was published by Scott in 1873, with the inscription "By the wife of a beneficed clergyman." Frank was outraged. According to Annie, he threatened to shoot her. She left, taking Mabel with her. In its time, this was an act that took the recklessness of a fanatic; without faith, home, husband, or reputation, she was nothing, an abject pariah. But she had truth on her side, as she saw it.

Struggling in London, Annie was devastated by another blow: Her mother died suddenly in 1874. She turned to work. Under the great dome of the British Museum Reading Room, she could stay warm, earn money, and forget hunger in busying herself on the series of pamphlets Scott commissioned from her. He was shocked by her next scheme—to become a public lecturer. But Annie was set on it: The platform was not just unwomanly—it was lucrative. Every aspiring orator, she was told, must hear the notorious atheist and republican Charles Bradlaugh speak at the Hall of Science. The experience was decisive. Within months, she was his lieutenant, rapidly elevated to vice presidency of the National Secular Society (NSS), writing for Bradlaugh's *National Reformer*, a convinced atheist, and a speaker of power herself, making her debut on February 25, 1875. Seeing the faces beneath her from the platform, she perceived herself as "ruler of the crowd, master of myself."

Very quickly Annie embroiled the "chief" in a scandal of national proportions. A dry and outdated pamphlet on birth control, *The Fruits of Philosophy*, had suddenly attracted prosecution for obscenity in Bristol. Against the wishes of her NSS colleagues, she persuaded Bradlaugh to undertake its republication, to test the law, and to assert the right of the poor to contraceptive information. Like Bradlaugh, she undertook to speak in her own defense in court—an unwarrantable self-display on the part of a woman. The case was won, on a technicality. Annie had become the first woman in history ever publicly to advocate birth control, claiming the right to knowledge that society forbade women, and in so doing had branded herself forever. The immediate result was a lawsuit with her husband and its inevitable result, her loss of her children: She was unfit to be a mother, ruled the judge, because "One cannot expect modest women to associate with her."

In 1880, Annie achieved another goal, becoming one of the first women to take a degree through London University, winning first-class honors in botany and animal physiology. In the same year, Bradlaugh commenced the greatest struggle of his career. Elected to Parliament from Northampton (at the fourth attempt), he was refused his seat because he could not swear a religious oath of allegiance. It was to take six years and three more elections to give it to him, years that would also lose him Annie's support.

Bradlaugh had opened the columns of the *National Reformer* and the platform of the Hall of Science to debate with the new socialist groups that had sprung into being in the wake of widespread disappointment with the Liberal government that had swept into office in 1880. In socialism's collectivist creed, which thus gained considerable publicity, Annie saw her ideal of brotherhood come to light, and in socialism's emphasis on social action a new arena for her talents. After much heart-searching—for socialists were bitterly hostile to Bradlaugh—she joined the Fabian Society, a high-minded group formed in 1883.

By 1885, she was at the forefront of the movement, a member of the executive, giving space in her own journal *Our Corner* to Fabian news, and sneered at by some of her new colleagues for her enthusiasm ("Joan of Arc of the Proletariat," one called her). Perhaps her greatest hour as a social reformer came with her heroic leadership of the Match Girls' Strike, in 1888, which won decent working conditions and a living wage for women whose employers literally had allowed them to rot away in close rooms full of dangerous phosphorus fumes.

Shortly afterward, Annie left the Fabians to join the more radical Social Democratic Federation. Partly at their urging, she stood for the new London School Board and won a landslide victory in the December, 1888, elections. She was the board's first woman member. "Ten years ago under a cruel law," she wrote, "Christian bigotry robbed me of my little child," but "now the care of the 763,680 children of London is placed in my hands." In the three years she served, she did sterling service in the cause of free and nonreligious education for the poor.

There was a lack in her life—of certainty, of personal ease, and of reconciliation between her sacrificial and apostolic spirit and her analytical mind. A new movement, half religious, half occult, and with deep roots in India, now claimed the ability to meet that lack, to establish the brotherhood of humanity, and—through secret knowledge of the secret laws of nature—to bridge the gulf between revelation and science into which so many Victorians had plunged despairing: Theosophy. Its charismatic Russian founder, Madame Blavatsky, had marked down well-known Annie Besant's as a mind destined to lead the movement and to lend it some of the credibility its beliefs defied: automatic writing, astral "Masters" ("Mahatmas"), "karma," and reincarnation. As Taylor explains, step by step, Annie first mocked, then read deeply in Blavatsky's *The Secret Doctrine* (1888), weighed the "proofs," felt the spell of Blavatsky's personality, and emerged to announce her conversion. In Theosophy she recognized "the means of realizing the dreams of childhood on the higher plane of intellectual womanhood."

It may be, too, that in Theosophy's ideal of celibacy she found a kind of peace. Taylor carefully unravels the tangled web of Annie's blighted love life, from the time of her marriage—when the facts of life and gender were first revealed to her with shocking abruptness. She argues convincingly that Annie's intensely close relationship with Bradlaugh remained platonic (despite outward appearances, and whatever more she may have wanted), and that her liaisons with figures such as playwright George

Bernard Shaw were modeled on a chivalric ideal. The one man to whom she was erotically attracted was W. T. Stead, campaigning editor of the *Pall Mall Gazette*, and he rejected her advances.

In 1889, Annie undertook a hectic lecturing tour in Ireland, speaking on three separate subjects: Theosophy, socialism, and secularism. A year later, Bradlaugh was dead, and she broke her ties with the socialists. In 1893, she set sail at last for India. She was met with drums and flowers, and she walked in procession behind two white bulls. The prophetess of many messages had found her home.

Established in the holy city of Benares, she rapidly proved to be a powerful force in the reawakening of Hindu pride, advocating Indian self-rule within the Empire. Her real objective was millennial and visionary: to bring about a Theocratic state under the firm and wise rule of which all people would live as brothers and sisters. She learned Sanskrit, established the Central Hindu College, and set up newspapers and a publishing operation. In 1909, the death of her coleader released her from his ban on political involvement. She was elected president of the Theosophical Society. Her position, her increasingly dogmatic belief, and the support of Indian associates now allowed her openly to pursue power. The same year, she adopted the boy Krishnamurti, encountered by chance on a beach, in whom she recognized Theosophy's new World Teacher.

She was received—and closely watched—by the viceroy of India; maverick and inflammatory politicking in the turbulent subcontinent, which England truly held only by consent, earned her the soubriquet "naughty Annie" from the governor of Bombay. She used the methods Bradlaugh had taught her—go to the villages, speak directly to the people. In so doing, she prepared the way for Gandhi, to whom she gave the title "Mahatma." She joined the Indian National Congress in 1913, was threatened with deportation in 1915, was interned in 1917, and for a few months after this "martyrdom," as the new president-elect of Congress, briefly had supreme power in India in her grasp. When she revealed herself to the crowds as priestess and lawgiver instead of democratic politician—as Taylor remarks, a huge miscalculation—they turned elsewhere. The hectic activity of the next ten years—extraordinary for a woman in her seventies—produced nothing of moment. When, in 1929, Krishnamurti rejected the role in which she had cast him, her life was over. Membership in the Theosophical movement, which had peaked at forty-five thousand in 1928, began to decline. Four years later, she died.

"She 'saw herself' as a priestess above all," said George Bernard Shaw. "That was how Theosophy held her to the end." As much as this, she was an orator in an age electrified by oratory, an age in which women, like children, were meant to be seen and not heard. Her public ambition disoriented and even disgusted her contemporaries partly because she was a woman, partly because it was difficult to predict what would be its next object. Above all, she meant a great deal to a great many people, especially in India, at a time when the initiatives and symbols she provided had crucial importance. For all her flaws, she deserves a better biography.

Although Taylor marshals her facts competently (some disquieting inaccuracies aside), a fundamental lack of sympathy with her subject drags this book down. The writing is lackluster. Taylor has a distaste for the romantic, the tasteless, and the dramatic, but these were all part of the person whose story she tells. When Taylor tells us that Annie was genuinely convinced of the truths of Theosophy, her tone invites us to suspect fakery; Annie is lashed for wanting to "gratify" a "desire for self-sacrifice"; and it seems both harsh and naïve, given the nature of late Victorian radical politics, backhandedly to condemn her for "allow[ing] her distress at losing Mabel to be paraded in the interest of propaganda for the secularist cause." It is also now unfashionable to respect outsiders who throw themselves into the life and affairs of another country: Because Annie Besant could not be an "authentic" Indian, it is implied, she was merely an intruder and a power-monger. The Indian verdict might be less negative. Finally, a new biography of Annie Besant requires a kind of contextualization that Taylor refuses to provide, in the situation of women from the 1870's to the 1890's, and demands understanding both for the dead ends they ran into and for their need for what Taylor derisively calls "masculine associates." It is not fair or helpful to judge Besant by the standards of the late twentieth century. Her peregrinations helped form those standards.

*Joss Lutz Marsh*

## Sources for Further Study

*The Observer*. March 29, 1992, p. 63.
*New Statesman and Society*. V, May 1, 1992, p. 38.
*The Times Literary Supplement*. June 19, 1992, p. 8.

# ARCHIBALD MacLEISH
## An American Life

*Author:* Scott Donaldson (1928-        ), in collaboration with R. H. Winnick
*Publisher:* Houghton Mifflin (Boston). 622 pp. $35.00
*Type of work:* Literary biography
*Time:* 1892-1981
*Locale:* The United States and Europe

*Archibald MacLeish was successful as a lawyer, a journalist, an administrator, and a government official, but he always thought of himself as first a poet*

> *Principal personages:*
> ARCHIBALD MACLEISH (1892-1982), a noted American poet
> MARTHA HILLARD MACLEISH, an educator, mother of Archibald
> ANDREW MACLEISH, a successful merchant, father of Archibald
> ADA HITCHCOCK MACLEISH, a professional singer, wife of Archibald
> MARY HILLARD, an educator, sister of Martha and aunt of Archibald
> MARK VAN DOREN, a poet, teacher, and close friend of Archibald

Archibald MacLeish was born into an upper-middle-class family in a suburb of Chicago, Illinois. He was the second son of Andrew MacLeish, president of a large Chicago department store, and Martha MacLeish, who before her marriage had been president of a college for young women. A fractious child, Archibald eventually was sent to an eastern prep school and then to Yale, where he won honors as a poet, scholar, and athlete. At Yale, he was chosen for the most prestigious of the secret societies, Skull and Bones. Determined to be a poet but knowing that he could not earn a living or support a family through poetry, he went to Harvard Law School and, after service in World War I, entered the practice of law in Boston. After a successful start on a career in law, he turned down a partnership in his firm and took his wife and child to Paris in 1923. Financial support from his father made it possible for him to spend the next few years writing poetry.

MacLeish at once became part of the expatriate American community in France, joining such other famous writers as Ernest Hemingway, with whom he had a long and sometimes difficult friendship, poet John Peale Bishop, and novelist F. Scott Fitzgerald. MacLeish and his wife, a soprano who became known for her skill with the music of such composers as Erik Satie and Igor Stravinsky, were social people who soon became intimate with the famous writers, painters, and musicians who made Paris their center of activity in the 1920's. MacLeish during this period established a reputation as a new voice among poets, although it was noted that his verse owed more than a little to that of T. S. Eliot and Ezra Pound.

The MacLeish family returned to the United States in 1928, buying an old farm in western Massachusetts which was to remain their permanent home for the rest of Archibald MacLeish's life. The stock market crash and subsequent depression made it necessary for MacLeish to find a way of making a living, and by 1930 he was working as a journalist for *Fortune,* a new business magazine being published by Henry Luce, the founder of Time, Inc., and like MacLeish a graduate of both Hotchkiss and Yale. The job provided MacLeish with a solid income and with enough time to write some of his most impressive poetry during the 1930's.

By the end of the decade, MacLeish was becoming restive with his responsibilities and disturbed at what he regarded as the pro-Fascist leanings of *Time, Fortune's* partner in Luce's stable of magazines. MacLeish left *Fortune* to become the first head of Harvard's Neiman Fellowship program for journalists. MacLeish had become very active politically, speaking and writing on behalf of the Loyalists in the Spanish Civil War and helping to produce the motion picture *The Spanish Earth* (1937), which some regarded as propaganda for the Loyalist cause. These activities led some people to regard MacLeish as sympathetic to communism.

These suspicions led to difficulties when President Franklin D. Roosevelt, in 1939, asked MacLeish to assume the post of Librarian of Congress. There was bitter opposition to the nomination from those who mistrusted MacLeish's politics as well as from professional librarians, who pointed out that he was entirely without experience as a librarian. After a hard battle, he was confirmed. He did an excellent job of reorganizing the Library of Congress and bringing it up to date, but as World War II progressed he became more and more active as an aide to Roosevelt, writing speeches and helping to orchestrate the flow of information about the war that was released to the public. Late in the war, MacLeish was appointed as an assistant secretary of state; the confirmation process was again acrimonious, but he was again confirmed. He worked primarily in the process of setting up the formal United Nations organization; he wrote the English version of the prologue to the U.N. charter.

MacLeish left the government after Roosevelt died in April of 1945. For several years, he devoted himself entirely to his poetry and to opposing the activities of those politicians who he believed were creating a "Red scare" like that which followed World War I. Eventually he would be attacked by Senator Joseph McCarthy as one of the many "Reds" or "pinkos" supposed to populate the faculty at Harvard. MacLeish had accepted a position at Harvard in 1949, teaching a writing course and another course in poetry on a part-time basis. He helped develop many poets and novelists who would become prominent, and he was very productive in his own work.

In 1958 MacLeish published *J. B.: A Play in Verse*, in which he recast the Book of Job in a modern setting. The play eventually was produced on Broadway, directed by Elia Kazan, and was a great success, winning a Pulitzer Prize and a Tony award. Other verse dramas MacLeish wrote subsequently did not fare as well. When MacLeish reached the age of seventy, he was forced to retire from Harvard. Over the remaining twenty years of his busy life, he lived at his Massachusetts farm, spending most winters at a house he and his wife had built on Antigua in the West Indies. He was the recipient of many honors, including three Pulitzer Prize awards; the Medal of Freedom, awarded by President Gerald Ford; the National Medal for Literature; the gold medal for poetry of the American Academy of Arts and Letters; and dozens of honorary degrees.

In writing about MacLeish, the veteran biographer Scott Donaldson is venturing into new territory; his previously published books deal with writers of fiction: Ernest Hemingway, F. Scott Fitzgerald, and John Cheever. Donaldson, perhaps unsure of his ground, seems somewhat reluctant to analyze his subject's poetry, choosing instead to print entire short poems and lengthy extracts from important longer poems, making a few brief comments on the subjects of these and leaving it to the reader to examine the poems, or not, at the reader's discretion. He does include, with reference to MacLeish's collections of poems or his best-known single works, the comments of critics, both favorable and hostile.

The result of this approach is that Donaldson provides the context in which poems were written and some sense of what MacLeish's contemporaries thought of him and his work. Donaldson seems at a loss to recognize what caused the differences of opinion; too often he simply explains negative comments about MacLeish's work as emanating from envy or personal animus. This is unfortunate, because it leaves Donaldson without a reasonable explanation for the fact that MacLeish's poetry was falling out of favor with critics and readers even while MacLeish was alive and has not recovered since his death. The reasons for this are not hard to find: MacLeish's style, during most of his career, relied heavily on rhetorical phrasing and language for its effects, and rhetoric does not usually wear well. Even the love poems, written to or about the succession of women who were his lovers or objects of his desire, have this quality. It is also true that the tone of many of his poems was preachy; he liked to tell his readers what they should think. The poems that attracted the most attention during his lifetime, and which are likely to last, are those in which emotion and language somehow came together: "Ars Poetica," "Not Marble Nor the Gilded Monuments," "You, Andrew Marvell," "Frescoes for Mr. Rockefeller's City," and a handful of others.

Donaldson is on the right track, however, when he argues that the work of MacLeish's later years has been unjustly neglected. As Donaldson's quotations show, once he passed out of public life at the age of seventy, MacLeish wrote a more personal verse in a less traditionally "poetic" style; his late poems are spare, written in language that approaches the tones of speech. It may be hoped that the attention Donaldson pays to these late poems will help make more readers aware of their virtues.

*Archibald MacLeish: An American Life* is a biography, however, not a study of the subject's poetry, and as a biography it is successful. Like so many recent biographies (Richard Ellmann's 1959 study of James Joyce and Leon Edel's five-volume work on Henry James set the style), it aims at completeness, with the result that some unnecessary information about meals eaten or the guest list at certain parties fills the pages. It does, nevertheless, provide a detailed and entirely believable picture of MacLeish and the people with and among whom he lived. It is a sympathetic portrait, for the most part, but Donaldson does not exclude material that shows his subject in an unfavorable light.

Archibald MacLeish was a charming and handsome man, but he was no paragon of virtue. His need for the approval of others was constant and intense. Many contemporaries mistrusted him, arguing that he changed his opinions and ideas too readily to suit the demands of the time. It was pointed out, for example, that he had been vehement in the 1920's in denouncing the falsity of World War I propaganda; in this he was part of the "Lost Generation" with Ernest Hemingway, John Dos Passos, E. E. Cummings, and many others. In 1940, however, in a book called *The Irresponsibles: A Declaration*, trying to stir up support for American involvement in World War II, he accused those writers of creating a generation of cynics who would not flock to the banner if war came. Further, as an aide to Franklin D. Roosevelt, MacLeish wrote a good deal of the propaganda he had earlier despised.

Donaldson does not emphasize this side of MacLeish's character, but he provides evidence that his subject was regarded as a difficult and distant friend, not always to be trusted. His marriage, placid on the surface, was troubled. He and Ada Hitchcock were engaged for two years, during which he had at least two affairs with other women; within months after the marriage he was pursuing other women and would do so for most of the rest of his life. His three children all believed that their parents were so concerned with their own relationship that they deprived their children of affection and attention. He was especially harsh with his older son, Kenny.

Donaldson explains most of MacLeish's failings and foibles, especially his thirst for approval, by the neglect he suffered as a boy. Second son of his father's third marriage, he longed for signs of his father's affection but rarely received them; since he had grown to be successful, he reasoned, he should treat his own children without warmth to make them better adults. His need for approval, Donaldson argues, led him to seek success in a variety of fields, rather than being content to be a poet. Donaldson, with only rare lapses, provides reasons for MacLeish's behavior without apologizing for his actions. *Archibald MacLeish: An American Life* is a thorough, entertaining biography, sympathetic to its subject but honest about his character. There should be no need for another study of MacLeish's life for a long time.

*John M. Muste*

## Sources for Further Study

*Booklist*. LXXXVIII, April 1, 1992, p. 1424.
*Chicago Tribune*. May 24, 1992, XIV, p. 1.
*Choice*. XXX, October, 1992, p. 296.
*The Christian Science Monitor*. May 15, 1992, p. 14.
*Library Journal*. CXVII, March 1, 1992, p. 92.
*Los Angeles Times Book Review*. June 28, 1992, p. 2.
*The New Leader*. LXXV, June 1, 1992, p. 20.
*The New York Times Book Review*. XCVII, July 12, 1992, p. 13.
*Publishers Weekly*. CCXXXIX, March 2, 1992, p. 55.
*The Washington Post Book World*. XXII, May 3, 1992, p. 3.

# ARIADNE'S THREAD
## Story Lines

*Author:* J. Hillis Miller (1928-      )
*Publisher:* Yale University Press (New Haven, Connecticut). Illustrated. 280 pp. $30.00
*Type of work:* Literary criticism

*Ariadne's clue becomes Arachne's tangled web in this investigation of several aspects of narrative in nineteenth and twentieth century European novels*

When Ariadne gave Theseus a thread at the entrance of the Cretan labyrinth, she knew that he could easily find his way in. The challenge was to help him find his way out. *Ariadne's Thread* makes the same assumption of its readers. This book is not an introduction to story lines or the lines of narrative theory. Rather, *Ariadne's Thread* assumes that the reader is already caught in a critical labyrinth, that the reader is aware of the many intellectual currents that converge in the multifaceted processes of literary criticism at the end of the twentieth century. *Ariadne's Thread* searches for a way out of this labyrinth by seeking approaches to the complexities of narrative theory.

Writing at the culmination of a distinguished career as professor of English and comparative literature, Miller merges the psychoanalytic theory of Sigmund Freud, Ludwig Wittgenstein's philosophy of the self, and the grammatology of Jacques Derrida in order to trace a twisted path through several pieces of long fiction, especially George Meredith's *The Egoist* (1879), Johann Wolfgang von Goethe's *Die Wahlver-wandtschaften* (1809; *Elective Affinities*, 1872), and Jorge Luis Borges' "La muerte y la brújula" (1951; "Death and the Compass"). The goal of this journey is a theory of narrative composition that sheds light not only on European long fiction but also on the process of literary theory itself. Indeed, Miller's attention not only is directed outward, toward the creative work of others, but also is directed inward, toward Miller's own process of critical thinking. Part of the labyrinth in this book consists of the critic tracing his own path through an intellectual maze of deconstruction and reconstruction, of interpretation and reinterpretation.

The journey begins with the ancient Greek myth of the labyrinth, a maze that serves as the central metaphor of Miller's examination of narrative. The twisted and tangled passageways of the labyrinth parallel the passages that a literary critic must unravel and interpret. Just as Ariadne's thread was the clue and the key to the Cretan labyrinth, so the word "thread," with semantic cognates such as "weave" and "line," becomes in this book the metaphoric key to the problem of literary criticism. Indeed, illustrations of labyrinths on ancient Cretan coins and on the wall of the cathedral in Lucca, Italy, suggest to Miller that Ariadne's thread merges visually with labyrinthine form. So, too, does thread converge with story line and written line in the labyrinth of literary criticism, in which the image of the line operates in a broad semantic field. Ariadne's line of thread represents not only the act of writing in phrases such as "to write a line" but also the written character, that is, the letter of the alphabet. Themselves composed of curved and crossed lines, alphabetic designs are transformed into the signs that these lines represent. Word and meaning, morphology and semantics, join via Ariadne's line, which is itself both a material and a symbolic thread. In the process, the distinction between signifier and signified blurs.

Ariadne's story does not end in the Cretan labyrinth. Fleeing her homeland with Theseus, the princess is abandoned by the hero on the island of Naxos, where she eventually is rescued by and married to the god Dionysus. Threads unravel and ravel again as Ariadne's story line merges with that of Dionysus. Miller uses well-known paintings by both Titian and Tintoretto to illustrate how the two are bound in the marriage knot via another line, the circular crown or ring of stars that Dionysus gives his bride. Noting that in Friedrich Nietzsche's *Also sprach Zarathustra: Ein Buch für Alle und Keinen* (1883-1895; *Thus Spake Zarathustra*; 1896) the god informs Ariadne that he is her labyrinth, Miller concludes that the thread is itself a labyrinth, that the story line is a complexity of linguistic and critical fields. Three of these theoretical paths are tracked in separate chapters of *Ariadne's Thread:* character line; "anastomosis," or the line of interpersonal relationships; and the figurative line. Each of these paths requires a detour into the *Oxford English Dictionary*, detours in which Miller examines the labyrinthine meanings of "character," "anastomosis," and "figure," and their linguistic links with the processes of plotting story line and narrative theory.

"Character," derived from the Greek word for "stamp," receives most of Miller's attention. Although the etymological and literary contexts of "character" suggest predictability and repetition, the word also harbors questions about the nature of selfhood and its relationship with the outside world. Is there any difference between the fictional "character" of a novel and the character of a living self? Are these characters and selves fixed? If so, where does that leave free will, the human ability to choose?

The distinction between inner and outer realities is obscured as Miller deconstructs self as it is portrayed in Nietzsche's *The Will to Power* (1910). Ariadne's thread takes another twist as the traditional unified and static self is posited against a multiple, changing self. This quest for character and self leads Miller through Walter Benjamin's "Schicksal und Charakter" ("Fate and Character") and Charles Baudelaire's writings on Edgar Allan Poe to Jacques Derrida's concept of an "other" within the self.

Various metaphoric definitions clarify and complicate the character line followed by Miller. In *An Autobiography* (1883), Anthony Trollope describes character in fixed genetic and sexual terms, while character in George Eliot's *Daniel Deronda* (1876) is seen as a physical alphabet combining both corporal and moral features. The act of reading a character becomes more hypothetical as it merges with astrology and palmistry in Maurice Blanchot's *L'arrêt de mort* (1948; death sentence) and with the exotic list of divining of the self via fire (pyromancy), geometry (geomancy), fish (ichthyomancy), and names (onomatomancy) in François Rabelais' *Gargantua and Pantagruel* (1653-1694). Edgar Allan Poe's rejection of such scientologies of character in favor of character as an indecipherable hieroglyph in "Autobiography" finally leads Miller to Ludwig Wittgenstein's *Philosophical Investigations* (1953), in which

language and character hover between two modalities, with the linguistic (or character) sign viewed as either intrinsic or mimetic, as an innate entity or a metaphoric
pointer.

From this maze of character lines, Miller emerges with the theory that, in realistic
fiction, character serves the double purpose of both affirming and questioning self.
Identification between character and self, between the world of imagination and the
world of reality, enables character to ward off a reader's loss of self by enacting such
loss in fictional characters. Miller illustrates this duality in an extended analysis of the
character of Clara in Meredith's *The Egoist*. In this novel, images of mirrors and broken
lines reinforce Clara's volatile nature as she struggles to free herself from her
engagement to Willoughby in order to marry Vernon Whitford.

Breaking a promise in order to make another promise places Clara's marriage vow
in epistemological and moral jeopardy. Can such an unstable character make a reliable
promise? In order to answer this question, Miller examines the sovereign man in
Nietzsche's *On the Genealogy of Morals* (1896), the individual who has acquired
through discipline and bitter experience the ability to make and keep promises. In the
end, sexual imagery associating Clara with chalices, vases, and vessels in *The Egoist*
persuades Miller that the female Clara cannot exactly fit the mold of Nietzsche's
sovereign man because she lacks the biological means. For Miller, Clara lacks will
because she is not male.

From an examination of the individual as self or character, Miller moves to paths
where "self" intersects with "other," to interpersonal relationships. These paths Miller
calls "anastomosis," a word that historically carries anatomical, botanical, and topo-
graphical associations. "Anastomosis" takes on special interpersonal connotations in
the works of James Joyce, in which the word refers simultaneously to human
copulation and to the ancestral line. The myth of Ariadne weaves together many such
pairings, which are particularly sexual (Ariadne and Theseus or Ariadne and Dionysus)
or generational (Ariadne and her half-brother, the Minotaur). In order to confirm the
explicitly sexual nature of such relationships, Miller cites an imaginary island in
Rabelais' *Le Quart Livre* (completed 1552; *Fourth Book*, 1694) where arbitrary
copulation has undermined kinship and inhabitants must seek new and bawdy terms
of endearment. Miller follows the complications of such I-Thou relationships through
the works of Joyce, in which intersubjectivity becomes a narcissistic attempt to find
self in others. In an extended analysis of Goethe's *Elective Affinities*, Miller reads
metaphoric references to mirrors, architecture, and landscape as traces of intersubjectivity in the adulterous relationships among four characters: Edward, Ottilie, Charlotte, and the Captain. Edward's self-centered love for Ottilie raises two contradictory
models of anastomosis, one in which fixed characters interact with each other and
another in which selves find meaning and substance only via the very act of anastomosis. Thus Miller's critical path leads through a maze in which two metaphysical
systems both unravel and define each other.

The final route that Miller follows in *Ariadne's Thread* is that of figure, which can
mean simultaneously an outline of a concrete object or its abstract, artificial repre-

sentation. The use of such figures in the narrative line is illustrated by Borges' "Death and the Compass," a sophisticated detective story in which maps, rhombs, and triangles operate in the undoing of the detective Lönnrot. In this labyrinth, the moment when the murderer is found is also an awful moment of self-discovery and self-destruction for his discoverer. By solving his murder case, Lönnrot causes his own death.

The narcissistic image of the mirror is a refractory motif through *Ariadne's Thread*. Reflecting back to Meredith's *The Egoist* and Goethe's *Elective Affinities*, mirror imagery in Borges' story line results in an ambiguously double-ended narrative that loses itself in the dizzying logic of Zeno's famous paradox. Just as Achilles never catches the hare via his infinite series of half-distance sprints, so the shot from Scharlach's gun lingers in a temporal neverland between narrative time and reality and never actually kills Lönnrot. Narrative is thus a distorted time capsule in which past, present, and future merge in the depths of the figurative, fictional labyrinth.

Theseus' labyrinth was perilous not only because it harbored the monstrous Minotaur but also because its intricate passageways made exit impossible. In the end, for Miller all narrative, like Theseus' labyrinth, is a dangerous catachresis, a linguistic misunderstanding in which words never quite mean what they appear to mean, in which narrative never leads where it seems to lead. Because the process is deconstructive, because there is always another critical path to follow, literary critic and discerning reader remain forever caught in the labyrinth of story lines.

In this process of endless wandering, it is Ariadne's thread that complicates the path. The narrative itself, with its ambiguous tension between character, anastomosis, and figure, becomes not a thread of escape but a thread of entanglement. Consequently, Miller, following the implicit suggestion of John Ruskin, conflates two Greek myths and identifies Ariadne's thread with Arachne's web. The thread of liberation and of solution becomes a web of multiple, self-contradictory interpretations.

As he follows Ariadne's thread through the labyrinth, Miller is not only Theseus. He is at once the Minotaur, consuming his readers in the dangerous maze of critical exegesis, and Daedalus, the skilled craftsman who plans out the many detours and dead ends of the labyrinth and who thus knows the way out.

*Thomas J. Sienkewicz*

## Sources for Further Study

*The New York Review of Books*. XL, March 25, 1993, p. 46.
*The Times Literary Supplement*. November 6, 1992, p. 25.

# ART IN THE LIGHT OF CONSCIENCE
## Eight Essays on Poetry by Marina Tsvetaeva

*Author:* Marina Tsvetaeva (1892-1941)
Translated from the Russian by Angela Livingstone
*Publisher:* Harvard University Press (Cambridge, Massachusetts). 214 pp. $27.95
*Type of work:* Essays and literary criticism

*Eight newly translated essays on the nature and art of poetry by one of the great masters of twentieth century Russian verse*

> *Principal personages:*
> BORIS PASTERNAK, a Russian poet and friend of Tsvetaeva
> VLADIMIR MAYAKOVSKY, a Russian poet who was defended by Tsvetaeva
> RAINER MARIA RILKE, a German poet and admirer of Tsvetaeva
> OSIP MANDELSTAM, a Russian poet and friend of Tsvetaeva

The generation of Russian poets that began to reach maturity in the 1920's is significant for a number of reasons. In its own right, their work extends and renews the poetic tradition of their native country, bringing to it new codes of verbal facility and emotional intensity. In translation, however, particularly during the Cold War period, the reception and perception of what this poetry represented, in terms of cultural value and self-expressive freedom, had a resonant impact on European and American poetry, particularly on those poets to whom such terms were in need of renegotiation in the light of their own historical experience. Beginning with the reception of the prose and verse of Boris Pasternak in the late 1950's and early 1960's, access to the poets of this generation has become increasingly available. Their significance also has been enhanced by the prominence received by various Russian émigré writers who have come to the West since the regime of Nikita Khrushchev. The overall result of this complex tissue of cultural transmission and assimilation has yet to be determined. There is no doubt, however, that, together with that of Pasternak, the poetry of his illustrious contemporaries, such as Anna Akhmatova and Osip Mandelstam, has come to be regarded as very much part of the body of enduring poetry produced in the twentieth century.

It is to this generation of poets that Marina Tsvetaeva belongs, not only by virtue of her intimate acquaintance with Boris Pasternak but also because of her outstanding merits as a poet. Overshadowed to some extent by the prominence conferred on her contemporaries, and by more than usually complicated issues concerning dependable texts, it was only in the 1980's that the distinctive qualities of her genius and the tragedy of her personal life began to be documented adequately. The essays in *Art in the Light of Conscience*, most of which appear here in English for the first time, provide a valuable supplement to the volume of essays published in 1980, entitled *A Captive Spirit: Selected Prose*. In addition to an introduction which is as impressive for its passion as it is for its impeccable and resourceful scholarship, *Art in the Light of Conscience* contains a chronology of Tsvetaeva's life, the original bibliographical provenance for each of the essays included, and an index which gives some elementary information on the often unfamiliar Russian and other writers whose names occur unglossed in Tsvetaeva's prose. As an added bonus, twelve poems by Tsvetaeva are also included, partly so that the reader may appreciate the essentially poetic origins of the essays' prose, but also as an introduction to the essayist's principal and proper claim to attention.

The scholarly apparatus that accompanies Tsvetaeva's texts is of particular importance, not merely for the factual information it supplies and for the fidelity and dedication that its provision exemplifies. The facts themselves, drawing attention to incompletenesses in the essays, and in some cases to their irrecoverable originals, become an eloquent testimony to the travails of Tsvetaeva's own life as a writer. Such a context is central to an appreciation of the author's strong insistence throughout these essays on her own authority, as well as providing a framework in which an essay such as "Poets with History and Poets Without History" may be fully appraised. Essentially, all of the essays in *Art in the Light of Conscience* are episodes in the complex history of the spirit's striving for utterance. In addition to the penetrating insights they provide, their reflexive relationship to Tsvetaeva's narrative of her own artistic and cultural significance is central to their distinctive reality, as well as being the basis for the innovative and somewhat difficult formal character.

The first essay in *Art in the Light of Conscience* can be regarded as prototypical in a number of different ways. It is an essay that expresses the author's commitment to, knowledge of, and enthusiasm for Russian poetry. That such an expression should be made by a poet of Marina Tsvetaeva's refined and passionate sensibility may not come as much of a surprise, yet such enthusiasm frequently is reserved for the institution of poetry and is articulated as an admiration for a certain poetic tradition. What distinguishes Tsvetaeva's approach is her candid exuberance for the poet. It so happens that the poet in question in this opening essay, "Downpour of Light," is Boris Pasternak. Tsvetaeva's report on her encounter with Pasternak's book of verse *My Sister, Life* (1922) can in a sense be misleading, since it may appear that her generous appreciation of the work is a testament to Pasternak himself. Although there may be a certain coloring of personal sentiment in the essay, it is much more to the point to bear in mind that in addressing the poet, Tsvetaeva intends to celebrate what she perceives as the spirit of poetry, an impersonal and quasi-divine, or at least unworldly, power whose spokesperson the poet quite adventitiously, and helplessly, is appointed to be. Pasternak is, therefore, in addition to being a clearly gifted writer, an occasion of the power of poetry entering into being and into consciousness.

Although it is generally the case that, for writers of Tsvetaeva's and Pasternak's generation in Western European literature, the writer, or "the artist," came to be regarded as a special citizen, the specification of specialness that Tsvetaeva's somewhat visionary prose provides is an intensification and rarefying of that Western shift in cultural emphasis. As such, it speaks most urgently to developments in Russian literary culture and to the manifestation and survival of certain inward and spiritual tendencies in the Russian—or, to be more accurate, the pre-Soviet—literary imagination. Much of the difficult, fragmentary, allusive, ramified character of the work in *Art in the Light of Conscience* comes from the apparently insistent pressure under which Tsvetaeva felt herself in attempting to substantiate a vision of imaginative adequacy in the light of historical reality.

Such a reading of this material is reinforced by two additional considerations. The first of these is the fact of Tsvetaeva's grotesque suffering, brought about by social and economic conditions in the fledgling Soviet Union. The second is that she is writing in exile. Both considerations give the activity of recuperation, to which these essays are devoted, a considerable urgency. Tsvetaeva adapts the fundamental quality of voice in poetry in order to establish the full register of her own presence as a celebrant in prose of what poetry provides. As the opening of one of the more important of these eight vivid testaments reminds the reader, the concept of "the contemporary," how it is constituted and what is its value, has particular resonance for the author.

This interest led Tsvetaeva to adopt some cultural and aesthetic positions that were thought to be controversial by some of her peers. The whole issue of contemporaneity has a cultural and personal significance that is on the same plane of importance as its historical meaning. It has a direct bearing on Tsvetaeva's exile, on the fact that these essays were written while she was in exile and were published in émigré journals, despite the fact that Tsvetaeva's sense of her Russianness lacked the narrow ideological tendencies of many of the publications in which her prose appeared. Thus the art of refining and crystallizing the poetry of her thought gained additional urgency, and perhaps a certain amount of its vehemence, from the cultural context in which it was written. The essay, "The Poet and the Critic," therefore, although on one level a fascinating working out of some of Tsvetaeva's critical principles, is also an unsparing attack on some of the literary and cultural redundancy she encountered in the work, and among the attitudes, of certain Russian émigré groups. Such an essay, apart from expressing Tsvetaeva's courage, integrity, and individuality, also makes a contribution to Russian cultural history, thereby sustaining one of the time-honored roles of the Russian writer, which is to keep alive the voice of independence and the right to personal judgment.

Tsvetaeva's attitude toward her native country was somewhat more complex than that of many of her contemporaries in exile, who seem to have identified Russia with the Bolshevik regime. It seems remarkable, for example, that she returned to the Soviet Union in 1938, when Stalinist terror was at its height, and when her friend Osip Mandelstam underwent the arrest that led to his death. Events in the Soviet Union, however, were not allowed to overshadow Tsvetaeva's commitment to poetry. Her position in this regard also led to controversy. In the essay, "Epic and Lyric of Contemporary Poetry," she carries out a critique of the poet Vladimir Mayakovsky, an enthusiastic supporter of the Bolshevik government (at least in the first ten years of its existence), with the same degree of attentiveness, and with the same degree of acceptance of the legitimacy of his art, as she had shown in the case of poets with whom the émigré community felt more at ease, culturally speaking. The treatment of Mayakovsky in this essay gains its momentum and insight from being carried out as a comparison between his work and Pasternak's, a daring and exemplary act of cultural history.

Despite the complexity of her involvement with Russia and the poets of her generation, it is inevitable that Tsvetaeva be linked with those poets who, in various ways, were victims of the Soviet authorities. This is the case because of the privileged status she accorded poetry, and the sense of sovereignty she believed the poet embodies. The relationship between somebody with those principles and ideals and his or her society will virtually by definition be awkward, all the more so in a society without well-developed traditions of free speech. Tsvetaeva's essay on Mandelstam, or rather her defense of his poetic talent, "History of a Dedication," while perhaps not quite so concentrated and brilliant as most of the other works in *Art in the Light of Conscience,* is a valuable, as well as an accessible, reminder of where her commitments essentially place her. It should also be noted that Tsvetaeva's Russianness does not limit her perspectives on other literatures, as her treatment of a Russian version of Johann Wolfgang von Goethe's "Erlkönig" ballad in the essay "Two Forest Kings" shows. Here her familiarity with, in particular, German literature comes impressively to the fore.

The title essay of this collection is at once the most complex and most rewarding of the pieces. Its complexity is addressed through its formal character, the fragmentary nature of which is a feature of Tsvetaeva's typically restless and exuberant sense of the possibilities of prose. This essay contains some of the author's most direct encounters with the great figures of nineteenth century literature, such as Nikolai Gogol and Leo Tolstoy. Her reaction to them, and to certain moralizing tendencies in their work and careers, once again enacts an illustrative instance in the transformation of Russian literature and in the clarification of the Russian imagination, which is one of the most important legacies of Tsvetaeva's generation of writers. It is in this essay that Tsvetaeva reveals in fundamental terms her own artistic conscience. The terms in which she characterizes this conscience are typically modern. Her devastatingly elemental faith is in the artist's responsibility to his genius, his spirit. The fundamental zone of conscience for the artist is the maintenance of his integrity, his willingness to identify with the risks of speaking his mind, regardless of the consequences. The essay's aphoristic style is a dramatic expression of the tendency toward the singular and the incontrovertible which is the essay's subject, and in which the intense and penetrating expressiveness of Marina Tsvetaeva achieves a maximum level of conviction.

*George O'Brien*

### Sources for Further Study

*Library Journal.* CXVII, May 1, 1992, p. 82.
*The Virginia Quarterly Review.* LXVIII, Autumn, 1992, p. S122.
*World Literature Today.* LXVI, Summer, 1992, p. 542.

# AT WEDDINGS AND WAKES

*Author:* Alice McDermott (1953-    )
*Publisher:* Farrar Straus Giroux (New York). 213 pp. $19.00
*Type of work:* Novel
*Time:* Mid-twentieth century
*Locale:* Brooklyn and Long Island, New York

*This beautifully written poetic novel about the misfortunes of a death-haunted Irish-Catholic family is at once poignant and deeply sad*

> *Principal characters:*
> MARY "MOMMA" TOWNE, the caretaker of her nieces
> VERONICA TOWNE, Mary's niece
> AGNES TOWNE, Mary's niece
> MAY TOWNE CASTLE, Mary's niece
> LUCY DAILEY, Mary's niece
> BOBBY,
> MARGARET, and
> MARYANNE DAILEY, Lucy's children
> BOB DAILEY, Lucy's husband
> FRED CASTLE, May's husband

The opening sentence of *At Weddings and Wakes*, a densely detailed 127-word description of a woman shutting the front door of her house and going out with her three children, serves notice that this is no conventional work of bare-bones realism. Instead, it is a family novel as prose poem, depending for its effects not on the piling up of quotidian detail, not even on plot in the conventional sense, but on finely articulated language, the cumulative effect of image patterns, a structure which at first may seem random but which in fact is intricately ordered. Everything is significant. The door Lucy Dailey closes in the opening sentence, for example, forms the "backdrop for every Easter, First Holy Communion, Confirmation, and graduation photo in the family album." The novel itself is like a series of photographs, artistic revelations of nuances of light and shadow, of a family whose life is deeply colored by Roman Catholicism. Lucy is described as giving "a brief but accurate imitation of a desperate housebreaker" as she wrenches the door shut; indeed, she has hardly more place in the emotional life of her family than does a burglar. Unlike a burglar, she is breaking out of the house, not into it, a symbolic act which has no counterpart in her real life.

Lucy's birth family is far more real to her—painfully, destructively real—than the one brought about by her marriage to Bob Dailey and the birth of her children. In fact, the children, through whose eyes a good part of the action unfolds, are rarely even referred to by name; her relationship with them, lightly touched on, seems superficial and distant, poisoned by her bitter discontent. It is to visit her sisters and the aunt who reared them, an obsessive twice-weekly summer ritual, that she is leaving her house in Long Island and journeying to Brooklyn at the beginning of the novel. Although crucial details remain to be revealed, this journey and visit, events which in the minds of the children take on a darkly inchoate mythic significance, establish the mood that the rest of the story goes on to elaborate.

Essentially it is a journey into the hell this death-haunted family has created for itself. The simplest action reveals Lucy's isolation: for example, her "subtle, sneaky way of finishing a smoke." She moves with "stunned hopelessness," aware of "time draining itself from the scene in a slow leak." When they pass a cemetery, a place littered with "ice-cream wrappers, soda cans, cigarette butts, and yellowed athletic socks," the children feel "the eternal disappointment of the people whose markers l[ie] so near the road": There is no peace even in death. A stonecutter's yard seems "in its chaos to indicate a backlog of orders, a hectic rate of demand." They get out of a bus "suddenly grown taller and louder and far more dangerous" and enter "an exotic and dangerous realm"—a subway station—through "bars, prison bars, a wall of bars, and, even more fantastically, a wall of revolving doors all made of black iron bars." At different times on this journey (in effect, it is all one journey) they have seen midgets; a woman with skin "as splotched as a leopard's"; the blind and the deaf; "toothless old crones straight out of nightmares, women with claws for hands and mournful, repetitive coos for speech." To the children, the journey has something of the deliciously terrifying flavor of a ride through a carnival spook house. In another sense it is all real, and it threatens them, given the life-lessons taught them year in and year out by their mother and aunts, in ways they cannot begin to understand.

As they approach the aunt's apartment, Lucy is "as happy . . . as she'd ever be," but again the signs are dark: She is eating "the kind of bread . . . that Christ ate at the Last Supper," an image picked up later by the death of another character on Good Friday. Nor, as the story circles through the year, is there any corresponding image of Easter. Rather, the unbroken pattern of anger and recrimination more closely suggests the circles of Dante's *Inferno*—the work, not coincidentally, of the greatest of Catholic poets. When Lucy's son rings the bell to the apartment building, one of his aunts drops the key from the fourth-story window, an action that echoes fairy-tale princesses imprisoned in towers and reiterates the prison image from the scene in the subway.

In the apartment live Lucy's aunt Mary Towne, known as Momma, and Lucy's unmarried sisters Agnes, May, and Veronica Towne. With its heat and heavy food, its grown-up furnishings and rituals and frustrations, it is a place of torture for the children and hardly better for the adults. Lucy speaks "in the stifled and frustrated tone she use[s] only here," endlessly lamenting that her husband is not the man she married. She brings her discontent "to Brooklyn twice a week in every week of summer and la[ys] it like the puzzling pieces of a broken clock there on the dining-room table before" the children. Later in the day, the "sudden anger" which overcomes the four sisters is "somehow prescribed, part of the daily and necessary schedule, merely the routine." When their father finally arrives to take them home, "the footstep on the stair [is] a fabulous promise three seconds long that burst[s] into miraculous fulfillment with their father's familiar rap at the door." The heightened language, followed in the paragraph by "delivered" twice repeated, gives the father's arrival religious overtones:

This is a deliverance from the land of the dead, to which, however, they must again and again return.

It is not until much later, midway through the novel, that the primary cause of all this anger is revealed; until then, the reader's puzzlement and unease parallel the children's. Lucy's mother, Annie Towne—Momma's sister—died within a day or two of the birth of Veronica; Momma then married her sister's widower, only to have him die in turn while she was pregnant with a son who grew up alcoholic, and whom she rejected when he was twenty-one. Lucy saw how, as a result of the early deaths, "anger seemed to straighten Momma's spine and set firm her face" and concluded that "given the muddle of life, loss following as it did every gain, and death and disappointment so inevitable, anger was the only appropriate emotion." With her religion giving her no solace, with her anger poisoning her, the failure of her relationships is inevitable.

The central event in the present time of the novel, coloring almost every other event, is the marriage and sudden death, four days later, of the children's Aunt May. May's response to the events of her childhood had been to become a nun, a vocation she followed for fifteen years. Now, the gentlest of the sisters, she habitually but futilely attempts to reconcile Lucy to her marriage; her stubborn belief in the possibility of change, against all the evidence around her, presages her openness to a new life built on love. Her shy midlife romance with shy, flower-bearing mailman Fred Castle reveals the depths of her relatives' hatred of life. Sister Agnes hides the flowers away; when May talks of moving out to Long Island, where there are grass and flowers and trees, Momma says that it "sounds like a cemetery." It is May's wedding to which the title of the novel refers, a ceremony and festivity richly depicted in the penultimate chapter. Unbeknown to the participants, it is a wake as well, the reason, presumably, why there is no dramatic presentation of the funeral itself.

The opening chapter of *At Weddings and Wakes* depicts a circular journey and circular lives, the same sad story endlessly repeated; with the second chapter, a corresponding movement in the novel itself begins. Annually, Lucy's husband takes her and the children on a two-week vacation to the tip of Long Island, "believing that the green trees and furrowed fields, the stretches of pale beach, the moonlight and the sea would . . . give his children a sense of wonder and beauty and whole life." (Lucy, hating life, maintains her umbilical ties twice weekly by telephone.) The particular trip described here takes place right after the wedding, as revealed by a little scene in which the children try the sugared almonds they received: a suggestive detail, for they look appealing but taste terrible when bitten into. The chapter stops short of the vital revelation that a predawn phone call will inform them of May's death.

The reader learns of it only a few pages later, however, less than one-third of the way into the novel, when Maryanne, the youngest girl, confides in her new teacher that she has "the saddest thing in the world" to tell her. Some of the succeeding chapters and events, set in the time before the death, are thus tinged with melancholy irony, the wedding itself most deeply. Some, set afterward, are extremely poignant, as when Fred, who had lost his mother earlier and is now alone in the world, continues to visit the family. All are shadowed by the arbitrary and capricious death of the most sympathetic adult character in the novel. As the year turns, there are fights and yet more fights in Momma's overheated apartment. Lucy goes to the church where, amid "terrible rows, right up until the morning of the wedding," she was married—and writes "her parents' names in the parish book of the dead." At Christmas, Momma's son John appears, a reformed alcoholic whose exemplary behavior on this occasion does nothing to assuage the years of hoarded bitterness. In winter, at the children's school, at the end of three weeks of rain, the incinerator burns "every botched effort of the day." Fred and May court in the spring, and Margaret, the older daughter, presents her unattractive teacher with a bouquet of flowers she has salvaged from the cemetery. In a spring long past, Agnes hides her mother's diary, the record of a life, in the foundation of a wall. In the summer, May is married and dies, and the novel ends with the arrival of the message at the vacation cabin on the tip of Long Island, that place of green trees and flowers which is also like a cemetery.

The problematic element of *At Weddings and Wakes*, the death of May, lies right at its heart. People do die unexpectedly, and writers, especially major writers, have never been bound by statistical probability. Nor is there anything wrong with a sad ending, as long as it is the right ending, rising out of character, event, and the natural laws of the fictional world with what comes to seem, at least in retrospect, true inevitability. Here, however, it is hard to avoid the suspicion that May dies simply because the author has decreed that she shall, in order to strengthen a pattern and heighten, or deepen, a mood. May, the only one of the sisters brave enough to break the circle, the only one potentially capable of a sustained loving relationship, is arbitrarily denied her chance. Either her death has no thematic significance at all, which would make it intrusive indeed, or it suggests that life in general (not merely the life of this particular dysfunctional family) is so cruelly capricious as to defeat every impulse toward the "whole life" the children's father desires for them. That would justify Lucy's idea that "anger is the only appropriate emotion"; but Lucy gives the impression of being seriously neurotic. It is a notion heavily at odds, as well, with the author's outpouring of poetic detail, which seems to imbue the world of the novel with a complex significance.

This formidably crafted novel reveals true literary intelligence and seriousness of purpose, both rare and welcome. It also reveals, perhaps, the difficulty of making large mythic meanings out of characters who, whether of their own failures of imagination and will or simply of circumstances, are essentially victims. *At Weddings and Wakes* might be thought of as a small, flawed masterpiece.

*Edwin Moses*

### Sources for Further Study

*Booklist.* LXXXVIII, March 1, 1992, p. 1197.
*Chicago Tribune.* March 29, 1992, XIV, p. 1.

*Commonweal.* CXIX, May 22, 1992, p. 15.
*Library Journal.* CXVII, April 1, 1992, p. 148.
*Los Angeles Times Book Review.* April 12, 1992, p. 3.
*The New York Times Book Review.* XCVII, April 12, 1992, p. 3.
*Newsweek.* CXIX, April 13, 1992, p. 69.
*Publishers Weekly.* CCXXXIX, January 27, 1992, p. 88.
*Time.* CXXXIX, April 20, 1992, p. 95.
*The Wall Street Journal.* April 30, 1992, p. A10.
*The Washington Post.* April 15, 1992, p. F2.

# BALANCING ACTS
## Essays

*Author:* Edward Hoagland (1932-    )
*Publisher:* Simon & Schuster (New York). 351 pp. $23.00
*Type of work:* Essays

*One of America's foremost essayists divides his attention between the world and those who write about it*

Edward Hoagland makes sentences a mimicry of encounters along a path never walked before. He can jolt a reader, or twine one perception along another, or release a wealth of endless details he has wrested from any man or woman he has talked to. His fame rests on the essays constructed of such sentences—about turtles, tugboat captains, mountains, and those countries outside America he believes Americans should welcome to their too-provincial awareness. Travel writing, it is called, but it could be defined more lucidly as preservation-of-humanity writing, both the subject matter, when it is humanity, and the reader, in whom the writing fertilizes dormant awareness. Hoagland's first travel book, *Notes from the Century Before: A Journal from British Columbia* (1969), revealed that part of Alaska where men lived time-capsule lives, reliant on skills such as trapping, fishing, and running dog sleds. The point was not "I want to live this way," but "Look at how humans did live and still can," close as these contemporary pioneers were to a threatening yet zestful life-style in contrast to freeway, suburb, and office routines.

For Hoagland, love for nature is indissolubly crossed with love for humanity. He is no cold Robinson Jeffers proudly separate from those without whom, since they read his words, he could not propose to pose as separate. Hoagland is aware of his gifts, his skill at seeing and saying originally, but he is also very intent on making a gift of his gift. His roots are in the circus, where he worked for six months in his late teens. His first novel, *Cat Man* (1956), was set in that now antiquated arena of live performers presenting spectacles to live audiences.

"I know that life is an abyss, among other things," Hoagland says, in the title essay of *Balancing Acts*, "and like other travel writers, I enjoy wire walking a bit, courting, in a sense, a catastrophe." What he leaves out of this formulation is the return to the ground, whether by pencil or word processor, where the only danger is lack of skill at telling, akin to a magician under the big top without enough sleeves from which to produce silks and rabbits. After forty years as such a performer, Hoagland can enunciate what it takes to stay interesting, which, it happens, is only as demanding as juggling china plates and riding standing on a horse while informing the audience about particle physics in easily understood hand gestures:

[W]e expect an essayist to be rather abrasive and yet quite gentle, female and yet male, regret-
ful, cool, exuberant, single-minded, paradoxical, quirky, balanced, passionate, and fair. He should
be a sort of man for all seasons, in other words, loafing attentively, seizing risks, mastering data,

summarizing what we'd nearly thought to say ourselves. He should know everything that two eyes can be expected to take in, yet make a virtue out of being a free-lance observer, operating solo, not as a committee.

So antiquated is the idea of the circus that readers might shrug at such demands placed on writers by themselves. Just tell us the story, they may say. But the idea of writer as artist-performer, and the peculiar nature of writers, is one marvel this impresario insists on exhibiting. Nearly half the essays in *Balancing Acts* are on writers or about writing and what costs are paid in its production.

For Hoagland, writers are not what they used to be, less concerned as they are with presenting the subject than with maintaining bank balances. In the essay "Holy Fools," he remembers a friend nicknamed "Jude the Obscure," who fainted from hunger, too intent on producing his novel to eat. When Hoagland's *Notes from the Century Before* was published, he slept with it under his pillow and could recite its three hundred pages from memory. When it sold little and was largely ignored by reviewers, he vomited blood. Writing, he says, is cheapened today by the abundance of writing courses offered in colleges and taught by talented writers who cannot face the rigors of independence. Real writers are those who endure the awful but necessary despair of following an independent course, true to their muse, shrugging off fastidious editors. Hoagland's own father asked the publisher not to print his boy's book because he found it obscene.

Without the ailments of loneliness and despair there would be no *Moby Dick, The Sun Also Rises*, or *The Sound and the Fury*, Hoagland says. Instead, readers would be stuck with the humorless, zestless presentations of minimalism. The writer is the he or she who knows a story to be told and tells it. Contemporary writers, Hoagland complains, do very little traveling, and the reading public suffers.

A recurring theme of *Balancing Acts* is wildness—writers who are less and less willing to be wild, writers who were and are famous for it, and places in America where natural wildness remains, such as Alaska and Okefenokee. Thoreau is the saint of wildness, and *Balancing Acts* contains an essay on the author of *Walden* (1854), as well as one on John Muir, the explorer of California's Sierras and champion of preserving Yosemite as a national park. Thoreau's penchant for finding something new with every step is clearly Hoagland's personal aesthetic. In "The Circus of Dr. Leo," an essay on a book published in 1935 by a writer named Charles G. Finney, Hoagland introduces a forgotten novel about an imaginary circus: "In a circus we see mostly what we are ready to see. There is no script but chance and hope and spontaneity."

*Balancing Acts* asserts the connection between truth—reality—and wonder. "One reason literary minimalism had only a short run of being in fashion recently is that life itself is maximal." Writers such as Herman Melville and Gabriel García Márquez, and all other writers in the genius category, Hoagland argues, come at reality in a style now termed "magic realism." The awesomeness of creation and what man is cannot be made too large, too strange. Hemingway, says Hoagland, decided prose style was overblown and that he would trim it. Genius that he was, his style simply allowed the finest registering of modern war and some of the best pictures of nature and animals ever written.

Hoagland reminds readers that they cannot escape nature. "Our ancestral wish as predators is that somebody be worse off than we are." And "in the same way that we dash sauces on our meat (Worcestershire, horseradish, A.1., or béarnaise) to restore a tartness approximating the taint of spoilage that wild meat attains," so we like our New York and Los Angeles with a small complement of misery and hopelessness. The reader may argue back, but will remember Hoagland the next time he or she reaches for the meat sauce, and will wonder what Hoagland might say about any number of other behaviors. A city, after all, that modern place, was created by man, the maker of marvels. City-lover to the core, just one of the paradoxes that "wild" Hoagland relishes about himself, he sadly admits the death of his image of a "wild" city. The problem is that we cannot encompass its dangers as well as we previously did. The city has become impersonal. "The most fundamental decencies must be enforced by litigation or legislation, it seems." Neighborhood is a form of nature from which, to Hoagland's regret, we are indeed escaping.

Hoagland's genius as an essayist lies in his various ways of presenting a subject such that his readers want to know what he will say next and, when finished, what his next subject will be. "An essayist stands in for the rest of us." What does he think about Conrad, feminists, Thoreau, going to college? Everything familiar can come to life, given this essayist's words—another paradox in Hoagland's case, because few would sit and listen to him talk; he is a stutterer. In Hoagland's essays, by contrast, the words gush onto the page. One can read the essay "In Okefenokee" only after resting from absorbing the previous essay, because the reader will absorb a line-by-line specificity of natural history seamlessly blended with descriptions of fellow canoeists, the plates used for eating, and moonshiners.

Okefenokee, though circumscribed by industrial modernity, is a place like Alaska, virtual wilderness, where the century-before people can still be found, people who still have memories of living as predators among predators. Hoagland, always intent on the food chain, intuits the volition of an alligator's patience:

> So much of nature's picturesqueness is really a series of relentless tests of stamina. This Jurassic beast, like hundreds of its toothy fellows in the Okefenokee that are just as big, floated unobtrusively or lounged on the bank night and day, waiting for hunger to operate irresistibly on the possums, coons, rabbits, deer, and bobcats living on various dabs of land surrounding this wet prairie so that they'd enter the water to swim from one to another to feed.

Such an observation skewering "nature's picturesqueness," extends to all creatures, including humans.

Hoagland is in the ranks of writers such as Peter Mathiessen, John McPhee, and Edward Abbey, bent on preserving archaic awareness, if not actuality, from the erosions of the late twentieth century. "Emerson would be roaring with heartbreak and Thoreau would be raging with grief in these 1990s." What distinguishes Hoagland is his practical oneness with regular people. *Balancing Acts* opens with a rambling narrative-essay on riding the train from New York to California. The people he sits with in the dining car are as surprising as any series of sights in Okefenokee. Here is Hoagland, the benign alligator-writer, feeding on what happens to fall his way; the mode is celebratory and affirming. These "ordinary" people have survived unique twists of fate. They come off sounder than the classmates Hoagland revisits at a Harvard reunion described in a later essay. Hoagland's voice is never strident. He is always checking his footing, as in his title. This will not sit too well with readers hoping for the gospel.

. But resist, disobey he does, and the reader is surprised to discover that Edward Hoagland was fired temporarily from Bennington College for disapproving of homosexual practices. He had written in an essay "that anal sex is dangerous because it's not provided for physiologically, not because it is morally wrong. . . . [I] had tried promiscuity and anal intercourse myself, and thought I'd earned the right to a few feisty words on the subject." Free speech, it turns out, is going the way of Okefenokee. The heir of Thoreau, father of civil disobedience, Hoagland at the end of the century could propose any number of assertions about life and be welcomed for being original. But condemning the politically correct view of gay practice with the same style of insight used in speaking of Alaskan salmon or swamp flowers got him fired. The intolerant behavior on the part of his accusers he casts in an evolutionary perspective, implying its extinction: "[W]e Americans seem not to be good with dissent. Even the tolerant are intolerant of unorthodoxy. Minorities are catching the hectoring tones of majoritarians toward heterodox opinions, and our colleges are turning inhospitable to diversity."

When a writer the likes of Edward Hoagland uses the word "diversity," it comes to life, beyond the context of "diversity of opinion." He is life's celebrant, creation's extoller. He goes as far as anyone can to teach readers to love the world.

*Bruce Wiebe*

### Sources for Further Study

*Booklist*. LXXXIX, September 1, 1992, p. 2.
*Boston Globe*. November 8, 1992, p. 14.
*Chicago Tribune*. November 29, 1992, XIV, p. 3.
*The Christian Science Monitor*. December 3, 1992, p. 11.
*Houston Post*. November 29, 1992, p. C6.
*Kirkus Reviews*. LX, September 1, 1992, p. 1105.
*Library Journal*. CXVII, September 15, 1992, p. 83.
*Los Angeles Times*. December 15, 1992, p. E12.
*Publishers Weekly*. CCXXXIX, October 12, 1992, p. 59.
*The Washington Post Book World*. XXII, November 15, 1992, p. 3.

# BARCELONA

*Author:* Robert Hughes (1937-    )
*Publisher:* Alfred A. Knopf (New York). Illustrated. 573 pp. $27.50
*Type of work:* History
*Time:* 228 B.C.-1990's
*Locale:* Barcelona, Spain

*Not meant for scholars, this work highlights the social, political, economic, artistic, and religious history of Spanish Catalunya's premier city, Barcelona, in an engaging, anecdotal manner*

*Principal personages:*
> GUIFRE EL PELOS (WILFRED THE HAIRY), a powerful warlord during the Catalan Dark Ages who made Barcelona a stronghold city
> RAMON LLULL, a prodigious author who transformed spoken Catalan into a literary language
> RUIS I TAULET, the mayor of Barcelona who engineered the opening of the Exposition of 1888, which brought the city considerable notoriety
> ANTONI GAUDÍ, the most celebrated of Barcelona's twentieth century architects, known for his curvaceous and at times grotesque buildings
> LLUIS DOMÉNECH I MONTANER, a promising modernist architect who, upon occasion, lived up to his potential for genius

Robert Hughes's *Barcelona*, a study of two thousand years of that city's history aimed at a general audience, gives considerable information about the city's physical, political, religious, artistic, and social development while supplying essential historical narrative necessary for an understanding of Barcelona's unique presence and allure. Hughes, however, makes it known early in the book that this is neither an in-depth nor a scholarly assessment of Catalunya's principal city, operating rather as a general introduction with a heavy emphasis on the painters, architects, musicians, and sculptors whose works have importance. In this way, it is an outgrowth of methods applied in Hughes's earlier works, such as *The Fatal Shore: A History of the Transportation of Convicts to Australia, 1787-1868* (1987).

The work is divided into two parts, one half being listed under the heading "The Old City" and the remainder under "The New City." The first section covers the period from the third century B.C. to A.D. 1713, and the second, from 1848—the year of European revolution and turmoil—to the late twentieth century, ending with a discussion of the significance of Antoni Gaudí's Sagrada Familia church.

In the Old City section of the book, one learns that Catalunya, a nation in its own right at one time, was not colonized by the same Romans who settled elsewhere in Spain (those who founded such cities as Granada and Valencia), Barcelona having been created by footloose common soldiers and other lower-caste types interested only in building modest dwellings and living off their own produce. Those who went south and west, on the other hand, were aristocrats who desired large villas and spacious holdings. Barcelona's settlers became small farmers—growers of grapes, olives, and wheat—whose down-to-earth ways contrasted with the cultivated, luxurious life-styles of the villa builders; this practical, earthy outlook they bequeathed to their descendants, allowing their city to become an industrial power during the nineteenth and twentieth centuries. As for the early settlers, their inherent ability to make an arid, hot place bloom led to Barcelona's outward colonizing push of the early Middle Ages.

In the early fourteenth century, the kingdom of Catalunya (also referred to as Aragon and Catalunya) became one of Europe's great powers, extending its reach far beyond the confines of the Iberian peninsula. This process of conquest began under King Jaume I, whose energy combined with bad temper and greed to create a monarch intent on making Barcelona queen of the Mediterranean world. In earlier times, Hughes demonstrates, the inhabitants of Barcelona and its environs would not have been interested in foreign escapades, for they were an inward-looking, provincial group, content with an agricultural life and unimpressed with their silt-laden harbor, their adobe structures mutely testifying to their love of things earthy and anchored. They knew that they could go to sea if they chose, and Jaume I and monarchs that followed him gave them a vision of new lands and opportunities. Chief among those monarchs were Queen Isabella and Prince Ferdinand, who sponsored voyages for their realm of Castile, Aragon, and Catalunya.

Thus, by the Age of Discovery in the fifteenth and sixteenth centuries, Barcelona had a long-established link with Mediterranean lands such as the Balearic Islands (Majorca, Minorca, and Ibiza), Sardinia, and Sicily, where previous conquests had taken Catalunya's language and culture.

Catalans, as Hughes takes pains to point out, inherited a rich culture from their Roman forebears, to which they added their own unique and sometimes bizarre touches, such as a love for discussions of human excrement and the depiction of it in paintings. The Gothic Age in architecture reached Barcelona and had considerable impact upon building design, yet Catalans took pride in their insistence upon a heavy Roman element that counteracted the soaring Gothic vaulting of churches and cathe-drals. The curious, elongated barrel ceilings of the Catalans were unknown elsewhere, except in countries where Catalan influence was strong. Their churches, because they lack the theatrical verticality of French and English counterparts, have a solid, majestic feeling of rootedness about them that mirrors the attachment to the soil Barcelona residents traditionally maintained.

For centuries, money from overseas possessions poured into Barcelona, and it continued to do so long after the Middle Ages ended as gold and silver came in from New World acquisitions. This money built cathedrals, cloisters, and convents, but also impressive residences still much in evidence throughout the city, outwardly Spartan but inwardly resplendent. Not only the rich fared well: The poor also were, from all appearances, better off than their European contemporaries.

As the author notes, Catalunya, once a nation unto itself, never really considered itself part of Spain, having little in common with the heavily Moorish regions to the south and the royal enclave of Madrid to the west. Resistance to Madrid, often of a roundabout nature rather than an active one, has been a constant in Catalan history, and out of the tension between what Catalans think of as Spain and Catalunya has come a desire to outdo Madrid—to be European rather than narrowly Spanish; open to foreign ideas; regressive, not reactionary; aggressive rather than passive in pursuit of industrialization and the fruits of scientific inquiry.

Beginning in the eighteenth century, Barcelona, as an outcome of its long history of trading with and being open to the ideas of foreign lands, saw the possibilities inherent in trade with nations that slowly were becoming industrialized, among them England and Germany. The Catalan readiness to learn from cultures with which they came in contact served them well. From countries more scientifically advanced came concepts and practical inventions that would turn Barcelona into a modern, forward-looking capital: fast-moving, progressive politically and culturally, and enlightened—in vivid, unmistakable contrast to staid, self-contemplating Madrid.

Progress was slow at times, ebbing and flowing along with political tides, the chief of which was the Bourbon conquest of Spain in 1714. Apparently this victory had no lasting impact upon Barcelona's factory development, for great cotton and silk mills were created, making the city a preeminent producer of those goods. As advanced as these mills were, however, other industries found themselves struggling without the investment capital necessary to outdo their northern competitors. As Hughes observes, even though Barcelona never became a threat to London or Berlin in terms of trade, it was relatively advanced in technology, though never on the cutting edge of it. An unfortunate result of industrialization was the undoing of Barcelona's craftspersons; their work was highly regarded for centuries, and the destruction of their guilds by the new factories was a large loss.

Never an especially clean city, Barcelona experienced a wave of reforms beginning in the nineteenth century and continuing into the twentieth. In the Middle Ages, it had been bordered by two of the most completely polluted streams in the world, and, for centuries, it possessed some of Europe's foulest streets—this at a time when streets everywhere on the continent were used as sewers. Reformers, however, were not numerous, though they did manage to correct some of the worst abuses.

Hughes—not surprisingly, since he is an art historian—pays much attention to the fine arts and their development, his overall impression being that prior to the nineteenth century, little in the way of great, world-class art had been produced in Barcelona, the city having been known for its handcraftsmanship and decorative arts rather than for its painting, music, and sculpture. This would change in the twentieth century, when the city could list as artists in residence the famed Pablo Picasso and Joan Miró, inspirations to hosts of painters around the globe, and important architects, such as Lluis Doménech i Montaner and Antoni Gaudí. In addition, there were a number of second-tier artists, such as Santiago Rusinyol and Lluis Millet, whose works sometimes approached brilliance. Barcelona residents took pride in their designers, whose often offbeat, sometimes grotesque lines made the rest of Europe take note.

Apart from the well-known medieval quarter and the sports complex constructed for the 1992 Summer Olympics, the architecture of Barcelona rests solely in reputation upon such works as Casa Mila and the unfinished Sagrada Familia of Gaudí and some of the grander residences designed by Doménech. There is, as Hughes points out, little or no sustained brilliance on display in Barcelona's plazas and streets, for too much urban planning was slipshod, resulting in uninspiring vistas and a sense of architectural sameness. In its zest for tearing down the old and replacing ancient structures with new buildings, Barcelona has lost too many noteworthy buildings, and the ones that survive often have been damaged by poorly thought out renovations. Despite these drawbacks, the city's splendid physical situation between mountain and sea alleviates any sense of banality one might otherwise harbor. The medieval quarter and the dockside area also help alleviate the sense of sameness.

Hughes finds that Barcelona is a city greater than the sum of its parts, an alluring, vibrant place very much at home in the world and which, though haunted by its lost position as the queen city of an empire, continues to hope for a return to greatness. Although a victim for centuries, buffeted as it has been by political movements beyond its control, Barcelona at heart believes itself to be the capital of its own country, not a vassal of Madrid. To Hughes, Barcelona is one of those cities, unique in outlook, that still maintains a distinctive personality; it has not been as thoroughly Americanized as other European cities, increasingly alike in their mass culture and sterile architecture. She still remains what poet Joan Maragall calls "the great enchantress."

Thus, *Barcelona* captures the city's persona in differing ways: through an engaging historical overview, startling, risible anecdotes, well-selected and positioned illustrations, and careful analysis. This work is a valuable contribution to art and cultural history as well as to the enhancement of Barcelona's reputation, a classic text.

*John D. Raymer*

## Sources for Further Study

*Booklist.* LXXXVIII, January 15, 1992, p. 905.
*Chicago Tribune.* February 23, 1992, XIV, p. 1.
*Europe.* May, 1992, p. 46.
*Library Journal.* CXVII, January, 1992, p. 152.
*London Review of Books.* XIV, May 28, 1992, p. 17.
*Los Angeles Times Book Review.* February 23, 1992, p. 4.
*The New York Review of Books.* XXXIX, June 11, 1992, p. 3.
*The New York Times Book Review.* XCVII, March 15, 1992, p. 1.
*Newsweek.* CXIX, March 23, 1992, p. 55.
*Publishers Weekly.* CCXXXIX, January 6, 1992, p. 59.
*Time.* CXXXIX, March 16, 1992, p. 70.
*The Washington Post Book World.* XXII, March 1, 1992, p. 1.

# BASHŌ AND HIS INTERPRETERS
## Selected Hokku with Commentary

*Author:* Makoto Ueda (1931-    )
*Publisher:* Stanford University Press (Stanford, California). Illustrated. 457 pp. $45.00
*Type of work:* Poetry and literary criticism

*This innovative and exemplary work presents 255 poems by Matsuo Bashō in English translation, accompanied by selected commentary by Japanese poets and critics from the late seventeenth century to the late twentieth century*

It was back-to-school night, and the high school English teacher was telling the assembled parents about the ten-week writing module that the class had just begun. Explaining that instead of writing essays, the students would be writing poems, she gave two reasons for this departure from convention. First, a diagnostic test had shown that the writing skills of the students were generally poor, and she believed that they weren't ready to attempt full-scale essays. Second, the class was very large, and it would be impossible for her to read and respond to so many essays every week. The parents received this explanation with perceptible unease. One ventured a question: Wasn't writing poetry actually more difficult than writing essays, demanding more highly developed and specialized language skills? "Oh, don't worry," the teacher answered; "we'll be doing haiku."

For American readers, haiku occupies an ambiguous position. On the one hand, there is a strong literary tradition running from Matsuo Bashō (1644-1694) and later Japanese masters of the form through twentieth century figures such as Ezra Pound to contemporaries such as Gary Snyder. While this tradition has never been well represented in college literature curricula, being largely restricted to specialists in classical Japanese, anthologies of Japanese haiku in English translation had an enormous impact on American poetry in the post-World War II period.

Haiku also played an important role in introducing elementary and high school students to poetry. In the 1960's especially, many children first encountered poetry in the classroom through haiku. Instead of seeing poetry as an exalted but remote art—whatever those exotic creatures called poets do—students were encouraged to write poetry themselves in the form of haiku, just as in an art class students would be encouraged to draw and paint and not merely look at pictures. In this connection it is worth noting that Bashō himself was by profession a teacher of poetry.

For many readers, the fascination with haiku was part of a larger interest in Eastern thought, and particularly in Zen Buddhism. R. H. Blyth, whose extensive translations of haiku were among the most widely available in the 1950's and 1960's, believed that the distinctive qualities of haiku were rooted in Zen, and that perspective shaped his translations and commentary.

On the other hand, the very popularity of haiku has worked against it. Today many readers associate haiku with kitsch and cuteness and phony profundities. In part this reaction can be attributed to snobbery, but not entirely. Haiku's ambiguous status also derives from questions raised by the form—questions that connect with larger debates about poetry.

Stripped of many of the formal conventions that governed the composition of traditional haiku in Japanese, haiku and haiku-influenced poetry in English have contributed to the now-dominant tendency to define poetry as a particular kind of perception or attention, with no reference to the forms and measures that have traditionally distinguished poetry from prose. At the same time, the radical simplicity of haiku focuses anxiety and skepticism about the nature of poetry (and the nature of art): "Is that all there is to it?"

For that reason, Makoto Ueda's *Bashō and His Interpreters: Selected Hokku with Commentary* deserves the widest possible readership. Obviously a must for anyone with an interest in Bashō and haiku, Ueda's book should also attract readers and students of poetry generally; it would make an excellent text for a course in poetics. Ueda is a scholar of Japanese literature whose previous books include an introductory study of Bashō for Twayne's World Authors series (*Matsuo Bashō*, 1970) and Modern Japanese Poets and the Nature of Literature (see Magill's Literary Annual, 1984). Editor and translator of *Modern Japanese Haiku: An Anthology* (1976), Ueda is himself a poet as well.

Ueda's concise introduction surveys the origins of haiku or hokku, the significance of Bashō's work in the development of the form, and the substantial tradition of commentary on Bashō's hokku in Japan. Hokku had its beginnings in the linked-verse form known as *renga*, which dominated Japanese poetry in the fourteenth and fifteenth centuries. The first verse of a renga sequence was called a *hokku* ("opening verse"); it was written in the 5-7-5 syllable pattern familiar to modern readers of haiku. The second verse, a *waikiku* ("accompanying verse"), consisted of two phrases of seven syllables each. The renga sequence would continue in this fashion, alternating between verses in the 5-7-5 pattern and verses in the 7-7 pattern; while the sequences varied in length, the most common length was one hundred verses.

Renga was court poetry, typically composed at festive occasions by a group of poets who took turns trying to outdo one another with the verses they contributed to the sequence. Like court poetry in many cultures, renga was a sophisticated form of entertainment, a literary game. As William J. Higginson observes in his indispensable guide, *The Haiku Handbook* (1985), "Games have rules. By the time of Bashō, three centuries later, one could buy a book of rules for writing renga." One such rule was that the opening verse had to specify the season of the year in which the poem was composed—the origin of the traditional requirement that every haiku must include a "season word."

In the sixteenth century, an offshoot of renga known as *haikai* ("playful style") became popular. While traditional renga was primarily court poetry, haikai was broader in its appeal. In Ueda's words, haikai poets helped to "democratize poetry"; in diction, imagery, and subject matter they were relaxed and often cheerfully vulgar, with an emphasis on humorous and incongruous juxtapositions.

Meanwhile, as anthologies of renga were compiled there was an increasing tendency to treat hokku as individual poems, detached from their original context in a renga or haikai sequence. In time, poets began composing hokku as autonomous poems.

It was the nineteenth century Japanese poet Masaoka Shiki who established the critical distinction "between the hokku as the opening verse of a haikai sequence and the hokku as an independent, self-contained poem. To make the distinction clear, Shiki gave the name *haiku* to the latter type of hokku." Shiki's distinction prevailed. The only problem is that many of Bashō's poems which we in the West have come to know as haiku were in fact originally written to open haikai sequences. Bashō, Ueda notes, did not sharply distinguish between the two varieties of hokku. Accordingly, and in keeping with current usage in Japan, Ueda uses the term "hokku" in this book "to designate all seventeen-syllable verses written before the end of the Edo period (1600-1868), regardless of whether they actually opened haikai sequences."

The body of *Bashō* and His Interpreters consists of 255 hokku by Bashō, with each poem accompanied by selected critical commentary. The poems are presented chronologically and are grouped by year from 1675 to 1694, the year of Bashō's death; poems written before 1675 (there are only a handful here) are grouped in larger units. Ueda provides a biographical summary preceding each year's selection of poems.

Ueda's procedure for each poem is to begin with his English translation, followed by a transliteration of the Japanese original and a corresponding "literal translation" that follows the original word-for-word, insofar as that is possible. Some poems feature a headnote by Bashō, given in italics. Following the poem in its various versions is the commentary, consisting of brief observations drawn by Ueda from a wide range of Japanese poets and critics; Ueda frequently prefaces the commentary with a note providing background information. (The commentators are listed with brief biographical sketches at the end of the volume; the end matter also includes a glossary, indexes of Bashō's hokku in English and Japanese, and an index of names.) Poem and commentary together rarely exceed a single page. In every respect this layout is well conceived, and it has been superbly executed by Stanford University Press.

These are conventional translations. Instead of a Poundian "making new," they offer flat, prosaic verbal surfaces and unarresting rhythms—presumably a result of hewing closely to the letter of the original. Still, short of reading the poems in Japanese, Bashō and His Interpreters may provide the best available opportunity to encounter Bashō afresh, shedding as much as we can the preconceptions and associations that have accreted around haiku. The combination of Ueda's translations with the commentary permits us to experience something of the native strangeness of these poems.

Here is a characteristic hokku, written by Bashō in 1686:

> Cold night
>
> the sound of a water jar
> cracking on this icy night
> as I lie awake

What is immediately apparent is the smallness of scale, both in the sense that the poem centers on a moment in time and in the sense that its subject is small, homely. Early forms of literature tend to emphasize the heroic, the marvelous. Interest in the everyday is a late development, as is the fascination with single, sharply observed moments.

Writing about the "particularist aesthetics" of Gerard Manley Hopkins, Walter Ong has observed that the "meticulously detailed, particularized description of something under direct observation is quite foreign to verbal expression in oral cultures across the world and it does not come early in the development of writing or even of print" (*Hopkins, the Self, and God*, 1986). While Bashō does not approach the extraordinary detail of Hopkins' poems and journals, the "meticulously detailed, particularized description of something under direct observation" is one of the defining qualities of his art. (Like Hopkins, Bashō often combined verbal descriptions with sketches or paintings; like Hopkins, he sought to achieve a "deep seeing" that went beneath the surface of things.)

This aspect of Bashō's hokku is frequently emphasized in the commentary, where again and again a critic or fellow poet remarks upon the novelty of Bashō's subject matter and the precision of his observation. For example, a hokku from 1694, "spring rain—/ down along a wasp's nest, water/ leaking through the roof," elicits praise for Bashō's discovery of a sight never previously registered in poetry, while a hokku of 1687, "the first snow/ just enough to bend/ the daffodil leaves," is praised for the accuracy of its perception.

For late twentieth century readers, steeped in what Ong calls the "total immersion of present culture in particularist aesthetics," it requires an imaginative leap to appreciate the novelty of such descriptions. The effort is worth making, however; it yields a fresh perspective, for example, on Pound and Imagism, William Carlos Williams, the Objectivists—that whole current of modern American poetry. These lines from Williams' "Nantucket,"

> Flowers through the window
> lavender and yellow
>
> changed by white curtains—
> Smell of cleanliness—

written some 250 years after Bashō, nevertheless share a sense of the novelty of his project in registering with fidelity the visible world.

The "smallness" of Bashō's hokku has another aspect. While few of his poems could be called cryptic, their telegraphic style requires the reader to do a certain amount of filling in. Moreover, it is clear from the commentary that the critical tradition in Japan encouraged a more freely associative reading than would be common in Western criticism: the poem becomes a point of departure for the critic's personal response. At the same time, the spareness of Bashō's texts in proportion to the bulk of commentary guaranteed ongoing debate.

Responding to the hokku "the sound of a water jar," quoted above, the eighteenth century haikai poet Hori Bakusui suggested that the cracking of the jar had reminded Bashō of his physical infirmity. In contrast, Kato Shuson, a twentieth century haiku poet who is also a prominent Bashō scholar, believes that the poem is intended to convey a mood of "intense loneliness." The commentary itself becomes the occasion for further commentary. One critic's speculation that Bashō was awakened by the cracking of the jar "in the middle of the night" prompts this rejoinder from another critic: "The hokku's concluding phrase suggests that the time was near dawn, the coldest time of night. I do not think it was midnight." Such juxtapositions, arranged by the compiler, confirm that, along with his many other gifts, Ueda possesses a Bashōesque sense of humor.

*John Wilson*


### Sources for Further Study

*Choice.* XXX, October, 1992, p. 308.
*Library Journal.* CXVII, May 1, 1992, p. 80.
*Monumenta Nipponica.* XLVII, Fall, 1992, p. 392.

# BASTARD OUT OF CAROLINA

*Author:* Dorothy Allison
*Publisher:* E. P. Dutton (New York). 309 pp. $20.00
*Type of work:* Novel
*Time:* Mid- to late twentieth century
*Locale:* North Carolina

*The moving story of a plucky girl, determined to survive in a world in which women are the victims of violent men and of their own despair*

    *Principal characters:*
        RUTH ANNE (BONE) BOATWRIGHT, an illegitimate child
        ANNEY BOATWRIGHT PARSONS WADDELL, her mother
        GRANNY BOATWRIGHT, her grandmother
        REESE PARSONS, her sister by Anney's first husband
        GLEN WADDELL, her troubled, insecure stepfather
        RAYLENE BOATWRIGHT, the unmarried aunt who becomes Ruth Anne's
          protector

Although Dorothy Allison's first novel, *Bastard Out of Carolina*, is a story of cruelty, violence, and child abuse, it is also a story of survival and of triumph. At the end of the novel, Ruth Anne Boatwright, or Bone, as she has been nicknamed, is not quite thirteen years old. She already has endured more than many adults, however, and, amazingly, she has emerged from her trials with confidence in herself and in her future. *Bastard Out of Carolina* is also the story of the Boatwright clan, a rough lot whose gift to Bone is not only a place of refuge from her abusive stepfather but also their capacity for loyalty and their zest for life.

As Bone comes to understand, her own misery is the result of a number of factors. One is the character of her mother, Anney. It is true that, like the other Boatwright women, Anney has great strength. In the first pages of the novel, she is shown defying a courthouse clerk who refuses to change Bone's birth certificate and insulting the preacher who urges her to submit to the fact of her own sin in producing an illegitimate child. After the death of her first husband, Lyle Parsons, Anney again demonstrates her strength of character by going to work at miserable, underpaid jobs, first in a mill and then in a diner, in order to support Bone and a younger child, Reese Parsons. There seems to be nothing soft about Anney but her smile. Indeed, her reputation for toughness is such that when the courthouse holding Bone's records burns down, only Anney's airtight alibi prevents her from being considered seriously as the arsonist.

Along with her strength, Anney has a great weakness, her desperate need for a man. When she was married to Lyle, this dependence represented no problem, for Lyle was a kind and loving person, as devoted to Bone as he was to his own daughter. Glen Waddell is a different matter, for he needs not only love but also an outlet for his own frustrations. When Anney brings him into her home as Bone's stepfather, all of the elements of tragedy are in place.

As Granny Boatwright observes, there is something wrong with Glen Waddell: He won't look anybody in the eye. This sharp-eyed old lady is able to see beyond Glen's superficial politeness, even beyond his obvious adoration of Anney, to his deep-seated and dangerous insecurity. As Bone comes to realize, Glen's uncertainty about his own worth is the result of his being the only unsuccessful son of a successful father, who clearly despises him. To his father, Glen's marriage to a member of the Boatwright family is just another proof of his utter worthlessness. When they are dragged to visit the Waddells, Bone and Reese both see how badly they are treated; both Anney and her children routinely are fed outdoors, as if their presence in the house would contaminate it. Unfortunately, Glen is not sure enough of himself to object, to reject his father's values, perhaps to make something of himself just to prove his worth. Instead, he continues to visit his father with great regularity, each time hoping for a miracle of acceptance that never occurs. Unable to defy his father, Glen strikes out at everyone else: his employers, his wife, and his stepdaughters. As a result, he loses one job after another, and with every failure at work, he becomes more violent at home.

In addition to his insecurity about himself, Glen is afflicted with an irrational jealousy. It is not clear why he resents Anney's love for Bone more than he does her love for Reese. Perhaps it is because Bone is older and, because of her illegitimacy as well as her complete lack of contact with a father for whom the Boatwrights have nothing but contempt, more totally her mother's child. At any rate, Glen soon reveals his hatred for Bone, first in words, then in physical abuse, and finally, inevitably, in sexual abuse as well. Because Anney is so besotted with Glen that she will not hear anything to his detriment, Bone cannot confide in her. Furthermore, Bone loves her mother, and she knows that if the secret comes out, the Boatwright men will have no compunctions about killing Glen. All she can do is avoid Glen and try to survive.

When Bone is approaching her thirteenth birthday, her uncles discover the truth. Their reaction is predictable. They beat Glen so badly that he requires hospitalization, and they support Bone in her decision to live with her relatives, rather than with Glen and her mother. This does not, however, end Bone's ordeal. By now, she has become a habit for Glen; he now needs to torture Bone as much as he needs to make love to Anney. In a horrifying climactic scene, Glen finds Bone alone, beats her savagely, and then rapes her. At the end of the story, Glen has disappeared, and after a farewell to Bone, Anney has joined him in exile. Bone's uncles continue to hunt Glen, planning to exterminate him as they would any other noxious creature. One rather hopes that they will succeed.

It would have been easy to dramatize or to sentimentalize such an account, particularly since the novel is written in the first person, not by a mere observer, but by the victim herself. Dorothy Allison skillfully avoids such excesses, primarily because in Bone she has created a highly intelligent protagonist who can distance herself from the events she is describing; who, in other words, has learned to be an observer. Bone often refers to her love of books. Perhaps they have helped her to see herself as a character in a story. It is evident that only the capacity to detach herself from her own body has enabled her to survive. At the same time, from a purely technical standpoint, Bone is thus an ideal narrator whose matter-of-fact tone serves to intensify the horror of the events she relates.

Because her narrator is so observant, the author can quite plausibly have her re-create remembered events in complete detail. As a result, the novel is filled with memorable scenes, some of which are hilarious, in the tradition of the southwestern humorists. One thinks of the description of Granny Boatwright supervising her grandchildren, laughing at the half-naked girls tumbling around the yard, carrying on several conversations at once, or of the scenes backstage on the gospel music circuit, when the male performers are swigging alcohol and pinching any available females, just before they head out to bring salvation to their audiences.

Nevertheless, while the author intends for her readers to depend heavily on her narrator's observations and perceptions of events, she also makes it clear that Bone is limited by age and by experience. At first reading, for example, one is tempted to accept Bone's judgment of the Boatwrights. From the beginning of the novel, she emphasizes their virtues. Bone admits that in their little South Carolina community, the Boatwrights are despised as much as they are feared. The men, for example, are noted for their drunkenness, their foulness of mouth, their casual fornications, and their violence, both toward their wives, whom they beat whenever the mood strikes them, and toward their enemies, whom they are capable of shooting on sight. Bone also sees nurturing qualities in her uncles, their willingness to spend time with the children in the family, teasing them gently, inventing games, telling them stories, and instructing them in the skills that they will someday need. She also sees their independence, their pride, and their sense of family. In contrast, middle-class men such as the Waddells seem pallid. They may have money, but they are not real men.

It is clear that, like Bone, Allison appreciates the virtues of the Boatwrights. Compared to Glen, they are angelic. Although they would never admit it, however, the Boatwrights are committed to the idea that women were put on Earth to be used by men. For example, when Aunt Alma is pregnant, Uncle Wade takes care of his "needs" elsewhere. For a while, she refuses to live with him. Eventually, though, Alma makes up with him, in essence admitting that because he is a man, Wade should not be expected to control himself. Her attitude is not very different from that of Anney toward Glen; the difference is that Wade is betraying his wife, while Glen is violating a child. In both cases, women are making excuses for men.

Bone also observes how hard the Boatwright women work and how rapidly they age. They marry young, have children young, and spend their lives waiting on their husbands. The men, on the other hand, expect to eat when they like, have sex when they feel the urge, quit their jobs if they get annoyed, and go hunting and fishing when the mood strikes them. If their wives express annoyance, they can always be beaten. In this kind of society, it is no wonder that the women grow old fast. Bone does not seem to question this pattern but accepts the prevalent attitude: that women have no existence without men. It is this attitude that causes Anney to desert her own daughter; without Glen, Anney believes that she would not be a real person. In her defense, it should be remembered that Anney was trained to believe that. She knows from her own childhood that Granny Boatwright valued her boys much more than she did her girls. It is not surprising, then, that Glen puts so much stress on Anney's having a baby boy for him. Although the naïve narrator does not realize it, there is a profound symbolic significance in the fact that the first time Glen used her sexually, he was in the hospital parking lot with the girls, hoping desperately that his wife, in a hospital room above, was managing to have a baby boy for him.

The only woman in *Bastard Out of Carolina* who is not an object for the use of men is Raylene Boatwright, the unmarried aunt who takes Bone into her home after the rape and ministers to her with love and understanding. Raylene understands Anney's behavior and Bone's hurt because Raylene, too, has been in love. Her lover, however, was a woman who would not leave her husband and baby for Raylene. Thus although she has escaped enslavement to men, Raylene has felt the effects of a social pattern that the narrator innocently accepts, even forecasts for herself, but which the author obviously abhors. At the end of the novel, Bone may find meaning in having the strength of a Boatwright woman, but it is clear that Allison does not think that that is enough.

In her short-story collection *Trash* (1988), Allison's characters were the same kind of people as those in *Bastard Out of Carolina*, described with humor and with compassion, but without sentimentality. Allison's fiction is all the more poignant because her characters, and especially her women, are only dimly aware of the hopelessness of their lives. This first novel is an impressive achievement.

*Rosemary M. Canfield Reisman*

## Sources for Further Study

*Kirkus Reviews*. LX, February 1, 1992, p. 126.
*Lambda Book Report*. III, May, 1992, p. 42.
*Library Journal*. CXVII, March 1, 1992, p. 116.
*Los Angeles Times Book Review*. August 16, 1992, p. 6.
*The New York Times Book Review*. XCVII, July 5, 1992, p. 3.
*Publishers Weekly*. CCXXXIX, January 27, 1992, p. 88.
*San Francisco Chronicle*. April 19, 1992, p. REV7.
*The Times Literary Supplement*. August 14, 1992, p. 18.
*The Washington Post Book World*. XXII, May 3, 1992, p. 11.
*Women's Review of Books*. IX, July, 1992, p. 15.

# BECOMING A MAN
## Half a Life Story

*Author:* Paul Monette (1945-    )
*Publisher:* Harcourt Brace Jovanovich (New York). 278 pp. $19.95
*Type of work:* Autobiography
*Time:* 1945-1991
*Locale:* The United States, England, and Europe

*A painfully honest account of growing up gay in a homophobic culture and of the struggle to escape from the claustrophobic world of the closet*

> *Principal personages:*
> PAUL MONETTE, a writer and gay activist
> BOB MONETTE, his brother
> "BIG" PAUL and
> JACKIE MONETTE, his parents
> ROGER HORWITZ, his first long-term partner

This powerful autobiography by novelist, poet, and acquired immune deficiency syndrome (AIDS) activist Paul Monette, winner of the 1992 National Book Award for nonfiction, is in many ways as much a gay morality tale as it is a narrative of Monette's particular life story. Personal history here becomes the means of illustrating the stultifying horrors of the closet and persuading the next generation of gays and lesbians to abandon this shadow existence of exile and self-denial for the freely integrated existence that coming out makes possible. As he recounts his difficult journey from darkness to light, from furtive acts of self-loathing to public acts of self-assertion, Monette regularly interrupts the chronology in the voice of the angry, dying forty-seven-year-old human immunodeficiency virus-positive (HIV+) gay man that he is, denouncing his oppressors and urging younger members of his "tribe" to embrace the liberating truth of their sexual identities. Part morality tale, part manifesto, the memoir is Monette's urgent attempt to testify to what he knows: the deadly reality of homophobia in America.

In spite of his clear intention to provide a map of the landscape for young homosexuals so that they "may not drown in the lies, in the hate that pools and foams like pus on the carcass of America," Monette's book does more than this. It is, finally, about becoming a man. Gays and straights alike will recognize the harrowing rites of passage he identifies, the fears and humiliations that every boy must face in an American culture that prizes violent games, denies male intimacy, and demands success while providing too few images of what a successful man should be. Readers of *Borrowed Time: An AIDS Memoir* (1988), in which Monette movingly chronicles the death of his lover, Roger Horwitz, will recognize the same fierce eloquence here, the same sure voice, by turns passionate and lyrical, documenting the loss and pain as well as the surprising strengths that came from suffering. In the earlier book, however, Monette wrote a love story; for all the grief at its core, *Borrowed Time* is a celebration of two men and their magical union, of their valiant fight against an unrelenting illness. In the present memoir he has written an angry account of the tortured road to that union and the need for a fight, not simply against AIDS but against all the forces that would sentence gays and lesbians to the coffin of the closet.

Anger colors much of the narrative. Like many political activists (and in spite of his admission that things are never simply black or white), Monette has divided the world into collaborators and resistance fighters. The bureaucrats and politicians and priests, the puritanical New Englanders of his childhood and hypocritical educators of his youth—all of these he skewers for their poisonous collaboration to legitimize hate and prejudice against gays. He attacks the Catholic church with particular savagery, partly because of its insistent policy of regarding homosexuality as an intrinsic evil, and partly because of his own formative grade school experiences with Irish Catholic thugs who gleefully bashed in the heads of "sissies" in school bathrooms. The smug demonization of "queers" and the blatant campaign to eradicate them amount, he suggests, to nothing less than genocide, something made increasingly possible by the alliance he sees between the Catholic hierarchy and the fundamentalist right. In the face of this bigoted assault on human beings and human rights, Monette advocates open defiance, refusing to retreat to the invisibility of a closeted existence. He repeatedly asserts that it is homophobia which is deviant, homosexuality which is natural (that is, naturally occurring as a transcultural phenomenon), even if it is not the norm.

Monette's posture throughout the book marks him, in the theoretical debate within gender studies, as an essentialist rather than a social constructionist. That is, he regards homosexuality as biologically determined, something constituted by nature and there-fore essential to an individual's identity, rather than seeing sexual identity itself as something unstable and provisional, a construct produced by social interaction and the play of power in any particular historical moment. Monette understands that the history of same-sex relations long precedes the nineteenth century concept of a homosexual identity; he recognizes that what he means by "gay" may have been incomprehensible to an Athenian in the fifth century B.C. Nevertheless, the research of sociobiologists and the oral histories of other gays and lesbians persuade him that homosexual orientation is not a so-called "life-style choice"; it is no more a choice than eye color or foot size. This is a view he spent much of his life ignoring or wishing away, until at the age of twenty-five, paralyzed by these exhaustingly futile efforts, he accepted it as true, not as a tragic truth demanding some sort of wilted resignation but as a truth suddenly apprehended as profoundly liberating.

Finally the whole man could come into play. He need no longer feel forced to be a ventriloquist struggling to make the right sounds, a chameleon forcing itself into the appropriate social color, inventing himself again and again in the attempt to appear "normal." Happily, he had managed through all the denial—the frustrations of therapy, of willed sex with women or desperate couplings with other closeted men—to maintain one deeply nourishing image of intimacy: "two men in love and laughing." It was this fantasy that came alive at last when he met Roger at a dinner party in Boston in 1974, stepping from the isolation of his closet into the light and warmth of a loving, openly gay relationship.

Young Paul's story actually begins in the years following World War II, just outside Boston, in Andover, where he was born the first son of working-class parents. He was unconscious of much beyond the radio and television worlds of Kate Smith and Howdy Doody until his brother Bobby was born with spina bifida, which introduced a crippling reality to the home and turned Paul into a "perfect" boy. His perfect grades and perfect Sunday school attendance became a kind of compensation for Bobby's obvious physical imperfection, at the same time isolating Paul from family and friends. He came to see himself as a bodiless little scholar, denying his physical being to make it seem less important, in effect adopting the paralysis inflicted on his brother. The insistent realities of his young body were unleashed, however, when at the age of nine he had his first sexual encounter with another boy. He did not yet feel guilt—that would happen later, when his mother discovered the boys together, and would persist for nearly two decades—but he did feel that he had a life to hide, a real life that somehow could not be regarded as normal. Once discovered, Monette plunged even more deeply into denial, striving to mask his secret by creating the persona of a courtier, "the Noel Coward of the junior division." His witty, self-deprecating verbal performance made him confidant to the most desirable girls, and his nonthreatening self-effacement made him equally accepted by the boys. He became popular, but the price was transforming himself into a charming eunuch, a role he would later play successfully with New England divorcées and Hollywood wives. He had learned how to become that necessary additional man, the amusing fourth hand at bridge, the presentable society walker, the attentive companion to gossip and "share a Chivas with at sundown." This was a useful, safe, and ultimately destructive position, Monette suggests, because it neutralized the force of the real man and became a way of apologizing for his very being.

The move from the local Andover grade school to Phillips Academy was a move up the ladder of social class from townie to preppie, yet Monette characterizes these years as lonely and lost. In the rigid caste system of the school he was a nobody, separated from the athletic Apollos about whom he fantasized yet avoiding connections with misfits like himself and fleeing in homosexual panic from any boy who recognized in him a trace of fellow feeling. In sports, in the quest for a girl, in just about everything he was living a big lie; his dreams were of Broadway stardom, his interests lay in compiling his white leatherette Elizabeth Taylor scrapbook, performing Latin plays, and writing poetry. It began to seem that only in art would he be safe to explore the passionate feelings that could not otherwise be expressed.

At Yale, where he had won a scholarship, Monette once again reinvented himself, first as a hearty, voluble, rock-climbing outdoorsman, and then, with more success and with a clarifying sense of self-awareness, as a writer. He went from clubbable man to isolated poet, yet now the isolation he had always felt as a shamming outsider was distinguished by the higher calling of Art. He could revel in his uniqueness, in this aesthetic world where the repressive laws of desire had no power. It was on a summer research trip to England to read Alfred, Lord Tennyson's letters that Monette, desperate to express years of bottled up sexual desire, met a man and had his first adult homosexual experience. Losing his virginity produced the predictable guilt, but beyond that it produced the appetite for more experience. Still, after a summer of traveling and writing and thinking, Monette returned to Yale unable to admit his homosexuality; instead he careened through his last year as a kind of crazed cultural czar, importing film critics, hosting poets, filling the calendar with nonstop artistic events as if the sheer pace of things would keep his subterranean needs silently in check. From there he went on to graduate school.

Armed with a graduate degree and a 4-F deferment (obtained, ironically, by publicly admitting his homosexuality for the first time, to the doctor who examined him for the draft-board physical), Monette turned to teaching, first at a grim prep school off the beaten path in Connecticut. In spite of being a big hit with the boys, who found his exotic, unruly poet act hugely entertaining, he was forced to leave after two years, barely averting a scandal over a messy affair with one of the students. He had succumbed to the boy's overtures and been thrown completely off-balance by the intensity and volatility of the relationship. As he fled to a new and better job at Canton Prep, he realized he could survive only if he remained lifeless below the waist and threw everything into his poetry and teaching. This, with great difficulty, he did for some time, before the suffocation of such a life nearly broke him and he handed himself over to a young therapist with the injunction to make him straight. Desperate to change, he willed himself into a number of sexual relationships with women, often simultaneous, all of which taught him something but none of which satisfied him. He began seeing a wealthy Village novelist, an older man who squired him to the opera, to restaurants, and on trips. After a year or more of this complicated sexual quadrille, Monette was no closer to coming out than he had ever been, though he kept hoping to meet the "laughing man" who would lead him out of his closet and make it look like the easiest thing in the world.

Not surprisingly for a man who was both a budding writer and a full-fledged romantic, this breakthrough to his "queer self" came as a result of a summer's slow reading of Henry David Thoreau. Walking around Walden Pond, text in hand, he soaked in Thoreau's words: "I went to the woods because I wished to live deliberately, to front only the essential facts of life." That summer he did try to simplify his life, to rid it of the poses and transparent deceptions, to pursue the deliberate quest for a man to love without guilt or shame. By early September he had met Roger Horwitz. The lonely years were finally over; another man had penetrated the darkness and pulled a frightened Paul Monette, feeling unloved and unlovable, into a world of windows, light, and air.

Is it possible to find the story too melodramatic, the shifts from anger to sentiment too abrupt? Perhaps. Occasional notes of self-pity intrude, as does an exalted sense of romance. Monette, however, reminds us several times that he is speaking only for himself, not for the tribe. His dream of two men together is *his* dream, not the ideal he would impose on all gays. Being known to the core by another man, seeing himself whole in another man's eyes—that is what he had waited for all those solitary years, and to him it is not merely a sentimental cliché. Even if the romantic pitch gets carried too high at times, the power of the narrative is never in question. Monette has done something astonishing in this memoir. He has described the shadow world of the closet, its dangerous, delusional reality, with a precision and a passion rarely seen before. He makes it plain just how deep are the sorrows of a life unnecessarily suppressed, how persistent the rage over wasted time and lost opportunities. His clear-eyed anatomy of this oppressive space dramatizes the insidious way that cultural homophobia gets internalized in young gay people, the way they are made to accept the lies and distortions that lead to self-loathing and despair. Again and again he returns us to the angry, perplexing questions he poses at the beginning: "Why do they hate us? Why do they fear us? Why do they want us invisible?" Although unable to provide complete answers, *Becoming A Man* does go a long way toward making these embattled gay lives less invisible.

*Thomas J. Campbell*

### Sources for Further Study

*Advocate*. June 2, 1992, p. 34.
*Booklist*. LXXXVIII, May 1, 1992, p. 1568.
*Kirkus Reviews*. LX, May 1, 1992, p. 594.
*Lambda Book Report*. III, September, 1992, p. 20.
*Library Journal*. CXVII, May 1, 1992, p. 92.
*Los Angeles Times Book Review*. June 28, 1992, p. 10.
*The New York Times Book Review*. XCVII, July 26, 1992, p. 5.
*Publishers Weekly*. CCXXXIX , April 20, 1992, p. 44.
*San Francisco Chronicle*. July 12, 1992, p. REV8.
*The Washington Post Book World*. XXII, June 21, 1992, p. 1.

# BEFORE AND AFTER

*Author:* Rosellen Brown (1939-    )
*Publisher:* Farrar Straus Giroux (New York). 354 pp. $21.00
*Type of work:* Novel
*Time:* The 1990's
*Locale:* New Hampshire, Massachusetts, and Texas

*A story of the ways in which the commission of an unpremeditated murder affects the adolescent killer himself and the family that loves him*

> Principal characters:
> JACOB REISER, a seventeen-year-old student
> CAROLYN REISER, his mother, a pediatrician
> BEN REISER, his father, a sculptor
> JUDITH REISER, his younger sister

In *A Voice of One's Own: Conversations with America's Writing Women* (1990), Mickey Pearlman points out that one of Rosellen Brown's major themes is the power of the irrational in the lives of even the most rational of human beings. This theme was evident in Brown's first two novels, *The Autobiography of My Mother* (1976) and *Tender Mercies* (1978). While the crucial events in these early works are simply tragic accidents, the central incident in *Before and After* is a murder, one that the relatives of the killer would like to believe was in some sense an accident. In their attempt to understand the crime, to diminish or excuse it, the murderer's mother, father, and sister come to recognize the fearful effects of irrationality, not only on other people but also on their own thought and conduct.

*Before and After* is set in Hyland, a small New Hampshire town where Carolyn and Ben Reiser have chosen to spend their lives and to rear their children. Their social acceptance has never been a problem. Their occupations are prestigious: Ben is a sculptor with some success, Carolyn a popular pediatrician. As a couple, they seem ideal. What the practical, rational Carolyn lacks in imagination, Ben more than makes up for. The tolerant, loving family atmosphere has been reflected in the conduct of the Reiser children. Neither seventeen-year-old Jacob Reiser nor his fourteen-year-old sister, Judith, ever has been in serious trouble. At home, their offenses run to chaotic housekeeping or thoughtless absence from meals, for which they are routinely rebuked by parents who, like all parents of adolescents, are considered peculiar by their offspring. Despite such minor disagreements, it is obvious that both of the young Reisers have a deep affection for Ben and Carolyn.

The "Before" of Brown's novel effectively is summed up in her brief prologue. There, the author describes a home movie evidently made when Jacob and Judith were much younger. In it, the four members of the Reiser family simply act foolishly for the camera. The fact that this was no special occasion, just a typical time in the life of a happy family, makes the events that follow even more shocking.

The rest of *Before and After* deals with what happens "After"—that is, after the brutal murder of Martha Taverner at Jacob's hands. Although she chooses to tell this story in the third person, the author does not serve as an omniscient narrator, nor does she use a single character as narrator. Instead, she changes narrators, chapter by chapter, thus at the same time effectively revealing character and presenting the story from different perspectives.

Interestingly, the author permits only Carolyn, Ben, and Judith to serve as narrators. When Jacob confesses to his family, more than halfway through the novel, his account is incorporated in Ben's narration. This is one reason for the fact that, as critics have complained, Jacob never does become a fully realized character. It may be that Brown eliminated Jacob from the work of narration for that very purpose. Certainly the agony of the other major characters stems in part from their uncertainty about who Jacob really is: a normal adolescent who has had a momentary lapse, or a sadistic person whose real nature has been concealed from his family and perhaps from himself.

*Before and After* is divided into three parts, each of which takes one phase of the dramatic action to completion. In the first part, the body of Martha Taverner is discovered, and the police chief comes to the Reiser home to question Jacob, who was one of Martha's boyfriends. Jacob, however, has disappeared. In the days that follow, his parents are torn between their fears that something might have happened to him and their realization that if he is safe, as they hope, his flight suggests that he is guilty of the crime. When they begin to receive postcards in his handwriting, mailed from various parts of the country, they are reassured but puzzled. Finally, the family is notified that Jacob is in Cambridge, Massachusetts.

The second part of *Before and After* begins with Jacob's arrest in Cambridge and his return to Hyland, where the attempts of the police to question him meet with no success. Jacob will not speak, either to the authorities or to his family. Despite his silence, however, most of the community considers him to be guilty, and as a result, Jacob and his family are treated as pariahs. Ben's friends suddenly have no time for him; Carolyn's patients disappear; and at her school, Judith is tormented and ostracized. Then, when Jacob does find his voice, it is only to confess to his family that he did indeed kill Martha. According to his story, she had goaded him mercilessly, but in any case, he admits that he struck her repeatedly. This new knowledge is even more troubling than his silence, which at least left some room for speculation.

Judith is the narrator throughout almost all the final section. After establishing the fact that the four Reisers have moved to Houston, she proceeds to explain what happened when Jacob was tried. Stubbornly, Ben refused to testify against his son. In contrast, Carolyn told the truth, thus becoming a reluctant witness for the prosecution. A talented defense attorney, however, negated her account of Jacob's confession by painting her as a jealous, fantasy-ridden mother. The result was a hung jury, a retrial, and another hung jury. Jacob was released. Ben was sentenced to six months in the county jail for his part in concealing the crime and obstructing justice.

Although *Before and After* has many of the qualities of a good mystery story, such as an initial murder, uncertainty about the identity of the culprit, the accumulation of clues, a confession, and a trial, the focus of this novel is quite different from that of

such works. In *Before and After*, none of the major characters is dedicated to a search
for the truth about the murder, nor do any of them achieve certainty as to what really
happened. Instead, each of them discovers two other truths: that human beings are at
the mercy of the irrational and that they are destined to be isolated, alienated exiles on
this earth.

Before the events of the novel, Ben could not have realized how much his pleasant
life depended on the rational structures created by society and by Carolyn. He took for
granted the community activities, the household routines, the easy solutions of minor
problems, all of which freed him to work at his own creations. In his sculptures, Ben
could let his imagination run loose. He could invent unrealistic, fanciful figures only
peripherally connected to the real world.

It is not surprising that when the real world comes to him, in the person of the police
chief, Ben's instinct is to reject it and, in the manner of an artist, to create something
to take its place. What he does, without thinking, is remove the evidence of murder
from the car trunk where Jacob had thrown it and, in an act that is symbolically
significant, hide it among the raw materials he uses for his sculptures. This time,
however, Ben cannot keep his creation separate from the world of reality. Although
his irrational action saves Jacob from being convicted, Ben himself is haunted by
feelings of guilt. For months, he is unable to work at his art. When at last he returns
to it, he has not lost his technique but he has lost his innocence. There is a new hardness
in what he produces.

In contrast to Ben, Carolyn is guided not by instinct and imagination but by her faith
in reason. Herself a rational, practical, and moral person, she expects other people to
behave as she would in their position. Therefore she, too, loses her innocence when
she discovers how irrational the people of her community can be. Carolyn cannot
understand why patients who seemed so attached to her no longer come to her, just
because her son is a suspect in a murder case. Surely, she thinks, whatever Jacob has
done, she herself is the same person and the same skilled doctor that she was before.
Her empty office, however, is evidence of the triumph of unreason.

It is Carolyn's very dedication to the pursuit of truth, the basis of both her character
and her training, that causes a breach between her and Ben, at a time when they most
need each other. Unlike Ben, Carolyn does not construct alternate worlds. Therefore,
she is shocked when Ben conceals evidence, appalled when he insists that the family
modify or forget Jacob's confession. Despite Ben's disapproval at what he considers
her rejection of her son, Carolyn bravely tells the truth at the trial, only to be attacked
by the defense counsel the family has hired, who, ironically, accuses her of inventing
her story out of an irrational maternal possessiveness. Carolyn has paid a high price
for her faith in reason, in other people, and in the truth. As Judith says, though the
lawyer compared her to spiteful Medea, she seems more like a heartbroken Jocasta,
plunged into despair by her knowledge of wrong.

In some ways, it is Judith who suffers most of all, primarily because she understands
her brother better than either of their parents do. A rulebound person like her mother,
Judith has long been torn between her love for Jacob, who can be so charming on

occasion, and her knowledge that he is a dangerous person. Only Judith knows how cruelly he once tortured a little dog, indifferent to its suffering; only Judith knew how insistent he was on involving her in sexual acts, performed in the absence of their parents. While Judith realizes that part of her distress stems from her feeling neglected while her parents are so concerned about Jacob, she is certain that, more profoundly, she is aware of living in a moral vacuum. Jacob has sinned, but he has not repented. He has not even been punished. When she realizes that Jacob will not ever have to pay for his crime, Judith loses the faith in a moral universe that has always been the basis of her admirable character.

As for Jacob, at the novel's end he is even more an unknown quantity than he was at the beginning. Before the murder, he had been impetuous and imaginative, like his father. Afterward, he has become withdrawn and passive. Although she does not know as much about Jacob as Judith does, Carolyn worries about his behavior. He is the kind of person, she thinks, who might one day murder all of them.

A less honest writer might have brought the Reiser family together in the final pages for a feast of forgiveness and the promise of a new beginning. It is to Rosellen Brown's credit that she avoids such a sentimental ending to this compelling novel. From the truths that the Reisers have learned, there is no turning back. Carolyn's faith in reason, Judith's faith in a moral order, and Ben's faith in the goodness of the imagination all have been shattered. Having discovered the power of the irrational to destroy them, they can never again feel safe. Having discovered the isolation that is the human condition, they can never again feel truly loved. The scene which concludes the novel, balancing the prologue, emphasizes their new, tragic knowledge. To a casual observer, it is another scene of family pleasure. The four Reisers are in a boat together, paddling along a bayou and enjoying a perfect day. What they now know, however, is that if they are together, it is only because they are bound by the same experiences. There are no real bonds between them beyond the memory of a tragedy and the fact of exile.

*Rosemary M. Canfield Reisman*

## Sources for Further Study

*Chicago Tribune.* September 6, 1992, XIV, p. 1.
*Houston Post.* September 20, 1992, p. E1.
*Los Angeles Times.* September 3, 1992, p. E4.
*The Nation.* CCLV, September 28, 1992, p. 333.
*The New Republic.* CCVII, November 2, 1992, p. 40.
*The New York Review of Books.* XL, January 14, 1993, p. 36.
*The New York Times Book Review.* XCVII, August 23, 1992, p. 1.
*Publishers Weekly.* CCXXXIX, August 31, 1992, p. 54.
*The Washington Post Book World.* XXII, August 30, 1992, p. 3.
*Women's Review of Books.* X, November, 1992, p. 5.

## THE BEGINNINGS OF WESTERN SCIENCE
### The European Scientific Tradition in Philosophical, Religious, and Institutional Context, 600 B.C. to A.D. 1450

*Author:* David C. Lindberg (1935-      )
*Publisher:* University of Chicago Press (Chicago). Illustrated. 455 pp. $57.00; paperback $19.95
*Type of work:* History of science
*Time:* 600 B.C. to A.D. 1450
*Locale:* Western Europe, North Africa, and the Middle East

*A survey of science in Western Europe from pre-Socratic Greece until the Renaissance*

*Principal personages:*
> THOMAS AQUINAS, the thirteenth century Italian philosopher who established "Christian Aristotelianism"
> ARISTOTLE, a Greek philosopher whose thought dominated both late antiquity and the thirteenth through fifteenth centuries
> GALEN OF PERGAMUM, the leading medical authority in antiquity
> IBN RUSHD (AVERROËS), a twelfth century Muslim commentator on Aristotle
> NICOLE ORESME, a fourteenth century Parisian philosopher and theologian

Research into the roots of modern Western science has flourished since World War II. Building upon the prewar work of Pierre Duhem, Charles Homer Haskins, and Lynn Thorndike, two generations of historians have compared, edited, translated, and interpreted texts. Their scholarship has been complemented by students of ancient and medieval philosophy, theology, pedagogy, and institutions. As a result, the understanding that specialists have of pre-sixteenth century science was altered greatly in the latter half of the twentieth century. Most of this scholarship, however, has been available only in scholarly journals and specialized monographs. The knowledge has not been synthesized, particularly not in a format accessible to the nonspecialist.

In this outstanding book, Lindberg, one of the most respected American historians of medieval science, provides that accessible synthesis in the first English-language history since World War II to integrate Greco-Roman (pre A.D. 500) and medieval (A.D. 500-1450) science into a single study. *The Beginnings of Western Science* is also the first postwar history to balance discussions of medieval mathematical and physical sciences with those of the biomedical sciences (previous surveys of science during the Middle Ages have emphasized the physical and mathematical sciences), and it is the first to blend analysis of scientific thought with concern for the larger intellectual and institutional context, especially the role of religion.

This multifaceted book will meet the needs of readers with varying goals. Those unfamiliar with the field, looking for an introduction founded in the latest scholarship, will benefit from a narrative presented with clarity, precision, and sensitivity. An experienced teacher, Lindberg frequently writes as if he were lecturing to a group of bright undergraduates who, he assumes, have little or no prior knowledge of the history of science, the history of philosophy, or medieval history, and do not have the time to immerse themselves in the ancient or medieval worlds. He recognizes that there is a great danger that such individuals will bring twentieth century values to bear in their interpretations of the thought or motivations of those who lived in those very different times. Time and again, carefully and cogently, Lindberg admonishes the reader not to judge the work of intellectuals who lived half a millennium or more ago by current standards of good or bad science.

Lindberg also warns that the usages of the word "science" in the twentieth century are very ambiguous. He identifies at least eight different meanings of the word, ranging from highly technical philosophical definitions to common everyday usage. Science has been defined in terms of patterns of behavior; bodies of theoretical knowledge; the form in which knowledge is presented, such as laws presented in mathematical formulae; a methodology (for example, experiments, or simply procedures characterized by rigor, precision, or objectivity); epistemological status; or content. "Science" has even become a term of approbation, used as a label to distinguish between activities that we esteem and those of which we do not approve, irrespective of the subject or content.

Faced with the imprecise nature of the word "science," Lindberg chooses to use the terms "science" and "natural philosophy" fairly interchangeably. Science is more familiar; natural philosophy more closely captures his meaning. He also distinguishes between the craft and theoretical aspects of science and limits himself to the latter. Hence, in the modern sense of the term "science," Lindberg's book is a survey of scientific theory. In ancient and medieval context, however, he is analyzing investigations of, and thoughts about, nature. He does not care whether the methodology used by the investigators and the definition of nature meet twentieth century standards for scientific research.

The first third of the book deals with the ancient world. Lindberg appraises Greco-Roman cosmology, philosophy, the mathematical sciences, and medicine. He provides insight into the educational systems, temples, and other institutional contexts within which scientific knowledge was created, disseminated, or sometimes opposed. The central figure in this discussion is Aristotle, whose thought dominated his successors in the ancient world and, after his rediscovery in the eleventh century, the medieval world. What distinguishes Lindberg's discussion is his emphasis on appreciating the power of Aristotle's insights and understanding Aristotle in context. Lindberg rejects the thesis that Aristotle was a dominant force in European thought simply through the authority of the Roman Catholic church. Instead, he argues that Aristotle's ideas were admired and followed because they successfully explained the way the world worked, at least the world as seen through the eyes of Europeans before A.D. 1600. If Aristotle was frequently "wrong" according to modern interpretations of nature, it was not because of stupidity or backwardness. His methodology was in concert with his worldview and the questions he asked of nature.

The second third of the book covers the first thirteen centuries of the Common Era. After discussing the transition in the West from the ancient to the medieval world,

Lindberg dedicates a chapter to the rise and fall of science in the Islamic world. He approaches Islamic science as the end product of the diffusion and assimilation of Greek science in parts of North Africa and Asia. In turn, Islamic science served as a means of transmission of Greek science back to Western Europe. The narrative then takes up the revival of learning in the West, especially during the twelfth century. Throughout this middle section of the book, Lindberg stresses the complex relationship between religion, whether Christian or Islam, and science. In both cultures, science had to serve as a handmaiden to theology. Scientific study usually was justified in terms of religious utility. Conflict with theology was to be avoided, especially conflict in which science was viewed as attempting to limit the power of God. This conception of science as handmaiden to theology goes back at least to Saint Augustine in the fourth century.

In the concluding third of the book, Lindberg surveys late medieval science. He provides separate chapters on astronomy, the physical sciences, and medicine and natural history. With the aid of figures and some wonderful contemporary illustrations (there are other fine illustrations scattered through the book), Lindberg summarizes the state of scientific knowledge in Europe at the birth of the Renaissance.

The historiography of early Western science has not been devoid of controversy. Lindberg integrates those debates over interpretation into his narrative. He summarizes the major historiographic issues that have confronted specialists in the field and the responses of those specialists. Although he has his own opinions, which he explicitly delineates, Lindberg is fair, judicious, and balanced in these historiographic discussions. He is especially good at portraying the factions and issues of the continuity debate. Throughout the twentieth century, historians have argued whether the scientific revolution of the sixteenth and seventeenth centuries—a shorthand reference to the thoughts and publications of Nicolas Copernicus, Johannes Kepler, Galileo, and Isaac Newton, to name a few—represented a break from, and even a repudiation of, medieval learning and traditions, or was built upon and can be viewed as a continuation of the teachings of the medieval scientists.

Lindberg manages to agree, in part, with both sides. He accepts the argument that there was discontinuity at the largest metaphysical and methodological level. Viewed from that perspective, the scientific revolution was all about change. It was nothing less than a rejection of the Aristotelian metaphysics that had dominated medieval thought. From the perspective of the history of individual disciplines such as optics, astronomy, physiology, and natural history, however, there was considerable continuity between the medieval and modern periods. Practices, objectives, and principles remained the same. In short, Lindberg warns the reader that historical study offers few simple, pat answers. Approach a historical question from a different angle and you will arrive at a different, equally valid answer.

For those readers wishing to go more deeply into the subject on their own, Lindberg's endnotes provide a critical commentary on the bibliography of the field. The bibliography itself runs thirty-five pages. There is nothing equivalent to it for publications in English.

This is not the last word on any particular aspect of early European science. For most of the topics, time periods, or disciplines, there are many other publications, each providing extensive detail and analysis not given by Lindberg. For those looking for an accurate, stimulating, insightful introduction, however, this is the book to which they should turn.

*Marc Rothenberg*

## Sources for Further Study

*Choice*. XXX, December, 1992, p. 642.
*Library Journal*. CXVII, July, 1992, p. 117.
*Nature*. CCCLX, December 24, 1992, p. 713.
*The New York Times Book Review*. XCVII, September 20, 1992, p. 49.
*Science News*. CXLI, June 27, 1992, p. 418.

# "BEYOND REASONABLE DOUBT" AND "PROBABLE CAUSE"
## Historical Perspectives on the Anglo-American Law of Evidence

*Author:* Barbara J. Shapiro (1934-     )
*Publisher:* University of California Press (Berkeley). 365 pp. $42.50
*Type of work:* History
*Time:* 1500-1800
*Locale:* England and the United States

*This intellectual history traces the evolution of contemporary standards of behavior for Anglo-American juries and criminal justice officials at the trial and pretrial stages, linking the development of legal notions of evidence and truth to those of science, philosophy, and theology*

In this book, Barbara J. Shapiro, a professor of rhetoric and author of two previous works on seventeenth century intellectual history, explores the roots of two key doctrines in contemporary Anglo-American criminal procedures: the standard mandating that criminal charges must be proved "beyond a reasonable doubt" and that prohibiting the arrest and prosecution of defendants without some minimum evidence to serve as "probable cause." Shapiro's interest is not with formal legal constructs regarding admissibility of evidence, right to bail, and the like. She seeks a fuller understanding of the guidelines informing juries in their decision making once trial evidence has been submitted and, similarly, those informing public officials and juries in their decisions whether to prosecute suspected criminals. These focal points are not easily researched. Jury behavior, for the most part, has been shielded from open observation. Likewise, the details of prosecutorial discretion are not easily recovered by means of even the most fastidious historical research. Still, through the examination of numerous practical handbooks of the times, formal treatises by dozens of theorists and commentators, and public records, Shapiro is able to construct a reasonably coherent account of and explanation for the emergence of "beyond a reasonable doubt," "probable cause," and related doctrines as fundamental principles of Anglo-American criminal justice.

Shapiro's research revolves around three basic themes. First, she seeks out the interaction between legal and other intellectual conceptualizations of evidence, probability, and truth. In this sense, Shapiro's study might be said to be "contextual," that is, one that strives to set legal ideas into a broader social and intellectual setting. Second, Shapiro examines the "migration" of evidentiary guidelines among various institutions and procedures in the criminal justice process. She wishes, therefore, to study the circulation of ideas within the criminal process as well as between the criminal process and broader society. Third, Shapiro is interested in any connections that might exist between English law and the Romano-canon tradition of evidentiary procedure.

Shapiro manages to make scholarly headway regarding all three of these themes. As is usually the case in histories of ideas, Shapiro examines a dizzyingly broad variety of tracts and authors. The latter include empiricists Francis Bacon and John Locke, social reformer Jeremy Bentham, and common law authorities Sir William Blackstone and Sir Edward Coke, as well as many less well-known figures. This research indicates a parallel, but often cross-pollinating, relationship between the secularization of thought (and ultimate emergence of empirical science) and rationalization of criminal procedures. Just as philosophers and enlightened theologians were sometimes anxiously, sometimes reluctantly separating the spheres of reason and faith, legal theorists and criminal justice officials were moving toward more objective, logical, and empirical procedures. The doctrines of "beyond a reasonable doubt" and "probable cause" emerged in the context of these interrelated intellectual quests. Like scientific method, they are based on an ideal of intersubjectivity. Whereas scientific conclusions are based on the empirically testable findings of a community of scholars, the modern doctrines of criminal procedure examined by Shapiro are based on evidence (preferably empirical, but also circumstantial) which, in the eyes of any reasonable person, would justify the trial and/or conviction of a defendant. It should be noted that neither standard claims infallibility or certainty. In science, all conclusions are open to future tests and revision. In criminal justice, conclusions are based on as high a level of probability as possible rather than on certainty. Following the epistemological findings of the times, legal theorists had to accept uncertainty in order to maintain public order. The doctrines of "beyond a reasonable doubt" and "probable cause" are designed to legitimate criminal justice decision making in the absence of either divine authority or secular certainty.

Shapiro's research also indicates a clear pattern of migration of doctrines among different criminal justice institutions and procedures. Most specifically, she follows the progression of "probable cause" from the stage of arrest to the processes of search and seizure, the preliminary hearing, and ultimately the American grand jury. In describing this migration, Shapiro does a good job of laying out the central problem addressed by the concept of "probable cause," that of devising a standard of evidence that would prevent capricious prosecution while avoiding duplication of the trial itself. Indeed, Shapiro believes that this problem is one that has never quite been solved. An exact point at which the evidence warrants a full-blown trial without clearly indicating guilt has proved most elusive.

Finally, Shapiro's findings indicate a fair amount of borrowing from the Romano-canon law and procedures of the European continent. English writers were loath to admit such borrowing, partly for chauvinistic reasons and partly to avoid association with such continental practices as the inquisition and selective torture (though in its most elevated form, even torture had to be based on some early version of "probable cause"). Nevertheless, Shapiro finds numerous examples of such borrowing, usually accompanied by creative fudging in the citation of sources. As a result, she suggests that the emergence of "beyond a reasonable doubt" and "probable cause" can be understood as a joint product of English common law and Romano-canon (or "civil") sources.

In addition to these significant findings on her chosen themes, Shapiro provides valuable insight into the processes of historical change writ large. Although "beyond a reasonable doubt" and "probable cause" are a familiar part of our social landscape, an observer of juries in the Middle Ages would have found far different standards of operation, ones that in all likelihood would offend a modern sense of justice. More specifically, while modern legal systems, at least in theory, try to exclude prejudice and subjectivity from criminal proceedings, medieval juries based their decisions in large part on previous knowledge, or opinions, of the crimes committed and persons allegedly involved. Modern standards of fact-gathering and evidence were relatively unknown. Shapiro does a good job of showing the untidy, seemingly glacial process of changing collective standards of behavior. This may seem utterly foreign to contemporary readers accustomed to highly visible, rapid-fire socioeconomic and political change. The constant, almost hourly, change of the sort covered on nightly television news broadcasts and in books on popular culture should not blind observers to that dimension of social evolution which lies below the surface. This latter variety of change is usually unplanned and may be difficult to identify, but it is often the most crucial for future generations.

One example of gradual change mentioned in Shapiro's study and highly pertinent to everyday life involves the response to allegations of witchcraft. To modern minds, the arrest, prosecution, and punishment of witches seems intolerably superstitious and brutal. It also offends a modern sense of criminal justice, since witches, by their very nature, were supposed to be able to elude ordinary measures in terms of evidence and proof. In fact, witchcraft was held to be in a special class of crimes for which the standards of evidence had to be lowered. (Interestingly enough, rape also was often accorded such a status because of its inherent privacy and lack of witnesses.) The rise of modern standards of evidence and proof gradually rendered the crime of witchcraft irrelevant, since it could not be prosecuted according to those standards. By the eighteenth century, witchcraft laws were being taken off the books. This occurred not because of some investigative reporter's undercover work or because of a mass demonstration, but because slowly changing standards of criminal procedure came to exclude the sort of tainted evidence needed to prosecute witches.

Shapiro's study also has some rather important and disturbing implications. Although it is easy and entirely appropriate to see her tale as one of progress, important caveats must be noted. First, progress toward a rational and fair criminal process has not been uniform or complete. As Shapiro makes clear, practice has not necessarily been in accord with theory or doctrine. The American criminal process in particular has been subject to severe racial discrimination. Although this has been somewhat alleviated in recent years, the cost of high-quality legal representation leads systematically to socioeconomic distortions of justice, with poor defendants substantially disadvantaged in the system.

There is a more fundamental problem, however. Even if incidental inequalities such as those mentioned above could somehow be eliminated, the standards of criminal justice studied by Shapiro have inherent weaknesses, since in many cases they lead to findings based on high probability rather than on the certainty one would like to have when depriving defendants of their freedom or even their lives. Eyewitnesses remain remarkably unreliable, and juries are notoriously fickle and unpredictable. Moreover, the system is far from free of mistakes. Guilty defendants seem routinely to go free while, and perhaps less routinely, convicted defendants are shown to have been innocent. In short, the modern criminal process, even at its very best, remains problematic and, all too often, unsatisfactory. This is even more true when one considers difficulties with the concepts of free will, determinism, social causation, and culpability that also challenge the basic tenets of criminal justice.

This failure to transcend fully the subjectivity and caprice of previous standards of criminal prosecution and jury decision making is magnified in a society such as that of the United States, in which criminal justice is mass-produced in order to serve as a primary source of public order. Examined in this light, the existence of a massive criminal justice establishment may itself be seen as a major social problem, particularly when widespread practices such as plea bargaining are clearly based on the presumption of guilt.

As Shapiro is well aware, this study has shortcomings. For one thing, as mentioned above, it is based on an examination of various published doctrines rather than on a record of actual practices, the latter being historically unrecoverable. Although Shapiro believes it is reasonable to presume the probability of a somewhat positive relationship between doctrine and actual practice, she is admittedly unable to demonstrate such a relationship with any degree of thoroughness. In addition, she spends relatively little time distinguishing between American and English procedures. Finally, because of its considerable breadth of coverage and multiplicity of sources, the book is not nearly as readable as one might like. These weaknesses, however, do not neutralize the book's assets. Shapiro has effectively explored a historical moment of note, one that helps in an understanding of the roots and reason of criminal justice procedures as well as their limitations.

*Ira Smolensky*

## Sources for Further Study

*American Journal of Criminal Law*. XIX, Spring, 1992, p. 519.
*Choice*. XXX, September, 1992, p. 218.

# BLACK DOGS

*Author:* Ian McEwan (1948-    )
*Publisher:* Doubleday (New York). 149 pp. $19.50
Type *of work:* Novel
Time: 1946-1989
*Locale:* Great Britain, France, Germany, Poland, and Italy

*An encounter with enormous dogs while on her honeymoon changes a woman's view of the world and puts a philosophical strain on her marriage*

> *Principal characters:*
> JEREMY, the narrator, an English publisher
> JUNE TREMAINE, his mother-in-law, a writer
> BERNARD TREMAINE, her husband, a politician
> JENNY, their daughter, Jeremy's wife
> SALLY, Jeremy's niece

Many of the themes explored in Ian McEwan's previous fiction are treated anew in *Black Dogs*: the pain and isolation of childhood, as in *The Cement Garden* (1978); the inexplicable, violent nature of evil, as in *The Comfort of Strangers* (1981); and the effect of political, social, and psychological forces on the individual, as in *The Innocent* (1990). *Black Dogs* combines these subjects with religious and political beliefs and the history of twentieth century Europe as McEwan creates another original view of contemporary chaos.

Jeremy, the narrator, grows up in London longing for replacements for his dead parents. Living with Jean, his older sister, Harper, her loutish husband, and Sally, their neglected daughter, Jeremy spends considerable time with his friends' parents. He hopes to find the stability, comfort, intellectual stimulation, and love missing from his life—except for the affection he attempts to provide to Sally, his honorary fellow orphan.

Jeremy remains partially dissociated from life until he, at the age of thirty-seven, marries Jenny Tremaine, adopting her parents as his own. June and Bernard Tremaine are Communists when they marry in 1946, but on their honeymoon in France, June undergoes a spiritual crisis. Although the couple remain in love until June's death in 1987, their philosophical differences mar their relationship. Bernard leaves the party after the 1956 Hungarian uprising, writes a well-received biography of Gamal Abdel Nasser, becomes a frequent guest on radio and television broadcasts, and is elected to Parliament in 1964. June lives in France most of this time, writing about wildflowers and mystical subjects.

When June's health forces her into an English nursing home, Jeremy visits her for interviews upon which he will base a memoir. McEwan offers only brief glimpses of the pivotal event in June's life until he presents Jeremy's memoir as the fourth and final major section of *Black Dogs*. By that time, he has masterfully created a mythic significance for June's battle with two black dogs.

*Black Dogs* is compelling on several levels. One is as a portrait of June, Bernard, and their unusual marriage. June's sensibility dominates the novel, with Jeremy almost as much in love with her, despite her difficult personality, as with Jenny, her daughter and his wife. Jeremy and June disagree about the focus of the memoir during the interviews, June wanting him to write a biography, Jeremy having in mind "more a divagation" in which she will be central but not dominant. In writing about June, Jeremy says as much about himself, tries to explain to himself the nature of evil and the spirit of his times.

Contributing to Jeremy's obsession with his mother-in-law is a photograph taken the day she and Bernard became members of the Communist Party of Great Britain. Jeremy seeks the woman's character in the picture, the woman she is to become. He wonders at how June could have been so profoundly altered by time, her face becoming long, her nose lengthened, chin curved, forehead amazingly creased. The wrinkled June resembles the elderly W. H. Auden: "In repose her face had a chiseled, sepulchral look; it was a statue, a mask carved by a shaman to keep at bay the evil spirit." Jeremy thinks that June's face changed to accommodate her belief that she has been tested by evil. Attracted to the younger June, he sees in her older self something "extraordinary."

Jeremy describes June's life as a spiritual quest, but Bernard, evolving from Communist outsider to liberal politician, is almost her opposite. Bernard is also a man of contradictions. Although a socialist, he disdains the working class. When a taxi driver attempts to enter his and Jeremy's conversation about the state of Europe, Bernard rudely ignores the man. In justifying his lack of a common touch by explaining that he is a man of ideas, Bernard illustrates the rationalism June abhors. The difference between the two is clear even while June is confronted by the dogs. Bernard is three hundred yards away, sketching caterpillars: "Bernard did not derive pleasure from sketching, nor did his drawings resemble what he saw. They represented what he knew, or wanted to know."

McEwan presents this marriage as one in which the partners share little but their love. June constantly ridicules Bernard to Jeremy, considering him "unreflective, ignorant of the subtle currents that composed the reality he insisted he understood and controlled." Bernard neglects visiting his dying wife, attempting to maneuver Jeremy into conveying "the illusion that he was perfectly intact without her" and that he loves her "despite her evident madness."

Bernard, at least, acknowledges his failings in their relationship: "I was cold, theoretical, arrogant. I never showed any emotion, and I prevented her from showing it. She felt watched, analyzed, she felt she was part of my insect collection." June attacks him for wanting to organize everything neatly. His political beliefs stem not from compassion for his fellow man but from a need to impose order on society. Bernard criticizes June for bending facts to fit her view of the world: "My wife might have been interested in poetic truth, or spiritual truth, or her own private truth, but she didn't give a damn for *truth*, for the facts, for the kind of truth that two people could recognize independently of each other." Jeremy accuses them both of loading each other with their own guilt.

Jeremy is fascinated by this couple not only because they are his substitute parents but also because he has lacked a system of belief: "there was simply no good cause, no enduring principle, no fundamental idea with which I could identify, no transcendent entity whose existence I could truthfully, passionately, or quietly assert." He represents the contemporary bourgeois European: materially comfortable, slightly cynical, satisfied with his disbelief. As a teenager, Jeremy is most at ease when playing with Sally, since he mistrusts and fears the outside world. He separates himself from his contemporaries by intellectual pomposity and disdain for their activities: "They could range freely because they were secure; I needed the hearths they had deserted." After leaving the University of Oxford without a degree, Jeremy establishes a drifter's pattern of leaving dwellings, jobs, friends, and lovers until he finds Jenny and commitment, then becomes a parent himself.

Comfortable with retreating into the family he and Jenny create, Jeremy remains mostly disengaged from the larger world until he visits the site of his in-laws' honeymoon. Seeing a boy mistreated by his parents in a hotel restaurant, Jeremy is challenged by the father and responds by beating him severely: "I knew that the elation driving me had nothing to do with revenge and justice." He sees in himself the savage potential lurking beneath the placid exterior of modern Europe.

This savagery is best exemplified by the dogs June encounters at St. Maurice de Navacelles. She sees two huge black dogs in the distance and immediately begins attaching greater significance to them: "they were the embodiment of the nameless, unreasonable, unmentionable disquiet she had felt that morning." She is frightened of them not because they are dogs but because they are so enormous and have appeared out of nowhere in this isolated setting. She falls, cuts her arm, and, terrified that the blood will provoke their attack, defends herself with rocks. When one leaps onto her, she stabs it with a penknife until both beasts run away.

June and Bernard later learn from the villagers that the dogs had been brought there by the Gestapo during the German occupation. The mayor claims that two men saw the dogs being forced to rape a woman, but Bernard refuses to believe this tale, saying that June trusts it because it fits so neatly into her interpretation of her experience. June considers her instinctive understanding of the dogs' evil to be the essence of her spiritual transformation. For June, her battle with the dogs "explained everything— why she left the party, . . . why she reconsidered her rationalism, her materialism, how she came to live the life she did, where she lived it, what she thought." Jeremy is skeptical about the overwhelming significance attached to one event until his beating of the brutish father. How June translates the evil of the dogs into what she calls "an infinite resource, a potential for a higher state of being, a goodness" is another matter.

When Jeremy visits Poland in 1981 as part of a cultural delegation and meets Jenny, she insists that he accompany her to the concentration camp of Majdanek. When she notices that the sign listing the nationalities of the victims does not mention Jews, she says to herself, "The black dogs." Jeremy, who accompanies Bernard to Berlin to see the collapse of the Berlin Wall only to be caught up in a potentially fatal mob scene, comes to see the dogs as symbolic of tyranny in Europe. The novel ends with his vision of the dogs moving "into the foothills of the mountains from where they will return to haunt us, somewhere in Europe, in another time."

The nature of belief is at the center of *Black Dogs*. Jeremy finds himself annoyed both by June's "optimistic prattle" and by Bernard's "sonorous platitudes." In an imaginary argument with them, Jeremy says, "It's not the business of science to prove or disprove the existence of God, and it's not the business of the spirit to measure the world." He finds Bernard's skepticism too arrogant and June's faith too smugly virtuous. To Jeremy, his in-laws "are the extremities, the twin poles along whose slippery axis my own unbelief slithers and never comes to rest."

Like all McEwan's novels, *Black Dogs* is a meditation on alienation. June retreats from it into spirituality, Bernard into socialism, Jeremy into family life. McEwan suggests that contemporary religion and politics offer no solutions to life's complexities and that sincerely caring for those closest to one is as good a defense against alienation as any. Jeremy states his humanistic belief "in the possibility of love transforming and redeeming a life." June admits that despite their philosophical differences, she and Bernard love each other deeply. Their love, however, is insufficient to create "a simple society" in which they can coexist easily.

*Black Dogs*, which lacks the irony and dark humor of most of McEwan's fiction, is an eloquently pessimistic view of the future of civilization. Nazism can be defeated, totalitarian dictatorships can collapse, yet new horrors will arise. Individuals cannot prevent or effectively combat such evil. They can only, McEwan implies, hope to hold off the chaos in their daily lives.

*Michael Adams*

### Sources for Further Study

*Booklist*. LXXXIX, October 15, 1992, p. 402.
*The Guardian*. June 18, 1992, p. 27.
*Library Journal*. CXVII, October 1, 1992, p. 120.
*London Review of Books*. XIV, June 25, 1992, p. 20.
*Los Angeles Times Book Review*. December 20, 1992, p. 3.
*The New Republic*. CCVII, November 16, 1992, p. 41.
*New Statesman and Society*. V, June 19, 1992, p. 26.
*The New York Times Book Review*. XCVII, November 8, 1992, p. 7.
*Publishers Weekly*. CCXXXIX, September 14, 1992, p. 103.
*The Spectator*. CCLXVIII, June 27, 1992, p. 32.
*Time*. CXL, November 16, 1992, p. 103.
*The Times Literary Supplement*. June 19, 1992, p. 20.
*The Wall Street Journal*. November 16, 1992, p. A8.
*The Washington Post Book World*. XXII, October 25, 1992, p. 4.

# BLACK WATER

*Author:* Joyce Carol Oates (1938-    )
*Publisher:* E.P. Dutton (New York). 154 pp. $17.00
*Type of work:* Novel
*Time:* July 4, 1991
*Locale:* Grayling Island, Maine; Boston; and Washington, D.C.

*In this taut novella based on recent history, a man identified only as "The Senator" drives a young woman away from a Fourth of July party for the night, only to plunge into a deep creek where he abandons her and she drowns*

*Principal characters:*
> KELLY (ELIZABETH ANNE) KELLEHER, a twenty-six-year-old writer living in Boston
> THE SENATOR, a powerful Massachusetts politician who meets Kelly at a Fourth of July party
> BUFFY ST. JOHN, Kelly's closest friend, who is staying at her parents' home in Maine

*Black Water* is a fictional tragedy that refuses to abandon its origins in personal political history. "The Senator," whose name is never given beyond this title, arrives at a Fourth of July party on Grayling Island, off Boothbay Harbor, Maine. During the course of the afternoon that he spends talking, drinking, and playing tennis with the younger people gathered at the party, he meets and captivates Kelly Kelleher, and the two of them leave that evening to catch the last ferry off the island, to have dinner in Boothbay Harbor, and, presumably, to spend the night at the motel where the senator is staying.

But something goes terribly wrong. The drunken senator misses the ferry road and ends up on a narrow and abandoned track. Kelly repeats several times, "I think we're lost, Senator," but it is Kelly who is finally lost. In the rush to catch the ferry, the rented Toyota skids and plunges into a deep creek. The car overturns in the water. The Senator escapes by crawling over Kelly, and the young woman, who is still pinned in the car, slowly drowns. The Senator stumbles several miles to call a friend for help; the accident, he yells into the phone, was the girl's fault.

If the events sound familiar, they should, for they follow closely the July, 1969, incident at Chappaquiddick, Massachusetts, when Senator Ted Kennedy left the scene of a similar accident and Mary Jo Kopechne was drowned. The major difference is time: The model occurred decades earlier, but Joyce Carol Oates brings this incident up to the fictional present. Still, readers are witnessing an imagined version of recent political, but very personal, history.

The model of the Kennedy character is only thinly disguised. Although his brothers are not mentioned, the senator is otherwise easy to recognize; described as separated from his wife of thirty years, he is a man with a "diminutive first name," "an exhausted middle-aged man beginning to go soft in the gut, steely-gray curly hair thinning at the crown of his head, his left knee . . . sprained back in January playing squash. . . ." As Kelly thinks as she heads toward her death "in the bouncing jolting car":

> Here was one of the immune, beside her: *he*, one of the powerful adults of the world, manly man, U.S. senator, a famous face and a tangled history, empowered to not merely endure history but to guide it, control it, manipulate it to his own ends. He was an old-style liberal Democrat out of the 1960s, a Great Society man with a stubborn and zealous dedication to social reform. . . .

The Senator "had been among the three leading candidates for the Democratic presidential nomination in 1988," Oates tells her readers, but he withdrew "in favor of his old friend the Massachusetts governor," Michael Dukakis. If Ted Kennedy is never named here, most of the other political players are; The Senator, for example, is "eleven years younger than George Bush." Not only the players but also the drama of contemporary politics gets this full Oates treatment:

> During the most recent presidential election Kelly had volunteered her services working for Governor Dukakis's doomed campaign. She had not known the campaign was doomed until the final weeks of the contest, each time she saw or heard George Bush it seemed self-evident to her that anyone who saw or heard him must naturally reject him, for how transparently hypocritical! how venal! how crass! how uninformed! how *evil*! his exploitation of whites' fears of blacks, his CIA affiliation!

Oates is using undigested political history here, as the people at the party

> spoke of the outrage of the recent Supreme Court decisions, the ideologically sanctioned selfishness and cruelty of a wealthy society, how systematic the dismantling of the gains of the civil rights movement, the retirement of Justice Thurgood Marshall, the end of an era.

The Senator tells the younger people around him that afternoon how "the Gulf War has given your generation a tragic idea of war and of diplomacy: the delusion that war is relatively easy, and diplomacy *is* war, the most expedient of options."

The center of the novel, however, is less the powerful senator and contemporary history than Kelly Kelleher, a naïve young woman who is the innocent victim of The Senator's political and sexual power. Ironically, Kelly wrote her senior honors thesis at Brown University on The Senator, and her collegiate idealism still thrives: She not only writes articles now on issues such as capital punishment for the liberal *Citizens' Inquiry* (an article that The Senator thinks he may have read), but she also teaches two nights a week in a literacy program in Roxbury, in inner-city Boston. Kelly is a young woman with a history of acne, but not much else; she will not talk about her one lover and has regularly starved herself as self-punishment for her imagined failures. The child of a rich suburban family, she ends up at the bottom of a creek with a fractured skull and a broken kneecap, trapped in a slowly sinking car, and abandoned by the man to whom she has been so powerfully drawn. The real tragedy in *Black Water* is hers.

> She was fighting to escape the water, she was clutching at a man's muscular forearm even as he
> shoved her away, she was clutching at his trousered leg, his foot, his foot in its crepe-soled canvas
> shoe heavy and crushing upon her striking the side of her head, her left temple so now she did cry
> out in pain and hurt grabbing at his leg frantically, her fingernails tearing, then at his ankle, his foot,
> his shoe, the crepe-soled canvas shoe that came off in her hand so she was left crying, begging,
> "Don't leave me!—help me! Wait!"
> Having no name to call him as the black water rushed upon her to fill her lungs.

The short novel is broken into two parts and thirty-two chapters. Part 1 opens with
a chapter that gives the core action of the book:

> The rented Toyota, driven with such impatient exuberance by The Senator, was speeding along
> the unpaved unnamed road, taking the turns in giddy skidding slides, and then, with no warning,
> somehow the car had gone off the road and had overturned in black rushing water, listing to its
> passenger's side, rapidly sinking.

The following chapters alternate between descriptions of the accident, The Senator's
escape, Kelly's slow drowning, and earlier incidents in the day (the doubles tennis
match he loses, for example, their first kiss, his suggestion that she join his staff) and
in her young life (snippets of scenes with her parents, with Buffy at Brown, with her
earlier lover). Much of the action is described from somewhere within Kelly's
fractured head, and, increasingly in part 2, readers get her fantasies of escape and/or
rescue. The first sentence of chapter 16, for example, which opens part 2, reads: "He
was gone but would come back to save her." Always, as a refrain in the novel, the
water is rising: "As the black water filled her lungs, and she died." This prose has an
intense poetic quality characteristic of Oates at her best; chapter 10, for example,
consists of one two-page sentence that provides tension to the writing and momentum
to the story.

It is a tribute to the power of this writing that, though the outcome of this story is
certain, Oates makes it as exciting as she does. In fact, as Ambrose Bierce did in his
famous 1891 short story "An Occurrence at Owl Creek Bridge"—in which readers
watch a convicted Confederate spy escape only to realize that it was all a dream in the
seconds before he was hung—Oates gives readers the hope that in *this* version of
history, at least, the innocent young woman may in the end escape.

*Black Water* is really a novella; it is only three times as long as "Where Are You
Going, Where Have You Been?", for example, one of Oates's many well-known short
stories. Like that story, or her more recent *Because It Is Bitter, and Because It Is My
Heart*—a 1990 novel nominated for the National Book Award—*Black Water* explores
the theme of what could be called "Death and the Maiden" (the original title for
"Where Are You Going, Where Have You Been?"). In work after work, Oates has
probed this situation of the naïve young woman seduced by some powerful, almost
demonic male figure. In "How I Contemplated the World from the Detroit House of
Corrections and Began My Life Over Again," another often-anthologized Oates story,
the villain is a seductive young drug addict. In "Where Are You Going, Where Have

You Been?", it is Arnold Friend (or "an old fiend," a thinly veiled representation of the devil) who lures Connie to her death. In *Black Water*, the antagonist is much more lifelike and fleshy—but just as evil. Selfish and greedy, The Senator thinks of nothing but trying to save himself. In the end, he does, but another Oates heroine has drowned in the waters of male power and selfishness.

Increasingly in American writing in the last decades of the twentieth century, the line between fiction and nonfiction has been harder and harder to find. Nonfiction writers such as Hunter S. Thompson, Michael Herr, and Gay Talese have invaded the territory of fiction and appropriated most of its weapons. Conversely, novelists— E. L. Doctorow and Kurt Vonnegut, Jr., for example—have felt perfectly legitimate in placing their fictional characters in real worlds peopled by historical figures. As Doctorow has remarked, there are no longer separate categories of fiction and nonfiction today, only narrative.

In *Black Water*, Joyce Carol Oates enters this tradition. There is no denying that the basis for the action in her novella is recent political history, specifically the events at Chappaquiddick. What Oates has accomplished is to make that history taut with terror in the retelling. But in dredging up this tragedy, Oates has made little attempt to disguise its origins, and the reader can only feel a kind of vague discomfort; the history is too recent, the players all too alive—or dead. Doctorow's *Ragtime* (1975), in contrast, uses historical personages at the turn of the century to flesh out the tale; Oates is using living people as the foundation for her fiction, and the difference leads to some elementary questions. If the focus is on Kelly, why use real people? But if the object is The Senator, then why write fiction at all? The fragile line between fiction and nonfiction here disappears.

*David Peck*

## Sources for Further Study

*Booklist*. LXXXVIII, February 15, 1992, p. 1066.
*Boston Globe*. May 21, 1992, p. 92.
*Chicago Tribune*. May 3, 1992, XIV, p. 5.
*Los Angeles Times Book Review*. May 10, 1992, p. 2.
*National Review*. XLIV, June 8, 1992, p. 51.
*New Statesman and Society*. V, October 30, 1992, p. 42.
*The New York Times Book Review*. XCVII, May 10, 1992, p. 1.
*Publishers Weekly*. CCXXXIX, March 9, 1992, p. 47.
*The Times Literary Supplement*. October 16, 1992, p. 22.
*The Washington Post Book World*. XXII, May 17, 1992, p. 11.

# BLUE CALHOUN

*Author:* Reynolds Price (1933-        )
*Publisher:* Atheneum (New York). 364 pp. $23.00
*Type of work:* Novel
*Time:* 1950's-1990's
*Locale:* Raleigh, North Carolina

Blue Calhoun *is Reynolds Price's* Lolita, *but with southern rather than Nabokovian verbal pyrotechnics*

> *Principal characters:*
> BLUFORD CALHOUN, a man the reader follows from the age of thirty-five
>    to his late sixties, as he atones for an early-middle-aged infatuation
> LUNA ABSHER, the sixteen-year-old object of Blue's obsession
> RITA ABSHER, her mother, a "good ol' girl" brought down by bad fortune
> MATTIE CALHOUN, Blue's daughter
> MYRA CALHOUN, Blue's wife

With each passing year, and thus with each new book, Reynolds Price's body of work becomes ever more distinguished. Although this latest effort has been severely criticized by reviewers—indeed, the narrative in this novel is somewhat grim, making it one of Price's darkest works—Price's style, his unique voice and compelling morality, redeem *Blue Calhoun*, the story and the character.

Lest any mistake be made about just whose story is being told, Price turns his tale over to the eponymous narrator, who at the beginning of this tale has all the trappings of a happy life: a fine, Catholic wife, an adoring and beautiful daughter, a wise, if crusty, mother, and a good job. Blue sells instruments in music-loving Raleigh, North Carolina. He is a reformed alcoholic whose daughter shamed him into abandoning the bottle and pills. Asked to leave Davidson College after only one year, he is a soldier home from the war where he killed men, not quite with the same reckless or unthinking determination that had characterized his own dissolute descent into addiction. All in all, as he says, the year between the Aprils of 1956 and 1957 were preceded by a time that "starts with the happiest I ever was, though it brought down suffering on everybody near me." Furthermore, "that one year was built like a story, whoever built it. It had a low start that stoked up fast to such a heat that hinges on doors were melting away; and pent up people were tearing loose and running for what looked like daylight till, at some weird invisible signal, everything started cooling again."

Blue is given to such hyperbole, but considering the circumstances of that year, perhaps he is justified in believing that fate marked him and his for a dark reckoning that is easier explained in such poetic, idiosyncratic language. Blue is a great talker, a great explainer. In this long epistle to his granddaughter, he can be forgiven if he exaggerates in order to escape the blunt truth. Such white-hot honesty burns in the memory.

On that day in 1956, an old school friend, Rita Absher, walks into the music store to buy an autoharp for her daughter. Even at sixteen, Luna, as beautiful and bright as her namesake, is every bit as beguiling and mysterious as the moon. Characteristic of Price's mastery of dialogue that crackles with hidden meaning while getting to the bare bones of truth is this first encounter with Rita and her child, Luna:

> That instant a stock boy passed, bumped me and said "Old *Blue*."
> Rita said "*Blue*?"
> I held in place.
> "Not Blue Calhoun?"
> I nodded and grinned. "—His cold remains."
> She stood a second, then made a little graceful skip and a glide, then took my hands. "If you're cold, child, then cool *my* skin."

Such elliptical but entirely understandable phrases are characteristic of Blue's recollections of events. He is writing this memoir many years later, and if the characters all tend to share his quirkiness of expression, it is because they speak with Blue's voice, one that he acquired naturally from his mother, whose matter-of-fact aphorisms are as piercing as they are original. Given Blue's manner of speech and thought, Luna's symbolic nature—child, daughter, woman, lover—is readily apparent. She is, in short, a dangerous but wholly desirable taboo. Blue Calhoun is an addict, although a reformed one, and Luna is every bit as potent and appealing as any drug: "[D]on't let any expert try to tell you that sweet warm bodies are any less of a maddog craving than all the liquor east of the Rockies or mainline coke."

In short order, he is lost, willing to give up wife, daughter, and home for the chance at another life, a new life with Luna. She is no ordinary girl, having suffered hideous abuse as a child and, consequently, all the more prone to accept Blue precisely because he is an older man and is kind to her. For the rest of that year—twelve months that take up the largest part of this story—Blue learns that his angel-child is also a girl-woman, blessed with sexual knowledge well beyond her years but with all the dreams and high-school ambitions of any other eleventh grader. Hating his guilt even as he is lying to his wife and deceiving his child, he is unrepentant; perhaps only his mother, whom he cavalierly calls Miss Ashlyn, knows the moral turmoil that this obsession stirs in his soul. Yet she is not entirely sympathetic: Moral quandaries are so many Gordian knots; if insoluble, they are to be cut to clear the way to proper conduct.

Blue is surrounded by such women of character. His mother is sharp-tongued and the very pillar of rectitude, blessed with "an absolute certainty of right and wrong." His wife, Myra, is pious to a fault; so patient and long-suffering is she, in fact, that she becomes real only in the tortured, hellish act of dying. Mattie, his daughter, is self-assured, almost smug in her Catholic faith and awful in the singular moment when she denies her father forgiveness. Rita has a gilded heart; her life has robbed her of any chance at gold except perhaps in the lyrical voice of her lovely daughter Luna. None of the characters, even Blue, is so simply depicted that he or she can be reduced easily to an abstraction. Even Luke, Luna's ex-convict half-brother with whom she possibly has an incestuous relationship, is not entirely evil. His shortcomings, whether hereditary or learned, are explicable and somehow hidden by "white trash" charm.

Throughout his writing, Price is given to such characterizations. At the same time that he sets up issues of morality as black and white, he shades his characters and situations with so much gray that the "right" choice, the honorable one, is obscured or ambiguous, so much so that a basically kind man like Blue muddles through as best he can. It is no accident in this novel that Blue is in such a quandary while the women around him suffer no such indecision. Miss Ashlyn and Myra have years of experience with Blue's dissipation, and they have unerring knowledge, they believe, of what is best in this situation: While Myra retreats with her rosaries, Miss Ashlyn, who, symbolically, is losing her eyesight, still sees clearly enough to speak the truth to Blue. "Your dreadful cruelty—that young girl and your wife and child. I will not watch you do it, Bluford. Forget my eyes. I mean to go blind and put myself in a nursing home with my own money and let you sow your meanness in the dark—my dark at least."

With Mattie, his daughter, Blue cannot escape the consequences of his actions. She is only a couple of years younger than Luna and a true innocent who believes in the power of prayer to effect reform. Thwarted by Blue's genuine love for both Luna and his family, Mattie turns away from him. In giving her undeserved pain, Blue commits his greatest sin. It is one for which he will have to pay many times over thirty years later.

Literary critics today are prone to talk about "issues" in literature and how an author "explores" them. They are all too often reticent to explain directly what the exploration involves, what authors are saying, what they mean, or why they deal with certain issues. Detractors of this novel believe that the female characters are one-dimensional, that they do not act like women but like women imagined by a man. Susan Wood even argues that in creating such idealized women Price loses all irony, and she compares Luna to other mysterious, enigmatic women of fiction—Henry James's Isabel Archer and Thomas Hardy's Tess. Whether the comparisons are apt, she misses the point, the "issue," as it were, of sexual abuse of children. Luna is no reserved maiden; nor is she a teenage harlot. Unlike another baby siren, Lolita, Luna is mature enough, honest enough, to send Blue back to his wife and child, not once but twice. She is also independent enough to spurn his money and to strike out on her own. Another critic, Robert Towers, condemns Price for character abuse: Miss Ashlyn is going blind, Mattie and Myra both suffer agonizingly dreadful deaths, and Rita is a slipshod excuse for a mother. Essentially, he sees the secondary characters as fate's foils, or more accurately as foils for Reynolds Price. They are better regarded and better understood as Blue's, who sincerely believes that the awful things that happen to them are his fault. His epistle is a long outpouring of guilt, and in two uncomfortable scenes, the careful reader will note that Price's "issue" of child abuse *requires* awful reckonings. In each case, a father sits at the edge of his daughter's bed and ponders incest. In such chilling fashion, the theme and narrative focus of this unsettling novel have an organic symmetry deeply rooted in the very characterizations of Blue and his coterie of women.

Blue is shy when it comes to the graphic depiction of sex; after all, this "letter" is intended for his grandchild, a young woman who cannot reasonably be expected to understand what has happened to her. He even leaves unanswered some questions that are perhaps too terrifying to answer. Did Luna and her half-brother have sex in Blue's dying friend's house? When Luna tries to explain, partly at least, her role in this relationship, Blue stops her; he does not want to hear exactly what he most needs to know, that he is basically taking advantage of an emotionally troubled girl who behaves like a woman seasoned in sexual knowledge and practice. Blue can hide behind or in southern circumlocution and hyperbole. He can use words to clarify as well as to obfuscate, and in several places, Price is clever in having a problem hinge on a misunderstanding of a phrase, or on one left unfinished. Blue wants his mother's counsel and introduces the subject of his yearning into a conversation, both amusing and revelatory:

> Mother said "Luna—that's a long lost name, haven't heard it for years. You remember Miss Luna Pittman? Turned wild at the end and called her preacher a son of a bitch at the church door on Easter morning. They hauled her off unfortunately, and none of us ever saw her again—I miss her still."
> This was our normal way to talk, a looping road with plenty of time to stop and stare.

It is also Price's normal way of writing: He gives his readers plenty of time to stop and stare, to laugh and to marvel at such wonderful handling of language. Blue is a fine narrator, and Reynolds Price is an exceptional writer, one who describes *himself* when Blue tries to figure out how he is going to tell a painful truth: "*But first I need a story to tell.* Like most of the humans born south of Baltimore, I was seldom without a story to meet the occasion."

The occasion in this disturbing novel is certainly a topical one. The reader is in no better hands than those of Reynolds Price when it comes to telling a story about it.

*William U. Eiland*

### Sources for Further Study

*Atlanta Journal Constitution.* May 10, 1992, p. N8.
*Booklist.* LXXXVIII, March 1, 1992, p. 1164.
*The Christian Science Monitor.* June 8, 1992, p. 14.
*Commonweal.* CXIX, May 22, 1992, p. 17.
*Los Angeles Times Book Review.* June 21, 1992, p. 12.
*The New York Times Book Review.* XCVII, May 24, 1992, p. 10.
*Publishers Weekly.* CCXXXIX, February 17, 1992, p. 45.
*Southern Living.* XXVII, September, 1992, p. 38.
*The Wall Street Journal.* June 26, 1992, p. A9.
*The Washington Post Book World.* XXII, May 10, 1992, p. 5.

# BLUE-EYED CHILD OF FORTUNE
## The Civil War Letters of Colonel Robert Gould Shaw

*Editor:* Russell Duncan
*Publisher:* University of Georgia Press (Athens). Illustrated. 421 pp. $29.95
*Type of work:* Letters
*Time:* April, 1861-July, 1863
*Locale:* Primarily northern Virginia and the coast of South Carolina

*In these letters written during the Civil War, Robert Gould Shaw describes the events that resulted in his being given charge of the Fifty-fourth Massachusetts, the most famed of the all-black Union troops, which he led in a failed but inspiring attack on the Confederate Fort Wagner, South Carolina*

*Principal personages:*
ROBERT GOULD SHAW, the young, idealistic commander of the Massachusetts Fifty-fourth Infantry
FRANCIS GEORGE SHAW, his father, a wealthy New England businessman
SARAH BLAKE STURGIS SHAW, his mother, an ardent abolitionist
ANNA SHAW CURTIS, his sister, married to publisher George William Curtis
JOSEPHINE "EFFIE" SHAW LOWELL, his sister, married to Charles Russell Lowell, Jr.
SUSANNA "SUSIE" SHAW, his sister
ELLEN "NELLIE" SHAW, his sister
ANNIE KNEELAND HAGGERTY SHAW, Shaw's fiancée, later his wife
COLONEL JAMES M. MONTGOMERY, a former associate of John Brown and leader of the Union Second South Carolina Infantry
JOHN A. ANDREW, the governor of Massachusetts
CHARLOTTE FORTEN, a black teacher and missionary with whom Shaw became infatuated in South Carolina

Robert Gould Shaw was, from any purely military standpoint, a minor figure in the Civil War. Nevertheless, his position as white leader of the Fifty-fourth Massachusetts, the premier regiment of Union African American troops, one of the first to fight in the war, brought him and many of his men a hero's death and earned them a magnificent monument created by the sculptor Augustus Saint-Gaudens on the grounds of Boston Common. Relegated to footnotes during most of the twentieth century, Shaw was brought back to public attention as the subject of the Academy Award-winning film *Glory* in 1989. Inspired by the film, Russell Duncan, a professor of history, undertook the collection and annotation of Shaw's Civil War letters, some of which had been published (and sometimes expurgated) by Shaw's mother, Sarah, in 1864. Bringing together other letters from additional sources, and restoring to original form letters Shaw's mother had edited, Duncan has made available an important and often compelling story of a young man's movement into legend. The title, *Blue-Eyed Child of Fortune*, comes from the oration of William James (who knew Shaw and whose brother, Garth Wilkinson James, served with Shaw in the Fifty-fourth) delivered at the 1897 dedication of the memorial. James had it right, for Shaw was a "child of fortune," caught up in a surge of history that carried him to a greatness beyond his own knowing or doing.

The son of a wealthy and prominent abolitionist family, Shaw had spent his youth enjoying the luxuries and advantages of the privileged few. His parents had been financial supporters of the Brook Farm communal experiment described by Nathaniel Hawthorne, an acquaintance, in *The Blithedale Romance* (1852) as well as other idealistic ventures originating during this period of great social change. They were also strong advocates in the American Anti-Slavery Society and the Boston Vigilance Committee, both of which helped runaway slaves find freedom in the North. Shaw grew up among many notable reformers and writers of the Transcendentalist period, among them Henry Ward Beecher, Harriet Beecher Stowe, William Lloyd Garrison, Lydia Maria Child, and Ralph Waldo Emerson. As a boy, he attended first Fordham and then the Roulet boarding school in Neuchâtel, Switzerland. During his years in Europe, he sometimes indulged himself in high living, but by the time he returned to enter Harvard, Shaw had become increasingly aware of the inevitability of war, a struggle, as he and his family saw it, primarily over the question of slavery. Following the secession of South Carolina from the Union, Shaw immediately joined the Seventh New York National Guard, among the first troops sent to Washington to protect the capital from capture by the Confederates, a very real possibility at this early point in the war.

Although Shaw admired his parents' social idealism, he was not himself a confirmed believer in all of their causes. The war gave him the opportunity to discover his own truths. Although he completely supported the Union, he often questioned the political and military leaders who commanded it. He also quickly found that the life (and death) of a soldier was not the adventure he had imagined originally. He wrote his mother after leaving with his regiment for Washington, "It is very hard to go off without bidding you goodbye, and the only thing that upsets me, in the least, is the thought of how you will feel when you find me so unexpectedly gone. But I know, dearest Mother, that you wouldn't have me stay, when it is so clearly my duty to go. . . . We all feel that if we can get into Washington, before Virginia begins to make trouble, we shall not have much fighting." Later he wrote, "It is a pleasant feeling to be here bullying the Southerners." Shaw and his fellow soldiers at first thought the worst of their enemy, accepting each rumor of Southern cruelty and barbarism. It was a mark of Shaw's growth as a soldier and as a man that he soon came to respect his Confederate opponent. He could write, "I long for the day when we shall attack the Rebels with an overwhelming force and annihilate them. May I live long enough to see them running before us hacked to little pieces," but a week later observe, "If the treatment of our prisoners depended on the officers and soldiers of the Rebel army, I think they would fare well, for those I have met seem to have no bitter feeling towards us. We can't help getting a feeling of respect for each other, after such a fight as the last."

One of the great pleasures of reading a collection of letters such as this one is to witness the development of the writer through a telescoping of time and events. The callow Rob Shaw who goes off to war is far different from the bloodied Colonel Robert

Shaw who prepares to lead his men into a desperate and doomed attack on Fort Wagner. The reader's foreknowledge that all Shaw's choices and chances over three years will ultimately converge into this final massacre lends a true poignancy, but also a real irony, to the letters. For example, his life is saved in May, 1862, when a bullet hits his pocket watch; later he is hit in the neck by a bullet that already has passed through another soldier and fails to penetrate his own body.

These letters challenge modern sensibility in a number of ways. Shaw was a true patriot, but he also was a victim of his—and his family's—patriotism. He never totally shared their abolitionist beliefs, and his attitude toward the black race could be as condescending as his initial feelings toward Southerners. When Sarah Shaw first published his letters, she removed the more offensive of her son's remarks on black people. Duncan, to his credit, has restored these lines and honestly examines Shaw's sometimes contradictory thoughts on the question of race. When offered the command of the Massachusetts Fifty-fourth, Shaw, who was not the first choice, turned it down, preferring to stay with his friends and fellow soldiers in the Second Massachusetts. He wrote his fiancée Annie Haggerty, "If I had taken it, it would only have been from a sense of duty; for it would have been anything but an agreeable task. . . . I am afraid Mother will think I am shirking my duty; but I had some good practical reasons for it." Within days, however, he had changed his mind, again writing Annie:

> It is needless for me to overwhelm you with a quantity of arguments in favour of the negro troops; because you are with Mother, the warmest advocate the cause can have. . . . You know how many eminent men consider a negro army of the greatest importance to our country at this time. If it turns out to be so, how fully repaid the pioneers in the movement will be, for what they may have to go through! And at any rate I feel convinced I shall never regret having taken this step, as far as I myself am concerned; for while I was undecided I felt ashamed of myself, as if I were cowardly.

Shaw certainly was never a coward—he often discussed the likelihood of his death in battle—but he clearly met his death, and thus gained his significance, in large part because of his desire not to embarrass his family, especially his mother, Sarah, and his young bride, Annie. As Duncan astutely puts it,

> The adrenaline of life and death on the field of battle brought Shaw closer to his comrades in a male world than he had ever been to his classmates at Harvard or to his boyhood companions. This universe of maleness helped him to pull at the strings of his female-dominated family, and helped him mature even though he had not been able to break free of his mother's dominance by the time of his death. In that sense, Shaw never got past his mother; the monument on Boston Common is much more representative of her ambition than of his.

Thus, Shaw's letters portray not only a soldier's military conflict in war but also the more personal conflict of a son and lover attempting to define and prove himself to those in a world he has left behind. "You must have thought, from my late letters, that I was degenerating sadly from the principles in which I was brought up," he wrote his mother in 1862, after having earlier questioned the ultimate worth of Lincoln's Emancipation Proclamation from a military standpoint, "but an ordinary mortal must be somewhat affected by his surroundings, and events which you look at in one way from a distance, often seem very different when you are in the midst of them. The man at a distance is more apt to be impartial." That Shaw could not be "impartial"—that he matured and questioned and searched for his own way of understanding—is one of the great strengths of this collection.

Although Duncan's editorship of Shaw's letters has much to praise, there are aspects that suggest that the book was rushed to capitalize on the interest in Shaw caused by the film *Glory*. Duncan's introduction, a seventy-page biographical essay of Shaw, is extremely useful and carefully documented but sometimes written in a pedestrian manner. The annotations to the letters are placed at the end of each letter rather than at the foot of the page, an arrangement that requires the interested reader to flip back and forth from letter to note, to the detriment of the reading experience. In addition, the annotations themselves are too frequently inadequate. Some figures are identified by birth and death dates and a brief description; others are simply designated by a full name, which adds little to the information already gleaned from the letter itself. For example, in the letter of May 13, 1862, Shaw writes, "I haven't seen Capt Perkins but believe he was detained in Washington by illness"; Duncan's footnote reads simply, "Captain Perkins," suggesting that he intended but failed to provide more discussion of this figure. There are numerous other people who also are insufficiently identified. At least one letter (June 6, 1862) has indications of footnotes within the text where none actually is given in the notes. Nevertheless, on the whole Duncan has done an impressive job of bringing together a great deal of information, and in his discussions of such figures as Colonel James Montgomery and Charlotte Forten, he has created significant portraits of fascinating historical personages.

Duncan surely overstates the case when he judges Shaw's letters as "written in what may be the most eloquent prose any soldier wrote home during any war," but Shaw was a gifted correspondent, one who grew in depths of feeling, judgment, and compassion as he neared his death. The early traces of the insecure martinet (Shaw believed in discipline and punishment, although he never went as far as Montgomery, who would shoot one of his own soldiers to prove a point) give way to the solemn determination of a man made haggard by the inevitable necessity of sacrifice. In one of his last letters, written on July 13, 1863, he thought of how different his life might be if he had never been offered or accepted command of the Fifty-fourth and had stayed with the Second Massachusetts, which had several days earlier fought in the pivotal Battle of Gettysburg:

> I should have been Major of the Second now if I had remained there, and lived through the battles. As regards my own pleasure, I had rather have that place than any other in the army. It would have been fine to go home, a field-officer in that regiment. Poor fellows, how they have been slaughtered! . . .
>
> My warmest love to Mamma and Clem. . . . That country place of ours is often before my eyes in the dim future.

Five days later, Shaw was dead, killed on the parapet of Fort Wagner. He was buried in a mass grave, the bodies of twenty of his black soldiers deliberately piled on top of him, "buried with his niggers" as some Southerners put it. Shaw's parents refused to have their son's body removed from the grave. "We do thank God that our darling . . . was chosen, among so many equals, to be the martyred hero of the downtrodden of our land," his father would write. What becomes clear from these letters is that Shaw was much more complex, more ambiguous and torn, than either of these roles would suggest. Nor was he totally the serious, earnest character portrayed by Matthew Broderick in the film *Glory*. His letters reveal an infectious sense of humor, even of the absurd. He was a fascinating and admirable man in his own right. Russell Duncan has done well by him in bringing his letters to public attention in such a respectful yet honest manner.

*Edwin T. Arnold*

## Sources for Further Study

*Booklist*. LXXXIX, October 1, 1992, p. 231.
*Boston Globe*. October 11, 1992, p. 16.
*Library Journal*. CXVII, October 1, 1992, p. 104.
*The New York Times Book Review*. XCVII, September 27, 1992, p. 34.
*Washington Times*. October 31, 1992, p. B3.

# THE BOY WITHOUT A FLAG
## Tales of the South Bronx

*Author:* Abraham Rodriguez, Jr. (1961-    )
*Publisher:* Milkweed Editions (Minneapolis, Minnesota). 115 pp. Paperback $11.00
*Type of work:* Short stories
*Time:* The 1990's
*Locale:* The South Bronx

*A collection of seven loosely related stories chronicling the lives of characters caught up in a world in which they are forced to come of age prematurely*

*The Boy Without a Flag: Tales of the South Bronx* is a first book of fiction from Abraham Rodriguez, Jr., a young Puerto Rican American writer whose greatest strength is his ability to capture the salsa-driven rhythms and late-night bodega rap sessions of a streetcorner posse in a quick-tongued prose style that is searingly raw and jagged-edged. These are gritty, graffiti-colored stories that reach right for the jugular, working gradually down toward the heart. Rodriguez showers light on those who live invisibly, shoved to the side, into the guttered margins, fallen between the cracks.

These stories, Rodriguez himself has declared, are "about the rancid underbelly of the American Dream. These are the kids no one likes to talk about. . . . I want to show them as they are, not as society wishes them to be." In at least two of these tales—the title story and "Birthday Boy," a story of adolescent awakening into a life of crack dealing and two-bit crime—Rodriguez goes a step further, delving deeper beneath the skin. Not only does he re-create the true-to-life brutality overriding the lives of these characters, but also he manages to illuminate the inner conflicts, the unspoken struggles, of those caught in the cross fire, those left scrambling, roachlike, for a few measly crumbs of that mythical American Dream pie. The "boy without a flag" and the cast of characters that flesh out the rest of this collection linger in the memory with the persistence of seemingly innocuous encounters with complete strangers that continue to haunt us.

The narrator of "The Boy Without a Flag" is a precocious eleven-year-old schoolboy who writes "unreadable novels" (including a biography of Hitler) and reads books as "fat as milk crates." He refuses to stand up to salute the American flag during a school assembly, an act of defiance that, he hopes, will impress his father, a frustrated poet and Puerto Rican nationalist who has planted the seeds of rebellion in his young son's highly malleable mind. As the American flag enters the auditorium, unfurling majestically (meanwhile, the lone-starred Puerto Rican flag "walked beside it, looking smaller and less confident. It clung to its pole . . ."), the narrator flashes back to a time when his father sat on the edge of his bed, yelling about Chile, cursing about what the CIA had done there. "I watched that Yankee flag making its way up to the stage . . . father's scowling face haunting me, his words resounding in my head. . . . Everyone rose up to salute the flag. Except me."

As it turns out, though, the plan backfires, and the boy's father, when summoned to the school by Miss Marti, the militant, pig-faced assistant principal, is nothing but meekly apologetic and self-critical for his son's "crazy" anti-Uncle Sam behavior. "I never thought a thing like this could happen," he says. "My wife and I try to bring him up right." His father, the one person the boy wishes to impress, to whom he looks for approval, abandons him. The boy is left alone to come to terms with his father's betrayal, which triggers his preadolescent passage into the disillusion that we are all strangers, both parents and children alike—that we are alone in this world, even when we are together. "I felt like I was falling down a hole," he says. "My father, my creator, renouncing his creation." Years later, though, he comes to the understanding that his father has, in fact, provided him with a most valuable lesson. He has learned that he must break away from his father's sphere of influence; that he must find his own means of independence. In the process of assimilating into that cauldron known as the melting pot, ethnicity, the salt-and-pepper seasoning of identity, is lost, washed away into a tasteless, watered-down broth. The narrator works his way up from this epiphany, and it is clear that he has pledged allegiance to no one but himself, "away from the bondage of obedience."

This is an eye-widening lesson in the young boy's life, and he is not alone. All the characters in this collection are, in one way or another, forced to grow up too fast. This loss of innocence happens, it seems, overnight: a wing-clipped flight into the cold-neon corridor of broken dreams, where compromise is the greatest common denominator, the lone exit, and the ideals of youth are bullied into silence.

In "Birthday Boy"—a recklessly fast-paced narrative that reads like a runaway train—thirteen-year-old Angel raps off a regressive account of a day two years earlier. One afternoon, home early from school, he nonchalantly "walked in" on his mother and his uncle. The secret is safe with him, at least for a while, but when his father finally finds out, the results are explosive. The father begins drinking heavily and repeatedly beats both mother and son, until one day the mother escapes. Angel sticks around, for a time, though it reaches the point, finally, that he has no choice but to leave. "[W]hen he said, 'I'm gonna kill you!' in his boiler-room Spanish, I made for the exit." From there, Angel goes to the streets, often sleeping in crack houses "cause sometimes you gotta sleep in strange places when friends can't come through with a crib." His mentor, a boy named Spider, apprentices Angel into a life of drugs, petty theft and burglary, and casual sex. As in several other stories in the collection, pregnancy is an unwanted accident, something that simply seems to "happen." Angel recounts that his "steady," Gloria, "lay a real bomb on me just last night"—the bomb being that she is pregnant. It is left ambiguous as to what happens to the "bomb" in this situation. What happens to Angel, though, is quite clear. After botching a robbery that his girl-on-the-sneak Miriam clues him in on, Angel ends up spending his first teenage birthday in jail. When it comes time for Angel to phone someone into whose custody he would be released, there was "only one person I could call": Spider. Angel's passage into adolescence is now complete, a full-fledged flight into a web from which there is no escape.

At the beginning of "No More War Games," Nilsa is, for the moment at least, still a child. Yet, as her best friend Cha-Cha reminds her, "God, you gonna be twelve next week. You gotta start growin' up. You can't keep playing war games forever." The war games to which she is alluding are the day-to-day child's play of a South Bronx tomboy, games that include hanging out in deserted lots "brimming with shattered glass and the odor of raw decay . . . peppered with swaying lanes of tall grass . . . growing wild and uncut," days spent ambushing the "NO GIRLS AL-LOWED clubhouse on the lot across the street." It is high time, Nilsa concedes, to start playing other types of games, the games grown-ups play, such as sex and wearing makeup. Cha-Cha had turned twelve the week before, and already Nilsa noticed the changes. "For starters, Cha-Cha hadn't come to the yard all week. She started seeing those older boys from as far away as Jackson Avenue. She painted her nails. Dark red. . . . She didn't want to get dirty."

Like the boy in "The Boy Without a Flag," Nilsa is a child straddling the invisible borderline dividing innocence from experience. She is caught in mid-stride, standing in limbo, searching for conviction, a sign to tell her which road will take her where she wants to go. She looks to Cha-Cha as her point of reference, a model, and she comes to the conclusion that "I guess I should dress up. I guess my pants should be tighta, I mean, these shorts are pretty tight, but they're not sharp. They're little girl shorts, like f' gym. Not sexy." Nilsa's migration into womanhood, into the world of skin-tight jeans and lip gloss, is dramatized as a sexual ambush in which she attempts to capture her first kiss. She corners her first conquest, Patchi, one of the neighborhood boys with whom she once played "war games," turns him into her "prisoner," and then tries to muscle him into giving her a kiss. The kiss never comes, however, and Nilsa is left unnerved, deadened even, by the experience. "The whole place looked and smelled different. Something was gone forever."

When Nilsa descends, fatigued, "broken and delicate," she is no longer a child with a voice "carried by the warm breezes." Her descent, her fall, into sexuality already is tainted by a sordid drugstore cheapness, and her realization that "there would be no more war games" is overshadowed by the inescapable fate of premature motherhood that seems to hover above, waiting to descend.

Motherhood's premature descent is the prevailing theme in three of the remaining five stories. "The Lotto" tells the story of Dalia, a young girl haunted by a recurring dream in which babies keep popping out of hats. The dream itself possesses a cartoonish quality, yet when viewed in the context of Dalia's situation, it is clear why she awakens in tears, screaming for her boyfriend Ricky, who has been nowhere to be found since Dalia, five days ago, had told him the news "about throwing up and being weak-kneed and dizzy and scared." Enter Elba, "a short, curvy girl with dark, curly hair" who "talked real loud, catty and chatty." Elba and Dalia had recently become close friends, "holding unofficial races to see who could get a boyfriend first." What they didn't expect is that they would both be forced to take a pregnancy test that, unlike a pop quiz in Geography, could possibly affect the rest of their lives. Dalia is blessed by the luck of the draw. She, in a sense, wins a lotto that has no monetary value, though it is, all the same, priceless. Elba is not so lucky. She "looked as if she had just lost fifty million dollars." What she has really lost is her innocence, her childhood, her future. The story ends as Elba descends into motherhood.

The last story in the collection, "Elba," picks up where "The Lotto" left off, forming somewhat of a diptych, a before-and-after framework that allows readers to follow the progression of Elba's demise, from a carefree childhood to single motherhood trapped in a window-perched world where she feels "old and lonely and abandoned, a lifer in a prison cell waiting for the chair," looking down at a world from which she is now distanced, a world lost, where "laughter would drift up to her while she . . . washed dishes or changed little Danny's diapers." Readers watch Elba struggle with her new role as mother, and her story recounts the steps leading up to "the baby," including her courtship with Danny, a courtship limited by a world in which romance is reduced to this: "Two days after entering the eighth grade . . . he lifted her up and carried her through dark hallways as he had seen men do in old movies on TV. He carried her down steps and over decaying planks of wood, nails sticking out of them like teeth. He carried her over a cracked threshold. . . . They didn't notice the rotting wood smell at all."

It comes as no surprise, then, that Elba, as a way of seeking symbolic retribution against the baby's father—against the imprisonment of motherhood—decides to "jet" back into the world that has been stolen away, feeling momentarily "satisfied . . . as she made her way down the creaking stairs in her high heels," leaving her wailing baby behind in her wake. This fade-away image of Elba's descent creates a resonating link with the last lines from "The Lotto," in which Elba races down the stairs from Dalia's apartment, "her sneakers thumping as if they belonged to a happy little kid on her way to play house." It is clear, though, that Elba's "house" is anything but happy. Rodriguez's use of this imagistic detail, the side-by-side contrast pairing a child's sneakers with the spiked high heels of a woman, is perhaps the most graceful, the subtlest stylistic touch in the collection. It is a beautiful stroke, a telling moment, on which note the book comes to a close, promising readers that, if anything, Rodriguez's craft in the art of fiction is on the ascent.

A first book of fiction can be expected to have its awkward moments, much in the way that Rodriguez's adolescent characters stumble haphazardly and oftentimes fall gracelessly into the adult world for which they are unprepared. Sentences such as "Her eyes bored holes through me" or "I went through the motions like a robot" are, it is true, hard to stomach. Still, the successes of this book—Rodriguez's sense of the South Bronx, a place that inhabits his characters, brought to life with an affection, a sympathy that is in no way sentimental—cancel out the scattering of stylistic shortcomings. Rodriguez's depictions of lost childhoods are true and brutal. He is a writer driven by the impulse to tell the stories belonging to those who are voiceless, whose lives have been snuffed out, sucked marrowless, ground to the bone. Their stories deserve to be heard.

*Peter Markus*

## Sources for Further Study

*Kirkus Reviews*. LX, April 15, 1992, p. 494.
*Library Journal*. CXVII, October 15, 1992, p. 103.
*Los Angeles Times Book Review*. September 27, 1992, p. 12.
*The New York Times Book Review*. September 27, 1992, p. 17.
*Publishers Weekly*. CCXXXIX, May 18, 1992, p. 63.
*World and I*. VII, October, 1992, p. 347.

# BREAD WITHOUT SUGAR

*Author:* Gerald Stern (1925-    )
*Publisher:* W. W. Norton (New York). 96 pp. $18.95
*Type of work:* Poetry

*Stern's restlessness—his constant turning things over, shifting perspectives, holding off closure—is the strain that runs through and is expressed by a meditative manner that embraces life even while pondering death*

Looking at his year of birth, one suddenly realizes that Gerald Stern is only a couple of years younger than James Dickey, who came to a "late" prominence in the 1960's. More striking, he is a year older than Allen Ginsberg, who first pelted readers' consciousness in the 1950's and was enshrined with his *Collected Poems, 1947-1980* (1984), a volume that reveals how little of Ginsberg's poetic energy lasted beyond 1970. Then one realizes that this active and fecund poet, Stern, is not even in many anthologies, not in his place between Dickey and Ginsberg, who seem now curiously dead as working poets while Stern goes on and on, getting better and better. Like Robert Peters, he is a late-bloomer, a long-distance runner. Only in the anthologies published in the twenty-first century will Stern find his place among the important voices of the last half of the twentieth century.

Preeminently Stern is a poet of sentiment and of a qualified nostalgia. Almost single-handedly, he gives a good name to artistic impulses that have been long out of fashion and against which weaker, less mature talents need to be warned. He is, like Saul Bellow's fictional Herzog, a man of heart, but his sense of humor is healthier than Herzog's. Stern's agonizings often end in smiles, or in tears of joy. No less a realist than anyone else, Stern nevertheless conjures redemption. In a poetic style formally reminiscent of Walt Whitman and Allen Ginsberg, Stern strikes a tone that has affinities with Isaac Bashevis Singer and Bernard Malamud—the bittersweet cantorial voice of blissful suffering and redemptive faith.

These references to Jewish writers are not meant to suggest that Stern is to be categorized neatly and thus defined by limitation. The Jewish feeling-tones in his poems are the cultural sails of a sprightly, adaptive vessel, not its anchors. Not traditionally religious, but reflecting a schmaltzy humanism, Stern's works add up to nothing less than the spiritual autobiography of a devout, gentle sensualist, a man whose God is in the juices of indulgence that trickle down our chins as well as in the very mysteries of appetite and deprivation that riddle human history. In his occasional clowning, Stern is no schlemiel. He does not imaginatively transform a situation to survive its pain. Indeed, Stern's historical sense, his feeling for the past, is rooted in a knowledge that allows for little idealization. His delight in history and memory is not so much a yearning to go back as a refusal or inability to abandon.

There are some standard ways of categorizing poets, ways that Gerald Stern defies. He is a master at evoking the urban ethos, but he is also a poet of great intimacy with natural processes and the botanical world. Sometimes he seems to be a poet of place, a regionalist, but then the place becomes places and the boundaries of time and geography vanish to leave the reader in a familiar home territory that covers much of the Western world. Most of Stern's poems begin somewhere and reach out across space and time—the time of one's life and the larger history that frames one's actions and being. Poems such as "Those Things" and "Red with Pink" should not make the unified impression that they do, so various in their images and impulses, so inclusive.

One of Stern's great talents is to give form to openness. He is a great elaborator, a writer who finds a language and cadence for the rhythms of imagination and memory. Some of his most impressive poems risk exhaustion, disintegration, or collapse. They maintain an improvisational quality, a teetering toward chaos, even while they find a permanent shape. The cohesive force is the power of personality, aided at times by the artful handling of such Whitmanesque devices of song as inventory, parallelism, and anaphora. Often, a strong narrative thrust is the bonding element. Stern's poems are not, however, primarily narratives or lyrics. Granting some leeway for Stern's protean poem-making, we can perhaps best categorize his work as meditative.

As a meditator, Stern is a questioner. A hallmark of his rhetoric is the interrogative. As a poet of the self, Stern risks an inward-turning examination of the universe and an abrasive egocentricity. In *Bread Without Sugar*, as in his earlier collections, Stern avoids the uglier excesses of the inward gaze. As Peter A. Siedlecki has observed (in "Mediation of the I and the I," found in Leonard M. Trawick's *World, Self, Poem*, 1990), "all of Gerald Stern's poetry is written both against egocentric isolation and against the cool acceptance of the perceived world." Facing and feeling mortality at every turn, Stern's celebrations of human experience are not made by escapist transformations (like the schlemiel) or by passively accepting or insulating the self from harshness and tragedy. The power of his yearning to feel his way to the end of the great questions—Why do we suffer? Should we despair? What can we truly know? What difference do we make in this universe?—is a unique dimension of Stern's poetic vision.

Much of Stern's writing is in the tradition of the great elegiac poetry that works toward the terms for reconciling the self to death. The occasion need not be the death of a loved one. In a poem such as "The Age of Strolling," Stern mourns the style and gestures of an earlier self, a youth not quite gone, a memory. Change may be growth, but it is also death: The doubleness of change, of becoming, weighs on the speaker. Seeing his youthful self positioned to absorb the world's secrets, even to feast on its gloom, Stern realizes that each stance and each perception remade him:

> When I stood there cupping my right hand
> and when I looked at the barges struggling up
> my river I was already changed. I spent
> a lifetime doing this, grieving and arguing.

Grieving and arguing are two sides of the Stern dialectic; or, as he puts it in "Brain of My Heart," the two voices that talk to each other and talk through him: "one is tormented, one/ is full of sappy wisdom." In his poems, he has invented himself as a wanderer, a restless walker who might find himself among the amusing detritus of Greenwich Village, among plants and flowers he knows intimately, among the figures and stones of history. As the receiving and responding center, Stern's persona organizes and interprets the scenes he walks through with a stride or shuffle that aspires to dance. Stern, the poet, aspires to dance, as he tells us in "Aspiring to Music," insisting jokingly that poetry and music are enemies.

"Two Daws" is a fine example of Stern's elegiac, meditative style and tone. Two crows—or "daws"—spur this entrancing mental play in which daws are transmuted to dawns, both true and false, and the insistence that there are two deaths. For Stern, there cannot be one of anything. One thing always leads to another; one image or experience or thought already announces the possibility of a second—and a third. There are always at least the two: the true and the false. These the restless, haranguing word-dancer can turn inside out and keep airborne, like a juggler's pins. The poem ends:

> . . . Shouldn't I sing then,
> breathing my last, fretting over my own death
> among the other birds? And shouldn't I sleep
> like a wise man through the false dawn even if the first
> thin blue is out there, even if there is a call
> from one or two creatures, even if the cardinal
> is making me moan, and even if the chickadee
> is hanging upside down and banging his head
> against the shiny glass—even if the worm
> is fighting for his life and the lily of the valley
> is bowing her head in shame, shouldn't I live on?

Among the many fine poems in this, Stern's eighth collection, is the title poem. "Bread Without Sugar" is a formal elegy, a remembrance of the poet's father. Printed first separately in a beautiful edition from Sutton Hoo Press (1991), "Bread Without Sugar" is reminiscent of Ginsberg's "Kaddish," though it is neither as excessively elaborated nor as self-consciously monumental. Stern's elegy gains, perhaps, from the poet's distance on the central event, his father having died two decades before the poem was written, though with Stern's prodigious memory, time vanishes.

The resemblances to "Kaddish" have to do with the way both poems open out from the occasion of graveyard thoughts to become personal, familial, and cultural rumi- nations. From the perspective of the 1980's, Stern recalls an event of the 1960's that ushers in the world of his father's generation, a generation whose neighborhoods were fixed in styles that preceded World War II and the worst years of Jewish catastrophe. Evocations of Stern's Depression childhood fade into a Diaspora catalog and a questioning of the father's and the son's connection to Jewish fate: "Where should my site be? In Texas? Arizona?/ I am more scattered than my father was,/ born in Kiev, died in Miami." This poem of astonishing detail and range is one of Stern's major achievements, a supreme example of the questioning, associational "grieving and arguing" that is his mighty tool for self-exploration and affirmation. All the ways in which the speaker is scattered—the wanderings that have brought him to savor so much of this globe, the hearing and attempting its many languages, the restlessness of mind and spirit that leave no corner unturned—receive a magnificent and ultimately prayerful orchestration.

The way Stern, in "Bread Without Sugar" and elsewhere, bashes together his most profound and trivial concerns ("Where would I eat—on a hot plate?") reminds one of Arthur Miller's notion of the modern hero defined by a constant struggle between self and self-image. Stern's persona resembles an intellectual, less guilt- or failure-ridden Willy Loman, whose free-fall Hegelian talking to himself is not a sign of deterioration but rather of constructive mastery—of establishing balance. The liberating swing into disorientation and then back to a tentative, poised resting place is the arc of Stern's meandering and the arc of experience that the reader shares. It is a dizzying, breathless ride, and the consolation is that we want to and can hang on. Frightened, we smile.

*Philip K. Jason*

## Sources for Further Study

*Boston Globe.* June 21, 1992, p. 107.
*Choice.* XXX, October, 1992, p. 302.
*The Georgia Review.* XLVI, Fall, 1992, p. 554.
*Library Journal.* CXVII, March 15, 1992, p. 92
*Los Angeles Times Book Review.* September 13, 1992, p. 15.
*Poetry.* CLXI, November, 1992, p. 99.
*Publishers Weekly.* CCXXXIX, April 27, 1992, p. 257.
*Times-Picayune.* April 26, 1992, p. D19.

# BRITONS
## Forging the Nation, 1707-1837

*Author*: Linda Colley (1949-    )
*Publisher*: Yale University Press (New Haven, Connecticut). Illustrated. 413 pp. $35.00
*Type of work*: History
*Time*: 1707-1837
*Locale:* Great Britain

*Colley analyzes the cultural and historical elements that promoted the ideal of British national unity during the Hanoverian period*

>  *Principal personages:*
>  KING GEORGE III, a king of England
>  KING JAMES I (KING JAMES VI OF SCOTLAND), a ruler who united the monarchies of England and Scotland
>  KING JAMES II, the son of Charles I; ruler of England
>  JOHN STUART, LORD BUTE, a prime minister of England under George III
>  HORATIO NELSON, a British naval hero
>  SIR ROBERT WALPOLE, FIRST EARL OF ORFORD, a British statesman
>  SIR ARTHUR WELLESLEY, FIRST DUKE OF WELLINGTON, a statesman and hero of the Battle of Waterloo

At a time when nations that have existed for generations are either disintegrating or threatening to disintegrate, Linda Colley, a professor of history at Yale University, has produced a book that explores how the United Kingdom, one of the oldest and most illustrious nations, formed itself into a cohesive political system. Beginning with the Act of Union in 1707, which united Scotland politically and economically with the rest of Great Britain, she chronicles the development of the nation up to the coronation of Queen Victoria in 1837. The period saw the last of the Stuart monarchs succeeded by the Hanoverians. This dynasty, from an obscure German principality, began in 1714 to fulfill the requirement established by the Act of Succession of 1689 that English monarchs be Protestant. Although the first two Hanoverians spoke no English and exerted little influence over national affairs, George III, whose reign spanned sixty years, became one of the nation's most revered monarchs. As Colley's account demonstrates, the Hanoverian period laid the groundwork for Great Britain's prominence as a European power and its domination of vast portions of the world during the nineteenth century.

The period 1707-1837 possesses a historical configuration all its own. For Great Britain, the distinguishing feature was a succession of minor wars with France, England's most significant continental opponent, conducted almost entirely outside Britain's borders. The first prolonged historical conflict with France, during the fourteenth and fifteenth centuries, was waged over territorial claims by England within France itself. The later struggle grew out of ideological and commercial rivalries between the two nations. In the religious conflict dating back to the Reformation,

France replaced Spain as the leader of European Catholic opposition to Protestant England. As Colley points out, the persistent foreign threat aided in creating a sense of national identity and purpose.

If France did not fully commit to war on its own, it lent assistance to those who sought to create difficulties for Britain, offering support to the two Stuart pretenders who led minor rebellions in 1715 and 1745 as well as to the American colonists. The American Revolution, occurring at about the midpoint of the period, was the only war that Britain lost, and Colley believes that the defeat brought a sense of national humiliation. Although the Americans enjoyed some French support, they were the only Protestant people that warred against the British during the period and the only enemies who prevailed. Renewed patriotism and more effective policies following the defeat prepared Great Britain to emerge successfully from the Napoleonic Wars. In the aftermath of Waterloo, Great Britain became the most powerful European nation. Only then could it turn its attention to long-deferred reforms such as the abolition of slavery in its colonies, electoral reform, and religious freedom for English Catholics. When the era ended, Britain was poised for additional developments that promoted national unity as it faced a revolution of a different sort in industrial production, transportation, and communications.

The roots of British nationalism extended deep into the past, and geopolitics accounted for many of the developments as well as the problems faced by the emerging nation. England stood in the vanguard of the historical movement toward nationalism, a movement that received its strongest impetus from the Reformation. By 1707, most of the island had formed a single unified monarchy. Historically, Wales, Scotland, and the far southwestern portions—areas Colley designates as the "Celtic Fringe"— remained somewhat isolated from the more populous central and southern areas of Britain. Reasons for this extend back many centuries. Beginning in the first century A.D., successive invasions and settlements by Romans, Anglo-Saxons, and Danes drove many of the Celts, the island's earliest known inhabitants, westward and northward into Wales and Scotland, where they concentrated. There, in sometimes forbidding terrain, they preserved their original language, customs, and culture, and because of their remoteness achieved a measure of independence. Following the Norman Conquest, English monarchs began to challenge the relative independence of these groups.

Monarchical motivation was simple enough to understand. Initially, the kings built castles along their borders to protect against marauders from less affluent areas. Later, as the historical movement toward nationalism gained momentum, territorial expansion became a major factor. The Plantagenet monarchs, particularly Edward I and Edward III, made the conquest of Wales a primary objective, and their Lancastrian successors furthered the objective by appealing to patriotism while severely repressing Welsh nationalism. Only the Tudors, invoking the Arthurian myths dear to the Welsh and citing the Welsh origin of Henry VII, the first Tudor monarch, succeeded in bringing Wales into a reasonably close bond with England.

Throughout the Middle Ages and the Renaissance, the Scots retained their own independent kingdom, despite periodic conflicts with their powerful southern neighbors. When James VI of Scotland also became James I of England in 1603, the two nations formed a single monarchy, although they retained separate parliamentary, judicial, and economic systems. During the seventeenth century, the Stuart monarchs themselves encountered extreme difficulty in their relations with Scotland, and following the Glorious Revolution, the allegiance of James II and his male heirs to Catholicism alienated staunchly Protestant Scots. Clear economic interest and opposition to the Stuart religion made the Scots willing to support official union in 1707, accepting the Hanoverian succession and uniting the two parliaments. Although sympathy remained for the Stuart Pretenders, particularly among highland Scots, the majority supported the national union. It is safe to assume that most Scots did not think of themselves as natives of Great Britain before 1707. Colley shows that throughout the following century a patriotic sense of nationalism developed among the Scots and other inhabitants of the Celtic Fringe, who accepted the concept of the larger union as secure protection against hostile outside forces.

Although her lucid, rational analysis suggests a traditional historical narrative, Colley's approach is far from ordinary. Hers is clearly not a history of heroes and heroism. Sir Robert Walpole, the Whig prime minister who dominated the first half of the eighteenth century, receives only brief mention. Arthur Wellesley, Duke of Wellington, who led the victorious British army at Waterloo, fares little better, and Horatio Nelson, England's greatest naval leader, is treated as a figure of popular political iconography. On the other hand, King George III is accorded lengthy treatment as a monarch who contributed to the patriotic spirit of the age and gained the affection of his subjects because, paradoxically, they identified with his human weaknesses. The very fact that English monarchs held estates all over the island, rather than having a central palace that served as an official residence, brought the monarchy closer to the citizens.

Instead of chronicling the deeds of heroes and the development of institutions, Colley addresses a much more elusive task, that of explaining how a patriotic sense of national identity developed within the British population over time, following the Act of Union. To put the problem in another light, she attempts to explain how the sense of local identity and loyalty among Welsh, Scots, and other somewhat isolated populations was replaced by a sense of national identification and loyalty. Insofar as she describes the idea of a nation, she writes intellectual history. As she characterizes the developing sense of nationalism among the people, she includes social and cultural history as well. She draws upon popular culture, particularly descriptions of epic paintings—calculated to instill a sense of national pride, self-sacrifice, and patriotism—and cartoons that satirically depict national enemies. The numerous illustrations in this volume are often accompanied by lengthy analytical descriptions. She also draws heavily upon contemporary newspapers, handbills, and popular books that shaped national taste. In addition, she examines the records of various local patriotic societies and clubs to show that patriotism was widespread among all classes. The practical results were sometimes comically mixed: During the Stuart rebellion of 1745, many patriotic clubs signed loyalty oaths and voiced strong support for the Hanoverian dynasty but clearly were willing to fight only if the conflict reached their local area.

In maintaining that Protestantism served to unite dissenters and members of the national church in a common cause, Colley uses in her defense religious and polemic tracts of the age. These influential writings show the English inclination to view themselves as chosen actors in a providential history. This inclination did not wane when France became a power more secular than religious at the time of the French Revolution. All Britons could look back to the Reformation and the defeat of the Spanish Armada in 1588 as indicators of the guiding hand of providence and omens of the future. History and culture combined to promote a strong sense of providence in human affairs.

Socially and economically, forces produced by the Act of Union brought a greater commonality of interests. During the period when Lord Bute, a Scot, served as prime minister, Scots moved to London to take positions in the government. Daughters and sons of wealthy landowners married and linked estates in England, Scotland, and Wales. In addition, thousands of less prominent Scots found positions in the colonial service and thereby hitched their economic fortunes to those of British companies.

In education, a subtle change served to reduce conflicts between classes. During the eighteenth century, English aristocrats, who previously had studied at home under tutors, began attending the established schools as a matter of course. Although the English public schools enrolled only a small elite and were by no means egalitarian, they assured that the offspring of nobility would mingle with students of different backgrounds and absorb the national and imperial values that were part of the curriculum. Although small by continental standards, the English upper class, like the monarchy, was closer to the lives of commoners than its European counterparts.

In her conclusion, Colley considers contemporary tensions marked by the reemergence of national separatist movements in Scotland and Wales. Given her analysis of the reasons the union was achieved in the first place, some countermovements are to be expected. As she observes, the influence of Protestant Christianity as a unifying factor has waned over time. No pressing threats from abroad are perceived, and the monarchy alone seems insufficient to preserve a passionate sense of national identity. Having suffered a relative decline in prosperity and an absolute decline in world leadership, Britons can no longer view themselves as agents appointed by providence to lead lesser peoples toward the light.

Although Colley acknowledges that no one can predict with assurance how the tendency toward disintegration will resolve itself, it would appear a mistake to become too pessimistic about Britain's prospects. Britain's finest hour is not, after all, so far in the past, and a tradition of national service and self-sacrifice in a just cause still resonates throughout the land. Monuments, works of sculpture, paintings, and museums, in abundance throughout the island, commemorate British contributions to national unity and preservation. A shared culture and language and tightly intertwined economic interests may preserve the national unity that has evolved over ten centuries.

*Stanley Archer*

## Sources for Further Study

*The Guardian.* September 17, 1992, p. 28.
*History Today.* XXXII, October, 1992, p. 56.
*Kirkus Reviews.* LX, August 15, 1992, p. 1030.
*Library Journal.* CXVII, September 1, 1992, p. 188.
*London Review of Books.* XIV, October 8, 1992, p. 6.
*New Statesman and Society.* V, September 11, 1992, p. 37.
*The New York Review of Books.* XXXIX, November 19, 1992, p. 35.
*The New York Times Book Review.* XCVII, October 11, 1992, p. 11.
*The Spectator.* CCLXIX, September 19, 1992, p. 32.
*The Times Educational Supplement.* October 16, 1992, p. S9.
*The Times Literary Supplement.* October 16, 1992, p. 5.

# THE BROKEN STAFF
## Judaism Through Christian Eyes

*Author:* Frank E. Manuel (1910-    )
*Publisher:* Harvard University Press (Cambridge, Massachusetts). Illustrated. 363 pp. $34.95
*Type of work:* History
*Time:* Renaissance to the late twentieth century
*Locale:* Europe and the United States

*A historical account of the influence that Jewish thought has had on the intellectual currents
of the Christian tradition and the manner in which Jewish scholarship was represented and
applied by Christian and secular thinkers*

Frank E. Manuel has broken new ground in the history of ideas. In *The Broken Staff:
Judaism Through Christian Eyes*, Manuel, historian and professor emeritus at both
Brandeis and New York universities, has taken up the task of writing a history of the
Christian appraisal of Jewish thought. Anyone familiar with the history of anti-Jewish
sentiment in Christian thought is aware that this is a difficult field in which to work
without bias. Manuel's extraordinary objectivity makes it appear to be easily within
grasp—an achievement facilitated by his forthrightly secular perspective. Manuel
displays abundant sympathy with both the strengths and novel contributions of
Christian scholarship and the contributions of Jewish commentary and philosophy.
His ability to travel easily between the world of books in both cultures gives the reader
a sense of participating in the arena of accomplished cosmopolitan scholarship.

This book is designed to overcome clichés held in Christian, Jewish, and secularist traditions concerning the relationship between Jewish and Christian intellectual
history, which necessarily includes the relationship between scholars of both groups.
As the title indicates, Christianity has had a varied record in its treatment of Jewish
intellectual sources, sometimes condemning them as corrupt or superstitious, the work
of the Antichrist, at other times praising them for their usefulness in understanding the
Gospels or as aids in facilitating the conversion of Jews. Specifically Manuel's title
alludes to the notion that God's covenant with the Jews was broken when they rejected
the messiah. What value was therefore left in the study of Jewish wisdom was
contested throughout Christian history, though Manuel focuses on the period from the
sixteenth century through the twentieth century.

This is a history of Christian ideas about Jews and Judaism, and of the scholarship
dealing with Jewish thought that circulated among the most literate in Christendom.
Many of these same ideas were later to be found among secular scholars who, though
critical of the Church, maintained medieval prejudices against the Jewish intellectual
tradition, and in some instances, such as that of Voltaire, held Judeophobic attitudes
that were significantly more vitriolic than those of the Churchmen.

One of the strengths of Manuel's careful research is his refusal to engage in
premature generalizations. Rejecting the categories of traditional Jewish historiography, which dichotomizes persons as either Judeophiles or Judeophobes, Manuel

instead records the complex history of Jewish-Christian interaction, the nuances of which often defy received opinion. Johann Gottfried von Herder, for example, sang praises to the genius of early Hebrew poetry yet argued against the emancipation of Jews in Germany. Similarly, seventeenth century Christian Hebraists whose praise of Jewish scholarship and personal acquaintance with Jewish scholars led to significant respect and tolerance, nevertheless defended their research as instrumental to the Christian conversion effort.

Manuel's precision and breadth allow him to review the question of how Christian scholars valued the Jewish tradition apart from mass-minded anti-Jewish sentiment. He steers away from analyzing popular hatreds because he is concerned with the world of books, and because extensive analysis of popular anti-Semitism already has been carried out by sociologists, psychoanalysts, and historians of mass movements. Manuel's concern is with the analysis of, and the perceived significance of, the Jewish faith and its intellectual achievements in the minds of the best Christian or ex-Christian (secularist) scholars in the centuries under consideration.

Two questions underlie his assessment of European and American scholars. First, how much and how well did they know the vast corpus of Jewish intellectual history—the Talmud and the Mishna, and the diverse contributions of commentators, historians, and translators (of the rich scholarship of the medieval Arab world)? Second, to what uses did they put this learning? The first question concerns not only the amount of material known but also the degree of mastery of original and secondary languages necessary for sensitive access to the Jewish corpus. The second question, concerning the application of this knowledge by Christian and, later, secularist scholars, leads to the most interesting material in the book.

Examples of how knowledge of the Jewish corpus was put to use in different ways at different times can be found in the medieval and Reformation desire to know in order to convert; the sixteenth century's search for the ideal polity; the seventeenth century's apologetic quest for uncovering the original and thus divinely sanctioned form of political organization; the eighteenth century's secularist attempt to undermine traditional Christianity by showing the barbarism and cruelty of its Jewish roots; and the eighteenth century's deistic search for "natural religion." Also illumined are the nineteenth century's various attempts to arrive at a "pure science" of religion apart from religious and philosophical agendas—a program that included dubious racial theories and the equally dubious search for the "essence" of a religion, presumed to remain the same throughout the history of a religion; the nineteenth century's secular attack on Jews under the aegis of Romanticism, exemplified by Johann Gottlieb Fichte's depiction of Jews as a malignant growth threatening the purity of the *Volk*; the twentieth century's attainment of a shared Jewish and Christian scholarship with an unprecedented degree of objectivity and an extraordinary variety of approaches; and, most significantly, the confessional acknowledgement by post-Holocaust Christianity of its participation in entrenched patterns of anti-Semitism, and its willingness to look at Jewish sources with fresh eyes.

Manuel's overarching method is one deeply established today by historians; he does not ask how one religion differs from another but considers the full variety of opinion in each age, country, and denomination, including conflicts of assessment within each denomination. This leads away from the facile conclusion that Christianity as a whole has maintained this or that attitude, and enables the author to indicate how a tradition or subset of a tradition held at time x to positions x, y, or z. Lutherans are distinguished from Calvinists, Catholics from Protestants, and French Catholics from Spanish Catholics. The notion that religions have an unyielding essence that is above the vicissitudes of time is not only rejected, but also its history is traced from Montesquieu to Herder and on to Oswald Spengler.

An aspect of the history of religions routinely overlooked in scholarly works is the history of one religion's life in the religious imagination of another. Although the images that religions hold of one another may or may not correspond to reality, such perceptions have enormous practical consequences for the way in which one religion treats another. Religions are as much about the history of projections as they are about empirical fact.

A number of the eleven chapters that make up *The Broken Staff* were first given as lectures and can be read as complete essays on their own merit. Researchers who wish to focus on specific topics will find this easy access invaluable. On the negative side, the organization of the volume leads to a degree of repetition; topics covered earlier are frequently summarized to set up a new progression. The reader might find this annoying, though it is a minor inconvenience. Another caveat is that readers of *The Broken Staff* must be prepared for voluminous references to works in their original languages in the main text. Manuel is a polyglot, and draws citations from several European languages to document his position. Happily for the average reader, he usually translates his sources.

In rediscovering the impact of Judaism on the thought of Western Christianity, Manuel tracks the evidence for influence, finding little in patristic or medieval times. The first dramatic appropriation begins with Pico della Mirandola's search for Cabbalistic truth in the Renaissance, but leaves little permanent mark in Christian history. Some quiet scholarship existed even earlier in the writings of the Victorine monastics in France, who used material from medieval rabbinical interpreters such as Rashi of Troyes for their biblical glosses. Serious Hebraic scholarship developed in the sixteenth century, and by the seventeenth the complete scholar was assumed to be skilled in Latin, Greek, and Hebrew.

The flowering of Christian Hebraism in the seventeenth century brought into the Christian tradition the full range of Hebrew classical learning, though Christian scholars showed little interest in contemporary developments in Jewish intermural discussion. The eighteenth century, despite its philosophies of toleration that led to eventual Jewish emancipation and citizenship, displayed a great negative animus to the Jewish tradition. The attacks of deists and philosophers in search of "rational religion" were so hostile that they reduced the study of things Jewish to the study of superstition and immorality, and thus to irrelevance. In the new religion of reason, Judaism lost even the negative raison d'être granted by traditional Christianity, wherein the Jews existed as an eternal testimony to their rejection of Christ. Even a secular "saint" such as Immanuel Kant, whose works so heavily influenced Reform Judaism, did not support the emancipation of Jews into equal citizenship unless they were willing to espouse an ethic that mimicked his own; that is, Jews must renounce the rabbinical tradition and the Talmud as an entrance price.

The nineteenth century saw the ideal of a scientific study of religion, even though it rarely attained it. At the same time, Romantic notions concerning the essential nature of a "people" or ethnic group often led to absurd and politically biased depictions of the "Jewish spirit," and at best to well-meant oversimplifications. Still, significant developments in history and ethnology opened up the study of Hebrew scripture and enabled it to be compared with other traditions, thus breaking down the sacrosanct status of scripture, a process begun in the eighteenth century but with limited ethnographic sophistication.

The twentieth century emerged with scientific historical research conducted by reform-minded Jews who had accepted the methods of inquiry established by the larger academic community and also the challenge of Protestant-developed biblical criticism. This led to a scholarship that has become transreligious and pluralist.

Any such summary of Manuel's account of this complex Christian, Jewish, and secularist interaction is doomed to fail, however, for it is the richness of detail that distinguishes his study, giving authority to his challenge to widely held assumptions. The author is one of a growing number of scholars who deny the existence of a so-called "Judeo-Christian tradition," an idea he traces to the writings of Ernst Renan in the nineteenth century. What instead has existed until recently is a Christian and secularist scholarship that has at times been influenced by Jewish thought, at other times not, and in most circumstances has reworked it to satisfy non-Jewish agendas.

Unlike many scholars, however, Manuel sees in the concept of the "Judeo-Christian tradition" a promise of mutual acceptance and appreciation. Modern scholarship has long since rejected the parent-child metaphor that for centuries was used to describe the Jewish-Christian relationship, a metaphor that most often found little of value in the Jewish tradition after the first century. In contemporary scholarship, early Christianity is understood as a Jewish sect, and the multiple bonds that connect Christianity with Essene, Hellenistic, Rabbinical, and Apocalyptic Judaism are explored with increasing depth. Gone is the notion that significant developments in Judaism stopped in the first century, or with the formation of the Talmud. In biblical research, in the study of early Christianity, in the study of each other's history, scholarship in the two traditions has attained significant convergence.

The early discourse that existed between Christians and Jews in the first centuries of the common era has been reconnected. Although always existing in some small degree, even if only in the reading of Josephus or Maimonides, and building since the sixteenth century, in the contemporary era it has become most significant. In ending *The Broken Staff* the author allows himself a hope for the emergence of an ecumenical Jewish-Christian tradition that will exalt the Sermon on the Mount, the Psalms, the book of Job, and various prophets for their vision of mercy and righteousness.

This work not only will remain memorable for its pioneering scholarship but also is likely to become an indispensable resource for anyone concerned with issues surrounding Christian-Jewish dialogue. If one criterion for the success of a work is that a given field has changed because of it, it is relatively easy to predict the success of *The Broken Staff*.

*Edward J. Hughes*

## Sources for Further Study

*Boston Globe*. June 14, 1992, p. 43.
*Choice*. XXX, October, 1992, p. 318.
*The New Republic*. CCVI, June 1, 1992, p. 49.
*The New York Times Book Review*. XCVII, August 16, 1992, p. 21.

# BUNTING
## The Shaping of His Verse

*Author:* Peter Makin
*Publisher:* Clarendon Press/Oxford University Press (New York). Illustrated. 370 pp. $79.00
*Type of work:* Literary criticism; biography
*Time:* 1900-1985
*Locale:* England, France, Italy, the Middle East, and North America

*One of the first book-length studies of Basil Bunting, this will be a work of lasting value*

> *Principal personages:*
> BASIL BUNTING, a poet, translator, conscientious objector, music critic, soldier, foreign correspondent, newspaper drudge, and reluctant visiting professor
> EZRA POUND, Bunting's mentor, with whom he frequently disagreed
> LOUIS ZUKOFSKY, a friend and fellow poet, also a highly independent protégé of Pound

"There are those who think that after 1945 the poetry of Bunting is manifestly better than any other poetry in English written in the same period. It is in a class of its own. But this was so far from received opinion that it could not be taken seriously." Thus Donald Davie, writing at the end of the 1980's, summed up the critical standing of Basil Bunting's poetry. The title chosen by Davie for the book from which this assessment is quoted, *Under Briggflatts: A History of Poetry in Great Britain, 1960-1988* (1989), alluding to Bunting's long poem *Briggflatts* (1965), leaves no doubt about his own high estimation of Bunting's verse. Similarly, in *A Sinking Island: The Modern English Writers* (1987), Hugh Kenner celebrated Bunting's achievement, noted the general incomprehension with which it was met, and suggested that in order to come to terms with Bunting "we must relearn our reading skills." Now, with the publication of Peter Makin's *Bunting: The Shaping of His Verse*, the case for Bunting has been made at book-length by a superb advocate.

One of the virtues of the much-publicized debate over the canon is that, potentially at least, it should prompt a wholesale reexamination of why we read what we read, why we deem certain works worthy of study. In practice what we have got has largely been argument at a very low level. On one hand there are the defenders of Western civilization, for whom the list of set books has the authority of the tablets on Mount Sinai. (And yet it was T. S. Eliot who asked, in 1918, "Who, for instance, has a first-hand opinion of Shakespeare? Yet I have no doubt that much could be learned by a serious study of that semi-mythical figure.") On the other hand there are the spokespeople for various groups (usually defined in terms of race, ethnicity, or gender) said to have been underrepresented in the canon. What the two sides have in common is a readiness to accept uncritically whatever ideal reading list their ideology endorses, a disinclination to form firsthand opinions.

In contrast, consider Bunting's answer when asked by an interviewer to name the poets he judged to be "world-class": "Homer, Ferdosi, Manuchehri, Dante, Hafez,

Malherbe, Aneirin, Heledd, Wyatt, Spenser, Sidney, Wordsworth" (*Paideuma*, Spring, 1980). Whatever else can be said about that pugnaciously unconventional response—a similar roster appears in the preface to Bunting's *Collected Poems* (new ed., 1978), with some variations—it is clearly a personal selection. Not a list sanctified by custom or promoted by any consensus of literary commissars, it reflects Bunting's firsthand opinions based on a lifetime of reading.

In Peter Makin, Bunting has found a reader whose judgments are as independent and as deeply grounded in firsthand knowledge and experience as his own. Anyone can have an opinion—the student, for example, who disliked Dostoevski because "the names of all the characters sound the same"—yet too often, literary study consists of replacing such laughably ignorant responses with a set of approved opinions which the student has not formed for himself or herself. That is one reason Bunting generally held professors of literature in low regard. He preached against excessive bookishness; writing needs to measure itself always against the real. One of his models was Sir Walter Raleigh: "a great poet, a pirate, a statesman, and a million other things. You can't write about anything unless you've experienced it."

Makin's book is divided into five sections. The first part, "Development," consists of a sketch of Bunting's life to 1965 interwoven with an analysis of his development as a poet. Chapters are devoted to "Villon" (1925), Bunting's free adaptation drawing from several of François Villon's poems, somewhat in the spirit of Ezra Pound's *Homage to Sextus Propertius* (1919); "Chomei at Toyama" (1932), another free adaptation rather than a literal rendering, this time based on an Italian translation of a thirteenth century Japanese poem; "The Well of Lycopolis" (1935), an anti-love poem that uses classical allusions to underline the poet's disgust with the sordid state of "modern life"; and "The Spoils" (1951), which reflects both his World War II experience and his intensive study of Persian poetry, begun in the early 1930's.

"The Spoils" was followed by a long hiatus, nearly fifteen years in which Bunting simply was not able to write. During the war he had advanced rapidly to a position of great responsibility. (In World War I, Bunting had been an uncompromising conscientious objector, as a result of which he was jailed and brutally mistreated. World War II, in contrast, he embraced with gusto.) "By 1946," Makin tells us, "he was in Baghdad as acting chief of Combined Intelligence, covering the further half of the Middle East from the Indian frontier to that of Palestine." But as the aftermath of the war played out, Bunting—who had married a Persian woman, his second wife—had to find work in the civilian sector. He served with distinction as a correspondent for *The Times* until he was expelled from Iran after anti-British rioting.

Back in England in 1952, with his wife, their two-year-old daughter, and a newborn son, Bunting, despite his wealth of experience, was not readily employable. Some of Bunting's partisans, writing of this period, have indicted a "system" that could find no place for a man of his gifts and achievements. Makin is more balanced, sharing that anger but also factoring in Bunting's character. Stubborn integrity, pride, pigheadedness, a distaste for cant but also for routine work of any kind, a disordered personal life: Bunting had always gone his own way, whatever the consequences. In his early fifties, he had to take a proofreading job that barely supported himself and his family: "reading unbearable English in a deafening print-room," Makin relates.

Excerpts from Bunting's letters from this period suggest his self-disgust, despair, and increasing sense of intellectual isolation. While he was able eventually to get a job as a subeditor for *The Newcastle Journal*, his circumstances were only marginally improved. Then, in 1964, an unemployed young poet, Tom Pickard, came to visit, having been told about Bunting by the American poet, publisher, and impresario, Jonathan Williams. Within a short time Bunting had begun *Briggflatts*.

Pickard and the circle of young writers and readers who came to know Bunting evidently restored his faith in himself. Still, as Makin observes, "the odd thing is that nothing had changed. It is true that he had fears about his eyesight, and felt that the years remaining to write poems were few. But he was not getting an hour more of freedom from the drudgery." Yet if outwardly nothing had changed, Makin suggests, something had changed within, allowing Bunting to find a new voice.

Makin's part 2, "Matter," is devoted to *Briggflatts* and to an exposition of the Northumbrian tradition in which Bunting believed that he was working. As soon as it was published, *Briggflatts* was hailed as a masterpiece by figures as various as Hugh Kenner and Cyril Connolly. This was the work that put Bunting back into circulation. It led to the issuing of his collected poems, first by the Fulcrum Press in 1968 and then, a decade later, with minor changes and four additional poems, by Oxford University Press. It led to a series of invitations to teach as a visiting professor at various North American universities—work that he disliked but accepted out of financial necessity. It gave him the impetus to begin another major poem, unfinished at his death in 1985, the stunning first stanzas of which appear as Ode 11 in his *Uncollected Poems* (1991), edited by Richard Caddel. It is the work by which he is likely to be remembered.

*Briggflatts* is an unusual fusion of the personal and the historical. As Makin notes, the poem "takes a considerable part of its substance from the Dark Ages: from the lives of St Cuthbert, the *Gododdin* poems, the Norse sagas, the Anglo-Saxon Chronicle." Yet it is also Bunting's most personal work. Subtitled "An Autobiography," it harks back some fifty years from the time of its composition, to Bunting's youth.

When he was twelve years old, shortly after he was sent to the Quaker school in Ackworth, Bunting was invited by a classmate to visit the small village of Brigflatts (one *g*, though Bunting preferred the alternate spelling). George Fox had stayed in Brigflatts in 1652, just prior to what is traditionally taken to be the founding of Quakerism. While there, Bunting met a girl, Peggy Greenback, whose father was the local mason. The poem *Briggflatts* is dedicated to her; she is the love whose abandonment by the poet sets this oblique "autobiography" in motion. (In Makin's very terse account, after their initial meeting "Bunting came back often. But when he was released from prison in 1919 he did not come back. . . .")

The first two sections take up the bulk of Makin's book. In part 3, "The Form of Poetry," Makin relates Bunting's fascination with an illuminated book, the Lindisfarne Gospels (c. 698), to his distinctive sense of "abstraction" in art; this leads into the following chapter, where Makin considers Bunting's emphasis on poetic form as being analogous to musical form. Part 4, "Theory," shows how Bunting's apparently naïve "literary realism" can withstand the challenge posed by contemporary literary theory. In part 5, "Coda," Makin briefly traces Bunting's post-*Briggflatts* career. The book concludes with several appendices and a bibliography.

Makin's frequent quotations from fugitive essays will make many readers yearn for a collection of Bunting's prose. (The extracts from letters are also enticing.) Makin has seemingly read every word Bunting wrote. He does not try to make all of Bunting's pronouncements consistent; as he remarks, "the critical theory of the mature author is largely a Distant Early Warning system for the protection of the writer's personality." Thus, while we will want to understand why the cult of experience was central to Bunting's art, we are not thereby committed to a universal principle. (Behind Bunting's insistence that one can write only about what one has experienced, Hugh Kenner sees "an honest, and desperate, rejection of much communality gone facile; Shakespeare could feel safe in being without the experience of watching sheep, of killing, of wearing a crown.")

Makin is particularly good on sound in poetry. Of all the themes in this rich study, it is the one with most general application, sufficient by itself to engage anyone with an interest in poetry. Makin's subtitle announces his interest in the shape of poetry. As he explains in his preface, "I assume, as Basil Bunting did, that the reason-for-being of a poem is its shape." When Makin speaks of "shape" he has in mind several different scales at once. One aspect of a poem's shape, for example, is the way in which it introduces a theme (such as the abandonment of love in *Briggflatts*), moves to other themes, then returns to the original theme. Most fundamentally, though, the shape of a poem is formed by the sounds its words make.

When the stir over *Briggflatts* brought Bunting's views into currency, he became notorious for his emphasis on the role of sound in poetry. "People sometimes suppose me to be saying that music is the only thing in poetry. Not at all. It is not the only thing. But it is the only *indispensable* thing." What is striking about most contemporary poetry, of whatever "school" or "movement," is the extent to which there is in it no "beauty of sound." Even the so-called New Formalists seem not to notice that, with all their reverence for "traditional forms," they rarely approach the densely patterned "sound-working" which Bunting sought in his own verse and in that of others worth emulating, the music of these lines from the "Coda" to Briggflatts:

> Blind, we follow
> rain slant, spray flick
> to fields we do not know.

*John Wilson*

### Sources for Further Study

*Durham University Journal.* LXXXIV July, 1992, p. 353.
*The Times Literary Supplement.* October 16, 1992, p. 26.

# THE BURIED MIRROR
## Reflections on Spain and the New World

*Author:* Carlos Fuentes (1928-     )
*Publisher:* Houghton Mifflin (New York). Illustrated. 399 pp. $35.00
*Type of work:* Social history
*Time:* The 1400's to 1992
*Locale:* Spain and Latin America

> *Celebrating the quincentenary of Christopher Columbus' journey to the New World, Fuentes explores the national identities of Latin American countries, relating the roots of these identities to their varied origins*

Spain had been in disarray for some decades before 1492, the year in which Italian explorer Christopher Columbus persuaded King Ferdinand and Queen Isabella to finance his efforts to find a route to India and the Spice Islands that did not necessitate a long, dangerous overland trip. The route around the Cape of Good Hope was not conquered by Vasco da Gama until 1498. Fuentes calls 1492 a watershed year for Spain, and few would quibble with that contention.

The Iberian peninsula, emerging from the Middle Ages, had been hard hit by the Black Death of 1350. Spain had a population in 1469—the year in which Ferdinand and Isabella married—of about seven million, half a million of whom were Jews, although Jews constituted about one-third of the country's urban population. A substantial Islamic community flourished south of Madrid, around Granada.

The kings of Aragon, Castile, and Navarre had preserved their separate boundaries jealously through the early fifteenth century, but the Castilian Isabella's union with the king of Aragon brought about a relaxation of the territorial imperatives under which Spain had lived, opening the possibility that the country could be unified. By 1492, it was evident that the peasantry, which previously had owed fealty to feudal lords, now saw its first duty as to the crown.

In the name of achieving a unity based on religious orthodoxy and racial purity, the monarchs in 1492 attacked Granada and drove the Muslims from it and into foreign exile. They also demanded that all Jews convert to Christianity or leave. This proclamation effectively robbed Spain of the most culturally active segment of its population. It also devastated the economy, because Jews were the tax collectors, the heaviest taxpayers, the bankers, and the professional people of Spain.

It was into this mercurial situation that Columbus came, begging assistance. The monarchs, desperate for a way to fill their shrinking coffers, agreed to provide the backing the young Italian needed. In so doing, they gave their tacit approval to an important and far-reaching hypothesis that challenged common sense. They gave their blessing—and their money—to someone who obviously did not accept the prevailing notion, confirmed by human perception, that the earth is flat. In doing so, they opened a new and significant chapter in the history of the human race.

Setting sail on August 3, 1492, in his three caravels, the *Niña*, the *Pinta*, and the

*Santa Maria*, Columbus sailed west for sixty-six days before he landed on the minuscule island of Guanahani, which he renamed San Salvador. He found the natives curious and friendly. They wondered whether the voyagers who had landed were men or gods. The strangers' clothing and jewelry fascinated the natives, who were soon subdued and enslaved.

The Spanish explorers who followed Columbus—Francisco Pizarro, Hernán Cortés, Pedro de Valdivia—had been brought up in a multicultural Spain that had, in 1492, tried to erase multiculturalism. Nevertheless, these early explorers understood cultural diversity. They came to the New World to gain riches, to convert the natives to Christianity, and to impose their ways upon the inhabitants they found there. They also intermarried, creating a new breed of Spanish Americans.

Although these early explorers served Ferdinand and Isabella, whose chief aim was to bring about Christian unity, and although these explorers shared these aims, they were still sufficiently a part of the tricultural society that Spain was before the expulsion of the Muslims and Jews to realize that they had to deal with the "Other," as Fuentes calls the non-Spanish, non-Christian group, when they began to colonize. Fuentes notes that when an outside group deals with the "Other," conflict is inevitable and both groups are altered irrevocably. Such was certainly the case in the development of Latin America, as the invaders "both destroyed and created the culture of the New World."

Fuentes traces the initial habitation of the New World to a period forty-eight millennia in the past, when a land bridge existed between Asia and the North American continent. The early entrants into this previously uninhabited land mass were nomadic. They hunted, following the animals they quested after, until, at some point between 7500 and 2500 B.C., they learned to cultivate crops, enabling them to settle in one place and lead a more settled existence than their previous lives had allowed. Out of this shift grew native cultures, some of which, such as the Mayan, Aztec, and Inca, were remarkably advanced scientifically, mathematically, and artistically.

With the coming of Europeans to the American continent after 1492, Fuentes points out, Latin America became multicultural, as Spain had been before Ferdinand and Isabella moved to eliminate multiculturalism from their empire. In its multiculturalism, however, Fuentes finds hope for Latin America. He believes that nations that practice exclusion betray themselves, whereas those that are inclusive, open to other cultures, discover themselves. He does not view multiculturalism as a divisive force.

Fuentes contends that a people are whole only in relation to other people who help to define them. By extension, cultural groups are whole only in relation to other cultures that provide the measure of what a culture really is. Because Latin America's beginnings were multicultural, essentially Indian and Hispanic, and have become more so with immigration from other parts of the world, the cultural fiber of the area is intricately interwoven with elements of many cultures.

Fuentes contends that the Latins who brought their culture to the Americas themselves represented a mix of cultures—notably Mediterranean, Islamic, and Jewish. Looking into the Latin American mirror that is his metaphor, he sees the reflection of a mother culture that was similar in fundamental ways to the cultures in which he lives. Using the mirror metaphor to project as well as to reflect, he prophesies a brighter future for Latin America than present conditions in much of the region immediately suggest.

One of the causes of early conflict between the native residents of Latin America and the explorers from Europe had to do with religious practices. Latin American Indian societies practiced human sacrifice. Fuentes explains knowledgeably how this practice became entrenched. Drawing from the Mayan bible, he shows how, according to this account of human genesis, the human race was spawned through sacrifice.

As the story goes, the gods met and decided that one of their company should sacrifice himself by leaping into a roaring fire. A handsome, important god hesitated, but one of the other gods, a dwarf, naked and covered with ulcers, leaped into the conflagration unhesitatingly and was instantly resurrected as the sun. At this point, the more recalcitrant god sacrificed himself and was resurrected as the moon. Based on this sort of holy writ, human sacrifice—with the expectation of instant transformation into something better than the person had been—became a central element in the religion of these people.

Obviously, this custom, understandable as it is in light of its background, was repugnant to the Europeans, almost exclusively Christian, who came to the New World. Sacrifice was a practical necessity for the Latin American Indians, who believed that four previous suns (creations) had been extinguished by the gods (natural forces) and that human sacrifice alone could prevent the destruction of the fifth sun. The outsiders were both appalled and threatened by what they viewed as a barbaric practice, and at times they used their repugnance as a justification for enslaving, deporting, and slaughtering the natives.

Some of those who came to the New World from Europe were changed incalculably by living among the Indians. Bartolomé de las Casas had resettled in Cuba and owned Indian slaves. His chief motive for coming to the New World appears to have been greed. His cupidity vanished, however, after he heard a sermon delivered by Father Montesinos at the Christmas mass in 1511 suggesting that the Indians were men who had "rational souls."

A conscience-stricken las Casas by 1515 had begun to disperse all of his holdings and release his slaves. He joined the Dominican order in 1524 and railed until his death in 1566 against the injustices the Europeans had visited upon the natives they found in the lands they claimed. As for the paganism of the Indians, he dismissed the matter by asking whether the Greeks, Romans, and Jews, who were certainly human, were not also pagans.

Although Fuentes focuses primarily on the period from 1492 to 1992, his book, in exploring the roots of the dominant cultures upon which he concentrates, delves into the earliest beginnings of Spanish culture, going back as far as the caves at Altamira. He explores as well the pre-European history of the Latin American Indians. This book packs into less than four hundred pages an incredible span, a remarkable feat considering the multicultural nature of its discourse.

The neatly interwoven thread that holds together a book that might easily have become unraveled is Fuentes' inherent understanding of the importance of continuity in all human activities and interactions. With a mighty sweep, Fuentes is able to relate the cave drawings at Altamira to the graffiti sprayed last night on a wall in Los Angeles or El Paso. What separates the ancient drawings from the more recent ones is merely time. Fuentes realizes that in both instances, people were expressing themselves, telling something about their lives, their needs, their aspirations.

It is in such a context, of course, that Fuentes finds more to unify humankind than to divide it. He is, however, less optimistic about politics than he is about art. He finds in art the release of a healthy imagination. In modern Latin American politics, he sees little to suggest imagination. Indeed, he sees politics and art as parts of opposing camps, with the politicians either trying to suppress artistic expression or bending it to their own propagandistic uses.

Art, on the other hand, holds the mirror up to society, as Fuentes demonstrates in his discussion of Pablo Picasso's *Guernica* (which is reproduced in the book) and Diego Rivera's depiction of General Antonio López de Santa Anna, in which the dictator looks like a comic strip character. Fuentes thinks such a depiction befits Santa Anna, whom he describes as a "comic-opera Latin American dictator." He tells of Santa Anna's pretensions and of his indifference to the needs of his people, as shown when he ordered yellow satin uniforms from Paris for his palace guards, dealing his country's treasury yet another blow solely for the purpose of feeding his own arrogant ego.

In essence, Fuentes, one of Mexico's leading novelists as well as a respected statesman who has served as Mexico's ambassador to France, is calling for a renewed emphasis in Latin America on the common cultural heritage that its people from Tijuana to Tierra del Fuego share. He sees art in all its manifestations as the linchpin for bringing about the kind of unity that, in his view, can offer hope to the nations of the Americas. He also calls for a democratization throughout Latin America that will replace revolutions as a means of bringing about the kinds of economic development and social justice that people crave.

Along with a stimulating text, this book provides more than 160 illustrations of excellent quality. The volume—an outgrowth of a five-hour television series on the Discovery Channel, for which Fuentes was the on-camera host—is as well designed as it is researched and written.

*R. Baird Shuman*

## Sources for Further Study

*ARTnews*. XCI, April, 1992, p. 20.
*Chicago Tribune*. April 19, 1992, XIV, p. 5.
*The Christian Science Monitor*. June 30, 1992, p. 13.

*Hispanic*. V, October, 1992, p. 80.
*History Today*. XLII, May, 1992, p. 59.
*Insight*. VIII, April 27, 1992, p. 23.
*Library Journal*. CXVII, March 1, 1992, p. 105.
*Los Angeles Times*. April 22, 1992, p. E4.
*The Nation*. CCLIV, March 30, 1992, p. 408.
*New Statesman and Society*. V, April 17, 1992, p. 41.
*The New York Times Book Review*. XCVII, April 26, 1992, p. 9.
*Publishers Weekly*. CCXXXIX, March 23, 1992, p. 58.
*Time*. CXXXIX, June 29, 1992, p. 78.
*The Washington Post Book World*. XXII, March 29, 1992, p. 1.

# THE BUSINESS OF FANCYDANCING
## Stories and Poems

*Author:* Sherman Alexie
*Publisher:* Hanging Loose Press (Brooklyn, New York). 84 pp. Paperback $10.00
*Type of work:* Poems, stories, and sketches

*The pieces in this collection of forty poems, five stories, and several vignettes by Sherman Alexie, a Spokane/Coeur D'Alene Indian, seek to define what it is to be a Native American with one foot in the reservation and the other in the outside world*

In this first collection of Sherman Alexie's work, the author presents a selection of his writing around a central theme: what it means for Native Americans living on the reservation to find themselves delicately balanced between their tribal traditions and an impinging modern world outside the reservation. The conflict that such a situation engenders extends far beyond the confines of the Spokane/Coeur D'Alene Indian Reservation at Wellpinit in eastern Washington, where Alexie lives and about which he writes. His writing has cogent meaning for members of all subcultures within American society, whether racial or religious or those dictated by such factors as age, gender, or sexual orientation.

*The Business of Fancydancing* is divided into three sections entitled "Distances," "Evolution," and "Crazy Horse Dreams." The most allegorical of these sections is certainly the last, which deals—fancifully at times—with the history of a native people. Elements of this history surface in the two other sections, although they are not as central to them as they are to "Crazy Horse Dreams," which, at thirty-one pages, is the book's longest section.

Fancydancing, from which Alexie derives his title, refers to the ritualistic tribal dances through which major elements of the history and tradition of Native Americans are communicated. These rigidly programmed dances are performed in elaborate costumes decorated with the feathers of rare birds and with ornaments made from seashells and from semiprecious jewels, often turquoise, topaz, or agate.

A picture of the author dressed in a typical fancydancing costume appears on the cover of the book. This costume cloaks all of his body save for part of the face and the hands. The legs are covered with chaps, the feet with soft, decorated slippers. The size and ornateness of the costume purposely minimize the fact that it covers a person, deemphasizing the performer—who is virtually lost in a flurry of feathers—in favor of focusing attention on the traditions that the dances convey: People are transient, tribal traditions eternal.

In most of the pieces in this collection, Alexie deals with the inherent conflicts of being a Native American in the late twentieth century. Some of the conflicts are overtly external. The police in eastern Washington discriminate against Native Americans, pulling their cars over threateningly and accusing them of infractions, often of drunk driving, as in "Traveling," the first selection in the book.

A more internal conflict is that between the Native Americans who live on the reservation and the tribal police—their own people—who have to enforce the laws. The most extended piece in which Alexie deals with this situation is "Special Delivery," perhaps the most psychologically and structurally complex story in the collection. It contains some of the most amazing writing in the book, mixing reality and fantasy in spine-tingling ways.

In this story, Thomas Builds-the-Fire, whose life generally follows an unwavering routine, leaves for the post office, as he always does, at 9:15 A.M. Eve, the reservation's postmistress, is supposed to open the post office at 9:30, but she is late and Thomas stands in the cold waiting for her. As he waits, his mind reverts to a conversation he had with a fellow tribesman, Simon, a whimsical character, often drunk, who makes a habit of weaving when he drives soberly so that the tribal police will not notice a change in his driving habits when he has been drinking.

Simon has caused Thomas to think about what he calls the politics of time, distance, and geography. Simon, in a talk with Thomas when they are both drinking, contends that Point A is where a person is and Point B is where that person ought to be: If Point A, for example, is drunk, Point B is drunker. What falls between the two points is, according to Simon, politics.

As Thomas stands in the cold musing about this insight, Simon comes weaving down the road in his car, stone sober, jumps the curb, plows through a shrub, and parks directly behind Mary Song's station wagon. Mary shrieks at him, telling him to get his truck away from her vehicle. He obliges, backing his truck all the way down the street until he hits a utility pole and disrupts electrical service. As sparks fly, "crawling along the grass like blind snakes," Simon observes profoundly that "electricity is just lightning pretending to be permanent," certainly one of the most memorable statements in the book, one that reflects the tie that Native Americans have to nature, using it freely and often in their similes and metaphors.

With electrical power to the tribal trading post interrupted, the tribal police are called and soon arrive. They begin to abuse Simon, picking him up by his braids and finally throwing him, unconscious, to the ground. They then turn their attention to Thomas, who has been taunting them. When they finish with Thomas, they direct their attention to Eve, who finally runs into the post office followed by Thomas, who locks the door behind them.

The tribal police then spread the word that Thomas is holding Eve hostage, which he clearly is not. He threatens to begin shooting, but the police know that Thomas does not have a weapon and tell him so. He responds that he has the idea of a gun and stays in the post office telling Eve a story that he wants to finish. When the room grows cold, Thomas suggests building a fire with the undelivered junk mail, but Eve reminds him that to do so would be a federal offense, so he abandons the notion.

The story Thomas needs to tell is that he has found his "vision animal," an allegorical beast who limps up to Thomas on three legs, the fourth pulled close to his chest. It asks for water, but Thomas has only whiskey to give it. It requests deer jerky, but Thomas has only the commodity cheese that the Bureau of Indian Affairs distributes on the reservation. Finally the vision animal tells Thomas, "You don't have a dream that will ever come true," which seems to be Alexie's statement about the plight of Native Americans living in the United States.

Besides the conflicts with police, Alexie's characters experience the greatest of all conflicts, the internal conflict that involves the self. Nearly every selection in this anthology contains elements of this conflict, but it is particularly prominent in a half-page vignette, "Dead Letter Office," in which the narrator receives a letter, written in his tribal language, that he does not understand and cannot read.

After seeking translators in a bar, he asks Big Mom to translate the letter for him, but she will not do so until he fancydances for her, reinforcing the importance of tradition. At closing time, Big Mom rises from her chair and leaves. The narrator follows her "for years, holding some brief letter from the past, finding she had never been here, she had never gone."

Such are the fantasies that work their way in and out of many of the stories and poems of this collection, the allegories of which deal with loss of identity through loss of tradition. It is the recognition of this conflict that embodies Alexie's statement about the internal conflicts that are the constant companions of Native Americans. He generally seems to be suggesting that attempts to preserve tribal identity are doomed in the United States of the late twentieth century.

The eleven Fausto poems that occupy three pages in the book are curiously interesting. Fausto is a Hawaiian, son of a mother from the Philippines and a father from Japan. He is the narrator's college roommate in the state of Washington and is a sort of outsider different from the narrator. Fausto makes assumptions about the narrator that turn out to be false; the narrator makes assumptions about Fausto that turn out not to be valid.

Fausto, going home with the narrator for Thanksgiving, wants to see him ride a horse. The narrator does not know how to ride, surprising Fausto, who thinks that all Indians can ride horses. Then, when the two are watching a televised show, the narrator asks Fausto how well he surfs. Fausto says that he does not know how to surf, whereupon the narrator says that he thought all Hawaiians knew how to surf. Alexie deals here with much deeper insights into human perception than the surface story suggests.

Fausto, who sometimes goes for long periods without talking, communicating instead by gesturing, creates his individual analogies based on the environment in which he grew up. Standing beneath a hundred-foot pine tree on which the snow is falling, he remarks that the snow is like cold sand.

One night, Fausto disappears, leaving his clothes and his best pair of shoes behind. The narrator tries to reach him by telephoning Hawaii several times, but he fails. He watches *Hawaii Five-O* to remind himself of his errant roommate. Finally he hears from Fausto, who has joined the U.S. Army, receiving letters from him with postmarks from various bases in the South. Fausto writes that he fixes helicopters, fixing them so everyone can fly again. The Fausto poems end on this note.

It is characteristic of Alexie's writing to avoid decisive endings. One cannot read any of these selections linearly; they are not so intended and to read them thus is to do them a significant injustice. The poems and stories in this collection are subtle in the way that Japanese art is subtle. Like Japanese art, they are uncluttered. They suggest more than they state.

Once read—and it is probably best not to read this short book in one sitting—the individual selections, which often warrant rereading, begin to grow in the reader's imagination. Allowed gentle repose in readers' minds, each story and each poem will swell into something much larger than its surface immediately suggests.

One might compare Alexie's work to Mary Mebane's vignettes about black society found in *Mary, Wayfarer* (1983) or to Julia Ortiz Cofer's depictions of Puerto Ricans caught between two worlds in *Silent Dancing* (1990). Such comparisons, however, are specious even though they may seem initially to be valid. Alexie is dealing with a very different set of conflicts from those that characterize other minorities in the United States. Native Americans are the original Americans. Other ethnic minorities derive their traditions from origins very different from those of Native Americans. Each set of traditions is important but not directly comparable.

In order to appreciate Alexie, whose work scintillates through some of its subtle insights that lead to striking epiphanies, one must suspend a great many preconceptions about literature. Alexie breaks new artistic ground—and a remarkably fertile ground it is. Not a product of writing workshops or college programs in creative writing, this Native American writer is an original, someone capable of turning over new furrows in literary acreage that has thus far been sparingly attended.

*R. Baird Shuman*

### Sources for Further Study

*American Book Review.* XIV, January, 1993, p. 8.
*Library Journal.* CXVII, October 1, 1992, p. 86.

# CAPITOL GAMES
## Clarence Thomas, Anita Hill, and the Story of a
## Supreme Court Nomination

*Authors*: Timothy M. Phelps (1947-    ) and Helen Winternitz (1951-    )
*Publisher:* Hyperion (New York). 458 pp. $24.95
*Type of work*: Current affairs
*Time:* Spring through Fall, 1991, with background and a brief epilogue
*Locale:* Washington, D.C., and the United States at large

*Two journalists, one of whom broke the news of Anita Hill's sexual harassment charges against Clarence Thomas, tell the story of Thomas' nomination to the Supreme Court and the subsequent battle for Senate confirmation*

*Principal personages:*
> CLARENCE THOMAS, a nominee to the U.S. Supreme Court
> ANITA HILL, a former employee who accused Thomas of sexual harassment
> GEORGE BUSH, the U.S. president who nominated Thomas
> BENJAMIN HOOKS, a civil rights leader who helped to blunt initial opposition to Thomas' nomination
> JOHN DANFORTH, Thomas' most avid supporter in the Senate
> ARLEN SPECTOR, a senator who took primary responsibility for cross-examining Hill
> JOSEPH BIDEN, the chair of the Senate Judiciary Committee
> TED KENNEDY, a key opponent to Thomas' nomination who largely withdrew from the process
> ANGELA WRIGHT, a potential witness for Hill who was not called upon to testify at the Senate hearings

Although coauthored, *Capitol Games* is narrated from the point of view of Timothy Phelps, who, as a reporter for *Newsday*, first made public Anita Hill's allegations of sexual harassment against Supreme Court nominee Clarence Thomas. Supplementing this vantage point with additional research, the authors explore the path by which Thomas came to be President George Bush's choice for the slot on the court vacated by Thurgood Marshall. They also explore the behind-the-scenes machinations of the confirmation process and the reasons for to Thomas' confirmation by a narrow margin. Along the way, evaluations of participants in the process, including President Bush, various prominent senators, and members of the mass media, are offered.

Phelps and Winternitz also reassess the performance of the principals themselves; neither Thomas nor Hill, however, cooperated directly in the writing of this book. Instead, the observations of relatives, friends, and acquaintances are used to reconstruct the course of events.

Thomas' path to the Supreme Court was an extraordinary one even before the controversy with Hill. Born in Pin Point, Georgia in 1948, Thomas lived in relative poverty with his mother until the age of six. His father had deserted the family to escape a paternity suit. When he was six, Thomas went to live with Myers Anderson, his maternal grandfather. A relative stranger to the boy, Anderson was a somewhat distant but powerfully positive role model for Thomas. Anderson was a strict task-master who inculcated in Thomas both a powerful work ethic and a firm commitment to civil rights. Thomas was a hard-working, talented student, ultimately earning a law degree from Yale University. Upon graduation from law school, Thomas had trouble finding the type of employment he wanted, in a field other than civil rights, until he went to work for John Danforth, the attorney general of Missouri and a Republican. Danforth, a fellow Yale graduate, allowed Thomas to specialize in tax work. It was his connection with Danforth that led Thomas to Washington, first as a legislative aide when Danforth was elected to Congress, then as a political appointee in the Ronald Reagan Administration.

Thomas' political views had changed quite drastically over the years. They had become more militant during his college years, when Malcolm X supplanted Martin Luther King, Jr., as a personal hero. After college, however, Thomas gradually became more conservative, tying his destiny first to Danforth, a moderate Republican, and later to more conservative elements in the Republican party. Although Thomas' motives may have been partly opportunistic, he seems also to have found the ideas of Thomas Sowell and other black conservatives highly compelling.

After going to work for Reagan, first in the Department of Education and then at the Equal Employment Opportunity Commission (EEOC), Thomas became even more rightist, fostering close connections with extremist groups rigidly opposed to sanctions on the apartheid government of South Africa, abortion, and affirmative action, among other things. Thomas' religious affiliation also changed during this time, from Catholic to a highly politicized antiabortion Baptist denomination.

In the eyes of Washington right-wingers, Thomas' ideological and racial credentials made him a supremely qualified nominee to replace Thurgood Marshall. Marshall, a legendary civil rights pioneer and all-around liberal, had been named to the Court by Lyndon Johnson in 1967, becoming the Supreme Court's first African American justice. Thomas could fill what was seen as the African American place on the court but promote conservative rather than liberal ideas.

In 1989, in preparation for his possible role as Marshall's successor, Thomas was nominated and confirmed as a federal appellate court justice. When Marshall retired two years later, Thomas was the consensus choice of right-wingers to replace him. Thomas' combination of African American status and avid right-wing credentials would, it was hoped, confound liberals and mainstream civil rights organizations. Such groups, smarting because of the rightward direction the Court was taking under President Reagan, had managed to block the confirmation of Robert Bork in 1987. The strategy of Thomas' supporters was to split the African American community so that liberal and Southern Democrats would hesitate to oppose Thomas, despite considerable pressure to do so. This scheme received a boost when Benjamin Hooks of the National Association for the Advancement of Colored People (NAACP) delayed and then modestly weakened the negative response of his organization to Thomas.

Thomas' first round of hearings before the Senate Judiciary Committee did not go particularly well. Thomas' lack of experience in judicial matters and vacillation on remarks he had made in his various speeches to right-wing groups made him seem evasive, if not downright deceptive. His credibility also was damaged by his claim that he had never discussed the merits of the landmark *Roe v. Wade* case (1973), which established a woman's reproductive freedom as a constitutionally protected right. Thomas had been in law school at the time, making this claim dubious.

The committee hearings resulted in a tie vote, mostly along party lines, with the committee recommending neither confirmation nor denial of Thomas' nomination. It appeared that the vote in the Senate as a whole would provide a comfortable, though not overwhelming, margin of victory.

Anita Hill's accusations of sexual harassment then became public. They were not a surprise, however, to most members of the Judiciary Committee. Democrats had been informed of the accusations by Joseph Biden, the Democrat who chaired the Committee. Strom Thurmond, the ranking Republican, also had been informed. Thurmond had not thought the charges serious enough to inform his fellow Republicans on the committee. Agents of the Federal Bureau of Investigation had been dispatched to Oklahoma to interrogate the reluctant Hill. After questioning both Hill and Thomas, they concluded that there was an insufficient basis for the charges. This investigation, however, did not exonerate Thomas or discredit Hill. In addition, the committee members had possession of a signed statement by Hill in which she claimed that Thomas had sexually harassed her while he was her superior at the Department of Education and later at the EEOC. With the charges made public, the committee and the Senate at large were forced to respond, though only reluctantly and only after Democrats agreed to a severe limitation on the time that would be taken to investigate the charges.

Hill was put in the position she had wished from the beginning to avoid, that of having to make her charges in public. Because of various compromises between Senate Democrats and Republicans, both she and Thomas, who denied all of Hill's charges outright, would be forced to defend themselves in an open, televised hearing marred by a circus atmosphere and the absence of any reasonable rules of due process.

The politics of the situation favored Thomas. His Republican supporters in the Senate, led by his mentor, John Danforth, launched an attack on Hill's character, integrity, and even mental health. Democrats, on the other hand, neutralized by Thomas' race or by desires to maintain a certain image, treated Thomas with deference and left Hill on her own to fend off her Republican interrogators, led by Pennsylvania's Senator Arlen Spector. The result was an unsavory, one-sided rhetorical spectacle in which winning public support for Thomas took precedence over the quest for truth.

Thomas, however, won Senate confirmation by only a 56-44 margin. Hill had spoken credibly and carried herself with dignity. Public opinion polls during the hearings favored Thomas by a sizable margin, but the figures shifted over the next year or so to the point where Hill actually was believed by more Americans than was Thomas. Testimony by third parties conclusively demonstrated that Hill was not part of a last-minute conspiratorial effort to discredit Thomas, as Thomas and a number of supporters asserted. Three different witnesses indicated that Hill had told them of Thomas' behavior at the time it occurred. Likewise, Republican allegations that Hill was a scorned woman or was given to fantasy remained unsupported. Nevertheless, the Republicans kept attacking Hill, as though the weakness of their arguments could be neutralized by sheer volume. That assumption, given the politics of the situation, proved correct. There was, however, a cost. Spector spent his 1992 campaign groveling for the forgiveness of women voters, beating a female opponent by only a narrow margin. Alan Dixon, an Illinois Democrat, was ousted in the Democratic primary by a relatively unknown black female opponent, largely because of his vote on the Senate floor to confirm Thomas despite Hill's allegations. The image of the Senate as a whole, in fact, was damaged badly.

The authors blame inappropriate handling of the investigation on Judiciary Committee members of both parties; on Biden for his confused handling of Hill's charges and the subsequent hearing, on Republican Committee members for elevating partisan loyalty over fairness and civility, and on Committee Democrats for allowing the Republicans to attack Hill for the sake of political expediency. The authors chastise the Senate as a whole for its insensitivity to the issue of sexual harassment.

Senators, however, are not the only ones criticized. President Bush is blamed for denying that race played a role in his selection of Thomas. In this case, competence came in a poor fourth behind race, ideology, and interest-group pressure. Phelps and Winternitz also criticize the hysterical behavior of reporters, though they defend Phelps's own action of reporting the news of Hill's accusations once he had confirmation that they had been formally lodged.

Thomas and Hill also come in for some criticism. The authors try to be even-handed, pointing out, for example, that Thomas appeared to be a force for moderation in the Reagan Administration until he was shunned by mainstream civil rights groups. Nevertheless, they are clearly unimpressed by Thomas' self-proclaimed martyrdom during the Hill hearings. Hill and her team of lawyers are taken to task for failing to realize the importance of Angela Wright as a witness. Wright, another Thomas employee who claimed to have been harassed mildly, was never called upon despite her willingness to testify.

Phelps and Winternitz do not speculate on whether Thomas or Hill was telling the truth. They point out evidence that Thomas displayed an avid interest in pornographic films during his law school and Washington years and that Wright would probably have had considerable credibility as a supporting witness for Hill. Their point, however, is that the truth of the matter became entirely irrelevant in the context of political maneuvering.

The authors also do not predict whether Clarence Thomas will be a good or bad Supreme Court justice. A relatively young man, Thomas should have ample opportunity to overcome the bizarre circumstances of his arrival on the Court.

*Ira Smolensky*

## Sources for Further Study

*Atlanta Journal Constitution.* July 5, 1992, p. N9.
*Business Week.* August 10, 1992, p.10.
*Chicago Daily Law Bulletin.* CXXXVIII, July 15, 1992, p. 2.
*Chicago Tribune.* August 17, 1992, V, p. 3.
*Los Angeles Times Book Review.* June 14, 1992, p. 2.
*The New Leader.* LXXV, October 5, 1992, p.17.
*The New York Times Book Review.* XCVII, October 25, 1992, p. 1.
*The New Yorker.* LXVIII, August 17, 1992, p. 7.
*San Francisco Chronicle.* June 5, 1992, p. REV13.
*The Washington Post Book World.* XXII, July 12, 1992, p. 1.

# A CASE OF CURIOSITIES

*Author:* Allen Kurzweil (1960-      )
*Publisher:* Harcourt Brace Jovanovich (New York). 358 pp. $19.95
*Type of work:* Novel
*Time:* 1780-1790
*Locale:* Tournay and Paris, France; and Geneva, Switzerland

*The ten divisions of this work, named for the objects in the* memento hominem *that the protagonist creates, trace the adventures of Claude Page during his second decade of life*

*Principal characters:*
> CLAUDE PAGE, the protagonist, a skilled artist and craftsman
> JULIETTE CORDANT PAGE, his mother, an herbalist
> JEAN-BAPTISTE-PIERRE-ROBERT AUGET, abbé and count of Tournay, Claude's patron
> ADOLPHE STAEMPHLI, a surgeon from Geneva, a collector of curiosities
> PAUL DOME, a coachman who befriends Claude
> SEBASTIAN PLUMEAUX, a Parisian hack writer and debarred lawyer
> LUCIEN LIVRE, a bookseller, pornographer, and Claude's employer
> ALEXANDRE HÉLÈNE HUGON, Claude's blue-eyed, blond mistress
> MARGUERITE, a nursemaid who marries Claude

Eighteenth century deists compared the world to a watch, an analogy well suited to this historical novel, in which the main character creates ingenious mechanisms, including timepieces. The book thus reflects the age in which it is set; it is also very much a postmodern text, as concerned with its own composition as with the story it has to tell. This duality pervades the work, which emerges as at once art and artifice. Like the devices that Claude Page creates, the novel delights in two ways. On the surface, one can enjoy the movement of the figures, the characters' actions, but one can also take pleasure in the elaborate construction, in a mechanism that produces life, or at least its simulacrum.

The twin aspects of the book expose themselves in the opening pages, in which the narrator describes his acquiring a case of curiosities at a Paris auction in 1983. In one sense, this case refers to a box in which a person places a collection of objects, often commonplace, that relate to important events in the individual's life. This case of objects inoculates the narrator with a case—in a medical sense—of curiosity, so that he spends the next six years studying the life of the young man who had assembled these items. The account that results, a history presented in "a novel manner," as Sebastian Plumeaux will punningly say late in the story, is itself about a character whose curiosity leads him into a curious life between the ages of ten and twenty.

The tale that follows unfolds in ten units. The decade of divisions corresponds to the number of years that elapse; it also reflects the decimalization that the French Revolution imposed on all facets of life, including time, which it sought to measure in ten-day weeks, ten-hour days, and hundred-minute hours. Numerology, especially relating to time, affects other aspects of the work as well. The book contains sixty chapters and 360 pages, though the last two are blank because Claude's story is unfinished. Kurzweil appears to have stolen a (blank) page from Laurence Sterne's *Tristram Shandy* (1759-1767), doubled it, and converted it to a representation of Page's blank. The story completes a circle of 360 degrees because in the last numbered chapter—there is an unnumbered postscript—Claude assembles the case of curiosities that the narrator buys in the preface. Claude completes his masterpiece, a talking head, in the year 1789; of its 2,199 parts, 1,789 are responsible for speech.

Each of the major divisions receives its title from one of the objects that occupy the box acquired at the Paris auction. The first item is a jar, which, like many other objects that Claude includes in the case, is object, metaphor, and pun. As the first, it represents the container holding the middle finger of Claude's right hand, which is embellished with a mole that resembles the head of Louis XVI. Believing that the mole causes Claude pain, Jean-Baptiste-Pierre-Robert Auget, the local count, summons Adolphe Staemphli, a Geneva surgeon, to remove it. Unhappily for Claude, Staemphli, too, is creating a case of curiosities and wishes to improve his collection with this blemish. To ensure its preservation, he removes the entire finger. The amputation foreshadows the fate of the real head of the king and of Claude's later curiosity, a head of another sort. More immediately, it jars Claude's life, resulting in his leaving home to live with the count. As Kurzweil writes in one of his many examples of word play, "Amputation had brought about attachment," the patronage of the abbé.

The title of the second unit, "The Nautilus," once more assumes multiple meanings. The abbé loves the helix: His staircases, gates, and pillars spiral; he even peels his fruit helically. His house has a chambered conception with increasingly secret compartments, and he sees his life as "a series of hidden chambers. There is always one more waiting to be entered." As Claude penetrates these physical and biographical compartments, he, too, grows, so that the nautilus serves as a metaphor for his life as well as the abbé's. The nautilus represents not only development but also shyness: it "recoils in moments of terror and delight." Claude and the abbé exhibit this characteristic, retreating rather than exposing their fears and hopes; this mutual concealment leads to misunderstanding and separation.

While Claude lives under the abbé's tutelage, he learns much about watchmaking, his great passion. To raise money, the abbé must produce mechanisms more in demand than mere timepieces, "Hours of Love" with erotic scenes. "Nautilus" may pun on the "naughty lass" these pictures include. Among the commissions is a request for a bawdy scene incorporating the face of a young woman painted on an ivory cameo. Claude falls in love with the image, which he encounters in the third unit, "The Morel." Morels move, appearing in different places each year, and the mushroom occupying the third compartment represents Claude's leaving the abbé's employment. In the most secret part of his house, the abbé is reported to harbor a mistress who is also his music student. Claude believes that he witnesses her murder when she refuses to play, and he flees Tournay. Actually, this Madame Dubois is, as her name indicates, a thing of wood, an imperfect automaton. Had Claude not reacted as a nautilus, he might have stayed to learn the truth and so not acted as a morel.

Instead, he finds himself in Paris without money or employment. Poverty compels him to work for Lucien Livre, a bookseller and pornographer who believes that name is fate. With his name he could do no other than sell books, and he had long believed that Page, too, belonged in a bookstore. A wooden mannequin stolen on the journey to the French capital marks Claude's migration and supplies the name for the fourth unit—the figure is also "du bois"; a "pearl," as Livre calls each of his written instructions, and fills the fifth compartment of the case. While working for the unpleasant Lucien—Claude could regard himself as a pearl cast to a swine—he meets Alexandre Hugon, the woman whose face had enchanted him in Tournay, and she seduces him. She cares nothing for his research into mechanics and sound, but she supplies him with money and buys his freedom from Livre by paying the bookseller for the services of his apprentice.

Although Claude recognizes Alexandre's indifference to his projects, he creates an elaborate mechanical tribute to her. It includes several birds, including a linnet nesting in a bed lined with Claude's own hair. Each bird sings its peculiar note. Claude invites Alexandre to his garret to observe his creation. She comes, and they make love; but she then dismisses him. Her marriage has been annulled because of her husband's impotence, and she wants to wed a rich widower. Claude loses his mistress and his freedom from Livre, but he blackmails the bookseller by threatening to expose the illicit trade in pornography unless Livre cancels the apprenticeship. At the age of sixteen, in the midst of the sixth unit, marked by the linnet freed or severed from its mechanism, Claude is free. He now prospers by selling mechanical toys.

When he hears of a fatal fire in Tournay, Claude returns home to find his mother and sisters dead, the abbé living but aged and impoverished. Claude also learns of his mistake about Madame Dubois, discovering that she was an artifact, a "kurzweil" or pastime (a play on the author's name). Claude is reunited with the watch that his father had left him, and that object will occupy the case's seventh compartment. "The Watch" represents not only this timepiece but also Claude's waiting to create his masterpiece and to secure revenge on Staemphli. In return for a manufactured container secretly filled with grubs that will destroy the surgeon's curiosities, the abbé and Claude secure for their project such necessities as reindeer tendons and the vocal cords of a monkey. Then they move to Paris, where Claude learns of Alexandre's death in childbirth. Her daughter—and Claude's—has survived, and the infant has inherited the bell that Claude had given Alexandre and that she had rung when feeling especially amorous. Claude takes the child home; her bell enters the case.

Her nursemaid, Marguerite, loves not only the girl but also the father. In a passionate moment she bites off the last button holding Claude's pants, and shortly afterward they marry. The button is the last object that Claude places in his box, and that ninth compartment represents the year of his greatest achievement. For a moment he is the very button on Fortune's cap. Happily married, he produces a talking automaton, the Miraculatorium, which says, "Vive le roi." The mechanism enjoys great popularity. Claude embarks on an international tour, and Sebastian Plumeaux, a hack writer whose name appears to be his fate, produces an account of the creation. His book has ten major divisions, each with a name that carries multiple meanings, and should run to 360 pages; but the printer's concern for paper reduces the number to 358. Plumeaux, who is "partial to narratives based on contrived structures," thus writes a book very much like the one that tells of his writing it; like a nautilus, *A Case of Curiosities* makes yet another self-reflexive turn.

The French Revolution creates a revolution in Claude's fortunes. Because of the talking head's royalist sentiments, it is sentenced to beheading. The tenth compartment remains empty as a sign of an unfinished life. Like the two blank pages, emptiness emphasizes the silence imposed on Claude's masterpiece and so on its creator. At the same time, it leaves space for expansion. Claude remains alive and may speak again; his story may allow a sequel.

*A Case of Curiosities* is a delightful kurzweil, an entertaining story ingeniously told. As a historical novel it offers much detail about late eighteenth century life. The abbé, for example, exemplifies anticlerical Enlightenment attitudes and pursues scientific research. He is a philosopher who corresponds with his counterparts in England and America and on the European continent. Claude's mother, an herbalist, reflects the simpler beliefs of the peasantry. Her talk is filled with proverbs and biblical quotations, and her chief scientific instrument is a fir-tree branch that serves as a barometer. Alexandre's cosmetics are made from bacon grease and vegetable puree. Generally the novel wears such learning lightly, but the details of M. Hugon's impotency trial, though a comic tour de force, add nothing to plot or characterization.

Because the novel is so immersed in its period, anachronisms are troubling. Among Livre's proofs that "name is fate" is William Battie's *Treatise on Madness* (1758). The book is real, but the joke is modern. According to the *Oxford English Dictionary*, "batty" did not acquire its link to madness until 1903. The abbé owns a book with steel engravings, which did not become popular until the nineteenth century; copper would have been more in keeping with the time.

Such slips are, however, few. Kurzweil has captured the sights, sounds, and tastes (in all senses of the word) of the age that produced the first novels. Henry Fielding and Laurence Sterne would appreciate the variations that Kurzweil plays on the form as he returns to the eighteenth century for his setting and many of his techniques.

*Joseph Rosenblum*

### Sources for Further Study

*Booklist.* LXXXVIII, October 15, 1991, p. 401.
*Chicago Tribune.* January 12, 1992, XIV, p. 7.
*Literary Review.* CLXVII, May, 1992, p. 41.
*London Review of Books.* XIV, May 28, 1992, p. 22.
*Los Angeles Times Book Review.* January 19, 1992, p. 3.
*New Statesman and Society.* V, March 27, 1992, p. 41.

*The New York Review of Books.* XXXIX, April 9, 1992, p. 35.
*The New York Times Book Review.* XCVII, January 26, 1992, p. 1.
*The New Yorker.* LXVIII, March 23, 1992, p. 99.
*Publishers Weekly.* CCXXXVIII, October 4, 1991, p. 80.
*The Times Literary Supplement.* March 20, 1992, p. 21.
*The Washington Post Book World.* XXII, January 12, 1992, p. 9.

# THE CHAIRMAN
## John J. McCloy: The Making of the American Establishment

*Author:* Kai Bird (1951-    )
*Publisher:* Simon & Schuster (New York). 800 pp. $30.00
*Type of work:* Biography
*Time:* Mid-twentieth century
*Locale:* New York and Washington

*A fascinating work that mixes biography and history in exploring the influence of Wall Street on American foreign policy*

*Principal personages:*
JOHN J. MCCLOY, the chairman of Chase Manhattan Bank
HENRY L. STIMSON, the secretary of war during World War II
KONRAD ADENAUER, the chancellor of West Germany
DEAN ACHESON, the secretary of state during the Harry S. Truman Administration
JOSEPH MCCARTHY, a senator from Wisconsin during the 1950's
HENRY KISSINGER, the national security adviser to Richard M. Nixon

The premise of this earnestly written, well-researched book is that during the middle decades of the twentieth century an elite group of Wall Street insiders known as the Establishment came to wield great political power, especially over the nation's foreign policy. In order to win the Cold War and expand the international operations of America's most powerful corporations, these self-proclaimed public servants helped transform their country (to its ultimate detriment, Bird believes) into a national security state, with most important operations carried out unobserved and uncontrolled by the larger body politic. They were dedicated to creating a counterrevolutionary world order, one that John J. McCloy labeled Pax Americana.

In May of 1962, journalist Richard Rovere published a satirical article in *Esquire* that used the word "Establishment" to describe a group of moderate Republicans who played a prominent role (official and unofficial) in Democratic administrations going back to 1940. Liberal economist John Kenneth Galbraith dubbed John J. McCloy "chairman of the Establishment." Although his name was little known to the general public, McCloy exerted more influence than most contemporary congressional or cabinet members. "Alone among his peers," writes Bird, "he managed to straddle for nearly five decades the interlocking directorships of corporate America, the federal government, and the country's leading public-policy and philanthropic foundations." Neither intellectually brilliant nor an original thinker, McCloy was a practical, persistent, uncharismatic conciliator (Henry Kissinger called him a genial gnome), frank and unafraid to tackle problems, with an open mind and yellow pad at the ready.

McCloy's portfolio came to include chairmanships of the Chase Manhattan Bank, the Council of Foreign Relations, the Ford Foundation, and the Advisory Committee on Arms Control and Disarmament. Among his corporate clients were the leading steel, insurance, automobile, and oil companies. They got their money's worth, as McCloy saw no conflict of interest in merging government and business, believing quite literally that what was good for Chase Manhattan Bank was good for the country.

*The Chairman* is a remarkably dispassionate, fair-minded, and even-handed "life and times" biography. Ten years in the making, it demonstrates the author's mastery over the burgeoning historical literature on such germane subjects as the internment of Japanese Americans, postwar Germany, McCarthyism, the Cuban Missile Crisis, and the Iran hostage crisis. The only primary topic getting short shrift is disarmament.

Bird does not probe deeply into the inner man, nor is McCloy's private life examined beyond occasional references to hunting and fishing trips, tennis matches, and demonstrations of marital compatibility. An assimilator possessing fewer insecurities than most social climbers, McCloy apparently was a solid family man and loyal friend, but his prejudices and degree of acquisitiveness could bear more scrutiny. How wealthy was McCloy? Did he become one of America's super-rich or remain merely their steward? These questions need to be answered before one can assess how disinterested was his public service.

Not quite the epitome of the Horatio Alger rags-to-riches American success myth, McCloy grew up on the wrong side of Philadelphia's "Chinese Wall," a Pennsylvania railroad viaduct separating the common people from their "betters." His father, a high-school dropout, rose to a chief clerkship at Penn Mutual Life Insurance Company but was himself denied a policy because of a heart murmur. His untimely death forced his widow, Anna, into a career as a hairdresser. Anna's wealthy clientele included the family of George Wharton Pepper, a prominent Main Line attorney who would become young McCloy's first role model.

With frugal planning, Anna was able to launch her son on a path of upward mobility. The first stop was New Jersey's Peddie Prep School, then on to Amherst College and Harvard Law School, with the summers of 1915 and 1916 spent with the right people at Plattsburg military training camp. Returning home after World War I, during which he missed most of the action, McCloy was advised by George Wharton Pepper to practice law in New York City, where his plebeian blood lines would not be so much a liability.

During the 1920's and 1930's, McCloy specialized in helping corporate clients avoid governmental regulations and, in some instances, file dubious bankruptcy claims that fleeced independent stockholders. When some of his colleagues were hauled before Senator Burton K. Wheeler's Committee on Interstate Commerce, it appeared to McCloy that big business was unfairly being scapegoated as criminally responsible for the Great Depression. No New Dealer, he helped prepare the Schechter "sick chicken" brief that nullified Franklin D. Roosevelt's National Recovery Administration.

The case that most enhanced McCloy's reputation and in many ways was the formative experience of his life was a decade-long effort to recover damages from the so-called Black Tom disaster. In 1916, at a munitions terminal located in New York harbor, German secret agents had blown up wagons full of high explosives awaiting shipment to France. McCloy's relentless pursuit of clues paid off in a lucrative 1939 settlement from the Mixed Claims Commission. Thereafter, he was an advocate of effective American intelligence capabilities.

In the fall of 1940, with sabotage stories in the news, McCloy became a consultant on Army intelligence under Secretary of War Henry Stimson, who would become even more a role model to him than Senator Pepper. An ardent interventionist, McCloy helped lobby for the Lend-Lease Act and put together the decoding operation that led to the *MAGIC* interceptions of Japanese secret messages. He also worked on contingency plans for creating a ten-million-man army and for coordinating strategy with the British. On September 19, 1941, he told the Michigan Bar Association, "We have as much chance of ignoring this war as a man has of ignoring an elephant in his parlor."

Moving up to a position as assistant secretary of war and operating as a virtual commissar, McCloy played a key role in the internment of more than 110,000 Japanese Americans living on the West Coast. McCloy later tampered with evidence sent to the Supreme Court to forestall an adverse ruling on the constitutionality of the concentration camps. The ease with which McCloy wielded power led Secretary of the Interior Harold Ickes to describe him as likable but "more or less inclined to be a Fascist."

McCloy supported opening a diplomatic dialogue with the French Fascist Vichy regime but dragged his feet at African American demands to desegregate the armed forces. Most egregiously, he turned a deaf ear to pleas to alter military policies in order to aid Holocaust victims. It would have taken little effort to bomb rail lines leading to Auschwitz, for example, but McCloy was skeptical of evidence that "pushy" Jews presented to him of Hitler's so-called final solution.

On the other hand, McCloy opposed dropping the atomic bomb on Hiroshima without first warning the Japanese. He believed that the Japanese were on the verge of surrendering but needed assurance that Emperor Hirohito would not be treated as a war criminal. McCloy's views on atomic diplomacy were influenced by Robert Oppenheimer, whom he deeply admired. McCloy would later lament the Red Scare excesses that resulted in the scientist's classification as a security risk.

McCloy was instrumental in the building and design of the Pentagon and the launching of the Central Intelligence Agency (CIA). Infatuated with covert operations, he later used his banking connections to set up conduits for the CIA. His advocacy of an independent CIA earned him the enmity of J. Edgar Hoover, director of the Federal Bureau of Investigation (FBI).

McCloy turned down President Harry S. Truman's offer to become ambassador to Moscow, but after a short stint as a partner in the Rockefeller family law firm, he accepted the presidency of the World Bank. He frugally augmented the bank's bond rating, but during his watch most loans to underdeveloped countries were rejected.

More controversial was McCloy's tenure as West German high commissioner. He got along well with the austere, authoritarian Chancellor Konrad Adenauer, who paid lip service to reunification but, like McCloy, was more interested in containing communism. Former Nazis such as Klaus Barbie were employed in clandestine activities and then spirited out of the country. McCloy granted clemency to industrialists such as Alfred Krupp, who had employed slave laborers, and physicians who had conducted experiments on death camp victims.

In 1953, McCloy became chairman of the newly merged Chase Manhattan Bank but remained, in Bird's words, "Ike's hidden vizier." His White House connections brought him into contact with Texas businesspeople who were keeping the president's freezer well stocked, buying him expensive suits, and even building him a summer cabin in Augusta, Georgia. McCloy helped two of them achieve a hostile takeover of the New York Central Railroad, a takeover that ultimately led to the Penn Central's bankruptcy.

President-elect John F. Kennedy sought McCloy's advice in making key cabinet choices, but the only assignment that McCloy would accept was as a part-time arms control czar. When the Russians would not forgo nuclear testing, McCloy urged a resumption of U.S. tests, not for scientific reasons but to avoid appearing weak. He shrugged off critics, saying "I don't believe in world opinion. The only thing that matters is power."

One of Kennedy's inner circle during the Cuban Missile Crisis, McCloy initially favored.air strikes but came around to supporting the naval quarantine. Even though he did not believe that the offensive missile sites would significantly alter the military balance of power, he worried about maintaining America's credibility with its allies and adversaries.

McCloy's first assignment for Lyndon B. Johnson (the only Democratic president he voted for other than Roosevelt in 1944) was to serve on the Warren Commission. Skeptical of the information provided by the FBI and CIA, whose investigations were slanted toward portraying Lee Harvey Oswald as the lone assassin, McCloy realized that the commission's unwritten purpose was to reassure the public that there had not been a conspiracy, foreign or domestic, rather than to solve the case.

An overconfident supporter of American military action in Vietnam, McCloy was offered the ambassadorship to Saigon. When he and other assembled "wise men" lost faith in the attrition strategy after the 1968 Tet offensive and recommended a negotiated settlement, President Johnson complained that "the establishment bastards have bailed out." McCloy appeared more perturbed by the disruptions of decorum at college graduations and monthly meetings of his beloved Council on Foreign Relations than by the continuation of the war under Richard M. Nixon. What he really lamented was how Vietnam shattered the bipartisan Cold War consensus.

During the 1970's, McCloy used his clout to get the so-called Seven Sisters oil companies exempted from antitrust prosecution, supposedly so that they could deal more effectively with the members of the Organization of Petroleum Exporting Countries (OPEC). The result was that the oil companies made windfall profits from skyrocketing oil prices, which were blamed on OPEC. After the fall of the shah of Iran, McCloy, Henry Kissinger, and David Rockefeller orchestrated a pressure campaign to persuade President Jimmy Carter to allow the shah to come to the United States. Against his better judgment, Carter gave in, because he needed Establishment support on such other matters as a second Strategic Arms Limitation Treaty

(SALT II). During the Iran hostage crisis, McCloy cynically blamed Carter for being caught off guard and said, "National honor is more important than American lives."

During the 1980's, McCloy endorsed the Ronald Reagan Administration's enormous defense buildup. He was a close friend of CIA director William Casey but worried that too much attention was being given to Central America and not enough to Europe. He was made an honorary German citizen in 1985 at a White House ceremony. Mourners at his funeral four years later included former German chancellor Helmut Schmidt and Secretary of State James Baker, who read a testimonial from President George Bush.

Ideally, the Establishment was a meritocracy and its leaders possessors of what McCloy called *gravitas*—probity of character, weightiness of judgment, and a balanced, realistic, practical understanding of life's complexities. The reality was less exalted. During the mid-1960's, for example, McCloy negotiated with Brazil's left-wing President Joao Goulart on behalf of a corporate client, all the while privy to a CIA "destabilization" campaign that would ultimately topple him.

Bird's book is a welcome antidote to the recent wave of nostalgic books about the Establishment. For example, Walter Isaacson and Evan Thomas' *The Wise Men: Six Friends and the World They Made* (1986) laments the passing of those good old days when statesmanlike captains of industry steadied the ship of state by their wise counsel. The Establishment's Cold War legacy, Bird concludes, was a costly national security state that left America "with an uncompetitive economy burdened with debt, high unemployment, low growth, and income levels more unevenly divided than at any time since the beginning of the Cold War."

*James B. Lane*

### Sources for Further Study

*Commentary*. XCIV, September, 1992, p. 58.
*Foreign Affairs*. LXXI, Fall, 1992, p. 194.
*Los Angeles Times Book Review*. April 19, 1992, p. 1.
*The Nation*. CCLIV, May 25, 1992, p. 694.
*The New Republic*. CCVI, May 11, 1992, p. 40.
*The New York Review of Books*. XXXIX, October 8, 1992, p. 22.
*The New York Times Book Review*. XCVII, April 12, 1992, p. 1.
*Political Science Quarterly*. CVII, Fall, 1992, p. 544.
*Publishers Weekly*. CCXXXIX, February 17, 1992, p. 52.
*The Wall Street Journal*. April 16, 1992, p. A22.
*Washington Monthly*. XXIV, March, 1992, p. 53.
*The Washington Post Book World*. XXII, April 12, 1992, p. 1.

# CHAMFORT
## A Biography

*Author:* Claude Arnaud (1919-    )
*First published: Chamfort: Biographie, suivie de soixante-dix maximes, anecdotes, mots et dialogues inédits, ou jamais réédités,* 1988
Translated from the French by Deke Dusinberre
Foreword by Joseph Epstein
*Publisher:* University of Chicago Press (Chicago). Illustrated. 340 pp. $27.50
*Type of work:* Literary biography
*Time:* 1740-1794
*Locale:* France

*A biography of a writer of the French Revolutionary era remembered primarily for his posthumously published epigrams and aphorisms much admired by Stendhal, Friedrich Nietzsche, Albert Camus, and other writers*

Principal personages:
SÉBASTIEN ROCH NICOLAS DE CHAMFORT, a French playwright and man of letters
JEAN-JACQUES ROUSSEAU, a French philosopher, political scientist, and novelist
HONORÉ GABRIEL VICTOR RIQUETI, COMTE DE MIRABEAU, a French orator and revolutionary leader
ABBÉ SIÉYÈS, a French clergyman and revolutionary leader
MARTHE BUFFON, a widow, Chamfort's lover
PIERRE-LOUIS GINGUENÉ, Chamfort's friend and literary executor

Literary history presents occasional examples of writers known more for their celebrated friendships and reports of their sparkling conversational skills than for their actual writings. This is very much the case with Sébastien Roch Nicolas de Chamfort (1740?-1794), a complex and contradictory man of letters who was both blessed and cursed to live during the most turbulent period of French history. A would-be member of the nobility (as seen in his affected use of "de" Chamfort) who never forgot his merchant foster parents and who eagerly embraced the egalitarian ideals of the French Revolution, Chamfort was born in Clermont-Ferrand, the principal city of the Auvergne region of France. He was the illegitimate son of Jacqueline de Vinzelles, a member of a noble family of Clermont-Ferrand who farmed Nicolas out to a grocer whose infant son had just died, thus concealing her indiscretion.

A brilliant student once destined for the priesthood, Chamfort, to use the name he adopted, developed early into a freethinker of legendary caustic wit. Aborting, at the last minute, an impulsive scheme to emigrate to North America, he made his way to Paris in 1760 and wasted little time in launching his literary career. He authored a verse comedy called *La jeune indienne* that so impressed the critic Jean François La Harpe that the latter showed it to no less a personage than Voltaire, who approved emphatically. Chamfort showed particular talent in forging alliances with prominent literary figures and *philosophes*, including Jean-Jacques Rousseau and Jean Le Rond d'Alembert. In later years, this circle would expand to include writers as ideologically diverse as the Marquis de Condorcet and François René de Chateaubriand.

Chamfort's successes as a playwright eventually attracted the attention of the royal couple themselves, Louis XVI and Marie Antoinette. The latter invited Chamfort to the royal box at Fontainebleau during the performance of his *Mustapha et Zéangir* on November 1, 1776. Marie Antoinette praised his talent and announced that the king had granted him a royal stipend for his work. Strictly observing the expectations of the theater-going public, Chamfort had openly modeled his tragedy on Racine. These last years of the *ancien régime* did not encourage dramaturgical innovation, and the aged Voltaire praised Chamfort for his skill at imitation, to the consternation of La Harpe, who by now had turned against Chamfort. Chamfort's willingness to flatter conventional literary taste had also earned him a place, at the tender age of twenty-nine, in the exalted *Académie française*. This was a result of his stunning triumph in a competition held for the purpose of penning a eulogy to the genius of Molière.

However great his literary fame, Chamfort was most widely known for his semi-scandalous role in society. As a young man, his amorous activities were legendary, and this aspect of the man is what clearly most interests his gossipy biographer, Claude Arnaud. A mysterious disfiguring disease (possibly syphilis) put a stop to his career as a lover when he was still in his twenties. Thereafter, Chamfort would be known best for his scathing wit and outrageous conversation. Like other biographers before him, Arnaud speculates that Chamfort sought revenge or compensation for his reduced physical circumstances through verbal bloodletting. All who knew him testified that his conversation was incessantly misanthropic, though nevertheless entertaining. Of all of his writings, the handful of maxims he left unpublished at his death provide the clearest indication of the impact he must have had on his friends and acquaintances, as in this characteristic epigram: "Living is an ailment which is relieved every sixteen hours by sleep. A palliative. Death is the cure."

Paradoxically, this fiercely iconoclastic man could skewer everyone in sight and still form strong friendships. For most of his life, he also had a keen ability to judge the direction of the prevailing political winds. As the revolution approached, he systematically distanced himself from all aristocratic associations, attaching himself to Mirabeau, the great orator of the revolution's opening phase, and the Abbé Siéyès, on whose famous manifesto *Qu'est-ce que le tiers état?* (What is the third estate?) he reportedly consulted. Having campaigned so determinedly to attain membership in the *Académie française*, Chamfort drafted a proposal, which death prevented Mirabeau from presenting in the National Assembly, that would dismantle that and other French academies. In 1791, Chamfort assumed direction of the newly "republican" Bibliothèque Nationale. At least until the September Massacres of 1792, Chamfort demonstrated great skill at weathering the changing storms of the revolution.

Chamfort's ally Siéyès, at the end of a long life, responded to the query "What did you do during the Revolution?" with the terse "I survived." Chamfort would not survive. He was openly contemptuous of Jean-Paul Marat whose denunciations and accusations published in his *L'ami du peuple* sent many to the guillotine. Chamfort was denounced to the Committee of Public Safety by a colleague at the Bibliothèque Nationale after he expressed his admiration for Charlotte Corday, Marat's assassin. Chamfort was arrested and briefly imprisoned. Shortly after his release, he received word that he was once again subject to arrest, and, firmly resolved to avoid further incarceration, he carried out a ghastly, and amazingly unsuccessful, suicide attempt. Attempting to shoot himself in the head, he managed to blow out his right eye and shatter the bridge of his nose. He then slit his throat with a razor. Dismayed at being yet alive, he slashed himself about the chest and wrists before passing out. This wretched man then lived another four months, finally succumbing to the infection festering in his improperly dressed wounds.

His devoted friend Pierre-Louis Ginguené became guardian of Chamfort's memory, publishing the first collection of his writings in 1795. From this point on, Chamfort's maxims and other brief thoughts or anecdotes (none of which he had wished to publish in his lifetime) came to overshadow the plays and occasional essays he published during his literary career. Through them, he has had a kind of second, more lasting career. Arnaud suggests that the aphoristic genre was the most successful for Chamfort because it offered resolution of the contradictory tendencies of his comedies and tragedies. As Arnaud also understands clearly, aphorisms present problems of classification. For that matter, Chamfort's literary career defies conventional classification, something true of many revolutionary-era figures who straddle the late Enlightenment and early Romanticism. As for his posthumous reception, nineteenth century French writers such as Chateaubriand and Stendhal as well as twentieth century writers including Louis-Ferdinand Céline and Albert Camus have been among Chamfort's admirers. Chamfort's most celebrated admirer, however, was Friedrich Nietzsche, who learned of the obscure French writer through his own reading of Arthur Schopenhauer.

Recent French criticism, in the wake of postmodern theories of literary signification, has been much taken with the nature of the literary fragment, such as the genre-defying aphorism. Roland Barthes was only the most notable example of a theorist/critic whose style harked back at least as far as Walter Benjamin, if not the *ancien régime* practitioners of the type of writing for which Chamfort is remembered. One reasonably might have expected such a recent biography appearing in French to exploit the possibilities afforded by postmodern literary theory for reading Chamfort's maxims afresh. These finely chiseled nuggets would seem tailor-made for contemporary preoccupations with language, meaning, and consciousness. There is also the subtext of Nietzsche's admiration of Chamfort's style—Nietzsche, whose very reinterpretation is at the heart of current literary debates in France and elsewhere.

Arnaud, however, misses the opportunity to ground any reconsideration of Chamfort's life and work in an appreciation of his relatively unique aphoristic style. He at least provides a useful appendix containing a sampling of Chamfort's fragments. The appearance of a major biography in English should certainly be deemed significant. For that matter, Arnaud's biography is only the third to be published in French during the twentieth century. Arnaud's flawed biography, however, adds very little to the admirable lengthy introduction to W. S. Merwin's anthology of Chamfort's writings, *Products of the Perfected Civilization: Selected Writings of Chamfort* (1969). Thus, however eagerly one may have awaited a new biography, this one is disappointing. Furthermore, since Arnaud provides only a fraction of the material made available in English in the Merwin edition, the latter will remain the better choice for introducing readers of English to Chamfort.

Arnaud's biography is flawed through excessive attention to gossip and absolute obsession with the virility or, in some cases, impotence of the principal masculine contemporaries. Quite a number of these speculations on or rumors about the sexual exploits or abject failures of everyone from Louis XVI to Mirabeau are set off in commas or hyphens. Deke Dusinberre's often eccentric translation renders them even more distracting and annoying through the use of parentheses. Scarcely has Arnaud introduced the *philosophe* d'Alembert before we read the qualifying phrase "impotent in bed." Mirabeau, by contrast, is described as more or less priapic. Recounting his final illness, symptoms of which included a peculiar stiffening of the muscles, Arnaud cannot resist telling us that Mirabeau had an erection when he died. Not surprisingly for a biographer so intent on phallic powers, Arnaud is quick to disparage the women who were part of Chamfort's intimate circle. They routinely become "tarts," the translator's choice for the derogatory sense of *filles*. A forceful, opinionated woman such as the Duchesse de Gramont, a sometime friend of Chamfort, is dismissed with the label of "termagant." No equivalently derogatory term appears in conjunction with any masculine counterpart.

Much of what is irritating or disappointing about *Chamfort: A Biography* is a matter of tone, to some extent the tone of Dusinberre's translation (as when *la garçonnière* becomes the anachronistic "bachelor pad"). Arnaud's tone is often simply too arch or inappropriately flippant for a biography presumably intended to win renewed interest for its subject. Perhaps this is an occupational hazard for a biographer of a writer known for his mordant wit. This sarcastic tone alternates oddly with such melodramatic flourishes as the borrowing of Céline's phrase "journey to the end of the night" to close out the chapter that precedes the grisly account of Chamfort's botched suicide attempt. Some of Arnaud's more brutal asides raise the question of the reason for his own interest in the subject. After recounting the vicious cabal Chamfort's literary rivals mounted against his *Mustapha et Zéangir*, Arnaud quickly rationalizes that Chamfort never really deserved much of a literary reputation, since most of his writing "doesn't even bear mentioning." After all, Arnaud confides, Chamfort "was born at the wrong time."

In the better half of Charles Dickens' famous formulation, the French Revolution was, for Chamfort, often the "best of times." As Arnaud makes clear, the advent of the revolution seemed like a real vindication for Chamfort for the wrongs his aristocratic and literary associators had dealt him. Chamfort comes across as a restless man torn by the conflict between the desire for acceptance and scorn for the undeserving souls in a position to confer acceptance. Like more than a few nobles and priests who cast their lot with the third estate, he could experience the exhilaration of renouncing even his own privileges in the name of republican ideals.

Arnaud's biography of Chamfort comes alive in the chapters that chronicle the years from 1787, as the winds of revolution began to stir, to 1793, when Chamfort could no longer keep pace with the acceleration of Jacobin zeal. Both in these pages and in the surprisingly scant space accorded the maxims and related literary fragments, Arnaud rescues Chamfort from the habit, cultivated ever since the days of Chateaubriand, of associating this author with the long tradition of aristocratic repudiation of revolutionary ideals. It is clear that Chamfort fervently embraced the ideals of 1789 and that he was even willing to follow Maximilien Robespierre, up to a point. Arnaud also distinguishes between the maxims of Chamfort and those of La Rochefoucauld and other aristocratic predecessors in that genre.

As a result, Arnaud's biography will help to challenge the view, fostered in part by an outmoded reading of Chamfort's admirer Nietzsche, that Chamfort's writings belong in the literary canon of reactionary elitism. Because of its limitations however, Arnaud's book should not be recommended ahead of the Merwin volume for readers who wish to be introduced to this anomaly in the history of French writing.

*James A. Winders*

## Sources for Further Study

*Boston Globe.* July 12, 1992, p. 38.
*Kirkus Reviews.* LX, March 1, 1992, p. 291.
*London Review of Books.* XIV, November 5, 1992, p. 3.
*New Statesman and Society.* V, July 31, 1992, p. 34.
*The New York Review of Books.* XXXIX, June 25, 1992, p. 3.
*The New York Times Book Review.* XCVII, August 9, 1992, p. 12.
*Publishers Weekly.* CCXXXIX, April 6, 1992, p. 43.
*The Times Literary Supplement.* June 12, 1992, p. 12.
*The Wall Street Journal.* June 19, 1992, p. A8.
*The Yale Review.* LXXX, October, 1992, p. 90.

# THE CHANGE
## Women, Aging, and the Menopause

*Author:* Germaine Greer (1939-    )
*First published:* 1991, in Great Britain
*Publisher:* Alfred A. Knopf (New York). 387 pp. $24.00
*Type of work:* Women's issues

*In this detailed exploration of how society and individuals experience and interpret female menopause, author Germaine Greer suggests alternatives for mature women who have been abandoned by youth-oriented cultures*

As medical science makes strides in the quest for human longevity, it is not surprising that the various stages of human physical and social life have come under scrutiny. The female reproductive system involves an intricate series of biological, psychological, and sociological events that are being studied more intimately than ever before, but only as they relate to the cycle of childbearing. Puberty and reproduction have thus far received the majority of attention paid to the normal female body by the scientific community. Now, as a result of the efforts of maturing female writers such as Germaine Greer, menopause—the catalytic event that marks the finite limits of the reproductive spectrum—is coming into sharper and more significant focus.

Greer's groundbreaking 1970 book *The Female Eunuch* launched her career as an international literary celebrity. Her enthusiastic exhortations for women to enjoy their lives regardless of their relationships with men conveniently coincided with the onset of "the sexual revolution." More than twenty years later, Greer is concerned with a different sort of sexual revolution, that of reclaiming one's body when pregnancy becomes impossible, of aging with grace and honor, of giving up the possibility of reproduction without giving up one's inner self.

Tribal ancestors revered their elders, male and female, as wise and experienced teachers whose gifts were appreciated by the community at large, but modern culture worships the innocence and elasticity of youth above all else. In women, this worship seems to encompass the physical and social adjustments taking place within the female anatomy between the onsets of puberty and menopause, from the first red spot of menstrual blood to the first hot flash. With this in mind, Greer believes that reverence for the female physiosocial experience should not turn to horror once the ovaries no longer release eggs each month. Most women do not shrivel up and fade away at the age of forty-five or fifty without society's inadvertent but negative assistance.

With modern life spans, barring accidental death, averaging well beyond eighty years at the end of the twentieth century, a full one-third of a woman's life remains before her at the point of menopause. Greer suggests that this transformation from childbearer to wise nurturer and teacher is pitifully neglected; it is time both women and men paid attention to its personal and societal value. Challenging the bondage of the stereotypical view of femininity, Greer calls for women to celebrate this critical passage, to see it as a return to innocence and freedom after suffering without choice the tyrannies of pregnancy and child rearing. "Women will have to devise their own rite of passage, a celebration of what could be regarded as the restoration of a woman to herself. The passionate, idealistic, energetic young individual who existed before menstruation can come on earth again if we let her."

Greer also attributes the public's newfound awareness of menopause as a public health issue to the growing desire for physical fitness among women of all ages. Although women have accepted that the body-and-mind-changing event of menopause is as unavoidable as death and taxes, they now want to know in advance how to transit its course with as little stress and discomfort as possible. "The increasing tendency of younger women to show an interest in menopause and to begin to ask for information about it is due in part to their growing awareness of their bodies and their understanding of the importance of being in good shape to handle whatever might be demanded of them. They exercised for efficient childbirth and they expect to be able to prepare for the stress of the climacteric."

Unfortunately, the physical changes of menopause are interwoven with the natural aging of the body, a condition society still treats as taboo. "As far as the individual woman is concerned, the symptoms of aging do not need to be separated out from the symptoms of menopause, for she experiences them together. They are not simply concurrent, however; they interact. . . . One of the commoner reactions to menopause is resentment that it has come so soon, when in fact it has come in its due season."

Greer reminds readers that the study of aging, ironically, has been spearheaded by and for men: "A woman who desires to remain vigorous for as long as possible, and take her leave quickly when she is too tired to go on, will not find much in gerontology that will help her devise a strategy. . . . The real impetus for the attack on aging came from the aging male elite, who wanted to enjoy the fruits of a lifetime's accumulated power, namely the love and adulation of young women."

Thus, the separation of menopausal symptoms from those associated with aging is especially difficult:

> The changes associated with aging have been summarized as a continuous decrease at the rate of a per cent or so a year of basal metabolism, vital capacity, maximal breathing capacity, glomerular filtration rate, standard cell water and nerve-conduction velocity. These are biologically more precise ways of saying what ordinary people mean when they say that when people age they "slow down" and "dry up."

She goes on to say that, conversely, the glands and connective tissues go through subtle changes and increase in their substance or function as one ages; for example, older people sweat less with a fluid less pungent than sweat manufactured by younger glands. These natural phenomena do not, however, cushion the impact of having passed the biological point of no return. Men can lose their hair or develop a hefty gut and still be considered virile; women who reach menopause sense death just around the corner.

The metaphor of death is particularly apropos in relation to menopause, as Greer says: "At menopause as never before, a woman comes face-to-face with her own mortality. A part of her is dying. . . . Nothing she can do will bring her ovaries back to life." She suggests that the grief that seems to appear on the heels of menopausal symptoms can be reduced to a momentary stress if a woman so chooses: "At the turning point the descent into night is felt as rapid; only when the stress of the climacteric is over can the aging woman realize that autumn can be long, golden, milder and warmer than summer, and is the most productive season of the year. . . . When the fifty-year-old woman says to herself, 'Now is the best time of all,' she means it all the more because she knows it is not forever." Greer goes on to say that "The human female is unique among living organisms on this earth because she can live twice the time of her reproductive span and more. . . . [H]aving served the species, [she] is the only one that can build a life of her own; it is too bitter a biological irony to think that she may not have the heart."

The bulk of Greer's exploration of the historical and contemporary treatment of the numerous physical and emotional changes experienced by women passing through menopause is devoted to detailing the biological symptoms and discussing the most prominent treatments. Although she is somewhat exhaustive and occasionally overly dry in her presentation, she makes cogent suggestions for alternatives that do not produce the drastic side effects that accompany Hormone Replacement Therapy (HRT), the medical establishment's preferred solution for delaying or preventing the menopausal ravages of the female anatomy and psyche. Greer cites the permutations of contemporary eating and work habits that mark society's progress as influencing "The Change" as well:

> It would be interesting to learn if middle-aged women who habitually sit on the ground rather than in chairs ever display the characteristic fracture of the head of the femur that costs health authorities so many millions each year. When the facts that such women do not eat red meat and do eat yogurt and green vegetables and walk for tens of miles each day, usually carrying loads on their heads, are taken into account as well, we would be surprised to find dowagers' humps among them. . . . Osteoporosis does have a genetic component, but it is also a disease of affluence.

It is affluent society that has thus far been lax in studying the complexities of the menopausal female. As today's maturing women demonstrate en masse through their influence on the business and creative realms that a woman's life is meant for more than just child rearing, their requests for medical assistance have begun to force the issue. It is no wonder that doctors faced with assertive female patients who want to experience menopause without it wreaking havoc on their lives try to fulfill their patients' desires by recommending the practice of HRT. As Greer says,

> Estrogen replacement, then, would seem to be turning the clock back for the menopausal woman by mimicking her earlier hormonal state, rather than helping her to accomplish the transition upon which her later health depends. What cannot easily be assessed is whether the use of exogenous steroids in the peri-menopause interferes with the establishment of the default system, in which estrogen secretion is taken over by the adrenal glands. Very few trials have so far attempted to establish the levels of the estrogen precursor, androstenedione, in the bloodstream throughout the climacteric, either with or without HRT, and the picture is far from clear.

In addition to Greer's detailed examination of the physical effects of menopause and medical responses to its discomforts, she explores the treatment of female aging through literature and the lives of prominent women. Somewhat encouraging yet oddly distressing, because of their dependence on men, is her citation as role models of postmenopausal courtesans and mistresses of centuries past, who easily seduced and influenced kings and noblemen far younger than themselves. As for today's role models, Greer finds women writers far more interesting than women in the media spotlight. Actresses and performers whose work demands an obsession with physical appearance and public presentation do not for the most part meet her criteria for positive, mature female images. Unfortunately, there are few mature or maturing scientists or political leaders, other than possibly the Queen Mother or Margaret Thatcher, who offer hope for younger women whose lives are more mundane than those of Joan Collins, Jane Fonda, and Helen Gurley Brown.

Greer's case for aging gracefully, with or without the support of medical and cosmetic sciences, sums itself up toward the end of *The Change*, when she reminds readers of the historical and literary images of female elders. Seen as crones or witches, these women traditionally have been in touch with the earth through gardening and herbology. They found solace and inspiration in the company of female peers who also discovered a spiritual sense of themselves once they were released from male domination through physical reproduction. Ironically, women who were considered "crones" in centuries past often were ridiculed or reviled rather than revered. The Salem witch hunts are an example, as are the pagan religions of Western Europe, which were primarily matriarchal in nature and content.

It is in Greer's final chapter, titled "Serenity and Power," that her personal hope for maturing women of the future is revealed. She uses writer Karen Blixen, better known by her pen name Isak Dinesen, who "took the art of aging to such heights of refinement," as an example of what postmenopausal women can do when they so desire:

> Karen Blixen used to say, "One must in this lower world love many things to know finally what one loves the best...." It is simply not true that the aging heart forgets how to love or becomes incapable of love; indeed, it seems as if, at least in the case of these women of great psychic energy, only after they had ceased to be beset by the egotisms and hostilities of sexual passion did they discover of what bottomless and tireless love their hearts were capable."

Thus it is through the love of humanity that comes through the acceptance of self, according to Greer, that women will continue to break through their "chrysalis of conditioning" and allow "the female woman finally to emerge."

*Barbara Elman Schiffman*

## Sources for Further Study

*American Health.* XI, October, 1992, p. 98.
*Booklist.* LXXXIX, September 1, 1992, p. 21.

*Library Journal.* CXVII, September 15, 1992, p. 86.
*Los Angeles Times Book Review.* October 18, 1992, p. 1.
*New Statesman and Society.* IV, October 11, 1991, p. 23.
*The New York Times Book Review.* XCVII, October 11, 1992, p. 1.
*The New Yorker.* LXVIII, November 2, 1992, p. 106.
*Newsweek.* CXX, November 16, 1992, p. 79.
*Time.* CXL, October 26, 1992, p. 80.
*The Times Literary Supplement.* October 25, 1991, p. 6.
*The Washington Post.* October 20, 1992, p. E2.

# CIVIL WAR COMMAND AND STRATEGY
## The Process of Victory and Defeat

*Author:* Archer Jones (1926-    )
*Publisher:* Free Press (New York). 338 pp. $24.95
*Type of work:* Military history
*Time:* 1861-1865
*Locale:* Primarily the Confederate states

*A study of the military thinking, North and South, that determined how the American Civil War was fought and decided*

> *Principal personages:*
> JEFFERSON DAVIS, the president of the Confederacy
> ABRAHAM LINCOLN, the sixteenth president of the United States
> ROBERT E. LEE, the commander of the Army of Northern Virginia
> ULYSSES S. GRANT, the Union commander
> WILLIAM T. SHERMAN, a Union general

No sooner had the American Civil War ended in the exhausted spring of 1865 than the second Civil War began. When the soldiers laid down their arms, the historians took up their pens, seeking answers to questions that perplex us yet. Why had the South lost? Could it have won? Why had the North prevailed, and what did its victory mean? One central question sums it up: Why did the war end as it did?

Along with the American Revolution itself and the presidency of Franklin D. Roosevelt, which carried the United States through both the Great Depression and World War II, the American Civil War stands as one of the three defining events in American national history, one that the American people, northern and southern, black and white, continually use as a reference and as a benchmark to national identity and purpose. So much treasure, blood, and emotion went into this struggle that it has become a central motif, a national epic, and it remains intensely felt even by Americans only slightly interested or learned in history. Its incidental symbols and basic causes, such as the Confederate battle flag or the abolition of slavery, stir feelings that can be explained only by reference to the words of Abraham Lincoln. Somehow these are linked to the present through the "mystic chords of memory," a memory that reverberates as strongly as ever.

Yet a central question remains: How did they fight this war, the generals and commanders, the presidents and the common soldiers? What did they think they were doing, how did they try to achieve it, and how, amid the confusion and carnage, did they judge their efforts? Those are the questions Archer Jones attempts to answer in his study, *Civil War Command and Strategy: The Process of Victory and Defeat.*

As the title implies, this volume approaches the war in terms of its political and military leaders, their backgrounds, and the plans they conceived based on those backgrounds and their situations. Jones underscores the importance of leadership and strategic plans to the outcome of the war, because he believes that the conflict could have ended much differently. As he explained in considerable detail in his earlier work with Richard E. Beringer, Herman Hathaway, and others, *Why the South Lost the Civil War* (1986), Jones believes that a Union victory, despite the North's preponderance in material advantages, was by no means inevitable.

The enormous extent of the Confederacy, the opportunities for prolonging the war until northern patience or endurance failed, the chance for foreign intervention, and the inherent advantages of the defense over the offense helped even the odds between the contestants. This being the case, leadership assumed a vital role. "because of the fairly even match between the antagonists," he writes, "much would depend on the quality of each's command and strategy."

In the American Civil War, command and strategy began at the top, since both Jefferson Davis and Abraham Lincoln sought to exercise the position of commander in chief to the fullest practical extent. To a large degree, therefore, the fortunes of their respective armies, and ultimately of their two nations, stemmed from actions and decisions made by these two leaders.

Both men were inclined to an activist presidency, not only by their own natures but also by the fairly recent example of James Polk, who had successfully managed military operations during the war with Mexico. Historians have often noted that military strategy and especially tactics in the Civil War were influenced by the earlier struggle, but Jones draws fresh attention to the political legacy perceived by both the Union and Confederate presidents. His analysis of their use of that legacy is incisive.

Davis, who had been graduated from West Point, had fought with distinction in the Mexican War, and served as one of the United States' most effective secretaries of war, possessed considerable military experience. His detractors and critics—and these have been legion, including many of his contemporary Confederates—believed that Davis' experience was not matched by talent or judgment. As a matter of fact, Davis' interference in military matters has sometimes been given as a prime reason for the South's defeat.

Jones clearly does not share in this view. Consistently, he rates Davis' performance as seldom less than competent and often as highly innovative. Faced with the problem of creating a military structure from the ground up, Davis acted with remarkable vision and often with genuine strategic flair. His two major mistakes, if they deserve to be labeled so harshly, stemmed from conditions beyond his control.

The first error with which Davis is often charged was his decision to adopt a cordon defense of the Confederacy, dispersing troops at many points along the contested border, including the South's enormously long coastline. Critics argue that it would have been far more effective to have concentrated the limited Confederate manpower, making its armies stronger and more potent. Some historians have argued that the Confederacy should have been more willing to trade territory for time, wearing down the invading Union forces in protracted defense of carefully chosen positions.

Jones rightly notes that this argument, though perhaps valid, clearly is anachronistic. For largely political reasons, the South was forced to adopt a cordon defense in order to assert its claim to sovereignty and independence. Further, voluntarily yielding land at the very outset of the war would have depressed southern morale. And, not to be omitted from the equation, Union conquest of southern land meant Union control of black slaves, raising the unacceptable possibility of their emancipation, which could have caused serious problems even after a southern victory.

In any event, Davis himself recognized the weakness of the cordon defense, and when it proved impractical, following the loss of central Tennessee in 1862, he largely abandoned it, admitting "the error of my attempt to defend all the frontier, seaboard and inland." Still, it is difficult to see what different course Davis, or any Confederate president, could have adopted in the early days of the war.

Davis' second failing, as cited by many military historians, was his reluctance to remove generals who would not fight, or who fought badly. Generally speaking, however, Davis' appointments to command were, as Jones judges them, "mostly sound." There were some disappointments perhaps, such as John Clifford Pemberton, whose less-than-brilliant counters to Ulysses S. Grant led to the loss of Vicksburg, but Davis generally chose well from his limited options.

Davis' counterpart, Abraham Lincoln, also pursued an active role in the conduct of the war, but his interventions were sparked less by a military background than a political wisdom that recognized the need for prompt, vigorous, and above all continual action by the Union forces. Lincoln understood that time played a paradoxical role in the American Civil War. On one hand, the longer the war lasted, the greater the chance that northern sentiment would turn against the struggle and allow the South to go its own way. On the other hand, each day of war weakened southern resources and strengthened those of the North. Lincoln recognized, perhaps better than most, that if the North remained in the battle, it eventually would prevail. The question was, would it stay the course?

Although the North's remaining in the war ultimately was a political decision, it was influenced directly by events on the battlefield, and Lincoln's major contribution to the Union strategy was less in telling his generals how to fight than in finding generals who would fight. This was a process which, unfortunately, had to be conducted through trial and error, especially in the eastern theater of operations, as the Army of the Potomac went through a succession of commanders.

In the western theater, which stretched from the Allegheny Mountains to beyond the Mississippi River, Lincoln seemed to have more success with his generals, quickly finding men such as Ulysses S. Grant and William T. Sherman to command the Union forces. Jones points out, however, that western generals enjoyed advantages of terrain, especially in having more room to maneuver, as compared to those in the East. Nor was the Union record in the West uniformly successful.

Below the political level, the military leaders practiced their arts of war. Although the Civil War produced some excellent generals, as well as a selection of incompetents, there was actually little variation in the strategic and tactical backgrounds and doctrines of the commanders involved. The very first battle of the war, Manassas, or First Bull Run, set the pattern for almost every encounter, large and small, that followed. For that reason, Jones aptly titles the engagement "a representative battle."

This representative battle was marked by three factors: the dominance of the defense, especially on the tactical or battlefield level; an outcome that left both victors and vanquished so disorganized that immediate renewal of the fighting was practically impossible; and a combination of the first two factors, which meant that no single battle would decide the war.

These lessons were learned quickly by both Union and Confederate commanders, and throughout the conflict there was a marked preference for "turning movements," both strategic and tactical, in which the offense tried to force the defender to retreat without engaging in a costly and often inconclusive frontal attack. On the tactical level, the surprisingly high level of discipline and drill of the armies prevented most turning movements, as Robert E. Lee, perhaps the best general of the conflict, had to admit in several battles, including the Seven Days and Gettysburg. On a strategic level, the turning movement had a much greater and more successful impact.

This was so because of the central and permanent role played by logistics and supply during the war. As Jones points out, most Civil War armies were larger than many American cities. When they could not live off the land, which was often the case, especially with Union forces, they were dependent on long and often fragile supply lines. If an opponent threatened a supply line, an army had to respond or face starvation. The Civil War, William T. Sherman noted, came down to "grub and mules."

With battles so often inconclusive, with supply lines so vital and tempting, it is little wonder that the raid, often on a grand scale, became one of the war's most frequent and effective strategies. Jones's work places special emphasis on raiding, bringing it a prominence that it often lacked in earlier studies of the conflict. In this, he advances knowledge of how the war actually was fought.

Such advances are frequent in this volume, which provides the serious student with fresh angles of vision and new, thought-provoking discussions of familiar facts. At the same time, the casual reader, even one unacquainted with military history, will find the work accessible and profitable, especially the discussions of how decisions are made in large, sometimes unwieldy organizations. That lesson can be applied to a variety of subjects, whether Civil War armies or modern corporations.

*Civil War Command and Strategy* will not end the debate over why the conflict ended as it did, nor does it supplant the excellent special studies and broad narratives that chronicle various aspects of the struggle. It does, however, provide a careful and valuable study of how the war was fought and what the war's leaders believed they were doing.

*Michael Witkoski*

**Sources for Further Study**

*Bookwatch.* XIII, June, 1992, p. 2.
*Kirkus Reviews.* LX, February 15, 1992, p. 234.
*Library Journal.* CXVII, March 15, 1992, p. 100.

# CLAIRE CLAIRMONT AND THE SHELLEYS, 1798-1879

*Authors:* Robert Gittings (1911-1992) and Jo Manton (1919-    )
*Publisher:* Oxford University Press (New York). 281 pp. Illustrated. $39.95
*Type of work:* Literary biography
*Time:* 1798-1879
*Locale:* England, Italy, Austria, Russia, Germany, and France

*This new biography of Claire Clairmont emphasizes her resilience, generosity, independence, and tenacity as it highlights her role in the Romantic literary movement*

*Principal personages:*
> CLAIRE CLAIRMONT, Lord Byron's mistress, friend of Percy Bysshe
>   Shelley, and half-sister of Mary Godwin Shelley
> WILLIAM GODWIN, a philosopher and writer, Claire's stepfather
> MARY GODWIN SHELLEY, the daughter of William Godwin and Mary
>   Wollstonecraft, wife of Percy Bysshe Shelley, and author of *Franken-*
>   *stein*
> GEORGE GORDON, LORD BYRON, a poet and Claire's lover
> PERCY BYSSHE SHELLEY, a poet
> PERCY FLORENCE SHELLEY, the son of Mary Godwin and Percy Bysshe
>   Shelley
> ALLEGRA, the daughter of Claire Clairmont and Lord Byron
> JANE ST. JOHN SHELLEY, the wife of Percy Florence Shelley

In December, 1826, Claire Clairmont wrote to Jane Williams Hogg,

> I am unhappily the victim of a *happy passion*. I had one—like all things perfect in its kind it was
> fleeting and mine only lasted ten minutes but those ten minutes have discomposed the rest of my
> life. The passion, God knows for what cause . . . disappeared, leaving no trace whatever behind it,
> except my heart wasted and ruined as if it had been scorched by a thousand lightnings.

The happy passion to which Claire refers was her love for George Gordon, Lord Byron, whom she had sought out in 1816. Byron at first rebuffed her epistolary courtship, then agreed on a night together outside London "by way of novelty," as he remarked. He was never as taken with Claire as she was with him; to Byron she was "that odd-headed girl—who introduced herself to me." As he wrote to Douglas Kinnaird, "I never loved nor pretended to love her, but a man is a man, and if a girl of eighteen comes prancing to you at all hours, there is but one way. . . ." The authors suggest that Byron wrote the lyric "There Be None of Beauty's Daughters" to Claire before she became his mistress, but others have been suggested as the inspiration for that poem. While Byron repeatedly insisted that he was not in love with Claire, she worshiped him: "I do not expect you to love me; I am not worthy of your love. I feel you are superior," she wrote to him. The liaison resulted in the birth of a daughter on January 12, 1817. Claire wanted to call the girl Alba, perhaps playing on the initials of Lord Byron, but in this matter, as in all others concerning the child, Byron had his way; she was christened Clara Allegra Byron.

Before Allegra's birth, Claire had agreed to surrender the child to Byron, who had promised to keep the girl with him. Allegra spent her first year with her mother in England, however, while Byron remained on the Continent. Despite her separation from the man she still loved, this year was happy for Claire. Gittings and Manton include a number of Claire's letters that demonstrate her joy. Writing to Byron of Allegra, Claire noted,

> she is so fond of me that I hold her in my arms till I am nearly falling on purpose to delight her. We sleep together and if you knew the extreme happiness I feel when she nestles close to me, in listening to our regular breathing together, I could tear my flesh in twenty thousand different directions to ensure her good.

The surrender of her daughter to Byron in Venice left Claire distraught; "[T]he chill of Death fell upon my heart," she wrote.

Byron was less faithful to his part of the bargain, placing Allegra in the convent of Bagnacavallo. The action was doubly distressing to Claire because it removed Allegra from both her parents and also meant that the girl would receive a Catholic education, an idea abhorrent to the then-atheistic Claire. On April 20, 1822, Allegra died of typhoid. Byron sent the body back to England for burial at Harrow but never told Claire the site of the grave, which remained unknown to her for fifty years.

In 1822, Claire lost not only her daughter but also her closest friend, when Percy Bysshe Shelley drowned in the Bay of Spezia on July 8. Claire had met the poet a decade earlier, when she was still Jane—she changed her name in 1814. When Shelley fled England with Mary Godwin in July, 1814, Claire accompanied the lovers to serve as translator. Later that year, Shelley began teaching Claire Greek. Whether she ever inspired Byron to poetic expression, she certainly did Shelley. "To Constantia Singing" responds to her extensive musical talents, and in "Epipsychidion" she is the comet, "beautiful and fierce." The authors do not believe that Claire and Shelley were lovers, but rumors at the time and subsequent speculation have suggested that they were. When Byron learned of Claire's pregnancy, Byron wondered whether he was the father.

Shelley was kinder to Claire than was Byron, leaving her a legacy of twelve thousand pounds in his will, the sum to be paid upon the death of Timothy Shelley, the poet's long-lived father. Shelley also paid for her music lessons. Claire's presence in the Shelley household must have been trying for her half-sister. On July 4, 1820, Claire wrote in her journal, "Heigh-ho the Claire & the Ma [that is, Mary Shelley]/ Find something to fight about every day." Later that year, Claire moved into the home of Professor Antonio Bojti of Florence, to assume the first of many posts as governess. As partial payment for room and board, she was to teach English to the Bojti children. Shelley and Claire continued to correspond, and he apparently missed her more than she missed him. "Your absence," he wrote, "is too painful for your return ever to be unwelcome." Claire was caring for Percy Florence, the only one of Shelley's children to survive infancy, when she learned of the poet's death.

Shelley had been her protector and closest friend in life; until her own death Claire remained faithful to Shelley's memory and principles. Although she never wrote a memoir of Shelley, late in life she assisted Edward John Trelawny with his biography. Trelawny was so impressed with her account that he urged her to undertake her own life of Shelley. She contented herself with praising Shelley in her journal. Among the entries cited by Gittings and Manton is Claire's comment that Shelley's "whole existence was visionary, and there breathed in his looks and in his manners that high and superhuman tone which we can only conceive as belonging to a superior being." When Tom Moore wrote unkindly of the poet, Claire responded angrily in her journal and expressed shock that Mary Shelley would continue to associate with the man.

This loyalty to Shelley she transferred to his son. When Trelawny had asked her for information about Shelley, she first had mistaken his meaning and had written back about Percy Florence, a misprision that Gittings and Manton ascribe to her devotion to the young man. Claire demonstrated this dedication in a number of ways. During a cholera epidemic in London in 1832, Claire sent money to Mary Shelley to allow mother and child to flee the disease. Claire initially had planned to send the money to her brother, who by a cruel irony died of the plague that the Shelleys were able to escape. In 1839, when Shelley became involved with a girl whom Mary Shelley disliked, Claire defended him. She even claimed to rejoice when she learned that he was getting fat, writing wittily that he would "become the greatest poet and the greatest philosopher England has ever produced." She continued more seriously, "he will follow the doctrines of his father and force by his truth and eloquence the blind and ignorant creeds that infect us to retire into obscurity." Unhappily for her hopes, Percy Florence Shelley demonstrated that genius is not necessarily inherited. Claire would remain more loyal to Shelley's principles than would his son. Repeatedly she had to force herself to remain silent when her employers voiced their conservative opinions, and she would flee an uncongenial Victorian England to spend the last years of her life in Italy.

Claire's relationship with her half-sister continued to be troubled throughout Mary's life. Periods of reconciliation were followed by periods of estrangement. The authors note that Shelley's legacy to her strained the family's finances and hence their feelings toward Claire. With the rest of her family, Claire was on better terms. Following the deaths of Shelley and Allegra, Claire joined her brother Charles in Vienna, where she hoped to secure a teacher's license. The weather did not agree with her, though—she later claimed that she nearly died in the winter of 1822-1823—and suspicions of her radical sentiments prevented her from securing permission to teach. Determined to earn her own way, Claire became governess in the Zotoff family of St. Petersburg. The authors dispute the view that Claire's years in Russia were relentlessly unhappy, but she hated the winters, and in 1827 she resolved to leave.

For the next decade, she served in various aristocratic households, returning to England in 1837 to care for her ailing mother. After Mary Clairmont's death, Claire returned to the Continent, probably living with a lover for several years. The early 1840's remain a blank—Claire did not confide even to her journal what she was doing.

The death of Timothy Shelley in 1844 freed Claire from financial worries. Claire used her money to help friends and family even when her own circumstances were difficult. She loaned two hundred pounds to Jane Hogg's daughter, a sum never repaid. She ill-advisedly bought a farm in Austria to be near her nephew, and after her brother Charles's death in 1850, she continued to support her sister-in-law to the extent that she denied herself her own apartment in Italy until the woman died in 1868.

The apartment Claire then took was in Florence, on the Via Valfonde, where Percy Florence Shelley had been born in 1819. Claire's niece Paula moved in with an illegitimate daughter, Georgina. To raise money for the girl's education, Claire tried to sell her Shelley manuscripts. Edward Silsbee, a New England seafarer, came to buy the papers; unable to pay Claire's price, he remained as a lodger and became Paula's lover. After Claire's death, he hoped to get the Shelley papers from his mistress, but the price was still too high—marriage, according to contemporary gossip. Claire's best-known contribution to literature stemmed from this episode with Silsbee: Henry James heard the story in 1887 and used it as the basis of *The Aspern Papers* (1888).

Despite the fictional rendition, the novel faithfully captures Claire in old age. Subsequent accounts, supposedly more factual, were influenced by Jane St. John Shelley's objections to Claire and, indeed, to the radical sentiments of the Shelley circle of the early 1800's. Biographies were sanitized, Claire marginalized. Gittings and Manton's readable, well-researched account has restored Claire to her proper place among the Romantic writers of the nineteenth century and reveals her talents, generosity, impulsiveness, passion, and independence. Even when she was living with her lover in France in the early 1840's, she paid her own way. The authors have a good story to tell, and they tell it well. In her old age, Mary Shelley wrote to Claire,

> When I think of your life—how left unexpectedly to your own resources you courageously took your fate on yourself—supported yourself for so many years—refusing to be a burthen to anyone— making dear and valued friends wherever you went through your own merit—I feel sure you ought to meet with some reward.

This biography may be the fulfillment of Mary Shelley's wish.

*Joseph Rosenblum*

## Sources for Further Study

*Choice*. XXX, December, 1992, p. 617.
*London Review of Books*. December, 1992, p. 617.
*New Statesman and Society*. V, April 17, 1992, p. 44
*The Observer*. April 5, 1992, p. 63.
*The Spectator*. CCLXVIII, April 25, 1992, p. 38.
*The Times Literary Supplement*. April 17, 1992, p. 5.

# CLOCKERS

*Author:* Richard Price (1949-    )
*Publisher:* Houghton Mifflin (Boston). 599 pp. $22.95
*Type of work:* Novel
*Time:* The 1990's
*Locale:* Dempsy, New Jersey

*Part detective story and part naturalist novel,* Clockers *is the most detailed and evocative account yet written—or likely to be written—about contemporary America's meanest, most drug-drenched streets*

*Principal characters:*
> RONALD DUNHAM (STRIKE), the supervisor in charge of a crew of "clockers," or street dealers, in a housing project in Dempsy, New Jersey
> VICTOR DUNHAM, his hard-working brother
> DAVID KLEIN (ROCCO), a homicide detective
> RODNEY LITTLE, a local drug dealer and, at the age of thirty-five, a father figure
> TYRONE, a young boy whom Strike first protects and later betrays
> THE FURY, one of the several narcotics squads assigned to Dempsy

Richard Price is one of those writers who keep the American Dream theme alive by tracing its demise. He is an F. Scott Fitzgerald without the lyricism, an Arthur Miller minus the overt politics and tragic grandeur. Price is closer in spirit and in some ways even in style to Theodore Dreiser, with whom he shares a detached but nevertheless evident sympathy for suffering humanity. Even more, Price resembles the slightly lesser but more recent Naturalists, James T. Farrell, Hubert Selby, and John Rechy. These chroniclers of America's urban underbelly differ markedly from Tom Wolfe, author of the best-selling *The Bonfire of the Vanities* (1987), with which *Clockers* (mistakenly) has been compared. Price has little interest in stridently proclaiming realism's second coming or in narrating the story of the age of greed and yuppie self-striving. His characters are too busy just trying to survive, both physically and psychically.

Survival is Price's abiding theme. His highly acclaimed first novel, *The Wanderers* (1974), is set in a Bronx housing project and centers on Richie Gennaro, the seventeen-year-old "warlord" of a local gang. The novel succeeds in large part because it reads like some strange mutation of naturalist fiction, the hybrid offspring of television's *Happy Days*, with its likable greaser The Fonz, and film noir in the American style of *The Blackboard Jungle* (1955). In Price's second novel, *Bloodbrothers* (1976), Stony De Coca, Jr., discovers that one's own family can be as dangerous and confining as any gang. At the age of eighteen, Stony has to decide whether to follow his father and uncle into the construction trades or strike out on his own. In *Ladies' Man* (1978), thirty-year-old Kenny Becker finds himself alone. Losing his girlfriend and his job in quick succession, he wanders Manhattan's singles scene only eventually to realize that

"All my moves were frauds, to get out of things, not into them." *The Breaks* (1983) received less praise than it deserved, perhaps because it is a "campus novel," a subgenre more loved in the United Kingdom than in the United States. Peter Keller is graduated from a college that seems suspiciously like Cornell (where Price studied as an undergraduate) but is rejected by Columbia Law School. The family's first-ever college graduate stays on hold for a year, unwilling to live out his parents' version of his future—as a lawyer with a family and a suburban home—but also unsure just what it is that he wants to do.

Having had his first novel made into a film, Price wrote two successful and highly acclaimed film scripts during the 1980's: *The Color of Money* (1986) and *Sea of Love* (1989). Both films offer additional evidence of Price's obsessive interest in survival, particularly in the seamy and often violent side of American life. As mystery thriller and police story, *Sea of Love* represents something of a change in direction in Price's work. Old preoccupations and new interests combine, often brilliantly, in *Clockers*, the novel that grew out of the research Price began doing for *Sea of Love*. Already teaching at a drug rehabilitation center in the Bronx, Price began accompanying New York City and Hudson County, New Jersey, police on their rounds, also hanging out with the "clockers," young, low-level drug dealers.

The two or more years of research that went into its writing give the novel its aura of authenticity and immediacy, but it is Price's highly personalized and deeply autobiographical vision that gives the novel its narrative drive and depth. At the opening of *Clockers*, Strike surveys his small corner of the two-square-block Roosevelt Housing Project in fictional Dempsy, New Jersey, located along the actual JFK Boulevard that runs from Bayonne through Jersey City and Union City. At 5'-7" and 125 pounds, Strike survives by a combination of luck and sense, living by his three golden rules: don't do drugs, don't get greedy, and don't trust anyone. He oversees a crew that sells $10 bottles of cocaine for Rodney Little, who in turn works for a dealer named Champ. The pay is good but in a sense worthless. Possessions only make a dealer conspicuous, a target for thieves and for "knockos" (narcotics police). It cannot even be used to buy one's way out of dealing, for dealing is the only skill clockers have. Having "no option but to do as he was told," Strike is reminded of his helplessness and hopelessness with each bout of stammering, with each ulcer attack, and with each humiliating police search. In a world in which the average clocker lasts about six months on the street, Strike is, at nine months, a survivor. Just as clearly, he wants something more, not so much more money as more recognition, especially from Rodney, a surrogate father. He also wants more responsibility and more freedom but less pressure and less vulnerability.

His chance comes when Rodney offers to promote Strike from his outside perch to an inside job dealing "weight," selling ounces out of Ahab's, a fast-food shop. All Strike has to do is "get" Darryl Adams, who has been cheating on Rodney, selling some of his own weight along with Rodney's, just as Rodney has been cheating on Champ. Strike agrees that Darryl has "got to be got" but cannot bring himself to do the deed. Strike's hard-working brother, Victor, strangely claims to know someone who will do the job, which Victor has been made to believe is a matter of honorable revenge, not a drug dealer's payback. That same night, Darryl is murdered. Although he stands to gain from Darryl's murder, Strike does not know who did it. Nor does he know until much later that by not doing it himself, he has put himself at greater risk, for if part of Rodney's plan was to punish Darryl and reward Strike, then another was to "bloody" Strike in order to make it impossible for him ever to betray Rodney without making it possible for Rodney to betray him. In the world of *Clockers*, betrayal is the norm. Betrayed by Rodney, whose power over him Strike both abhors and admires, Strike will in turn betray twelve-year-old Tyrone, the younger and still innocent version of himself.

Strike is only one of the novel's two main characters. The other is David "Rocco" Klein, the officer investigating Darryl's murder. Born and raised in Dempsy, Rocco now lives across the river in New York with his wife, twenty years his junior, and their two-year-old daughter. At forty-three, Rocco is six months from the retirement he both longs for and fears. When Victor confesses to Darryl's murder, Rocco quickly assumes he is "taking the heat" for someone else, presumably his brother Strike.

Proving Victor's innocence and Strike's guilt, even at the risk of his own job, becomes Rocco's "mission." Rocco is, as the reader already knows, wrong about Strike, but as the reader will eventually learn he is also wrong about Victor. Rocco's mission is, however, as much about saving himself as it is about saving Victor. Each of the novel's characters—cops, clockers, parents, and kids alike—has his or her own salvation fantasy.

Escape or just plain survival, much less salvation, seems to be an increasingly remote possibility in a world in which power rules, betrayal is a fact of life, and the cycle of fear and failure is perpetual. As one knocko explains to Rocco, curious about the circumstances behind Victor's one brush with the law, the shouting match in which Victor got involved with a police officer

> "was all about *dis*. The kid disrespected me by raising up in my face. I dissed him by throwing him up against the fence and doing the Johnson check. He dissed me by walking off. I dissed him by flicking his hat in front of his people. He dissed me by giving me a shove. The mother comes along, she disses me by snatching the keys. I dis her by making fun of her wheeze. Everything's *dis*."

The officer comments later that everything soon cooled down, and that "life goes on." But life will not go on for Darryl, or for Victor, who prefers thirty years in prison with all of its horrors, to thirty years in the projects, with all of their frustrations. Eventually even Rocco can understand why Victor says he killed Darryl in "self-defense."

*Clockers* is a vivid and compelling but by no means perfect novel. Price's use of parallelism is insistent and obtrusive, and his symbolism, Strike's ulcer and stutter in particular, is heavy-handed. Price's language occasionally slips from its usual register of sympathetic detachment to something closer to sentimentality and purple prose. (Rocco at one point "experienced a stuporous surge of anxiety" and elsewhere "sat in his car spasming with fatigue.") The happy ending—Strike clutching a handful of

Greyhound tickets as he boards the bus that will take him on the first leg of his See America tour—seems similarly willed and unconvincing, even distracting. As Frank Norris warned a century ago, realists must confine themselves to the probable and avoid the merely possible. (The ending seems made for a film, and Universal Pictures has paid $1.9 million for the rights to make it.)

The ending fails to convince for yet another reason. Even though the author succeeds extraordinarily well in making virtually all of his characters compelling and empathetic, Strike never seems to merit the concern for his future that a number of other characters and certainly the author express. Call this the "Radio Rahim" problem: Viewers of Spike Lee's *Do the Right Thing* (1989) know that the police have wrongfully killed Radio Rahim, but those same viewers find it hard to care about this particular character's death. Far more effective is the overall structure of *Clockers*, its alternating chapters devoted to clockers and cops, to Strike and Rocco. In the long final chapter, alternating sections come in a breathless rush much like the words that pour from Strike's mouth when he finally tells Rocco all that he knows.

Price's treatment of his characters and his volatile material is eminently fair, sympathetic but never overtly judgmental in a novel that is as much about self-deception on all sides as it is about Jersey's meanest streets. The depiction of that meanness is *Clockers'* greatest achievement. Price knows the routines of cops and clockers alike, everything from examining a murder victim at the crime scene to the complexities of the drug trade on the local and street level. Above all, Price knows Dempsy, the projects and hangouts, the squad rooms and holding centers. He also knows the pathos—half humorous, half horrific—behind the kid who proclaims himself "the black Jesse Owens," the grandmother who screams "Hat don't do drugs" as her grandson is thrown to the floor, not knowing that what "Hat" does do is kill people. Price even knows the pathos of places and the people to be found in them, the Anne Donovan Pediatric Center, for example, "a spectacular ruin, a Depression-era monolith abandoned in the 1970's for a variety of reasons" but still drawing the sick, the dopers, and AIDS victims who scavenge pipes, porcelain, and anything else of value. Price knows the shakedowns and strip searches, the payoffs and procedures, and above all the tacit agreements that make life on the street for clockers and knockos something more and something less than President George Bush's platitudinous War on Drugs. Not even Strike's escape, his happy ending nearly four hundred pages later, can quite erase Price's depiction of this "spectacular ruin" and the many others like it in this immensely readable, immensely affecting, brilliantly claustrophobic novel.

*Robert A. Morace*

## Sources for Further Study

*Booklist.* LXXXVIII, April 1, 1992, p. 1411.
*Chicago Tribune.* May 17, 1992, XIV, p. 5.

*Los Angeles Times Book Review*. June 14, 1992, p. 3.
*The Nation*. CCLIV, June 1, 1992, p. 755.
*The New York Review of Books*. XXXIX, July 16, 1992, p. 23.
*The New York Times Book Review*. XCVII, June 21, 1992, p. 10.
*Publishers Weekly*. CCXXXIX, March 9, 1992, p. 47.
*Time*. CXXXIX, June 8, 1992, p. 89.
*The Times Literary Supplement*. June 26, 1992, p. 21.
*The Wall Street Journal*. July 3, 1992, p. A5.
*The Washington Post Book World*. XXII, May 24, 1992, p. 2.

# A CLOSED EYE

*Author:* Anita Brookner (1938-    )
*First published:* 1991, in Great Britain
*Publisher:* Random House (New York). 263 pp. $21.00
*Type of work:* Novel
*Time:* 1939 through early 1990's
*Locale:* London and Switzerland

*Anita Brookner, winner of England's prestigious Booker Prize, presents an ironic and tragic tale of a docile woman whose life closes without her having fully lived*

> Principal characters:
> HARRIET LYTTON, a docile daughter and wife
> FREDDIE LYTTON, her husband, contemporary of her parents
> MERLE AND HUGHIE BLAKEMORE, Harriet's parents
> IMOGEN, Harriet and Freddie's daughter
> TESSA, a lifelong friend of Harriet
> JACK PECKHAM, Tessa's handsome husband
> ELIZABETH "LIZZIE" PECKHAM, Tessa and Jack's daughter

Harriet Lytton, the protagonist of Anita Brookner's eleventh novel, is, like her creator, the daughter of parents adversely affected by World War II, whom she feels she needs to please and protect. Consequently, as Brookner said of herself, she becomes "an adult too soon and paradoxically never" grows up (*Paris Review*, Fall, 1987). *A Closed Eye* is Harriet's story, from her birth in 1939 and childhood with Merle and Hughie Blakemore, two people "too young, too feckless" to be parents, through a loveless marriage with a man her parents' age, motherhood, and ultimately lonely widowhood. An intimate study of Harriet's feelings and moral development, the novel offers an ironic, tragic portrait of a woman who has chosen to keep self-knowledge "at bay for half a lifetime" and who, once awakened, finds despair. Indeed, because Harriet has obeyed and acquiesced to others her entire life, she has been both untrue to herself and inauthentic in all her relationships.

Taking its title and epigraph from Henry James's novella *Madame de Mauves* (1874), *A Closed Eye* is a novel James himself might have written. Moreover, midway through, the reader imagines that had James written *Mrs. Bridge* (1959), Evan S. Connell, Jr.'s masterpiece, the result may well have been *A Closed Eye*. Brookner's heroine feels as desperate in her "truce with painful truth" and her stultifying, conventional middle-class marriage as did Connell's Mrs. Bridge, yet the style and pace of Brookner's novel, its concern with moral decision, and its use of confrontation scenes followed by extensive rumination by the main character are typically Jamesian. Structurally, *A Closed Eye* is retrospective fiction, apart from two opening chapters that set the stage for what will follow. The opening chapter, in fact, evokes a mystery. Harriet is writing an invitation to Lizzie, later revealed to be the daughter of Harriet's deceased friend Tessa. One name, Harriet writes, must be avoided at all cost. It is only much later in the novel that the reader discovers this name is Imogen, Harriet's own daughter, who has been killed in an automobile accident. From this opening epistle and the chapter that follows, *A Closed Eye* explores Harriet's relationships with all the major characters: her parents, her girlfriends, her husband, and her friend's husband—Jack Peckham, who opens Harriet's closed eyes—as well as Imogen and Lizzie. Although Harriet remains the center of consciousness through most of the novel, Brookner shifts the point of view occasionally to provide insights from others, particularly Freddie, Merle Blakemore, Imogen, and Lizzie. Thus the novel's main point of view is omniscient, though Brookner refrains from the nineteenth century device of direct authorial commentary on her characters. Others' views of Harriet, however, provide an essential contrast to her own shame-filled judgments of herself.

What characterizes the relationships in *A Closed Eye*, as in other Brookner novels, is contrast: contrast, for example, between the self-assured and often selfish and the docile and obedient; between those of sanguine and those of melancholy temperaments. Harriet Lytton fits decidedly in the latter categories in the above examples, but this is not to suggest that Brookner takes a simplistic view of her characters. On the contrary, her focus is the struggle of the melancholy, obedient type to take action—a conflict evolving from their keenly developed moral consciousness—and their failure to grasp what comes easily to the more self-confident. That it is pleasure, sensation, and feeling that define life is made clear throughout *A Closed Eye*. The self-assured know this and grasp for what they want. (Tessa, Harriet's friend, wants the handsome Jack, her lover, as husband, and so gets pregnant.)

Harriet comes to realize the value of the sensory life through the course of the novel, though she is never able to find physical fulfillment. Ironically, she is born to people who know the pleasures of active sociability. Harriet's father, permanently damaged by his experiences as a prisoner of war, is a perpetual boy, "frozen at the age of immaturity, and curiously unlined," yet he delights in the sensory ritual of toast and tea. Harriet's mother, who supports the family with a dress shop prior to Harriet's marriage, cares for her husband but finds passion with the landlord, Mr. Latif. Such compromises, usually the result of careful calculation, are everywhere evident among Harriet's associates, including her own daughter, yet Harriet keeps her eyes closed for much of the novel, choosing, instead of the path of pleasure, a more virtuous and morally arduous life. Significantly, Merle and Hughie's frivolity allows them to marry off their only daughter to a man her father's age, a wealthy buddy of Hughie from World War II. The compromise causes some pity for Harriet, but not enough to discourage either Merle or her husband. Indeed, Harriet's marriage provides both financial and social ease for her parents.

Other sets of contrasts in *A Closed Eye* include the marriage of Tessa and Jack and that of Harriet and Freddie, as well as the children of those marriages, Lizzie and Imogen. A ruthless though appealing cad, Jack Peckham has the vitality and sexual magnetism Freddie lacks. He becomes for Harriet the handsome stranger of her fantasies, "the villainous hero of romantic fiction, the cruel lover who breaks hearts and thrills women." So powerful is Jack's effect that Harriet instinctively hides her splotchy red facial birthmark when she first meets him. The gesture, Brookner writes, is "symbolic, as if she were hiding more than her face, as if she were hiding herself," her sexual, passionate self. Additionally, while Jack marries Tessa for their child's sake, he continues to live in his own flat and keep a mistress, even taking her to his wife's funeral. Freddie, in contrast, is a dull, reasonable man. Although a "careless," "even violent" and "foul-mouthed" lover, he is Harriet's "protection, her support, her very respectability." Harriet, moreover, unlike her girlfriends, including Tessa, is unable to actuate an adulterous affair, though Jack Peckham clearly invites such a relationship.

Ironically, Lizzie and Imogen are so unlike their mothers that they might be changelings. Like Harriet, Lizzie is guarded, composed, a lover of books and solitude. She has neither Jack's nor Tessa's beauty. In contrast, Imogen, the astonishingly beautiful daughter of dull Harriet and aging Freddie, is high-spirited, imperious, and "adept at imposing her whims." Moreover, while the two girls are infants together and spend hours under the care of Harriet, the central issue in Lizzie's life is her absent father, whom she longs to make proud. Imogen sees her faded father as "too old . . . and too graceless to be accepted." Her behavior deeply hurts Freddie, but Imogen remains distant and cold. Ironically, she functions as her mother's alter ego, not only in her rejection of Freddie, but in her freedom and love of adventure, so much a part of Harriet's fantasies yet consistently repressed.

In one early scene shortly after her marriage, Harriet watches the silhouette of a figure shadowed on the window shade of a flat opposite her back garden. "The mysterious window" where the figure appears is "always closed yet always lit up" and the figure always agitated, "like a prisoner, for whom she [Harriet] felt a terrified sympathy." The scene introduces one of the subtler themes in *A Closed Eye*: that of the darker, concealed shadow self. For Harriet, this shadow is her sexual, adventurous self, the antithesis of her respectable self, which she represses for the sake of her marriage. The shadow and dream motifs in *A Closed Eye* are psychological devices that grant depth to Brookner's characterizations. The more ostensible theme of the novel is feminist: Harriet, like her mother Merle and her three female friends, has suffered a disappointing marriage. They all have sacrificed youth, happiness, freedom, even a closeness they once had. To protect the dignity of their husbands, the women now retain secrets, replacing the transparency of their girlhood friendship with adult opacity. As in other Brookner novels, women pay dearly for marriage.

Other dominant themes in this novel are *memento mori* and its corollary, *carpe diem*: all is decaying; seize the day. A renowned art historian and former lecturer in art at London's Courtauld Institute, Anita Brookner knows the *memento mori* images of Dutch art and uses them in her novel, particularly in her portrayal of Freddie, a frequent gallery visitor. In one scene, he encounters a "sinister" picture with a foreground of "split fruit, a peach or a nectarine" with a fly on "the lip of the fruit . . . breeding corruption." Startled, Freddie realizes "that the picture was meant to remind him of his own decay." Harriet, too, must face corruption and death: the growing fragility of her parents, Tessa's cancer-caused suffering and demise, Freddie's ill health and eventual death, her daughter's accidental death. All the people closest to Harriet die in this novel, with the exception of her aging parents, leaving her life empty. Like the Dutch painter of the canvas Freddie observes, Brookner seems to say to her reader: "There is no escape. . . . [O]ur substance is being consumed." The only salvation is to seize the moment and live.

Literary allusions abound in *A Closed Eye*, particularly to nineteenth century novels. Aside from the epigraph from Henry James's *Madame de Mauves* and reference to Harriet's reading *What Maisie Knew* (1897), Brookner establishes parallels between Harriet and the heroine of Charles Dickens' *Little Dorrit* (1855-1857), another novel Harriet is reading. Like Amy Dorrit, Harriet is a devoted daughter, ends with a "wreck of a husband," and is good, always wanting "to be good, believing that if one wished it so one could become perfect." Jack Peckham too, in Harriet's imagination, is a hero of romantic fiction: Mr. Rochester of Charlotte Brontë's *Jane Eyre* (1847), who is uncontrollable until dependent and blind. Allusions to T. S. Eliot's "The Love Song of J. Alfred Prufrock" (1915) also appear, emphasizing Harriet's inability, like Prufrock's, to communicate her true feelings. In a clear echo of Prufrock's words, at one point in the novel Harriet thinks, "Oh no, that was not what I meant at all." The last and most extensive allusion is a lengthy quotation from the work of the French writer Stendhal. Occurring in the last pages of the novel, this passage from an unidentified work is translated for Harriet by Lizzie and emphasizes the importance of sensation and the life of the senses, without which there is only death.

Paralleling many of the novel's themes, moreover, is "a sort of progressive darkening" in the imagery, imagery designed to match the closing of Harriet's life with the deaths of her husband and daughter. Indeed, Brookner uses light and darkness throughout the novel to reflect her characters' moods. In one scene, for example, sunshine coming through a dusty window parallels Harriet's hope for passion glimmering amid the dust of her marriage. Like any observer of art, Brookner also has an eye for painterly detail and interior decor. She depicts the Blakemore's Brighton apartment, Jack's Judd Street flat, and Harriet and Freddie's various homes in London and in Switzerland in masterly, vivid detail, from carpets to drapes to furniture. Natural scenes too are evocatively sketched, one rendered like a nineteenth century Impressionist canvas:

> The air shimmered; in the boat basin the little craft were motionless on the tideless waters. Tiny brown waves spread over the cobbles below the wall on which they leaned, momentarily dazzled.

That such descriptions match her heroine's moods adds irony and depth to Anita Brookner's work.

Since 1981, Anita Brookner has published a novel every year, each a subtle, ironic, and carefully written portrait of isolated, melancholy protagonists struggling with the moral dilemmas the more frivolous never consider in their pursuit of personal pleasure. Harriet Lytton, like heroines before her, is such a protagonist, yet her life seems particularly bleak. The reader can only hope by the end of the novel that, with her husband dead and Lizzie agreeable about visiting Switzerland, Harriet will reestablish her ties to Lizzie's father, the man who awakened her life. Brookner's beautiful novel deserves a less stark ending.

*Stella Nesanovich*

## Sources for Further Study

*Chicago Tribune.* March 22, 1992, XIV, p. 7.
*The Christian Science Monitor.* July 10, 1992, p. 11.
*Library Journal.* CXVII, February 1, 1992, p. 121.
*Los Angeles Times.* March 27, 1992, p. E4.
*New Statesman and Society.* IV, August 23, 1991, p. 35.
*The New York Review of Books.* XXXIX, May 14, 1992, p. 25.
*The New York Times Book Review.* XCVII, April 12, 1992, p. 12.
*The New Yorker.* LXVIII, April 27, 1992, p. 106.
*Publishers Weekly.* CCXXXIX, January 13, 1992, p. 45.
*The Times Literary Supplement.* August 23, 1991, p. 20.
*The Wall Street Journal.* March 30, 1992, p. A14.
*The Washington Post Book World.* XXII, March 22, 1992, p. 6.

# COLLECTED SHORTER POEMS
# 1946-1991

*Author:* Hayden Carruth (1921-     )
*Publisher:* Copper Canyon Press (Port Townsend, Washington). 417 pp. $23.00; paperback
$12.00
*Type of work:* Poetry

*Carruth has a powerful ability to recognize and register with precision the course of the*
*development of his spirit and its relationship to the world*

Hayden Carruth's *Collected Shorter Poems: 1946-1991*, winner of the 1992 National Book Critics Circle Award for poetry, provides an overview of the life's work of one of the most important contemporary poets of the United States. Through his wide publication (twenty-two previous books), various editorial roles at *Poetry*, *Harper's*, and *The Hudson Review*, his anthology *The Voice That Is Great Within Us*, and his teaching career, Carruth has had a central role in influencing American poetry.

Throughout his career, Carruth has explored the self's ambivalent relationship to the world. It becomes apparent in the volume's first section, poems from *The Crow and the Heart*, that destruction and violence are key elements in the release of the self from its mundane and merely incidental incarnation. After the train wreck, in "Wreck of the Circus Train" it is clear that "life remained, at work to detain spirit." Such is the case for the collection; it is the dramatic wreck, of spirit and poet, that allows the natural and primitive self to escape into the imaginative and loving landscape as the lions of the train wreck wander off to the hills. A great tension builds between this all-important natural self and the encumbered societal self as it is alienated and exposed to a harsh human and natural world in poems such as "On a Certain Engagement South of Seoul": "Nor could we look at each other, for each/ was a sign of fear, and we could not conceal/ Our hatred for our friends." This tension is maintained throughout the collection.

With the destruction of the incidental and entrapping self, the natural, purely subjective self is free to experience a renewed right relation to its universe. The resulting language (as in poems such as "The Snow") is frequently a friendly subjectification, if not outright personification of the self's environment in I-Thou terms. Thus, the very nature that is often the destructive agent for the incidental self is a companion and home to the natural self.

Throughout the collection Carruth explores the relationship of self to world within a loose system of symbolism established in these early works. In poems such as "The Snow," "Birth of Venus," and "The Fact of the Matter," Carruth focuses much attention on images of birds. In "The Fact of the Matter" Carruth writes:

> A visitant aloof and lone,
>> The phoenix comes on swooping wings;
>> The wind against his feathers sings
> A song that stays when he is gone.

As the bird actualizes its existence in the natural, often stormy and chaotic, often loving world in song, so the poet writes. Once the destructive world has stripped the self of the incidental, it is the song, the poem, that establishes the reconnection between the natural self and the natural world—the phoenix rises from the ashes. In "Mild Winter," Carruth refers to Edgar Allan Poe's "metaphysical bird," who spreads word of agonizingly incomplete mortality, "I peer/ through gray air but the raven is not visible; only/ a voice is there, guttural bad news penetrating/ the thickness of spruce trees." Yet in "The Loon on Forrester's Pond" Carruth recognizes the bird's song, and the poem, not only as the "cry of the genie inside the lamp" but also as that which overcomes the otherwise damning silence of the disconnected self:

> the loon
> broke the stillness over the water
> again and again,
> broke the wilderness
> with his song, truly
> a vestige, the laugh that transcends
> first all mirth
> and then all sorrow
> and finally all knowledge, dying
> into the gentlest quavering timeless
> woe.

The poet remarks that the bird's song seems "the only real sanity to me." The poem, then, is at once a lament of alienation and destruction and an agent of reconciliation and unity.

Carruth's language reflects his passion for the natural, unencumbered self. While expanding the range of his poetic voice to match the scope of his emotional and philosophical concerns, he recurs to a conversational manner that serves as the pattern against which his more extravagant flights of language are counterpointed.

Carruth's use of conversational language is particularly effective in his examination of rural characters in poems such as "Johnny Spain's White Heifer," "Lady," "Regarding Chainsaws," and "Marshall Walker." These are people whose glory comes not in false idealization but in their hands-in-the-dirt connections to their environment. And if it is Carruth's project to show us the inner experiences of such people, he is successful primarily in the language of these poems, which is bold and unadorned. Here Carruth's voice has the directness of natural speech, driving straight to the reality of these rural people and the beautifully harsh landscape that shapes their lives. The language creates a connectedness, an unpretentious and honest tone, as in "Marvin MaCabe," where the speaker, with ironic clarity, ponders his supposedly poor speech and resulting inability to communicate a thought. He asks if the listener knows how it is to have a thought "that's clear and shiny inside your head come out/ like a mouthful of mud." These are characters who, in their natural language, speak for natural man, connected to himself with the same ease that he is connected to the earth he farms.

To be sure, Carruth experiments with an immense range of language and usage. His contemplative poems such as "R.M.D.," "In Russia," and "Unnatural Unselection" are unapologetically philosophical in their determination to explore concepts and open cognitive space. These are poems that grow from a more intellectual creative process, and in their reflection they often become startlingly self-aware. In "Une Présence Absolue," the importance of the very imagination from which Carruth is writing manages to escape from the bonds of tight, logical language: "Imagination, let me pay more attention to you,/ You alone have this letting power; give me your one gift, which is the one/ absolution." The power of these poems results from the combination of intellectual, formal language which explores a philosophical position, and subversive emotion which at last breaks the objective tone. Thus, the natural self reveals itself also in Carruth's more linguistically philosophical work when the academic concerns are finally grounded in the human. If these poems are less successful than those of a more offhand linguistic style, it is perhaps only because they lack the colloquial charm of voice and personality found in so much of the collection, and not because they fail to convey the truth of the authentic, natural self.

Despite the abundance of natural violence in the collection, despair comes most frequently from society. In "Sam and Poll Go Back to the City," "Living Alone," and "Essay on Death," those who have stripped the incidental and become human are attacked by a society that destroys the authentic connections of natural self to environment. In the key poem "Paragraphs," Carruth sees modern society as diminishing the individual in right relation to his surroundings to the extent that the "national mean taking over" has squelched even his abilities to achieve a clear power of poetic imagination. He wishes himself a romantic, with all the accompanying glory of the visionary landscape, but he sees modern society as all but prohibiting this:

> Wordsworth!
> thou should'st be living in this hour:
> Vermont hath need of thee
> Carruth
> being at all events not up to it;
> the ancient power
> of that vision is gone.

Encroaching society encumbers the natural self, and in turn the poet as voice of that natural self is diminished.

As the collection progresses into work from the 1980's. Carruth draws on an ever-widening spectrum of formal technique, and thus avoids falling into narrow classifications of structure as well as language. His formal ability allows him a flexibility in approaching his subjects that is not common among late twentieth century writers. His choices are his own, not mere reflections of poetic fashion. That Carruth could write (and choose to include in the collection) a section of numbered sonnets that are often directly philosophical and grow strongly from tradition is a testament to his versatility and freedom from fashion.

Thematically the sonnets explore, if not reconcile, tension and apparent contradiction between poetry and silence, love and isolation, and knowledge and futility. The tension between the sonnet tradition and the desire to break structurally free, and the various resolutions that Carruth achieves (abandoning or modifying the line and rhyme pattern), punctuate the themes in a way typical of the structures of poems throughout the collection.

Carruth's experimentation is certainly not limited to manipulating established poetic form, but frequently involves borrowing structure from music, whether in the specific musical movements of a sixteen-bar theme and stop-time chorus in "The Cowshead Blues" or the soulful echoes of "Eternity Blues," in which he writes "Long ways from home is how they say it./ Long ways from home, boys, long long ways from home." This use of a wide structural repertoire is evident as well in Carruth's more typical poems, such as "Song of Two Crows," in which the structure is much looser, but the rhythm and balance form a strong undercurrent to what would otherwise seem an unmanageably wandering poem.

The true value of this collection lies in the view it offers of the process and development of Carruth's poetry. The inclusiveness that characterizes his work is perhaps most evident in the poems in the later sections of the collection, including those in the last section, *New Poems (1986-1991)*, comprising thirty-three poems not previously published in book form. These poems continue to deal with existential issues of the incidental versus the natural self and the possibility or impossibility of connection to the world outside that self.

Carruth's treatment of these themes reflects the forty-five years of evolution and ever-increasing dexterity that the collection traces. The offhanded voice of "Songs About What Comes Down: The Complete Works of Mr. Septic Tanck" conversationally explores a fascination with the connection between the physical (especially the brain) and the natural self as if simply commenting from everyday thought. And the colloquial "Pa McCabe" communicates the complex struggle for actualization and connection that was so much the concern of Carruth's cognitive poetry, but does so by means of a direct narrative line and decidedly unphilosophical language. The result, in this poem as well as in "Living Alone," "Essay on Death," and "The Way of the Conventicle of the Trees," is perhaps the most natural and personal voice of the collection, yet it is a voice that speaks unashamedly in contemplation and abstraction.

In "The Way of the Conventicle of the Trees," Carruth writes of the trees:

> I have looked at them out the window
> So intently and persistently that always
> My who-I-am has gone out among them
> Where the fluttering ideas beckon.

Carruth has never more fully reconciled his independent, natural self and his encompassing, loving environment than he does in this late poem, and at the same time has never more directly recognized his authentic poetic imagination as the agent of unity.

*Jonathan Johnson*

## Sources for Further Study

*Booklist.* LXXXVIII, April 1, 1992, p. 1425.
*Library Journal.* CXVII, April 1, 1992, p. 121.
*The Nation.* CCLV, November 16, 1992, p. 600.
*The New York Times Book Review.* XCVII, December 27, 1992, p. 2.
*Publishers Weekly.* CCXXXIX, February 17, 1992, p. 58.

# COMPANY MAN

*Author:* Brent Wade (1959-    )
*Publisher:* Algonquin Books of Chapel Hill (Chapel Hill, North Carolina). 219 pp. $18.95
*Type of work:* Novel
*Time:* The late 1980's
*Locale:* Baltimore, Maryland

*A black man trying to make it in the white-dominated corporate world, William Covington is "Billy" to his black friends and "Bill" to the whites he works with; therein lies the tale*

*Principal characters:*
> WILLIAM COVINGTON, who knows he is the token black on the white corporate executive ladder but does not realize what he has lost in his push to "make it" in the corporate world
> PAULA COVINGTON, William's wife, who projects the perfect image of spouse to a corporate executive but who actually prefers a child and a contented husband and father
> JOHN HAVILAND, Covington's patron, who withdraws his support when Covington refuses to help put down the machinists' demand
> NANCY MARUSKI, Covington's secretary, who tries to seduce him and then threatens to charge him with sexual harassment
> CARL RICE, a second black man in a highly visible position, though a dead-end one
> PAUL WALKER, Covington's closest friend, though they parted in anger seventeen years ago

In this first novel, Brent Wade explores the question of ego identity as it relates to a black man trying to make his way up the corporate ladder in white America. The questions are those of identity, centering on alienation and assimilation. William Covington, the protagonist of the novel, has carefully done everything right so as to assimilate himself into the "old boy" patronage network of the corporation he works for. As director of marketing communications at Varitech Industries, Covington has a fine salary, a beautiful wife, a handsome house, and a red Jaguar XJ-6, the kind of car he had always dreamed of having. In addition, Covington has the patronage of the company's chief executive officer. Covington is unsteady in his position, however, haunted by his grandmother's admonitions on one hand and by the loyalty he believes he owes to his corporate patron on the other. When he is asked by a black employee, Carl Rice, to take the side of machinists in a company dispute, Covington's tensions begin to increase, building to the point that he attempts to kill himself with a gunshot in the head. He is successful in blowing off a side of his head, thus paralyzing himself so as to affect his speech and movement and maim his facial muscles.

The novel is told in a series of journal entries set up as though they were letters written to a man who was Covington's best friend in high school, a man whom Covington had carelessly rejected, breaking not only a close and loving relationship but also a dream of lifelong friendship and male bonding. This loss of friendship hounds Covington throughout his ordeal as he seeks answers to what, just beyond his grasp, is preying on his mind. Covington's friend, Paul Walker, apparently has been estranged not only from Covington but also from childhood friends, hometown, and home state. Walker and Covington have not seen each other since they were seventeen, just before their high school graduation. The boys were swimming, and Paul chose that time to reveal his homosexuality. Not strong enough in his own sexuality to accept Paul's situation, Covington turned away from the best friendship he had and the only person he knew who matched his own cleverness and ambitions. In many ways Paul is a mirror for Covington's validity, his existence. Without Paul, Covington has only his grandmother's advice not to be "niggerish" and the poses that he knows will be demanded of him by his boss. In his journal notes, Covington addresses Paul directly, trying not only to apologize and thus attempt to remedy damage done to Paul and their friendship but also to find that mirror of himself that he needs before he can find himself.

Not surprisingly, one of the first symptoms of Covington's state of mind is his own impotence. His wife, Paula, is the very model of a young executive's spouse, with manners suitable to cocktail parties and conversational skills to match any member of the corporate group. Paula is also blessed with the ability to function at elegant dinners. Her light skin color is another asset suited to young black executives on the rise who desire assimilation over anything else. Indeed, Covington's grandmother certainly would have approved of Paula, who represents for Covington in the corporate world proof both of his own potency and of his good salesmanship.

As the corporate officers begin to learn about the demands of the black machinists Covington is called upon by John Haviland, his patron, to bring information to him. As claims on him become clearer, Covington loses more of his rational self, since he is being pulled in two directions at the same time. What parts of himself should he sacrifice for the privilege of entering mainstream society? Will black people ever be more than "alien" to America? Is it possible that white America will ever escape from its racist heritage? Or will more and more blacks enter into the old boy network becoming what Covington calls "Pavlov's Negroes"?

The novel, however, is about more than alienation and loss. The author explores their opposites—inclusion and redemption. Here is where the structure of the novel seems most relevant. The journal becomes an extended letter to Paul Walker, answering questions Paul ostensibly has asked in correspondence with Covington, explaining the mental turmoil resulting from being pulled in opposite directions, or recording the musings of the recovering man. In form then, the novel can be categorized as epistolary, an organizational structure restricted in nature, allowing only first-person ruminations after the fact of occurrence. Because the journal/letter writer is recovering from traumas leading to a suicide attempt and resulting in maiming of the face, those ruminations could be considered suspect, lacking in credibility. The opposite is true. The suicide attempt seems to have resulted in damage to the left half of the body, allowing for healing to take place and for the strengthening of the right side.

In reaching for recovery, however, Covington reaches for two people: Donna, his nurse, and Paul, his former friend. Donna sings island music for him. Her favorite is

"Redemption Song." To Covington, she seems to offer hope in a rigorous ascetic life, in an appreciation for unadorned things. With Paul, Covington needs to dissipate his anger, to ask why Paul insisted on telling him about his sexual preference. Why did Paul force him to confront a fact he could not accept if it were openly broached, if Covington could accept Paul and even love him if words were left unspoken? These questions bring on counterquestions. If one must tell someone, why not a best friend? The answer is not apparent but is half understood. Covington realizes that he has been treating his wife, Paula, badly and that only love and friendship make life bearable.

Sexual potency is a theme running throughout the novel. It is the reason for Covington's withdrawal from Paul; impotency is the result of Covington's interactions with Varitech and the demands made on him. He is unable to complete the sexual act with Nancy, one of the few women in the corporate structure, though she seduces him (and later threatens him with charges of sexual harassment). Once he chooses sides, however, once he clearly abrogates the corporate world, Covington is able to impregnate his wife and at the end of the novel, he looks forward to the birth of their child.

In an interview after the publication of *Company Man*, author Brent Wade acknowledged that he intended to write perhaps two more novels with Bill Covington as protagonist. Wade makes this intention clear in the closing chapter of the book. Covington tells Paul that he is engaged in a new project. The project involves travel to exotic places and exploration of ancient ruins. The last sentence of the novel sounds like an invitation to Paul to accompany Covington in his journeys. Other intriguing points will perhaps be followed up in subsequent books: the similarity of the names Paula and Paul, sexist as well as racist themes, injury to the left side and the role of the noncognitive in the developing man.

Wade has made the point in interviews that much of the fiction by black writers that he has read and liked concerned black people in different stages of development, both socially and emotionally. The corporate has not been explored in fiction by many black writers. Black society is not a monolith. Most black people go to work every day and try to make a living. Their life is no longer that of a sharecropper or a runaway slave or even of a person on welfare and living in the projects. In *Company Man*, Wade testifies to the diversity and complexity of the black experience.

*Mary Rohrberger*

## Sources for Further Study

*Black Enterprise*. XXII, June, 1992, p. 26.
*Chicago Tribune*. March 15, 1992, XIV, p. 3.
*Essence*. XXIII, July, 1992, p. 42.
*Los Angeles Times Book Review*. March 29, 1992, p. 3.
*Newsweek*. CXIX, March 9, 1992, p. 61.
*San Francisco Chronicle*. April 5, 1992, p. REV6.
*The Washington Post Book World*. XXII, February 9, 1992, p. 12.

# COMPLETE COLLECTED ESSAYS

*Author:* V. S. Pritchett (1900-    )
*First published:* 1991, in Great Britain
*Publisher:* Random House (New York). 1319 pp. $35.00
*Type of work:* Essays; literary criticism

*V. S. Pritchett, England's leading man of letters, has collected his literary essays and reviews in this massive volume*

V. S. Pritchett has had a prolific and distinguished career as a travel writer, novelist, biographer, memoirist, short-story writer, reviewer, and essayist. He has been most highly praised as a composer of short stories and as a literary critic. His stories describe the lives of everyday people subjected to surprising disruptions that show how little they know about their own desires. Seven of his short fiction collections were recently gathered in a 1,232-page tome, *Complete Collected Stories* (1991).

*Complete Collected Essays* is a companion volume. Equally massive, it includes 203 essays of literary interpretation that originally appeared in eight works: *In My Good Books* (1942), *The Living Novel and Later Appreciations* (1946), *Books in General* (1953), *The Working Novelist* (1965), *The Myth Makers: Literary Essays* (1979), *The Tale Bearers: Literary Essays* (1980), *A Man of Letters* (1985), and *Lasting Impressions* (1990). This definitive collection of one of the English-speaking world's most distinguished contemporary critics covers English, American, European, and Latin American texts and ranges in time from such eighteenth century writers as Edward Gibbon and Samuel Richardson to modernist authors such as Gabriel García Márquez, Bruce Chatwin, and Salman Rushdie.

Pritchett's essays concentrate on a writer's life, era, and works. A shrewd and adroit psychologist who is intensely curious about people, he is quick-eyed, precise, pragmatic, vital, blunt, and generous. He disdains psychoanalytic clichés and elaborate critical methodology. He is remarkably free of jargon, witty, and informal in his tone, thereby dissociating himself from the most influential critical vogues of his time: the New Criticism and the French-led schools of structuralism, poststructuralism, and deconstruction. Nor does he invoke the perspectives of Marxism, Freudianism, or any other dogma. In his urbane and chatty manner, he resembles such nineteenth century literary essayists as William Hazlitt and Charles Augustin Sainte-Beuve, demonstrating that discussion of literature can be pleasurable and stimulating in the manner of sparkling conversation. His nearest American peers are probably Edward Wilson and Gore Vidal, but Pritchett avoids their granitic egotism and score-settling malice.

As himself a writer of fiction, Pritchett approaches his subjects with the sympathy of a fellow toiler. He knows how to convey a narrative synopsis and a sense of character with remarkable encapsulating skill. Describing Benjamin Constant's confessional novel *Adolphe* (1816), he talks about the difficulty of dispelling the author's ghost while reading his work, of life laying its subversive hands on fiction. This book, he states, is "as melodiously and mathematically clear as the phrases of a Mozart quartet." He pictures a copiously weeping Constant beating his literary omelette so that his wives and mistresses could not unmistakably identify themselves with the characters. Pritchett does not particularly like Constant, deploring his morbidity, narcissism, emotional fatigue, and general weakness of will, yet he is fair-minded enough to admire *Adolphe* as a great treatment of the intellectual who creates love out of his head only to discover that his heart embraces emotional enslavement.

In an essay on Émile Zola's *Germinal* (1885), Pritchett notes important distinctions between English and European novelists. Such authors as Charles Dickens are emotional about characters but averse to ideas about society. English nineteenth century writers were amazingly indifferent to the political and scientific thoughts of their time. Not so French novelists. Zola knew his Karl Marx and Charles Darwin, Pierre Joseph Proudhon and Mikhail Bakunin, the struggle for life and the struggles between classes. He had the temperament, will, and curiosity to write the great working-class novel *Germinal*. Moreover, adds Pritchett, Zola was free of the fallacy that people who are starved and oppressed are good and noble simply because they are starved and oppressed. His preoccupation with human corruption and its resulting nightmares shows that poverty can lead to degradation, that souls do become exhausted, and that people can form bestial and brutal mobs. Pritchett paints a vivid picture of Zola as a timid and plump bourgeois, fussing with pencil and paper as he documented the lives of miners for six months before writing his book. Zola's fortifiying and melodramatic imagination, however, far transcends his powers of factual observation. His belief in the presence of evil in all humans enabled him to make the central labor leader, Étienne, not only an ideologue but also a completely realized person, not only a self-serving exploiter of the miners but also an idealist who, though he does sacrifice the workers' welfare, seeks to lead them to their socioeconomic emancipation.

Pritchett takes Nikolai Gogol's unfinished *Dead Souls* (1842) as a springboard for discussion of the disorderliness of masterpieces. He observes the frequent carelessness, lethargy, or bad taste of fictive genius, its liability to accident, its slovenliness. Thus Miguel de Cervantes' *Don Quixote de la Mancha* (1612-1620), Stendhal's *The Charterhouse of Parma* (1895), Leo Tolstoy's *War and Peace* (1865-1869), and the works of Charles Dickens and Fyodor Dostoevski all escape tight structures. Gogol's burning of the second part of *Dead Souls* is not altogether surprising, and Pritchett is somewhat relieved, fearing that Gogol might have violated in the sequel the comic tone of the first part. He admires the springs of the novel's plot, involving the protagonist Chichikov's plan to buy the ownership of dead serfs, called "souls," take the title deeds to the bank posing as the owner of so many thousand serfs, raise a large mortgage on an apparently thriving estate, and end up making a rich marriage. He hails *Dead Souls* as a great picaresque novel of travel in which the episodic adventures of a single character open up the world. The picaresque mode, Pritchett remarks, depends on the existence of social disorder, on an epoch of lethargy, cynicism, and disillusionment in which wry laughter at roguery becomes people's only sane outlet.

Reviewing a new biography of Honoré de Balzac, Pritchett calls him the most egotistical writer in literary history, sharing the illusions of the early nineteenth century's money grubbers and pleasure grabbers, buying up houses and antiques, obsessed with money, a natural speculator and often bankrupt. In a vividly compelling analogy between literature and life, Pritchett regards Balzac as "the Micawber for whom things were only too continuously 'turning up,' a Micawber who worked." He focuses on Balzac's "poor relations" novel, *Cousin Pons* (1847). It is a typically French text insofar as Gallic writers deal with passions as though they were legal traits, insisting that each particular attribute has its prototype, each human experience its category. In an English novel, the poor, ugly, asexual bachelor Pons would have been treated as an eccentric, with no general laws to pin him down. For Balzac, however, Pons's every characteristic suggests some aspect of the society he inhabits, with Balzac complicating and recomplicating his plot so as to have Pons's misfortunes illustrate society's appetites and rapacities. Pritchett declares, "Balzac knew his people as few novelists ever know their characters." No one has ever surpassed Balzac in revealing the crucial role of money in middle-class life, with Balzac's historic role being dramatization of the establishment of the quest for money as the foundation for middle-class morals.

Pritchett loves to celebrate significant fictive characters. Ivan Goncharov's Oblomov, after whom the profound 1859 novel is named, is called a personage ripe for canonization. He is a saintly martyr for opposing cultures of energy, expansiveness, and productivity with his sluggishness, sleepiness, sloth, and slovenliness. Pritchett admires the author for having created one of literature's gentlest and most lovable personages who is yet given to frantic despair beneath the cover of his torpor. Pritchett is also candid in appraising Goncharov as not only a writer of genius but also a man eaten up by malice and jealousy who developed a persecution mania concerning Ivan Turgenev's supposed plagiarism of his plots.

Few critics can equal Pritchett in describing the pace of a work of art, the way in which a writer imposes a rhythm and tone as well as a vision. The reader of Dostoevski's *The Possessed* (1872) is often in a melodramatic fog of crisis upon crisis, previewing one of Franz Kafka's nightmares. The fog is dispelled by comedy featuring the tottering scholar Stepan Trofimovich Verkhovensky and his domineering companion, Varvara Stavrogin, who mocks his feebleness but is awed by his intelligence. The humorous interludes are, in turn, intercepted by nightmares of political and personal intrigue. Because he considers the writing of literature primarily a social act, Pritchett deems Dostoevski as expressing the confusion of Russia's middle class in its ideals and practices. The fog that envelops a novel such as *The Possessed* is minor compared to the fog of Dostoevski's own indecisions and strivings for self-control. Pritchett concludes that Dostoevski "was a spiritual sensationalist, a man of God somewhat stained with the printing ink of the late night final." Depending on newspaper reports of sensational cases, Dostoevski had the talent to convert topical events into universal truths.

Discussing Joseph Conrad's work, Pritchett reveals dislike for the Malayan novels, such as *Almayer's Folly* (1895) and *Lord Jim* (1900), as so many bad, muddled dreams, filled with half-lights, tortuous incidents, unreal major characters, and "insectile" minor ones. He prefers Conrad's "straightforward daytime manner" that created *Youth: A Narrative, and Two Other Stories* (1902) and *Typhoon and Other Stories* (1903), all lacking the exotic elaboration that baffles and irritates Pritchett. He is uneasy about Conrad's penchant for prophecy, whereby his characters tend to be souls rather than persons. The English, Pritchett insists, reject prophets, who turn out to be disappointed and frustrated people inordinately conscious of failure. D. H. Lawrence was angry about sexual failure; Conrad, Pritchett asserts, was angry about failures of loyalty or honor. Lord Jim was not, as Conrad insisted, a good man gone wrong, but a compulsive neurotic "running away from job after job." With a typical love of matter-of-factness, Pritchett rejects Conrad's "dubious Romantic over-world" and instead espouses "his real observation . . . his feeling for real life." For him, Conrad's genius lies in his capacity for rendering the contrast between people's intense inner lives and the slack and ragged circumstances in which they find themselves.

Even though Pritchett may be unfair to Conrad's metaphysical and spiritual side, he is generously appreciative of the accomplishments of a writer who shares Conrad's preoccupation with failure, betrayal, and evil: Graham Greene. In a long essay titled "Disloyalties," Pritchett does more than salute Greene's skills as a cutter of mosaics, an evoker of loneliness, ugliness, transience, and shabbiness. He praises Greene for his mastery of the subjects of pain, betrayal, and tormented conscience, for his alertness to ironies of desire and self-pity, for his freshness of precise description, and above all for his sympathetic portrayal of people's painful journeys into self-knowledge. Curiously, many of the qualities that disturbed Pritchett in Conrad's fiction delight him in Greene's.

Because Pritchett insists on linking the writer to his time, the self to society, he is at his best when evaluating a realistic-to-naturalistic novelist such as John Updike. Rabbit Angstrom, the protagonist of Updike's cycle of novels set in Pennsylvania, is a former athlete turned automobile salesman who marries the boss's daughter and takes over a Toyota dealership. Pritchett approves of Updike's decision to place Rabbit in the car business in a small city, since automobile traffic is responsible for much urban decay. As a verisimilar chronicler, "Updike has the extraordinary gift of making the paraphernalia of . . . the Sears Roebuck catalogue sound like a chant from the Book of Psalms turned into vaudeville." Pritchett admires Updike's skill as a genre painter of contemporary America, a chronicler of provincial and domestic manners. Moreover, he extols Updike's control of allusive narrative, which blends Rabbit's and other characters' past guilts and follies with the demands of their ongoing worlds. He salutes Updike as both a true historian of his era and a finely lyric poet of personality. Pritchett himself is both historian and poet, a level-headed and vivacious interpreter of fiction and an eloquently sympathetic appreciator of the variety and complexity of human nature.

*Gerhard Brand*

## Sources for Further Study

*Boston Globe*. May 27, 1992, p. 51.
*Chicago Tribune*. June 21, 1992, XIV, p. 6.
*National Review*. XLIV, August 3, 1992, p. 19.
*New Statesman and Society*. IV, December 6, 1991, p. 44.
*The New Yorker*. LXVIII, July 27, 1992, p. 72.
*The Spectator*. CCLXVII, November 23, 1991, p. 36.
*The Times Literary Supplement*. January 17, 1992, p. 27.
*The Washington Post Book World*. XXII, June 14, 1992, p. 1.

# THE COMPLETE POEMS OF C. DAY LEWIS

*Author:* C. Day Lewis (1904-1972)
Edited, with an introduction, by Jill Balcon
*Publisher:* Stanford University Press (Stanford, California). 746 pp. $49.50
*Type of work:* Poetry

*This collection presents, for the first time, all of C. Day Lewis' published poems and includes those published posthumously as well as the occasional verse written as poet laureate*

Throughout his career, in his writings as well as in his personal life, Cecil Day Lewis revealed himself only selectively and even then only reluctantly. In part, this stemmed from a conviction he shared with W. H. Auden, his fellow student at the University of Oxford, that a poet's voice should be universal and disembodied from any persona. Day Lewis shared Auden's righteous indignation when their colleague Stephen Spender published his autobiography *World Within World* (1951) to popular acclaim. Part of Day Lewis' reticence, however, also must have arisen from an awareness that his fame, and indeed his notoriety as well, came from involvements other than the composing of verse. It was as Nicholas Blake that Day Lewis wrote the detective novels that freed him from prep school teaching after 1935 and allowed him to become a full-time writer. His own autobiography, *The Buried Day* (1960), is a rejoinder to Spender, both in the wordplay of its title and in the similarity of its purpose: the search for the hidden self.

Even so, the autobiographies of both Day Lewis and Spender obscure much more than they reveal. Day Lewis, for example, says next to nothing about the failure of his idyllically described marriage to Mary King and nothing at all of his second, to Jill Balcon, who edited (without credit on the title page) this complete collection of poems. Day Lewis is similarly chary about the reasons for his estrangement from his father, an Anglican curate. Indeed, Day Lewis says nothing in *The Buried Day* of events between 1945 and 1960, the year of the book's publication. In this respect as well, its title proves appropriate.

One can infer that Day Lewis' proclaimed agnosticism and his membership in the Communist Party of Great Britain did not draw his father closer to him. Day Lewis includes these facts in *The Buried Day*, and though he does not see them as such, they clearly were reasons for his departure from teaching and important motives for his verse from 1931 through at least 1943. Like many intellectuals who reached their maturity in the 1930's, Day Lewis was drawn to Communism for essentially altruistic reasons; nevertheless, the Marxist line of *From Feathers to Iron* (1931), *The Magnetic Mountain* (1933), *A Time to Dance and Other Poems* (1935), and *Noah and the Waters* (1936) gashes across the development of a distinctive poetic voice. *Overtures to Death and Other Poems* (1938) anticipates World War II, and once the war begins, Day Lewis finds himself with precious little in his poetic corpus between his Oxford juvenilia *Beechen Vigil and Other Poems* (1925) and *Country Comets* (1928), both of which are classically inspired collections recalling Theocritus, Vergil, Horace, and Catullus, and his dreary homage to Marxist ideology. This is the essential tragedy of Day Lewis as a poet, that the admittedly derivative but bright promise of *Beechen Vigil* and *Country Comets* should be effaced by any ideology.

It is tempting to infer that Day Lewis desired this effacement. Just as he made his reputation among general readers by writing detective novels under one of his mother's family names, he became known to classicists not through scholarly publications but through his masterful translation of Vergil's *Georgics*, which he began at the onset of World War II in 1939. Vergil's respect for the life of the farmer and the dignity of manual work held special meaning for this idealist intellectual who had little firsthand experience of either beyond clearing the garden of a neglected estate he had just purchased at Mumsbury, Devon. After the war, Day Lewis' reputation as a translator would grow with his verse editions of Vergil's *Aeneid* (1952), the Roman national epic that notably acknowledges the futility of war as much as it does the desirability of patriotism, and Vergil's *Eclogues* (1962), a collection of ten pastorals modeled on Theocritus but with decidedly Roman settings and motifs.

Here then, in essence, is the real Day Lewis: a gifted poet of Anglo-Irish stock who hated his first name and never used it; who dropped the hyphen in his last name because it appeared too aristocratic, yet continued to call himself Day Lewis; who made his living under a pseudonym drawn from his mother's name; who became known in the academic world as a translator rather than as an original poet; who became a communist out of personal conviction, but to the detriment of his own development as a poet; and who accepted both the chair of poetry at Oxford and the position of poet laureate despite the demands that both of these honors made on his independence as a poet.

Twelve years before his death, while writing his autobiography, Day Lewis recognized this pattern and candidly accepted it. He notes that in rereading his *Collected Poems* (1954) he sees many good starts but few continuations. He seems to himself a poet who is always beginning yet never deepening. Day Lewis may be judging himself too harshly here, but several examples from poems composed early and late in his career might cause a reader to agree. His postwar collection *An Italian Visit* (1953), written after his first trip to Italy, represents a return to the classicism of his youth and marks a blessed end to the political poems. *Pegasus and Other Poems* (1957) is a modern reworking of classical legends. Despite what Day Lewis says, one can see a maturity in these two collections that the political poems lack. The essential difference is the humanity, the personal involvement Day Lewis allows in his later work that he never would have tolerated when speaking on behalf of the masses. As he writes in "Flight to Italy" in *An Italian Visit*, and as he increasingly understands in his later verse:

> This land is nothing
> But a mythical name on an outline map
> For us, till we've scaled it to our will's dimensions,
> Filled in each wayward, imperious route,
> Shaded it in with delays and chagrins,
> Traced our selves over it, foot by foot.

Making the poetic territory one's own, foot by foot, had become as important to Day Lewis in his later career as eliminating the personal had been for him in his early years.

*Transitional Poem* (1929) is the one work of Day Lewis' early poetry that remains to some degree unscathed by the poet's political involvements of the period. As its title indicates, the poem marks a change, though more accurately, changes: in the poet's style as he leaves behind his juvenilia; in the poet's philosophy as he sees the need to adopt a social consciousness; in the world at large which roughly corresponds to that of T. S. Eliot's *The Waste Land* (1922), but with the significant acceptance of personal agnosticism. If anything, its landscape is even more barren than that of Eliot's poem; yet, welcome elements of the personal save *Transitional Poem* and make it the most important example of Day Lewis' early period. Notably, all these elements concern the poet's wife, who assumes the identity of a lover and a beneficently erotic feature of an otherwise hostile or indifferent cosmos:

> My love is a tower.
> Standing up in her
> I parley with planets
> And the casual wind.
> Arcturus may grind
> Against our wall:—he whets
> A tropic appetite,
> And decorates our night.

The style is still derivative, but it is a clever jumble of Andrew Marvell, Matthew Arnold, Sigmund Freud, and of course Eliot.

*Transitional Poem* seemed the making of young Day Lewis. At least Virginia and Leonard Woolf thought so when they accepted it for The Hogarth Press, but the bleak Marxist poems followed it. Indeed, it was only with publication of *Noah and the Waters* that Day Lewis himself began to recognize the stasis that follows from adopting a political program as a substitute for a distinctive poetic voice.

*Noah and the Waters* essentially is an absurdist allegorical drama. Day Lewis originally intended it as the libretto for a choral ballet. What eventuated was a Marxist morality play. The burghers of England, representing every segment of the established political order, come to Noah to ask his help in turning aside the waters that threaten to engulf the country. Since Noah has been through a similar experience in the biblical past, he will, presumably, know what to do. After the burghers have offered their arguments for keeping things as they are, Noah decides that a second flood is by far the better alternative. The burghers, who include among their number a representative of the Church of England, promptly turn on Noah. The verse play thus asserts the need for tides of change as well as the degree to which those entrusted with upholding moral standards have strayed from their trust. There is a quirky humor in much of this poetry, which resembles that of Bertolt Brecht and Kurt Weill. Brecht had written the libretto for Weill's *Der Aufstieg und Fall der Stadt Mahagonny* (1927, rev. 1930; English translation *The Rise and Fall of the City of Mahagonny*) only a few years before, and

Day Lewis' verse play follows in its tradition.

Day Lewis, the Anglo-Irish minister's son and Oxford classicist, could never become an English Brecht. *Noah and the Waters* marks an extreme to which he would not return. In truth, Day Lewis' career bears an uncanny resemblance to that of Spender, who was his Oxford contemporary, also a somewhat unwilling academic, and another intellectual carried along by the socialist tide of the 1930's. It is interesting to note that at the end of their lives both Day Lewis and Spender became part of the Establishment: Day Lewis as poet laureate in 1968, Spender as knight-commander of the British Empire in 1982. The ambivalence with which each accepted these honors is characteristic. Day Lewis obviously knew that at least since Alfred, Lord Tennyson, the poet laureate writes verse on demand. Spender confides in his *Journals 1939-1983* (1985) that part of him wants to turn down the K-C.B.E. in no uncertain terms, but part of him thoroughly enjoys the pomp and circumstance. This vaulting ambition, ever checked by guilt, characterized many English intellectuals of 1930's vintage.

One senses that Day Lewis tries repeatedly in his verse to distance himself from Spender and, failing to achieve an absolutely distinctive poetic voice, moves closer to Auden. Spender's poetic oeuvre is only about one-third the size of Day Lewis', yet it is more consistent in its quality. Even so, Auden is a better poet than either because his verse is distinctive yet universal. Day Lewis had begun to find this distinctiveness in the early 1960's, when he started to employ mythic themes extensively. In "Travelling Light" from *The Gate and Other Poems* (1962), Jason's voyage becomes Day Lewis' design for living:

> Our type of sailor
> May tell you that he also lives
> For landfall, profit, whores and spivs:
> This is not so. To him, the thing
> You voyage for is voyaging—
> Purely that.

Readers coming to Day Lewis' poems for the first time should probably read them in reverse chronological order, leaving the political poems and the laureate occasional verse for last. Admittedly, this creates a rather jarring juxtaposition, but it also underscores how far Day Lewis had to travel before he discovered he had come home.

*Robert J. Forman*

## Sources for Further Study

*Choice*. XXX, January, 1993, p. 790.
*The Observer*. July 26, 1992, p. 54.
*Publishers Weekly*. CCXXIX, September 21, 1992, p. 78.
*The Times Literary Supplement*. August 28, 1992, p. 10.

# COMPLEXITY
## Life at the Edge of Chaos

*Author:* Roger Lewin
*Publisher:* Macmillan (New York). 208 pp. $22.00
*Type of work:* Science
*Time:* 1989-1991
*Locale:* North America, Central America, and England

*A popular account of the development of what might turn out to be one of the most revolutionary theories of twentieth century science*

> *Principal personages:*
> BRIAN GOODWIN, a molecular biologist who is exploring the origins of biological form
> STUART KAUFFMAN, a biologist who has played a pioneering role in the study of self-organization
> JAMES LOVELOCK, a biologist, the originator of the Gaia hypothesis
> TOM RAY, a biologist engaged in the study of artificial life and computer modeling

According to its proponents, complexity theory will change the way humans think about the biological and the social worlds. Relationships to nature and to each other could be altered. The theory will demonstrate the great unity that underlies apparently disparate spheres of human and nonhuman behavior. It will prove the power of computer modeling even in the very messy and resistant realm of human social organization. Even Charles Darwin's theory of natural selection will be put on the trash heap of history, next to vitalism and natural theology. Much of the accepted knowledge in the fields of ecology, economics, political science, anthropology, and evolutionary theory will become obsolete. In short, complexity theory will be the vehicle for a great scientific revolution, one perhaps unequaled in the twentieth century.

The science of complexity is an attempt to explain the observed self-generated order that permeates natural systems. Examples of this self-generated order include the ordinal emergence of life, the development of a forest, and the evolution of a national economy. The science has been described as the point at which physics meets biology to create a new science. It might also be thought of as the arena of the application of mathematics and computer modeling to natural history. From the lay perspective, there are two points to remember. First, many aspects of the natural world—molecular behavior, the development of organisms, the rise and fall of civilizations, even the balance of nature on the planet—can be viewed as different forms of the working out of complex systems. Second, if the supporters of the theory are correct, there is a set of relatively simple rules underlying all these systems. Local changes lead to global properties. Discovering the rules governing complexity would provide a grand unified theory of the life and human sciences, analogous to the cosmological Grand Unified

Theory for which Stephen Hawking is searching.

The eye is a case in point. William Paley, a nineteenth century natural theologian, used the eye as his starting point for his argument that the world was the result of action by an almighty creator. The existence of such a complex, well-adapted organ as the eye has been a problem to evolutionists going back to Darwin. They explain it as the result of a series of random mutations; successful mutations survived because they improved an organism's ability to survive. Complexity scientists reject this view. Having identified some forty instances when eyes developed in different organisms, they question how this could be the result of chance mutations. They argue that the form of the eye is actually highly probable, given the observed dynamics of tissue development. The same computer model that explains the morphology of a species of algae can explain a human eye. Put more technically, "Eyes are the product of high-probability spatial transformations of developing tissues." To complexity scientists, there is nothing mysterious or unlikely in their existence.

*Complexity* is both a travelogue and a series of dialogues between the author, an experienced science writer with a Ph.D. in biochemistry, and many of the key figures in the field. It opens and closes with picturesque descriptions of the archaeological remains of the pre-Columbian Anasazi society in Chaco Canyon, New Mexico, highlighting an effort to apply complexity theory to the rise and fall of that society. In between, the author visits rain forests in Costa Rica, laboratories and offices in the United States and England, and the center of research on complexity, the Santa Fe Institute in New Mexico, a multidisciplinary research center preoccupied with artificial intelligence and computer modeling of the natural world. Lewin also provides a selective but excellent bibliography. The quoted conversations are better described as dialogues rather than as interviews, because they include almost as much of Lewin's thoughts and reactions as they do of the scientists'. Essentially, Lewin takes the reader along during his very personal odyssey towards an understanding of complexity.

Most of the dialogues are with supporters of the theory, scientists united by a belief in a set of ideas that have been ignored or attacked by most biologists for two decades. There is Brian Goodwin, at England's Open University, a molecular biologist interested in coupled oscillating chemical systems. In 1963, Goodwin tried to show how molecular control systems gave rise to global patterns. A few years later, his book was read by Stuart Kauffman, now of the University of Pennsylvania, who, as a second-year medical student in 1965, decided that the order visible in the natural world was the result of a natural property of genetic systems. He labeled this property "order for free."

James Lovelock may be the most famous—or infamous—of the complexity scientists. In the late 1960's, he invented the Gaia hypothesis, which argued that the biosphere—life on Earth—maintained aspects of the physical environment, including the climate and atmospheric composition, for its own benefit. The hypothesis remains highly controversial and suspect among many biologists. In 1981, Lovelock created Daiseyworld, a relatively simple computer model that, he contends, demonstrates the coupling of the biological and physical worlds as well as showing that complex ecological systems can result from relatively simple rules. Biologists were not convinced.

Tom Ray's experience, on the other hand, demonstrates the more recent respectability of these scientists. A field ecologist turned proponent of artificial life and computer models, Ray in 1990 created a computer model, called Tierra, of an ecological system. In his model, many of the textbook patterns of ecology were reproduced from a few simple rules. As a result, he was granted tenure at the University of Delaware.

Although Lewin can present technical detail about Daiseyworld, Tierra, or Kauffman's theory with clarity, his chattiness can get in the way of understanding. So can his jumping back and forth between scientists, following a logic that is neither chronological nor thematic. Having to follow Lewin's thought processes as he attempts to clarify issues by thinking out loud quickly loses its charm. There are other distractions. For example, Lewin's conversation with the taxicab driver on the way to visit James Lovelock is colorful but not relevant. For a relatively short book, there is too much extraneous material, particularly Lewin's musings. Areas of complexity theory, on the other hand, are sometimes slighted. For example, a clear definition of the subject area in the opening pages would have been helpful in making some of the later discussions more intelligible.

Because Lewin has created such a personal book, some areas of complexity receive more attention than others. Its impact on evolutionary theory and ecology are discussed in detail, because these issues are of central concern to him. The social sciences receive relatively short shrift. Chaco Canyon is described more than it is analyzed. The possibility that complexity theory might become part of the repertoire of the economist or political scientist is mentioned only in passing.

The history of complexity science supplies a number of general lessons about the history of science in general. None of these are new to historians or sociologists of science, but they do challenge popular myth and bear repeating. First, new and controversial ideas are not always immediately considered by the scientific community or even granted recognition as important. Aspects of complexity theory had been discussed for twenty years before they were taken seriously. The explanation is sociological. The status of the scientist, as well as the medium and format in which an idea is presented, can play a part in the hearing that a new idea receives. Many of the early supporters of complexity were on the margins of the scientific world. Kauffman's receipt of a MacArthur Foundation "genius" fellowship led others to look at his work in a new light. An institutional base also helps. Not until the establishment of the Santa Fe Institute in 1984 did complexity scientists find a favorable institutional home.

Second, scientists accept theories both because of their explanatory power and because of considerations that might be called metaphysical, psychological, or even mystical. Belief and the search for evidence go hand in hand. This is not to say that a scientist in such a situation deliberately misreads data, only that attachment to theories can be emotional as well as cerebral. In 1965, Kauffman had no evidence supporting his theory, but he "had this unshakable conviction that [I] was right." This is a conviction he still holds. No wonder Lewin describes him as having "proselytizing passion." The parallel with religion is apt.

Third, and related to the previous two points, no evidence self-evidently proves the correctness (or even incorrectness) of a theory. Different scientists looked at the same computer models and came to very different conclusions about the explanatory power of these models. For whatever psychological or sociological reasons, some scientists are more predisposed than others to accept complexity theory as the next great scientific revolution. Others are neutral or even hostile.

What about the reader? By the end of the book, Lewin describes himself as having "become something of an enthusiast" but admits to some uncertainty. Because readers have viewed complexity essentially through the filter of Lewin's eyes, they too will likely come to the same conclusion: It is a very interesting theory, with great potential, but is not yet proven. Complexity theory provides an ongoing story, with the most important chapters yet to be written.

*Marc Rothenberg*

## Sources for Further Study

*Boston Globe*. December 27, 1992, p. 13.
*Kirkus Reviews*. LX, November 1, 1992, p. 1358.
*Library Journal*. CXVII, November 1, 1992, p. 114.
*The New York Times Book Review*. XCVIII, February 14, 1993, p. 12.
*Publishers Weekly*. CCXXXIX, November 9, 1992, p. 69.
*San Francisco Chronicle*. November 15, 1992, p. REV3.
*Science*. CCLIX, January 15, 1993, p. 387.
*The Washington Post Book World*. XXII, December 20, 1992, p. 1.

# COMPULSORY FIGURES
## Essays on Recent American Poets

*Author:* Henry Taylor (1942-    )
*Publisher:* Louisiana State University Press (Baton Rouge). 318 pp. $29.95
*Type of work:* Literary criticism

*A collection of critical essays by a distinguished poet that consider the work of seventeen relatively recent American poets from the perspective of their development as artists and with specific attention to particular poems*

The opening of the field of American poetry in the twentieth century has led to a richness of invention and a variety of possibility arguably the equal of any other era in the history of the English language. It has also resulted in an energized and frequently fractious debate about the nature of poetry itself, a continuing dispute among poets and theoreticians in which positions have been determined as much by a desire to protect and justify a style of expression as by an interest in the "sullen art" and the craft of its composition. This has generated an often useful confusion that tends to prevent the establishment of restrictive orthodoxies and to promote the publication of a genuinely diverse range of voices across a poetic continuum. There also has been a tendency toward criticism devoted to disparaging and condemning what the authors regard as unpoetic and misguided rather than concentrating on the merits of preferred poems. Henry Taylor's *Compulsory Figures* is an impressive addition to the work of other critic/poets such as Charles Molesworth (*The Fierce Embrace: A Study of Contemporary American Poetry*, 1979) and Donald Hall (*The Weather for Poetry: Essays, Reviews, and Notes on Poetry, 1977-81*, 1982) who have been able to combine their carefully considered convictions about poetry with an enthusiasm for the accomplishments of poets whose approaches are singular and various. As Hall has observed, a love for the poetry of Robert Frost does not require a resistance to the poetry of Charles Olson, and while Taylor is quite definite about why he likes a certain poet's work, the criteria upon which his judgments and choices are based are not exclusionary.

Taylor, whose *The Flying Change* (1985) won the Pulitzer Prize in poetry, published these essays in their original form during the 1970's and 1980's. They are linked by an evolving critical aesthetic that includes a close scrutiny of a poet's development that he calls "the record of a triumphant progress." His concern for a "lifelong process" is connected to his choices for inclusion, as he explains that these are people who have written poetry he has returned to "countless times over the past twenty-five years." His method is to discuss individual poems in enlightening detail within the context of the poet's goals and means of reaching them. A major source of strength in his consideration of a particular poem is his sensitivity to the nuances of a word. The title of the book is both a register of this responsiveness and an indication of the direction of his most fundamental critical thinking. The multifold meaning conveys his claim that his subjects command attention as important figures necessary for an understanding of American literature, that their best work is driven by a compulsion to achieve artistic excellence, and that the formal requirements of the poetry he admires calls for a discipline akin to that of a champion skater perfecting the movements of a previously determined form so that the "continued flow . . . arouses suspense" while "its graceful conclusion gives pleasure." Taylor is careful to point out that he is not a proponent of "rigid allegiances to open or closed form," but he is quite clear about the importance of form. The initial essay, on J. V. Cunningham, whose "work and advice" he cites as a debt beyond measure, sets out a kind of poetic credo that will be applied throughout the volume.

The placement of the Cunningham essay at the onset of the volume and one about James Wright at the conclusion create a frame for the entire endeavor. Taylor pointedly acknowledges his gratitude to Cunningham for showing him that he could write "free verse" by choice when appropriate, not "by the ignorance of metrics that many young poets have considered sufficient equipment." The emphasis on metrics is at the heart of his conception of poetic form. Aside from a glancing reference to Charles Olson, a hugely influential figure for many poets who have an entirely different conception of form, Taylor generally avoids any argument with opposing views and chooses instead to explain why he believes that metrical regularity is essential to provide a basis for variation or "irregularity," using Cunningham's work to show how "metrical patterns perform subtle modulations." The idea of order recurs in essay after essay, often supported by quotes from poems such as William Jay Smith's "A Sculptor, Welding," which talks of the artist bringing "out of life's formlessness, now form." This venerable position, Taylor understands, has been less than congenial for postmodern poetics, but he is never deterred by unfashionable convictions. He develops his case by its application to poet after poet, noting in the essay on William Meredith that "form is a method, not a barrier," and asserting in the essay on James Wright that there is an infinite number of ways of doing things within the "mastery of traditional forms."

If Taylor's idea about metrical form is determinedly traditional, his philosophy about the place of literature in human civilization is so conservative as to seem nearly radical in its contrast with current academic literary theory. Cunningham contends that

> our purpose in the study of literature, and particularly in the historical interpretation of texts, is not in the ordinary sense to further the understanding of ourselves. It is rather to enable us to see how we could think and feel otherwise than as we do.

Taylor calls this "as succinct and clear a statement of the value of literary study as I have seen." Taylor stresses Cunningham's reliance on "principles of morality" as a basis for "the understanding of an author in the scholarly sense." The sort of scholarship he has in mind is clarified by the essay on Anthony Hecht that immediately follows. He describes Hecht writing at "an extremely high level of what is now, alas, called cultural literacy." In spite of the vulgar popularization of the term, Taylor is still convinced of the value of shared cultural assumptions and experiences, or a sound classical education. He admires Hecht's ability to move "securely among art treasures, classical myths, neoclassical literature, history" and to write poems that "exist in a timeless state, somewhat remote and durably elegant."

Because he has espoused several traditionalist principles, Taylor has been praised enthusiastically by cultural commentators distressed by the forceful pronouncements about poetry in collections such as Donald Allen and Warren Tallman's well-known *Poetics of the New American Poetry* (1973) that present an alternative approach to the entire issue of form and structure. The enduring power of the essays in *Compulsory Figures*, however, is not that they offer a rebuttal to "the opponents of traditional form" who in the twentieth century "have produced the stronger propaganda," as Taylor asserts in the Wright essay. Rather, it is that they offer incisive, illuminating examinations of the poems Taylor uses to illustrate and support his claims for each poet, and that they do so without ever employing the neologic technical terminology temporarily in vogue in some academic precincts. Taylor writes in a consistently engaging manner in the spirit of those who have shaped the language of discourse through centuries, with a respectful attention to what has been done well before and an enlivening feel for the pulse and rhythm of contemporary English. The essays are accessible for anyone with what has been generally regarded as a solid education in the humanities.

The range of the poets Taylor covers is not exceptionally wide. He is drawn to the work of only two women—Gwendolyn Brooks and May Sarton—and the "madmen of language" are notable by their absence. The affinities and similarities among his subjects do not prevent him from locating and rendering the singular voice and distinctive attributes of each poet. In considering the "substantial portion of a poet's body of work," as his publisher claims, Taylor is able to build toward a succinct summary that captures the essence of a style. In William Stafford's poetry he finds "certain qualities of calmness and unpretentious gravity." He demonstrates how they operate in the poem "Adults Only" by identifying and explaining Stafford's use of "discursiveness, directness, delicacy of meter, specificity of description, definitiveness of general statement." His conclusion that Stafford's poems "occupy a relatively narrow range" but one "sufficient to the creation of explosions that many other poets would need far more energy to reach" offers access to Stafford's work that does not depend on complete agreement with Taylor's claims. David R. Slavitt and George Garrett, both celebrated for a "defiant individualism" as well as "generous erudition," are revealed as writers better known as novelists whose poetry is "among the treasures of contemporary literature." Both men are friends of Taylor, and the thoroughness of his knowledge of their work and their motives informs discussions of their poems, particularly in terms of the shift between colloquial and elevated language and the poet's capability with "the power of narrative to transform the events it recounts."

Not all the poets about whom Taylor writes are equally suited to his explorations. He seems to be somewhat less excited about Louis Simpson's work, fair-minded but a bit distant from Brooks, and not inspired by Robert Watson. A poet such as John Hall Wheelock is probably more significant as a figure in literary history than as an important poet, which Taylor acknowledges by calling his essay "a tribute to a long career." Brewster Ghiselin may have had "a steadily increasing impact on American letters," but it may be an excess of enthusiasm to call him "one of America's finest poets." Still, Taylor's considerations of Wheelock and Ghiselin offer the opportunity to become familiar with their work through the guidance of an excellent advocate. When Taylor adopts the stance of one discovering a neglected genius while talking about John Woods, an initial skepticism about claims such as Woods's "unobtrusive yet absolute mastery of sound" or his "extraordinary subtlety" begins to dissolve as Taylor's close, clear, and systematic analysis gradually captures and displays the tremendous power of the spare, economic diction of Woods's work. The book's one real surprise is the essay on Jackson Mac Low, an "experimental" poet and composer of performance pieces. Taylor admits that "many widely held convictions about the nature of poetry make it easy to dismiss such work." In an effort to remain open to "honest exploration," Taylor gives Mac Low's work the same careful scrutiny he has provided for some much more congenial artists. The unexpected result is an enlightening evaluation of Mac Low's technique, qualified by Taylor's reassurances to his core constituency that "plenty of sensible people will deny that this kind of thing is poetry."

Although there are numerous poets whose work and poetic philosophy Taylor prefers to ignore, he is determined to avoid a reflexive dismissal of a poet since "it does not greatly matter . . . whether a poet is, by some reckoning or other, distinctly loyal to older traditions or notably interested in exploring frontier territory." One of the reasons he handles Mac Low's work so well is that Mac Low has a very elaborate method behind his compositions, and Taylor is attracted to the operations of any device that might maintain order or help to shape a poem.

Even for those readers who are drawn primarily to the poets who were inspired by "the commandments that came down from the Black Mountain," as Taylor characterizes the thinking of Charles Olson, these essays are provocative in the best sense, challenging the reader to think about what a poem is and can be. The qualities that he finds in Cunningham—"Great care, great patience, and steadfast attention to the craft and tradition of poetry"—are clearly Taylor's aims as well. What he says of William Meredith's *The Wreck of the Thresher, and Other Poems* (1964) can stand as a fine summary of his own work:

> The book consistently offers the voice of a civilized man, a man with good but not exclusive manners, engaged in encounters with matters of inexhaustible interest.

*Leon Lewis*

## Sources for Further Study

*Library Journal.* CXVII, August, 1992, p. 101.
*The Washington Post Book World.* XXIII, January 3, 1993, p. 9.
*Washington Times.* November 15, 1992, p. B10.

# DARWIN

*Authors:* Adrian Desmond (1947-    ) and James Moore (1947-    )
*First published:* 1991, in Great Britain
*Publisher:* Warner Books (New York). Illustrated. 808 pp. $35.00
*Type of work:* Biography
*Time:* 1809-1885
*Locale:* England and South America

*A life study of the influential scientist whose theory of natural selection revolutionized ideas about the development of species and caused significant controversy among scientists and religious thinkers in the nineteenth century*

*Principal personages:*
CHARLES DARWIN, a naturalist and geologist
EMMA WEDGWOOD DARWIN, his wife
CHARLES LYELL, a geologist whose work influenced Darwin's thinking about the process of evolution
THOMAS H. HUXLEY, a disciple of Darwin whose lectures and debates with clergy and creationists popularized the older scientist's ideas

In the history of science, only a few men and women can be said to have cast a very long shadow. Surely among them is Charles Darwin. No one can now study biology or geology without feeling the impact of the work of this retiring English gentleman whose painstaking analysis of the animal kingdom led to the publication of the most controversial theory about the development of species: natural selection. After Darwin, in the minds of intellectuals, God took a backseat to natural forces as the shaping force for the world.

Adrian Desmond and James Moore's comprehensive biography helps readers understand how a young, middle-class Englishman from Shropshire could have become such a renowned scientist. Arguing that any new biography of Darwin "must take account of the recent upheaval in the history of science, and its new emphasis on the cultural conditioning of knowledge," they provide in Darwin a healthy blend of "history"—the story of Darwin's life—with an analysis of the intellectual "doings" that characterized the turbulent century in which he worked.

Darwin was a man of great contradictions and complexities. Desmond and Moore bring into sharp focus the multifarious nature of his life: father, husband, brother, son, friend, enemy, patient, correspondent, community activist, political lobbyist, public leader (even town magistrate), and most of all man of his times. What Desmond and Moore provide is a wider context in which to view Darwin's discoveries. Stressing the human qualities of their subject, the authors refute convincingly the myth that scientists are people sealed away hermetically in their labs, concocting abstract theories based on experiments untainted by the messy realities of everyday life.

In his professional life, Darwin was a student of Jean Baptiste Pierre Lamarck, of his own grandfather Erasmus Darwin, and especially of Thomas Malthus—all influential thinkers who paved the way for the more radical science of the nineteenth century. He was a friend of Charles Lyell (author of *Principles of Geology*, 1830-1833), a reader of Robert Chambers (author of *Vestiges of the Natural History of Creation*, 1844), an acquaintance of eminent scientist J. F. W. Herschel, and a mentor for a host of scientific promoters, the most famous of whom, Thomas H. Huxley, made his reputation popularizing Darwin's ideas among the English and taking on Darwin's chief enemies, the scientist Richard Owen and the Anglican clergyman Bishop Samuel Wilberforce. Through his work Darwin expanded the frontiers of zoology, botany, geology, and genetics. Nevertheless, he was also a devoted father (some of the most poignant passages in this biography recount his grief over the premature death of his daughter Annie) and a devotee of sentimental novels, listening attentively as his wife read from them in their evenings at home.

Influencing Darwin's thinking was the political and social climate in which he and his family lived. The Darwins were strong supporters of Whig politics; his liberal tendencies were formed early, and he never lost the spirit for reform. Not surprisingly, his scientific theories resembled advanced Whig social thinking; small wonder the Tory establishment reacted most violently to On the Origin of Species (1859) when it appeared. For years before Darwin published his notions about transmutation of species, the idea had been bandied about by radical elements of society and was associated with "riot and revolution," as a tool in the hands of radicals who angrily eyed "the islands of gentrified opulence."

Beneath many of Darwin's scientific pronouncements was a firm belief that progress was possible and that people had responsibilities for taking care of the less fortunate. More than a century before "multiculturalism" became a buzzword in academic circles, Darwin was expressing concern for peoples of other colors and life-styles. Naïvely, he thought he could help less privileged communities improve by bringing European civilization to them; unlike his more imperious countrymen, he did not favor conquest and colonization as methods for effecting improvement.

The political implications of Darwin's research are stressed repeatedly, and with good reason. For Victorian Britons, geological and biological discoveries had implications for domestic and foreign policy. Findings that supported the differences in human species fed the fires of imperialists who believed that conquest of "inferior races" was not only permissible but ordained by the deity who created all men unequal. As Desmond and Moore note, Darwin's theory "threatened the ideals so cherished by the geological gentry: human dignity and accountability."

Popular legend has suggested that Darwin rushed to print with his controversial On the Origin of Species to ward off publication of the theory by Alfred Wallace, who had arrived at similar conclusions independently. The authors of *Darwin* dispel such myths, noting that the scientist from Shropshire actually had worked out the outlines of his controversial theory some twenty years before *On the Origin of Species* appeared. Fear of public castigation—and its effect on his young family as well as on himself—caused him to keep his radical ideas private. Slowly, between 1839 and 1859, he revealed his observations to a few close friends. Most saw the serious implications of Darwin's position; nevertheless, more than one encouraged him to come forward, believing that the world's cultured elite were ready for an explanation of the natural world that did not posit the constant intervention of a divine creator. Darwin, who relished his privacy and loathed the idea of having to engage in public debate over something so controversial as natural selection, respectfully declined to follow their advice. Instead, for more than twenty years, he lived a "schizoid existence," watching more vocal radicals suffer reproachment and ignominy for proposing less revolutionary ideas than his. His "double life" brought about an "inner conflict" that manifested itself in stomach disorders that often kept him from working and that restricted his socializing throughout his life.

Not even his status as an internationally respected scholar could shield Darwin from the firestorm of criticism he had predicted and feared upon publication of *On the Origin of Species*. The reasons for the furor were complex. Contrary to the beliefs of many twentieth century readers, Darwin's public—especially the scientific public— was ripe to receive a comprehensive theory to explain the changes in species that the natural record so clearly demonstrated. His contemporaries saw science as having a moral dimension, however, and any theory that challenged the idea of fixity in nature suggested the overthrow not only of government but of the deity itself. A few enlightened scientists and religious leaders saw evolution as a sophisticated way for God to operate in nature; most, however, found the notion simply anathema. Darwin's radicalism was not in proposing evolution (others had done so before him) but in challenging the pillars upon which society had rested its comfortable notions of both theology and natural philosophy. Not only did Darwin's portrait of natural selection eliminate a beneficent God; it also removed whatever might have been viewed as beneficent in the natural processes, substituting instead a Nature "ruthless, sifting and selecting, picking the most 'profitable'" from among the species and turning a damning glance on all others.

The buildup to the appearance of *On the Origin of Species* has the place of central interest in this narrative. Less attention is paid to the great debates staged during the pivotal decade between the publication of that work and the appearance of *The Descent of Man, and Selection in Relation to Sex* (1871), perhaps because Darwin himself shied away from the public eye. His younger colleagues, led by Huxley, carried on that fight. The proponent of natural selection preferred to continue his scientific inquiries away from the limelight. Ever the introvert, he remained outside the public eye, tending to the affairs of his family and community and corresponding with the hundreds of scientists and dilettantes who sent him materials for his continuing studies.

The life study of this retiring radical proffered by Desmond and Moore is remarkably free of the pretensions that cloud many academic biographies. At the same time, Desmond and Moore have marshalled an impressive body of scholarship, and their speculations are based on an intuition steeped in the available evidence. The pursuit of science as an exciting venture gets a welcome boost, too, as the authors dramatize Darwin's exploits in the wilds of South America. Images of film hero Indiana Jones may well come to mind as readers come across the young explorer Darwin, attired as a gaucho, riding over the rough terrain of the Brazilian plains, copying notes as he sits beside a fire where his dinner of wild game is roasting. The authors re-create the excitement Darwin felt as he worked through his notebooks and examined thousands of plants, animals, and rocks he had taken with him from the landfalls he made in his five years aboard the *Beagle*. Readers see the young scientist—not yet thirty as he formulated his thoughts about the reasons for differentiations among species—struggling to reconcile older theories with the evidence he had accumulated.

Like so many Victorian prose writers (John Ruskin comes immediately to mind), Darwin was both polymathic and prolific. *On the Origin of Species* is just one of more than a dozen multivolume studies and detailed monographs, composed on subjects as varied as the geological formations in South America, the variations of domestic plants and animals, and an extended essay on earthworms. Never a polished stylist, he struggled to gain control over paragraphs that seemed to wander from example to example while the train of his argument became lost. Throughout his life, he relied on friends and family to help him recast his ideas in ways that the general public could understand and accept. On several occasions Desmond and Moore make disparaging references to Darwin's prose, and anyone who has tried to read *On the Origin of Species* or *The Descent of Man* knows they are not always wrong.

Desmond and Moore's own prose fares somewhat better. The science is explained clearly for the general reader, who needs only modest familiarity with biology, geology, and the sister sciences to follow the many examples cited to show how Darwin progressed toward his understanding of the natural world. One does get a sense, however, of Darwin's prodigious interests and his insatiable curiosity about the natural world. The story of Darwin's struggle to refine his ideas about natural selection and to preserve his theory from usurpation recalls James Watson's account of the race to describe the deoxyribonucleic acid (DNA) molecule, told with the excitement of a novel in *The Double Helix: A Personal Account of the Discovery of the Structure of DNA* (1968). Perhaps this book goes on too long with too much detail for nonspecialists, but the authors can be excused for wanting to reveal all sides of a personality too long thought of as a disembodied scientific intellect.

*Laurence W. Mazzeno*


## Sources for Further Study

*The Christian Century*. CIX, August 26, 1992, p. 776.
*London Review of Books*. XIV, March 12, 1992, p. 14.
*Los Angeles Times Book Review*. July 26, 1992, p. 1.
*Nature*. CCCLV, January 16, 1992, p. 215.
*New Scientist*. CXXXII, October 26, 1991, p. 54.
*The New York Times Book Review*. XCVII, August 2, 1992, p. 10.
*Science*. CCLVII, July 17, 1992, p. 419.
*The Times Literary Supplement*. September 13, 1991, p. 3.
*The Washington Post Book World*. XXII, July 5, 1992, p. 5.

# DAUGHTERS OF ALBION

*Author:* A. N. Wilson (1950-    )
*First published:* 1991, in Great Britain
*Publisher:* Viking (New York). 287 pp. $21.00
*Type of work:* Novel
*Time:* The mid-1960's
*Locale:* England, primarily London

*Rice Robey, author of several visionary novels when a young man, is apparently an aging charlatan who is writing a novel about Jesus and Saint Paul; he repels and fascinates Julian Ramsay, the narrator*

Principal characters:
> RICE ROBEY, who wrote novels under the name of Albion Pugh and is now
> a civil servant who angers his superiors
> JULIAN RAMSAY, the narrator, who wrote a single novel and now makes his
> living as a radio actor
> FELICITY RAMSAY, Julian's older cousin, sharer of his house, and eventually
> his lover; an admirer of Rice Robey
> MILES DARNLEY, an old schoolmate of Ramsay, editor of *The Spark*, a
> scandal magazine that prints Robey's vicious gossip
> ROY RAMSAY, an Anglican priest, Felicity's father and Julian's uncle, who
> reared Julian after his parents were killed in an air raid
> MRS. PAXTON, the "Great Attachment," Robey's mistress for many years
> SARGENT LAMPITT, a onetime friend of Roy Ramsay, uncle of Julian's
> former wife, Anne
> VERNON "ERNIE" LAMPITT, a radical Labour Party politician
> RAPHAEL HUNTER, a writer, nemesis of Julian, and author of a biography
> of James Petworth "Jimbo" Lampitt, an earlier writer

Julian Ramsay, a graduate of the University of Oxford, hoped to be a writer, but after publishing a single novel he has had to make his living as a radio actor, playing a character in a popular British Broadcasting Corporation serial. In this third novel in A. N. Wilson's series dealing with a large group of characters (see *Magill's Literary Annual*, 1990 and 1991, for reviews of the first two novels in the sequence, *Incline Our Hearts* and *A Bottle in the Smoke*), Julian continues to be interested in the Lampitts, an old established family with considerable power; he has been married to Anne, who is connected to the Lampitts, but the marriage is over. Julian's uncle Roy, an Anglican priest who reared Julian after his parents were killed in an air raid, is obsessed with the Lampitts, and Roy's special friend has been Sargent Lampitt, from whom he has been estranged for a number of years. Julian mocks his uncle's obsession, but it has infected him as well.

Sargent, with the approval of Ernie Lampitt, tries to interest Julian in writing a book which will be a history of the Lampitt family but which will have as its principal aim the revising of popular opinion about James Petworth Lampitt, a member of an earlier generation whose life had been the subject of a scurrilously inaccurate book by

Raphael Hunter, a longtime rival of Julian. Julian is reluctant to undertake the task but does agree to serve Sargent as a kind of part-time secretary.

Julian's interest in the Lampitt family becomes connected to his fascination with Rice Robey (always referred to by his full name), a dominating man he meets at a luncheon given by Miles Darnley for people connected in some way with *The Spark*, a not very successful magazine that tries to serve too many interests. Rice Robey, it develops, is the source of the gossipy items appearing in *The Spark* that deal with the sex lives of the rich and famous; *Daughters of Albion* is set in the period when the Profumo scandal rocked the British establishment and led to the loss of an election by the Conservative Party, and such gossip was very popular. It also turns out that Rice Robey, under the name of Albion Pugh, wrote four novels during World War II which are generally forgotten but are the object of admiration by some of Julian's friends.

Julian's cousin, Felicity Ramsay, with whom Julian shares a house, works with Rice Robey in the Ministry of Works and brings him home with her frequently, making it inevitable that Julian will know the man and hear his proclamations. Rice Robey is an expert in ancient archaeological sites around Great Britain, and because of their religious significance he tries to prevent their destruction. Both Felicity and Miles Darnley are enthusiastic supporters of Rice Robey, regarding him as a kind of guru; Felicity is clearly in love with him, although he seems never to become involved in sexual relationships with her or with other young women who find him fascinating. Felicity's admiration for Rice Robey is especially significant, since she was a brilliant don at Oxford, specializing in philosophy before taking a leave to become a civil servant. Julian, who has had little interest in sex since his divorce, suddenly finds that he is strongly attracted to Felicity, so that sexual jealousy enters into his feelings toward Rice Robey.

Julian regards Rice Robey's habit of collecting and publishing scurrilous gossip as reprehensible, but he finds that what Rice Robey says about the subjects of his gossip generally is accurate. He also knows, however, that Rice Robey tells his admirers that the burden of his life and the reason for his failure to achieve great heights as a writer is his "Great Attachment" to Mrs. Paxton, the wife of his onetime employer with whom he eloped and with whom he has lived for many years. She is a dragon, according to Rice Robey, insanely jealous, terribly demanding, and unable to care for herself. When Julian accidentally meets her, delivering some books to Rice Robey's home, he finds that the stories are nonsense; Mrs. Paxton knows all about and does not resent Rice Robey's relationships with other women, she is entirely capable of caring for herself, and she seems to Julian to be anything but a dragon.

Two of Rice Robey's actions become central in the novel. One is his project of writing a novel, in the vein of his earlier mystical works, about the relationship between Saint Paul and Jesus. He begins his novels in verse, for some reason, and later turns them into prose; large segments of both poetry and prose are included in *Daughters of Albion*. They are undistinguished in style and idea except for Rice Robey's notion that some of Saint Paul's actions were caused by an almost sexual attraction to Jesus. They also include the not very original idea that the life of Jesus parallels that of sacrificial figures from earlier mythologies, including the Celtic. The long poetic segment printed in the novel concerns a trip to England that Jesus might have taken as a boy in company with his cousin, Joseph of Arimathea. This connection is based on a hymn by the visionary eighteenth century British artist and poet William Blake, whose spirit hovers over Rice Robey and over the novel.

The more public action that becomes the center of action in the later stages of *Daughters of Albion* is Rice Robey's accusation, published in *The Spark*, that James Petworth Lampitt had not died accidentally or by suicide but had in fact been murdered by Raphael Hunter, who, it is claimed, pushed him off a balcony. The Lampitts are generally agreed that Hunter lied about the extent of his acquaintance with James Lampitt. Sargent Lampitt's estranged wife, Cecily, who had been James Lampitt's lover, delivers some damaging testimony against Hunter, but there seems to have been no motivation for murder. Hunter sues Miles Darnley, *The Spark*, and Rice Robey for slander. Darnley's family convinces him to settle out of court and he offers to pay a settlement for Rice Robey, but the latter refuses and the case goes to court.

Rice Robey's defense is based on Pontius Pilate's words, "What is truth?," which offends the judge. When Rice Robey acts as his own attorney and tries to bring abstract ideas into the trial, he is rebuked by the judge, who shows great sympathy for Hunter's attorney. The jury quickly decides in favor of Hunter, fining Rice Robey a substantial amount of money. The fine is paid by Mrs. Paxton, who sells a nearly forgotten painting by an artist who has lived all his life as a clerk but whose hobby of painting has suddenly made him famous and whose works are now very valuable. Rice Robey is dismissed from his job with the Ministry of Works.

In the novel's closing stages, Rice Robey makes a living guiding tours and giving lectures. Mrs. Paxton has died. Rice Robey devotes his time to an attempt to save a ruin that is a smaller version of Stonehenge. His former employers in the Ministry of Works intend to remove the ruin to make way for a new highway. Julian, out for a drive with Miles Darnley and his wife (another Lampitt), happens upon the site. Julian joins Rice Robey, another of the latter's young female admirers, and a group of protesters in a sit-in. They are forcibly removed by police as bulldozers approach. It turns out that the site was, in fact, an important one, repository of numerous relics and artifacts from the pre-Christian era.

The question at the heart of *Daughters of Albion* is the character of Rice Robey: Is he simply a liar and *poseur*, or is he in fact some kind of seer? On the negative side, there are his apparent lies about the "Great Attachment"; the fact that he is pretentiously bombastic in speech (despite his lack of formal education), employing a high-flown vocabulary rich in Greek words (*episkopos* for "bishop," or *neaniskoi* for "young men," for example), spoken in a Cockney accent; his obvious dependence on the adoration of young women; and the fact that he is resented by his superiors in the Ministry of Works not for his genius but for his careless performance of his duties. On the positive side are his knowledge of and sensitivity to the ancient British ruins he tries to protect; his foolish but somehow noble decision to act as his own attorney when sued by Raphael Hunter; the fact that he attracts the loyalty of people as intelligent as

Felicity and Darnley; and his willingness to go to jail to protect the ancient ruin. The puzzle is never resolved: In the end, he can be seen as both something of a fool and something of a hero.

The disparate elements of Rice Robey's character are at once the most interesting aspect of *Daughters of Albion* and the source of its most serious problems. Julian's reasons for resenting the man make the narrator's observations an unreliable source of judgment, and Rice Robey remains a mystery. Presenting long swatches of his poetry and prose is of doubtful value; its quality is such as to cast doubt on whether Rice Robey deserves to be called a literary genius, or even a good writer. In a novel written as well as this one is, mannered purple prose like Rice Robey's does not make a favorable impression, and notwithstanding an impressive vocabulary, his ideas are not especially original. In the end, *Daughters of Albion*, despite its focus on Rice Robey, has more to say about Julian Ramsay's disappointing life than any other subject.

*Daughters of Albion* is interesting for its picture of British society at a time of change. It is even more interesting for its portrayal of a number of distinctively British eccentrics. The novel paints sharp and fascinating portraits of its many characters, most of whom are odd or unusual, sometimes to extremes. The many Lampitts, Aunt Cecily, Mrs. Paxton, and other acquaintances of Julian are amusingly depicted, and their interactions create considerable interest. This is a fitting continuation of A. N. Wilson's fictional history of Julian Ramsay, and its ending suggests that other volumes may follow.

*John M. Muste*

## Sources for Further Study

*Booklist*. LXXXVIX, December 15, 1991, p. 731.
*Boston Globe*. January 19, 1992, p. 16.
*Chicago Tribune*. January 5, 1992, XIV, p. 1.
*Library Journal*. CXVI, December, 1991, p. 202.
*Los Angeles Times Book Review*. January 19, 1992, p. 6.
*The New York Review of Books*. XXXIX, May 14, 1992, p. 41.
*The New York Times Book Review*. XCVII, January 26, 1992, p. 9.
*Publishers Weekly*. CCXXXVIII, October 11, 1991, p. 50.
*Time*. CXXXIX, February 10, 1992, p. 73.
*The Times Literary Supplement*. August 30, 1991, p. 19.
*The Washington Post Book World*. XXI, December 15, 1991, p. 3.

# DAYS OF OBLIGATION
## An Argument With My Mexican Father

*Author:* Richard Rodriguez (1944-    )
*Publisher:* Viking (New York). 230 pp. $21.00
*Type of work:* Essays

*This collection of ten provocative essays presents the author's reflections on his own life and on the complex fabric of cultures that he has inherited as a Californian of Mexican descent*

In *Days of Obligation*, Richard Rodriguez pushes the poetic style of his much-acclaimed memoir *Hunger of Memory: The Education of Richard Rodriguez* (1982) to even more ambitious literary and cultural limits. In the earlier book, Rodriguez dramatized how his successful academic education as a "scholarship boy" painfully but inevitably alienated him from his immigrant parents, and he surprisingly argued against affirmative action and bilingual education. In contrast, *Days of Obligation* presents a much wider range of personal experience and cultural issues: historical, religious, educational, and racial. His title refers to Catholic feast days of such importance that the faithful are obligated to remember and attend them, and his essays at their most powerful focus on days of the past—in his own life and in history—to which he and the reader must attend.

Although he subtitles the book as an "argument," Rodriguez pursues neither a single consistent argument nor an unbroken autobiographical line. Rather, he plays numerous variations on the contrasts he derives from an argument he had at the age of fourteen with his father:

> "Life is harder than you think, boy."
> "You're thinking of Mexico, Papa."
> "You'll see."

For Rodriguez, the contrast between Mexican and Californian sensibilities expresses the tensions in himself and in American life between Catholicism and Protestantism, communalism and individualism, cynicism and optimism, past and future, age and youth—between a tragic and a comic view of life. As Rodriguez uses "tragic" and "comic," the words take on rather specialized meanings: The tragic view emphasizes the inescapability of sin, limitations, compromise, failure, and death; while the comic view emphasizes the limitless possibilities of new beginnings, new ideas and ideals, and new sorts of people and societies.

Although Rodriguez claims in his introduction that the purpose of his book is to explore the "wisdom" of both perspectives, the weight of his sensibility tends to fall on the tragic Mexican side, and his tone is usually ironic. This tendency toward a Mexican attitude is fortunate for the reader, however, for the prevailing sense of irony and tragedy helps to keep the reader oriented through a book whose structure and style are sometimes bewildering. Although the general progression of chapter topics is from the old to the young (from the first chapter, on the Indians of sixteenth century Mexico, to the closing chapters, on Rodriguez's youth in Sacramento, California), shifts back and forth in time are common, both from one chapter to the next and within particular chapters. This structure of the book can be accounted for partly by its disparate origins in a number of essays that Rodriguez had previously published in journals, magazines, and other books. But the bold manner in which Rodriguez frequently changes voice, time frame, and focus within individual essays suggests the serendipitous method of his quest for truth, which may appear with surprising immediacy and directness, or with an unexpected paradoxical twist. Although the variety and exhilaration of Rodriguez's writing can therefore be appreciated fully only from page to page, an overview of the book's ten chapters may help to clarify the continuities that tie the book together.

"India" begins with Rodriguez looking in the mirror, wondering how he should feel about his conspicuously Indian face. He sardonically considers attitudes in the United States and Mexico that place the Indian in the past or outside history while denying the presence and diverse character of Indians who live in the present day. Rodriguez then reverses this tragically exclusionary view. He seeks to reclaim the honor of contemporary Indians, beginning with an imaginative interpretation of the legend of the Virgin of Guadalupe. According to Rodriguez, the appearance in Mexico in 1531 of the Virgin Mary as a dark-skinned Indian symbolizes "the absorbent strength of Indian spirituality." Mexican Indians have not merely passively accepted Europe and Catholicism; they have transformed it and, along with other Latin Americans, are in the process of taking it over through sheer force of numbers. Rodriguez praises Mexico City, the most populous city in the world, as "the capital of modernity" for its fecund miscegenation, which represents the renewal of the European Old World in the spiritual and sexual embrace of the New. Rodriguez's conceit might be criticized for ignoring the numerous problems caused in Latin America by overpopulation, poverty, and political powerlessness, but it has the charm of a refreshingly original viewpoint.

"Late Victorians" presents a beguiling and poignant portrait of San Francisco, its gay community, and, of all things, its architecture. Rodriguez presents himself as a homosexual who was drawn into San Francisco's gay community in 1979 and witnessed its blossoming in the gay liberation movement of the early 1980's. In exploring the implications of the city's architecture, Rodriguez notes how gays took over the Victorian houses that once had been bastions of the heterosexual family, compares the many-storied richness of these buildings to the many-"storied" richness of the Victorian novel, and contrasts the playful personality of Victorian houses with the chilly soullessness of downtown San Francisco skyscrapers and suburban tract houses. On a more melancholy note, Rodriguez recalls how he was skeptical of the utopian optimism of the gay liberation movement and held himself back from participating in its libertine sexuality. He mourns the fact that the acquired immune deficiency syndrome (AIDS) epidemic confirmed his forebodings, but he finds an unexpectedly heartening soulfulness in the ways that San Francisco has formed a supportive community around its dead and dying.

"Mexico's Children," the longest and most richly elaborated chapter of the book, presents a compelling portrait of the opposing pulls felt by Mexican Americans toward the United States and toward Mexico. Rodriguez characterizes the United States as a land oriented toward the future, toward optimism, individualism, and financial opportunity. In contrast, Rodriguez imagines Mexico as a warmhearted but demanding mother, drawing her children back into the land of memory and communal intimacy. The irony of California's futurist orientation is in its amnesia: It forgets that it was once Mexico, and in tightening its borders it forgets that it once encouraged the seasonal immigration of Mexicans as cheap agricultural labor. The ironic tragedy of the choice facing contemporary Mexicans and Mexican Americans is that they are in danger of succumbing to Californian amnesia. They may go to California intending only to make money and then return to Mexico, but they underestimate the power of Californian values to transform them and cut them off from individual and cultural memory.

"In Athens Once" further develops the contrasts of the previous chapter in an ironic dual portrait of Tijuana and San Diego. What fascinates Rodriguez about these proximate cities is how each maintains its national character yet at the same time has developed radically contrasting qualities as a result of the influence of the city just across the border. Tijuana, once a magnet of sinful escapism for the United States, still possesses a shady side in its essential cynicism, but it ironically has developed a beaming Yankee face. American families flock to "El Main Street," the fifth most popular tourist attraction in the San Diego-Tijuana region, and manufacturing flourishes in a large industrial park of sweatshop assembly plants on the outskirts of town. San Diego, on the other hand, in some ways fits Rodriguez's image of forward-looking America: "San Diego is the future—secular, soulless," a "postindustrial city of high-impact plastic and despair diets." San Diego, however, ironically has developed Mexican qualities: Part of the city has taken over Tijuana's former role as a center for drugs and other vices, while another part identifies with "the past, guarding its quality of life" in memory of better days.

"Asians," "The Latin American Novel," and "Nothing Lasts a Hundred Years," the final three chapters in the book, all intertwine Rodriguez's memories of his Sacramento boyhood with his reflections on the dilemmas of American immigrants. "Asians" reiterates the argument from "Mexico's Children" that Americanization means loss of memory, of cultural identity and communal tradition. Rodriguez sympathizes with immigrant parents who want to believe that their children can become successful in America yet resist Americanization, but he pessimistically believes that the power of America's adolescent popular culture ultimately is irresistible. Curiously, however, the educational solution that Rodriguez proposes is not the way of multiculturalism, which holds with the immigrant parents that children should explore and preserve their ancestral heritages. "If I am a newcomer to your country," he asks, "why teach me about my ancestors? I need to know about seventeenth-century Puritans in order to make sense of the rebellion I notice everywhere in the American city." Rodriguez holds that what will bring America together is the study of a "common culture," focusing on such key Americans as Benjamin Franklin, Thomas Jefferson, Andrew Jackson, and Mark Twain—the historical and literary figures who contributed the most to the dominant culture and to the primary ideas and forces that continue to shape it.

"The Latin American Novel" begins by considering the question, Why are evangelical Protestant churches having such success in recruiting members among traditionally Catholic Latin Americans? Historically, according to Rodriguez, Catholicism has been a communal religion most suited to the rural village, while Protestantism has been the religion of the individual, the city, and the literary form of the novel (since it deals with the individual standing out from the communal group). Rodriguez relates this religious contrast to his high-school friendship with Larry Faherty, a rebellious freethinker—and thus in some sense a Protestant and an ideal character for a novel—in contrast with Rodriguez himself, an "obedient schoolboy" and a Catholic. Ironically, Rodriguez comes to realize that his closeness with Larry ultimately resulted from his friend's Catholic qualities of forgiveness and communal exuberance. Similarly, Rodriguez believes that the success of evangelical Protestantism among traditional Catholics is that they have revived the warm communal spirit of traditional Catholicism: "The small Protestant church revives the Catholic memory of the countryside. In the small evangelical church, people who are demoralized by the city turn to the assurance of community."

"Nothing Lasts a Hundred Years," the poignant concluding chapter, considers the numerous tragedies concealed behind the optimistic American façades of Sacramento, Rodriguez's hometown. There is the tragedy of his father, who preferred San Francisco but yielded to family pressures and in Sacramento lost his hearing and much of his capacity to find pleasure in life. A tradesman who makes dentures, the melancholy father ironically spent his working days "surrounded by shelves of grinning false teeth." There is the tragedy of the Irish nuns and priests in the Sacramento schools and churches, who like Rodriguez's father and mother felt sadly cut off from their homelands far away. There is the tragedy of Rodriguez's Uncle Raj, who came from India as a skilled dentist but then had to endure the humiliation of patients recoiling from him ("No nigger dentist is going to stick his fingers in my mouth!"). There is the historical tragedy of Johann Sutter, who in the mid-1800's hoped to establish an insulated European settlement in the Sacramento Valley until his dreams were trampled by the gold rush of 1849, a symbol of the onrushing soulless American culture that Rodriguez deplores for its destruction of memory and communal spirit.

Upon finishing the book, the reader may pause to wonder what personal satisfactions Rodriguez has gained by attending to his days of obligation. At several points in the book, the author makes the ironic claim that tragic Mexican culture, with its acceptance of life's limitations, is actually happier than comic American culture: "Tragic cultures serve up better food than optimistic cultures; tragic cultures have sweeter children, more opulent funerals," and "Catholics have better architecture and sunnier plazas and an easier virtue and are warmer to the touch." Rodriguez rarely seems happy himself, however, and he repeatedly characterizes himself as drawing back from the cultural qualities and pleasures he extols. In Mexico, he recoils from the food and drink; he declines an invitation from a priest he admires to go to Easter mass in a village outside Tijuana, opting instead for brunch with friends in La Jolla, California. In San Francisco, he berates himself for his "unwillingness to embrace life" with his libertine friend César and for his detachment as a "barren skeptic" at the AIDS memorial service that ends the chapter. In Sacramento, he believes that he ends up betraying Larry Faherty by failing to extend "the fervor our past demanded" when he meets him under difficult circumstances. Ultimately, writing the book may have been a way for Rodriguez to reconcile with his father, to concede that his father was right in emphasizing a tragic view of life. Or, like many a hero and heroine in the fiction of Henry James, Rodriguez may have found satisfaction in believing that he has seen the entire rueful truth about the situations he has lived through and that he has not spared himself from seeing the rueful truth about himself. Whatever Rodriguez's satisfactions may have been, the reader's satisfactions in his keenly sardonic company are many. It is interesting that the title of Rodriguez's high-school newspaper column was "The Watchful Eye," for that seems the role he is destined to play in literature and in life. Perhaps the ultimate irony of *Days of Obligation* is that it helps Richard Rodriguez, advocate of Catholic communal values, to come closer to earning an honored place in the Protestant individualist tradition of American literature, next to other detached observers of life such as Ralph Waldo Emerson, Henry James, and fellow Californian Joan Didion.

*Terry L. Andrews*

## Sources for Further Study

*Booklist*. LXXXIX, October 15, 1992, p. 397.
*Insight*. VIII, November 30, 1992, p. 23.
*Kirkus Reviews*. LX, September 1, 1992, p. 1115.
*Los Angeles Times Book Review*. November 15, 1992, p. 1.
*National Catholic Reporter*. XXIX, November 20, 1992, p. 33.
*The New York Times Book Review*. XCVII, November 22, 1992, p. 42.
*Newsweek*. CXX, December 14, 1992, p. 80.
*Publishers Weekly*. CCXXXIX, September 7, 1992, p. 84.
*San Francisco Chronicle*. November 1, 1992, p. REV1.
*The Village Voice*. XXXVII, December 29, 1992, p. 91.
*The Washington Post*. November 28, 1992, p. F1.

# DEATH WITHOUT WEEPING
## The Violence of Everyday Life in Brazil

*Author:* Nancy Scheper-Hughes (1944-    )
*Publisher:* University of California Press (Berkeley). 614 pp. $29.00
*Type of work:* Cultural anthropology and current history
*Time:* 1964-1989
*Locale:* Northeastern Brazil

*A nontraditional ethnographic account of the effects of culture and poverty on morality, mother love, and child death in northeastern Brazil*

Nancy Scheper-Hughes was among the first group of Peace Corps volunteers to work in northeastern Brazil following the military coup in that country in the spring of 1964. It is an area of great poverty, high infant mortality, short life expectancy (forty years), malnutrition, illiteracy, and joblessness. The introduction to the book is Scheper-Hughes' story: how she came to Brazil, her life there, subsequent visits, and the profound effect Brazil has had on her life and career.

She begins by telling how—as a twenty-year-old community health and development volunteer—she served briefly in a large public hospital in the sugarcane plantation zone, then lived and worked for two years in a shantytown of five thousand rural workers in the state of Pernambuco. Her frequent encounters with political corruption and repression, violence, poverty, sickness, and death—especially in children, from diarrhea and dehydration—made an indelible impression on her. She developed a strong relationship with the community and, in addition to working in health promotion, became actively involved in raising the political consciousness of the peasants through Paulo Freire's adult literacy programs, programs associated by many with leftist or communist agitation.

Fifteen years later, in 1982, when the military regime in Brazil had become more "open," Scheper-Hughes, now an anthropologist, returned to the community where she had worked as a Peace Corps volunteer. Between 1982 and 1989, using a phenomenologically grounded anthropological approach, she conducted four field expeditions, for a total of fourteen months of fieldwork.

This book is a report of her research, a subjective, sometimes fragmented, record of the lives of mothers and their children, living (and dying) in the midst of abject poverty and violence. It incorporates the study of documents, interviews, and observations, as well as scholarly literature reviews and citations from anthropology, sociology, psychology, political science, philosophy, and literature. It also contains emotional, highly personal anecdotal narratives and observations, spanning the twenty-five years of Scheper-Hughes' intermittent contact with the community.

The scope of the book is tremendous. Topics such as poverty, hunger, rural medicine, death and illness, body image, and maternal-infant bonding, are explored in depth. Scheper-Hughes' research has been driven by the connection she perceived, as a young Peace Corps worker, between the high infant mortality rate in the community in 1965 (from dehydration, hunger, and neglect) and the military takeover in Brazil in 1964.

The social conditions that prevailed and the mothers' acceptance (routinization) of day-to-day suffering and violence had a profound impact on her. To her amazement, the death of a baby in the shantytown did not appear to be the great tragedy it would have been in the United States; mothers were calm, almost casual, and indifferent. This impression was to haunt her and shape her anthropological research.

Scheper-Hughes chronicles the sufferings of almost one hundred women through family and reproductive histories, migration and employment histories, domestic and conjugal liaisons, and anecdotal commentaries. The central theme of her work is the relationship between chronic psychological and material poverty, illness, and child-loss and a mother's ability to practice moral judgment and to express maternal love. She hypothesizes that the expectation of child death actually jeopardizes the lives of certain children. In both the public and private sectors, the death of a child is not seen as a serious or urgent problem. It is the norm for poor families. Scheper-Hughes doubts that the modern "bourgeois" notion of mother love is a universal phenomenon. The basic research and current thinking about mother-infant interaction and "human nature" are called into question. In *Death Without Weeping*, she proposes that when conditions of high fertility and high infant mortality prevail, which is the case among the shantytown mothers, women distance themselves psychologically from their weak and vulnerable infants and withdraw love and care. They give birth to many children and invest only in those most likely to survive; they do not experience a deep sense of loss or grieving when a fragile child dies. This is the major thesis of the book.

The first six chapters present a broad perspective of the region in Brazil that is the context of Scheper-Hughes' work. In chapter 1, she traces the colonial history and sugar economy of northeastern Brazil up to the present time, giving an ethnographic tour of the large sugarcane plantation and mill just outside of the principal market town of the region (called by the pseudonym of Bom Jesus da Mata in the book). The social and cultural institutions that were a part of the sugar plantation society romanticized by Brazil's leading sociologist, Gilberto Freyre, have left their mark on present-day northeastern Brazil in modern-day versions of the landed aristocracy, paternalism, and slavery. Greedy landlords have forced peasants and sharecroppers off the land, driving them to seek work in urban slums. "Racial democracy," the apparent lack of social friction between the races in Brazil, has long been attributed to miscegenation between master and slave in the colonial period. It is only a myth, according to Scheper-Hughes. Agrarian reform proposals, protests, and any attempts by workers to organize are treated with contempt and violence by those in power.

In chapter 2, Scheper-Hughes discusses the significance of the chronic droughts (*secas*) in northeastern Brazil. Water is precious—the misery of hunger cannot be compared with the misery of thirst—and thirst becomes a metaphor of the "dry lives" of the people whose basic needs go unmet in the interior of northeastern Brazil.

In chapter 3, Scheper-Hughes describes the shantytown "Alto do Cruzeiro" that is the focus of the study and the larger market town "Bom Jesus de Mata" which, together, make up a complex social world. There are three social stratifications that coexist and interact in the social drama Scheper-Hughes describes. The old feudal world of the plantation (categorized by the *casa* or "big house") is represented by the upper class; the new world of commerce and capitalism found in the streets, factories, and supermarkets (categorized as the *rua* or "street") is represented by the middle class; and the world of poor, disenfranchised squatters (categorized as *matutos* or "backward country people") is represented by the lower class or common people. The poor are subdivided into even more stratifications: the respectable working poor, the struggling seasonal workers, and the wretched poor who literally live from hand to mouth. Scheper-Hughes presents vignettes depicting people from all walks of life in this complex social realm, believable to anyone familiar with northeastern Brazil. Servants and workers are locked into personal relationships with their patrons and bosses that foster dependency and compromise their humanity.

Chapters 4 and 5 deal with the problem of constant hunger and malnutrition. Two-thirds of all children in the area show evidence of undernutrition and stunted growth. The hunger endemic to the sugarcane region, however, is not the same as the fabled, cyclical, acute hunger of the drought-plagued backlands, (*o sertão*). With chronic hunger, rage and passivity alternate as bipolar rhythms, described in the literature as a Brazilian type of "manic-depressive" personality. Hunger and deprivation are manifested as irritability and nervousness. In recent years, the folk idiom of nervous hunger or "madness of hunger" (*delirio de fome*) has been translated into the ethnomedical idiom of "nervous frenzy" (*nervos*), a condition treated with tranquilizers and sedatives in a blatant misuse of medicine.

Chapter 6 discusses the random and institutionalized violence that occurs every day in the shantytown. During the years of military rule, the sudden "disappearance" of the poor or dissidents was commonplace. More recently, death squad "disappearances" continue and evoke a sense of powerlessness and pervasive anxiety in the population.

Chapters 7 through 12 describe Scheper-Hughes' research and the central thesis of her work. Chapter 7 explores the environment in which child death is accepted as ordinary and expected. When the author wondered why the church bells rang so often in Alto do Cruzeiro, she was told that it was "just another little angel gone to heaven." She gradually came to the realization that babies presumed destined to die are neglected, a practice contributing, in part, to the high infant mortality rate. She explores in chapter 8 the many meanings of motherhood, maternal thinking, and morality, and concludes that mother love is not a universal, natural phenomenon, but is culturally conditioned. It is a mistake to impose one's own cultural expectations on mothers of other cultures. Chapter 9 rejects classical bonding theory, likening the shantytown mothers' relationships with their infants to their relationships with husbands and boyfriends; these are often temporary attachments that result in disappointment, and disappointment leads to a failure to mourn. There is "death without weeping" because the infant's happiness is certain in heaven. It is only considered appropriate to express attachment and grief for older children.

Chapters 10 and 11 follow the life histories of three half-sisters, Antonieta, Lordes, and Biu, whom Scheper-Hughes knew for the entire twenty-five-year period covered by the book. The lives of these women demonstrate the resilience to adversity of many women of Alto do Cruzeiro who still find life worth living, despite the hardships they face on a daily basis. The three sisters were fathered by different men within six years of each other, and each was partly raised by their aunt. Antonieta, the oldest, was fortunate enough to marry into a "good" family and managed to leave the shantytown. Several of her children survived, and she even raised a number of foster children. She refused to be overwhelmed by life's experiences, recasting problems in the past in a favorable light and actively working to overcome the obstacles to happiness in her life. Biu, the same age as Scheper-Hughes, is hard-working, independent, and spirited. She had ten pregnancies, three miscarriages and seven live births, and was able to raise four children. She is able to forget her numerous problems, for a while, by celebrating carnival. Lordes, the youngest sister, gets by in ways that are fairly typical of women in the Alto. She has had several bad lovers, infant deaths, and illnesses, but eventually was able to form two stable relationships with older men.

The conclusion, chapter 12, reflects on how shantytown residents are able to "get by," "make do," and endure by "relying on their wits, playing the odds, and engaging in the occasional *malandragem* of deceit and white lies, gossip and rumor, feigned loyalty, theft, and trickery." Religious rituals and various personal dramas enrich their lives and provide hope for a better world. The author describes the history of attempts to politically organize the people of Alto do Cruzeiro (more recently by the Catholic church, enlightened by the theology of liberation). The most recent attempt to revive the shantytown association was aborted by fighting within the association, the radical rhetoric of a few of the leaders, and bureaucratic obstacles. The book ends on a somewhat ambivalent note, acknowledging the power of poverty and oppression but also celebrating the resilience of people able to survive under such conditions.

*Death Without Weeping* is a splendid book. The narrative moves from the scholarly exploration of one topic to another, provides wonderful descriptions of life in the shantytown, relentlessly drives home the thesis of the book, and punctuates the discussion with indignation and moral outrage. Scheper-Hughes, in a departure from conventional ethnography that refuses to "engage" with its subjects, challenges the basic assumptions of her subjects and offers assumptions of her own. For her, anthropology is an ethical and radical project that demands the compassionate and crusading involvement of the researcher in the lives of the people studied. She believes that traditional anthropological methodology has been an intrusion into the lives of peoples exploited by Western imperialism and argues that anthropology should try to free itself from Western cultural assumptions. She replaces those assumptions with another set of assumptions—those of a Marxist theoretical perspective. She is dogmatic in her convictions about human nature, the causes of human misery, and solutions to the problems. At times, her conclusions seem more informed by her biases than by her observations. Nevertheless, she makes a powerful case for another view of maternal-infant attachment and a significant contribution to an understanding of what it means to be a woman and a mother in an impoverished, violent society.

*Edna Quinn*

## Sources for Further Study

*The Chronicle of Higher Education*. XXXVIII, June 10, 1992, p. A7.
*Commonweal*. CXIX, September 25, 1992, p. 24.
*Kirkus Reviews*. LX, April 1, 1992, p. 451.
*Library Journal*. CXVII, April 15, 1992, p. 102.
*The New York Times Book Review*. XCVII, August 30, 1992, p. 11.
*Publishers Weekly*. CCXXXIX, April 13, 1992, p. 50.
*San Francisco Chronicle*. August 23, 1992, p. REV1.
*Women's Review of Books*. X, October, 1992, p. 6.

# DEFENDING BILLY RYAN

*Author:* George V. Higgins (1939-    )
*Publisher:* Henry Holt (New York). 245 pp. $21.95
*Type of work:* Novel
*Time:* The 1990's
*Locale:* Massachusetts

Defending Billy Ryan *provides a close-up view of the process and principles of criminal law, as the narrator successfully defends a public servant accused of corruption*

> *Principal characters:*
> JERRY KENNEDY, a defense attorney, the narrator and protagonist
> BILLY RYAN, a Massachusetts public works commissioner, Kennedy's client
> EDWARD "CADILLAC TEDDY" FRANKLIN, Kennedy's friend
> JOHN "JACK BONNIE" BONAVENTRE, a prosecution witness

*Defending Billy Ryan* is George V. Higgins' third novel about the exploits of Jerry Kennedy, "The classiest sleazy criminal lawyer in Boston." Although it can stand on its own, readers familiar with the first two in the series—*Kennedy for the Defense* (1980) and *Penance for Jerry Kennedy* (1985)—will likely find more to enjoy in it. Numerous characters and events from the earlier books are referred to in passing; whether or not Higgins was deliberately writing for his faithful fans, they will experience a pleasing resonance in details that new readers will find merely tantalizing.

Higgins is a terrific writer, justly famous as a raconteur whose dialogue, especially when the voices are those of small-time crooks, jumps off the page. *Defending Billy Ryan* is an entertaining novel, far more rewarding than most of the fiction published in any given year. Nevertheless, it is relatively thin, lacking the tremendous variety and vitality of its predecessors.

The title alone is a danger signal. From *The Friends of Eddie Coyle* (1972) onward, Higgins in his best work has eschewed tight, narrowly focused plots. Seemingly insignificant details do indeed tend to come together by the end, bringing about revelations which, however, are far less important than the leisurely, convoluted process of getting to them. In the earlier Kennedy novels there is, quite simply, a lot more going on. Kennedy is involved in several cases in each: some appear in a single, often hilarious episode; others surface, submerge, and pop up again just when Kennedy (but not the reader) hopes he has seen the last of them. Woven through the professional episodes, and contributing greatly to the emotional warmth of the books are scenes from Kennedy's personal life. For him and for the reader, there is never a dull moment. In *Defending Billy Ryan*, as the title suggests, Kennedy devotes himself to a single case. He is divorced from his wife; his daughter has grown up and moved far away; with a single exception, everyone else he cared about has died. No new love interest or even a new friend has appeared to fill the void, a negative detail that at least confirms

Higgins' independence and originality. By gambling on a linear story short on human interest, sustained almost entirely by inside detail about the practice of criminal law, he has slighted his own great strengths.

Higgins essentially is a comic novelist, reveling in the paradox of characters doomed by their own folly yet stubbornly vital. His best books celebrate life in all of its glorious absurdity. *Defending Billy Ryan,* colored by the terrible losses Kennedy has sustained, is darker in tone, equivocal in theme. From the beginning, as Kennedy sets out to tell the story of the commissioner of public works whom he successfully defended against corruption charges, the mood is elegiac. It is six years later, and Billy Ryan, the defendant, is dead. In the present time of the novel, Kennedy is driving with another client to Ryan's wake and "bargain diamonds and battered Boston lawyers don't look good under strong white light . . . the question isn't whether they really need repairs, but whether their value justifies the certain cost."

Kennedy, however, is perhaps being disingenuous here. Before the Ryan case (turned down by five other lawyers as an invitation to professional suicide) comes his way, he is pretty much down and out, his secretary coming in only three days a week. Then Ryan pays him a hundred thousand dollars in cash. Six years later, as a result of the publicity from the successful defense, he is driving a new Thunderbird and has more business than he can handle. That reversal of his material fortunes, as he is wise enough to know—having had ups and downs enough in the courtroom, after all—is nothing that can be counted on to last. What sustains him is his deep understanding that what he does is indeed of value, and that therefore it is necessary to do it well. That virtually all of his clients, including Billy Ryan, are guilty as charged is beside the point; it is due process that he defends with all his heart, mind, and soul. Kennedy's convictions, which provide the book with its moral center, sustain the readers as well. If *Defending Billy Ryan* had no other virtues, it would still be worth reading for its defense of the value and honor of work. In the fiction of the late twentieth century such a viewpoint, rendered through a central character of intelligence and integrity, is close to unique.

Kennedy's (and by inference his creator's) interest in process is revealed by a critically important narrative strategy: that Billy Ryan was acquitted is revealed on page 1. Higgins writes about lawyers and the people they defend or prosecute because, having been a criminal lawyer himself, he knows them intimately. His novels, however, are not conventional mysteries or thrillers; rather, they are comedies of manners or, as in this case, serious social commentary. There is a sense in which Billy Ryan, who remains somewhat showy, exists primarily to test a hypothesis. Higgins here offers a character deliberately unsympathetic, entirely lacking the flamboyant charm of, say, Edward "Cadillac Teddy" Franklin, the long-standing friend and client with whom Kennedy drives to Ryan's wake. It is difficult for the reader to care whether Ryan is convicted; in fact, inasmuch as he clearly is guilty not only of the charge against him but of numerous others never brought, over a span of many years, justice in the abstract hardly is served by his acquittal. The acquittal itself comes about because, and only because, without Kennedy's knowledge the key prosecution witness has been intimidated. Despite all that, is Kennedy right to defend Billy Ryan to the hilt? The answer is a resounding and convincing yes, because it is a noble system for the implementation of justice, flawed though it inevitably is in application, that he is defending. In the process Kennedy himself, however battered and in some ways cynical, gains greatly in stature and sympathy.

The plot reveals his legal expertise, his intelligence, his principles—everything except his deepest feelings, about which, in common with so many fictional heroes, he remains reticent. Summarizing the plot of a Higgins novel can be tedious, misleading, and in this case positively discouraging, since the salient fact about the story, as Kennedy says very early, is that practically everything he does—the dogged investigation, in particular, which fills many pages—turns out to be irrelevant to the defense.

Billy Ryan is accused of authorizing an unneeded road, acquisition of the land for which enables his cronies, particularly John "Jack Bonnie" Bonaventre, to make a quick killing in real estate. That in turn makes Jack Bonnie the key prosecution witness, since the prosecution can put him in prison for a long time if he refuses to cooperate. Carefully hidden before the trial though he is, however, someone gets to him—a bit of skullduggery engineered by Kennedy's friend and client, Cadillac Teddy—and as a result his testimony is just vague enough for Kennedy, with an eloquent closing argument, to get his client off. The acquittal, then, is anything but the logical outcome of a rational defense. Rather it is the final link in a quirky, essentially political chain of causality. Kennedy, by once helping a policeman accused of brutality, caught the eye of a shadowy Mafia don; therefore when Cadillac Teddy calls this man, he helps. But that is an enormous oversimplification. The overlapping spheres of influence and crosscurrents of motivation in a typical Higgins novel make three-dimensional chess sound simple; in this one, unfortunately, the behind-the-scenes wheelings and dealings remain almost entirely offstage, denying the reader the giddy pleasures of trying to work it all out.

What the author offers instead is, first, a series of essays—mercifully brief—about the techniques of criminal defense and the inner workings of the law. Thus the reader will learn the importance of, and techniques for, getting truth and cooperation out of clients; the definition of "bill of particulars," and why caution is necessary when asking for one; the ways in which criminal law applies differently to different social classes; and so on. Although this is a fairly obtrusive approach (Higgins taught law more subtly and enjoyably in the earlier novels), the typical reader presumably will push on for the modest pleasure of feeling like an insider, and in hope of arriving soon at a good anecdote. These Higgins provides in roughly equal numbers; too few and too brief to make up for the lack of a broad comic plot, they nevertheless give this relatively dark and serious book a degree of zest.

One such story provides, as well, the only real insight into the desert that is Kennedy's personal life. It is apparent from the beginning that his work is all he has. He lacks family and friends; his wife took their year-round house, leaving him the beach house in which he now permanently camps; when engaged in a case he survives on fast-food hamburgers. The pain he reveals when he tells of how he came to be divorced, however, suggests that he works so hard and well in part to uphold the system of laws he venerates; in part to bolster his self-esteem but also, perhaps more than he knows, as an anodyne. A weakness of *Defending Billy Ryan* is that, without reference to the earlier books, one can only infer the depth of his loss.

Kennedy's emotional deprivation seems arbitrarily imposed. Weldon Cooper, the neighboring attorney with whom he shared an office wall, frequent lunches, and his innermost thoughts, has died in the prime of life of a heart attack (or really of a broken heart, brought on by the breakdown of his family) between the second and the third books. Kennedy's marriage ended because he could not bear his wife's adultery, of which by the end of *Penance for Jerry Kennedy* (though that book had chronicled some marital hard times) there had been no foreshadowing. Those characters, who along with Kennedy's daughter contributed greatly to the richness of the first two novels, disappeared for one of two reasons: as a matter of convenience, out of the author's desire to write something relatively pure and simple; or out of a darkening of the author's vision. In either case, the result is a paradox: By focusing on Kennedy's work, exploring both its methods and its rationale, Higgins has written a highly original novel. By presenting him as incapable of sustaining a lifelong relationship, or at least as living in a world that makes such a relationship impossible, he has echoed and to a degree evoked the typical, tedious anxiety that colors (or washes the color out of) so much fiction of the late twentieth century.

*Kennedy for the Defense* opens with Cadillac Teddy telling Kennedy, in his own delirious words, how he steals Cadillacs and why he steals only Cadillacs; it ends with Kennedy's family together, about to go shopping. *Defending Billy Ryan* begins with a description of Kennedy alone, down and almost out, and ends with Billy Ryan's wake. As clearly as anything else, those changes reveal the altered mood and purpose of this new novel. Higgins has taken the risk—doubly great for a popular author working with an established character—of trying something new. The result is that some of his readers will surely feel cheated, and with some reason. Clearly Higgins possesses the mastery to have rendered Kennedy's (and by inference his own) devotion to the honorable practice of law in a richer fabric. The novel is challenging and interesting nevertheless: Higgins at less than his best is still better than most. His work continues to break down the artificial distinctions between genre and mainstream, popular and literary fiction. *Defending Billy Ryan* deserves and will repay attention.

*Edwin Moses*

## Sources for Further Study

*Atlanta Journal Constitution.* October 11, 1992, p. K13.
*Booklist.* LXXXVIII, August, 1992, p. 1972.
*Boston Globe.* September 7, 1992, p. 21.
*Chicago Tribune.* September 6, 1992, XIV, p. 4.

*The Christian Science Monitor.* September 22, 1992, p. 12.
*Kirkus Reviews.* LX, July 1, 1992, p. 801.
*New York Law Journal.* CCVIII, December 1, 1992, p. 2.
*Publishers Weekly.* CCXXXIX, August 10, 1992, p. 52.
*The Wall Street Journal.* September 22, 1992, p. A16.
*The Washington Post Book World.* XXII, September 20, 1992, p. 5.

# DE GAULLE
## The Ruler, 1945-1970

*Author:* Jean Lacouture (1921-    )
Translated from the French by Alan Sheridan
*Publisher:* W. W. Norton (New York). 640 pp. $29.95
*Type of work:* Historical biography
*Time:* 1945-1970
*Locale:* Primarily France

*The story of France's greatest statesman of modern times from the Allied invasion of France to his death in 1970*

*Principal personages:*
> CHARLES DE GAULLE, a French general and statesman, president of the Fifth Republic until his resignation in 1969
> KONRAD ADENAUER, a German statesman after World War II
> WINSTON CHURCHILL, a British prime minister
> MAURICE, COUVE DE MURVILLE, a French prime minister and foreign minister during the Fifth Republic
> MICHEL DEBRE, a French prime minister, finance minister, and justice minister during the Fifth Republic
> DWIGHT D. EISENHOWER, a president of the United States
> JOHN F. KENNEDY, a president of the United States
> HAROLD MACMILLAN, a British prime minister
> FRANÇOIS MITTERRAND, a French Socialist politician and opponent of de Gaulle, later president of France
> GEORGES POMPIDOU, a French prime minister during the Fifth Republic and later president of France

Charles de Gaulle, leader of the Free French during World War II, returned to his beloved country from London in 1944 after the successful D-Day landings. Still not free from Allied control, de Gaulle struggled not only against his German opponents but also against his British and American allies, and even against his fellow Frenchmen. From the end of war until his final resignation from politics in 1969, de Gaulle continued his crusade to raise France once again to what he believed she should and could become. When he died in 1970 he felt defeated, having failed to fulfill his vision of France, but in crucial matters he had succeeded in changing France and affecting the world beyond her borders. De Gaulle's story is the subject of Jean Lacouture's magnificent biography, the sequel to his 1990 *De Gaulle: The Rebel, 1890-1944.*

The author, biographer of political figures such as Leon Blum, Pierre Mendès-France, and Ho Chi Minh and of the writers André Malraux and François Mauriac, was a journalist and foreign editor of *Le Monde* during the last thirteen years of de Gaulle's career. He was not a Gaullist, and at the time he generally was unsympathetic to much of what de Gaulle did and stood for. In this work, however, Lacouture concludes that de Gaulle largely was correct in most of his decisions, although this biography is not hagiography. Lacouture's de Gaulle is portrayed as one of the most insightful and prescient statesmen of the twentieth century, but he could also be blind to current realities and future possibilities. De Gaulle was at times ruthless toward not only his enemies but also his friends and supporters, personally difficult, often abrasive, and autocratic in his dealings with everyone and everything, including France and its citizens.

In 1944, de Gaulle's task was more political than military, although the two were inseparable. To restore France to its past glory—not just to free France from German occupation—required that the French participate militarily in the liberation of the country. From a purely military viewpoint, French arms were not a major factor in strategic considerations. De Gaulle's relations with the Allies remained difficult; he was always on guard for any slight against his dignity and France's sovereignty—for him they were indivisible—and even more friction might have resulted without the political astuteness of General Dwight Eisenhower and Winston Churchill.

Within France, de Gaulle faced great problems. His position as head of France generally was accepted, but not without dissenters. He had to satisfy the major resistance leaders, many of whom were communists and whose ideological ties were to the Soviet Union. In addition, there was the question of the status of the Third Republic and the discredited wartime regime of Vichy and its leader, Philippe Pétain, de Gaulle's mentor after World War I. In spite of the difficulties and his own occasional missteps, by the end of 1945 he was seemingly turning France into something closer to his own vision of her: free, secure, and with greater self-confidence than during the interwar years. But in January, 1946, he resigned, surprising friends and foes alike. His reasons were obvious. Always the student of history, de Gaulle predicated his actions on the past. Strong executive leadership had been characteristic of French politics from Louis XIV to the two Napoleons, and de Gaulle believed that France's present difficulties, domestically and internationally, were the result of the dominant position of the legislature, coinciding with the destructive competition between political parties, over a weak executive. De Gaulle's inability to change those prewar conditions as quickly as he hoped led to his resignation. Lacouture concludes that de Gaulle expected that he would return to power quickly at the head of a presidential regime when the assembly, the politicians, and the people realized that there was no other choice in the task of returning France to greatness. When that did not immediately happen, he organized his own political movement to restore him to power, but by 1951 that too had failed.

De Gaulle and his causes continually polarized people. Many would follow wherever he led, but opponents saw him as a threat to liberty and equality, another Napoleon Bonaparte who would become a dictator. De Gaulle was never enamored of Napoleon; he believed in democracy and that the people were the fount of political power. For him, there was no contradiction between democracy and strong leadership.

The 1950's saw de Gaulle as the man in reserve, waiting to be recalled. He retired to his country home, La Boisserie, in the village of Colombey-les-Deux-Églises, where he wrote his memoirs, a major literary work. There he waited and planned his return. The call finally came in 1958. The crisis that brought him back to power was Algeria. The winds of change had been sweeping through the colonial world, and although de Gaulle's own attitude toward imperialism was complex—he had supported the French return to Indochina after World War II—he was a realist when it came to continued political control over peoples who no longer wished to remain under France. Algeria was a particular problem. Its proximity to mainland France, its sizable European population, and its historic ties to France posed complex difficulties. A bloody and bitter rebellion had broken out against French rule. The French Algerians, long in a privileged position, were fearful of being abandoned, and the French army, already suffering from diminished morale after its forced withdrawal from Indochina, in the mid-1950's, was reluctant to accept a second defeat. As France appeared to be on the brink of civil war, de Gaulle returned to power. Lacouture notes that de Gaulle was privy to information regarding dissident plots within the military against the Fourth Republic, but power was his goal, not for its own sake but to form France to correspond to his vision of her.

The Algerian crisis also gave de Gaulle the opportunity to dispose of the Fourth Republic and its legislative and political party dominance. The new Fifth Republic brought with it a strong executive. De Gaulle was elected president, and he controlled both the assembly and the prime minister. Despite the reservations of some politicians and against the wishes of many in the military, he used the technique of the plebiscite, which allowed him to bypass the assembly and appeal directly to the people, to bring French opinion around to granting independence to Algeria and freeing France from its North African debacle. It has been argued that de Gaulle sold out the European Algerians, and Lacouture claims that additional guarantees could have been obtained from the rebels if de Gaulle had been more patient during the negotiation process, but his actions showed his ruthless decisiveness when the opportune moment arrived.

On the world stage, de Gaulle proved difficult for most foreign governments, particularly that of the United States. When he returned to power in 1958, he made known his disagreement with many aspects of American foreign policy. Although he admired Dwight Eisenhower and John Kennedy, he objected to their policies. He was convinced that the Vietnam imbroglio would prove to be a disaster for the United States. He resented the manner in which American policymakers did not discuss the crises of the Cold War as equals with their European allies; he worried that America would strike its own agreement with the Soviet Union, and that Europe's, and France's, defense rested too much on America's wavering whims. He withdrew France from the North Atlantic Treaty Organization (NATO), the military cornerstone of the Atlantic Alliance. His decision to make France a nuclear power was deplored in the United States, but was in keeping with his determination to make France again a great power. Whether nuclear weapons made France more secure is debatable, but given de Gaulle's desire to restore greatness to France, they were inevitable.

His relations with his fellow Europeans were also stormy. Great Britain remained a rival. In the past, Britain had often been the great opponent of France, and de Gaulle was influenced by history. He admired Churchill and many British institutions, but he feared British policy. His initial doubts about the development of a European Community—he first envisioned a Europe in which the various nations were only loosely tied together—changed in favor of an integrated common market. When Britain applied for membership, however, de Gaulle vetoed her application, believing that Britain must be resisted, particularly if she retained her special relationships to the United States and to the British Commonwealth. His attitude toward Germany also changed radically. At the end of the war, he hoped that Germany would be broken up into her nineteenth century components. When he returned to power in 1958, however, it was to West Germany and to its president, Konrad Adenauer, that he turned. He hoped to develop an alliance between France and West Germany to counterbalance the special relationship between the United States and Great Britain. De Gaulle and Adenauer became close, but West German policy remained anchored to NATO.

De Gaulle deplored the Soviet regime, and in times of need he stood with the West, such as during the Berlin Wall and the Cuban Missile crises. Unlike many American policymakers, however, de Gaulle did not interpret the Cold War and the Soviet threat from an ideological perspective. For him, history was the story of nations; ideologies were transient but the nation-state remained to achieve greatness or to lose it. His vision of a Europe from the Atlantic to the Urals was seen by many to be either naïve or a deliberate attempt to subvert American leadership against an opponent whose ideologies were in total opposition to Western values. Lacouture claims that de Gaulle too readily ignored ideological considerations and that his nationalistic interpretation of past and present was inadequate. Within a decade of his death, however, his vision of a Europe driven by nationalism appeared more accurate than those of his critics.

Reelected president in 1964, he resigned in 1969. The turbulence of the late 1960's affected France as elsewhere in the West, and de Gaulle was caught unprepared by student uprisings and labor demands in 1968. He survived that outbreak, but just several months later, in a badly conceived plebiscite over regional development, his government was defeated by the French voters. De Gaulle, almost eighty years old and perhaps believing that his day was done, resigned and returned to his country home, again to write his memoirs. He died suddenly on November 9, 1970. Always the rebel, his funeral was private, and the great gathering of dignitaries who descended upon France to pay their last respects had to settle for a memorial service in Paris.

Lacouture's two-volume biography of de Gaulle will not soon be surpassed, and not until all the papers of the participants of the events are released to scholars. As could be expected from a journalist of Lacouture's experience and ability, *De Gaulle: The Ruler, 1945-1970* is well written. There are, however, two major criticisms to be made. First, at times the wealth of detail threatens to overwhelm the general reader. The second criticism is of the publisher, not Lacouture. Originally published as a three-volume work in France, the American edition of the work was reduced to two, and the second volume has been drastically condensed. In particular, de Gaulle's years in political exile in the 1950's are told very briefly, and the private life of this private man is absent. Nevertheless, this is a superb study of a major world figure whose like will not soon be seen again.

*Eugene S. Larson*

## Sources for Further Study

*Chicago Tribune.* April 12, 1992, XIV, p. 6.

*Choice.* XXX, October, 1992, p. 363.

*Europe.* January, 1992, p. 53.

*Foreign Affairs.* LXXI, Summer, 1992, p. 165.

*Library Journal.* CXVII, February 15, 1992, p. 178.

*New Statesman and Society.* V, January 10, 1992, p. 39.

*The New York Review of Books.* XXXIX, April 23, 1992, p. 18.

*The New York Times Book Review.* XCVII, May 10, 1992, p. 3.

*Publishers Weekly.* CCXXXIX, February 17, 1992, p. 53.

*The Times Literary Supplement.* April 24, 1992, p. 23.

*The Washington Post Book World.* XXII, April 19, 1992, p. 4.

# DEVOLVING ENGLISH LITERATURE

*Author:* Robert Crawford (1959-     )
*Publisher:* Clarendon Press/Oxford University Press (New York). 320 pp. $22.00
*Type of work:* Literary history
*Time:* 1780-1990's
*Locale:* Scotland, England, and the United States

*Crawford demonstrates the continuing influence and presence of Scottish literature within British literature and thereby revises and expands the accepted boundaries of British literary history*

*Principal personages:*
> SIR WALTER SCOTT, the influential poet and novelist who established the popularity and prestige of the historical novel in the nineteenth century
> TOBIAS SMOLLETT, an eighteenth century novelist who showed the troubled relationships between the English and the Scots
> ROBERT BURNS, a Scottish Romantic poet who used both Scots dialect and standard English in his poems
> THOMAS CARLYLE, a nineteenth century writer whose unconventional style and views influenced many American writers, including Ralph Waldo Emerson

*Devolving English Literature* attempts to deconstruct the received literary history that posits an "English Literature" that somehow would include Scottish, Irish, and Australian elements within it. Crawford wishes to redirect critics and readers to the provincial aspects of literature, especially Scottish literature, that remain embedded in what is called "English Literature." He is a professor of modern Scottish literature, and his major interest seems to be in restoring Scottish literature to a separate and honored place distinct from English literature, although he does deal with the provincial aspects of American literature and sees modernism as a more provincial and eclectic movement than has been realized by most critics. Some readers will have expectations of a different sort of book from the title; it might better have been called "The Presence of Scottish Literature in English Literature."

*Devolving English Literature* discovers, as the first culprits in the creation of "English Literature" as a subject, certain Scots bent on improving culture during the eighteenth century. The teaching of Thomas Stevenson and Adam Smith, and later that of Hugh Blair, of university courses in "Rhetoric and Belles Lettres" was a precursor to courses in English literature. Before this, only the Greek and Roman classics were judged to be literary subjects worthy of study within a university. Now "English Literature" would be studied in Scottish universities—and later English and American universities—and it would include such classic English writers as William Shakespeare and Joseph Addison. The native writers in Scotland were to take their models and styles from approved texts included in the area of "English Literature." There was to be no respectable Scottish literature but rather an Anglocentric one that would include Scottish works only if they conformed to "English" standards. Another aim of this group was to improve the culture of their native land by purging the spoken and written language of distinctively Scottish elements. Ambitious Scots were to remove any traces of "Scotticisms" and other signs of provinciality. Adam Smith was especially important in this area, since his own example of an "un-Scottish" style influenced many aspiring young Scots. These activities were attempts at "improvements" in the culture of Scotland; they are typical, Crawford suggests, of the cultural imperialism that drives out or subsumes native or provincial literature and language.

Crawford claims that the Scots also were responsible for creating "British Literature." This is a reaction by Scottish writers to the lumping of their distinctively Scottish writing into an "English" literature. Crawford cites such writers as James Thomson, Tobias Smollett, James Boswell, and Robert Burns as being the main figures who undermined Anglocentric qualities in their poems and novels. James Thomson's poem "The Seasons" affirmed Scottish ways by celebrating the romantic landscape of Scotland. This obviously points to the special glories of a land that had not earlier been seen as beautiful. More significantly, Thomson stressed the use of the term "Britain" in order to include the distinctly Scottish elements into a new and expanded culture. "And thus united BRITAIN BRITAIN make/ Intire, th' imperial MISTRESS of the day." "Britain" was no longer merely England but an amalgam that prominently featured Scotland. Scotland would not be buried under England but would become a significant part of an inclusive Britain.

The novels of Smollett go beyond Thomson and are especially interesting for their attack upon prejudice against all Scots and their Scottish ways. The characters who are prejudiced against Scottish manners and ways are portrayed negatively and finally exposed as inadequate in *Roderick Random* (1748) and especially in *Humphry Clinker* (1771). Crawford claims that *Humphry Clinker* is "about" anti-Scottish prejudice on the part of the unthinking English. Crawford suggests that the union of characters of different nationality mirrors the union of England and Scotland. That political union, of course, created "Britain" as an entity.

Boswell, on the surface, would not seem to belong in this group, since he put aside his Scottishness in the presence of the formidable Samuel Johnson. Crawford claims, however, that Boswell defused the anti-Scottish prejudice of Johnson by showing how arbitrary and absurd it was. Crawford asserts this without much evidence or discussion, and many readers who are amused at Johnson's quips about Scotland and the Scots will not be convinced. The "Britishness" of Boswell, according to Crawford, lies in his attempt to have "access" to England while preserving his Scottish culture.

Robert Burns contributed more to this program of destabilizing the work of the eighteenth century improvers by actually opposing them in his retention of Scots dialect in his poems. Burns essentially wrote in a bilingual manner, infusing the standard language with the freshness of Scots dialect: The culture and language of the Scots was not denied or hidden in the new entity of "English Literature" but came to take its place in a British one.

The chapter "Anthropology and Dialect" deals primarily with the work of Sir Walter Scott. Scott, according to Crawford, created an "eclectic" text in *Waverley: Or, 'Tis*

*Sixty Years Since* (1814), the first of his important novels. Crawford honors the presence of the eclectic as a breaking down of unitary views; eclecticism is a key concept in his deconstruction of the received literary history. The novel is an anthology, including poems and observations on the Scottish landscape. It is also a mixture of languages, from standard English to Scots dialect. The end of the novel celebrates a union of Scotland and England, and the eclecticism creates a British perspective rather than an exclusively English one. Crawford also sees an anthropological aspect to Scott's work, since he consciously collected the work of earlier Scottish poets in his *Minstrelsy of the Scottish Border* (1802-1803). This was an act of recovering the lost or ignored cultural tradition of Scotland.

Crawford also deals with the work of Carlyle, a Scot who seems on the surface to have turned his back on Scottish elements in his life and work. Crawford suggests that Carlyle was the successor to Sir Walter Scott. Carlyle's *Past and Present* (1843) continued the work of Scott in portraying the life of the medieval period with warmth and sympathy. The contrasts that Carlyle makes between the unity of the Middle Ages and the fragmentation of modern life are devastating. In addition, Carlyle's unconventional style seems out of place in the decorum of "English Literature," and Crawford describes that strange style as a kind of Scottish dialect.

The last section in the chapter deals with the work of James G. Frazer, a Scot who wrote the influential *The Golden Bough* (1890-1915). This is more obviously a work of anthropology. The book has had an enormous influence on twentieth century writers such as T. S. Eliot, but it is not usually classified as a literary work. Crawford, however, discovers in this anthropological work a "narrative device," the travelogue, that makes it literary and directly links it to the use of such a device in the fiction of Sir Walter Scott.

The chapter on "Anthologizing America" may be of more interest to general readers than are those dealing with Scottish concerns, but Crawford is interested primarily in tracing Scottish influences upon American writers. He goes so far as to label America "another Scotland," since it too had a separate culture and literature. In addition, he shows the Scottish influence on specific writers. For example, James Fenimore Cooper's novel *The Pioneers: Or, the Sources of the Susquehanna* (1823) was, Crawford claims, influenced by Thomas Campbell's *Gertrude in Wyoming: A Pennsylvania Tale, and Other Poems* (1809). He traces specific passages from a number of Cooper's novels and shows how they are similar to various aspects of the Scottish writer's work.

Carlyle's Scottish influence on American writers is more important and widespread. The works of Ralph Waldo Emerson are filled with the views—if not the style—of Carlyle. Of special importance is Emerson's adoption of "expansion and *re*composition," from Carlyle. As Carlyle brought together various sources in a new composite form, so did Emerson, especially in his work on the new American world.

When Crawford comes to Walt Whitman, he has a difficulty that is not present in his treatment of Emerson. Whitman's poems are insistently "ensemble," composite, and eclectic, and Crawford suggests that this obsession of Whitman comes from

Scott's *Minstrelsy of the Scottish Border.* Emerson's debt to Carlyle has long been documented and acknowledged, but the claim of Scott as a primary source for Whitman is new, startling, and unconvincing. Scott's poems may have been "composite," and aimed at a national epic, but that hardly proves the alleged connection to Whitman.

"Modernism as Provincialism" may startle readers who are used to seeing modernism as a distinctively international movement that spurned all provincial thinking. Crawford claims there are benefits in "decentering" Modernism to look at its use of provincial elements, and he finds provincial writers at the heart of the movement. It was, claims Crawford, "the un-English provincials and their traditions which contributed most to the crucially provincial phenomenon which we now know as Modernism." Ezra Pound did come from Idaho and T. S. Eliot from St. Louis, but both of them buried those origins and chose instead a European cultural model. Crawford can cite a few references to Pound praising Whitman or acknowledging his Idaho origins, but most of his work is from such sources as the Italian Renaissance, Confucian China, and the Rome of Propertius, so the insistence on Pound's American and provincial origins does not get one far in redefining Modernism. Crawford's claim for Eliot's provincialism persisting in England is also only partially successful. Eliot succeeded in making himself more English than the English, and to label him a "savage" or provincial "alien" is to distort what Eliot accomplished in his poetry and criticism.

Crawford also deals with the work of Hugh MacDiarmid in this chapter. He convincingly shows how the eclectic and provincial aspects of this writer became important in the creation of Modernism. It is interesting to note that MacDiarmid wrote in a Scots dialect that immediately called attention to his provincial origins. MacDiarmid's significance has been neglected or underrated, and Crawford is helpful in calling attention to this writer.

The last chapter, "Barbarians," deals with the work of recent writers who maintained a provincial perspective in their work. Philip Larkin rejected Modernism for a plainer and simpler style and poetic form, but Crawford finds traces of such Modernists as T. S. Eliot in Larkin's work. Crawford's examples of Eliot's influence on Larkin are not convincing. Larkin's "Breadfruit" is nothing like Eliot's "Sweeney Agonistes," and Eliot's "Boston Evening Transcript" is not similar to Larkin's "The Whitsun Weddings." Crawford is on surer ground when he describes the "barbarian" elements in the work of such Scots poets as Douglas Dunn and the northern English poet Tony Harrison. These poets do not efface their origins but call the reader's attention to it in their style and subject matter.

Robert Crawford uses the deconstructive enterprise not to reread specific works of literature but to question and redefine the received version of the British literary history of the last two centuries. In order for this to be fully effective, however, Crawford's limited vision needs to be expanded. It is useful to call attention to the importance of Scottish literature, but what of the importance of Irish writing in the twentieth century? Surely, James Joyce and William Butler Yeats are more important to Modernism than Hugh MacDiarmid. The project of *Devolving English Literature* needs to be expanded and revised so that the redefinition of the British literary tradition can come more fully into being.

*James Sullivan*

## Sources for Further Study

*London Review of Books.* XIV, July 9, 1992, p. 10.
*New Statesman and Society.* V, August 21, 1992, p. 41.
*Poetry Review.* LXXXII, Fall, 1992, p. 42.
*The Times Literary Supplement.* January 1, 1993, p. 5.

# DIDEROT
## A Critical Biography

*Author:* P. N. Furbank (1920-    )
*Publisher:* Alfred A. Knopf (New York). Illustrated. 524 pp. $30.00
*Type of work:* Literary biography
*Time:* 1713-1784
*Locale:* France

*Furbank provides a critical biography of this polymath of the Enlightenment, interspersing details of Diderot's life with analyses of his works*

*Principal personages:*
DENIS DIDEROT, an encyclopedist and philosopher
ANNE-TOINETTE (NANETTE) CHAMPION DIDEROT, his wife
JEAN LE ROND D'ALEMBERT, coeditor with Diderot of the *Encyclopédie*
JEAN-JACQUES ROUSSEAU, a political philosopher and writer
PAUL-HENRI THIRY (BARON D'HOLBACH), a patron of the *philosophes* and
    major contributor to the *Encyclopédie*
FRIEDRICH MELCHIOR GRIMM, a German man of letters resident in France;
    a commentator on the Enlightenment
LOUISE-HENRIETTE (SOPHIE) VOLLAND, the mistress and confidential cor-
    respondent of Diderot
LOUISE DE LA LIVE D'ÉPINAY, a protector and friend of Rousseau, later of
    Diderot; a mistress of Grimm
FRANÇOIS-MARIE AROUET DE VOLTAIRE, a philosopher and man of letters;
    a contributor to and supporter of the *Encyclopédie*
CATHERINE II (THE GREAT), the empress of Russia; a supporter and protector
    of Diderot

P. N. Furbank's admirable *Diderot: A Critical Biography* surveys virtually every aspect of the fascinating period of secular intellectual ferment known as the Enlightenment. Broadly viewed, this movement swept Europe, accelerated the development of colonial America, and reflected a response to the conservatism of church and state that prevailed in Europe through the end of the seventeenth century. Its real impetus, as Furbank's study makes eminently clear, came from the rise of popular science, though its transmission occurred through popular philosophy. The massive undertaking that came to be known as the *Encyclopédie* (1751-1765) represents the underlying diversity of the Enlightenment, and Denis Diderot, the polymath who shepherded the work from inception to completion, typifies the versatile intellect that eighteenth century France produced.

Diderot's life spanned those years of the century that produced the most important aspects of the Enlightenment. Even in his youth he had adopted as his own one of its fundamental tenets, that the only limit on inquiry should be the bounds of the human intellect. Born in the provincial town of Langres, he might at another time have followed the trade of his father and become a master cutler. As it happened, his apprenticeship lasted a total of five days. The Jesuits of his boyhood school considered him unruly and undisciplined, while his father, Didier, became so exasperated by his son's apparent irresponsibility during his student years in Paris that he refused all financial support.

Diderot's student years, 1728-1732, initiated a pattern of events important in his development. Having matriculated at the strongly Jansenist Collège d'Harcourt, Diderot would finish his student period at the University of Paris, from which he obtained a master of arts degree. It may be that Diderot's vague goal of obtaining a doctoral degree in theology originated during his Sorbonne period, but it is clear that his revolt against dogmatic thinking dates from this time.

Events moved swiftly for him thereafter. Denied the family financial support he required to maintain his studies and his excessive personal expenditures, Diderot did not hesitate to convince a Carmelite friar that he had a vocation to the religious life. This audacity paid his debts, though it did not produce a Carmelite novice; indeed, it enraged Didier and further estranged him from his son. More than a decade would pass before Diderot would be reconciled with his family. This prolonged period of residence in Paris would provide Diderot's introduction to many in the intellectual vanguard that came to be known as the philosophes. All these individuals ranged far beyond their original areas of expertise, and all were united in their conviction that the human mind would triumph if left unfettered by dogmatic institutions. This conviction gave their writings a decidedly political cast and necessarily placed them in opposition to the positions espoused by the French government and the Roman Catholic church. It is both significant and inevitable that what began as intellectual contention in virtually every discipline—the sciences, philosophy and theology, and even music and art—would develop in the political sphere and emerge in the American and French revolutions.

Diderot responded to this ferment. By 1741, Diderot had married Anne-Toinette (Nanette) Champion. He established a bohemian *ménage* with her, her mother, and the two children who would be born to them in the years immediately following their marriage. Both these children would die in infancy, and only a third child, a daughter named Angélique, would survive to adulthood. Perhaps this offers one indication of how precarious Diderot's personal circumstances would remain until publication of the first volume of the *Encyclopédie*. It is certainly true, however, that Diderot's acquaintance with Jean-Jacques Rousseau and Diderot's first independent work, *Pensées philosophiques* (1746; philosophical thoughts), had attracted attention in official circles. In the summer of 1749, amid rumors of national bankruptcy and sexual scandal in high places, Diderot was arrested by royal warrant and imprisoned with others considered dangerous in the prison fortress of Vincennes, six miles east of Paris. Diderot would remain imprisoned through that summer, and it was only by written repudiation of writings the authorities considered objectionable that he managed to obtain his release.

Vincennes, then, did not reveal a particularly idealistic or courageous Diderot, but his release from prison and his conspicuous welcome by Rousseau did wonders for the *Encyclopédie* project, then in its infancy. André-François Le Breton, one of the leading French publishers, had envisioned it as early as 1745, but various obstacles, including the resignation of its first editor, had caused it to become hopelessly stalled. Le Breton boldly named Diderot and a philosophe mathematician, Jean Le Rond d'Alembert, as replacements for the resigned abbé. This change of editorship would provide the philosophes with what would become one of the most important vehicles of Enlightenment thinking.

Diderot and d'Alembert, from the first, conceived of a comprehensive encyclopedia that would also serve as a dictionary. It would be modern and emphasize technology and philosophy; by eighteenth century definition, this meant it also would be controversial and potentially subversive. Diderot would always be the moving force behind the *Encyclopédie*, and though he would have the support of some of the most impressive intellects the century produced, he would spend the twenty years of his mid-career struggling to incorporate Enlightenment ideas while evading censorship or suppression of what he published.

Two centuries before another group of French scholars, the deconstructionists, began to consider the subversive nature of language, Diderot had mastered the art of injecting heterodox points of view into his encyclopedia. In places he did this merely by featuring discussions of topics such as materialism, religion, determinism, perception, or nature; even more revealing, however, are his puckish cross-references. His primary cross-references for "anthrophagy" (eating human flesh) are "eucharist," "communion," and "altar," in that order. Such depersonalized inclusions and offhandedly heterodox references offered a means of evading censorship even as they provided an outlet for Diderot's own points of view.

It is fortunate that Diderot was able to attract outstanding support for the *Encyclopédie* but also ironic how many of these alliances led either to estrangement or to outright enmity. His publisher, Le Breton, recalling the royal suspension of publication that had taken place in 1759, bowdlerized many of the more controversial entries without consulting Diderot in order to make them more acceptable to the censors. The result was that Diderot finished this twenty-year project from a sense of duty rather than with real enthusiasm. His coeditor, d'Alembert, originally entrusted with the articles on science and technology, broke with Diderot over an article d'Alembert had written on the city of Geneva. Rightly, d'Alembert emphasized the Swiss city's paradoxical stance on free thinking. On one hand, it was home to François-Marie Arouet de Voltaire, the preeminent philosophe, but it also had been home to John Calvin and Calvinism. D'Alembert argued that this placed an indelible stamp of provincialism and closed-mindedness on the city. Diderot, who was caught between Le Breton's desire to modify the article and his allegiance to d'Alembert, found himself estranged from his friend after d'Alembert withdrew from active involvement with the entire encyclopedia project.

Diderot would himself irrevocably terminate the friendship by writing a dialogue on what he imagined to be his old friend's innermost thoughts. This work of irreverent presumptuousness, entitled *Le rêve de d'Alembert* (1769; d'Alembert's dream), was Diderot's serious consideration of created matter's wholeness, but it was also invasive.

Not only did the work place Diderot's ideas in d'Alembert's sleeping consciousness, but it also compromised Julie de l'Espinasse, d'Alembert's mistress. In fairness to Diderot, he was careful always to print privately those of his works that named living persons; even so, the limited circulation they received (usually in the private journal of Friedrich Melchior Grimm known as *La Correspondance littéraire*) reached those most closely acquainted with the individuals named.

Although Diderot often alienated those closest to him through this unusual technique of mixing reality and fiction, it was the most distinctive feature of his nonencyclopedic writing, and it served as a vehicle for exposition of his own philosophical positions. Elements of this ingenious technique also appear in his *Le neveu de Rameau* (Rameau's nephew), a dialogue written between 1762 and 1763 but not published until 1805, more than twenty years after Diderot's death and even then in German translation. It would be 1821 before Diderot's countrymen would read a reconstituted French version.

*Le neveu de Rameau* is essentially a discourse on genius and celebrity that features the eccentric and ne'er-do-well nephew of famed composer Jean-Philippe Rameau. Jean-François Rameau was also a musician, though a mediocre one. The book places Rameau in a conversation with Diderot at Paris' Café de la Régence, a haunt for chess players. Rameau argues with Diderot for the necessity of mediocrity, since hundreds of mediocre persons must exist to produce one individual that the world would categorize as a "genius." He contends that geniuses are limited in all respects other than the area in which they excel; they are, therefore, at a disadvantage and often incapable of dealing with the larger world in which they exist. Genius and fame do not, according to Rameau, provide the means to a happy or well-lived life.

Diderot surely was thinking of his own situation when he wrote *Le neveu de Rameau*. The relative anonymity of his work on the encyclopedia, the vast amount of time he had devoted to editing, revising, and occasionally rewriting works that would bring others fame, must have weighed heavily upon him. Friends whom he had served, among them Rousseau, deserted and repudiated him. Others, such as the wealthy Paul-Henri Thiry (Baron d'Holbach), supported the encyclopedia project but fell away from Diderot after its completion. Grimm, however, remained faithful, and it is upon him that Diderot's life settled following completion of the *Encyclopédie*.

Grimm was a German with connections to Frederick the Great. It was he who encouraged Diderot first in the writing of plays, then in the area of criticism. Diderot's art criticism is particularly ingenious. Like his fiction, it shares the characteristic of authorial involvement. Diderot believed that the person perceiving a work of art (as much as a reader of a book) was essential to the artistic experience. For this reason, Diderot's salon reviews, published in Grimm's *La Correspondance littéraire*, frequently place the critic in the paintings he critiques. Diderot often imagines himself as a part of the narrative the painting describes; in doing this, he recognizes the highly personal experience of all the arts. In one respect, the viewer, auditor, or reader of a work of art requires greater, more flexible sensitivity than does the artist, since one who appreciates must see the conception of its creator in purely personal terms.

Likewise, an appreciative member of a theater audience will, according to Diderot, feel the impact of drama more keenly than either the playwright or the play's actors, who already have come to terms with their emotions and are thus concerned with effective transmission of a work.

Grimm's appreciation of Diderot's critical talent ultimately would assure Diderot's financial security. Grimm's diplomatic connections secured Diderot a subvention from Catherine the Great, empress of Russia. Through this unusual arrangement, Diderot became curator of his own library, which Catherine purchased but left in place for Diderot's continued use. At Catherine's behest, Diderot advised on and purchased many of the paintings that would form the basis of the Hermitage collection.

Catherine's subvention provided a dowry for Diderot's only surviving child, Angélique, whom he reared, much against the wishes of his wife Nanette, as an atheist and freethinker. In part, it was Nanette's lack of sympathy for Diderot's theological and philosophical views that led him to long associations with Louise de la Live d'Épinay and Louise-Henriette (Sophie) Volland. D'Épinay originally was Rousseau's protector and later was Grimm's mistress. Like many of Rousseau's friends, she was badly treated, and this drove her to a more stable friendship with Diderot. She became one of his major correspondents, and it is likely that Diderot found in her the intellectual sympathy he had never discovered in his wife, Nanette. Volland provided Diderot with a sexual relationship he also lacked in his marriage, but even here the intellectual alliance was more important. Their correspondence is far-ranging and amazingly sophisticated. It indicates that Diderot valued her reactions to his ideas on aesthetics and critical theory.

Furbank's study reveals a Diderot whose greatest importance exists in the influence he had upon the aesthetic standards of ensuing generations. This critical emphasis is its greatest single difference from the biography written by Arthur Wilson in 1957. Furbank demonstrates that Diderot provides important linkages in a variety of the arts: in fiction between Laurence Sterne and the modern psychological novel; in theater between the static drama of Carlo Goldoni and the realism of the nineteenth century; and in criticism on the role of the audience as participants in the artistic process, a position that finds its fullest development in the deconstructionism of the twentieth century. In philosophy, Diderot foreshadows the materialists even as he reflects the Enlightenment and the antistate, anticlerical sentiments of his own period. In every sense, Diderot was thus a polymath, and it was the time in which he lived as much as his own genius that made this possible.

*Robert J. Forman*

## Sources for Further Study

*Library Journal.* CXVII, November 1, 1992, p. 90.
*London Review of Books.* XIV, August 20, 1992, p. 7.

*Los Angeles Times Book Review.* November 15, 1992, p. 3.
*New Statesman and Society.* V, May 8, 1992, p. 40.
*The New York Times.* November 25, 1992, p. C20.
*The New York Times Book Review.* XCVIII, January 24, 1993, p. 9.
*Newsweek.* CXX, October 12, 1992, p. 80.
*The Observer.* April 26, 1992, p. 57.
*Publishers Weekly.* CCXXXIX, September 21, 1992, p. 81.
*The Times Literary Supplement.* May 1, 1992, p. 5.
*The Wall Street Journal.* December 17, 1992, p. A16.

# THE DIVERSITY OF LIFE

*Author:* Edward O. Wilson (1929-    )
*Publisher:* The Belknap Press of Harvard University Press (Cambridge, Massachusetts).
424 pp. $29.95
*Type of work:* Science

*Wilson provides a review of current views on evolutionary theory and ecology and pleads for the preservation of the world's biological diversity*

Edward O. Wilson is an entomologist specializing in ants, the recognized leader of biodiversity studies, the founder of sociobiology, and a talented writer. Combining impeccable scientific credentials with the ability to communicate with the lay public, Wilson pleads for the reversal of what he calls "the sixth great extinction spasm," the destruction of a large fraction of living species within a single human generation.

As a student of ants, Wilson looks at issues of preservation, ecology, and biodiversity in ways different from many people, even different from many biologists. He does not focus only on the possible disappearance of the spotted owl, or large mammals, or majestic birds of prey, although he understands the appeal of such animals to the public. When he speaks of a diverse biosystem, he includes all plants and animals, no matter what their size, aesthetic attraction, or apparent usefulness. He is just as concerned about the thirty species of feather mites that live exclusively on the feathers of a particular species of parrot as he is about that bird or the tree in which the bird lives. From tiny parasite to huge tree, all living things are parts of ecosystems.

The problem he brings before the reader is that 90 percent of all species now living on the earth have never been described by scientists. For all intents and purposes, no one knows they exist. Many may become extinct before they are understood. At first glance, this might seem to be strictly an academic issue, of interest only to biologists. Why should the lay public worry about obscure and undescribed fungi or insects? Wilson's answer is twofold. First, some of these species may have economic value, either as food sources or sources of medicine. Humanity cannot risk destroying a possible natural cure for cancer out of ignorance. Second, the loss of a species or a number of species may lead to the collapse of an entire ecosystem. The consequences of human actions may be far more widespread than anticipated.

Wilson begins with a discussion of small-scale and large-scale annihilations of life, ranging from the fall of a tree in a rain forest to the destruction of an island by volcanic eruption and finally to the five great extinctions of the last half billion years, extinctions in which 90 percent of all species living at the time may have perished. The lesson he wishes the reader to draw from these accounts is that nature easily recovers from localized destruction. It can even rebound from a great extinction. Biodiversity can be restored. The time required for such a restoration on a planetary scale, however, is measured in the tens of millions of years. Unlike localized destruction, which can be restored within a few years, the global destruction that humans could inflict on the planet Earth in a single human lifetime cannot be repaired in millions of lifetimes.

The second section of the book is an excellent popular account of current views of evolution and related theories in biology. To understand the significance of biodiversity, one must first understand taxonomy, classification, evolutionary theory, and ecology. Aided by clear illustrations, Wilson provides a series of lessons in biology worthy of the great teacher he is. In doing so, he also acknowledges the limitations of scientific truth. Sometimes, the best that science can offer is a concept that is provisionally acceptable to a majority of scientists. Wilson makes clear when and if he is presenting the consensus view or his own personal opinion. He also provides the alternative theories. The provisional nature of science is brought out most explicitly in his discussion of the definition of species, the most fundamental concept for biodiversity and systematic biology. He concedes that the currently accepted working definition of a species as "a population whose members are able to interbreed freely under natural conditions" may be at best a pragmatic compromise that works most of the time. Scientists are not as certain about truth as some journalistic accounts imply.

In his final section, Wilson writes about the impact of humans on biodiversity. The history of human effect is dismal. No matter what their culture or race, the introduction of humans to a new ecology has led to the mass destruction of large mammals and flightless birds. This was true for North America, Madagascar, New Zealand, and Australia, whether the humans were Paleo-Indians, Polynesians, or Dutch sailors. More recently, habitat destruction has become the most significant cause of extinction, with the introduction of exotic animals into ecosystems second. Overharvesting is relatively insignificant. One example consists of fresh-water fish species. When habitat destruction is defined as either the physical destruction of the habitat or pollution of the habitat to an extent that it becomes unusable by a species, habitat destruction has been a significant cause in more than 90 percent of known fish species extinctions within recent historical times.

What makes the problem of habitat destruction so complicated is that solutions are necessarily international. An example is Bachman's warbler, a bird that bred in the riverine swamplands of the southern United States and that is now thought to be extinct. Its habitat in the United States is abundant; however, it winters in the forests of Cuba, which have been destroyed for sugarcane agriculture. Likewise, the habitat of Kirkland's warbler in Michigan might be preserved, but its wintering grounds in the Bahamas are still under threat.

Complicating matters even further are two realities of human population and resource distribution. The most biodiverse regions of the earth are the tropical rain forests, which happen to be in some of the poorest countries that also have the fastest-growing populations. In North America and Europe, habitats can be saved by declaring them as parks and closing them off to commercial exploitation. In the rain forests, the solution is more complicated. Any solution must recognize that the first obligation of humans is to feed themselves and their children. Second, the human population will triple by the middle of the twenty-first century. The pressure upon habitats will be tremendous, even in environmentally sensitive societies.

Wilson's solutions are in the context of what he calls the "New Environmentalism," a recognition that there is practical value in wild species. Perhaps overoptimistically, he claims that "there is no longer an ideological war between conservationists and developers." According to Wilson, both sides recognize that a healthy economic return is dependent upon a healthy environment. Accompanying this economic approach to the environment is a shift in attention from the so-called "star species"—those that attract media attention, such as pandas, tigers, or redwoods—to the environments in which these star species live. Simply because the star species become extinct is not a reason to abandon preservation of the ecosystem. There are many species of equivalent significance still in the ecosystem, even if not of equivalent beauty, size, or cuteness.

Wilson's plea ends with a set of very specific recommendations for both the very near future and two generations hence. First, Wilson calls for a survey of the world's flora and fauna, to be carried out over the next fifty years. The realities of economics and politics make it difficult to preserve until it is known what exists to be preserved. This will require, among other things, increased funding for the training of systematists as well as support for their research and publication. Second, bioeconomic analysis must become part of routine land management. Better knowledge of the wealth that species represent must become more widely known. Third, sustainable development must be promoted. The inefficient exploitation of natural resources in the Third World must be reversed. Blame can be divided among both the wealthy nations, which exacerbate the situation with their trade and other economic policies, and the poorer nations, which desperately need population-control policies if the human species is not to overwhelm all others. Fourth, Wilson promotes saving what species remain, whether in the form of seed or gene banks, genetic stock in zoos or gardens, or (when and where possible) in natural ecosystems. Wilson's last recommendation is to restore the wildlands. Underlying all of his recommendations is the belief that biodiversity is a public resource, to be defended not simply by ethical pressure or economic incentives but by force of national and international law.

For those readers wishing to explore particular issues more deeply, Wilson supplies notes that double as a bibliography. As an aid to those readers whose grasp of the vocabulary of biology is limited, he provides an excellent glossary of technical terms, that also includes very brief biographical sketches of important scientists.

Wilson's book is very optimistic. The villain, to the extent Wilson identifies one, is ignorance, not greed. Greed is a very difficult motive to overcome. Ignorance, on the other hand, can be overcome. If Wilson is correct and the New Environmentalism is the wave of the future, if education can reverse current economic policies among the industrial nations and resource exploitation policies among the developing nations, and if the human race will stabilize its growth during the next two generations, then there is hope. If not, then the sixth great extinction spasm will continue and biodiversity on this planet will end in a wink of geological time, perhaps never to be restored.

*Marc Rothenberg*

## Sources for Further Study

*Audubon.* XCIV, November, 1992, p. 124.
*The Christian Science Monitor.* October 22, 1992, p. 11.
*Library Journal.* CXVII, November 1, 1992, p. 114.
*New Scientist.* CXXXVI, November 14, 1992, p. 43.
*The New York Review of Books.* XXXIX, November 5, 1992, p. 3.
*The New York Times Book Review.* XCVII, October 4, 1992, p. 1.
*Newsweek.* CXX, October 19, 1992, p. 69.
*Science News.* CXLII, September 26, 1992, p. 194.
*Scientific American.* CCLXVI, March, 1993, p. 146.
*Time.* CXL, November 16, 1992, p. 101.
*Washington Monthly.* XXIV, October, 1992, p. 56.
*The Washington Post Book World.* XXII, September 27, 1992, p. 1.

# THE DOUBLE LIFE OF STEPHEN CRANE
## A Biography

*Author:* Christopher Benfey (1954-    )
*Publisher:* Alfred A. Knopf (New York). Illustrated. 294 pp. $25.00
*Type of work:* Literary biography
*Time:* 1871-1900
*Locale:* New Jersey, New York, Florida, Cuba, Greece, and England

*This brief biography suggests a reinterpretation of the relationship between Crane's life and his work*

*Principal personages:*
STEPHEN CRANE, an American fiction writer
JONATHAN TOWNLEY CRANE, his father
MARY HELEN PECK CRANE, his mother
CORA TAYLOR, his common-law wife

This life of probably the most original and possibly the most enigmatic of America's major fiction writers shatters the rule that literary biography runs long. Discounting index and notes, white space, the twenty-six superb photographs, and the copious quotations from Crane and other sources, fewer than two hundred pages of text remain. The volume also raises the question of just how much biography can do to elucidate literature. The answer depends less on the erudition and skill of the biographer than on the nature of the subject. The fiction of Charles Dickens, for example, is so deeply embedded in his time and place and in the author's own well-documented social concerns, springing so clearly out of the traumas of his childhood, that biography is critical to understanding it. The case of Stephen Crane could not be more different. For most of his brief lifetime he was an outsider, a social and cultural exile, despite his lionization for *The Red Badge of Courage* (1895). At crucial times he was actually an expatriate. Moreover, whereas Dickens' life is revealed almost day to day by thousands of letters and by the periodicals he edited, few of Crane's letters are preserved and most of those are unrevealing. For long stretches, not only during his childhood, he virtually disappears. The challenge he offers a biographer is formidable.

It is so formidable, in fact, that Crane's early biographer Thomas Beer, in his *Stephen Crane: A Study in American Letters* (1923), met it by invention. According to articles published in 1990 and 1991, which Benfey cites, Beer himself forged many of the letters from which he "quotes." Thus "half the clues to Crane's life have gone up in smoke." It would have been interesting to learn more about the extent of and evidence for the forgeries; in any event, the situation Benfey reveals suggests something of the nature of his own contribution. Inasmuch as biographers since 1923 have drawn heavily from Beer, Benfey is able to do a good deal to clear the air. If he himself at times goes fairly well out on speculative limbs, at least he is engagingly tentative about it. The informal and undogmatic tone of this biography, in fact, is one of the most enjoyable aspects of it.

*The Double Life of Stephen Crane* is by no means thesis-bound. The author adopts the sensible course of tracking down clues as he comes to them, even if sometimes into blind alleys. The volume does, however, proceed from a basic premise: that Crane, instead of writing about experience, "did the reverse: he tried to live what he'd already written." The biographer's challenge, therefore,

> is to make sense of Crane's fascinating attempts to live his fictions, to make his life an analogue of his work. . . . This doesn't mean we can dispense with psychological explanations in making sense of Crane's life and work. On the contrary, we must deal with a psyche so powerful that it shaped events according to its own, mainly literary, patterns.

In demonstrating that this pattern exists, Benfey clearly succeeds; the evidence is irrefutable. Inevitably, he is less successful in answering the difficult analytical questions to which it points: why did Crane live this way, and what are the implications for appreciating his work?

Since little is known directly of Crane's childhood, Benfey begins by deducing what he can from the lives of Crane's parents. Crane's father was a Methodist clergyman "opposed to dancing and the reading of fiction"; his mother, a "lecturer and pamphleteer for the Women's Christian Temperance Union." Crane, growing up in this household in New Jersey and rural New York, would seem to have experienced a straitlaced but fairly ordinary childhood. Benfey, however, speculates convincingly on the later effects of a variety of traumas. Crane, to begin with, was the last of fourteen children, of whom the four preceding him had died in infancy. Given the emotional exhaustion inherent for his mother in such a situation as well as her interest in the Temperance Union (founded in 1874, just as Crane turned three), Crane may well have had very limited mothering. When Crane was four, his father was demoted to the itinerant ministry as a result of a question of doctrine. The demotion probably caused familial stress. Crane's father died when Crane was eight years old. "Crane's works," Benfey points out, "are notable for their absent fathers, their harassed and difficult mothers." Crane's mother, in fact, "suffered some sort of mental breakdown in 1886." Benfey makes no pretense of defining the precise effects of these events. If art is an attempt to exorcise ghosts or heal wounds, however, Crane was surely in no want of either.

Crane's formal education began late and ended early. Benfey suggests that he associated the written word with grief: His father died when he was learning to read, around the age of eight; his mother, in 1891, when he was learning the writer's craft. Certainly the mood of *Maggie: A Girl of the Streets* (1896; privately printed, 1893) supports that hypothesis. The compelling external evidence Benfey presents, moreover, indicates that most of this first short novel was drafted just before her death and before Crane arrived in New York in the fall of 1891. Thus he would indeed have written it first, and only later verified the details of life in the slums.

With Crane, the boundaries between fact and fiction, life and work, tend to blur. Inspired in part by the sensationalistic journalistic traditions of his time, but surely as well by his obsessive desire to create his life by writing, he "reported" a spectacular fire that he had in fact made up. His sketch "An Experiment in Misery" (1894) is exactly that: He spent a night in New York's underworld. Although Benfey's attempt to date the writing of *Maggie* by internal evidence is speculative, he makes, in the process, a fascinating point: "In his idealized portrait of a prostitute he was already imagining the kind of fallen woman whom he later sought out, first in the streets of New York, and then in the aptly named Hotel de Dream." The second reference is to Cora Taylor, who became Crane's common-law wife.

Much has been made of the fact that Crane, born six years after the Civil War ended, wrote *The Red Badge of Courage* with no direct experience of war. He had had some military training in college and presumably listened to veterans' stories, yet "the greatest war novel written by an American still seems, in essential ways, to come out of nowhere." Crane researched the book by reading a series of pieces by veterans published in *Century* magazine but complained that none of the authors revealed what they felt. That remained the work of the brilliant speculative artist. Crane, as Benfey points out, then made obsessive—ultimately successful, in Greece and in Cuba near the end of his life—efforts to experience war for himself, to see, as he told his friend Joseph Conrad, if *The Red Badge of Courage* was "all right."

*The Third Violet* (1897), a novel that followed *The Red Badge of Courage*, is according to Benfey "among Crane's unfairly forgotten works." Such a statement about a work that, given the fame of its author, has had every opportunity to be remembered is necessarily suspect. Whatever its literary interest, however, it holds (as Benfey convincingly argues) the key to Crane's love life. The story of a rustic artist caught between his interest in a remote socialite and a physically immediate model, it "established and predicted the terms of Crane's own sexual activities and proclivities during the rest of his life." In the novel the model, though not a prostitute, has something of that aura; Crane was soon to become involved with the prostitute Dora Clark and later to marry the madam of a brothel. It is the inaccessible socialite, however, whom the character ultimately desires. Crane later fell in love with such a woman seemingly by a pure act of will, since he had met her only once. In his letters to Nellie Crouse of Akron, Ohio, from which Benfey quotes extensively, he painfully attempts to create a self that she will find acceptable. His inevitable failure reveals something of the psychic hazard of attempting to invent one's life through literary art.

The story of Crane's involvement with Dora Clark—a crucial episode in that it led to a feud with the New York Police Department, culminating in his withdrawal from the city—has long been misleadingly told, in Benfey's view, "as a tale of gallantry and coincidence, with Stephen Crane coming to the rescue of a woman wrongly accused of prostitution." Crane was working for a newspaper that encouraged its writers to make news rather than merely reporting it; his deep tendency, moreover, was to create the terms of existence, in life as in art. Benfey's argument that he stage-managed the whole affair is, like so much else in this book, unprovable but suggestive.

Cora Taylor, whom Crane met in Florida in 1896, while covering the Cuban insurrection, "stood for adventure, the sea, the great world—everything Crane was in quest of." That too is speculation, since whatever letters he wrote to her have never surfaced. Benfey therefore is able to reveal little of the nature of their relationship. At least it is evident that Cora was herself adventurous—accompanying Crane to Greece, for example, to cover the war there—and in that sense a good match. Crane's wanderings in his last years, perhaps in search of his own "red badge of courage," seem to have been limited only by the wars available to cover and by his failing health. Benfey effectively documents the frenetic urgency of this period, during which Crane wrote his greatest stories. He is unable, however, to say when Crane became aware that he was dying of tuberculosis; thus he can only speculate as to the ways in which Crane's sense of onrushing mortality colored his art.

This biography is in general least satisfying in the passages devoted to literary interpretation. The odd chapter entitled "Ominous Babies," for example, applies Freudian theory at length to several of Crane's early city stories while begging the question of the source of their real power: Accurately observed social realism is commonplace and tends to date, but Crane, his imaginative genius striking deeply inward, raised his to an art form. In *The Red Badge of Courage*, Benfey claims, the army is all body whereas the hero is all mind, the task of the story being to bring the two together. That is a dressed-up commonplace: Henry Fleming's movement, obviously, is from abstract theory to physical reality. And Benfey's dismissal of *The Red Badge of Courage* as antiwar novel is too offhand; there are strong arguments for that reading which need to be examined if the subject is opened at all. He argues plausibly for veiled religious motifs in "The Blue Hotel" (1989) but is less convincing in his assertion that "Crane means the Last Supper to serve as an analogue for the story he is telling about the Swede"; this is in keeping with the largely unenlightening approach of an earlier generation of critics to *The Red Badge of Courage*. In general, quotations seem unnecessarily drawn out; at times they resemble padding.

The brevity of *The Double Life of Stephen Crane* is a significant issue. The valuable information and insights it contains could fit easily into a monograph or into three or four articles. Its publication in this form may have something to do with the prestige value of books, as opposed to articles, in the world of literary scholarship. Nevertheless, the result is that Benfey's research is conveniently accessible to the general reading public—along with the wonderful and moving photographs of Crane, a sufficient reason in themselves to read the book. This biography is by no means indispensable to an appreciation of Crane's fiction; unless a great many more clues turn up, no biography will be. It is, however, lively, engaging, and consistently interesting.

*Edwin Moses*

**Sources for Further Study**

*Booklist*. LXXXIX, September 1, 1992, p. 25.
*Chicago Tribune*. September 13, 1992, XIV, p. 1.

*The Christian Science Monitor.* September 28, 1992, p. 15.

*Kirkus Reviews.* LX, July 15, 1992, p. 890.

*Los Angeles Times Book Review.* September 27, 1992, p. 3.

*The New Republic.* CCVII, December 21, 1992, p. 40.

*The New York Times Book Review.* XCVII, September 6, 1992, p. 10.

*Newsweek.* CXX, October 12, 1992, p. 80.

*Publishers Weekly.* CCXXXIX, July 20, 1992, p. 241.

*The Washington Post Book World.* XXII, September 20, 1992, p. 3.

# DOWN FROM TROY
## A Doctor Comes of Age

*Author:* Richard Selzer (1928-    )
*Publisher:* William Morrow (New York). 300 pp. $20.00
*Type of work:* Memoir
*Time:* 1928-1992
*Locale:* Troy, New York; and New Haven, Connecticut

Down from Troy *presents a poignant account of Richard Selzer's childhood as a doctor's son in Depression-era Troy*

> *Principal personages:*
> RICHARD SELZER, a surgeon and writer
> BILLY SELZER, Richard's older brother
> GERTRUDE SELZER, Richard's mother, a singer/soubrette
> JULIUS SELZER, Richard's father, a general practitioner in Troy, New York
> JON, Richard's son, a sculptor
> DUFFY, a wounded war veteran and storyteller

In his memoir *Down from Troy*, surgeon-writer Richard Selzer revisits his childhood home of Troy, New York, where he grew up during the Depression years. Selzer describes his transformation from a frail, bookish child to an eager assistant to his father's general medical practice among the working-class Irish families of Troy. His parents were temperamentally very different—his father a tolerant, humane, skeptical physician and his mother a volatile, emotional cabaret singer and soubrette. His parents, of Russian Jewish background, had moved south from Montreal and settled where his father could open a general practice. Richard, his parents, and his older brother Billy lived above his father's office, in a three-story red-brick building with a high stoop and curved wrought iron railings. The building burned when Richard was seven years old.

Selzer's memoir is very personal, even painful at times, as he recalls the emotional tensions in his highly charged family. His parents did not get along and often quarreled about his future. His mother wanted him to be a writer and his father preferred that he become a surgeon. Richard became the prize in their struggle, their family's version of the Trojan War. His father was rational and skeptical, his mother emotional and impulsive; each saw the world very differently. His father was content with his work and location, his mother restless and discontented in upstate Troy. His mother would fill the house with her silvery soprano voice, singing opera arias, while his father would quietly come up to dinner after his six-to-eight o'clock evening office hours were over.

As a child, Selzer loved the shabby children's room of the Troy Public Library. His mother encouraged him to read, despite his father's objections. Selzer was a voracious reader of fairy tales, myths and legends, fantasies, and epic adventures, especially Homer's *Iliad* and *Odyssey*. Selzer plays the mythic, heroic Greek allusions of the city's namesake against the harshness, disorder, and violence of his childhood world.

He mythologizes the commonplace landscapes of his native town by associating them with the Trojan War, even personifying the Hudson River as a river god that demanded its share of sacrifices each year through accidents and drownings.

In his memoir, Selzer pays tribute to the enormous formative influence of his father, an old-fashioned small-town physician who healed through touch, by his careful and compassionate examinations—sometimes all he could do for his patients. "His idea of doctoring," Selzer recalls, "was to treat the symptoms and trust the sickness to become discouraged and go away." His father believed in courtesy, even to his poorest and most destitute patients. He would make the rounds in the county jail, encouraging the poor, alcoholic, tubercular inmates with his cheerful greetings. He would never give up on his patients, treating them as tenderly as he did the spindly cyclamen plant that he kept alive for fifteen years. During World War II, when there was a shortage of practice, Selzer's father took on a second, country practice outside of Troy and kept such long hours that he collapsed and died from overwork when Selzer was twelve years old. His father's final influence came through his death, which motivated Selzer to emulate him through the career he chose.

There is much that is gothic, even morbid, in Selzer's reminiscences, which are always suffused with an aura of death. He seems torn between his desire, as a physician, to heal the wounded and battered humanity that he encounters, and his fascination, as an artist, with the mechanics of sickness, disease, and death as entities unto themselves. Surgery and writing have much in common, Selzer claims, since they involve either healing or creating. One spills blood or ink, sutures flesh or words, and predicts or imagines various outcomes. From early childhood, he was torn between his fascinations with doctoring and storytelling. Although he chose surgery as a profession, his creative urge remained unsatisfied until, at the age of forty, he began to write gothic short stories based upon his experiences as a surgeon. His mentor as a storyteller was the garrulous Duffy, a wounded World War I veteran and regular patron at Troy's Central Tavern who regaled patrons with his extravagant stories. One of Duffy's favorite tales was of the Mohawk Indian who fell from a girder during construction of the Watervliet bridge and was entombed in the freshly poured concrete of a bridge pillar. When the young Selzer challenged his veracity, the indignant Duffy replied, "We are not a liar. We are a storyteller."

Selzer's memoir makes use of an interrupted chronology to move back and forth between anecdotes and memories as child, medical student, surgeon, and writer. His prose evokes the dirty, sooty, grimy ethos of Depression-era Troy, with its winter coal smoke, dirty snow, and frozen Hudson River. He offers lush descriptions of the local bars, jails, hospitals, and whorehouses to which he followed his father on medical calls. Selzer seems to have a penchant for grotesque memories and recollections, from the brutal beating of an aging prostitute by some gangsters outside his house, to the gustatory delights of three immensely fat women exclaiming over their dinner, to the varicose veins of a now-elderly childhood friend whom he visits after she sends him a sentimental "Dear Dicky-bird" note.

Selzer tells everything in this memoir, from the embarrassment of his sexual initiation in a Troy brothel; to his mother's many affairs after his father's death; to his own brief infatuation with a young Korean girl whom he met while he was stationed in Korea and met again thirty years later, accompanied by her husband, in a Texas hotel; to a malpractice suit that forced him to defend his professional integrity.

Selzer always thought that people respected physicians, but in 1986, two years after his retirement from Yale Medical School, he faced an unexpected lawsuit. Eight years earlier he had performed a routine operation, a cryohemorrhoidectomy, upon an elderly woman named Marina. It was minor surgery, but the patient claimed that the operation left her ill and incapacitated, requiring eight to ten enemas a day. She took her grievance to one lawyer after another, even filing papers and serving as her own counsel, until an attorney finally agreed to take up her case. Six years later, she died of causes unrelated to her operation, but her husband decided to continue her case. Through misleading newspaper accounts of Selzer's retirement ceremony, the plaintiff had gotten the wrong impression that Selzer was a wealthy author and celebrity surgeon who would be fair game for a lawsuit.

Through his diary account of the six-day trial, Selzer presents a sympathetic account of the emotional and psychological trauma of a physician facing a malpractice suit. He is forced to endure the tedium, boredom, and humiliation of a highly publicized trial, with the judge berating him, the opposing lawyer aggressively cross-examining him, and newspaper photographers hounding him for publicity shots. His problems are compounded by the sensational and inaccurate reporting of the trial in the *New Haven Register*. He sticks to his defense, however, and finally wins his case when the plaintiff decides to withdraw his suit.

Not long after his retirement, Selzer was invited to teach for a week at the Ranger's School at Yellowstone National Park. Each morning one of the rangers took him on a tour of the park, which he was later asked to "reinterpret" for students in terms of the human body. Selzer's most memorable impression of his stay at Yellowstone was an incident at Floating Island Lake. Selzer evokes the ruthless efficiency of three coyotes in bringing down an elk calf and the dogged determination of the mother in standing guard for hours over the dead body of her calf until, panting and exhausted, she gives up her vigil and trots off, yielding to the coyotes and ravens. Predator and prey; life and death: Selzer had often witnessed the same struggle as a surgeon, and with the same unequal odds. The incident reminds him of the first time he witnessed death when, as a boy, he accompanied his father on a house call and watched a patient's last few labored gasps, as blueness crept up the patient's extremities.

Much later in life, Selzer faces the ethical dilemma of whether or not to assist in hastening the death of a patient terminally ill with acquired immune deficiency syndrome. Selzer is asked by the patient's friend to prescribe a lethal dose of narcotics. He indignantly refuses, but after several visits to the patient, a young Colombian public health doctor named Ramon whose condition is rapidly deteriorating, Selzer's professional scruples begin to weaken. Ramon takes a sublethal dose of barbiturates and is rushed to the hospital, where, after having his stomach pumped out, he takes twelve agonizing days to die.

Having spent much of his professional career in hospitals, Selzer has some interesting thoughts on the relationship between hospital architecture and the degree of patient comfort in a hospital. Recognizing that most people associate hospitals with death, since admission to a hospital was once tantamount to a death warrant, Selzer wonders how they could be designed to be more appealing to patients. Condemning the dreariness, monotony, and sameness of many large medical centers, Selzer proposes that his ideal hospital should face west, with hallways and corridors opening to the sunlight; it should have an interior courtyard with the healing sounds of a fountain and wind chimes; and it should be constructed of natural materials such as brick and wood, so that it might rise out of the earth like a living creature. A hospital should be a place to nurture life and send it forth healed and renewed by the spirit of the place. These, he admits, "are the fantasies of a mere scribbler who cannot even read blueprints."

From St. Mary's Hospital in Troy, Selzer could see smoke rising from the crematorium that had frightened him as a child. A grim Victorian stone structure, the Gardner Earl Crematorium stands on a ridge overlooking the city of Troy. The building cast a dreary spell over his childhood, when Richard and his brother Billy used to sneak across the grounds and peer through the windows, hoping to catch a glimpse of the dreaded furnace and flames. Peering in, the boys would terrify themselves with morbid fantasies of how the dead felt as they were being burned. In Selzer's imagination, the crematorium became a crucible in which the transformation from life to death was enacted. Fifty years later, Selzer returns to Troy to confront his childhood fears and witness an actual cremation. He is taken on a tour of the grounds by the genial and accommodating director, who is full of bland reassurances. Selzer peers into the furnace where, inside the burning coffins lined up side by side, a hellish vision appears of flaming skulls and boiling remains. Having confronted his worst fears and made his peace with the dead, Selzer decides to be cremated there after his own death.

Richard Selzer's *Down from Troy* is a medical memoir rich with the memories and associations of an extraordinarily good writer who manages to convey the magic of a Depression-era boyhood in upstate New York. Troy is transformed through his imagination from a dingy collection of taverns and brothels to the site of a Homeric epic, where in Selzer's formative years his parents fought an epic battle to shape his character and interests. Fifty years later, as Selzer returns to haunt the streets of his boyhood, he discovers, ironically, that his father's former medical office has been transformed into a funeral home, where not wounds but bodies are dressed and laid out for burial. His mother would have appreciated the irony.

*Andrew J. Angyal*

## Sources for Further Study

*Booklist.* LXXXVIII, May 15, 1992, p. 1652.
*Chicago Tribune.* July 19, 1992, XIV, p. 5.

*JAMA: Journal of the American Medical Association.* CCLXVIII, October 21, 1992, p. 2107.
*Kirkus Reviews.* LX, May 15, 1992, p. 660.
*Library Journal.* CXVII, June 15, 1992, p. 84.
*Los Angeles Times Book Review.* July 19, 1992, p. 6.
*The New York Times Book Review.* XCVII, July 26, 1992, p. 1.
*The New Yorker.* LXVIII, August 17, 1992, p. 87.
*Publishers Weekly.* CCXXXIX, May 18, 1992, p. 52.
*The Washington Post Book World.* XXII, September 6, 1992, p. 2.

# DREAMING IN CUBAN

*Author:* Cristina Garcia (1958-   )
*Publisher:* Alfred A. Knopf (New York). 229 pp. $20.00
*Type of work:* Novel
*Time:* The 1930's to 1980
*Locale:* Cuba and the United States

*Three generations of Cuban women relate themselves to their country and to each other through dreams, letters, interaction, and imagination*

*Principal characters:*
CELIA DEL PINO, a supporter of Fidel Castro's revolution
LOURDES PUENTE, Celia's elder daughter, who owns a bakery in Brooklyn
FELICIA DEL PINO, Celia's younger daughter who has remained in Havana
PILAR PUENTE, Lourdes's daughter, who is especially close to her grandmother, Celia
LUZ AND MILAGRO VILLAVERDE, Felicia's twin daughters, in school in Cuba
IVANITO VILLAVERDE, Felicia's youngest child, closest to his mother

Cristina Garcia's first novel, *Dreaming in Cuban*, dramatizes the profound interconnections between three generations of Cuban women. Their memories, dreams, and hopes are gradually revealed and interlinked, and the importance to them of Cuba and what it means to be Cuban is explored. The voices of the three generations are presented in short, clearly labeled segments that move backward and forward in time to tell their life stories. Gradually their lives are interwoven and their interdependencies become apparent, although historical events have separated the family members geographically.

For Celia del Pino, and for her three children and her grandchildren, Cuba is a complex construct of memories and realities. Celia's story frames the novel. Sets of her unmailed monthly letters to her first love, a Spaniard who returned to Spain in 1935, just before the Spanish Civil War, are included at regular intervals throughout the book, in chronological order. The book concludes with Celia's last letter, in which she tells Gustavo that "The revolution is eleven days old. My granddaughter, Pilar Puente del Pino, was born today. It is also my birthday. I am fifty years old. I will no longer write to you, *mi amor*. She will remember everything." The novel is structured as Celia's transmission to Pilar of all she knows. The family members are introduced in the immediate present of 1972, and their various stories gradually mesh and explain each other as they recount the events of the next eight years. Celia and her daughters, Lourdes and Felicia, are described in an intimate third-person voice, and the grandchildren tell their tales in first-person segments, with the strongest voice being that of Pilar.

Celia in 1972 is an enthusiastic supporter of Fidel Castro (El Líder in the book), and she is proud to be part of the revolution. As the novel opens, she dresses up in her best housedress and drop pearl earrings to keep watch from her porch swing, but instead of a hostile invading force, she sees the image of her husband and knows that he has died in New York City, where he had gone for medical treatment. She thinks back over her life, and the displacements and passions that have shaped it.

Everyone in *Dreaming in Cuban* has been displaced: some by exile, some by madness, some by family crises. The novel reveals the similarities of their different experiences, and the family ties, intuitions, hallucinations, and dreams that bind them together. For Celia, displacement occurred when her mother put her on a train when she was four, to go live with her Tía Alicia in Havana. She loved one man but married another, feels out of touch with her children, and yearns especially for closer contact with her first grandchild, Pilar, in Brooklyn; in Cuba, Celia "closes her eyes and speaks to her granddaughter, imagines her words as slivers of light piercing the murky night."

Celia's daughter Felicia has stayed in Cuba but is indifferent to the revolution, in touch only with her passions and the melodramas of daily life. Infected with syphilis by her first husband, a merchant sailor, she struggles with bouts of dementia, violent behavior, and amnesia, described with sympathy and wonderful humor, as when Felicia is assigned to a special attitude-reforming brigade in the mountains as a corrective for having tried to commit the antirevolutionary act of suicide.

For Celia's other daughter, Lourdes, the revolution has meant being violently dispossessed of family land and being raped by a revolutionary soldier, followed by migration to Miami and then to Brooklyn. Her husband is unable to adjust, but Lourdes thrives. She runs one bakery successfully and then opens a second one. "Immigration has redefined her, and she is grateful. Unlike her husband, she welcomes her adopted language, its possibilities for reinvention." While Celia communes frequently with the sea, wading into the water by her house, immersing herself in its tides and rhythms, for Lourdes, it is winter that makes her feel alive. She loves "the cold scraping sounds on sidewalks and windshields, the ritual of scarves and gloves, hats and zip-in coat linings. Its layers protect her. She wants no part of Cuba, no part of its wretched carnival floats creaking with lies, no part of Cuba at all, which Lourdes claims never possessed her."

For Pilar, Lourdes's daughter, Cuba represents all she longs for: warmth, identity, family connectedness, and the presence of her beloved grandmother. Pilar's first-person account is a story of growing up and becoming aware of adult realities. She tries to run away to Cuba when she discovers her father with a lover, but she gets only as far as her uncle's house in Miami. She struggles with her strong-willed mother, tries out art school and boyfriends and punk rock, and despairs at her parents' right-wing politics, scoffing that her mother's "Yankee Doodle bakeries have become gathering places for these shady Cuban extremists who come all the way from New Jersey and the Bronx to talk their dinosaur politics and drink her killer espressos." Pilar yearns for the Cuba she has never known, fearing that "Every day Cuba fades a little more inside me, my grandmother fades a little more inside me. And there's only my imagination where our history should be." She believes that a return to Cuba will put all the pieces of her life together. When she and Lourdes do return to Havana, impelled by Pilar's sense of urgency (and indeed they do find Celia in despair after the death of Felicia), Pilar does reconnect with her grandmother; as she listens to Celia's stories, she says that "I feel my grandmother's life passing to me through her hands. It's a steady electricity, humming and true." Celia passes along to Pilar her unmailed letters to her Spanish lover, along with the volume of Federico García Lorca poems that have meant so much to her and that have been woven into the narrative. Pilar begins to dream in Spanish. In Cuba, she says, "I wake up feeling different, like something inside me is changing, something chemical and irreversible." But she knows that however deeply important it has been to her to experience Cuba, she eventually will need to return to New York: "I know now it's where I belong—not *instead* of here, but *more* than here." For Lourdes, reencounter with the past is painful. She cannot forgive, and she rants about the failures of the revolution and the question of retribution: "Who will repay us for our homes, for the lands the Communists stole from us?" She shouts "*Asesino!*" at El Líder himself and engineers the emigration of her nephew Ivanito, although this distresses Celia and Pilar.

Only with her husband in New York has Celia been able to dedicate herself to the revolution. She has replaced her bedside portrait of her husband with a photo of El Líder (which Lourdes throws into the sea when she visits), volunteers for sugar cane harvesting and vaccination campaigns, keeps watch over her stretch of the coast, and serves as a civilian judge in the People's Court. *Dreaming in Cuban* is full of the specific realities of Cuban experience, from food rationing to idealism, but it is primarily a novel about the fragile balances between passion and obsession. Passion for Cuba, for lovers and family, for expression in music and painting and dance, and for the emotional fulfillment possible through belief in *santería* (the Cuban fusion of Catholicism and traditional Yoruba religion) and herbal holistic medicine, are all tied together by a vital tide of sexuality and sensuality that pervades every aspect of life.

Celia's voice is lyrical and connective, but her three children represent radically different ways of dealing with Cuban reality: Each one is driven to extremes by personal unbearable pain. All three inherit Celia's dangerous dedication to passion, but in each of the three it is realized differently. Javier so identifies with the Communist affiliation of the revolution that he moves to Czechoslovakia, returning to Cuba in utter despair when deserted by his wife and child. Felicia hardly notices the revolution, absorbed as she is in life's immediate melodramas, moving from one excess to another, as she falls in love, slips in and out of madness, dancing "for days to her Beny Moré records, her hands in position for an impossibly lanky partner, to 'Rebel Heart,' her slippers scraping the floor, to 'Treat Me As I Am,' a buoyant *guaracha*." For a whole summer, she feeds her children nothing but coconut ice cream, to purify and heal them. She demolishes the men she loves and is finally totally absorbed by the rituals of *santería*.

Lourdes is just as voracious and just as obsessive. She, too, lives out her vengeance and her painful memories, coping with her father's illness by indulging her almost unlimited appetites for sex and food, her personal anguish translated into ferocious entrepreneurship as she runs her bakeries, firing off snapshots of her pastries to Celia in Cuba: "Each glistening éclair is a grenade aimed at Celia's political beliefs, each strawberry shortcake proof—in butter, cream, and eggs—of Lourdes's success in America, and a reminder of the ongoing shortages in Cuba."

For all their differences, the parallels between the experiences, emotions, and imaginations of the various family members are emphasized. They are instinctively in touch with each other: her dead husband appears to Celia, and Lourdes carries on a series of conversations with her dead father; Pilar and Celia converse mentally; they are all able to sense one another's well-being or danger across distances. These magical communications are closely allied with spiritual beliefs. The Catholic rituals of childhood spill into later reliance on the rituals of *santería*, with its predictions and atonements and complex rites. Celia seeks the *santera* in times of stress, and Felicia finally is absorbed altogether into the ceremonies that connect her "to larger worlds, worlds alive and infinite" and is a novice *santera* herself when she dies. In New York, Pilar consults an herbalist, explaining that "I'm not religious but I get the feeling that it's the simplest rituals, the ones that are integrated with the earth and its seasons, that are the most profound. It makes more sense to me than the more abstract forms of worship." These beliefs are part of *Dreaming in Cuban*'s powerful network of repeated symbols and images: recurrent references to the songs of Beny Moré, the poems of García Lorca, shells, Tía Alicia's peacock brooch, the colors blue and green, and Celia's pearl drop earrings are effectively interwoven to connect the generations and unify events over the fifty-year span of the novel. Magic and imagination and historical reality fuse in the musical rhythms of *Dreaming in Cuban*.

*Mary G. Berg*

## Sources for Further Study

*America*. CLXVII, July 18, 1992, p. 39.
*Belles Lettres*. VIII, Fall, 1992, p. 15.
*The Christian Science Monitor*. March 24, 1992, p. 13.
*Los Angeles Times*. March 12, 1992, p. E10.
*Migration World Magazine*. XX, Number 2, 1992, p. 39.
*The New York Times Book Review*. XCVII, May 17, 1992, p. 14.
*The New Yorker*. LXVIII, June 1, 1992, p. 86.
*Publishers Weekly*. CCXXXIX, January 13, 1992, p. 46.
*Time*. CXXXIX, March 23, 1992, p. 67.
*The Washington Post Book World*. XXII, March 1, 1992, p. 9.

# ELEANOR ROOSEVELT
## Volume I: 1884-1933

*Author:* Blanche Wiesen Cook (1941-     )
*Publisher:* Viking (New York). 587 pp. $27.50
*Type of work:* Biography
*Time:* 1884-1933
*Locale:* New York, Hyde Park, and Albany, New York; and Washington, D.C.

*Roosevelt's dramatic evolution from an unhappy society matron to one of the most powerful figures of the twentieth century provides a compelling exemplary model for contemporary women*

> *Principal personages:*
> ANNA ELEANOR ROOSEVELT, a political activist, mother, writer, teacher, and wife of the thirty-second president of the United States
> ELLIOTT ROOSEVELT, her father
> FRANKLIN DELANO ROOSEVELT, husband of Eleanor, governor of New York, and president of the United States
> SARA DELANO ROOSEVELT, Franklin's mother

For men and women who reached adulthood during the years following World War II, Eleanor Roosevelt often seemed an indestructible and numinous figure. That she had had a public life before the death of her husband was vaguely known, but often the more naïve students of contemporary history were shocked to learn that only a decade or two earlier, Eleanor Roosevelt had been a figure of violent controversy, the subject of bitter jokes and vicious caricatures, mocked as radical and unfeminine and lampooned on posters and campaign buttons.

It has been the task of Blanche Wiesen Cook, a journalist, editor, and professor of history and women's studies, to rescue Eleanor Roosevelt—not from oblivion, but from the secondary position that some historians and biographers have assigned to her. Presenting this energetic wife of a powerful president of the United States as a political and intellectual being worthy of scrutiny in her own right, Cook does not pretend to solve the enigma of Roosevelt's complex personality or to resolve the contradictions that occasionally blur the historical record. Rather, drawing on interviews of those who knew her and previously unavailable papers of several of her friends and associates, Cook successfully and persuasively provides for the contemporary reader a fully rounded figure whose dilemmas and choices are both illuminating and exemplary. "To appreciate the struggles that Eleanor Roosevelt faced," Cook explains, "enables us to understand the struggles we continue to face, the political alternatives available, and the fact that on the road to political decency and personal dignity there have been no final victories."

*Eleanor Roosevelt* is not a polemical biography, but it is certainly a feminist one; it draws heavily and openly on the concerns and energies of the ongoing struggle for the recognition of women's full humanity in which Eleanor Roosevelt was herself engaged. Roosevelt's personal bravery, her determination to act on her beliefs, her commitment to causes, and her consciously undertaken course of political education are presented—convincingly—as the stuff of heroism. Her friendships, some of them passionate and intense, are allowed a major role in the drama of her personal and political growth. Even more important, her life work, largely undertaken only after the completion of her fourth decade, is seen as a career, a course of political action that was independent of her role as a politician's wife and that had a direction and logic of its own.

Anna Eleanor Roosevelt—always known by her middle name or its diminutives and referred to as ER throughout this book—was the child of a troubled marriage. Her mother had married the dashing Elliott Roosevelt at the age of nineteen and given birth to her daughter a year later, too early perhaps to continue to enjoy the pleasures of dances and parties that she still craved. Elliott, the younger brother of the future president, Theodore, was handsome, mercurial, and unstable. Although he professed to adore his wife and children, particularly Eleanor, he was a philanderer and a destructive alcoholic. "Little Nell," who remembered as an adult feeling increasingly rejected by her unhappy mother, worshiped her father in return for his attentions and his imaginative extravagance but saw him only between the bouts of institutionalization and semi-exile that his family imposed as his behavior deteriorated.

Her mother's death from diphtheria when Eleanor was ten years old increased the child's isolation. Sent to live with loving but strict and emotionally distant relatives, she developed a strong fantasy life built around her father's occasional letters. Within two years, he too died, leaving Eleanor and her much younger brother, Hall, in her maternal grandmother's care. Privately educated, she spent her time with her mother's younger siblings rather with than her contemporaries and developed in this company of women an inner reserve and strength that would serve her well later on.

Outside her family, the person who had the greatest impact on Eleanor's early life was Marie Souvestre, the founder and headmistress of the distinguished British school for girls, Allenswood, where Eleanor was sent as a boarder in 1899 and where she would spend three of her happiest years. A "feminist of bold conviction" whose rigorous scholarship and pedagogical methods had attracted the attention of the most liberal English intellectuals of the period, Mme. Souvestre picked Eleanor as a favorite almost immediately. She trained Eleanor in philosophy and conversational debate, nurtured her capacity for independent thought, and eventually took her on holiday journeys to Italy and France, where the young girl was encouraged to take over travel arrangements and the organization of tours and meetings, tasks generally restricted in that class and period to men. Her death in 1903, shortly after Eleanor's return to the United States, robbed the young woman of a valuable mentor and guide.

Mme. Souvestre's influence, however, seemed for a time to be of little value in Eleanor's life. Lonely and out of place in the world of New York City debutantes that she entered upon her return, she continued to spend time with her socially active aunts, now in their thirties, and with her uncles who were, like her father, out of control alcoholics. Eleanor's susceptibility to the attentions of her handsome distant cousin,

Franklin Delano Roosevelt, who was then still an undergraduate at Harvard, was therefore perhaps not unexpected. After a long engagement, kept secret at the request of Franklin's mother, the two Roosevelts were married on March 17, 1905.

Cook makes it very clear that Franklin and Eleanor, however distinct their lives and interests later became, were very much in love when they married and that they maintained, throughout their respective careers, respect and affection for one another. The differences in temperament and interest that would separate them were not at first apparent. Their major problem at the beginning—and in fact for many years—was Franklin's mother, Sara Delano. Wealthy, clannish, and above all ambitious for her son, Sara had no intention of relinquishing control over her only child: She bought and furnished his house, took over much of the education of his children, and withheld approval of any action on the part of the couple that did not have a place in her vision of the Roosevelt destiny. For nearly fifteen years, Eleanor resigned herself to her mother-in-law's tyranny, developing her own interests only when she was away from New York. With three children in the first four years (there would be two more later) and Franklin's blossoming career as a politician to encourage and support, she had little energy for rebellion or dreams of independence.

Franklin's election to the New York Senate in 1910 changed Eleanor's life. Listening quietly on the periphery of conversations, she quickly learned enough about the political process to participate. Eleanor became an effective political hostess, organizing parties with the right members of the opposition and calling on the right people to ease the passage of crucial legislation. She overcame her natural shyness and recalled her Allenswood lessons, reporting to Franklin on legislative debates and issues and speaking to constituents on his behalf. She supported her husband in his break with her uncle's Bull Moose progressivism in the election of 1912 and, when Franklin's loyalty to candidate Woodrow Wilson was rewarded with the post of assistant secretary of the Navy, she went with him to Washington eagerly, ready to perform the arduous duties of an official's wife but interested and increasingly astute on her own.

Cook's account of the future president's early years in Washington remind the reader that scandal, corruption, witch hunting, and bigotry were as prevalent during World War I and its aftermath as at any time in history. Franklin's affair with his social secretary Lucy Mercer, which everyone in Washington seemed to know about before Eleanor did, was surprising only because it was so public. Eleanor forthrightly offered Franklin a divorce. Sara Delano, foreseeing the end of her son's political career, forbade it, and Franklin agreed. The marriage would continue, but the terms of it were not yet clear.

For more than a year, Eleanor struggled to find direction. She appears to have become anorexic, purposeless, and depressed. Cook describes her many visits to the memorial to Marion Hooper Adams erected at Rock Creek Park by her husband Henry after her suicide. Speculating about the parallels between the two wives, Cook uses the visits to this enigmatic statue as the fulcrum of her volume. From this point on, Eleanor's life would develop a direction of its own.

Eleanor Roosevelt, like many others of her generation and class, was reticent about her most deeply felt emotions. Relying on the record of Eleanor's daily activities, on the testimony of her surviving friends, and on the surviving correspondence of her intimate acquaintances, Cook has constructed a moving story of Roosevelt's recreation of her public self, a re-creation that ironically coincided with the years when her psychological and then physical support of her husband were most in demand. Assaulted first by the threat of political scandal in Washington, then by the Democratic Party's loss of power in 1920, and finally by paralytic poliomyelitis in 1921, Franklin had to rely increasingly on Eleanor and others to keep up his strength and commitment and to maintain his viability as a candidate for public office.

It was at this time that Eleanor's new strength and energy began to emerge. Although still supportive of Franklin's career and willing to manage the complex problems involved in organizing three separate houses, five children, and a disabled husband with an active public career, Eleanor moved on a course of her own. Supported by several independent and politically minded women who were passionately committed to the amelioration of urban poverty and the empowerment of their own kind, Eleanor participated visibly and forcefully in the most important social welfare battles of her day. Popular myth depicts Eleanor as simply holding Franklin's place in the political arena in the years before his return to active campaigning, but Cook points out that, on the contrary, by 1928 Eleanor had assumed "the most powerful positions ever held by a woman in party politics": director of the Bureau of Women's Activities of the Democratic National Committee and head of the Women's Advisory Committee, formed "to develop Al Smith's presidential campaign organization." She was also an editor of the widely circulated *Women's Democratic News*, a position she had to drop when Franklin's election as governor of New York curtailed her political activity. In addition, from 1927 on she was a popular teacher at the private Todhunter School for Girls in Manhattan, commuting for four years each Sunday, returning on Wednesdays to preside over the weekly official tea.

During this active period, Eleanor tirelessly involved herself in her husband's career. Despite professional commitments, occasional political disagreements, and, increasingly, the divergence of their personal lives, Governor and Mrs. Roosevelt in public were united and supportive allies. In private, however, although they shared advisers and friends, they maintained separate social spheres. Eleanor openly encouraged Franklin's relationship with the younger Marguerite "Missy" LeHand, and herself became involved in lively and passionate friendships with various male and female members of the extended Roosevelt household. Cook leaves the question of physical or sexual intimacy between the parties up to the reader. It is clear that the relationships, however defined, played an important role in Eleanor's busy but essentially lonely life.

The volume ends with the inauguration of Franklin as president in 1933—a moment of triumph for Franklin, of course, but not necessarily one for Eleanor, who, it is clear, must renegotiate the terms of her independence. The reader is left in suspense, eager for the next chapter in this heroic and complicated life.

Cook's biography is powerful and persuasive. Through her careful use of sources and exhaustive explanatory footnotes, she enables the reader to understand the historical context of this extraordinary individual and the issues she confronted. Eleanor Roosevelt emerges, free from the stereotypes and sentimental distortions that have shaped her popular image for several generations, a complex and often unhappy human being who, against the expectations of her class and background, had a profound impact on the life of her time.

*Jean Ashton*

## Sources for Further Study

*America.* CLXVII, September 19, 1992, p. 169.
*Chicago Tribune.* May 3, 1992, XIV, p. 3.
*The Christian Science Monitor.* May 19, 1992, p. 13.
*Library Journal.* CXVII, February 15, 1992, p. 176.
*Los Angeles Times Book Review.* April 19, 1992, p. 1.
*The Nation.* CCLV, July 13, 1992, p. 58.
*The New Republic.* CCVI, May 25, 1992, p. 36.
*The New York Review of Books.* XXXIX, September 24, 1992, p. 49.
*The New York Times Book Review.* XCVII, April 19, 1992, p. 1.
*Publishers Weekly.* CCXXXIX, February 3, 1992, p. 68.
*The Washington Post Book World.* XXII, April 19, 1992, p. 5.

# THE END OF EQUALITY

*Author:* Mickey Kaus (1951-    )
*Publisher:* BasicBooks (New York). 293 pp. $25.00
*Type of work:* Current affairs

*A liberal commentator advocates "civic liberalism" and "social equality" over "income liberalism" and "money equality" as goals for the Democratic Party and the nation*

Depending on how one looks at it, the title of Mickey Kaus's first book, *The End of Equality*, is either annoyingly deceptive or hauntingly clever. This is because of the double meaning of the word "end." In his book, Kaus discusses the nature of equality as an end (or goal) of contemporary liberalism. He wishes to convince liberal Democrats—and, ultimately, an electoral majority of Americans—that they should pursue "social" rather than "money" equality.

Kaus believes that Democrats should accept the growing disparity of income that emerged during the Reagan-Bush years as an inevitable result of the globalized, postindustrial economy. The emphasis on skills needed to compete in the global economy and dramatic stratification of incomes even within the skilled professions (what Kaus calls the "Hollywood effect") make the attempt to level incomes quixotic at best, and, quite possibly, economically disastrous. Moreover, income equality, according to Kaus, is not a crucial element in American democracy as popularly conceived. Indeed, the quest for extraordinary wealth has always been a part of the American Dream. Correspondingly, equality of opportunity has always been emphasized over equality of result.

Kaus does believe, however, that social equality is a crucial element in American democracy. As a result, he is troubled greatly by the social disparity and separation of economic classes that have been developing in the United States since the end of World War II. Social inequality, Kaus asserts, has resulted from a number of factors quite independent of income disparity. Suburbanization has led to the physical separation of habitats along class lines, affecting the nature of schools and public places. The inequitable system of selective service during the Vietnam War and subsequent formation of a volunteer army have removed the socially democratizing impetus of military service that existed, for example, during World War II. Badly designed welfare programs have damaged a work ethic that used to cut across class lines, lending dignity to work endeavors no matter what the size of the resulting income. These developments have produced a society in which economic inequalities are no longer ameliorated by a transcendent public sphere. What the United States most needs is restoration of such a sphere, one in which wealth simply does not count, at least not for very much.

In order to combat social inequality, Kaus recommends an aggressive and comprehensive application of what he calls "civic liberalism." The goal of civic liberalism is to reconstruct and maintain a meaningful, shared public sphere insulated from the divisive effects of income inequality.

Kaus proposes three stages of reform. The first would be to narrow the gaps between classes immediately by restoring an equitable system of mandatory military or civilian national service, instituting campaign finance reform designed to minimize the influence of monied interests on elections, and developing a national health care policy designed to avoid segregation of patients based on their ability to pay. Mandatory national service would replicate the egalitarian aspects of universal conscription during World War II (something voluntary programs would not achieve). Public financing of political campaigns would reduce the corrupting effects of economic power on the democratic process. Universal health care that permitted less wealthy patients access to the same doctors and facilities used by those who are well off would ensure a certain minimum of human dignity and also put people with disparate incomes into contact with one another as equals.

Stage two, the most costly and complicated, would retrieve public space in inner cities and lower class barriers by legislating the urban "underclass" out of existence. This would be accomplished by substituting a relief program based on work rather than welfare. All able-bodied recipients of public aid would be given jobs at a pay rate just below the current minimum wage. According to Kaus, this would extinguish the culture of poverty, reduce crime, and return cities to a condition in which they can provide an abundance of public space for various kinds of interclass activities.

In the third and final stage, residential and educational segregation according to class would be addressed by a strategy designed to bring about an "ecology of equality." Communities would be offered incentives to become more economically diverse. This would be less difficult than it sounds, according to Kaus, once there is no longer an economic underclass with which to deal. One result of a policy designed to bring about such an ecology of equality would be to redemocratize schools, bringing together students of disparate income to interact as civic equals.

Kaus closes with a chapter on whether this agenda for change can be made into an electoral winner. His answer is twofold. First, who cares? The agenda should be pursued because it is the right thing to do. Second, yes, it can be a winner, or at least as much as money equality has been for Democrats. Just how much currency Kaus's theory achieves will probably depend on analysis of what voters had in mind as they cast their ballots in the 1992 election. Contrary to some of the book's blurbs, Kaus's ideas did not play a central role in the Bill Clinton campaign. Clinton's victory may well weaken the urgency of Kaus's message for many liberal Democrats. It may, on the other hand, open the way for a number of experiments aimed at alleviating problems of social equality.

There is a lot to argue with in this book, from just about every perspective. Economic conservatives and free-market advocates will feel uncomfortable with the government activism inherent in Kaus's approach. Even though Kaus wishes to reduce the emphasis on redistributive policies, he still is expanding the role of the federal government with his programs to provide employment and quality health care for all Americans. Moreover, he does not put these goals into the context of the seemingly uncontrollable annual budget deficit at the federal level and growing fiscal pressures at the state level. Social conservatives and perhaps some people who are not so conservative will also question the omission from Kaus's analysis of any discussion about religion or ultimate moral values. One source of social equality in the United States has been a common belief in equality before a higher power. If religion is now irrelevant to social equality, Kaus probably ought to have the forthrightness to say so. In addition, Kaus seems oblivious to the phenomenon of "culture war" espoused by Patrick Buchanan and other critics from the political right wing. Whether these critics have rightly discerned which side God is on, their relevance to American politics and the nature of American democracy would seem undeniable.

The main target of Kaus's analysis is not conservatism. It is liberalism. Here, too, there are a number of criticisms that can be aimed at Kaus's conception of the problem as well as his solutions. To begin with, traditional liberals might well point to Kaus's portrayal of their position as a "straw man" designed to make his own ideas seem fresher and more compelling than they actually are. After all, with the exception of a small democratic-socialist fringe, liberal Democrats have only gone so far as to advocate relief for both short- and long-term economic distress as well as for the empowerment of workers through organized labor. They have not challenged the central position of the free market and capitalism in American society. They have accepted income inequalities as necessary for the maintenance of a free society and also as a tool for increasing overall productivity, so that all Americans can enjoy a higher standard of living. Thus, there are precious few examples of strict money egalitarians. Moreover, Kaus's own proposals are redistributive in a number of respects. His health care plan would have the effect of providing equal care to those with low or middle incomes. His jobs program, while taking people off the dole, still is paid for by redistributing income from those who are gainfully employed to those who would otherwise be unemployed. Finally, Kaus's proposal to "means test" some Social Security benefits (reducing benefits to those who are well off) also links money equality to social equality and has a redistributive dimension.

As this last proposal suggests, it is not clear that social and money equality are, indeed, entirely or even fundamentally separable. Political philosophers going all the way back to Plato and Aristotle have warned against the destabilizing influences of luxury and want, particularly where they exist side by side in the same polity. There are, in other words, sociological and political ramifications of money inequality that cannot realistically be disassociated from social equality. Kaus, however, seems to believe in a golden age of social equality prior to the end of World War II. Although the war may have been fought in a wonderfully egalitarian way (except, of course, in racial terms), prewar America was subject to many different forms of social inequality: class snobbery, elitism, and breaches of dignity linked to income disparity. Intermarriage between classes, for example, has always served well as the stuff of romance in American literature and cinema because it is relatively rare. For all the democratic pretense, privilege, poverty, and disparity between "haves" and "have nots" traditionally have marred the American legal system with regard both to civil and criminal justice. In short, it is difficult to deny that income inequalities have been translated into important social inequalities throughout American history.

Even if a golden age of social equality did exist, it is likely that money inequality was mitigated by belief in the possibility of upward mobility and, later on, the guarantee of economic security. Although Kaus's jobs program might be seen as addressing the latter issue (though perhaps not well, since it would still allow for rapid fluctuations of income), he does not directly address the issue of upward mobility. Many observers will see this as an important omission since Americans of modest means traditionally have coped with their situation by seeing their hardships as stepping-stones for children and grandchildren.

Kaus also ignores the point of view of those liberals who believe it is economic growth itself that tends to kill off civic values and the public sphere. They see emphasis on greed and success as leading to a kind of empty individualism, one that results in economic, environmental, and spiritual frustration. Kaus also seems to gloss over the enormous difficulties attendant to legislating his program. Almost every part of it will meet with stern opposition from one powerful group of Americans or another. Many parts of his program will be tremendously expensive, costing money that simply is unavailable given the fiscal pinch in which federal and state governments find themselves. This leads to the final criticism many observers will aim at Kaus's book: an overall sense of superficiality. Very often, Kaus's ideas seem ingenious but facile. His extensive endnotes show that he is able to support many of his views in considerable depth, but there is a fantasy-land quality to this book. This sense of unreality applies not only to the solutions Kaus suggests but also to his diagnosis of problems and assessment of what really makes American democracy—and Americans themselves—tick.

Nevertheless, Kaus's book raises innovative questions about the future of American politics, the Democratic Party, liberalism, and, by implication, the Republican Party and conservatism as well. At the very least, Kaus has raised a stern challenge for conventional political strategists as the United States approaches the twenty-first century. As such, a wide range of readers will find *The End of Equality* provocative and interesting.

*Ira Smolensky*

## Sources for Further Study

*Chicago Tribune*. August 23, 1992, XIV, p. 3.
*The Christian Science Monitor*. October 2, 1992, p. 10.
*Commonweal*. CXIX, October 23, 1992, p. 20.
*Fortune*. CXXVI, November 2, 1992, p. 143.
*Los Angeles Times Book Review*. August 2, 1992, p. 1.
*The New York Times Book Review*. XCVII, July 12, 1992, p. 1.
*Time*. CXL, July 27, 1992, p. 70.
*The Wall Street Journal*. July 17, 1992, p. A10.
*The Washington Post Book World*. XXII, July 12, 1992, p. 1.

# THE END OF HISTORY AND THE LAST MAN

*Author:* Francis Fukuyama (1952-    )
*Publisher:* Free Press (New York). 418 pp. $24.95
*Type of work:* Current affairs; philosophy

*With the demise of Soviet communism and the end of the Cold War, the author argues that human history has reached its completion with the victory of liberal democracy and capitalism*

> Principal personages:
> GEORG WILHELM HEGEL, a nineteenth century German philosopher
> FRIEDRICH NIETZSCHE, a nineteenth century German philosopher
> ALEXANDER KOJEVE, a twentieth century Russian interpreter of Hegel
> PLATO, an ancient Greek philosopher
> KARL MARX, a nineteenth century German philosopher
> THOMAS HOBBES, a seventeenth century English philosopher
> JOHN LOCKE, a seventeenth century English philosopher

In 1989, a year that saw the fall of the Berlin Wall and other events signifying the end of the Cold War, Francis Fukuyama published a sixteen-page article titled, "The End of History?" in *The National Interest*, a journal with a circulation of about six thousand. Surprisingly, he and his article quickly became widely known and very controversial. Policymakers and politicians both within the United States and elsewhere debated his assertion. University academics and ordinary readers of popular news magazines discussed the question Fukuyama asked. *The End of History and the Last Man* is both a response to his many critics and an elaboration of the ideas found in his original article. Arguing that the end of the Cold War and the collapse of communism in the Soviet Union and Eastern Europe left the West in sole command of the political and economic landscape, Fukuyama claims that liberal democracy and capitalism have triumphed, that there are no alternatives or remaining ideological challengers, and that history, defined as the evolving competition between political, social, and economic ideologies, has come to an end.

Most critics vehemently disagreed with Fukuyama's original article. History cannot simply end; billions of human beings are living their lives, struggling for their existences, and reproducing themselves. Wars are still taking place, political battles are being fought, and even capitalistic economies can suffer depressions. The brutality of the Chinese communists in crushing the democratic student demonstrations at Tiananmen Square and Saddam Hussein's invasion of Kuwait showed that history obviously was not over. Fukuyama states, however, that he was not suggesting that wars would not be fought, that major events could no longer take place, that all controversies have ended. As he notes in *The End of History and the Last Man*, he was not referring to the ending of events but rather of history as a single, coherent, and evolutionary process. Fukuyama believes that history is teleological; it has a goal and a meaning, and these have been fulfilled in the victory of liberal democratic capitalism over all of previous human history, and not just over authoritarian communism.

Western society in the late twentieth century is the culmination of all that has come before.

*The End of History and the Last Man* is a work of large ideas and broad interpretations, and Fukuyama tackles them with considerable ingenuity, if not always with complete success. He begins his argument with the ideas of two nineteenth century historical philosophers, Georg Wilhelm Hegel and Karl Marx, both products of the Enlightenment. They agreed that universal history was directional and purposeful and that recent history evolved from, or was a reaction to, earlier stages of human society. For Marx, the end of history was to be the victory of pure communism, which would consequently see the withering away of institutions, such as the state and governments, that had been the product of and the means by which the economic haves controlled the economic have-nots. Hegel saw the final synthesis of history as the development of the liberal state, and Fukuyama argues that it was Hegel, and not Marx, who had the accurate vision of human historical development.

There are a number of factors that led to the victory of liberal democratic capitalism. The scientific method and the Industrial Revolution are crucial among these. With modern science, history could no longer be either merely random or cyclical. Now it could only be, Fukuyama claims, cumulative and directional. Luddites might resist the inevitability of technology and Rousseauists might long for a state of uncorrupted nature, but nothing could reverse the scientific-industrial-technological process once it began. Science and industry effectively modernized society in a forward direction, and in order for any human society to survive, much less progress, there is no alternative.

The economic system that best responds to the scientific and industrial implications of history's evolving direction is free-market capitalism. Fukuyama argues that the history of the twentieth century proves the triumphant efficiency of capitalism over socialism or communism as economic systems. Only capitalism can provide the greatest economic satisfaction to the greatest number. In the postindustrial age of computers and a worldwide integrated economy, the planned economies of socialist or communist states are simply beyond the abilities of government bureaucrats to control. Fukuyama points to the growth of the market economy even in communist China as well as the fall of the Soviet Union as evidence for his claim. As exemplified in the title of one of his chapters, "The Victory of the VCR," Fukuyama sees free-market capitalism as the only possibility for a global economy in a scientific and technological era.

Although capitalism and science can produce the material goods to satisfy the economic desires of most people at the end of the twentieth century, this is not in itself a sufficient explanation for the ending of history with liberal democracy. There is often, as Fukuyama notes, a high degree of correlation between successful capitalist economies and liberal democratic political systems. To answer why liberal democracy as a political and social system has triumphed over all challengers at the end of history, Fukuyama again turns to Hegel. Hegel argued that one of the key elements in the development of human history is the human desire to be recognized. This desire for recognition led to the origin of the first man and his aristocratic warrior society. The aristocratic warrior was willing to risk death for recognition, beyond mere economic gain. In the drive for recognition, the aristocratic warrior enslaved opponents, who in turn sought their recognition in their work. Christianity, originally a religion that appealed to slaves, preached the equality of humanity before God, but in the afterlife. It was the French Revolution, Hegel claimed, that brought to this life the possibility of a society in which all were recognized, and as equals.

Fukuyama also points to Plato's threefold division of the human soul to help explain the ultimate success of liberal democracy. In *The Republic*, Plato argues that human nature is divided into three parts, a desiring part (food and sex), a reasoning part (the quest for knowledge and the truth), and a third part, *thymos*, which Fukuyama defines as self-esteem and which he says is similar to Hegel's desire for recognition. A free-market capitalist society can produce all that is necessary to satisfy the desiring part of human nature. In turn, liberal democracy provides Hegel's recognition or Plato's *thymos* for all, which Fukuyama calls "isothymia," the desire to be recognized as equal to others. Aristocratic societies, hereditary monarchies, fascist nations, and communist states could allow for recognition for a few at the expense of the majority of slaves. "Megalothymia," the desire to be recognized as superior, would have a place among warriors, kings, leaders, and communist party bureaucrats, but not for the majority. Only liberal democracy fulfills that need for all humans.

*The End of History and the Last Man* is not just a paean to liberal democracy and capitalism. Fukuyama, a onetime student of Alan Bloom, author of *The Closing of the American Mind: How Higher Education Has Failed Democracy and Impoverished the Souls of Today's Students* (1987), might be broadly designated as a social conservative. He is not enamored of the libertarian right, which he castigates as a logical evolution from Lockean liberalism, with its emphasis upon rights rather than upon responsibilities. What concerns Fukuyama is what kind of a society there is at the end of history. He refers to Friedrich Nietzsche's prediction that a world of equality, be it Hegelian or Marxist, could only be a world in which the victorious slave has submerged and eliminated the aristocratic master and destroyed the values of the latter. Nietzsche argued that human excellence was possible only in an aristocratic society. Fukuyama seems to fear that the modern human has been subverted and seduced by values that are possibly necessary requirements in liberal democratic societies but ultimately are deleterious to the human spirit, values such as excessive tolerance, the abandoning of moral choices, and the imposition of destructive relativism, which Fukuyama condemns in modern education. The "last man" knows that history has been too often the story of meaningless battles—religious, nationalistic, and class conflicts—that ultimately led to nothing. Can there be anything in life at the end of history other than making money, acquiring things, or running for a political office? Is the last man content like a dog to lie in the sun, knowing that its next meal will be provided at the end of the day? In spite of his praise of liberal democracy and capitalism, Fukuyama seems to believe so, and he argues that the Chinese students facing the tanks in Tiananmen Square, the Russians defending their parliament and president, and the Romanians toppling the Ceaucescus were the most free and thus the most human. Paradoxically, in their valorous seeking of liberal democratic capitalism, they were planting the seeds of their decline.

*The End of History and the Last Man* is a book of its time. The struggle against German fascism and Soviet communism gave a transcendent meaning to much of the twentieth century, real evils to confront, opponents larger than life who threatened civilization, perhaps even history itself. The collapse of the Soviet Union and the ending of the Cold War initially resulted in elation and rejoicing, but after that came a vacuum. What is there now to strive against, what evil to overcome, what worlds to conquer? The West has won, but for Fukuyama it appears that there is only ennui and weariness at the end of history, or the sordid delights of the consumer society. He admits that there might be new and unforeseen challenges to the victory of liberal democracy, but he seems doubtful of their ultimate significance. In time, he predicts, religious fanaticism and national and ethnic rivalries will also pass away, perhaps neither immediately nor totally, but they too are part of history, and history is over.

Historians could argue that *The End of History and the Last Man* is not really about history. Is history only the conflict of ideologies? Does history have a pattern to be worked out? Most historians would doubt it. Also, it might be argued that Fukuyama's vision is too Western in its analysis and concentration. Students of Hegel, Plato, and the other seminal thinkers who form the core of Fukuyama's work might possibly quarrel with his interpretation of their writings. For example, is Hegel's nineteenth century liberal state the same thing as Fukuyama's liberal democracy? Free-market capitalism is prospering in much of the world in the later twentieth century, but in Asia capitalism often coexists with more authoritarian politics than in the West. Finally, it seems almost an act of hubris to predict the decline and ultimate disappearance of religion and nationalism as ideologies for which humans will give their lives and the lives of others.

*Eugene S. Larson*


**Sources for Further Study**

*American Historical Review.* XCVII, June, 1992, p. 817.
*Commonweal.* CXIX, June 19, 1992, p. 25.
*Current History.* XCI, April, 1992, p. 184.
*Los Angeles Times Book Review.* January 19, 1992, p. 2.
*The New York Review of Books.* XXXIX, March 26, 1992, p. 7.
*The New York Times Book Review.* XCVII, January 26, 1992, p. 14.
*Publishers Weekly.* CCXXXIX, January 1, 1992, p. 41.
*Society.* XXX, November, 1992, p. 116.
*The Times Literary Supplement.* April 24, 1992, p. 6.
*The Washington Post Book World.* XXII, January 12, 1992, p. 1.

# ENGLISH MUSIC

*Author:* Peter Ackroyd (1949-    )
*Publisher:* Alfred A. Knopf (New York). Illustrated. 399 pp. $23.00
*Type of work:* Novel
*Time:* Approximately 1920-1992
*Locale:* London and nearby areas of England

*This novel presents the growth to manhood of a boy with paranormal powers, interwoven with a series of dreams or visions which present characters from English literature and English musical history*

> *Principal characters:*
> TIMOTHY HARCOMBE, a boy with unusual powers
> CLEMENT HARCOMBE, a medium and healer, Timothy's father
> MARGARET, a dwarf, a member of the Harcombe circle
> GLORIA PATTERSON, Clement Harcombe's mistress
> WILLIAM BYRD (1538?-1623), composer of the first English madrigals

*English Music* is a work with a double structure. In its odd-numbered chapters we follow the development of Timothy Harcombe from childhood to manhood, opening with Timothy, now an old man, looking back on the much-altered scenes of his youth and reflecting on them. In the even-numbered chapters, by contrast, we are repeatedly plunged into a succession of strange worlds in which the authors and the characters of English literature, or English culture more generally, come alive and appear to Timothy in visions.

The contrast between these two strands is striking on every level. Timothy's life is unusual, but nevertheless drab if not dull. He has no mother, and has especially to begin with a particularly close relationship with his father, an undistinguished medium and healer practicing his trade among poor people in the back streets of London. Clement Harcombe uses his son in his business, and seems to treat the small boy Timothy is in the beginning almost as an adult, talking to him at an unusual level of sophistication. In spite of this close relationship, however, as the book develops Mr. Harcombe forms the habit of going off on his own affairs, leaving Timothy to be brought up in haphazard fashion by his grandparents, with further influences on him from members of the "Harcombe Circle," those people, themselves rather undistinguished, who believe in his father's powers. In this fashion Timothy grows up, goes to school, discovers that he too has unusual psychic powers of divination, finds a job in an art gallery, and in the end is caught up in World War II. It is easier, however, to say what does not happen to Timothy than what does. He shows no career ambition, makes no use of his psychic powers, remains sexually uninitiated, and from an early age seems more interested in remembering the past than in experiencing the future.

Color and life are added to the novel by the strange events interposed in odd-numbered chapters. These are easier to describe than to analyze. At the start of chapter 2, for example, the reader is told that as Timothy slept he "must have dreamed a dream"—an allusion to the opening words of *The Pilgrim's Progress* (1678-1684), by

John Bunyan. But the figure whom Timothy sees running toward him is not Bunyan's Christian but a young girl in a white dress. "Why," says Timothy to himself, "that's Alice," the heroine evidently not of Bunyan's *The Pilgrim's Progress* but of *Alice in Wonderland* (1865-1871) by Lewis Carroll, the pen name of Charles Dodgson. Yet what Alice says as she runs past him is the cry of Bunyan's Christian, "How shall I grapple with the misery that I must meet with in eternity," while when Christian appears (as he does on the same page), he is muttering a version of the White Rabbit's complaint from Wonderland, "Won't He be savage if I'm too late!" Why cross Bunyan with Carroll, Alice with Christian? At first sight they seem to have nothing to do with each other at all, the one pair preoccupied with questions of religion, predestination, and Hell, the other pair part of a child's fable. Yet as this chapter progresses, one realizes that both stories are for one thing nonrealistic in rather similar ways. Christian falls into the Slough of Despond, Alice finds herself almost drowning in her own tears. They are also both works containing a deep anxiety, overt in the case of Bunyan, covert in the case of Carroll. They feel similar, even if the authors come from almost totally different backgrounds and address different issues.

In brief, this is the mode of the succession of visions which Timothy sees through his young life. The second of them, chapter 4, is a collage of snippets from the works of Charles Dickens, in which Dickens himself mingles with his characters and with quotations from *Great Expectations* (1860-1861), *David Copperfield* (1849-1850), *The Mystery of Edwin Drood* (1870), and other novels. In chapter 6 we run into Sherlock Holmes, the great detective created by Sir Arthur Conan Doyle, in chapter 8 we find both Robinson Crusoe and Gulliver, from the works by Daniel Defoe and Jonathan Swift respectively, while the five further "visionary" chapters present allusions to or rewritings of works by a whole string of authors, including William Blake, Geoffrey Chaucer, Sir Thomas Malory, and a dozen others, some relatively little known. There is a certain sense that as the novel proceeds we are going back further in time, in contrast to the movement forward of Timothy's own life, but this never reaches total consistency. If there is a rule governing appearances, it is one of unexpectedness, connection by feel or style (as with Alice and Christian) rather than formal literary history.

What is the point of this proceeding (a question which Timothy asks himself more than once)? The answer perhaps lies in the phrase "English music," employed repeatedly in the novel. Timothy's father, with his lecturing style of conversation, uses the phrase to mean not only English music and its history, but also English literature, history, and painting. Why call all these things music? One answer suggested is that all of them are capable of being transposed without undergoing fundamental change. The same tune can be played by different instruments. Or it can be made into a series of variations. Or it can be absorbed into some other work. In each case it will remain in a sense "the same," while being discernibly different, and an educated listener will be conscious at once of the original tune and the way that it has been altered. All this is evidently true of Ackroyd's "variations" on the themes he borrows from his predecessors in English literature.

There is also a biological aspect to the idea of "English music," through the notion of descendants and relationships. Timothy, as one might expect from a boy with no strong familial roots, is fascinated by the idea of ancestry, of recognizing himself in his grandparents and in the unknown generations beyond them. His name is Harcombe. But his grandparents live in Upper Harford. Could the element *Har-* in both indicate some connection? Have the Harcombes *always* lived in Harford? In England, where a high proportion of the population carries surnames derived from places, and where the places are often identifiable, the speculation is not especially fanciful. Yet it is extended to something close to fancy in chapter 6, where one character discusses Sherlock Holmes, and wonders aloud whether there is any connection between the *-lock* in the detective's name and the English philosopher John Locke. The suggestion has never been made before; Locke and Conan Doyle are normally kept in entirely separate literary compartments, and Conan Doyle is at the very least most unlikely to have thought of the philosopher when creating his great detective. And yet there is a certain similarity, as with Alice and Christian. Both the author and the character were dedicated to reason, both believed firmly in the powers of analysis; perhaps one could say that they share a certain cold-bloodedness. Is "English music" then not, as another character suggests, rather like the English language, capable of continuous historical change without losing an underlying unity, and perhaps like English faces, all different but bearing the mark of some original gene pool?

At this point one could say that at least one strand of Ackroyd's intention is visible. He means to create a sense of English "ethnicity." This is in itself a slightly paradoxical goal, for the reason that English culture generally, like the English language, has through its transference to North America and the subsequent dominance of American culture, become in a way common to the entire developed world. Charles Dickens is read from Hong Kong to Vladivostok. English-language "pop music" is familiar the world over. Even the English Victorian gentleman's regulation dress of suit-coat, trousers, shirt and tie is as obligatory for business in Tokyo as in London or New York. In this process the sense of "ethnicity," of culture being the particular possession of a group or nation, has vanished. One might say that someone in a tartan kilt is asserting Scottishness. Someone in a Savile Row suit, however, is asserting nothing, except maybe wealth. Ackroyd wants to regain the sense of Englishness. He does this by stressing the quirky, the visionary, and above all the sense of a simultaneous historical continuity and individual eccentricity that he regards as typically English.

In this the idea of music has a special place. English culture is not famous for its music (or at least not until very modern times, with which Ackroyd does not deal). If one were to rate the European nations for their contribution to classical music, England would be well behind Germany, Italy, and probably France, at least. Nevertheless, in chapter 10 Ackroyd centers a whole scene on William Byrd, a composer now almost forgotten, but the originator of the madrigal, a distinctive English form. At the end of the chapter, the elderly Byrd and his disciples break into a string of traditional songs and dances, at least a score of titles being given from "Lady, Lie Near Me" to "Jack Pudding" and "Chirping of the Lark." The image they create is of a lost pastoral

England full of a kind of folk culture at once innocent and skillful. This is what England has to offer, and this is what has been lost in the imperial and postimperial expansion from Byrd's lifetime to Timothy Harcombe's.

A doubt which one may have about this portrayal is its heavy reliance on nostalgia. English culture is often accused of living in the past, and Timothy Harcombe suffers the same accusation. In both cases it seems self-evidently true, and in both cases the risk is that by living in the past one finds it impossible to move forward into the future. Timothy's sterility on several levels is particularly marked when one remembers that he is supposed to have paranormal powers. He is capable of seeing a malevolent spirit afflicting a woman whom his father is trying to heal. He is capable of reading his grandfather's mind unerringly. Given these powers, one would think it only natural that a normal person would try to use them, well or badly, not simply accepting and leaving them. Yet this is what Timothy does. He is more interested in understanding than in acting, remains passive under almost all provocations. Arguably he is there only as an eye, as a thread on which to hang the many visions and juxtapositions of Ackroyd's history. Arguably he is also there, in "postmodernist" style, to call up ideas about the involvement of the observer with the observed, the author with the character—for in *English Music*, as has been said, characters are liable to escape from their books and fraternize with their authors. Is Sherlock Holmes John Locke come back? Is Timothy Harcombe a reincarnation perhaps of William Blake, greatest of English visionaries and both a poet in his own right and an illustrator of others, Bunyan included? If so, his vision of twentieth century London, like a transposed tune, both hints at the London of Blake 150 years before and shows its own changes; at the very start of the novel Timothy is staring at places he once knew and observing how unrecognizably changed they are, while still being, of course, "the same place."

These considerations may help one to understand *English Music* intellectually, and may encourage one also to admire Ackroyd's skill in creating the feel and the language of many periods and many different authors; in all his books to date he has showed great skill in the writing of pastiche, and a cultivated historical sense. *English Music* is, however, not an easy book to approach, demanding for one thing the ability to recognize many references and allusions without warning or explanation. There is also a strong feeling in it of private reference, of complication for its own sake. Above all one has to say that the central story, and the central character, have been made quite deliberately bland, small-scale, and uninteresting. In this Ackroyd is following in a distinguished tradition of ironic writing, which takes in works as diverse as James Joyce's *Ulysses* of 1922 (the work of an Irishman), or Marcel Proust's deeply nostalgic *À la recherche du temps perdu*, whose English title *Remembrance of Things Past* (translated 1922-1931) would do excellently as a subtitle for Ackroyd's work. Nevertheless, Timothy Harcombe remains a shadowy and unmemorable character. Readers of Ackroyd's novel must draw their inspiration from the interaction of a complex background in the past and a drab foreground in the present.

*T. A. Shippey*

## Sources for Further Study

*Chicago Tribune.* November 1, 1992, XIV, p. 6.
*Library Journal.* CXVII, September 15, 1992, p. 92.
*London Review of Books.* XIV, July 9, 1992, p. 7.
*Los Angeles Times Book Review.* October 25, 1992, p. 3.
*New Statesman and Society.* V, June 5, 1992, p. 38.
*The New York Times Book Review.* XCVII, October 11, 1992, p. 7.
*The New Yorker.* LXVIII, November 23, 1992, p. 142.
*The Observer.* May 24, 1992, p. 60.
*The Times Literary Supplement.* May 22, 1992, p. 29.
*The Washington Post Book World.* XXII, October 18, 1992, p. 7.

# THE ENGLISH PATIENT

*Author:* Michael Ondaatje (1943-    )
*Publisher:* Alfred A. Knopf (New York). 307 pp. $21.00
*Type of work:* Novel
*Time:* 1945
*Locale:* Italy

*A novel that describes the experiences of four people brought together in a deserted Italian villa near the end of World War II*

*Principal characters:*
HANA, a Canadian nurse
THE ENGLISH PATIENT/COUNT LADISLAUS DE ALMÁSY, an ostensible explorer and adventurer, later revealed to have been a spy for the Axis
DAVID CARAVAGGIO, an Italian thief
KIRPAL SINGH, a Punjabi member of a British bomb-disarming unit
GEOFFREY CLIFTON, a British adventurer
KATHARINE CLIFTON, the wife of Geoffrey Clifton and onetime lover of the English patient

Michael Ondaatje is a Sri Lanka-born novelist who lives in Canada. He is a writer, consequently, whose work writhes with the tensions inherent among races, cultures, and nationalities. Personal and political histories are Ondaatje's concerns, particularly as they intertwine and work to shape the emerging individual consciousness. In *The English Patient*, which shared the 1992 Booker Prize with Barry Unsworth's *Sacred Hunger*, Ondaatje multiplies these histories and makes of his novel a four-stranded narrative that moves between love story, history, and mystery. Any story of love involves itself naturally in mystery, and Ondaatje here deftly takes his reader in and out of the often dark and crossing passages of his characters' lives.

The physical locus of this narrative is the Villa San Girolamo, a former nunnery set in the hills of Tuscany north of Florence. Once occupied by the Germans, the battle-ravaged villa more recently has served as an Allied field hospital. With the war in Italy near its end, the hospital has been abandoned, except for a patient—the English patient—and a Canadian nurse, Hana, who has refused to evacuate the villa with the rest of the hospital staff.

The dramatic locus of this narrative begins in the exchange of stories between these two figures. Each possesses a private history that demands slow and significant telling, and Ondaatje gives them time at the start of his novel to begin those tellings. These stories take the reader back in time and move about in space; they are effective and sometimes inaccurate histories. That, says Ondaatje, is exactly the point.

The English patient is a man without a name, without a face, without an identity, with barely a temporal existence at all: He submerges himself in a cherished anonymity. His body lies blackened and immobilized by burns received in a plane crash in the Libyan desert; that body, in fact, is the wrecked emblem of his story and is that story's starting point. Memory moves where the body cannot, and the English patient uses a voice sweetened by morphine to take Hana to the desert, to that "place of faith" and ultimate mystery. The English patient is one of a group of explorers who in the 1930's sought to map the desert of northern Africa. Most of them were upper-class Englishmen, members of the Royal Geographic Society and representatives of a specific British political consciousness. They moved in foreign cultures as aliens seeking to pierce the deep heart and history of place; their cartographies were scientific, political, and emotional.

The English patient pays a severe price for his engagement. Working backward from his plane crash and his rescue by a Bedouin tribe, he unravels slowly the intricate lines of his relationship with the wife of adventurer Geoffrey Clifton. Just as he seeks to understand the desert and the profound attraction it holds for him, so the English patient labors to comprehend his love for Katharine Clifton, mapping her body as if it were strange and powerful terrain. He finds himself eventually "disassembled" by Katharine, and after her death in the plane crash that chars the English patient's body beyond recognition, he spends his days and nights piecing together a history and a self from the fragments.

Hana listens to that narrative knowing that she, too, has been "disassembled" by events. Like the English patient, she has been marked by the war in cruel ways: She has lost her father (also badly burned) to the war, and as a nurse she has witnessed close-up the various, inventive, and tragic activities of death. She craves narrative, incomplete though it might be, for it proffers a route back from her own partial madness: narrative functioning as a psychic cartography, of sorts.

Much of Hana's history remains locked, however, until an element of that history appears—a virtual reality—in her present. David Caravaggio had been Hana's "uncle" in her childhood in Toronto, her father's best friend and a professional thief. An expatriate Italian, he had returned to his country to work for the Allies, putting his profession to political and historical use. Betrayed not by his art but by the accident of a photograph, Caravaggio is caught and dismembered by Italian fascists: his thumbs are lopped off, the thief left "disassembled" and recuperating in a field hospital. There he hears of Hana's circumstance, and he sets out to locate her in the Tuscan landscape. What he has in mind is his own rehabilitation, but what he actually recovers is more than one truth of the past.

Caravaggio's relationship with Hana drives part of the mystery of Ondaatje's narrative, for what is superficially avuncular carries with it the suggestion of sexual desire, at least on the part of Caravaggio. Hana, it seems, sparks the thief's own memory of his marriage and of his wife, now dead. The erotic tension runs near the surface and with special strength from Caravaggio toward Hana; reciprocation is not forthcoming.

That tension is aggravated by Caravaggio's concern over the relationship between Hana and the English patient, a concern that begins in emotional doubt and evolves into political suspicion. Himself an intimate of the network of intelligence and espionage, Caravaggio comes to a nagging certainty that the English patient is in fact a known and presumed-to-be-dead spy: Count Ladislaus de Almásy, one of that circle of desert explorers. Caravaggio turns his art to the purpose of stealing the English patient's secret from the history that he tells, simultaneously lifting the English patient's anonymity and filling a historical blank with the substantiality of fact.

Incomplete itself, though, is Ondaatje's quartet of storytellers. With the appearance of Kirpal "Kip" Singh at the villa, the compass of narrative is made whole. Kip—the name is meant to evoke thoughts of Kipling and of *Kim* (1901), a book that floats through Ondaatje's narrative—is a Punjabi Sikh who, through natural art and adeptness, has become an almost magical defuser of mines. He is part of a British sapper unit moving through Italy in the wake of the German retreat, mapping a terrain made suddenly deadly and "disassembling" the hidden landmarks of that terrain. The villa and the Tuscany hills are part of that geography, as is the "miniature world" within the villa itself. Kip seems to search for the fuse that would leave that group in pieces. Kip's art is in disarming.

It is an art he learned from the British, and that education is the very thing that sets him apart from the other members of the quartet. Conscious of color and of culture (and ironically linked to the English patient both by his knowledge of armaments and by the darkness of his skin), Kip involves the world gathered within the villa in the politics of racial and cultural differentiation. His own history works both with and against the larger historical pattern. Born in India, taken in by the British and appreciated for his artistry but exploited for that talent and magic, Kip struggles to resolve the question of character: individual, romantic, and geopolitical character. One knows, too, that Ondaatje is working to resolve the question of his character-as-artist as well. Character, as Kip perceives it, is "a map of responsibility" that he must learn to read. Charted successfully, that map yields power, power bought uncomfortably with one's anonymity. This is a realization that hits Kip in situ—at both a bomb site and at the villa, for the two are varieties of the same landscape.

> He knew he was for now a king, a puppet master, could order anything, a bucket of sand, a fruit pie for his needs, and those men who would not cross an uncrowded bar to speak with him when they were off duty would do what he desired. It was strange to him. As if he had been handed a large suit of clothes that he could roll around in and whose sleeves would drag behind him. But he knew he did not like it. He was accustomed to his invisibility. In England he was ignored in the various barracks, and he came to prefer that. The self-sufficiency and privacy Hana saw in him later were caused not just by his being a sapper in the Italian campaign. It was as much a result of being the anonymous member of another race, a part of the invisible world. He had built up defences of character against all that, trusting only those who befriended him. But that night in Erith he knew he was capable of having wires attached to him that influenced all around him who did not have his specific talent.

Kip Singh, defuser of mines, stubbornly resists his own disarming. That task falls to Hana, with whom Kip falls in love—or at least a form or degree of love. Love is problematic, making manifest the invisible and the anonymous. Kip, who sees in all things the "choreography of accident," reluctantly embarks on the "treacherous and complex journey" of romantic revelation and dependence. He looks for reliable maps, charts to the territory; the phrase "drawn by desire" suddenly takes on special resonance.

Disarmed and vulnerable, fleshed out by love and the relinquishment of self, Kip is dramatically brought up short by historical fact. In August, 1945, bombs are dropping, dropping on people of color, on people who are one minute visible and the next minute ghosts. These are bombs whose magnitude exceeds Kip's art. The reality of these events, however, shocks Kip into a greater kind of consciousness and sends him on a journey of a different sort. He escapes the villa, its community running down toward implosion, and heads east, immersing himself on the way in one more river.

Time leaps ahead. Fourteen years later, Kip Singh has returned to India. He is married and has become a father and a doctor. The English patient has died; Caravaggio has vanished (it seems); Hana, "at even this age, thirty-four, has not found her own company, the ones she wanted. She is a woman of honour and smartness whose wild love leaves out luck, always taking risks." She is a woman recalled now to Singh by the slightest of physical movements, an occasionally disturbed stone in the river of memory.

Rivers and water flow throughout the novel, alternating images of fluidity and turbulence, cleansing and death set against the arid landscape of the desert. Ondaatje positions his characters in precise relation to these elements, establishing the locations of those characters within the cartography of both his narrative and their fictive histories. The world, in time, reveals itself as invention, as product of belief and imagination and experience. People design, says Ondaatje, a choreography to fit that accumulation of belief, imagination, and experience. One can map, at best, a world in flux. Those particularly skillful at such mapping—writers with the poetic power and enduring vision of Michael Ondaatje—provide the less able with the visual and verbal documents needed for survival. *The English Patient* is one such excellent document, a map constructed in language too potent and too eloquent to be ignored.

*Gregory L. Morris*

## Sources for Further Study

*Booklist.* LXXXIX, September 15, 1992, p. 124.
*Chicago Tribune.* October 25, 1992, XIV, p. 5.
*Library Journal.* CXVII, September 1, 1992, p. 215.
*Los Angeles Times Book Review.* October 11, 1992, p. 3.
*New Statesman and Society.* V, September 18, 1992, p. 39.
*The New York Times Book Review.* XCVII, November 1, 1992, p. 7.
*Publishers Weekly.* CXXXIX, July 20, 1992, p. 220.
*Time.* CXL, November 2, 1992, p. 71.
*The Times Literary Supplement.* September 11, 1992, p. 23.
*The Wall Street Journal.* October 16, 1992, p. A12.

# EVELYN WAUGH
## The Later Years, 1939-1966

*Author:* Martin Stannard (1947-    )
*Publisher:* W. W. Norton (New York). Illustrated. 523 pp. $29.95
*Type of work:* Literary biography
*Time:* 1939-1966
*Locale:* Primarily England

*The second, concluding volume of what is likely to be the definitive biography of one of the twentieth century's foremost English writers*

     *Principal personages:*
          EVELYN ARTHUR ST. JOHN WAUGH, a novelist
          LAURA HERBERT WAUGH, his second wife
          ALEC WAUGH, his brother and also a writer
          LADY DIANA COOPER, a friend of Evelyn Waugh
          NANCY MITFORD, a fellow writer and confidant
          A. D. PETERS, Waugh's literary agent

In a preface to the first volume of this intricately researched two-volume biography, Martin Stannard claims he is attempting "something which no other biographical study of Waugh has done: to forge a relationship between the crucial events of Waugh's life and his developing aesthetic." Certainly Stannard, a lecturer in English at the University of Leicester and editor of a collection of critical essays on Evelyn Waugh (*Evelyn Waugh: The Critical Heritage*, 1984) offers insights into Waugh's "developing aesthetic." Among the many valuable things this biography provides is a rich context for Waugh's writings that can help readers to a fuller appreciation of his work, especially of such novels as *A Handful of Dust* (1934), *Brideshead Revisited* (1945), and *The Ordeal of Gilbert Pinfold* (1957). Another attraction of this biography is the glimpses it affords of the many well-known people who were in Waugh's circle—Graham Greene, Henry Yorke, Ian and Ann Fleming, Nancy Mitford, Lady Diana Cooper, and a number of other luminaries. What is most likely to engage readers of this volume is not the "developing aesthetic" mentioned by Stannard but rather the developing portrait of the artist as obnoxious human being—or is the sometimes truly odious person who emerges from these pages merely (as some have claimed) another of Waugh's masks adopted for self-protection, or perhaps out of boredom? The only certainty is that Stannard has produced a complex and controversial study of one of the twentieth century's masters of English prose. As biography, it is of the kind known as exhaustive; it is also of the kind known as unauthorized and is in fact regarded by Waugh's son Auberon as offensive to his father's memory.

    Two authorized biographies exist. *Evelyn Waugh: Portrait of an Artist*, published by Frederick J. Stopp in 1958, is too early to be comprehensive. The second, *Evelyn Waugh: A Biography* (1975), written by Waugh's friend Christopher Sykes, is also partial in several senses. As an intimate friend, Sykes was unable or unwilling to take a candid picture of his famous subject, and his book has been criticized therefore as being inaccurate. In addition, the sheer quantity of research materials has increased greatly since Sykes's writing. Even if Sykes had wished to write the kind of carefully researched biography that Stannard has produced, he would have been unable to do so. Waugh increasingly withdrew from the world, refusing to answer his telephone and conducting his friendships and his life through correspondence. As Waugh's friends have published their own letters, diaries, memoirs, and biographies, a wealth of material has become available. Stannard has been able to draw on these materials as well as on the large number of unpublished sources to produce this doubtlessly definitive biography.

Stannard's first volume, *Evelyn Waugh: The Early Years, 1903-1939* (1986), covered Waugh's upper-middle-class childhood, his career as rebel and aesthete at Oxford, his early literary successes (as biographer, novelist, and travel writer), his brief and disastrous marriage to Evelyn Gardner, his conversion to Catholicism, his second marriage to Laura Herbert, and throughout it all, his shameless social climbing and snobbery. The second volume begins with Waugh at the age of thirty-six, an aging although idealistic volunteer officer-trainee in the Royal Marines during World War II, determined to repulse the barbarians at the gates in order to conserve the best of Western civilization: monarchy, aristocracy, and the authoritarianism of a privileged (mainly Catholic) elite. He soon realized that he was not cut out to be a soldier, the barbarians were inside the gates, and the "cause" for which he fought was something other than what he thought. In fact, the end of the war ushered in all that Waugh abhorred—democracy, socialism, and the age of the common man, for him a new dark age.

According to Stannard, Waugh's political views evolved into "a jumble of Catholic Action, nineteenth-century *laissez-faire* and the values of the Whig gentry." The contrast between the free-spirited youthful radical of the first volume and the increasingly tyrannical, crabbed old reactionary of the second volume is confounding. Stannard himself appears nonplussed, observing that Waugh "seems to have moved from the boyish to the decrepit, omitting middle age altogether." French philosopher Blaise Pascal observed that "there is no man who differs more from another than he does from himself at another time." Waugh's life is a fascinating illustration of this precept. As Stannard makes clear, the relentless direction of Waugh's mature thought and life was back to the past. "Everything he had hated in his youth, Waugh now cherished. Soon he would be Victorian. By the end of his life he was back where he felt he belonged: in the Counter-Reformation and finally, the catacombs."

Stannard has a theory to explain Waugh's steady regression. He believes that Waugh's desperate need for discipline, authority, and order caused him to look to institutions such as the military, the church, and the aristocracy as embodiments of unified meaning. Waugh's strongly individualistic personality, however, was at odds with the modern hierarchies that made up these institutions and prevented him from ever fitting in. Additionally, his own perfectionist tendencies were constantly affronted by the flaws and failings of these merely human institutions. The Catholic church let him down when it adopted liturgical changes, especially when it abandoned the Latin for the vernacular mass. The aristocracy, England's ruling elite, rebuffed him in many ways but terminally outraged him by offering not the expected knighthood but the lesser Commander of the Order of the British Empire, an award that Waugh refused even though he coveted national honor more than wealth. After this, Waugh's veneration of the ruling class diminished. In Stannard's view, Waugh was "always a solitary in search of a club," but by his own temperament and expectations he was doomed to exclusion.

Much more perplexing is this biography's impression of Waugh as husband and father. Although Waugh was in love with Laura Herbert when he married her, he proved to be an insensitive, egocentric husband, usually choosing to be absent during her many pregnancies, never hesitating to indulge his own legendary appetite for champagne, cigars, and first-class travel. He seemed to be a remote father to his six children: "My children weary me. I can only see them as defective adults," he wrote. Even allowing for Waugh's self-dramatizing, hyperbolic style, there is some truth here. Waugh could be callously indifferent, as when he refused to visit or write to his seriously injured son, or when he did not see his newborn daughter Harriet until nine days after her birth because he was busy writing. The mystery is that his family and many of his friends seemed to have infinite tolerance for his brand of rudeness and abuse. To Laura, Stannard ascribes an attitude of forbearance and hero worship: "If Laura had much to endure from her husband, she endured it gladly," he observes.

It is deeply ironic that the intensely private Waugh whose shibboleth was "never apologize, never explain" is the subject of such minute public scrutiny, but the irony does not stop there. Inevitably, a biography as detailed as this one leaves a reader with more questions than answers. Was Waugh irretrievably damaged as a child by his father's favoring of brother Alec (also a writer)? Did this drive Waugh to become too close to his mother? Did his first wife's infidelity permanently wound him? How deep were his Catholic convictions, and how could he preach asceticism "with a cigar in one hand and a glass of champagne in the other?" Finally, how can one so gifted be so defective in so many ways?

Stannard declares that he is no analyst, but he does not shrink from analysis, nor does he hesitate to use clinical terms such as "manic-depressive," "schizophrenic," and "paranoia," to describe his subject. Of Waugh's famous "breakdown," which became the basis for the novel *The Ordeal of Gilbert Pinfold*, Stannard believes the "voices" ("traumatic aural hallucinations") that Waugh experienced were released by drugs Waugh had been taking, or perhaps by the withdrawal of those drugs. Either way, according to Stannard they were authentic expressions of Waugh's self-loathing and fears that he was normally able to control or repress. The way in which Waugh transformed this nightmarish experience into fiction, ultimately denying any relevance to his own life, is an example of Waugh's genius for creating masks and false public images. The problem was to distinguish and keep separate the mask from the authentic self, something that Stannard believes Waugh found increasingly difficult.

In a summary statement, Stannard presents his own view of Waugh succinctly: "I see Waugh as a brilliant but awkward, isolated, and neurotic man, with many intimate friends and few lovers, almost frightened but with dauntless bravado, a scintillating manic depressive . . . dispossessed, alienated." As a reader struggles to follow (through a plethora of detail) the unfolding narrative of Evelyn Waugh as writer, husband, father, aspiring aristocrat, dedicated Catholic, disappointed idealist, and prematurely aging man, it seems that "alienated" becomes the operative word. It seems an inadequate word, however, to convey the extent to which this brilliant man was out of sympathy with the twentieth century, and with humanity in general. Waugh's entire life seemed to be a largely futile search for something or someone in which wholeheartedly to believe. Stannard's biography is the record of that search and of Waugh's progressive and tragic disenchantment with all the things of this world.

*Karen A. Kildahl*

## Sources for Further Study

*Chicago Tribune.* September 20, 1992, XIV, p. 1.
*The Christian Science Monitor.* September 11, 1992, p. 12.
*Commonweal.* CXIX, August 14, 1992, p. 32.
*Los Angeles Times Book Review.* September 27, 1992, p. 3.
*National Review.* XLIV, November 2, 1992, p. 56.
*The New York Times Book Review.* XCVII, September 13, 1992, p. 1.
*Newsweek.* CXX, October 12, 1992, p. 80.
*Publishers Weekly.* CCXXXIX, June 29, 1992, p. 45.
*Time.* CXL, September 21, 1992, p. 65.
*The Washington Post Book World.* XXII, August 30, 1992, p. 1.

# THE FAMISHED ROAD

*Author:* Ben Okri (1959-    )
*First published:* 1991, in Great Britain
*Publisher:* Nan A. Talese/Doubleday (New York). 500 pp. $22.50
*Type of work:* Novel
*Time:* Mid-twentieth century
*Locale:* Nigeria

*A novel that suggests why much of the best contemporary fiction is coming from postcolonial writers*

*Principal characters:*

AZARO, the narrator and protagonist, who chooses the world of the living over the spirit world, "the liberty of limitations" over "the captivity of freedom"

DAD, Azaro's father, an embittered laborer and would-be champion of the poor

MUM, Azaro's mother, patient, practical, and loving

MADAME KOTO, the owner of the local bar

ADE, Azaro's friend, another *abuki* (spirit child)

JEREMIAH, who unwittingly takes photographs that get him into trouble with those in political power

THUGS, who work chiefly for the Party of the Rich

The awarding of the 1991 Nobel Prize for literature to Nadine Gordimer served to remind readers of the importance and vitality not only of this one writer's work but of African writing in general. Major new novels by her South African countrymen J. M. Coetzee (*Age of Iron*, 1990) and André Brink (*An Act of Terror*, 1991) reinforced the Nobel Prize message, as in its own way did *Mating*, the novel that won the 1991 National Book Award for fiction and that is set in Botswana, where its author, Norman Rush, lived for a number of years. What these four writers share is immense talent, a political as well as literary interest in Africa, name-brand status among American readers, and race: All are white. Few American readers will be nearly as familiar with writings by black African writers. The publication of *The Famished Road* by émigré Nigerian Ben Okri, who lives in London, should change all that. Winner of the 1991 Booker Prize for fiction, *The Famished Road* compares favorably with the novel that won the same prestigious award exactly one decade before, Salman Rushdie's *Midnight's Children*, which put contemporary Indian writing on the postmodern literary map. *The Famished Road* may also, and again favorably, be compared with the novel that seems to have influenced Rushdie most, *One Hundred Years of Solitude* (1967), by yet another postcolonial magic realist, Gabriel García Márquez of Colombia. In *One Hundred Years of Solitude*, García Márquez manages not only to mesmerize readers with his dreamlike, labyrinthine narrative but also, just as important, to compress the history of his fictional Macondo so that the Garden of Eden and the United Fruit Company seem to be separated by at most a few years.

Okri, a different but equally adept magic realist, proves a bit more allegorical but no less expansive: "In the beginning there was a river. The river became a road and the road branched out to the whole world. And because the road was once a river it was always hungry." *The Famished Road* is not merely a Nigerian version of *One Hundred Years of Solitude*, however; it is a novel that resembles many but is ultimately unlike any other, one in which two postcolonial styles and sensibilities meet, the narrative lushness of García Márquez and the rhythmical simplicity of Chinua Achebe. The same is true, though less conspicuously so, in the six stories collected in the *Stars of the New Curfew* (1988), Okri's fourth book but the first to appear in the United States, in 1989. Here characters have names, settings are clearly defined: Nigeria during the 1970's and 1980's. *The Famished Road* does not so much lack these specifics as avoid them. As in *Midnight's Children, One Hundred Years of Solitude*, and Jerzy Kosinski's *The Painted Bird* (1965), the novel possesses a dreamlike vagueness in which the primitive and the modern are startlingly juxtaposed, in which the reader's sense of time and place blurs, and in which transformations become the norm (rivers become roads, roads become devouring mouths). A car, a few vans, several trucks, the distribution of powdered milk, the electrification of the local bar-turned-brothel, and the single passing mention of "Independence" (Nigeria's independence from Britain in 1960) are about the only signs that the action takes place in modern times. What is clearly a village setting near the beginning of the novel is just as clearly part of a city—one of its many ghettos—later on, but exactly how this transformation occurs, and when, is never made clear, purposely so. The why, on the other hand, is clear, for although *The Famished Road* is not at all sociological in approach, it is, at least in part, deeply political.

"We carry in our worlds that flourish/ our worlds that have failed." These words, drawn from the Nigerian poet Christopher Okigbo, serve as the epigraph to *The Stars of the New Curfew* and apply equally well—in a way, even better—to *The Famished Road*. Only one of the six stories collected in the former deals with the folk beliefs and spirit world that figure much more prominently in the novel, in which it is not only the main character but the reader too who always seems to be stepping into "another reality," a "different world," and who often finds it impossible to tell where and when the phantasm ends and reality begins. This uncertainty is especially appropriate to the novel's larger purpose, for *The Famished Road* is very much about change. Nothing in this novel is immune to change and nothing is without its opposite, including change itself. Okri deftly plays mutability against a half-horrific, half-comforting sense of eternal recurrence that is part Nietzschean, part Nigerian. There are no celebrations without accompanying devastations in a novel marked not by the specifics of time and place but by certain elemental differences: male and female, black and white, power and powerlessness, wealth and poverty, the modern and the primeval, and above all the spirit world and the world of the living, all occurring within the seasonal cycle of drought and torrential rains.

Lacking the omniscience of *One Hundred Years of Solitude*'s anonymous narrator and the self-conscious literary skills of Rushdie's Saleem Sinai, Okri's young narrator is an *abuki*, a spirit child, who breaks his pact with the other spirit children, choosing not to return to the *abuki* world as quickly as possible after one of his reincarnations but to remain among the living. His choice entails forgoing the freedom and joy of the *abuki* for the limitations and enigmas of earthly life. Self-discovery and selfless love (for the parents whom he does not abandon for the pleasures of the spirit life) characterize his choice. So does persistence. Several times separated from his parents by riot, by kidnapping, by visions, by nearly fatal fevers, and once by death itself, he is renamed Lazaro. As a spirit child in human form, Azaro (as he comes to be known) possesses special, and to those around him, disconcerting, powers: the ability to read minds, to see people's dreams, to communicate with animals, and to hear the half-seductive, half-menacing voices from the other side. Being completely neither of one world nor of the other, he suffers a kind of double existence, caught "somewhere in the interspace between the spirit world and the living." He is beset by voices and visions that may, at least some of the time, be nothing more than hallucinations brought on by fever, fear, or the folk stories that are the greatest of gifts passed down to him by his otherwise impoverished parents.

One of these stories is his father's tale of the King of the Road, a giant who at first lives in the forests but then, as human settlements make the forests disappear, lives on the roads, demanding sacrifices from the people, who become so oppressed that they band together to kill him. Instead of killing the giant, the poisoned meal they prepare gives him a stomachache that makes him even hungrier—so hungry that he begins to eat himself, until only a stomach is left. Seven days of rain wash it into the road, making it part of the road. "What had happened was that the King of the Road had become part of all the roads in the world. He is still hungry, and he will always be hungry. That," Azaro's father concludes, "is why there are so many accidents in the world" and "That is [also] why a small boy like you must be very careful how you wander about in this world." The story of the King of the Road is a cautionary tale, but while *The Famished Road* may resemble it stylistically, the novel offers a different and less didactic lesson, one that is closer to the spirit, than the letter, of this and other stories and songs "of recurrence told down through generations of defiant mouths."

The novel's political dimension does not surface until the second of its eight parts. Politicians arrive, making promises, in effect buying votes by distributing the powdered milk that, because contaminated, results in a "refrain of vomiting." Caught in the act, these very same politicians claim that it was not they, the Party of the Rich, but their opponents, the Party of the Poor, disguised as the Party of the Rich, who were responsible. Not convinced, the people riot. The politicians' thugs prove more persuasive, renewing the old division between the haves and the have nots, Azaro's family and those like them on one side and the landlord, the bar owner Madame Koto (one of the very few characters in the novel to have a name and the only one to have both a name and a title), and other supporters of the Party of the Rich on the other.

Azaro's parents represent complementary ways of responding to the poverty and political powerlessness that is their condition. Believing that "there is too much suffering on this earth," Azaro's mother is at once fatalistic and determined, gentle yet practical. The father is no less contradictory and is, in his own way, noble: strong,

stubborn, abusive, but also idealistic, an odd mixture of the quixotic and the belliger-
ent, willing to fight for what is right but just as often, at least in the novel's first half,
ready to strike his wife or beat his son. His work (unloading trucks) leaves him bitter
and bent, but when he turns his strength to boxing, fighting a series of surreal
opponents, winning victories that leave him battered and near death for days at a time,
he not only achieves a measure of personal fame and dignity, but also begins to concoct
his "grand schemes" for improving ghetto life. Madame Koto resembles Azaro's
parents in important ways. She fights to protect what is hers (her business) and several
times cares for Azaro (and on one occasion nurses his mother back to life). She is,
however, a more ambiguous figure, dispensing her potent pepper soup with one hand
and the palm wine of weakness and forgetfulness with the other. Worse still, as she
becomes rich she becomes contemptuous, growing fatter as Azaro's mother grows
leaner, becoming more and more powerful as those around her grow "weaker, more
accepting, more afraid." Rumored to be pregnant (according to Azaro, with three
monsters), she becomes a vampire, the King of the Road in one of his many
incarnations. She becomes what, as Azaro discovers in one of his many visions, all
followers of the Party of the Rich are, only "part-time human beings"; wolves, as it
were, in suits and dresses.

   *The Famished Road* ends appropriately enough with yet another vision, that of
Azaro's father, a sleeping giant (another and far more beneficent King of the Road)
"redeeming the world as he slept," who mistakenly thinks himself "alone because he
didn't see the others, the multitude of dream pleaders, invading all the courts of the
universe while struggling in the real hard world created by the limitations in the minds
of human beings." When he finally awakens from his long sleep, brought back to life
by his wife's love, he tells one last story, the narrative of the dream he has had in which
his father, the Priest of Roads, admonishes him to keep his door and his heart open
even though "it is more difficult to love than to die." At once simple and profound,
magical and mannered (not least in its homage to the native oral tale tradition), *The
Famished Road* affirms the justice, dignity, and wholeness that elude Azaro's parents
without becoming naïvely optimistic about their future chances, least of all in its
closing lines:

> And then it was another morning. The room was empty. Mum and Dad were gone. And the good
> breeze hadn't lasted.
> A dream can be the highest point of a life.

And so too can a novel, at least a novel like *The Famished Road*.

*Robert A. Morace*

### Sources for Further Study

*Chicago Tribune.* June 14, 1992, XIV, p. 1.
*The Christian Science Monitor.* July 10, 1992, p. 10.

*Essence.* XXIII, September, 1992, p. 58.
*The Guardian.* October 4, 1991, p. 23.
*Los Angeles Times.* June 8, 1992, p. E6.
*The Nation.* CCLV, August 3, 1992, p. 146.
*New Statesman and Society.* IV, March 22, 1991, p. 44.
*The New York Times Book Review.* XCVII, June 28, 1992, p. 3.
*The Observer.* October 21, 1991, p. 61.
*Publishers Weekly.* CCXXXIX, March 30, 1992, p. 87.
*The Times Literary Supplement.* April 19, 1991, p. 22.
*The Washington Post Book World.* XXII, May 24, 1992, p. 1.

# THE FATHER

*Author:* Sharon Olds (1942-     )
*Publisher:* Alfred A. Knopf (New York). 70 pp. $20.00; paperback $11.00
*Type of work:* Poetry

*Poems that explore the myth and reality of the father-daughter relationship from the perspective of the father's death*

The Father is a devastating book, consisting of poems almost too painful to read. Moreover, one must read them all: This is not a collection for browsing, shot through with random epiphanies for the dilettante poetry reader with a pile of collections beside an armchair. This series is an organic whole, each poem drawing its power from the others and from its position in the series, despite the fact that many of them were first published separately in such venues as *The New Yorker, Poetry*, and *Antaeus.*

Sharon Olds' poetry is known for its candor and its lyric intensity. Earlier collections, including *Satan Says* (1980), *The Dead and the Living* (1984), and *The Gold Cell* (1987), demonstrate a daring that is more an invasive form of psychological realism than it is a confessional mode. Olds's poems function as psychodramas that lure the reader in to play parts in the family story he or she would avoid or sentimentalize or gloss over in any way possible. The previous collections are more heterogeneous, though, and allow the reader more respite from the realities of death and loss.

The poems of this book narrate the death of the poet's father (and the reader must surely be able to say she is speaking directly of her own father's death, because the distinction between speaker and poet is dissolved in the dedication). The chain of events is retold in minute detail, from the final days in the hospital through the death and funeral to the voice of the introjected father years later speaking to his daughter in dream and reverie. The reader is spared nothing but is given the particulars of hospital life, details of the subtle changes that encroaching death brings, nuances of relationships that are revealed in a gesture, word, or touch. What comes forth most strongly is the physical, the importance of the body in all relationships. The series of poems is a familial love story, leaving the bereaved poet (and the reader) with only the consolation that the earth provides, that of memory and familial continuity. In the last poem, "My Father Speaks to Me from the Dead," the introjected father says,

> Of course I love
> your breasts—did you see me looking up
> from within your daughter's face, as she nursed?
> I love your bony shoulders and you know I
> love your hair, thick and live
> as earth.

The daughter accepts that her father is now a part of her, existing in her flesh and nerves. As he explains at the end of the poem, this kind of material continuity will have to suffice.

> ... I am matter,
> your father, I made you, when I say now that I love you
> I mean look down at your hand, move it,
> that action is matter's love, for human
> love go elsewhere.

It seems fair to begin at the end in discussing this book, for this is what Olds does: The father's death serves as a lens through which the lifelong relationship between father and daughter is viewed and interpreted. There are only two important figures in the book, the father and the daughter. Other figures appear—the father's wife, usually referred to as "his wife," and, peripherally, the poet's daughter, seen as a continuation of the father. The intense focus, however, is on the father and the daughter as he disappears into her: his words taken in by her ears, his smell by her nose, his changing image by her eyes. Finally, he is wholly there, contained inside her.

His death is a kind of unbirth, and the imagery that surrounds it is physical and sexual. The equation of death is made explicit in the second poem, "Nullipara," and then carried throughout the book. "Nullipara" would mean "she who gives birth to nothing." The poem concludes, "He knows he will live in me/ after he is dead, I will carry him like a mother./ I do not know if I will ever deliver." The death-birth imagery becomes more sensual as the poems progress. In fact, what stands out most in this collection is the uncompromising presence of the physical, from the beginning to the end of this narrative of dying. The father is the body of the father, inhabited or uninhabited. Others take comfort in religion, but the daughter cannot. "The Feelings" describes the scene in which the death becomes officially recognized when "the intern listened to the stopped heart." The woman is estranged from the others in the room, who are able to accept the dualism of traditional religious belief while she alone is a materialist:

> ... everyone else in the room believed in the Christian God,
> they called my father *the shell on the bed*, I was the
> only one there who knew
> he was entirely gone, the only one
> there to say goodbye to his body
> that was all he was

She transfers the cycle of birth-ripeness-decay to herself at the end of the poem, where she compares herself to "some soft thing, some fruit" under her husband's body the next morning. She cannot escape from living, loving, grief and dying. The conclusion is an acceptance of the laws of nature:

> Yes the tears came
> out like juice and sugar from the fruit—
> the skin thins and breaks and rips, there are
> laws on this earth and we live by them.

The harshness of natural law is not the only motif of these poems. It is counterbalanced by the images of light, which cluster around the figure of the father through the scenes of his dying. These images give the impression of a dying man surrounded with light, emanating light: a saint. There is irony in the sanctifying, as it is clear that during his life the father's relationship with his daughter was flawed. He apparently did not know how to speak with her or accept her, and thus it is only after he is dead that she can feel accepted by him. The situation calls to mind another, better-known set of poems dominated by the death of the father: those of Sylvia Plath. Plath's poem "Daddy" in particular establishes a communication between the living daughter and the dead father, a "black telephone" that she in the poem is desperately trying to disconnect, because his voice is calling her to her death. Olds's father's message is mixed, but much of it is a call to life, instructions on how to participate in life fully.

It is his dying that translates Olds's father, that makes him into a kind of holy and healing text. That this luminosity is physical is constantly underscored, but its mystery constantly intrigues and troubles the reader by suggesting interpretations that are specifically ruled out by the poems. For example, in the "The Last Day" the hospital personnel turn the father toward the window, and

> The daylight was shining into his mouth.
> I could see a flake, upright, a limbless
> figure, on his tongue, shudder with each breath.

The physical acquires metaphysical suggestions through the mysterious exactness of the image, bringing to mind the medieval beliefs about how the soul exits from the body—although the reader is told repeatedly in one way or another that the father's soul is composed of body. Instead of a traditional dualistic philosophy, these poems seem to suggest that the physical transcends itself through love, so that the body becomes a sacred text to be learned, so to speak, by heart.

The style of these poems contributes to their mythic luminousness. The simple names of the poems narrate and universalize. Titles (in the order of appearance) include "The Waiting," "The Pulling," "The Lumens," "His Stillness," "Last Words," "His Smell," "The Dead Body," "The Urn," "His Ashes," "One Year," and "My Father Speaks to Me from the Dead." The images are strung together in sentences often connected by commas, giving a sense of seamlessness to each poem and to the whole. Falling rhythms predominate in these free-verse poems. The trochaic foot is found more frequently than usual; the word "father" itself is a trochee. There is little masking; the "I" is always present, a natural voice, and some poems begin with this direct "I": "I wish I could wash my father's face. . . ."; "I wanted to be there when my father died. . . ." The poems contain very few proper names; the father is referred to by his relationship to the speaker, not by his name, and the wife is called "his wife" although the father uses her name. There are few allusions, and there are fewer similes and metaphors than one would expect. The paucity of tropes makes each comparison Olds does use stand out, as when she describes her father's last three breaths as being "lined up like a woman's last three eggs." Olds's style has the overall effect of primal simplicity. Each detail is of equal value in this loving leave-taking.

Sharon Olds is a poet without a school, her individual vision taking the reader places he or she would rather not go but profits immeasurably from visiting. One strangely attractive poem, "The Underlife," illustrates the fierce pull of these poems. The poet spots a rat in the subway pit. "I see a section of grey rail de-/ tach itself. . . ." Her initial reaction is repulsion, but then she thinks of her son's mice and investigates the rat, which is "small, ash-grey,/ silvery, filth-fluffy." The rat's strangeness is gentled through association with his tamer, smaller brothers, and he becomes almost beautiful: "You can see/ light through the ears." Later, in a very similar scene, she sees "an amber lozenge in the sheet's pattern/ begin to move," and the movement turns out to be that of a cockroach. She addresses roach and rat as familiars, claiming that she knows their deathworld and the immutability of natural law. Their response is direct, immediate, physical:

> And the
> roach and rat turn to me
> with that swivelling turn of natural animals, and they
> say to me We are not educators,
> we come to you from him.

The poem, like so many others in the collection, has a spooky rightness to it. One could say that these poems are of the roach and rat, who speak for and of the underlife, that they are natural animals, that they come through her from him.

*Janet McCann*

## Sources for Further Study

*American Health*. XI, July, 1992, p. 100.
*Belles Lettres*. VIII, Fall, 1992, p. 30.
*Booklist*. LXXXVIII, April 15, 1992, p. 1498.
*Boston Globe*. October 4, 1992, p. 37.
*Library Journal*. CXVII, April 15, 1992, p. 96.
*Los Angeles Times Book Review*. September 13, 1992, p. 15.
*The Nation*. CCLV, December 14, 1992, p. 748.
*Publishers Weekly*. CCXXXIX, April 6, 1992, p. 57.
*Salmagundi*. No. 97, Winter, 1993, p. 169.
*Washington Times*. July 19, 1992, p. B8.

# FATHERS AND CROWS

*Author:* William T. Vollmann (1959-    )
*Publisher:* Viking (New York). 990 pp. $30.00
*Type of work:* Historical novel
*Time:* The sixteenth to the eighteenth centuries
*Locale:* Eastern Canada

*A dramatized history of the colonization of eastern Canada by French explorers, trappers, soldiers, and missionaries*

> *Principal characters:*
> SAMUEL DE CHAMPLAIN, the military commander of New France
> BORN UNDERWATER, a fictional character, daughter of a Frenchman and a Native American woman
> SAINT JEAN DE BRÉBEUF, a Jesuit missionary tortured to death by the Iroquois; canonized in 1930
> SAINT IGNATIUS DE LOYOLA, the founder of the Society of Jesus (Jesuits)
> ROBERT PONTGRAVE, a French explorer and adventurer, father of Born Underwater
> KATERI TEKAKWITHA, an Algonquin woman converted to Catholicism now generally known as St. Catherine

In the introduction to this long, intricate, often cryptic historical novel, William T. Vollmann writes:

> This book is the story of how the Black-Gowns [Jesuit missionaries] and the Iroquois between them conquered the Huron people. With its weight of antecedents and obscurities, as I admit, the tale is an ungainly one. . . ."

That is a pretty good capsule description of *Fathers and Crows*, a rambling narrative accompanied by an introduction, glossaries, and other reference material.

Although most of the principal characters are actual historical figures, the author has inserted imaginary characters to flesh out his scenes. He has also traveled backward and forward in time, going as far into the past as A.D. 30 and as far forward as 1989.

Vollmann himself calls his work a "dream." It is part of a projected series of novels about the conquest of North America by Europeans that will carry the omnibus title of *Seven Dreams: A Book of North American Landscapes*. The first volume in this series was *The Ice-Shirt* (1990), a much shorter but no less impressionistic book that covered the arrival of the Vikings in North America in the tenth century.

Vollmann, a young writer, has amazed critics with his literary talents and his passionate dedication to his craft. *Fathers and Crows* contains exhaustive reference material showing how deeply he has immersed himself in the period he is attempting to re-create. He persists in calling himself "William the Blind," and this cognomen may refer to the effects of all the research he has already done along with all that still lies ahead of him before he completes his monumental task.

What attracted the French to Canada was the apparently inexhaustible wealth of animal furs, especially beaver furs, which were much in demand in Europe to be made into hats. The fur trappers were followed by soldiers, and the soldiers by missionaries. The foremost soldier-explorer in Canadian history was Samuel de Champlain, who founded the city of Quebec and courageously ventured as far west as the Great Lakes in quest of a route to China. He is the most interesting character in the book, and this may be because he was motivated not by greed but by humane consideration for the native inhabitants as well as a dedication to the enrichment of human knowledge through exploration.

Unfortunately for the Native Americans, the fur trade also attracted the British and the Dutch. They began pitting the various indigenous tribes against one another and against their European competitors. At first, the Europeans were understandably cautious about providing the Native Americans with guns; later, however, the Iroquois obtained large quantities of guns and ammunition from the Dutch, with disastrous results for Native Americans and Europeans alike.

The main highway of exploration and exploitation was the mighty St. Lawrence River. As the omnibus title of Vollmann's work suggests, he loves natural beauty; his descriptions of American landscapes are perhaps more appealing than his descriptions of the people who inhabited them. Champlain followed the St. Lawrence to the Huron country, bordering what is now known as Lake Huron. His reports on the wealth of furs available in this virgin territory incited the greed of traders, because the existing supply of animals was being devastated by uncontrolled extermination.

There apparently was no understanding whatever of such matters as the ecological balance of nature or environmental protection. Canada seemed like an endless forest full of animal wealth. Champlain himself believed that it stretched all the way to China. Greedy European investors demanded maximum returns on their investments, not unlike many corporate shareholders of the late twentieth century. Fur trading was big business. Vollmann details the quantities of cheap trade goods brought in and beaver furs taken across the Atlantic in the sailing ships that required several months to make the hazardous crossing.

Champlain and a Jesuit missionary named Jean de Brébeuf are the only two characters in the entire book who are developed fully by the author; the others, whether they are real or imaginary people, make only cameo appearances. *Fathers and Crows* was not conceived or executed as a conventional historical novel such as the popular *Black Robe* by Brian Moore, published in 1985 and brought out as a motion picture in 1991. Moore's book focuses on a single fictitious character, a Jesuit priest, who has a single motive, which is to travel up the St. Lawrence River in order to reach two of his colleagues in the Huron country.

In contrast, Vollmann's *Fathers and Crows* is broken up into myriad fragments, almost like the bits of stained glass in a cathedral window. The text is not evenly divided into chapters but composed of innumerable short sections, some of which are less than a page long. At one point, Vollmann interrupts his disjointed narrative to present a forty-three-page biography of Saint Ignatius de Loyola, founder of the

Society of Jesus. This quixotic arrangement suggests a lack of planning or perhaps even some sort of neurosis. It has led one critic to complain: "The hundreds of pages of historical background included to bulk up the narrative subvert rather than enhance this novel of faith, desire and the tragedy of spiritual imperialism."

William the Blind often talks about the "Stream of Time" as an entity on which he and the reader can travel backward and forward at a much greater rate of speed. The effect of his repeated and deliberate violations of Aristotle's unities of time, place, and action is to destroy the book as a novel. The reader may get caught up in a dramatic episode and experience the illusion of being in another world; however, the illusion is sure to be dispelled by an abrupt change of scene or by one of the author's many intrusive interjections, of which the following is a typical example:

> She admitted that she'd considered herself an eternity of times as the cruelest of mothers, but begged him to remember that life was short, so that soon she would be reunited with him forever to rejoice in the glory OF GOD. (As a matter of fact, she had another quarter-century left to live.)

Here is another example of a kind of self-conscious intrusion that seems deliberately intended to jar the reader out of the illusion that the conventional historical novelist tries so hard to create: "But the Iroquois would have their revenge in 1649, reader; just be patient and you will see!"

Vollmann himself apparently regards his work as a "dream" about history. All this probably means is that he has read a lot of history books and documents and has imagined what the reality must have been like. It might most accurately be described as a dramatized or "colorized" panorama of history. This is what makes the book appealing and at the same time vexatious. Vollmann is more imaginative and poetic than the typical historian but less disciplined and less reliable. If it were not for Vollmann's undeniable gift with language, the book would hardly be worth reading, because it is not fact and not fiction.

The Hurons were anxious to trade furs for European manufactured goods. Vollmann's graphic narrative is useful in helping the reader understand the motivations of the various groups involved. Iron and copper cooking utensils made life much easier for the Native Americans (whom the French always referred to as "the Savages"). Prior to the introduction of these metals, the standard means of cooking soups and stews consisted of dropping heated rocks into scooped-out wooden containers. Iron arrowheads were also far more effective than stone ones in killing animals and human beings. Steel knives were much better than sharpened clam shells for slicing food, skinning animal carcasses, and cutting off the fingers of captured enemies.

A large part of *Fathers and Crows* has to do with the deadly rivalries among the various native peoples. The most ferocious and most feared group was the Iroquois confederation, made up of the Mohawk, Seneca, Cayuga, Oneida, and Onondaga nations. Their archenemies were the Hurons. Long before the arrival of the Europeans, Iroquois and Hurons had been conducting a bloody feud. Typically, invaders from one side would carry off captives, whom they would kill with fiendish torture. Women and children would take part in these festivities and contribute their own creativity to making the prisoners suffer as much and as long as possible. Naturally the other side would feel compelled to retaliate, and this had been going on since time immemorial.

The arrival of the Europeans gave the Iroquois and Hurons greater incentive to kill one another, not that they really seemed to need it. Now they were competing to exchange their furs for manufactured goods. The Hurons had an advantage because they were closer to the original trading posts; however, other trading posts operated by Dutch and English entrepreneurs complicated the situation. The French and English were wary about providing Native Americans with guns; the Dutch, however, had no qualms about doing so because they evidently did not believe they had any chance of establishing permanent colonies in this part of the New World.

When the Iroquois obtained large quantities of guns and ammunition, the balance of power among the Native Americans was destroyed. Iroquois killed Hurons faster than the Jesuits could baptize them. The biggest killer, however, was not the Iroquois but the microscopic smallpox virus, against which the native inhabitants had no genetic resistance. Father Brebeuf and the other Jesuit missionaries exploited the terror aroused by the recurring epidemics to win converts to Catholicism.

The Jesuits' interest in death and the afterlife won them the reputation of being evil sorcerers. When the Iroquois finally captured Father Brebeuf, they had a gala time baptizing him with boiling water, cutting strips from his flesh and devouring them, broiling him with a collar of red-hot iron axeheads, and finally putting him out of his misery with their tomahawks after torturing him for more than fifteen hours. Foremost among his tormentors were Native Americans he had converted to Christianity.

Half the population of the Huron confederacy was wiped out by epidemics between 1634 and 1640. The confederacy was totally destroyed and the survivors dispersed by the Iroquois between 1649 and 1650. This represents the end of Vollmann's main story, although he travels forward on his Stream of Time to describe present-day Canada and the conflicts that exist among the Native Americans, the French Canadians, and the dominant Anglo culture.

No one can deny that William T. Vollmann is a remarkable writer. He has a wisdom beyond his years and a genius for description. In addition to possessing the talents of a gifted creative writer, Vollmann has the passion for research of a dedicated scholar. He reminds the reader of the Jesuits themselves in his single-minded dedication to his craft. *Fathers and Crows* is an impressive work that evokes feelings of pity and terror, even though the reader might wish the Stream of Time had been less convoluted and the ride less bumpy.

*Bill Delaney*

## Sources for Further Study

*Booklist*. LXXXIX, September 1, 1992, p. 35.
*Chicago Tribune*. July 26, 1992, XIV, p. 3.
*Library Journal*. CXVII, August, 1992, p. 153.

*Los Angeles Times Book Review.* August 23, 1992, p. 2.
*The New York Times Book Review.* XCVII, September 6, 1992, p. 14.
*Publishers Weekly.* CCXXXIX, July 13, 1992, p. 36.
*Time.* CXL, August 31, 1992, p. 69.
*The Times Literary Supplement.* October 23, 1992, p. 21.
*USA Today.* August 13, 1992, p. D4.
*The Washington Post Book World.* XXII, August 2, 1992, p. 1.

# FOUNDING THE FAR WEST
## California, Oregon, and Nevada, 1840-1890

*Author:* David Alan Johnson (1950-    )
*Publisher:* University of California Press (Berkeley). Illustrated. 474 pp. $35.00
*Type of work:* Political history
*Time:* 1840-1890
*Locale:* California, Oregon, and Nevada

*The evolution of these three territories into states is traced through a study of the men who wrote the original constitutions and of the political, social, and economic forces that guided, or often controlled, them in their deliberations*

*Principal personages:*
Delegates to the 1849 California Constitutional Convention
WILLIAM MCKENDREE GWIN, a former Mississippi congressman, the most prominent member of the convention
JAMES MCHALL JONES, a former Louisiana lawyer, a consumptive
CHARLES TYLER BOTTS, a former Virginia agricultural reformer
HENRY WAGER HALLECK, a New Yorker and West Point graduate
LANSFORD HASTINGS, a legendary Missouri trail guide
MORTON MATTHEW MCCARVER, a Kentucky-born pioneer and antislavery advocate

Delegates to the 1857 Oregon Constitutional Convention
LA FAYETTE GROVER, a native of Maine, a soldier and lawyer, later a U.S. senator and governor of Oregon
GEORGE WILLIAMS, the chief justice of the territorial supreme court, later a U.S. senator
MATTHEW DEADLY, a member of the territorial supreme court, later of the U.S. district court
DELAZON SMITH, a noted orator and U.S. senator
THOMAS JEFFERSON DRYER, the editor of the Whig *Oregonian*, later U.S. minister to the Kingdom of the Sandwich Islands
DAVID LOGAN, a brilliant but alcoholic lawyer, son of Abraham Lincoln's law partner

Delegates to the 1864 Nevada Constitutional Convention
JOHN NEELY JOHNSON, a former governor of California, the convention's president
JOHN ANDERSON COLLINS, a former abolitionist, subsequent socialist and suffragist
THOMAS FITCH, a newspaper editor and orator, coauthor of the utopian novel *Better Days: Or, a Millionaire To-morrow* (1891)
CHARLES E. DE LONG, an attorney and politician, later U.S. minister to Japan

In this political history of the founding of the states of California, Oregon, and Nevada, David Alan Johnson has attempted to combine a study of ideology and culture with individual biography. Using as his focal points the movement into statehood of three territories—California in 1849, Oregon in 1857, and Nevada in 1864—he examines both the society found in each area and the people who brought their individual beliefs and visions with them to this frontier land. Johnson's study covers the years 1840 to 1890, half a century centered around the Civil War. Although most of the primary fighting was confined to the eastern half of the country, Johnson shows how the war's causes and its outcome directly influenced the political development of these western lands. Nevertheless, he also makes the case that these three contiguous regions had their separate political and cultural agenda, that each was an individual state with an identity based on social beliefs and economic realities.

Johnson constructs his study on three "considerations." First, because the creation of the state constitutions of each of these regions occurred before the end of the Civil War, "the early charter societies and the political charters of California, Oregon, and Nevada were the creation of antebellum Americans" bringing with them "similar cultural baggage," including a common sense of national identity, symbols, and allegiances. The second consideration is that despite these "commonalities," the writers of the constitutions were nevertheless "representatives of distinct, self-selected 'fragments' of antebellum American culture and society." Each area drew, for various reasons, different kinds of immigrants who brought with them distinctive attitudes and rationales, which were then incorporated into the philosophies of the constitutions themselves. Johnson's third point is that these authors represented a generation whose lives were "divided, not ended, by the Civil War era": "In writing constitutions they left detailed records of their individual ideologies and common political culture at the threshold of the Civil War. Because their lives extended into the 1880's and even beyond, they confronted the long-term consequences of both war and industrial revolution."

These three considerations help to establish the overall structure of the book. Johnson has divided his work into three sections, with each section containing separate chapters on each of the chosen states. The first section, "Politics and Society," concentrates on the prestatehood era of each territory: California from 1769 to 1849; Oregon from 1835 to 1857; and Nevada from 1849 to 1864. The second part, "Personality, Ideology, and Political Culture," details the writing of the individual constitutions, in Monterey, California; Salem, Oregon; and Carson City, Nevada. In this section, Johnson introduces the selected authors whose lives he finds representative or significant, although he quite rightly makes the point that he is not subscribing to the "great men" approach to history in doing so. "I have not chosen these individuals in order to resurrect reputations or claim greatness; rather, I have reconstructed the lives of ordinary men in politics because one finds in the details, where experience, personality, and ideology intersect, a key to political culture," Johnson writes. His claim is supported by these mini-biographies, which effectively illustrate how a variety of personages from different backgrounds formed the kind of political identity each state came to assume. The third section, "History and Memory," traces the aftermath of the historical moment of statehood, the success or failure of each state to hold to the goals and ideals put forth in its constitution. He also follows the lives of the selected individuals examined in section 2 beyond this event, for many of them their one moment of importance.

Each of these regions, in Johnson's study, assumes a kind of personality, caused in part by its settlers but also by its physical environment and social history. The land of California, originally a Mexican province, was in the early part of the 1800's "a land of isolated regions, imposing geography, and poor communications" populated by native-born "Californios." The region had a strong Hispanic culture. The first wave of Anglo settlers were soldiers of fortune, New England merchants, and hopeful farmers. By 1847, the Americans had conquered the Mexican natives and taken control of the land, but the military rule that followed proved to be an unacceptable form of government to these Anglo-American settlers. When the California gold rush began in earnest in 1848, the need for order became even more evident. Johnson describes the prevailing social view as "*Lockean liberalism*—the position that men who maximize their private satisfactions serve the common good," but the desire for self-gain led to conflict and power struggles. The delegates to the convention came from all over the region, and there was immediate dissension between newcomers to the territory, the native-born Californios, and the pre-gold rush settlers. Although Robert Semple, an old settler, was elected president, the influence of men from other regions of the country, bringing with them their own views, was strongly reflected in the constitution itself.

Oregon, on the other hand, was a land of tradition. As Johnson writes,

> At the time of statehood, Oregonians looked back on a generation of relatively slow, incremental American settlement, initiated by Methodist missionaries in the 1830's and then recast in the 1840's by succeeding waves of farming families from the Ohio and Mississippi River valleys. In contrast to California, the people of the Oregon Country were a homogeneous lot.

More farm than frontier, more native-born than immigrant, this region had different expectations and needs in the devising of its constitution. Oregon had moved quietly from local government to provisional government in 1843 and to territorial government thereafter. The men who came together to create a state were "a familiar cast of local characters, old settlers themselves, who stood at the head of organizations to which the men of Oregon devoted their spirited allegiance. The constitutional convention thus had a definite air of familiarity." The gold rush in California had drawn people away from Oregon, but those who remained preferred their contrasting way of life. Unlike the California explorers, who hoped to strike it rich, the farmers of Oregon wanted comfort and security but not great wealth. The chief political division in the territory was between the Democrats, whose lead spokesman was Asahel Bush, the editor of the *Oregon Statesman*, and the anti-Democrats (grouped as Whigs, Know-Nothings, and Republicans), led by Thomas Jefferson Dryer. For different reasons, both groups favored the idea of statehood, although their concepts of a state constitution were quite different.

The Nevada experience was closer to that of California. In fact, many settlers of

Nevada, and thus many of the men who would write the constitution, were "old Californians," miners who had played out in the gold rush and were looking for new hope in the neighboring region. Although the sense of liberal individualism that had motivated the California authors could still be found in their Nevada counterparts, these men had the benefit of California's experience to guide them in their vision. "These 'old Californians' convened in the midst not of boom times reminiscent of 1849 but, rather, during a sudden depression that forced them to confront the emerging industrial character of their society and, perforce, revise the liberal vision they had hoped to redeem," Johnson writes. The solitary miner of California had been replaced by the powerful corporate mining industry in Nevada, the individual subsumed by the group.

In his discussion of the writing of the California state constitution in 1849, Johnson makes several significant observations. The diversity of the authors was extreme: only six had been born in California, whereas the rest came from fifteen other American states and even from five European countries. More than half of the delegates to the convention were men for whom "California was but the most recent stop in an ongoing series of moves." Thirteen of the delegates came from New York and New Jersey, eleven from the Midwest, and nine from the South. The issues they discussed were influenced in part by their regional backgrounds and beliefs, and on four of these issues—banking, suffrage, the rights of free African Americans, and the state's boundary—they argued strongly. Although slavery was outlawed quickly, the questions of citizenship and suffrage for African Americans, Native Americans, and "other objectionable races" were not so easily resolved. Indeed, as Johnson concludes, the constitution authors were men of deep beliefs who could not, ultimately, find ways of resolving their conflicts, which were, in essence, the conflicts besetting the antebellum nation as a whole. The constitution they created merely repeated the received wisdom without fixing solutions.

Whereas the Californians had used the state constitutions of New York and Iowa as models, Oregon turned to midwestern models for its own. The diversity found in the California delegation was absent from Oregon's 1857 gathering. Moreover, these were permanent inhabitants, farmers and lawyers, not men ready to move on to new explorations. The split between Democrats and anti-Democrats, however, prevented peaceful consideration of the constitution. The Democrats, led by La Fayette Grover, omitted religious sentiment that the anti-Democrats supported. Similar disagreements arose on the questions of suffrage and immigrant rights. Both parties agreed, not surprisingly, on larger questions of race, with the result that no people other than pure white men were granted the full rights of citizens. Chinese, Native Americans, African Americans, and women of any race were prohibited from participation in the business of the state.

The 1864 convention in Nevada occurred in the last months of the Civil War, during a severe economic crisis. The delegates argued in favor of statehood, in part to support the Union during this time of national division. The economic problems centered on the mines, the primary industry in the territory. The writers of the constitution were greatly concerned with the financial problems besetting the region. The questions of railroad subsidies and taxation of the mines meant that railroad and mining interests were at the heart of the philosophical debates held during the convention. The chief railroad man was Thomas Fitch, a Republican, who linked the idea of the transcontinental railroad with that of national loyalty and unity. The railroad was also connected to the mining interests in that support for railroads was traded for support for taxation of mines. Corporate mining supporters, led by Charles E. De Long, argued that "it was incumbent on the constitution writers to recognize that their and their constituents' self-interest was subsidiary to, even subsumed within, the interest of the supra-individual corporation." Thus, the concerns of the individual were less important than those of the corporation, a direct contrast to the decisions made in California at their earlier convention.

The last section of the book discusses the results of these political decisions as each state moved toward the twentieth century. The end of the Civil War brought many changes and challenges, which in some cases directly confronted the ideologies set into law by these three constitutions. Johnson follows the selected individual writers of the constitutions as they played out their own careers, in many cases determined by the same national political and social forces. Some of these men went on to greater fame, but most did not. Indeed, Johnson makes clear that these were, for the large part, ordinary, common folk—in some cases less than ordinary—who took part in the creation of great works.

Johnson's study is a hybrid in its combination of biography with social, economic, and political matters, but it is a mixture that largely works. The individual histories give personality to the larger picture, which, examined alone, could be rather dry, despite the inherent political drama. Some readers might wish that Johnson had employed a different structure for his presentation. Given the large cast of personages, it is sometimes disconcerting to move from one state to another within each separate section of the book; the discontinuous discussion can cause temporary confusion. As Johnson indicates, the reader could choose to read the three chapters on each of the three states one after the other and more easily maintain the narrative thread. Moreover, the alternating structure Johnson uses has its advantages, enabling him to draw immediate parallels or contrasts among the states and their ideologies. In all, *Founding the Far West* is a thoughtful, perceptive study, an accumulation of good scholarship employed in the telling of a rewarding story.

*Edwin T. Arnold*


## Sources for Further Study

*Library Journal*. CXVII, April 15, 1992, p. 106.
*Publishers Weekly*. CCXXXIX, March 23, 1992, p. 51.
*The Washington Post Book World*. XXII, August 16, 1992, p. 13.

# FRANK CAPRA
## The Catastrophe of Success

*Author:* Joseph McBride (1947-    )
*Publisher:* Simon & Schuster (New York). Illustrated. 768 pp. $27.50
*Type of work:* Biography
*Time:* 1897-1991
*Locale:* Primarily Los Angeles, California

*An extensively researched revisionist biography treating the life and career of Frank Capra, who wrongly came to be associated with the central figures of his most popular and beloved films*

*Principal personages:*
> FRANK RUSSELL (FRANCESCO ROSARIO) CAPRA, a Sicilian American who became America's most popular film director during the 1930's
> ROSARIA (SARIDDA) NICOLOSI CAPRA, his mother, who worked hard to help her son better himself through education
> SALVATORE (PAPA TURIDDU) CAPRA, his father
> MACK SENNETT, the "King of Comedy," who hired Capra in 1924 as a gag man and eventually allowed him to direct the silent comedian Harry Langdon
> HELEN HOWELL, a comedic ingenue whom Capra married in 1923 and divorced in 1928
> HARRY COHN, the head of Columbia Studios, who hired Capra in 1927 and was quick to recognize and encourage his talents as a gifted director
> LUCILLE WARNER REYBURN, Capra's devoted second wife
> ROBERT RISKIN, a screenwriter, Capra's collaborator at Columbia Studios
> JIMMY STEWART, the romantic lead whose career was advanced by his collaboration with Frank Capra and whose acting talents helped Capra create an endearing emblem of the common man

Joseph McBride's *Frank Capra: The Catastrophe of Success* is sure to disturb the Capra cult that chooses to valorize Capra as the embodiment of the American success story, an immigrant artist who surely must have shared the innocence, goodness, and humane virtues of the screen heroes who populate his best films, a man who symbolized the best qualities that American culture produced during the twentieth century. The book begins with a bitter and negative account of Capra's return visit to his birthplace in Sicily in 1977, to a town he no longer remembered, to see relatives for whom he had no feelings, nearly declining an invitation to a dinner in his honor organized by his nephew, and finally spending only an hour in the company of kinsmen who had looked forward to his arrival.

This book is iconoclastic in the truest sense of the word. It fractures and attempts to demolish the image of Frank Capra that the director had so carefully cultivated during the years following a long and productive Hollywood career as not only a great director, whose films seemed to capture the best values that American society had to offer, but also as a "great guy." The autobiography (described by one reviewer as "autohagiography") *Frank Capra: The Name Above the Title*, published by Macmillan in 1971, was the stuff of legends. In fabricating the Capra myth, the director tended to slight the contributions of the many collaborators who had worked with him, according to McBride, who went out of his way to interview as many of those collaborators as possible. On the other hand, Capra's book (written with Eugene Vale, whose contribution the director also slighted after the book was published) helped to remind readers of a wonderful body of cinema that had been neglected during the period of Capra's decline after World War II, from *Mr. Deeds Goes to Town* (1936), *Mr. Smith Goes to Washington* (1939), and *Meet John Doe* (1941). *It's a Wonderful Life* (1946), which was not a box-office success, later came to be considered "the quintessential Christmas movie," though McBride calls it "essentially reactionary" and suggests that it later became popular because it was "the perfect film for the Reagan era."

McBride's book weighs in at 768 pages, answering Capra's book, which ran to 513 pages. McBride contends that Capra's book was more mythic than factual. It was produced with the help of others who were allowed to share neither the credit nor the glory. Chet Stricht retyped and corrected the manuscript, for example, but within three years of the book's publication, Stricht was let go "on six weeks notice after thirty-nine years of loyal service." Capra's book was a Book-of-the-Month Club selection, read by thousands and generally taken as factual. McBride's unauthorized biography tells a truer story, based in fact and unadorned by mythic embellishment. Only a fraction of those who read Capra's book will read McBride's, good as it is, so the legend is likely to survive.

Joseph McBride is a working journalist and film critic who has written substantially on several of America's greatest film directors, including books on Orson Welles, John Ford, and Howard Hawks. As a reporter for *Daily Variety*, he has covered Los Angeles as an industry insider for twenty years. He first began having doubts about the "real" Frank Capra when he was assigned to write the American Film Institute's Life Achievement Award tribute to Capra in 1981. Research on his Capra book began in earnest in 1984, and it took the author seven years to sort out the conflicting evidence produced by that research. Hundreds of people are cited and named in his "Acknowledgments," not only Hollywood figures but also Capra's classmates and dozens of family members no one else had bothered to contact. McBride's methods and thoroughness seem downright compulsive, and the "truth" he unearthed may seem distasteful to some.

Although McBride offers a major and substantial reevaluation of Capra's career, there can be no doubt that Frank Capra was a major director. His career flourished during the 1930's, when he was the top talent at Columbia Studios and seemed to encompass the spirit of the times. Even so, the success of Capra's Columbia pictures resulted from a fruitful collaboration with gifted screenwriters, particularly Robert Riskin, who worked successfully with Capra during the 1930's, even though the two men shared very different sensibilities and political attitudes. This situation recalls the reevaluation of Orson Welles and his collaboration with Herman Mankiewicz on the classic *Citizen Kane* (1941), debated during the 1970's by Pauline Kael, defending Mankiewicz, and Peter Bogdanovich, who championed Welles. McBride argues that films that are now considered "Capraesque" could just as easily and as accurately be called "Riskinesque." He also asserts that neither Capra nor Riskin worked as well separately as they did together.

Another less savory issue concerns the man behind the artist. After Alfred Hitchcock's death in 1980, Donald Spoto raised disturbing questions about the director's character in *The Dark Side of Genius: The Life of Alfred Hitchcock* (1984) and then offered more astonishing revelations in *Laurence Olivier: A Biography* (1992). Unlike Spoto, McBride is not simply selling sensationalism and smut, but the tarnished image of Frank Capra the man that emerges from McBride's book is likely to disappoint Capra's fans and admirers.

Frank Capra came with his family to Los Angeles at the age of six in 1903, before Hollywood was the center of motion picture production, indeed, before films had advanced much beyond the nickelodeon stage. The boy grew up in relative poverty and worked hard to put himself through school, but he apparently was ashamed of his immigrant antecedents, and, later, even of his family. Young Capra appears to have been runty, crude, and insecure at first, but smart enough to get into the school that was later to become the California Institute of Technology, where he became more popular than he had been in high school, perhaps because Pasadena was a bit distant from East Los Angeles, the old neighborhood, and his family. At college it was easier for Capra to disguise his insecurities. Although he claimed a degree in engineering, he in fact earned a less rigorous general degree. The tendency of Capra's autobiography was toward distortion and exaggeration, and this tendency carries forward to his early film career as gag man and later director. By his own account, Capra took full credit for the silent comedian Harry Langdon's screen success. Capra claimed that Langdon was not clever enough to design or even to understand his own comic persona. McBride gives clear evidence to the contrary.

Capra's first substantial success in pictures resulted from his work with Harry Langdon and Arthur Ripley at the Sennett Studio. When Langdon signed with First National Pictures in 1925, Capra was one of the Sennett gag men Langdon took with him to work on *Tramp, Tramp, Tramp* (1926), directed by Harry Edwards. (In his autobiography, Capra elevated his role to "codirector," but Capra admitted to McBride in 1984 that he was "just helping" on that picture.) Capra did direct *The Strong Man* (1926), now considered a silent comedy classic, which he brought in ahead of schedule and under budget. On the next Langdon comedy, *Long Pants* (1927), Capra directed but quarreled over the design with Langdon and writer Arthur Ripley and was fired just before the film's first preview. While the film was being made, both Langdon's and Capra's marriages broke up. Capra wrote in his autobiography that Langdon's career went downhill after *Long Pants* because Langdon did not understand his comic persona and could not maintain his success without Capra's guidance. In fact, McBride asserts, Langdon had invented his comic character on the vaudeville circuit before going to Hollywood. Arguably, Langdon might have damaged the film by cutting the seventy-minute Capra version down to sixty-one minutes.

Because the Langdon-Capra feud was public knowledge and Langdon claimed that Capra did not really direct the picture, Capra wrote to film columnists that Langdon was conceited, egotistical, and impossible to work with. By 1931, as Capra's star was beginning to rise, Harry Langdon was bankrupt and back working in vaudeville.

McBride's Capra always worked to put himself in the best possible light. Later in his career, when it was expedient to show his true political colors, he did, but during the Depression years, while working with writers who had either liberal or communist leanings, Capra claimed to be apolitical. McBride points out that Capra was not a supporter of Franklin D. Roosevelt or of the New Deal programs, that he was not necessarily in sympathy with the poor and the needy during those years (the capitalist characters in his films are not exactly beyond redemption, for example), that his ambition kept him loyal to the Academy of Motion Picture Arts and Sciences at the time the Screen Directors Guild was forming, that he admired Francisco Franco and Benito Mussolini, and that he even had anti-Semitic leanings. This was not the Frank Capra of legend.

Capra was very protective of his reputation and worked hard to maintain it during his later years. He made scores of campus tours and was generous in sharing his time with friendly interviewers, encouraging their respect and admiration. After the publication of his book, he was impressed by the power of the printed word. "Intellectuals threw verbal stink bombs at my films at the time they were made," he wrote to a journalist in 1972. After writing his book, in which he told the world how great his films really were, he found that "Academia believes me." Perhaps some of the films were great and deserved to be rediscovered, but certainly not all the academic critics were bamboozled by Capra's self-promotion.

Academic critic Charles J. Maland, the author of two critical works on Capra, has remarked, "I admire Capra's films a great deal, but I did not see him as a man without faults." He went on to enumerate some of those faults: Capra's need for acceptance, his oversized ambition and ego, and his quest for fame and reputation, faults also enumerated by McBride.

Capra fell fast and hard between 1938, when he made the cover of *Time* magazine and was the highest paid director in Hollywood, and 1948 and beyond, as his earlier immense popularity became a mere memory. It must have been difficult for a man who had served as president first of the Academy of Motion Picture Arts and Sciences and then of the Screen Directors Guild to pass into relative obscurity.

Capra's defenders will surely consider McBride's book unfair and one-sided, the "evidence" contained in McBride's interviews being used to fit his iconoclastic thesis. Maland believes that McBride was "harder on Capra than the evidence deserves," that another researcher might have used the same evidence to reach conclusions that were less harsh.

In fact, at times McBride seems to be trying too hard to demolish the Capra myth. The book begins with a negative account of Capra's return in 1977 to Bisacquino, the Sicilian village where he was born, to visit relatives he did not remember. The title of chapter 1 says it all: "I Felt Nothing." Reading further, one finds a brash and arrogant young man mainly interested in self-betterment, a man embarrassed by his family, his dreamy and impractical father, his immigrant status, his poverty, and his ethnic heritage. His American relatives were offended by the distortions they found in Capra's autobiography, which created its own reality in order to make Capra look as good as possible. Frank Capra was always his own best publicist.

To a degree, of course, this is understandable. Writing one's autobiography can be an act of intense egotism, and it is only human that a man might try to improve the reality of his own success story. McBride's intent is to demythologize the hero, to cut him down to size, to explain how he was not universally loved by his family, his classmates, and his closest associates whom he habitually slighted, to psychologize Capra's frustrated love life (including lurid details about a dose of gonorrhea and a badly executed circumcision performed by a quack), and to expose Capra's autobiography as a partly fictive, distorted pack of lies.

One doubts that McBride's own motives were self-serving here. He had already established his credentials long before this book was written. His industriousness cannot be faulted, and he must have cared deeply about Capra's work to justify a seven-year period of intensive research. The book is exhaustively researched in its attempt to set the record straight. It is an impressive work of revisionist biography, carefully written, eminently readable, and fascinating. One is convinced that it comes nearer to the truth of Frank Capra than Capra's own book, and one finishes it with a better understanding of Hollywood and its political pressures from the 1930's through the 1950's.

*James M. Welsh*

**Sources for Further Study**

*Booklist.* LXXXVIII, April 1, 1992, p. 1423.
*Chicago Tribune.* June 2, 1992, V, p. 3.
*Library Journal.* CXVII, May 1, 1992, p. 84.
*Los Angeles Times Book Review.* May 17, 1992, p. 2.
*The New Republic.* CCVI, June 8, 1992, p. 44.
*The New York Times Book Review.* XCVII, May 3, 1992, p. 3.
*Premiere.* V, July, 1992, p. 26.
*Publishers Weekly.* CCXXXIX, March 2, 1992, p. 59.
*Variety.* CCCXLII, June 1, 1992, p. 84.
*The Washington Post Book World.* XXII, April 12, 1992, p. 3.

# FRANK LLOYD WRIGHT

*Author:* Meryle Secrest (1930-    )
*Publisher:* Alfred A. Knopf (New York). Illustrated. 634 pp. $30.00
*Type of work:* Biography
*Time:* 1867-1991
*Locale:* Primarily the United States

*A biography of America's greatest architect that concentrates on his life and slights his work*

*Principal personages:*
FRANK LLOYD WRIGHT, an outspoken, nonconforming, arrogant, and brilliant architect
ANNA WRIGHT, his self-reliant mother
WILLIAM CAREY WRIGHT, his weak father
CATHERINE WRIGHT, his gentle first wife
MAMAH BORTHWICK CHENEY, his beguiling lover
MIRIAM NOEL WRIGHT, his destructive second wife
OLGIVANNA LLOYD WRIGHT, his resourceful third wife

Meryle Secrest is a British-born reporter, editor, and biographer who has written books about Romaine Brooks, Bernard Berenson, Kenneth Clark, and Salvador Dalí. In producing this text, she not only consulted Frank Lloyd Wright's family and associates but also pored over a depository of more than one hundred thousand items indexed by the Getty Center Archives for the History of Art and Humanities in Santa Monica, California. Her printed notes span thirty-eight pages, her selective bibliography five, and her acknowledgments eight.

The result is a lively life story that features the five women who played prominent roles in Wright's career and provides a number of vivid anecdotes. Regrettably, however, Secrest's expressed knowledge of her subject's achievements is severely limited, even though the publisher's blurb calls her an art critic. She makes little effort to analyze Wright's buildings in detail or to assess his national and international place in his profession. As a romantic narrative of a complex, zestful, willful, and indomitable individual, however, Secrest's book often makes for good reading. It succeeds as a popular biography even as it falls short as a scholarly and critical interpretation.

On his maternal side, Frank Lincoln Wright was descended from a Unitarian clan committed to freedom of thought and stubborn insistence on what were often considered to be renegade opinions. His mother, Anna Lloyd Jones, tall and handsome, loved to ride horses and impressed people as impulsive, erratic, and headstrong. She married William Carey Wright, a gifted and alluring man who lacked staying power in the pursuit of any calling. The oldest of four children, Frank received the full force of his mother's starved emotions. She convinced him that he was destined for greatness and excused him from such mundane tasks as making his bed or picking up his clothes. Such treatment bolstered the boy's self-confidence but also encouraged an egotistic unconcern for the feelings of others.

In 1884, when Frank was seventeen, his ill-matched parents were divorced. He never saw his father again and failed to attend his funeral in 1904. The Lloyd Joneses became his family, and in the late 1800's he changed his middle name from Lincoln to Lloyd. After one year of studies at the University of Wisconsin, he found his first architectural job with a Chicago firm, starting at eight dollars a week.

Catherine Lee Tobin was sixteen years old to Frank's twenty when they met. She was tall, stately, elegantly slim, well-bred, gentle, and dependent. Against Anna Wright's wishes, the couple was married in 1889. Frank moved to Louis Sullivan's flourishing firm that same year, absorbing his employer's "form follows function" philosophy, learning from the group's talented architects, then establishing his own practice in 1893. By 1895, when Wright had finished building his own house in Oak Park, Illinois, his style had become unified, minimal, and boldly uncompromising. Secrest liberally quotes various authorities rather than providing her own analysis of Wright's work. She does vividly describe Wright's extraordinary, mesmerizing charm, which often procured clients even though they considered his buildings somewhat bizarre. Throughout his life, Wright was willing to spend extravagant sums for clothes, cars, and horses even as his bills for necessities often went unpaid for months. In his twenties, he adopted the costume he was to don for the rest of his life—cane, swirling cape, and broad-brimmed hat, to suit his aquiline face.

Between 1894 and 1911, Wright designed 135 buildings, lectured widely, published many articles, and became world-famous. Secrest declines to describe many houses in detail, stating that it is beyond the scope of her book and has been done elsewhere. She does say that Wright "was able to weave house and grounds into a single flowing and interpenetrating design" and that he rejected the concept of rooms as a series of boxes, instead positioning them on the diagonal and turning the corners of houses with windows. He loved to open up interior spaces with cathedral-ceilinged living rooms while avoiding both attics and basements, with a strong bias against storage space. He built long and wide roofs that often extended far beyond their masonry support, angling them so as to protect the house from the harsh summer sun while letting winter's sunlight come in. Aesthetic considerations predominated.

In 1908, Frank Lloyd Wright, at the height of his success and influence, decided to end his marriage, abandon his wife and six children, and leave Chicago. Secrest suggests several explanations. His wife's absorption in her children caused her to neglect her husband's needs; moreover, she had begun to assert herself against his close control, as she changed from an insecure young woman into a confident matron. The architect also had fallen in love with Mamah Borthwick Cheney, the wife of one of his clients. He saw himself as a reincarnation of Taliesin, a legendary Welsh seer and magician, the artist as a superman above ordinary laws and customs. In 1909, Wright and Cheney left for a long European trip that became front-page news. Wright returned to his family in 1910, but the reunion lasted only a few weeks. Both Catherine Wright and Edwin Cheney consented to divorces, though Catherine hoped for many years for a reconciliation.

Wright began to build a new home, which he named Taliesin, in Spring Green,

Wisconsin. In 1914, while Wright was in Chicago supervising work on his fabulous Midway Gardens, he received word that Mamah and six others had been murdered at Taliesin. A crazed servant had set the house on fire and had then plunged a hatchet into the heads of Mamah and several others; two of the seven victims died from burns.

Wright spared no expense to restore Taliesin, but his temperament hardened. He often took sharp and sarcastic exception to people and actions. His pattern was to strike hard whenever he sensed hostility and to become convinced easily that former students of his were undermining his work with buildings that were sordid travesties. Always in need of feminine companionship, he became enamored of Miriam Noel, a beautiful but dangerously self-deluded society lady and amateur sculptor whose morphine addiction often undermined her sense of reality. Soon they were living together at Taliesin yet quarreling bitterly at times, with Miriam subject to pathological jealousy and lightning shifts of mood. Meanwhile, Wright's restless pursuit of work landed him an enormous project, the Imperial Hotel in Tokyo, that he spent six years building. It withstood a 1923 earthquake that took 150,000 lives. His triumph with the Imperial made him perhaps the world's most famous architect. Another distinguished achievement of that time was the Hollyhock House, built for a Los Angeles oil heiress, Aline Barnsdall. It resembled a Mayan temple in Yucatan in its fortresslike appearance.

Despite his many misgivings about her instability, Wright married Miriam Noel in November, 1923. Six months later, she left him after a series of bitter quarrels during which she threatened him with a knife and gun and he beat her. Wright was convinced that Miriam's morphine use had resulted in severe emotional disturbance. He devoted himself increasingly to his projects, many of them in Los Angeles, Hollywood, and Pasadena, and he attracted a number of able assistants, including Rudolf Schindler and Richard Neutra, both of whom were to become eminent architects in their own right.

In 1925, Wright met Olgivanna Lazovich, who was to be the great love of his life, third wife, and eventual widow. She was a Montenegro-born dancer, beautiful, cultivated, and attracted to men who were commanding and magnetic. Soon after she moved into Taliesin, a second fire broke out there, causing half a million dollars worth of damage. Wright was able to save his studio and workrooms.

Again he rebuilt Taliesin, with his appetite for life renewed now that Olgivanna was sharing it. Miriam Noel put an enormous number of roadblocks in the way of the divorce Wright desperately desired. She had him and Olgivanna followed by detectives, obtained adultery warrants for their arrests, and sought his arrest on Mann Act charges of transporting an unmarried woman across state lines for "immoral purposes." She also sought to have Olgivanna deported from the United States as an undesirable alien. Wright finally was able to obtain a divorce decree from Miriam in 1927; in September, 1928, he and Olgivanna were married. Miriam died of several degenerative diseases in 1930, and in 1932 her book-length version of her unhappy life was published.

The battles with Miriam as well as his own extravagance plunged Wright into severe financial difficulties. He hired Philip La Follette, who succeeded in the arduous task of keeping his client out of both jail and the bankruptcy courts, though Wright showed him little gratitude and continued to spend beyond his means. Anecdotes of Wright's indifference to the feelings of others, even if they were clients, proliferated. One customer, whose flat roof leaked whenever it rained, called the architect and cursed, "Dammit, Frank, it's leaking on my desk!" Wright simply replied, "Richard, why don't you move your desk?"

Frank and Olgivanna Wright began the Taliesin Fellowship in 1932 as a school for architectural students who would live as well as learn on the estate. There was plenty of work for them, with Olgivanna imposing a vigorous schedule of not only drafting building plans but also hoeing the fields, cooking, painting, weeding, digging, and other manual tasks. The school brought out Wright's best side, with many students attesting his kindliness, patience, and willingness to praise. The students and the Wrights were bound by intense loyalty and camaraderie. Wright was ambivalent about what he wanted them to become. If they were too good, he would resent their competition and withdraw his support from them. If they failed, he would feel like a failure.

In the mid-1930's, Wright built what many people came to consider his most beautiful home: Fallingwater, above a splendid waterfall and ravine in Connellsville, Pennsylvania. He built the house directly above the fall, as an interlapping series of reinforced concrete trays supported by piers and anchored to a central masonry core, with the floors of quarried stone and a rocky outcropping incorporated into the hearth. One's feeling was of being deep in a cave, with a background splash of water. In the late 1930's, Wright built Taliesin West on the slope of a range overlooking Scottsdale, Arizona, and also established a fellowship there.

The last twenty years of Wright's life were spent largely in a state of embattlement, from such minor incidents as refusing to let Russian border guards inspect a roll of his drawings to extended quarrels with such leaders of the International Style as Walter Gropius, Philip Johnson, Mies van der Rohe, and Le Corbusier. Wright obtained the enthusiastic support of the great architectural critic Lewis Mumford, who hailed him as "undoubtedly the world's greatest living architect." Even Mumford was distressed by Wright's isolationist opinions before and during World War II and his refusal to recognize the evils of Hitler's Germany.

Wright's greatest and most controversial commission in his last years was Manhattan's Guggenheim Museum, which opened two months after his death. His design of the museum was an enveloping, enclosing curve, flowing and asymmetrical, influenced by the Assyrian ziggurat, with spiraling balconies and rounded walls. Critics objected that the building was a mismatch for most modern art with its large canvases that would be tilted backward. James Johnson Sweeney, the museum's director, became Wright's bitter opponent on aesthetic grounds; most of New York's building officials opposed the project on legal grounds, as it failed to conform to city codes. The impasse finally was broken by Robert Moses, commissioner of all city and state public construction. He told the appropriate appeals board, "Damn it, get a permit for Frank. I don't care how many laws you have to break. I want the Guggenheim built."

It was built. Harry Guggenheim tactfully organized the June, 1959, dedication ceremony so that neither Sweeney nor Olgivanna Wright was called on for a speech. The architect himself had died on April 9, 1959. Mumford hailed him as "the Fujiyama of American architecture, at once a lofty mountain and a national shrine."

*Gerhard Brand*

## Sources for Further Study

*Booklist*. LXXXVIII, August, 1992, p. 1971.
*Chicago Tribune*. September 27, 1992, XIV, p. 6.
*The Economist*. CCCXXV, November 28, 1992, p. 104.
*Los Angeles Times Book Review*. October 4, 1992, p. 1.
*New Statesman and Society*. V, November 27, 1992, p. 45.
*The New York Times Book Review*. XCVII, December 13, 1992, p. 1.
*Publishers Weekly*. CCXXXIX, July 20, 1992, p. 237.
*Time*. CXL, October 5, 1992, p. 86.
*USA Today*. October 2, 1992, p. D5.
*The Washington Post Book World*. XXII, September 13, 1992, p. 1.

# GENIUS
## The Life and Science of Richard Feynman

*Author:* James Gleick (1954-     )
*Publisher:* Pantheon Books (New York). Illustrated. 532 pp. $27.50
*Type of work:* Biography
*Time:* 1918-1988
*Locale:* New York City; Cambridge, Massachusetts; Princeton, New Jersey; Los Alamos, New
  Mexico; Ithaca, New York; and Pasadena, California

*This biography of physicist Richard Feynman presents not only the details of his life and
character and his scientific achievements but also descriptions of the atmosphere in which he
lived and worked and the colleagues with whom he interacted*

> *Principal personages:*
> RICHARD FEYNMAN, a physicist
> MELVILLE FEYNMAN, his father, who encouraged and supported his son's
>   early interest in science
> ARLINE GREENBAUM FEYNMAN, Feynman's first wife
> GWENETH HOWARTH FEYNMAN, his third wife, mother of Carl and Michelle
> JOAN FEYNMAN, his sister, also a physicist
> FREEMAN DYSON, a close friend and fellow physicist
> JULIAN SCHWINGER, cowinner of the Nobel Prize in Physics with Feynman
> MURRAY GELL-MANN, an associate at the California Institute of Technology

Richard Feynman was a well-known and highly esteemed theoretical physicist, a
member of a new group of theoreticians who came to the forefront in the years
following World War II. Their backgrounds differed from those of previous generations of theoretical physicists in many ways, among which were their American
nationality, their Jewish ancestry, and their early childhood experience in New York
City. This group included J. Robert Oppenheimer, Julian Schwinger, Murray Gell-
Mann, Sheldon Glashow, and Steven Weinberg. All of them, except Oppenheimer,
became recipients of the Nobel Prize in Physics.

Feynman publicly revealed in anecdotal fashion many details of his personality and
activities, in and out of physics, in two autobiographical books, *"Surely You're Joking,
Mr. Feynman!": Adventures of a Curious Character* (1985) and *"What Do You Care
What Other People Think?": Further Adventures of a Curious Character* (1988). Both
of these books were transcribed by Ralph Leighton, a personal friend and associate,
from tape recordings made by Feynman. The second of these books was published
after Feynman's death from cancer on February 15, 1988.

The use of the word "curious" in the subtitles of these books can be understood in
two senses: as the description of Feynman's own curiosity and as the way that he was
perceived by others, as being different or unusual. When British physicist Freeman
Dyson first became acquainted with Feynman, he wrote home to his parents that
Feynman was "half genius, half buffoon."

Despite the jocular tone of the titles of these books and the many amusing stories they include, they revealed that Feynman could speak seriously. Fellow physicist Philip Morrison wrote in a review of the first, "Generally Mr. Feynman is not joking; it is we, the setters of ritual performance, of hypocritical standards, pretenders to care and understanding, who are joking instead. This is the book of a powerful mind honest beyond everything else, a specialist in spade-naming." Many readers will enjoy and profit from reading the above books before the biography reviewed in this article.

James Gleick's biographical study, *Genius: The Life and Science of Richard Feynman*, is an ambitious, well-researched, and skillfully written treatment of Feynman's life from his boyhood in Far Rockaway (a part of New York City remote from Manhattan) in the years between the two world wars, to his formal training in physics at the Massachusetts Institute of Technology (MIT) and Princeton University, to his work on the atomic bomb at the Los Alamos Laboratory during World War II and his postwar academic professional experiences at Cornell University and at the California Institute of Technology (Caltech).

Gleick says that he never met Feynman. It is clear, however, that before undertaking the writing of this book, he researched all available relevant sources of information. These included all of Feynman's own publications (popular, technical, and educational), archival materials located at many institutions, oral history interviews with Feynman and others previously conducted by historians of science, and his own interviews with Feynman's colleagues who were still accessible. In addition, after Feynman's death, Gleick was granted access to personal papers in the hands of Feynman's widow, papers which have proved singularly illuminating.

The extent of the resources tapped by Gleick is evident from the notes he has provided to his writing, page by page. In these, he scrupulously lists the source or the basis for each statement he makes, thereby assuring the reader of the reliability of his narrative. He also has appended "A Feynman Bibliography" as well as a bibliography of relevant material by other authors. The book is indexed well and includes numerous photographs of Feynman, ranging from showing him with his first bicycle to his final public appearance in 1986, before the presidential commission to investigate the accident of the space shuttle *Challenger* that took seven lives.

The details of Feynman's life, outside his achievements in physics, make an interesting story in themselves. Furthermore, Gleick has been careful to describe the atmosphere in which the various stages of that life progressed; for example, Feynman's family background, his life as an undergraduate at MIT living in a fraternity house, the wartime secrecy in force at Los Alamos, and a sabbatical year spent in Brazil, learning to play bongo drums among other activities social and scientific. In addition, there are details of his romantic involvements, starting with the sad case of his greatly beloved first wife, Arline, who died of tuberculosis in an Albuquerque sanatorium while her husband was working at Los Alamos, less than five years after their marriage. Many years later, after several temporary relationships, he married his third wife, Gweneth, who became the mother of his children and who survived him.

When dealing with Feynman's scientific achievements, Gleick makes an earnest and largely successful attempt to give the historical context of the twentieth century physics into which Feynman plunged after 1945. It was a time when new ideas and fresh minds were needed to solve the dilemmas of electromagnetic field theory that grew out of the quantum mechanics that was first introduced in the mid-1920's. He also has provided vignettes about many of the well-known physicists with whom Feynman interacted, such as John Wheeler at Princeton University, Hans Bethe at Los Alamos and at Cornell University, and Murray Gell-Mann at Caltech.

Feynman had impressed the older physicists with whom he came in contact at MIT, Princeton, and Los Alamos as a bright and talented newcomer from whom much could be expected. One of his first outstanding achievements was the invention of his "path integrals" to cope with the difficulties of quantum electrodynamics. For this he shared the Nobel Prize in Physics in 1965 with Julian Schwinger and the Japanese theoretician Shin'ichir Tomonaga, both of whom had approached their task with rigorous mathematical techniques. Feynman's style was mathematically sound but involved visualization in diagrams that were especially welcomed by students and have since become widely used by physicists at all levels. Incidentally, another theoretical physicist, Freeman Dyson, a longtime friend and associate of Feynman, showed that the Schwinger/Tomonaga and Feynman approaches were equivalent to each other.

Feynman's rivalry with Schwinger became evident in the late 1940's, starting with a series of conferences on contemporary theoretical physics that were organized to bring together, by invitation only, older established physicists and the young newcomers to the field. Gleick describes a particularly interesting episode involving the conversion of Oppenheimer from the Schwinger approach to that of Feynman and Dyson.

In describing Feynman's scientific work, Gleick has avoided virtually all mathematical language, carefully trying to give the reader the conceptual content and the innovative style employed by Feynman. These sections, interspersed with the general narrative and easily recognizable by readers, will be read with varying degrees of satisfaction depending on the individual reader's previous acquaintance with the vocabulary of modern physics (a topic that has received considerable attention by popular authors) and present level of mathematical sophistication.

Feynman did not often collaborate with others. In fact, he rarely read the usual scientific literature, and he advised his students not to do so. He preferred to read enough to comprehend the problem at hand and then work out the details of the solution in his own terms. He wanted his students to develop their own original methods of attacking a problem area. This approach often proved troublesome for those with meager originality. At one time, Feynman published a group of papers with his Caltech colleague, Murray Gell-Mann, when they were wrestling with elementary particle theory. It was not a true collaboration, however, as they thought so differently about the task at hand.

Feynman's characteristic curiosity, in at least one instance, led him away from the focus of his colleagues in theoretical physics. He tackled the problem of the strange behavior of liquid helium and achieved, single-handedly, a significant breakthrough in that area. His curiosity also reached beyond physics to encompass other areas, such as languages, sketching, drum playing, and biological research. Whatever he did, he did with natural talent and complete dedication, achieving respectable results.

Gleick chose *Genius* as the principal title for this biography in clear homage to Feynman's personality and achievements. About three-quarters of the way through his book, Gleick essays a somewhat digressive but thought-provoking dissertation on the nature of recognized geniuses of the past in science and other disciplines. He quotes mathematician Mark Kac's often-cited distinction between "ordinary geniuses" and "magicians." The former are like their coworkers but much better at some things. The latter are basically different from their colleagues and cannot really be understood. For Kac, Feynman exemplified the magician type. Readers must decide for themselves to what extent they agree with Gleick's analysis. In Feynman's case, genius was characterized most strikingly by originality and intuition, coupled with great intellectual capacity and self-confidence.

Feynman received many honors during his lifetime, some of which necessitated his traveling abroad to participate in award ceremonies and deliver lectures. Most of his life, energy, and interests, however, were focused on America. He was regarded, especially by European colleagues, as being quintessentially American. He struck Freeman Dyson as "uproariously American—unbuttoned and burning with physical energy." His public service included advising the state of California on matters of curriculum in mathematics and science and the federal government in determining the cause of the *Challenger* disaster. His simple demonstration, during hearings in Washington, of the effect of ice water temperature on the brittleness of the O-rings that failed on the *Challenger* will long be remembered as a prime example of the direct simplicity with which Feynman approached nature in various contexts.

*Katherine R. Sopka*


## Sources for Further Study

*Fortune.* CXXVI, November 30, 1992, p. 149.
*Library Journal.* CXVII, October 1, 1992, p. 96.
*Los Angeles Times Book Review.* November 1, 1992, p. 1.
*New Statesman and Society.* V, October 30, 1992, p. 39.
*The New York Times Book Review.* XCVII, October 11, 1992, p. 3.
*Newsweek.* CXX, October 19, 1992, p. 70.
*Publishers Weekly.* CCXXXIX, November 2, 1992, p. 43.
*Science News.* CXLII, October 17, 1992, p. 258.
*The Wall Street Journal.* November 3, 1992, p. A14.
*The Washington Post Book World.* XXII, October 11, 1992, p. 1.

# THE GREAT DEEP
## The Sea and Its Thresholds

*Author:* James Hamilton-Paterson
*Publisher:* Random House (New York). Illustrated. 300 pp. $23.00
*Type of work:* Travel; science
*Time:* The 1990's
*Locale:* Oceans and islands around the world

*A wide-ranging meditation on the oceans of the world and the influence they have on human beings*

There is an excellent tradition in literature, especially English literature, whereby an author takes a subject less as the guiding topic of his or her book than as the starting place for a wide-ranging series of intellectually and emotionally connected observations and meditations. During the Renaissance, Robert Burton's *The Anatomy of Melancholy* (1621) virtually established the genre, creating a form that essentially had no form, except for watching the author's mind at work. Almost all of Sir Thomas Browne's writings fall into this category, and the famous quotation from his *Urne-Buriall* (1658) might serve as the epitome of what delights this particularly intriguing sub-branch of literature provides: "What songs the Sirens sang, or what name Achilles assumed when he hid himself among women are not beyond all conjecture."

To this distinguished tradition James Hamilton-Paterson adds a new and valuable contribution with *The Great Deep: The Sea and Its Thresholds*, a volume that librarians may catalog under "oceanography" but which, like the very seas themselves, ranges so widely and freely that it defies classification. This book is about the oceans of the world, the mysterious creatures they contain, the islands they form, and the reefs they hold, but its true theme is the hold these things have upon the human imagination, and how over the centuries men and women have responded to that grip, sometimes with poetic inspiration; sometimes with scientific precision; and, all too often, with ecological destruction. As Hamilton-Paterson shows so clearly, the sea is not simply there as an objective fact; it is part of us, a subjective reality that is carried in our existence as human beings on planet Earth.

In pursuit of that theme, Hamilton-Paterson packs the pages with curious facts, resonant in their isolated selves. There are "low frequency waves with swells so long they might take half a day to pass," and the reminder that the Great Barrier Reef off the coast of Australia is the largest single structure on Earth. Human beings naturally add to this collocation of oddities. During World War II, the British government wished to learn the most likely frequency bands of hull and propeller noises, the better to detect German U-boats. Lacking technology later developed, they turned to scientists and musicians with predictably wry results:

Ernest Rutherford also took a colleague with perfect pitch out in a small boat as part of the war effort. At a prearranged spot one of the great names in atomic physics took a firm grip on his companion's ankles while this man stuck his head into the Firth of Forth and listened to the enginenote of a British submarine. Hauled back into the dinghy and toweling his head he announced it was a submersible in A-flat and he would recognize it anywhere.

*The Great Deep* takes observations such as these—and there are many others scattered throughout the work—and weaves them into a coherent but free-flowing tapestry that takes the reader through humanity's eons-old encounter with the oceans. What do we know about this mysterious three-fifths of our planet? How do we react to it, both in our daily lives and in our imaginations? What have we learned, and what have we merely imagined we know? Perhaps most important, what have we done to this ancient cradle of life? It is in answering those questions that Hamilton-Paterson finds the structure of his book. The answers take *The Great Deep* from observation to meditation and provide its greatest pleasures.

The earth has its seven seas, so *The Great Deep* has seven chapters, each concerned with a different aspect of the world's oceans. It begins, appropriately enough, with "Charts and Naming," reprising the human compulsion to possess the landscape (or in this case the seascape) by giving names to features. Aboard the research vessel *Farnella*, Hamilton-Paterson observes scientists at work charting and cataloging the unseen ocean floor thousands of feet below them. Using sophisticated sonar devices, the team builds up a painstaking picture of the seabed by bouncing soundwaves from the bottom and plotting them on computer-calibrated devices. Nothing is seen, nothing is touched, but total accuracy is assured by modern technology.

Or is it? In the second chapter, "Islands and Boundaries," Hamilton-Paterson subtly undercuts the assurances of scientific observation, indeed all human observation, by simply noting what has happened to islands both now known and others once assumed to be known. Their existence, both in the metaphysical and actual senses, is more problematic than commonly assumed.

Take Tiwarik, a real island with a fictitious name, lying less than half a mile off the coast of the Philippines. Uninhabited because it had no fresh water, it long served as a convenient pausing place for nomadic fishermen, wandering traders, and even errant Englishmen such as Hamilton-Paterson. Bought by a Japanese organization, it has been converted into an exclusive pleasure dome whose ultimate effect denies its very existence as an island, making it a mere extension of the electronic, air-conditioned global village. Is Tiwarik the island it was? Is it an island at all?

Some islands vanish by being bought and developed (Hamilton-Paterson and others might prefer more graphic verbs), and some islands vanish because there no longer is a need for them. Perhaps knowledge of the globe has increased, or the need for mystery diminished; perhaps both. "Until remarkably recently the North Atlantic was full of islands which have now disappeared. They constituted another type of vanishing island, one whose loss is due to the redrawing of maps, to improved cartography and navigation, but also to changed expectations."

Since they were there, at least on the maps, they have names, often magical and haunting ones: Antilla, or Seven Cities; Brasil; St. Brandan; Buss; and Mayda. They also have romantic histories. Antilla was discovered by Christian refugees, among them several bishops, who fled Spain during the Moorish conquest. Later travelers who claimed to have found the isle were supposed to have brought back sand that was one-third gold dust. Despite the obvious incentive to locate Antilla, it has never been found again.

The sunken island of Buss was recorded in 1578 by the English explorer Martin Frobisher as he attempted to find the Northwest Passage. A ship of his small fleet, the *Emmanuel*, known as a buss, was separated from the expedition by a storm and alone sailed past a great island, "the land seeming to be fruitful, full of woods . . ." The island did not simply vanish—it sank. Hamilton-Paterson quotes a 1745 chart which states authoritatively that "The submerged land of Buss is nowadays nothing but surf a quarter of a mile long with rough sea." So islands come and go, and if human beings cannot always rediscover what they claim to have found and named, often they cannot understand what they have before them. Such is the case with coral reefs, as Hamilton-Paterson explains in "Reefs and Seeing."

For millenia coral was used in jewelry, medicine, and furniture making and other crafts, with no one knowing what it was; in fact, it was not until well into the nineteenth century that it was definitively decided whether coral was animal, vegetable, or mineral. As to the growth of coral reefs— including that largest single structure on Earth, the Great Barrier Reef—World War II was over before scientists reached common agreement, and much doubt still lingers. Hamilton-Paterson's account admits there were a number of difficult problems to solve, but he also clearly demonstrates that what comes between human beings and the truth is less the object itself than our subjective viewpoint—our way of seeing.

How we see determines in many cases what we see, and nowhere is this more true than in "Wrecks and Death." Fetch up broken pottery from an Athenian trading ship off the coast of Asia Minor and you are an archeologist; recover golden coins from a Spanish galleon in the Florida Channel and you are a treasure hunter; but carry off dinner plates from the *Titanic* and you become—what? A looter? A profiteer? A ghoul? Hamilton-Paterson raises such questions, making them real with his insightful, careful use of detail and example, but he leaves the final moral equation up to the reader.

In a sense the sea has always been, in T. S. Eliot's term, an objective correlative to the moral vision of human beings. We fill it with many things: mermaids and monsters, blessed isles, and dangerous reefs. In the distant depths, where until very recently we could hardly imagine, much less go, it was supposed to be dark, silent, and devoid of life. "Deeps and the Dark" is the appropriate title of the chapter in which Hamilton-Paterson reveals the gradual awakening to the beauty and mystery of the life that has adapted to an environment where sunlight is like something glimpsed from another planet. He quotes from the great American oceanographer, William Beebe, who invented the bathysphere, that simple, dangerous globe of steel with a glass porthole for viewing, lowered fathoms deep with an observer curled inside. "In effect, it was an eyeball on a string. It could do nothing of itself but carry man's sight into unseen regions." In 1934, Beebe was lowered 3,028 feet off Bermuda, deeper than human beings had ever gone into the ocean. When he returned, he wrote the words that could be the theme of this book:

> If one dives and returns to the surface inarticulate with amazement and with a deep realization of the marvel of what he has seen and where he has been, then he deserves to go again and again. If he is unmoved or disappointed, then there remains for him on earth only a longer or shorter period of waiting for death.

Going down into the depths, recording sights never seen by man, a record of what the earth can provide by way of wonder, is counterpoised by the penultimate chapter, "Fishing and Loss," in which Hamilton-Paterson gives a sober and sobering vision of what humans can do by way of plundering the wonderful bounty of the seas by overfishing, waste, and sheer stupidity. The bounty of the sea was something once thought inexhaustible. That thought may be wrong, Hamilton-Paterson warns, and exhaustion may happen sooner than we realize.

To close, Hamilton-Paterson turns his gaze upon those who chose, long ago, to return to the sea, whether as fisherfolk, traders, nomads, or pirates. Bit by bit, our ancestral home is being denied us, bought by foreign companies and polluted by our own industries. The sea dwellers among us—and by extension, all of us—have been impoverished by our lack of respect, our failure of awe, before the great deep which once gave us life and even now sustains us. In a sense, this book leads up to the story of the sea dwellers and their tragedy. It is the story and the tragedy of all humanity as well.

So many themes in such a relatively short book might have made for incoherence, a seascape choppy and broken by waves. This does not happen with Hamilton-Paterson's *The Great Deep*. Early in the work, he quotes Vladimir Nabokov, who wrote that "the precision of the artist should accompany the passion of the scientist." It is an appropriate quote, for that is what he has brought and given in *The Great Deep*.

*Michael Witkoski*

## Sources for Further Study

*The Atlantic.* CCLXX, September, 1992, p. 122.
*Booklist.* LXXXVIII, July, 1992, p. 1907.
*Chicago Tribune.* September 13, 1992, XIV, p. 5.
*The Guardian.* September 13, 1992, p. 22.
*Kirkus Reviews.* LX, June 1, 1992, p. 705.
*Library Journal.* CXVII, June 15, 1992, p. 97.
*The New York Times Book Review.* XCVII, August 9, 1992, p. 6.
*Publishers Weekly.* CCXXXIX, June 15, 1992, p. 93.
*USA Today.* November 13, 1992, p. D5.
*The Washington Post Book World.* XXII, August 9, 1992, p. 2.

# THE GREAT MELODY
## A Thematic Biography and Commented Anthology of Edmund Burke

*Author:* Conor Cruise O'Brien (1917-    )
*Publisher:* University of Chicago Press (Chicago). Illustrated. 692 pp. $37.95
*Type of work:* Biography
*Time:* 1729-1797
*Locale:* England and Ireland

The Great Melody *attempts to reconcile Burke's shifting ideological ground in relation to Ireland, America, India, and France by identifying the abuse of power as the motivation of all of his great political crusades*

> *Principal personages:*
> EDMUND BURKE, an Irish author and member of the British Parliament
> CHARLES WATSON-WENTWORTH, Second Marquess of Rockingham, a Whig prime minister (1765-1766, 1782) and Burke's patron
> GEORGE III, the king of Great Britain and Ireland
> FREDERICK, Lord North, a parliamentary agent of George III who headed the Tory administration (1770-1782)
> WILLIAM PETTY, Second Earl of Shelburne, a Whig opponent of Lord North
> WILLIAM PITT, the Younger, a Tory prime minister (1783-1801, 1804-1806)
> CHARLES JAMES FOX, a Rockingham Whig and strong opponent of North and Pitt

Edmund Burke has suffered from having said too many wise things. In ardent support of the American colonists in 1774, he argued that "general rebellions and revolts of a whole people were never *encouraged*, now or at any time. They are always *provoked*." Sixteen years later, he was giving notice to the French that they could hardly be congratulated for letting loose the madman of revolution when they knew so little of the "new power in new persons, of whose principles, tempers, and dispositions, they have little or no experience." Understandably, Burke has been claimed by subsequent generations of both liberals and conservatives as a fundamental expositor of their deepest precepts. All polemicists love effective aphorism, and Burke was its master. The more prescient his observations across time, however, the more he opened himself to the charges of inconsistency which have ever plagued his reputation. In one of his most memorable formulations, Burke observed that "circumstances . . . give in reality to every political principle its distinguishing colour, and discriminating effect." Circumstances do change, as he knew and had the courage to say, and so should opinions follow. But this piece of wisdom makes it all the more difficult to identify those principles that were essential to Burke.

Burke is not an easy figure to study. There is little evidence of his early motivations. It is known that he came from a prominent, impoverished, Roman Catholic gentry family, that his mother remained a Catholic while his father converted to the Anglican church, and that he was throughout his life accused of crypto-Catholicism. For the period from 1748, when he was graduated from Trinity College, Dublin, until 1757, virtually nothing is known. When Burke fully reemerges during the 1760's, he has acquired both a reputation for oratory and an influential patron, the Marquess of Rockingham, upon whom he exerts considerable influence. The political scene was confused, however, and no means could be guaranteed to deliver success. Corruption was rampant, both the Whig and Tory parties were divided into factions, and the royal influence of George III was unusually potent. Thus, no matter where the scholar turns, there are shadows. In an Ireland bitterly torn over Catholic disabilities, how far had Burke personally distanced himself from his homeland? Burke is virtually silent. In Parliament, how much difference did his classic speeches really make? There were few obvious converts, and even Burke's warmest admirers were altogether willing to break with him on policy differences. Given the fact that he never held high office from which he could wield power directly, the nature of his immediate influence has remained shrouded. In this work, Conor Cruise O'Brien sets out to rescue Burke from critics who have minimized his political effectiveness, and seen in his fine phrases little more than the philosophical underpinnings of political opportunism.

O'Brien is unusually well qualified to get to the bottom of Burke's political character. First, he is Irish. Although Burke went to great pains to minimize his Irish past, it is clear that he never shook free of it, so that a sympathetic understanding of Burke's Irish consciousness is significant. Second, O'Brien, like Burke, has personally faced the dilemmas of practical politics, serving as a United Nations representative in the 1960's and in the Irish government during the 1970's. Third, he is a proven historian who made his mark during the 1950's. Finally, he has worked specifically with Burke before, admirably editing the Penguin Classics edition (1969) of Burke's *Reflections on the Revolution in France* (1790). During the period between 1960 and the publication of *The Great Melody*, O'Brien's reputation grew as wide experience enhanced his considerable skills as a social critic and scholar. It would be difficult to find anyone more suited to write Burke's life.

At once, however, the reader will realize that this is no ordinary biography. When O'Brien set out to write *The Great Melody*, he started from a clue supplied by a poet. In "The Seven Sages," William Butler Yeats had written a couplet that haunted the author: "American colonies, Ireland, France and India/ Harried, and Burke's great melody against it." The said "it" against which Burke performs his "great melody" is the abuse of power. In this metaphor, O'Brien finds the secret to reconciling so many otherwise contradictory political attitudes. At a personal level, he finds the secret to Burke's motivation in the ambivalence Burke felt, but seldom displayed, in having been forced by circumstances to renounce his Irishness. In order to support his thesis, often at odds with the accumulated wisdom of recent scholarship, O'Brien takes a large step off the historical path. "I was required," he writes, "by the very nature of my enterprise, not to set too tight a rein on such powers of imaginative insight as may have been granted me."

In a ten-page preface, O'Brien traces the development of his fascination with Burke, his frustration in attempting to make sense of Burke's life, and the evolution of the thematic approach that he employs. Once the "day-to-day clutter" of Burke's life was discarded, according to the author, the great, disinterested nature of his life emerged through a careful and detailed examination of the four causes to which he committed himself: equity for Ireland (throughout), freedom for the American colonies (1766-1783), justice for India (1777-1795), and opposition to the French Revolution (1789-1797). The "great melody" that is raised under O'Brien's orchestration is a consistent attack on abuse of power, and should be understood as "implying the existence of a profound inner harmony" in Burke's work.

Before coming to terms with Burke, however, O'Brien delivers a forty-three-page historiographical review, supplemented by dozens of references throughout the narrative, to demonstrate the extent of Burke's neglect. He shows how respect for Burke remained strong during the nineteenth and early twentieth century, with great Whig interpreters of history such as T. B. Macaulay, John Morley, G. O. Trevelyan, and Winston Churchill rightly appreciating his large and subtle qualities of influence. The villain of the piece, Sir Lewis Namier, clouds the horizon in 1929 with the publication of *The Structure of Politics at the Accession of George III*. It would be possible, O'Brien concedes, to read Namier's early works without noticing that Burke was the particular enemy, but "the rigorous historian—and Namier radiates rigour—does not take Burke seriously, and lets this be known, *en passant*." This is especially damaging, according to O'Brien, because Namier's work influenced virtually all studies of the late eighteenth century written before the 1970's. Even authors of the 1970's and 1980's, generally more favorable to Burke, are given stripes for their "vestigial Namierism."

From the beginning, then, a martial tension pervades this work, and one never quite loses the feeling that it is more about O'Brien's intellectual development than Burke's life. There are the obvious examples, such as the seventy-five pages of introductory material, frequent references to self-serving exchanges of letters with Sir Isaiah Berlin and Owen Dudley Edwards, and the incredible note, to an extract from Burke's *Letter to a Noble Lord* (1796), in explanation of why his "hair sat up": "I have also before me as I write a copy of the first edition of this work . . . with 'from the Author' in manuscript on the half-title page. . . . [It] is my most treasured possession." Hence, O'Brien's dedication of the book: "For Deirdre Levinson Bergson who brought the Message from the Master." Such inspiration makes it clear that the author refuses to be bound by the rules of ordinary scholarship.

Excusing the easy manner of the man of letters, who has perhaps earned in three-quarters of a century a right to constant self-reference, the value of the book remains to be tested in the author's treatment of Burke's life. Has O'Brien dispelled the shadows that previously surrounded his subject? The answer is "maybe." In a personal sense, Burke's actions are given unity, in O'Brien's estimation, by a deeply felt Irishness, with its multiple reminders that he was no Englishman. The difficulty here is that Burke publicly did minimize his Irish background. O'Brien, then, begins to interpret Burke's silences. Whenever there is "an unexpected silence, a failure to refer to something obviously relevant, or a cryptically guarded formulation," O'Brien is too ready to believe that the explanation is at " 'the Irish level': the suspect and

subterranean area of emotional access to the forbidden world of Roman Catholicism."
He may be on to something here, but there is much to indicate that the "message from
the master" has blinded him to the possibility of any interpretation but his own. As in
all closed systems, reductionist tendencies are all too apparent.

O'Brien depends too much upon "authentic whiffs," "cryptic asides," and "psychic
energies" in arguing for the "Irish level" being fundamental to an understanding of
Burke's life. It is a plausible theory, but in the absence of more information it should
hardly be held quite so high. O'Brien constantly makes inferences on the least premise,
simply "knowing" that Burke must have done this thing or that. Informed conjecture
is a necessary part of all historical writing but cannot alone be made the basis for
fundamental reassessments. If many of O'Brien's inferences are harmless, some are
fundamentally noxious, as in his determination that Burke was humiliated by his
father's conforming to the Church of England out of fear and by the knowledge "that
his own achievement would be based on the consequences of that act of conforming."
Perhaps he is right, but the evidence seems to tell otherwise, and no number of dark,
Burkean silences should be allowed to displace more substantial signs of reconciliation.

O'Brien's self-contained vision explains everything. Burke is not allowed to be
inconsistent, for there is always a deeper level that explains an apparent inconsistency.
When Burke's words and actions fail to fit neatly into a coherent angst-driven
"melody," they are not to be trusted and must be seen as the Whig persona that he has
been forced to adopt. He is always in control of his rhetoric. As a result, there is even
a consistency in what he chooses not to say. Burke is assumed to be intellectually
superior to his colleagues, with a corresponding assumption that he must have
influenced them greatly. Rockingham is a dunce, Charles James Fox a disciple, and
William Pitt, the Younger a mere practitioner. O'Brien fails to mention, however, that
intellect is seldom a key to success in politics. Pitt undoubtedly exaggerated when he
wrote that in Burke's writing there was always "much to admire and nothing to agree
with," but Pitt *was* prime minister for two decades. Unwittingly and understandably,
Pitt emerges as the master of the political side of this piece.

There is a great deal of worth in *The Great Melody*, most notably the careful
attention that the author pays to Burke's speeches and writings. His argument in favor
of Burke's self-conscious Irishness is interesting and deserves attention, but the nature
of the work makes it clear that O'Brien is altogether carried away by the Burke he
wishes had lived. Ultimately, *The Great Melody* fails because it unsuccessfully
attempts to reconcile the divergent demands of biography, history, and literary criticism. The worth of Burke's words says very little, in reality, about his life. O'Brien's
ideas are nevertheless suggestive. When properly edited and adorned, they would
make an excellent article for *The New York Review of Books*.

*John Powell*

## Sources for Further Study

*Booklist.* LXXXIX, November 15, 1992, p. 577.
*The Guardian.* September 10, 1992, p. 25.
*Library Journal.* CXVII, October 15, 1992, p. 76.
*Los Angeles Times Book Review.* November 22, 1992, p. 3.
*New Statesman and Society.* V, October 9, 1992, p. 33.
*The New York Review of Books.* XXXIX, December 3, 1992, p. 37.
*The New York Times Book Review.* XCVIII, January 3, 1993, p. 11.
*The Times Literary Supplement.* December 4, 1992, p. 3.
*Washington Times.* November 15, 1992, p. B10.

# THE GYPSIES

*Author:* Angus Fraser (1928-    )
*Publisher:* Basil Blackwell (Cambridge, Massachusetts). Illustrated. 359 pp. $24.95
*Type of work:* History
*Time:* The eleventh century to 1990
*Locale:* Europe

*The history of a people who have preserved their identity despite centuries of attempts to force their assimilation or to annihilate them*

It is appropriate that Angus Fraser was selected to author this volume in the series called *The Peoples of Europe.* Fraser's earlier scholarly work focused on George Borrow, the nineteenth century British writer whose fascination with Gypsies was evident in such accounts of his life and travels as *The Zincali: Or, An Account of the Gypsies in Spain* (1841) and *The Romany Rye* (1857). In writing his own book, Fraser had to acknowledge the fact that writers such as Borrow combined valuable observations with rumors and inventions. Even without such romantic testimony, it is particularly difficult to sort out the facts about Gypsies from the fictions that have grown up concerning them. The chief problem is that although they always have had a sense of identity, Gypsies themselves have kept no formal history, either oral or written. In writing his comprehensive study, Fraser had to rely on contemporary comments by outsiders, whose attitudes might vary from antipathy to romantic gullibility, as well as on the work of other scholars, who because of conflicting evidence have been unable to reach agreement on a number of central issues. Despite the difficulties of his task, in *The Gypsies* Fraser has produced a superb history that presents his extensive findings and some tentative conclusions in a balanced and highly readable manner.

Fraser's thoughtful approach is illustrated in the first chapter of the book, in which he discusses the various methods scholars have used in attempting to ascertain when and where Gypsies came into being as a people. The best-known of these methods is the study of linguistics. Since their language, Romani, is similar to Indian languages, it can be assumed that the Gypsies originated in India. As Fraser notes, however, because so little is known about the early development of Indian dialects, several theories as to the geographical home of the Gypsies are equally plausible. Even the one conclusion that linguists of both major schools had agreed on recently has come into question. Their assumption that the Gypsy exodus from India took place shortly before the ninth century A.D. has been challenged by a new argument, placing their entrance into Persia as early as the fourth century B.C.

More briefly, Fraser surveys studies in physical anthropology and in genetics that confirm the conclusion of the linguists as to the Indian origin of the Gypsies. The studies once again provide no hint as to the reason for the Gypsies' departure. Even modern Gypsies with scholarly training, after themselves investigating these historical problems, seem no better able to answer these perplexing questions.

In the chapters that follow, Fraser cites references to Gypsies in written texts of the tenth and eleventh centuries, proving that they first entered Persia and Armenia, then moved into the Byzantine Empire and the Balkans. Although there are now historical records to document the diaspora, the reason for the movement still is unclear. Even more mysterious than this historical question is a practical one. As Fraser points out, · unlike the Jews, the Gypsies had no historical tradition, no religious mandate, no prophetic tradition, no priestly regulations, in short, no structure to maintain their common identity after they had scattered in different directions. Their lack of a common history is reflected in the fact that no leaders ever attained the importance of folk heroes. The Gypsies had no David, no Moses, no Joshua. Their lack of a common religion is evidenced by the fact that various Gypsy groups eventually adopted different faiths, taking on the convictions of the people among whom they were living. Whatever their religion or location, however, throughout the centuries the Gypsies have maintained their sense of identity, their consciousness of being different from everyone around them.

It was inevitable that a people so distinctive would be extremely vulnerable to persecution. The documents Fraser cites suggest that these exotic people, who were called by a name suggesting that they had come from Egypt, at first attained a kind of security because their skills were needed by the people they visited. For example, skilled artisans, such as smiths and cobblers, were too valuable to be driven away. Moreover, the coming of Gypsy entertainers—of snake charmers, bear handlers, acrobats, and jugglers—must have provided much excitement to the inhabitants of small medieval villages. Early in their history, Gypsy women began to specialize in soothsaying, or fortune-telling, a talent much in demand even if Christian churchmen considered it suspect. Because they were needed, the Gypsies were given a certain latitude. Even though they were developing a reputation for sharp dealing, even for thievery, they were tolerated and even welcomed.

In feudal society, however, no person or group without a protector could be considered truly safe. Again, the fact that there were no records kept by the Gypsy people themselves is frustrating. Although the actions of the feudal lords who granted protection to Gypsy bands are fully recorded in their own histories, the negotiations that were undertaken by the leaders of the Gypsies, often even their names, are omitted. One can only assume that there were some brilliant diplomats in the bands, since they did manage to preserve their people. Undoubtedly, the greatest of these victories over the *gadže* was "The Great Trick," which Fraser considers interesting enough to merit a chapter of its own. In the fifteenth century, he explains, some unnamed genius among the Gypsy leaders found a way to utilize the piety of those around them for the benefit of the Gypsies as a whole. A story was formulated that cast the Gypsies, whose origins, fortunately, were so cloaked in mystery, as "penitents" sentenced by God to wander the earth in expiation of some past sin or apostasy committed in "Little Egypt." With this and similar stories confirming their status as pilgrims and thus making them sacrosanct, the Gypsies procured safe-conducts not only from local lords but also from assorted bishops and from the Holy Roman Emperor himself.

With the Reformation, however, came changes in attitudes that threatened the

Gypsies and their way of life. More indulgent societies could accept them as long as they were useful and entertaining, but the dour Calvinists, with their dedication to the work ethic, could see the Gypsies only as lazy, thievish vagabonds who needed to be reformed or exterminated. In three grim chapters, Fraser traces the new intolerance toward Gypsies that characterized the next three centuries. The methods of repression and rejection varied from town to town, country to country, and year to year. Sometimes the Gypsies were paid to leave the towns or cities in which they hoped to ply their various trades; sometimes they were forcibly driven away. It was not unusual for them to be turned back at frontiers they were attempting to cross, often because they were suspected of being spies. On the other hand, sometimes reformers attempted to assimilate Gypsies into conventional society and decreed that they must settle in one place. One of the most appalling of these efforts to destroy the Gypsy way of life concentrated on the children, who in the name of progress were abducted from their families and absorbed into "normal" society, to grow up without any knowledge of their real heritage. In addition, there were brutal massacres and wholesale executions. Seemingly, the laws that protected others did not apply to Gypsies. They could be killed without having committed any crimes; their offense was simply in being Gypsies.

In the chapter entitled "Forces for Change," Fraser points out how the new movements that began in the period of the Enlightenment affected the Gypsy people. The expansion of intellectual efforts created a new interest in their language and in their culture. Unfortunately, the most influential of the scholars who set themselves to write about Gypsies, the German Heinrich Grellman, accepted as fact such rumors as their being sexually depraved and their indulging in cannibalism. The result of his publications was assumptions that, for the next century and a half, were used to justify persecution.

When the more enlightened aristocrats discovered that Gypsies had an interesting musical tradition, their music became the vogue and some of the musicians attained fame and fortune. In addition, the emancipation movements of the Enlightenment meant that other Gypsies, for example in Wallachia and Moldavia, finally could be released from slavery. Similarly, the Gypsy people, always footloose, were affected by the general impulse of Europeans to emigrate. Fraser outlines the various waves of migration. Early in the nineteenth century, to Britain, then to the United States, and later in the century, directly from Eastern Europe to the United States.

This crucial chapter on migration concludes with a detailed description of the social system that prevails among the Rom, who, according to the author, insist that they are the "true" Gypsies, as do many competing groups. By comparing the customs of the Rom with those of other Gypsy communities, Fraser arrives at some interesting conclusions. When all the divergent customs are eliminated, he points out, there are left two traditions that are shared by all these people: the fear of the dead, which is reflected in various burial ceremonies, and the fear of contamination, particularly by females as sexual creatures, which makes it imperative that Gypsies limit their contacts with the *gadže*, who, observing no such taboos, must inevitably be unclean. As Fraser points out, these deep-seated convictions have been important forces in determining Gypsy work patterns and in separating them from non-Gypsies.

Ironically, as Fraser points out in his last two chapters, although the twentieth century has produced some legislative efforts to protect the Gypsies, it also has been the period of the most thorough and systematic attempt to exterminate them. Led by German enthusiasts for racial purity, Europeans began to talk about eradicating this people early in the century. By the time the Nazis came to power, the Gypsies were seen as a people who, like the Jews, were a source of contamination for the Aryan race and therefore must be eliminated. It is impossible to know exactly how many Gypsies perished in this Holocaust. Fraser cites estimates ranging from a quarter of a million to half a million, perhaps even more, out of a population of less than a million people. Even more appalling than these totals is the fact that in the postwar period Gypsy victims have had unbelievable difficulties in obtaining compensation. The custom of centuries seems still to prevail: labeled as "criminals" or "threats to security," they have been denied their rights by authorities who, if not Nazis by name, share the racial antipathies of their predecessors throughout centuries of oppression.

In his concluding chapter, Fraser summarizes recent trends in the treatment of Gypsies by outsiders, as well as developments within Gypsy society, as this people moves toward the twenty-first century. There is considerable material on the situation of Gypsies under communism as well as on the attempts of Western legislators to protect them while providing them with benefits such as education that can provide them with more opportunities to earn a living in a world no longer in need of tinkers or horse-traders. Fraser also surveys present-day linguistic studies, that have enabled scholars to classify Gypsy bands into larger groups. More important, he points out that for the first time in their history the Gypsies themselves have discovered the need to band together into associations that can work to preserve their culture and to exert pressure on political leaders. Since their emergence from India, at a time that probably will never be ascertained, this people has survived by strategic retreat. As Fraser comments, it will be interesting to see what a new policy of unity and activism will achieve.

*Rosemary M. Canfield Reisman*

**Sources for Further Study**

*The Guardian*. December 8, 1992, p. 8.
*Publishers Weekly*. CCXXXIX, November 2, 1992, p. 60.

# HEMINGWAY
## The American Homecoming

*Author:* Michael Reynolds (1937-    )
*Publisher:* Basil Blackwell (Cambridge, Massachusetts). Illustrated. 264 pp. $24.95
*Type of work:* Literary biography
*Time:* 1926-1929
*Locale:* Western Europe and the United States

*The third of a projected five-volume biography of Ernest Hemingway, which sees him move from relative obscurity and minimal success in 1926 to a deserved reputation as a fiction writer in 1929*

> *Principal personages:*
> ERNEST HEMINGWAY, an American expatriate and major novelist
> HADLEY RICHARDSON HEMINGWAY, his first wife (to 1927)
> PAULINE PFEIFFER HEMINGWAY, his second wife

Michael Reynolds' excellent biography of Ernest Hemingway from 1926 to 1929 follows two earlier volumes that bring Hemingway, born in 1898, up to 1926: *The Young Hemingway* (1986) and *Hemingway: The Paris Years* (1989). Reynolds is also the author of the critical work *Hemingway's First War: The Making of "A Farewell to Arms"* (1976). In all these works, as in the present volume, he has not only a firm grasp of the relevant facts but also a telling feeling for the moods and imaginative life of his subject.

The three years here covered are important ones for Hemingway; in the course of them he moves from a relatively unknown, struggling artist in Paris who had published only short fiction, principally in *In Our Time* (1925), to a novelist and short-story writer well known in Europe and America, with two novels to his credit, a second collection of short fiction, and a third novel in the hands of his editor. This volume of the biography is the record of how all this came to be. In the course of these three short years, Hemingway also divested himself of one wife and acquired a second. He signed a favorable contract with the prestigious firm of Charles Scribner's Sons. He prepared for his return to America by, consciously or unconsciously, cutting himself off from many of his former friends and associates, among them Sherwood Anderson, Gertrude Stein, and Louis Bromfield. Thus he arrived at Key West, Florida, accompanied by a pregnant wife, in April, 1928, only to return to Europe after a bare thirteen months, unable to settle in America, having been changed irrevocably by his long stay in Europe.

The first year of the biography is devoted to the contrapuntal themes of Hemingway's divorce from his first wife, Hadley, and his revision and rewriting of *The Sun Also Rises*, published in October, 1926. By April, 1927, his divorce from Hadley was final, and he married Pauline Pfeiffer in May. It took Hemingway almost a year to make final plans, earlier begun, to go to America, where he would meet his new wife's parents and revisit his own in Oak Park, Illinois. Neither trip would be a great success, for Hemingway was restless and unable to reconcile himself to small-town Arkansas or to the company of his own parents, especially that of his father. One of the constant themes through the book is the old one of the relationship between the father and the son; even if the father rarely appears in the work, he is a constant presence in the mind and imagination of the son.

This part of Hemingway's life also sees him introduced to Key West and the sport of deep-sea fishing, items that would play important roles in Hemingway's future. The year in the United States also saw the composition of _A Farewell to Arms_, which was handed over to Maxwell Perkins in February, 1929. Perhaps of most importance, even more than the literary success, for Hemingway was the death of his father, who shot himself in December, 1928. Hemingway, who certainly had earlier mused on suicide, could not understand his father's act, regarding it as cowardly. Reynolds does not need to comment on Hemingway's own escape from life by the same means in 1961. The moods of depression and physical failings of increasing years were shared by both father and son.

Reynolds relates these three years, a life full of incident, in impeccable detail. This biography shares many of the qualities of a good novel. It has a strong and complex character at its heart; it surrounds him with a cast of interesting, even eccentric characters. It is narrated with a wealth of significant detail and features the enduring themes of love and passion, the struggling artist true to his craft, and the attainment of success in one's chosen field, along with subthemes of suicide and virile masculinity.

As with any good novel, this work evokes a time and a place. Hemingway is seen clearly against and amid the expatriate life of Jazz Age Paris. The stock characters are all there: Sylvia Beach, Maxwell Perkins, Ezra Pound, Archibald MacLeish, Gertrude Stein and Alice B. Toklas, Ford Madox Ford, and Zelda and F. Scott Fitzgerald. The cafes and bistros of Paris and Spain are important places of resort and refuge, and the drinking often extends into the small hours of the morning. The moods of raffishness, the flying in the face of convention, the living for the moment, the search for sensation, are all made to come alive for the reader of this biography, and thus the reader can better appreciate the spirit and imagination of Hemingway in, so to speak, his natural habitat. This work can be satisfyingly read as an evocation of those years, whether or not one is particularly interested in Hemingway.

Just as the work evokes those things associated with the 1920's, so it also evokes the puritanism and repressive morality, especially in the United States of the same period. Examples include the reactions of Hemingway's parents to his divorce, the misgivings of his second wife's relatives, the editing of some of his writings to remove "offensive" material before publication, and above all the objections from many quarters to the sort of life depicted in his works and in those of a number of writers of the day. The protests to much of the literature of the 1920's may strike today's reader as making much of little, but it is useful to be reminded that virtually complete literary and artistic freedom is a fairly recent condition.

Reynolds also evokes the feel of many of the places in which Hemingway found himself. These three years see almost constant movement by Hemingway; clearly Hemingway is searching for something, even if he is not always sure what it might be. Readers are given the wind and the rain and the sweat and the smell and the feel of places as diverse as Paris, which acts as a sort of center to which Hemingway frequently returns; to Madrid, Pamplona, Valencia, and Zaragoza in Spain; Schruns and Gaschurn in Austria; Juan les Pins, Antibes, and Hendaye in France; Rapallo, La Spezia, Pisa, and Rimini in Italy; and Gstaad in Switzerland. Even during his year in the United States, Hemingway paid visits to or lived in Key West (which he came to fancy greatly); Piggott, Arkansas; Chicago; New York; Kansas City; and Sheridan, Wyoming. As Reynolds points out, wherever Hemingway was, he was homesick for somewhere else.

Although Hemingway frequently complained about a lack of money, he was far from being the starving artist of legend. His income, like that of many writers, was often irregular and uncertain, but he was never really hurting for funds, as evidenced by his sorties to Spain for the bullfighting and to Switzerland for the skiing. In addition, his second wife had a trust fund that contributed a steady income, and friends frequently came to his aid with loans and gifts. Perhaps the greatest benefactor was Pauline's Uncle Gus, who, in the space of two years, paid the rent on one of the Hemingway flats and bought two new cars for Hemingway. After 1929, Hemingway was well able to make his way by his pen.

As a writer, Hemingway's work habits are worth noting. When in his best form, he would write in the morning, go skiing or fishing or to watch bicycle races in the afternoon, and devote the evenings to drinking and conversation; it seems to have been the best of two or three worlds. The book also records that Hemingway possessed a power of work. For example, Hemingway corrected and returned the galleys of *The Sun Also Rises* in less than a month while spending at least ten days in Antibes and having to find separate residences for himself and his first wife upon returning to Paris. He wrote more than ten thousand words of *A Farewell to Arms* in less than a month after his return to the United States; within two months he had 279 pages written, and in a bit more than a month more had finished 477 pages. Another month and the first draft was complete—in all, the entire novel was written in just under five months. He did this while living in Piggott and Kansas City and seeing his wife Pauline through the birth, by cesarean, of her first child. Whatever the image of Hemingway as a sportsman and keeper of late nights, he was a dedicated artist and worked strongly at his craft. It is also clear that the famous Hemingway style was not arrived at by accident or on the first try. Reynolds amply documents the hard work that Hemingway put into revising and rewriting his fiction. Typically, the revisions turn out to be excisions; Hemingway pared his material again and again, attempting to remove the unnecessary, the sentimental, the arty. It is also recorded that Hemingway saved virtually every scrap of paper that passed through his hands, ultimately providing a vast resource for Reynolds.

Above all, this book has what any good story should have—pace and momentum.

Scenes and details build to climaxes; important scenes are highlighted, and Reynolds makes judicious use of foreshadowing. The high points of the work are Hemingway's divorce and remarriage, his return to the United States, and the difficult birth of his second son. Each of these moments marks a decisive turn for Hemingway's personal or professional career, and each is made a fascinating story by Reynolds.

What is said above, however, should not deceive the reader of this biography: This is not a literary biography in the sense that it supplies extensive readings and analyses of the creative works of the subject. Reynolds certainly has not neglected Hemingway's works and offers valuable insights, but he has concentrated on the life of his subject. What he has done is to supply a detailed account of the external facts of Hemingway's life during these three years, coupled with the imaginative life represented in the fiction. At the simplest, one might say that Reynolds has shown how Hemingway's experiences appear in his fiction, but it is much more complex than that. Reynolds has concentrated on how Hemingway's feelings and emotional and imaginative states are not only reflected but also used in the fiction. For example, Reynolds sympathetically juxtaposes Hemingway's experiences and moods while in the United States awaiting the birth of Pauline's child with the feelings and problems of Frederick Henry and the pregnant Catherine Barkley as Hemingway struggled with the writing of *A Farewell to Arms*. The result is entirely convincing and gives the reader a greater sense of reality and "feel" for Hemingway the man than even greater quantities of detail could. It is the accomplishment of this biography that it makes Hemingway real and alive, with an inner life of his own.

The reader should not, however, think that this is a biography full of the all-too-common "He certainly thought . . ." or "He must have said . . . " or "No doubt he felt . . ." The record of Hemingway's moods and feelings is not imagined or made the subject of guesswork, however inspired. When the reader asks how Reynolds could possibly have known something, the answer is supplied. Reference to the notes in the back of the book reveals that Reynolds has mastered his subject. He has at his disposal and uses great quantities of letters, notebooks, and interviews. He even consults when necessary such things as library tickets, the records of several governments, and appropriate meteorological records. Conclusions and interpretations are firmly rooted in fact and physical reality. The volume is further bolstered but not burdened by an index, maps, and a chronology.

The "Homecoming" of the title, then, though it lasted only some thirteen months, was for Hemingway both a success and a failure. It was a success insofar as his writing and professional reputation were concerned, but it could be deemed a failure on the level of personal relationships. He was even more estranged and irritated by his own family than he had been before his father's death. His new wife's family bored and frustrated him, however much they liked him. In general, he was uncomfortable, both as artist and person, with the America to which he returned, and he was glad and satisfied to be leaving again.

One small problem remains: If it takes Michael Reynolds three volumes to get Hemingway to the age of thirty, it is difficult to see how he can cover more than thirty additional years in two more volumes. Whatever the number of volumes it may take, on the evidence of this book, they will be well worth waiting for.

*Gordon N. Bergquist*

## Sources for Further Study

*Kirkus Reviews*. LX, October 15, 1992, p. 1300.
*Library Journal*. CXVII, October 1, 1992, p. 88.
*Publishers Weekly*. CCXXXIX, November 9, 1992, p. 70.

# HENRY JAMES
## The Imagination of Genius

*Author:* Fred Kaplan (1937-      )
*Publisher:* William Morrow (New York). Illustrated. 620 pp. $25.00
*Type of work:* Literary biography
*Time:* 1843-1916
*Locale:* New York City; Newport, Rhode Island; Cambridge, Massachusetts; London; Paris; Geneva; and Rome

*A psychologically revealing portrait of Henry James, based on an examination of more than twelve thousand unpublished letters of the James family*

> *Principal personages:*
> HENRY JAMES, the author of *The Portrait of a Lady* (1880-1881) and *The Golden Bowl* (1904)
> HENRY JAMES, SR., his father
> MARY JAMES, his mother
> WILLIAM JAMES, his older brother
> GARTH "WILKIE" JAMES, his younger brother
> ROBERTSON "BOB" JAMES, his younger brother
> ALICE JAMES, his sister
> MINNY TEMPLE, his cousin
> CONSTANCE FENIMORE WOOLSON, an American novelist and close friend
> HENDRIK ANDERSEN, a sculptor and close friend
> EDITH WHARTON, an American novelist and close friend

Fred Kaplan's biography of the expatriated American novelist bills itself as "the first to be conceived in light of late-twentieth century attitudes about feminism and homosexuality." A more condensed work than Leon Edel's magisterial five-volume *The Life of Henry James* (1953-1972), Kaplan's work is also more sharply focused on the two levels of James's life: the emotionally charged atmosphere of the James household, in which a controlling father maintained order even during intense out-breaks of sibling rivalry; and the more rarefied world of James's artistic and literary acquaintances. Such a context is perfect for a strict Freudian interpretation of the life of Henry James, and Kaplan delivers a readable and often entertaining account of a writer whose interests and fame spread across continents, cultures, and centuries.

Henry James was a descendant of a noteworthy if somewhat unstable New York family. James's grandfather, William James of Albany, New York, was an Irish immigrant who amassed one of the largest fortunes in the young republic. James's father, Henry James, Sr., was (for the most part) disinherited by his father after a scandalous career at Union College in Schenectady, New York, which included gambling and heavy drinking. After William James's death in 1832, Henry James, Sr., successfully challenged the will that penalized both himself and his mother, though the case was not decided until 1843, the year of Henry James, Jr.'s birth. In 1844, Henry James, Sr., experienced a form of mental breakdown that became known in the family as the "vastation"; he eventually found the answer to his problems in the writings of the Swedish mystical theologian Emanuel Swedenborg and in political radicalism. Kaplan finds many of the subjects of Henry James's later works in what Freud called "infantile experience," the impressions a child receives in the early years, and in the first component to Freud's famous method of dream analysis outlined in *The Interpretation of Dreams* (1900). James soon found himself in competition not only with a strong-willed older brother, William, but also with a quick-witted, though chronically ill, younger sister, Alice, and two impulsive younger brothers, Garth "Wilkie" James and Robertson "Bob" James. Henry adopted the role of the introvert and peacemaker; he was dubbed by his mother as "the angel of the house."

Kaplan's best analysis is found in the early chapters, setting the stage for James's later literary concerns. The James family traveled continuously in both North America and Europe; the children received at best a haphazard education at a number of schools, each utilizing a different progressive approach. Both Henry and William enjoyed the years spent at Newport, Rhode Island, where they delighted in the company of talented young men like themselves and a number of young female cousins, the most notable being the tragically fated Minny Temple, later the model for both Isabel Archer in *The Portrait of a Lady* (1880-1881) and Milly Theale in *The Wings of the Dove* (1902). The idyllic Newport existence was shattered by a series of moves brought on by Henry James, Sr.'s wanderlust and by a series of illnesses that Kaplan takes as a sign of a psychically wounded family. Henry suffered from an "obscure hurt" to the lower back incurred while fighting a fire in Newport in 1861. The disability effectively kept him from serving in the Civil War. William experienced a number of bouts with depression and psychologically induced illnesses. Alice's compensation was in neurological illness, from which she suffered more acutely than any other member of the family. Only Wilkie and Bob suffered actual physical injuries. Wilkie was critically wounded while serving as adjutant to commander Robert Gould Shaw during the attack on Fort Wagner, South Carolina, by the African American Fifty-fourth Massachusetts regiment; Bob became ill while serving with another African American regiment, the Fifty-fifth Massachusetts. The pain of the Civil War served to bring an end to the union of the James family, as the two elder brothers subsequently moved on to careers of their own.

James already had become a short-story writer and an established reviewer of books for *The North American Review* and the newly founded *The Nation* by the time he traveled alone to Europe in 1869. Kaplan sees this escape from the family as necessary for James as an aspiring artist. By removing himself from the emotional strain of family life, James was able to redirect his energy into the shaping of his fiction. Kaplan interprets most of the early fiction as heavily autobiographical, often with Oedipal and homoerotic subject matter. He somewhat predictably reads James's sensationalistic first novel-length fiction, *Watch and Ward* (serialized in *The Atlantic* beginning in 1871), as an Oedipal narrative. More convincing is Kaplan's interpretation of the short story "Master Eustace," and the little-known one-act play *Still Waters*, both also from 1871. The first is an Oedipal story of a son who returns from England to discover that his mother has remarried his supposedly dead father. The melodramatic discovery of the secret leads to the death of the mother and the lifelong impotence of the son. In *Still Waters*, a love triangle between two men and a woman is destroyed when one of the men realizes that he actually is in love with the other man. The sexually adventurous material from the early part of his career brought James criticism from several quarters, particularly from the prudish William Dean Howells at *The Atlantic*. When faced with criticism, as Kaplan insightfully notes, the young writer's response was to increase his natural inclination for misdirection. James's bluntness subsequently took a second place to his desire to create an audience for his fiction.

The climax of James's secession from his family came in 1875 with his permanent self-exile overseas, first in France and Italy, and then with permanent residence in London beginning in 1876. At this point in his career, James's subject matter became based less on family experience and more on what Freud called "the day's residues," the second component of dream analysis. James wrote his first popular novel, *The American*, published serially in 1876-1877, while living in Paris; notably, the novel deals with the clash of cultures occasioned by a wealthy American, Christopher Newman, courting a widowed aristocratic Frenchwoman, Claire de Cintré. Kaplan reads the novel as James's "affirmation of the preferability of American strength to European corruption, of the superiority of the values of the New World in regard to honesty, love, marriage, class relations, the idealization of the commonwealth of talent and virtue rather than the rigid hierarchy of birth." As such, the novel established the paradigm for much of the remainder of James's fiction. The clash of cultures is irreconcilable, so no marriage can take place; likewise, the suppression of anger on Newman's part was to be repeated by many other characters in James's fiction.

After the permanent move to London, James entered a period of intense productivity, culminating in the publication of *The Portrait of a Lady*. James's first masterpiece, it is concerned with the career of Isabel Archer, an energetic young American woman who travels to Europe to experience the world. Against all the warnings of friends and relatives, she marries Gilbert Osmond, an expatriated American, only to realize too late that Osmond is not what he appears to be. Kaplan reads the novel more in terms of James's family life than the issues found in the move to London; he describes the text as a "nightmare" novel. Unlike his perceptive placing of *The American* in the context of James's European travels, Kaplan neglects placing *The Portrait of a Lady* in a similar social context, preferring to concentrate almost exclusively on the text as a projection of James's childhood fears and fantasies. Kaplan returns to the societal context in the chapter, "The Great Money Question." Following the deaths of both Mary and Henry James, Sr., in 1882, James found himself more concerned than ever with his economic situation. Although he had been largely self-supporting since his move to London, the absence of a parental safety net caused a great deal of anxiety for the now-famous young writer. In this and subsequent chapters, Kaplan relies heavily on the excellent scholarly work done by Michael Anesko, among others, who has documented extensively James's dealings with publishers and literary agents. After the relative failure of two long novels, James turned almost exclusively to writing short fiction, which proved to be a remunerative enterprise. After gaining little money from the phenomenally successful "Daisy Miller" (1878), James made certain that his publishing rights were protected during the remaining decades of his career. Socially, James helped care for Alice, his invalid sister, who had moved to England, and kept his literary ties to France active, especially with the naturalist writers Léon Daudet, Émile Zola, and Edmond and Jules de Goncourt. He mourned other deaths in addition to those of his parents, including those of Ivan Turgenev, the Russian realist novelist; Constance Fenimore Woolson, James's closest female friend, apparently a suicide victim in 1894; and his sister Alice, who died in 1892. Alice's substantial bequest to James allowed him to spend the remainder of his career working only on projects he believed to be worthy and effectively provided him with an answer to the money question.

Kaplan notes that James's fixation with gaining a larger fortune eventually proved to be disastrous. Although freed from the necessity of writing short fiction, he turned to his one get-rich-quick scheme, writing for the stage. The culmination of the experiment was his public embarrassment after the 1895 premiere of *Guy Domville* (1894), when he was greeted during a curtain call by a hissing audience. Kaplan also emphasizes that James established several intense homoerotic friendships with a number of younger men during the 1890's. This happened against the backdrop of one of the greatest scandals of the decade, Oscar Wilde's trial and subsequent conviction on charges of sodomy. Although Wilde and James shared some acquaintances, including Morton Fullerton, the future lover of Edith Wharton, James declined the opportunity to sign a petition arguing for Wilde's pardon. Ever the believer in the private life, James could see no good coming from public pronouncements of support.

In 1896, James moved to Lamb House in Rye, Sussex, a house he eventually purchased and lived in for the remainder of his life. He began to dictate his work during this period, which saw the birth of his famous late style. Although he published three complete novels between 1902 and 1904, *The Wings of the Dove* (1902), *The Ambassadors* (1903), and *The Golden Bowl* (1904), he had relinquished the desire to be a popular writer. In an 1860's review of the novels of George Eliot, James had written that "the writer makes the reader very much as he makes his characters." James was finally writing for a reader of his making instead of for a popular audience, utilizing a masterly style created through decades of struggling with publishers and audiences. The revision of his novels and tales for the seventeen-volume New York edition, published in 1907, further showed his dedication to the craft of writing. Often ill in his later years, James continued working on a series of autobiographical volumes. On his deathbed in 1916, he began a series of dictations in which he saw himself as Napoleon and the James family as the Bonapartes. He believed that the work of his family would be immortalized, and through the work of skilled biographers such as Fred Kaplan, it appears that the prophecy may come true.

*Jeff Cupp*

## Sources for Further Study

*Booklist*. LXXXIX, October 1, 1992, p. 229.
*Chicago Tribune*. December 20, 1992, XIV, p. 5.
*Kirkus Reviews*. LX, September 15, 1992, p. 1167.
*Library Journal*. CXVII, September 15, 1992, p. 64.
*Los Angeles Times Book Review*. January 3, 1993, p. 4.
*New Statesman and Society*. V, December 11, 1992, p. 38.
*The New York Times Book Review*. XCVII, November 22, 1992, p. 12.
*The New Yorker*. LXVIII, November 2, 1992, p. 119.
*Publishers Weekly*. CCXXXIX, September 21, 1992, p. 84.
*The Spectator*. CCLXIX, November 21, 1992, p. 44.

# HIGH COTTON

*Author:* Darryl Pinckney (1953-     )
*Publisher:* Farrar Straus Giroux (New York). 309 pp. $21.00
*Type of work:* Novel
*Time:* The 1960's through the 1980's
*Locale:* Primarily Indianapolis, Indiana; and New York City

*A novel tracing the youth and maturation of an American middle-class black man as he comes to realize the high cost of integration and middle-class status*

> *Principal characters:*
> THE UNNAMED NARRATOR, followed from his school days through college to his first years as a working adult
> GRANDFATHER EUSTACE, an Ivy League graduate who spent most of his life as a minister
> UNCLE CASTOR, grandfather's brother, a musician
> AUNT CLARA, a light-skinned mulatto from a dying age and culture
> BARGETTA, the narrator's flamboyant college friend living in Paris

In his first novel, Darryl Pinckney provides the reader with a careful examination of a world not often explored by African American writers, the world of the black middle class. The family at the center of *High Cotton* represents four generations of college graduates who have gone from rural Georgia to the major cities of America and Europe. These are the "Also Chosen," as Pinckney calls them, W. E. B. Du Bois' "Talented Tenth" and their descendants, the "upper shadies," the privileged yellow-skinned doctors and teachers of the Old South, the members of the prestigious black social clubs of the 1950's and 1960's, inhabitants of the "Golden Ghettos" of America's suburbs in the 1960's and 1970's, and the contemporary affluent urban professionals. Pinckney demonstrates in this novel that achievement of middle-class status may come at too high a personal and cultural price.

The unnamed narrator provides the single perspective from which this story is told. The novel traces a period from the narrator's adolescence in the mid-1960's to his young adulthood following college graduation in the 1980's, from his boyhood in the urban neighborhoods of Indianapolis to the white suburbs where his is the first black family. It takes us from his home to relatives' homes in Louisville, Kentucky, and Opelika, Alabama, to his exploration of London, New York City, Harlem, Amsterdam, and Paris, leading him finally to his roots in his grandfather's birthplace in Augusta, Georgia. In following this young man's journey to adulthood, readers see the difficulties not only of growing up but also of growing up black and middle class in America. It is a context of mixed signals and contradictions, of opportunities glimpsed but often denied, of material gains at the cost of cultural loss. Pinckney's often funny, sometimes naïve, sometimes cynical, sometimes emotionally numbed narrator ultimately discovers that the journey he and his family embarked upon, toward the status and success inherent in the American Dream, obscures what is really important—family, ethnic identity, and self-awareness.

Family abounds in this novel. The narrator's early life is overwhelmed by the countless "old-timers" who "seemed to be all there was. They far outnumbered their younger relatives." In their looming shadows, the young man struggled to discover his own identity. The strongest member in this family pantheon is the narrator's paternal grandfather, Eustace, Brown and Harvard educated, a man whose presence "sucked up the air," a man completely at ease in the heady world of Cambridge academia but lost in the black southern world to which he returns. Contemptuous of his own siblings and children for failing to match his own scholarly accomplishments, disdainful of his parishioners for their unwillingness to show him what he considers proper respect, Grandfather Eustace spends his life disappointed, bitter, and distant from everyone, including his own wife (the "beige" stepgrandmother) and family. At once his antagonist and his defining fire, Eustace informs the narrator's young life, always edging him toward that "paradise of integration" the old man believed in but could not live.

The narrator tells his reader, "No one sat me down and told me I was a Negro. That was something I figured out on the sly." His maternal Aunt Clara and paternal Uncle Castor contribute to but complicate the boy's personal and racial awareness.

His train trip south to Aunt Clara's home in Opelika, Alabama, shows him a contradictory world in which skin color, even among African Americans, determines power and privilege. The narrator puzzles over the old woman's pride in describing her father as "seven-eighths white" and repeating family legend of an uncle whose mother had been rumored to be a white girl from one of the South's best families. Clara's "transparent" skin, through which the boy could detect her green veins, aided her high social position. Educated and married to the "Negro doctor," Clara had been served first by the darker-skinned woman renting Clara's shotgun shack and later by her daughters. Although the boy witnesses at first hand the poverty of her tenants (his newfound ruffian playmate Ezell and his little brother eating greasy fish from a newspaper makes a lasting impression upon him), Aunt Clara knows nothing of that world. In fact, that Opelika summer of the mid-1960's was undisturbed by news of Selma (he only hears the name later and thinks it is a woman), civil rights, and racial equality. Later, "Television added tear gas, gasoline bombs, University of Mississippi at Oxford," but the "Old Country" Aunt Clara inhabits is "a sort of generalized stuffy room" where time does not pass and nothing changes.

Whereas most "old-timers fell silent whenever [the boy] entered the room," Uncle Castor is not one of them. Uncle Castor reveals what Eustace finds too indelicate to discuss—the family's slave heritage, their father and grandfather "dark as tar," Ku Klux Klan "necktie parties," and the racism of Eustace's beloved Boston in the 1920's. Castor recalls for the boy the New England Conservatory of Music's regret that "a black boy could not hope for a concert career." Joining a "black and white" jazz band in the 1920's, Castor abandons his hopes for a classical career, sets off on a luxury liner for Europe, and writes about his life and music in a four-hundred-page manuscript the narrator later discovers hidden in the dust bag of his grandfather's vacuum after the old man's death. That manuscript, juxtaposed to the narrator's memories of Castor sitting late at night at his family's piano, silently depressing the keys as he worked on his "apotheosis," "an oratorio based on Shango cult themes," steels the narrator against his grandfather's condemnation of Castor. Having abdicated the white world Eustace insisted they could master, and eking out a living in piano bars and at race tracks, Castor becomes an object of Eustace's scorn and a further source of the narrator's confusion regarding his blackness.

Although the old-timers permeate his world, the narrator believes his only hope to define himself is to reject his family and heritage. He begins by identifying with all things British. When the family moves to the white suburbs, he feels as if "real life was beginning." He claims, "I couldn't allow myself to look back, having presented myself to myself as one who had never been anywhere but where I was." Purposely separating himself from his past and from the other black children at school, the narrator re-creates himself in the image of white suburbia—journalism club, white friends, and summer camps. Not until high school, when he dabbles in a splinter group of the Black Panthers, does the narrator give any thought to the black struggle. Even then, his activism is almost thwarted because of his lack of a black turtleneck and a driver's license. Only a white friend who is willing to drive him to his meetings and follow him in his car as he distributes militant propaganda saves him—until he grows bored with the group's pettiness and his own lack of conviction. At Columbia University, the narrator's friends again are mostly white. When he ventures into nearby Harlem, to the "Valley of the Shines," as his grandfather calls it, he is humiliated and incensed that two "brothers" almost con him.

In isolating himself from his past, the narrator creates an empty present. Graduation from college finds him alone in New York City with the regulars at the Melody Coast Bar—his dormitory security guard, the tough white bar owner Betty, and Jeanette, the black backup singer always waiting for her agent's call and a free vodka gimlet. Days and weeks pass, and only his parents' checks from home sustain him. A young white man's stabbing death in the bar's doorway awakens the narrator momentarily from his ambivalent existence, but like many children of the ambitious, upwardly mobile generation of the 1950's and 1960's, the narrator seems paralyzed, living only at the margins, unable to claim or create a life.

In a seedy room overlooking a line of no-longer-respectable row houses, he keeps watch over the old widows tending window boxes, the transients, and others as dispossessed as himself. He slips from one secondhand bookstore job to another, doing odd jobs for a petulant Djuna Barnes, until he lands his first legitimate job as a secretary to an insecure editor at a barely solvent publishing firm. Again he finds himself among mostly white people, save for another secretary or two, a janitor, and an angry managing editor, Maurice. While wanting to fit in and do well enough not to get fired (but hardly more than that), the narrator becomes increasingly aware of the company's implicit racism through its "token" treatment of Maurice. When Eustace is again rebuffed after asking to meet his grandson for lunch during his employ here, the old man inquires, "What's the matter? Don't you want them to find out your grandfather is a Negro?" The young man's personal and racial ambivalence becomes clear: He feels comfortable in neither the black nor the white world.

When he quits his job and temporarily escapes to Europe, the narrator enters yet another ambiguous world, that of African Americans abroad. In a chapter entitled "A Handbook of Interracial Dating," Pinckney presents Bargetta, the narrator's only friend from Columbia, an African American woman who dates only white men. She shares with the narrator their families' social aspirations, especially their common membership in the Jack 'n' Jill club, an exclusive black social organization requiring children's attendance at cultural outings, luncheons, and fashion shows. Like the narrator, Bargetta had no black friends at Columbia (other than the narrator). She followed her French artist lover to Paris, meeting the disapproval of Pierre-Yves's aristocratic mother. Her acquaintance Gilles "liked to be the only 'shine' in the room and resented the presence of other black men." Disconcertedly, the narrator recognizes much of himself in these two.

The confusion and even denial of one's race, family, and history inevitably leads to a crisis, and the narrator's is prompted by two events: his acquaintance with "black preppies" Trip and Rayburn, and the death of Grandfather Eustace. Trip, a collector of rare books whom the narrator meets in one of his used bookstore jobs, is a thoroughly integrated black man who "lived completely free of entanglements of racial identity" with his Wall Street job, his Jewish vegetarian girlfriend, and their expensively ostentatious apartment. Together with his friend Rayburn (Yale, NYU law school, and MBA), Trip forms a " 'wholly black-owned' firm of corporate troubleshooters" to sell "computer solutions" to African nations. The hypocrisy of these men in claiming minority preference without having the slightest understanding of, or sympathy with, their race sickens the narrator. "I cultivated an indifference," he claims, nagged by an unidentifiable "funny feeling," an emotional numbness. When Grandfather Eustace, who had been in a nursing home since the death of the beige stepgrandmother, dies, the narrator's emptiness directs him to his grandfather's birthplace in Georgia. In looking at the faces of his grandfather's people, the narrator no longer sees "old darkies" but "revealed texts, guides to a great landslide that would tell me what to feel about this ode in a shell called blackness when the time came." He experiences no epiphany in tracing the steps his grandfather took across the Savannah River to the integrated North, but among these people the narrator discovers "the emotion [he had] been looking for all those years." The narrator recognizes himself among these African American people and states proudly, "One day—if it comes—I may be someone's old darky." He understands the black past and people that he, his parents, and his grandfather have betrayed and the joy that their embrace can bring. He truly has come home. He has found himself.

Readers who come to *High Cotton* expecting yet another story of African Americans' struggle with poverty (whether urban or rural) and the injustice of American society will be disappointed. Darryl Pinckney, as part of the new tradition of African American writers that includes Paule Marshall, Gloria Naylor, and Terry McMillan, offers a new vision. He shows that an individual's gain in social class and status cannot come at the price of personal, racial, and cultural sacrifice. Pinckney's narrator demonstrates that only in understanding one's past and making it part of the present can true selfhood be achieved.

*Laura Weiss Zlogar*

## Sources for Further Study

*Chicago Tribune.* March 3, 1992, V, p. 3.
*The Christian Science Monitor.* February 28, 1992, p. 13.
*Los Angeles Times Book Review.* February 23, 1992, p. 3.
*The Nation.* CCLIV, May 18, 1992, p. 667.
*The New York Review of Books.* XXXIX, March 26, 1992, p. 13.
*The New York Times Book Review.* XCVII, February 2, 1992, p. 3.
*Partisan Review.* LIX, Spring, 1992, p. 282.
*Publishers Weekly.* CCXXXVIII, December 6, 1991, p. 55.
*The Times Literary Supplement.* August 14, 1992, p. 17.
*The Washington Post Book World.* XXII, February 23, 1992, p. 1.
*The Yale Review.* LXXX, July, 1992, p. 198.

# A HISTORY OF THE JEWS IN AMERICA

*Author:* Howard Sachar (1928-    )
*Publisher:* Alfred A. Knopf (New York). 1051 pp. $40.00
*Type of work:* History
*Time:* 1492-1991
*Locale:* The United States

*In a detailed yet fast-moving text, a prolific historian records the arrival, absorption, socioeconomic status, and cultural contributions of the Jews in the United States throughout their five-hundred-year history in North America*

> *Principal personages:*
> ISAAC LEESER, the founder of the Jewish Publication Society
> ISAAC MAYER WISE, the founder of the Union of American Hebrew Con-gregations and Hebrew Union College
> JACOB SCHIFF, a financier
> LOUIS D. BRANDEIS, a Supreme Court Justice and early Zionist leader
> LOUIS MARSHALL, a president of the American Jewish Committee and president of the Jewish Agency
> STEPHEN S. WISE, the founder and president of the Jewish Institute of Religion and the American Jewish Congress

Finally, amid a plethora of publications dealing with specific aspects of the American Jewish experience, Howard Sachar's monumental *A History of the Jews in America* has filled the need for a solid, comprehensive text reviewing the entire sweep of the Jewish experience in the United States since the Spanish first reached the New World, five hundred years ago. Written for a general audience, it stands as the finest effort to date to present a one-volume history of American Jewry.

There have been other efforts to record the Jewish experience in America, all of them troubled by fundamental weaknesses. Many of the first efforts, including Peter Wiernik's *History of the Jews in America* (1912) and Oscar Handlin's *Adventure in Freedom: Three Hundred Years of Jewish Life in America* (1954), use old scholarship and rely on limited sources. *Zion in America: The Jewish Experience from Colonial Times to the Present* (1974), by Henry Feingold, represents excellent research, but it is outdated and devotes a scant twenty pages to the twenty-five years following World War II, while Sachar's book devotes roughly four hundred pages to the same period.

Perhaps the most important previous history, published only three years earlier and an obvious source for comparison, is Arthur Hertzberg's *The Jews in America: Four Centuries of an Uneasy Encounter, a History* (1989). Hertzberg's book does not act entirely as a history, however, because it presents his vision of the Jewish American experience through supportive descriptions of select historical events. Thus, Hertzberg omits any mention of trade unions, perhaps the most powerful institutions created by Jews in America, because they contradict one of his central theses, that Jewish immigrants came to the United States as the poorest, least educated, least cultured, and least ideological Jews in Europe. By omitting such significant contributions to American society as the trade unions, and by ignoring such leaders as the anarchist Emma Goldman and the socialist Morris Hillquit, Hertzberg reveals the distortion-effect of his thesis.

In the midst of this impoverished historiography emerges another major work by Sachar, a talented chronicler of events in the history of world Jewry. In 1976, Sachar's *A History of Israel: From the Rise of Zionism to Our Time* filled a similar void by detailing the Jewish nationalist movement and the emergence of Israel. It is still possibly the most widely used text for courses on the history of Israel. Sachar's ability to organize diverse themes into dense yet fascinating chapters has allowed him to write numerous comprehensive texts for college courses.

*A History of the Jews in America*, unlike Hertzberg's book, attempts to trace the experiences of American Jewry without a predetermined thesis. The details of history speak for themselves. While Hertzberg juxtaposes anti-Semitism with assimilation as the central issues of Jewish identity, Sachar views both of them as simply a part of the American Jewish experience, which continues to evolve. Such a presentation gives Sachar intellectual honesty and the freedom to present details that either would be ignored by Hertzberg or that he would think contradicted his arguments.

In fact, Sachar records both positive and negative elements of the Jewish American experience, choosing to mention the nearly antiabolitionist stance of Isaac Mayer Wise along with the social activism of Stephen S. Wise, the prominence of such political leaders as Louis Brandeis and Henry Kissinger along with the case history of Abraham Ruef's political graft. By devoting many pages to the prostitution, arson, and even murder in New York's immigrant communities, to the organized crime of Meyer Lansky in the 1940's, to the insider trading of Ivan Boesky and Michael Milken, and even to "a kind of Soviet-Jewish Mafia," Sachar shows that he has presented an impartial portrait of Jewish life in the United States.

All fundamental elements of the Jewish American experience can be found within this masterful volume. Anti-Semitism, Zionism, and assimilation have shaped the course of Jewish history in America, and Sachar combines elements of economic, intellectual, political, and social history to describe the arrival, absorption, and expressions of culture of the many waves of immigrants that coalesced to form today's Jewish community. Each group experienced different hardships. Sachar does not hesitate to describe the intragroup tensions that led the established Central European leadership, for example, to express its superiority over the impoverished, supposedly backward East Europeans of the Lower East Side in New York City. He also notes that, for example, the son of David Sarnoff (a very successful East European immi-grant) married the granddaughter of Jacob Schiff (a prominent German immigrant) at Temple Emanu-El, the largest Reform Congregation founded by Central European Jews, showing that a more uniform Jewish community removed the ethnic factional-ism that plagued the first decades of the twentieth century.

Sachar provides the historical context for each wave of immigrants along with their difficulties entering the United States. By presenting the European backdrop for the immigrants' decision to come to America, as well as their attitudes toward their former homes, Sachar explains the context for various intellectual movements that arose out of immigrant communities. He argues that the 90 percent voter support for Franklin D. Roosevelt in 1940, for example, and the radicalism of the garment industry derived from the immigrants' "intellectual emancipation" and their exposure to "the dynamic new Socialist-revolutionary ideologies sweeping through Central and Eastern Europe." For some East European immigrants (who numerically overwhelmed the earlier Central Europeans), "the visions of humanitarianism, brotherhood, and progress, in all their Socialist and Judaic connotations, blended almost indistinguishably on the Lower East Side." For Sachar, the importance of political ideology defines the poetry of the nearly forgotten Yosef Bovshover, the treasonous aid Julius Rosenberg gave to the Soviet Union, and Jonathan Pollard's efforts to help the Israelis via espionage. Sachar dares to go further by presenting those intellectuals whose response to their Judaic origins was complete rejection and self-denial of their ethnic identity, such as Bernard Baruch and Walter Lippman, labeling their ideology as anti-Semitic.

Sachar's astute concern as a political historian turns his attention to the relationship between the American Jews and the presidents on whom they have depended. Each crisis facing the Jewish community, particularly in the twentieth century, is presented with the corresponding president's attitude toward the Jews and their perceptions of him. According to Sachar, whereas Woodrow Wilson, the Roosevelts, Lyndon B. Johnson, and John F. Kennedy supported the Jewish community, William Howard Taft and Harry S. Truman equivocated their allegiances, and Dwight D. Eisenhower and Richard Nixon were adversarial toward Jewish causes.

For each Jewish communal issue, such as the anti-Semitic scapegoating of Leo Frank, the establishment of Israel, and racist restrictionism, Sachar gives the community's response. This effective technique of presenting a cycle of crises and responses allows Sachar to demonstrate the varying strength of Jewish communal leadership over time. As a result, the reader makes an implicit comparison between early efforts to combat anti-Semitism and restrictionism and later communal responses. In addition, Sachar implicitly contrasts the Jewish community's ability to mobilize funds for the creation and early defense of Israel with its relative inability to meet its financial goals for the 1982 Lebanon war and for the absorption of Soviet Jews in the 1990's. He also notes the redundancy and waste that characterized the multiple Jewish agencies, especially in the late 1940's when Robert MacIver documented the tremendous overkill among Jewish organizations.

Another unique contribution to the historiography of the Jewish American experience is Sachar's focus on Jewish women's distinct contributions to and influence on life in America. In addition to mentioning essential figures such as Rebecca Gratz, Henrietta Szold, and the founders of the National Council of Jewish Women, he adds Lillian Wald (a "pioneer of American feminism"), Ernestine Rose (an Owenist), Julia Richman (the first female New York superintendent), Rose Schneiderman and the garment worker organizers, Rae Frank and Martha Newmark (students at Hebrew Union College years before it ordained a woman), and Betty Friedan (founder of the

National Organization for Women). By their inclusion in his book, he affirms women's contribution to American life.

Readers will find the various plans for Jewish colonization throughout the United States somewhat amusing. Beginning with Mordechai Noah's plans in 1820 to turn Grand Island, New York, into "Ararat," American Jews have questioned their ability to fit into a wider, often hostile society. In addition to efforts to promote Jewish agrarianism by Isaac Mayer Wise and others, such ideas as the Galveston Plan of 1907 and project "M" in 1945 were geared toward relieving restrictionist sentiments and xenophobic attitudes toward Jewish immigrants. Thus, while most American Jewish historians (such as Hertzberg) may choose to leave some or all of these plans out of their texts, their inclusion strengthens the reader's understanding of the political efficacy of restrictionist forces.

Although the bulk of his text provides an impartial description of the Jews' history in America, Sachar does not refrain from periodically providing the reader with his personal perspective. In particular, he expresses his anger at the U.S. government (especially the State Department) for ignoring the plight of the Jews during World War II. Even more compelling is his observation that Zionists spoke of "the need for a—post war—Jewish commonwealth in Palestine" and that the Jewish community did not press hard enough for a Palestinian refuge when it could have saved thousands of Jews from the gas chambers. With a wealth of details to support his thesis, Sachar's arguments are convincing.

The density of Sachar's book demonstrates his arduous work, but some may find that his ample examples are overwhelming. For example, in his chapter "The Americanization of German Jewry," Sachar presents both the background and the success stories of an endless list of German Jewish Americans. This proliferation of examples may actually obscure an understanding of the plight of German Jewry in America, although their inclusion certainly reinforces the idea that German Jews succeeded economically in establishing a place for themselves in society.

Indeed, for the novice reader of American Jewish history, the sheer length of this extensive, comprehensive text may make it difficult to keep track of Sachar's overarching themes. (Sachar's sterling prose and logical presentation alleviate this problem, but it remains a necessary evil, given the scope of his project.) Moreover, without a general knowledge of world Jewish history, the general reader can be misled about the American contribution to the history of Israel. For example, while Sachar emphasizes the role of Louis Brandeis and Chaim Weizmann in early Zionist history, most Israelis see their contributions as minimal. Also, Sachar gives the impression that American military contributions to the war effort were quite substantial when in fact they were overshadowed by the more significant Czech weaponry sent to the newborn land.

Finally, in light of the 1992 Council of Jewish Federations survey of American Jewish life, which focuses on the Jewish community's shrinking numbers and troubled institutions, Sachar's attention to the crisis of assimilation and intermarriage is clearly inadequate. In contrast with Hertzberg's study, which depicts a shrinking Jewish community suffering from the lack of a strong identity, Sachar's book understates one of the main crises of the American Jewish community of the 1980's and 1990's.

Even with these minor weaknesses, Sachar's masterful *A History of the Jews in America* stands as a monumental compilation of historical details into a comprehensive and comprehensible text for the lay student of Jewish American history. His sixty-three-page bibliography attests that his book consists almost entirely of data collected from other sources. Sachar's contribution is less scholarly and more educational, filling the historiographical need for a thorough yet general history of the Jewish experience in the United States. It is well worth reading.

*Jonathan D. Klein*

### Sources for Further Study

*Booklist.* LXXXVIII, March 15, 1992, p. 1314.
*The Guardian.* July 5, 1992, p. 20.
*Kirkus Reviews.* LX, March 15, 1992, p. 379.
*Library Journal.* CXVII, July, 1992, p. 103.
*Los Angeles Times Book Review.* May 31, 1992, p. 11.
*The New York Times Book Review.* XCVII, June 28, 1992, p. 29.
*Publishers Weekly.* CCXXXIX, March 16, 1992, p. 68.
*San Francisco Chronicle.* May 24, 1992, p. REV7.
*The Washington Post Book World.* XXII, May 17, 1992, p. 1.
*Washington Times.* June 14, 1992, p. B7.

# A HISTORY OF WOMEN IN THE WEST
## Volume I: From Ancient Goddesses to Christian Saints

*Editor:* Pauline Schmitt Pantel (1947-      )
*First published: Storia delle donne in Occidente,* Volume I: *L'Antichità,* 1990
Translated from the French by Arthur Goldhammer
*Publisher:* The Belknap Press of Harvard University Press (Cambridge, Massachusetts). Illustrated. 572 pp. $29.95
*Type of work:* History
*Time:* Prehistory to c. A.D. 500
*Locale:* Greece, Rome, and Western Europe

*A group of distinguished European and American historians examine the history of women in Western European societies from the earliest recorded literature and nonfiction through the advent of Christianity, showing how men's attitudes toward women influenced and retarded full female participation in societies*

Distinguished historian Michael Howard has observed that the "first lesson that historians are entitled to teach is an austere one: Not to generalize from false premises based on inadequate evidence. The second is not more comforting: The past is a foreign country; there is very little we can say about it until we have learned its language and understood its assumptions." Such advice has been more disregarded than heeded by many modern theorists, whose penchant for seeing patterns in the intricate carpet of the historical record has led them to make intriguing but sometimes wrongheaded pronouncements about the meaning of past events.

Therefore, it will not be surprising if many contemporary scholars, especially feminists, greet the volumes of *A History of Women in the West* with mixed emotions. The five collections of essays by distinguished European and American historians are committed to writing the history of women as it actually was, not as theorists wished it had been. According to scholars Natalie Zemon Davis and Joan Wallach Scott, whose brief introductory note to volume 1 is provocatively titled "A New Kind of History," the first group of essays is a kind of encyclopedia, surveying the lives of women in classical times and the attitudes toward women held by men, whose portraits of women form almost the only source modern historians have for determining what those lives were like. These authors offer an appropriate cautionary note, too: the approach taken by the writers of essays in this volume is "more eclectic and open-ended than might be the case if an Anglo-American team had been organizing the project." They warn readers that mainstream topics such as "domesticity, heterosexual families and religion, and internal state policies" are more fully treated than are the more controversial topics of "sexual practice and homosexuality, ethnicity and colonialism"—topics of much greater interest to feminist scholars.

Carefully edited by classical scholar Pauline Schmitt Pantel, the essays in this collection stress a pluralistic approach to women's history. The general editors of the series, Georges Duby and Michelle Perrot, note that their focus is on Western women, most of whom are white, but they are not apologetic. In fact, they address the issue of gender head-on, asserting that "[n]either feminism nor the representation of the feminine are universal values." Hence, anyone looking among the essays in *A History of Women in the West* for a feminist critique of male-dominated representations of women in classical times is in for some disappointment. The essayists in this volume are historians first, theorists only second (if at all). Most of the work is descriptive rather than political. Even in essays that deal directly with politics, such as Yan Thomas' "The Division of the Sexes in Roman Law," little editorial commentary intrudes on the author's narrative of the way things were in Roman society. The effect is actually salutary; one needs little exhortation to see that women were kept under tight rein by laws that promoted patriarchal domination and prohibited women from taking roles as citizens in the society at large.

Pluralism and interdisciplinary interests, however, are evident throughout volume 1. The essays range from Claudine Leduc's highly technical sociological analysis of marriage in ancient Greece, based on the different forms of dowry associated with the giving of a woman to her husband, to François Lissarague's lengthy examination, copiously illustrated, of images of women on Greek pottery and sculpture. A few provide speculations about the impact of various laws and practices on women who were subjected to restrictions not of their own making; others simply let the record speak for itself. The authors working with Pantel examine the images of women in Greek and Roman society, ranging freely between what scholars now classify as myth and more conventional sources of history. They cite the writings of such diverse authors as Homer and Pliny to capture a sense of how women were perceived by others (both male and female) and how they are captured in the literature, art, and political and medical writings of almost twenty centuries. Specialists may already know, but general readers may need to be cautioned, that ancient writers—even those who called themselves historians—were less concerned about the differences between fact and fiction, differences modern historians consider crucial for interpreting the documentary record and preparing an accurate portrait of the past.

Repeatedly, readers of *A History of Women in the West* are reminded that the modern view of women in classical times is necessarily a distorted one, since the historical record has been written almost exclusively by men, many of whom—including the intellectual giants of the age—were openly disdainful of the opposite sex. Plato, Socrates, and Aristotle were dismissive, even contemptuous, of the accomplishments of females, whom they considered defective forms of the male. Seen as objects—of lust, worship, or wealth—women were essentially voiceless, unable to tell their own stories about lives circumscribed by customs that inhibited females from entering public life. As Giulia Sissa notes, however, "our critique of a tradition from which women were excluded is nonetheless indebted to the positive accomplishments of that very tradition."

If the focus of this volume seems confined—examinations focus almost exclusively on religious practices and a few domestic matters—the reason is simple: There simply is not enough written evidence for historians to make conclusive judgments about life in antiquity. Hence, it is no surprise that much of the commentary in this volume contains some degree of speculation. This study reminds readers how difficult it is to construct an accurate history of women, because they were excluded for so long from the documentary record. Until the nineteenth century, little attention was paid by historians (almost all of whom were male) to daily life or domestic relations, areas in which women played a role equivalent to that of men. Confined to the private sphere or limited to the periphery in public life, women offered little to the major events captured in the chronicles of ancient or even pre-Enlightenment historians.

The authors of these essays are careful, however, to separate fact from hypothesis, and to let readers know when they stray from the historical record into the realm of theory. In this they are sometimes at odds with more militant practitioners of theoretical analysis, who are on occasion wont to offer as fact what is only a convenient construct. The problem has been exacerbated by demands of modern feminists who want the historical record revised so that women's place in history can be properly understood and appreciated. The zeal of some to correct the imbalance has led to new distortions. As Pantel herself points out, "Because women have been deprived of their history, it is tempting to recreate one for them in response to today's aspirations." A number of theorists are projecting modern conceptions and political premises onto the ancient world, and the result is a history based more on myth than on fact.

Writers in Pantel's collection are quick to eschew such an approach; in fact, on more than one occasion an author takes pains to point out the fallacies of such an approach. One of the finest pieces of scholarship in the work is Stella Georgoudi's critique of Swiss anthropologist Jacob Bachofen's theory of matriarchy, an idea embraced by those wishing to demonstrate the inherent rights of women to claim an equal place in society. In "Creating a Myth of Matriarchy," Georgoudi effectively debunks Bachofen's notion that there once existed a matriarchal system in which women had power over men, and that patriarchy is a later invention that won out over matriarchy at some time in the distant past.

The book is not feminist in small matters, either. The editor allows one of the authors to make the following observation about Roman law: "[I]t would be missing the point if the historian of law were to content himself with describing these surface changes [in Roman laws regarding the guardianship of women] while neglecting the forms . . . that these changes in practice had to take. . . ." The statement has no special relevance to feminism; however, the form of the pronoun used to describe the historian does. In this age of hypersensitivity to the gender of descriptive pronouns, to refer to a professional as "himself"—intending to include both men and women in this inclusive masculine term—is hardly permissible. One can only speculate that Pantel was too busy preparing the headnotes that bind the disparate essays together to catch this faux pas.

This is not to say that the authors are antifeminist. Quite the contrary is true. Lest the ultimate aim of this study be obscured beneath the specialized analysis of specific phenomena, Pantel uses her intercalary commentary to remind readers that "inequality" was the "fundamental feature of ancient society." Women in Rome, Greece, and other societies bordering the Mediterranean were expected to be wives and mothers, and to absent themselves from matters of government. Laws and social practices were designed to foster what was seen as women's essential (and sometimes sole) role: serving as vessels for reproduction and preservation of the race. What the authors consistently aim at, however, is to represent the past free of modern distortions of all kinds. In the process, they provide some unusual and provocative reevaluations of historical periods and the impact of the times on women. For example, if the authors in *A History of Women in the West* are to be believed, Christianity actually gave women greater opportunities to gain some form of independence and status; they were far from equal with their male counterparts, but many of them were able to make contributions to society through personal work and through charitable activities within the church. There is a certain irony in this observation, of course, since the church— especially the Roman Catholic church—is seen today as one of the staunchest patriarchal organizations in the world, treating female members as second-class members relegated to subservient roles as helpmates and assistants and denying them advancement within either the religious community (none can be priests) or laity (especially in countries other than the United States).

If volume 1 is any indication, the series will be of great value to historians who want to reconstruct the past so it can be understood and appreciated for what it really was. The scholarship demonstrated by Pantel and her team of essayists is nothing short of remarkable. In addition to important prior works of history, the contributions of anthropology, sociology, philology, and philosophy are examined and incorporated into the essays that compose this volume. The copious notes and bibliography occupy more than seventy-five pages in the volume. The authors have searched widely among sources in many languages to provide readers with a comprehensive reference list for further, more specialized reading. The result is a volume that is informative, provoca- tive, and enlightening—marks of a true contribution to what has become for twentieth century scholars of all disciplines an important and ongoing dialogue.

*Laurence W. Mazzeno*

**Sources for Further Study**

*Belles Lettres.* VIII, Fall, 1992, p. 47.
*Choice.* XXX, December, 1992, p. 677.
*The Christian Century.* CIX, August 12, 1992, p. 752.
*New Directions for Women.* XXI, July 1992. p. 32.
*The Times Literary Supplement.* June 19, 1992, p. 12.
*Washington Times.* May 10, 1992, p. B8.

# HITLER AND STALIN
## Parallel Lives

*Author:* Alan Bullock (1914-    )
*First published:* 1991, in Great Britain
*Publisher:* Alfred A. Knopf (New York). 1081 pp. $35.00
*Type of work:* Biography
*Time:* 1879-1953
*Locale:* The Soviet Union, Austria, Germany, and Western and Eastern Europe

*A definitive political biography, demonstrating in detail the parallel but quite different paths to power taken by Hitler and Stalin, grounded in the dense detail of historical research and in an immersion in the profound issues provoked by these lives*

*Principal personages:*
> ADOLF HITLER, the chancellor and political leader of Germany
> JOSEPH STALIN, a Soviet political leader who led territorial expansions and tried to develop industry and agriculture through collectivization
> HERMANN GÖRING, Hitler's second-in-command
> HEINRICH HIMMLER, the head of the Schutzstaffel (S.S.), charged with running Hitler's concentration camps
> ERNST RÖHM, the head of the Sturm Abteilung (S.A.), Hitler's private army used to intimidate his political opponents
> ALBERT SPEER, Hitler's architect, in charge of various government departments; tried to moderate the excesses of Nazism in the last days of World War II
> LEON TROTSKY, Stalin's rival in the fight to succeed V. I. Lenin
> VYACHESLAV MOLOTOV, Stalin's deputy, a dour diplomat
> LAVRENTI BERIA, the only chief of security to escape death at Stalin's hands
> NIKITA KHRUSHCHEV, a Stalin loyalist who later exposed Stalin's crimes to the Communist Party
> SVETLANA ALLILUYEVA, Stalin's daughter, who observed at first hand his paranoid, suspicious personality

Bullock's subtitle is borrowed from Plutarch, whose biographical essays are studies of parallel figures, from which the biographer draws certain moral conclusions and generalizations about public lives. Bullock is no moralist, though he cannot avoid making certain moral judgments about the heinous crimes of these two world historical figures, but like Plutarch he aims to reveal aspects of each life that may be apparent only by comparing these two careers in detail.

Bullock's method is that of the political biographer who concentrates on those personality traits that clearly manifest themselves in public; by and large he eschews intimate, psychological explorations of character, finding that a psychohistorical interpretation is mostly speculative and inconclusive.

Bullock's analysis of Hitler and Stalin appears not only in separate chapters but also in the excellent amassing of details that prove his thesis that both men were master politicians who carefully built up their power over years of patient manipulation and strategy. If Hitler ultimately failed, it is because, in Stalin's words, he did not know when to stop. His final aim was to establish a slave empire in the East (in most of what was then the Soviet Union), and he overreached himself. If Stalin succeeded, it was because his aim was to consolidate his power at home; his ventures abroad (compared to Hitler's) were timid, though in his own country he established a reign of terror and death rivaling that of Hitler.

Bullock's overall portrayal of Hitler and Stalin will provide few surprises to anyone reasonably familiar with the literature on these two figures, yet his comparison freshens the facts, making it necessary to think carefully through how Hitler and Stalin found themselves in quite different circumstances and with quite different personalities and nevertheless managed to acquire absolute power in the face of innumerable obstacles that made it seem extremely unlikely that either one would succeed.

Although Stalin was a member of the original revolutionary circle headed by Lenin, he by no means cut a distinguished figure in the Russian Revolution. Lenin found him dependable for various administrative jobs dealing with the rank and file. Although Stalin occasionally disputed Lenin's policies, he was absolutely loyal to them. Unlike many of his fellow revolutionaries, Stalin spent no time abroad. Between the failed revolution of 1905 and the successful one in 1917, he was in prison most of the time. After the revolution, he was known for his rough tongue and taciturn disposition. Stalin never let anyone know what he was thinking or plotting. He was slow in debate, a competent but not brilliant writer, and an indifferent speaker—clearly no match for the intellectual Leon Trotsky, who was renowned for his building of the Red Army, which kept the Communists in power during the Civil War in 1918. Moreover, by the early 1920's, as Lenin was dying, he let it be known in his final testament that he had grown to distrust Stalin, and he urged that Stalin be removed from his powerful position as general secretary of the Communist Party.

How was it, then, that by 1930, less than six years after Lenin's death, Stalin was in a position to transform the Soviet Union radically in the 1930's through his collectivization of farmland, massive investment in industry, and purges of the party membership and of the army, leaving him in an invincible position? Stalin prevailed because he cloaked himself in the mantle of Leninism, twisting Lenin's words when it was necessary, or getting his cronies to do so. Stalin did what Trotsky did not deign to: Stalin cultivated party members, installed them in positions beholden to him, and shrewdly pitted his enemies against each other, sowing suspicion so that he never faced the combined force of his opponents. Slowly, one by one, Stalin picked off his rivals after they had weakened each other and after he was assured of the votes necessary to drum his adversaries out of the party. Stalin never allowed his ambition to show, never bragged, and never admitted to having a plan to capture the leadership for himself. On the contrary, he always presented himself as the servant of the Communist Party.

Hitler, on the other hand, had no illustrious predecessor, no Lenin by whom he could chart his course. Until he was thirty years old, Hitler, a disaffected and unemployed veteran of World War I, had no idea of what his life's work should be. What he sought was some equivalent of the joy he had found on the battlefield, when he could feel at one with the national spirit, ready to sacrifice everything for his beloved Germany. A master of no trade or profession (though he deluded himself into thinking he had talent as an artist), Hitler gravitated to politics, the one field in which his fierce convictions could be channeled into spellbinding oratory. Unlike Stalin, Hitler had no patience for party bureaucracy. Compared to Stalin, he had no ideology, except for his belief in a master race, the Aryans who must destroy the Jews. Communism and Christianity were both Jewish-inspired plots in Hitler's mind.

Hitler's ideas were crude and vulgar. He believed in a nineteenth century philosophy called Social Darwinism. The strong and the pure of race should dominate the world, which meant to Hitler that the Germans ought to be the inheritors of the Roman Empire's legacy and take up arms against Soviet Russia, destroying the country and enslaving its subhuman population—as Hitler regarded it. Shortly after World War I, Hitler set about establishing a movement, National Socialism, that would convince Germans of their greatness and reverse the humiliating conditions foisted on Germany by the victorious powers, England, France, and the United States. Contemptuous of democracy, Hitler tried in 1923 to take over the government, failed miserably, and was jailed. When he came out of prison a year later, he was faced with the task of rebuilding a party that even before his prison sentence was nothing more than a very minor factor in national politics.

How is it, then, that Hitler became chancellor of Germany in 1923, and within six months totally dominated the country? His rise began with a courtroom speech in 1923 in which he excoriated the weakness of the Weimar government. Rather than denying his role in attempting to overthrow it, Hitler played to the public discontent with a government that had failed to control a ruinous inflation that had wiped out the savings of the middle class. He identified himself with the national cause of saving Germany, and he wrote a testament, *Mein Kampf* (1925-1927; English translation, 1933), that represented a plan for restoring his country to greatness.

From 1923 onward, Hitler professed to work within the political system. The Nazi party ran for seats in the Reichstag (parliament), and like other parties propagandized its policies and sought to increase its membership. Hitler tended to moderate his racial opinions, stressing instead his anti-Bolshevism and presenting himself and his movement as a counter to the growing concern over the spread of Communism in the labor movement in Germany and in other parts of Europe. He played to conservative elements of the electorate who were not Nazis but who were distrustful of democratic government because it seemed weak and unable to solve economic problems.

Like Stalin, Hitler consistently was underestimated. By 1930, his party was the largest in Germany, yet it could not gain a majority of seats in the parliamentary elections. In early 1933, it was thought by Germany's president, Paul von Hindenburg, and his advisers that naming Hitler chancellor in a coalition government would be a way to control him, especially since it was thought that his party had reached its peak of popularity and would soon lose votes. A government without Hitler seemed impossible, since no other party was large enough to govern, and the only alternative was the emergency powers that could be invoked for a limited period of time, so that the president and chancellor could govern on their own. It was these various emergency powers that Hitler turned to his advantage, especially after von Hindenburg, a military hero of World War I, died the next year. No one had the prestige or the power to oppose Hitler's rapid takeover of the entire country.

Until 1939, however, when Hitler's invasion of Poland began World War II, Hitler was careful to claim pacific intentions. He was out to reclaim German lands lost in World War I and to restore Germany as a major power. He did not want war, he said in speech after speech. He had to proceed carefully—as Stalin had done in his rise to power—slowly rearming Germany, taking possession of and remilitarizing the Rhineland, absorbing Austria into Germany, and claiming parts of Czechoslovakia that had a German population. Altogether it took six years for Hitler to create the conditions that made him feel strong enough to begin a war. In the same period, Stalin was wiping out all opposition in the Communist Party, equating any disagreement with him with treason and consequently ordering the executions of thousands of Communist Party members and millions of peasants who stood in the way of the collectivization of agriculture, the huge state farms and industrial projects that Stalin hoped would bring a rural, backward Soviet Union into the twentieth century as the equal of Germany and the other Western powers.

Bullock shows that all through the 1930's, Hitler and Stalin were quite aware of each other's ascent to power. Stalin made the mistake of thinking he could appease Hitler until Stalin himself had built an invincible military machine. Hitler, on the other hand, saw his pact with Stalin in 1939 as a temporary measure, to be honored only until he could finish off England and then launch an invasion of the Soviet Union.

Each dictator believed in the sovereignty of his own will. Stalin refused repeated requests to observe the catastrophic consequences of collectivization, the millions who suffered and died; Hitler never saw a concentration camp, never visited his soldiers at the front, and died in a bunker that literally became a tomb, the concrete manifestation of his belief in the superiority of his will. No less confident of his own rightness, Stalin died suspicious of even his closest associates and family, his daughter recalling that in his final moments he opened his eyes and raised his hand in a gesture that seemed to condemn everyone in the room with him.

*Carl Rollyson*

### Sources for Further Study

*The Christian Science Monitor.* May 5, 1992, p. 13.
*Foreign Affairs.* LXXI, Summer, 1992, p. 165.
*London Review of Books.* XIII, September 26, 1991, p. 20.
*Los Angeles Times Book Review.* March 29, 1992, p. 4.
*The New York Review of Books.* XXXIX, April 9, 1992, p. 3.
*The New York Times Book Review.* XCVII, March 22, 1992, p. 3.
*The Times Literary Supplement.* July 5, 1991, p. 4.
*The Washington Post Book World.* XXII, May 3, 1992, p. 4.

# HOPKINS
## A Literary Biography

*Author:* Norman White (1937-    )
*Publisher:* Clarendon Press/Oxford University Press (New York). Illustrated. 531 pp. $45.00
*Type of work:* Literary biography
*Time:* Primarily 1844-1889; but, briefly, afterward
*Locale:* England, Wales, and Ireland

*This massive biography traces the life, career, and religious struggles of the brilliant but profoundly alienated Victorian poet*

> *Principal personages:*
> GERARD MANLEY HOPKINS, a poet and Jesuit priest
> KATE HOPKINS (NÉE SMITH), his mother
> MANLEY HOPKINS, his father, an insurance broker and writer
> ROBERT BRIDGES, a poet and editor, Hopkins' friend

The poetry of Gerard Manley Hopkins presents enormous challenges to the reader; its complex rhythms and odd linguistic constructions often defy easy interpretation. Similarly, the curious, even perverse, life of Hopkins can shock and confuse, even as it compels. Norman White has accumulated an impressive array of factual materials and provides revealing selections from diaries and letters in order to make sense of a peculiar, tragic life story. Although he admits in his preface that Hopkins' was a life without a coherent pattern, he does illuminate many of its mysteries. White's great care in exhaustively documenting every step in Hopkins' career and extreme reticence to speculate beyond the boundaries of the strictly provable make this an eminently trustworthy, if never inspired, reference work on the late Victorian poet.

White is first and foremost a literary critic whose interest in Hopkins' biography stems from the ways it can help in understanding Hopkins' poetry. Thus in his opening chapters, White pays close attention to the literary output and aspirations of Hopkins' father, Manley, in order to trace their influence on Gerard, the son. Manley published both prose and poetry that, when placed side by side with the work of Hopkins himself, demonstrates some clear similarities in rhythm and tone. Of equal importance during these early years was the dynamic artistic community present in Hopkins' childhood home of Hampstead, where William Makepeace Thackeray, John Everett Millais, Anthony Trollope, Robert Browning, and George Meredith visited often. In this intellectually rich and stimulating environment, Hopkins grew up as an intelligent, creative child whose aesthetic sense was highly developed from an early age.

White nearly overwhelms his reader with data concerning Hopkins' years at school in Hampstead, Highgate, and later Oxford. He describes carefully the atmospheres and physical environments of the institutions and draws on numerous contemporary accounts of school life in order to give a sense of the day-to-day routine of Hopkins, the student. White's extraordinary care in documenting and supporting every statement that he makes leads to an unfortunate reticence to speculate beyond the wholly provable. He admits that Hopkins was a difficult child and lonely young man; he carefully reports Hopkins' passionate friendships with other boys and awareness of his sexual desires for them but never places the development of Hopkins' unstable self-image and ascetic life-style into the obvious context of a socially pervasive and finally internalized homophobia. White tells us the precise layout of Hopkins' rooms at school and describes carefully the view from his Balliol college window, but we find little insight into the inner struggles of Hopkins the confused young man, tortured by sexual yearnings that both church and state severely condemned.

Certainly White is at his best in tracing the development of Hopkins' aesthetic sense. From letters written during Hopkins' years at Oxford, White draws numerous quotes that demonstrate the poet's sensitivity to the natural world and love of beauty. White lingers over the language of the letters, drawing attention to its rhythm and variety. In one of his finest chapters, "Vital Truths of Nature: Hopkins and Ruskin," White places Hopkins' early observations of nature into a Ruskinian context, finding in Hopkins' attention to diversity in plant life and texture in scenery a translation of Ruskin's aesthetic theories into practice. Even before Hopkins began writing poetry (he was considering a career as a painter during these early years), his close observation and thorough appreciation of both words and natural beauty anticipated later expressions of sensual delight in poems such as "Pied Beauty" and "The Windhover."

The difficulty of poems such as the latter stems partially from Hopkins' eccentric use of language; he jammed words together without respect for grammar or syntactical clarity. Hopkins was fascinated throughout his life by words with similar sounds and possibilities for assonance and alliteration. White quotes from the many lists of favorite words that Hopkins accumulated during his Oxford years, compelling readers to hear their echoes in later poems. He quotes from Hopkins' letters, in which prose descriptions gradually gave way to poetic meters and rhythms, tracing the difficult birth of Hopkins the self-aware poet. White gives numerous examples of the immature but fascinating poems and scraps of poems that Hopkins slowly began to produce during his years at Oxford, pieces that capture the despair, loneliness, and tremendous talent of the quiet, introspective student.

Hopkins' process of coming to awareness as a poet is paralleled by his religious struggles but ends temporarily with his final conversion to Catholicism. This transition is one of the most difficult to explain or understand, for as White notes, Hopkins' family was not particularly religious and certainly his society was still profoundly suspicious of, even paranoid concerning, the Catholic faith. In his tenth, eleventh, and twelfth chapters, White attempts to account for Hopkins' decision in late 1866 to embrace Catholicism. He reports, but again barely analyzes, Hopkins' admissions concerning his sexual attraction to other males in his diaries, his profound guilt over his many "sins" (which he listed on paper and which included such petty matters as idleness and inattentiveness), and his final gravitation toward the most rigid of Catholic orders, the Jesuits. Although White never says so explicitly, it becomes clear to the reader that Hopkins desperately sought to control his own desires by seeking a stern and relentless agent of control outside himself. White does finally admit that Hopkins' choices seem "masochistic." In 1867, Hopkins was graduated from Oxford and briefly accepted a teaching post in Birmingham; in 1868, he decided to become a Jesuit priest and burned the poetry that he had written over the previous four years.

The period between 1868 and 1875 was a bleak one for Hopkins. He worked obsessively at his studies for the priesthood, avoided all poetry writing because of its potential for awakening "sensuality" in him, and spent many hours each day in silent reflection on his own perceived sinfulness. A man extraordinarily attracted to beauty from earliest childhood, Hopkins chose and led a life of startling, almost inconceivable, asceticism. White impresses readers with the painful deprivations that Hopkins endured by quoting amply from Jesuit documents and the memoirs of former Jesuits. In quotes from Hopkins' letters from the early 1870's, White shows the extreme distress and depression that Hopkins endured throughout these years, as he languished under the stern rules and rigid daily schedule of the order. In journal entries from the same period, however, White locates Hopkins' repressed but still vital aesthetic sense, as landscapes, clouds, and sunsets evoked profound emotions and guilty, because sensual, appreciation.

An important transition in Hopkins' life, occurred in 1874: In August, he was sent to St. Beuno's College in Wales to begin his theological studies. He was struck profoundly by the beauty of the Welsh countryside, and his interest was piqued by the difficulty and strange rhythms of the Welsh language. His church-approved studies of classical Welsh poetry naturally included translations, which in turn led to his own experimentations with Welsh poetic forms and schemes. As White makes abundantly clear, Hopkins found confirmation among Welsh writers of his own innate feeling that poetry should be spoken aloud, and that repetition and alliteration can help convey the "inscape," or internal, defining texture, of poetry and human consciousness. White shows that this was just the push that Hopkins needed to return to writing and resulted in the composition of some of the strangest, most beautiful poems in English literary history.

In his fine twenty-first chapter, White documents amply the many influences on Hopkins' brilliant first poem of his artistic maturity, "The Wreck of the *Deutschland.*" Setting up the historical and personal contexts that account for the shipwreck's profound effect on the poet, White constructs a powerful close reading of the poem itself; he traces the pessimism and disenchantment that are echoed in a poem that questions the existence of evil in a divinely ordered world. Not only does White trace Hopkins' confusion in response to the shipwreck itself, he also probes into the personal consequences of the poem's rejection by a respected Jesuit publication, a crushing blow for Hopkins, but fortunately one that did not result in his renewed silence.

In the years that followed, Hopkins produced one masterful poem after another, usually to the complete indifference of all but his very closest acquaintances. From these poems White quotes amply, relating the carefully chosen images and complex rhythms to Hopkins' own insecurity and desire for both spiritual self-renewal and the renewal of his audience. "God's Grandeur," one of his most beautiful and famous poems, is read against the backdrop of Hopkins' religious doubt and perception of widespread alienation during the late nineteenth century. Later White interprets "The Windhover," another of Hopkins' masterpieces, as a confession of Hopkins' profound inability to participate in the displays of life surrounding him. With admirable attention to nuance and artistic precedent, White proves himself time and again to be a careful and sensitive literary critic.

Hopkins' Welsh years ended in 1877 and were succeeded by various postings around England, often at dreary urban schools where his loneliness, alienation, and sense of failure became excruciating. In an 1883 letter quoted by White, Hopkins writes, "I have long been Fortune's football and am blowing up the bladder of resolution big and buxom for another kick of her foot. . . . [T]here is no likelihood of my ever doing anything to last." As White reveals, Hopkins did finally come to rest in one place, though it was hardly a fortuitous landing. In 1884, he accepted a position as a fellow in classics at the Royal University of Ireland and professor of Greek at University College in Dublin. As White makes immediately apparent, the urban posting was a disastrous one for Hopkins. The squalor of the city appalled him, and the isolation from his very few friends in England exacerbated his loneliness. Furthermore, Hopkins was not an inspired teacher, wholly unable to keep discipline in the classroom and mercilessly tormented by rowdy students. Finally, he began to suffer from terrible headaches and withdrew completely from his colleagues, most of whom never even knew that he wrote poetry.

These were the years of Hopkins' darkest poetic visions. In quoting from pieces such as "Carrion Comfort," "To Seem a Stranger Lies My Lot," and "No Worst, There Is None," White explores the painfully disturbed consciousness of a defeated man, one who chose a disastrous path for himself and was unable to change it. As described by acquaintances who knew him in Dublin, Hopkins was frail and haggard looking, seeming to incarnate the melancholy that he felt. White's narrative is a somber one as he takes the reader through these years, leading up to the final and greatest tragedy of his story. In 1889, Hopkins contracted typhoid, probably from contaminated food or water or the faulty plumbing of the college. He lingered a few weeks and died on June 8. Since at the time Hopkins was no more than an obscure teacher and cleric, his passing was barely noticed, except by his few friends and remaining family members.

White does not end his biography with Hopkins' death, for most of the poet's works were unpublished and scattered among friends and relatives. In his concluding chapter, "Post Mortem," White traces the gradual growth of Hopkins' reputation as a poet after his death. Although an entire book of his poems was not published for almost thirty years, a few choice pieces did appear in anthologies during the 1890's and the first years of the twentieth century. Hopkins' work gained a powerful ally when a friend and admirer, Robert Bridges, became poet laureate in 1913. In 1918, he used his influence to bring out the first edition of Hopkins' poems. As White's ample bibliography demonstrates, Hopkins' reputation has grown steadily since then, far surpassing those of most of his contemporaries and even that of the once popular, but now ignored, Bridges.

White's is an eminently useful biography of a strange and unfortunate man. He chooses his quotes judiciously to reveal the beauty of Hopkins' language and the misery of Hopkins' life. After finishing *Hopkins: A Literary Biography*, one is left with the feeling that there is still another story to tell, another level of exploration and explanation that needs to be reached. White makes abundantly clear the pain of Hopkins' existence but never places blame for it. Hopkins' tale is one that begs to be used as a basis for a critique of nineteenth century repression and homophobia; this is not the task that White takes on. Rather, he is committed to making sure that the facts of Hopkins' life are clear and that appreciation of his poetry is quickened. He does both admirably. The reader comes away from this work with a feeling of enormous loss over a man whose career was cut so short, as well as profound gratitude for the gems that he did produce during a life beset by worry and insecurity. For his effectiveness in evoking those feelings, White certainly deserves praise.

*Donald E. Hall*

### Sources for Further Study

*London Review of Books*. XIV, June 11, 1992, p. 19.
*The Observer*. March 22, 1992, p. 63.
*Poetry Review*. LXXXII, Fall, 1992, p. 64.
*The Spectator*. CCLXVIII, March 28, 1992, p. 30.
*The Times Literary Supplement*. March 27, 1992, p. 3.

# HOTEL LAUTRÉAMONT

*Author:* John Ashbery (1927-    )
*Publisher:* Alfred A. Knopf (New York). 157 pp. $23.00
*Type of work:* Poetry

*An almost haunted house of near art*

John Ashbery's latest collection of more than eighty poems is a remarkable achievement, particularly because each poem is a formulation against formulation, an act of would-be meaning that resists coherence and meaning. The tentative quality of Ashbery's poems is nothing new to his readers. This particular collection adds some new tinctures to the Ashbery oeuvre, something about the limits of an individual's dream and the need to negotiate with others. These poems seem to reflect upon the difficulty of creating meaning alone.

Ashbery announces a number of motifs in the first poem, "Light Turnouts," perhaps a play on turning out the lights before sleep and dream. Here the title suggests a tentative or light escape or moment of order. Addressing some emanation of the spirit, the speaker asks "Dear ghost, what shelter/ in the noonday crowd? I'm going to write/ an hour then read what someone else has written." If writing is a kind of shelter for the individual from the crowd, the individual is often carried back to others by reading. If there can be said to be a unifying theme in these poems, it is something like the negotiation between the imaginative flight of the individual in his own subjectivity and the need and reality of discourse with others and an admission of the influence of others in our thought. The second stanza suggests the way in which the adventure of the individual can be stopped, even if in nothing so certain as a mansion: "You've no mansion for this to happen in./ But your adventures are like safe houses,/ your knowing where to stop and adventure/ of another order, like seizing the weather." The flight of the imagination, shifting and elusive as weather, needs at times to be stopped or seized.

The "safe house" or "mansion," in which it might be possible to connect to those from the past who inform and give the present adventurer meaning, is both desired and haunted in these poems, something to be fled and something to be sought. In "The Phantom Agents," these mansions are like "decrepit cinemas/ whose balconies were walled off decades ago . . . where yellowing lobby cards announce/ the advent of next week's Republic serial: names of a certain importance once, names that float/ in the past, like a drift of gnats on a summer evening." This view of the past is depressing, equating the record of human effort with fleeting projections, insignificant as tiny insects. It evokes what Robert Lowell called "the horrifying mortmain of ephemera."

At other points, Ashbery seems willing to concede the necessity of some public place in the house of the self, as he does in "From Estuaries, From Casinos": "And though I feel like a fish out of water I/ recognize the workmen who proceed before me,/ nailing the thing down." Always sensing the lack of a central public stage, Ashbery seems uncompelled to speak or to "nail down" meaning in a recognizable edifice. Nevertheless, the building materials remain ready as a last resort: "Who asks anything of me?/ I am available, my heart pinned in a trance/ to the notice board, the stone/ inside me ready to speak, if that is all that can save us." There are a variety of metaphors in those phrases, "notice board," "pinned," "stone," which suggest building materials, school, the cliché of getting water from stone; Ashbery's forte is an ability to create a stream of figures which almost but do not quite cohere into a mythos or a meaning.

The title poem, "Hotel Lautréamont," is constructed as a loose villanelle and does somewhat illuminate the thematics of the book. The Comte de Lautréamont was the pseudonym of a late nineteenth century surrealist author Isidore Ducasse, who died at the tender age of twenty-four. His primary work, a prose poem entitled *Les Chants de Maldoror* (1868, 1890), was taken as an exemplar by the Surrealists. Ashbery's poetry shares some of the fluid and wild texture of that meditation on despair and evil. At one point Maldoror proclaims his loneliness: "I sought a soul that might resemble mine and I could not find it. I rummaged in all the corners of the earth: my perseverance was useless. Yet I could not remain alone. There must be someone who approved of my character; there must be someone who had the same ideas as myself." Ashbery has decided, it seems, to stop seeking and to dwell in the hotel of the isolated imagination: "Not to worry, many hands are making light work again,/ so we stay indoors. The quest was only another adventure." The individual imagination appears threatened by what Ashbery calls "collective euphoria" and decides to evade the quest for meaning under such degrading circumstances. Rather than travel into the "maze of time," Ashbery prefers to be sedentary in a house of transients and "in so doing deprive time of further hostages." Ashbery seems to want to come to terms with "our commonality," which is not to be found in seeking the mirror of our individuality but in dwelling in the changing mansion of the imagination.

One of the leitmotif words of this collection is "season," a word used powerfully by Arthur Rimbaud, whose inspiration is tacitly acknowledged in *Hotel Lautréamont*. Rimbaud saw us looking in vain for some fixed, eternal moment and living instead in seasons, stretches of time that have rough borders and are subject to unexpected openings and closings. One of the most comprehensible poems in this collection is entitled "Seasonal," a meditation on the elusiveness of meaning. A "lengthening season" is "the halo around a single note," as though spots of time were created by a solitary sound from the self. For Ashbery the answer to "what does the lengthening season mean?" seems to be the act of projecting form onto blankness rather than ascertaining a coherent meaning from writing: "Blunt words projected on a screen/ are what we mean, not what we wrote." What a "lying writer knows/ is pleasure, hallowed by attrition," an act of fading pleasure rather than a meaning.

Loneliness created by disconnection from meanings from the past and an uncertain audience in the present is evident everywhere in this book and occasionally receives more direct expression than one commonly finds in Ashbery's work. In "By Forced Marches," there is a recognition that the world dances to various tunes but that the postmodern skeptic refuses to participate: "And there is dancing under the porches—

so be it./ I am all I have. I am afraid./ I am left alone." This eloquent expression of the fear of isolation quickly mutates into a compromised sense of narcissistic fulfillment: "Yet it is the way to a certain kind of satisfaction./ I kiss myself in the mirror./ And children are kind,/ the boardwalk serves as a colorful backdrop/ to the caprices acted out, the pavanes and chaconnes/ that greet the ear in fragments." The conclusion is a vague and tentative phenomenology of satisfaction, a dim remembrance of the feeling of meaning: "And the old sense of a fullness/ is here, though only lightly sketched in." It is virtually impossible to tell whether this or any poem in the collection is ironic; the coordinates of theme, context, and drama are missing. Elegant phrases, clichés, and silly bric-a-brac are served up in a deadpan monotone which makes interpretation virtually impossible.

One always wonders how Ashbery goes on and on writing if he assumes, as it appears he does, that meaning is a crass fiction, and that poetry is an endless stream of evasions. Ashbery has expressed admiration for the romantic poet John Clare. In a telling couplet, Clare proclaimed the inadequacy of language for the task of expressing love: "Language has not the power to speak what love indites/ The soul lies buried in the ink that writes." Ashbery may keep on writing to keep his soul from being buried in ink. If the love is there it is inaccessible to just about anyone except as a shadow on the wallpaper that is his poetry. Ashbery's poetry, to play on a line from one of Seamus Heaney's sonnets, is the almost music of what does not quite happen.

*Robert Faggen*

### Sources for Further Study

*Booklist*. LXXXIX, September 1, 1992, p. 26.
*Library Journal*. CXVII, September 1, 1992, p. 179.
*Los Angeles Times Book Review*. August 30, 1992, p. 6.
*New Statesman and Society*. V, December 4, 1992, p. 39.
*Publishers Weekly*. CCXXXIX, August 10, 1992, p. 58.
*San Francisco Chronicle*. October 11, 1992, p. REV3.
*The Times Literary Supplement*. December 4, 1992, p. 10.
*Washington Times*. October 4, 1992, p. B8.

# HOUSMAN'S POEMS

*Author:* John Bayley (1925-    )
*Publisher:* Clarendon Press/Oxford University Press (New York). 202 pp. $49.95
*Type of work:* Literary criticism

*John Bayley's critical analysis of Housman's poems is an attempt to redefine the pleasures and thematic interest to be found in the work of this once-fashionable poet*

John Bayley's *Housman's Poems* attempts to reestablish the once high critical reputation of A. E. Housman. Bayley analyzes the poems to discover new ways of reading and appreciating the poems. He uses not a New Critical or formalist approach but instead a combination of thematic, comparative, and genre criticism. Bayley is very good at discovering Housman's elusive poetic strategies and revealing some of the ways the poems work and have an impact on the reader. He shows that Housman is not a failed formalist poet but one with a different way of creating significant poetic structures. *Housman's Poems* is a work marked by Bayley's affectionate and reasoned regard for the continuing values and delight to be found in a supposedly outdated poet.

The first chapter of *Housman's Poetry* deals with "Death and Endings." Housman killed his poetic speakers or subjects at such early ages and with such regularity that it became an immediate sign of his poetry. Death was, however, for Housman, a necessary act that relieved man of the burden of existence in a world of suffering. In "To an Athlete Dying Young," for example, the young man who dies early does not live on to decay and see his records "cut." He expires at a moment of completion. Bayley compares this type of Housman poem to Paul Celan's poems on the Holocaust, one of which tells the victims of the concentration camp: "Read no more—look!/ Look no more—go." Housman, in the last two lines of "An Epitaph," describes the providential place of the dead man. "Here, with one balm for many fevers found,/ Whole of an ancient evil, I sleep sound." The "ancient evil" is the pain inherent in life. Man, in Housman's view, is better off in the peaceful sleep of the grave; to struggle against human misery only increases the pain.

The next chapter in Bayley's defense of Housman is on "Love." To Housman, love was based on failure; he had one great love in his life, with a college contemporary, Moses Jackson. Jackson soon rejected Housman's declaration of love. Housman's poems are filled with descriptions of the state of failed love. For example, in *More Poems* xii, his "unlucky love" has "its sure foundation of despair." In Horace's *Odes* 4.7, a poem that Housman thought to be the finest in ancient literature, the hero Theseus cannot rescue his friend Pirithous from Hades, since he is "in the chain/ The love of comrades cannot take away." Love is seen in terms of loss that does not diminish the intense feelings of love but points to the imposed distance between the loved one and the lover. *More Poems* xxxi, which was published after the poet's death, describes the failure of the relationship between the poet and Moses Jackson. "Because I liked you better/ Than suits a man to say,/ It irked you, and I promised/ To throw the thought away." The moment of failure is reduced to a bare exchange in which promises are made that last a lifetime. The doomed relationship is reduced to the simple word "irked," and the stoic speaker ends by both declaring his love and keeping his promise: "And say the lad who loved you/ Was one that kept his word."

The chapter "Sex and the Soldier" points to an area that many ignore in Housman's work. Bayley cites a number of poems dealing with soldiers; some deal with patriotism and the dangers of the soldier's trade while others hint at or make clear a personal relationship between the soldier and the poet. Poem xxii in *A Shropshire Lad* deals with a silent exchange between the "single redcoat" and the speaker. The last stanza sorts out the delicate relationship that is based on a meeting of eyes: "What thoughts at heart have you and I/ We cannot stop to tell;/ But dead or living, drunk or dry,/ Soldier, I wish you well." An extension of this relationship can be found in poem xxxii of *A Shropshire Lad*, in which the soldier conveys his meaning to the poet speaker. "Speak now, and I will answer;/ How shall I help you, say;/ Ere to the wind's twelve quarters/ I take my endless way." The exchanges are minimal, but they bear great emotional weight and even suggest the possibility of a true connection being made in spite of the differences in class and situation.

"Personae" is one of the most interesting chapters in the book. Bayley contrasts the continual self-change and development in William Butler Yeats's poetry to that of Housman and Philip Larkin. Bayley makes the distinction very clear. Yeats "makes himself, style and poems, and they become true for us and for him in the act of creation. For the youthful Housman the discovery of self was so disturbing and disconcerting that poetry came as a way of disclosing it." Housman creates the self in the poem, and it remains a self-discovery. The reader is not encouraged to take part in the discovery; yet the enactment of that changed consciousness, Bayley asserts, changes the reader. Housman uses a more personal and less public manner of displaying consciousness, but the impact on the reader may be very great. In *More Poems* xiii, for example, Housman describes an "involuntary memory" of "my kind and foolish comrade/ That breathes all night for me." When Housman speaks of dreams he is, according to Bayley, the dreamer, in contrast to the fabulous inventions of a poet such as Yeats. Bayley finds less "collusion" with critics in Housman's poetry, so the reader and an unprejudiced critic must discover ways of perceiving the value and power of a less direct poet.

"The Romantic Personality" once more explores aspects of Housman's poetry that are usually disregarded. Housman did not show the triumph of the imagination as the great Romantics have done; more often his poems speak of failure and death. Bayley sees in Housman and Larkin a balance of the Romantic's temperament and classical stoicism. Housman's poetry avoids the extremes of both modes and discovers a middle way between the assertion of self and its destruction. In *More Poems* x, for example, Housman contrasts the mourning of nature to the response of the abandoned lover. "The weeping Pleiads wester,/ And the moon is under seas"; the first two lines of description collide with the last two, in which the speaker reveals his situation: "The weeping Pleiads wester,/ And I lie down alone." The active and emotional "Pleiads" contrasts with the inactive and stoic human speaker.

The chapter "The Straitening" is less about Housman than about the poetic strategies of such poets as Paul Celan and Thomas Hardy. Once more, Bayley contrasts this type of poet, who found strength by facing adversity, to such confessional poets as Sylvia Plath and Robert Lowell. The essential difference between these poets is that Celan and Housman do not "will" the terrible description of events that make up the poem. Instead of an obsession, it is a revelation of a fact. It is communal, Bayley suggests, not personal.

"The Name and Nature of Poetry" deals with Housman's critical theories of poetry. Housman remains a very unfashionable critic. He spoke of recognizing true poetry by a sudden chill down the spine. Such an affective response is nowhere to be found in the New Criticism, which consequently found little value in Housman's poems. Bayley analyzes various passages of poetry from Samuel Daniel, John Milton, and George Darley cited by Housman in his lectures on poetry to discover the special power they held for Housman. Housman could, for example, be powerfully moved by one line in Milton: "Nymphs and shepherds, dance no more." The line is a command that indicates the end of a pastoral world, and yet it is captured in memorable verse. Housman's own poetry combined just this sad sense of loss with the sweetness of the verse, Percy Bysshe Shelley's "sweetest songs" that "tell of saddest thought."

"A Voice in Opposition" is an attempt by Bayley to acknowledge and refute the negative criticism of Housman's poetry. The primary offenders were the New Critics. They questioned Housman's use of metaphor and brought down what once had been a great reputation. Bayley effectively refutes the inadequate or incomplete analyses of such critics as F. R. Leavis and Cyril Conolly by directing readers to an appreciation of the special unexpected and original qualities and unusual pleasures found in Housman's poetry. Bayley shows that Leavis is not fully reading Housman but only finding deficiency in parts of the poems. For example, Leavis' analysis of Housman's "Reville" concentrates only on the poetic first two stanzas; he completely misses the irony and the simple language that follow the deliberate flowery opening. The poem, in fact, ends with an injunction to be up and doing; it completely reverses the poetic beginning.

"Jokes" points to a favorite poetic strategy of Housman. Humor is used in the most unlikely places, especially in connection with death. In *Last Poems* xx, for example, Housman describes the fate of "Dick," who hates the cold. "Fall, winter, fall; for he/ Prompt hand, and headpiece clever,/ Has woven a winter robe,/ And made of earth and sea/ His overcoat for ever,/ And wears the turning globe." The protective "overcoat" Dick wears in death is both amusing and touching. Dick is made familiar and ennobled by his homely garment as he "wears the turning globe."

"Hell Gate and Parnassus" looks at two aspects of Housman's art. "Hell's Gate" is one of the most revealing poems he wrote, about a relationship with a rebellious guard. The Parnassian, or more consciously poetic, side of Housman's poetry can be found in the outwardly less personal and more formal poems such as *More Poems* xliv, on the rebuilding of the campanile in Venice. The "belfry" is rebuilt; it "stands again." The speaker bids farewell to "Andrea" and declares, "The tower that stood and fell/

Is not rebuilt in me." The outer renewal of a Venetian monument is not mirrored by the personal renewal of the speaker, who must bid farewell to a love.

"Contacts and Reversals" is the last chapter of the book. Bayley compares the use of "reversals" in the poetry of Celan, Larkin, and Housman. Housman often has a balance of sadness and joy, and in many poems he turns bitterness into delight. Especially important in Housman is what Bayley describes as "reversed heroism." The usual heroic tone is rejected for a more defiant mode; in "The Chestnut Casts Its Flambeaux," for example, the solution to being in an unjust universe is to "bear them we can, and if we can we must./ Shoulder the sky, my lad, and drink your ale." The Housman speaker advises both a superhuman effort and the retreat of homely drinking.

John Bayley's *Housman's Poems* makes a cogent argument for the continuing value of this poet. The book places Housman in a context of poets such as Celan, Hardy, and Larkin and helps establish a tradition in which readers might more truly understand Housman's poems. Bayley is very good at sorting out the poems in Housman's many books that are still of interest. The book is clearly written and economical, and it contains a good deal of wit and insight. It provides readers, above all, with methods of coming to terms with a poet who has been discredited in the last thirty years. *Housman's Poems* may not be the definitive book on A. E. Housman, but it may well speak a revival of interest in this unusual poet.

*James Sullivan*

### Sources for Further Study

*Choice*. XXX, January, 1993, p. 788.
*The Guardian*. July 16, 1992, p. 25.
*London Review of Books*. XIV, July 9, 1992, p. 8.
*The Observer*. May 10, 1992, p. 54.
*The Times Literary Supplement*. October 30, 1992, p. 11.

# THE IMAGINATIVE LANDSCAPE OF
# CHRISTOPHER COLUMBUS

*Author:* Valerie I. J. Flint (1936-    )
*Publisher:* Princeton University Press (Princeton, New Jersey). Illustrated. 233 pp. $24.95
*Type of work:* History; biography
*Time:* The fifteenth and sixteenth centuries
*Locale:* The entire world as it was thought to be in Columbus' time: Europe and the Atlantic, the newly discovered lands first thought to be Cathay, and the "Terrestrial Paradise"

*The author reconstructs Columbus' view of the world, and of the new lands he discovered, on the basis of his writings, known readings, and the maps of his time, stressing what she calls their "medieval" aspect*

For generations the historians of North America have presented exploration of the continent as a progressive endeavor. The blank, white spaces on the early maps were slowly filled with information as a result of expeditions led by Europeans—the Spaniards, French, English—and later by the Americans themselves. A representative study was John Bartlett Brebner's influential *The Explorers of North America, 1492-1806* (1933), which presented the exploration of the North American continent as a quest both heroic and scientific at the same time. Exploration continues to exert a powerful attraction, and it was often dramatic. Traditional narrative accounts usually were based on a potent metaphor: the unknown, or the white spaces on the map, gradually succumbed to the exploratory expeditions, with their technical expertise and scientific curiosity, which named the new territories. A second popular metaphor was that of creation—as the explorers saw the lands "for the first time," these were conjured into existence, it seemed from nothing. In historiography, the narratives of exploration usually merged with narratives of the creation of new states. Exploration, and independence, were two of the basic founding myths of many countries on the American continent.

Recently this entire framework for exploration, with its many assumptions, has been challenged. Christopher Columbus is a key figure in the history of almost every nation on the American continent, and the traditional interpretations and evaluations of Columbus' role have come under increasing attack in the past decade. They have been called narrowly Eurocentric, ethnocentric, imperialist, or simply untrue.

The anniversary of the voyages by Columbus (1492-1504) has coincided with an increasing awareness that they were far from beneficial for the people who already lived on the American continent. They brought enslavement, disease, intolerance, and destruction, some say genocide. Historians have claimed they only brought a Pandora's box of European evils, and that Columbus did not "discover" the American continent in a meaningful sense at all. During his first two voyages, he thought he had found Cathay—hence he was deluded and simply lost. When he encountered Indians, he kept asking them where the "Great Khan" was. As Columbus sailed along the coast of Cuba, he was certain that the harbors he could see were used by the Khan's ships;

he was equally convinced that the fragrances he smelled and spices he tasted were those of Cathay.

During the third voyage he changed his mind but did not do much better—he believed that he had discovered not Cathay but the "Terrestrial Paradise" marked on many of the maps of the time. In addition, the world was not round as so many people had thought, but was shaped like a pear, rising to a high, nipple-like point where the Terrestrial Paradise was located. Was this, then, a "discovery"? The term, handed down in so many textbooks and works of popular history, would seem to be unacceptably narrow and uncritical. For Native Americans and the descendants of those who greeted Columbus, it is an impertinence.

Valerie Flint, a history professor from the University of Auckland in New Zealand, is not a "revisionist" who seeks to deny the accomplishments of Columbus. She admires his basic talents; she writes in her summing-up at the end of the book that he "remains one of the most talented and, perhaps above all, one of the most imaginative human beings ever to have lived." Her portrait is careful, well-balanced, and scrupulously researched. She does not dismiss Columbus because he did not understand the real nature of his "discovery," nor does she indignantly condemn him because he sought wealth and self-promotion. As a man he was better than many, worse than some. He was complex, and her psychological portrait of Columbus has real depth and subtle shading. She does not believe that Columbus was the person described in portraits by some other scholars, for example Samuel Eliot Morison, who called Columbus a dualist and "scientist-mystic," or J. L. Phelan, who described Columbus as a follower of the millennial teachings of the Franciscans. Nor, on the other hand, does she believe that Columbus was motivated by detached, objective curiosity. He was not a representative of progress, nor was he a "Renaissance man."

Her portrait of Columbus is based on two kinds of research: an analysis of everything that Columbus read and wrote, and a thorough acquaintance with his fifteenth century background. She is the author of an earlier study on the rise of magic in early medieval Europe, and this research on the Middle Ages is in evidence in her study of Columbus.

The different interpretations of Columbus recall an earlier quarrel between two historians about the interpretation of the Renaissance. Jakob Burckhardt described the period in a famous book, *The Civilisation of the Renaissance in Italy* (1890), while Johan Huizinga, in an equally famous book, described the period as *The Waning of the Middle Ages* (1924). Like Huizinga, Flint emphasizes the medieval background of the fifteenth century; she associates Columbus more with this background than with the humanism slowly emerging in parts of Europe. She divides her book into two sections: Part 1 is entitled "The Medieval Background," and part 2 is "The Imprint on Columbus." The last chapter of the book, which contains her conclusions on Columbus' psychology, is significantly called "Columbus and his Christian World."

Flint does not believe that Columbus' "discovery" of America represented "progress" or the dawn of a new epoch. Earlier geographers such as Ptolemy had postulated long before that the earth was round—this was almost fourteen centuries before

Columbus. If the Ptolemaic world map was a "discovery"—that is, a rediscovery—of the fifteenth century, it was also a shock; and Columbus, who was devoted to the medieval Christian tradition, rejected Ptolemy. On the other hand, Columbus had a number of individual traits that did not make him an entirely conservative figure either: He read widely, made good use of his reading, and possessed considerable navigational skills. He was characterized by a high degree of what she calls "creative tension." Unlike Morison, Flint finds that Columbus' reasoning was logical and understandable, given the nature of his reading; he did not express any "duality" between science and mysticism.

The key to understanding any period in history is to understand it in its own terms, not in contemporary terms, which are anachronistic when applied to the past. The same applies to a historical personage such as Columbus. The author of *The Imaginative Landscape of Christopher Columbus* first tries to understand his period, which was radically different from the present—far more different than most people realize.

In her introduction, she disarmingly describes her method as a quest for "fantasy" rather than "fact": "I shall attempt . . . to reconstruct, and understand, not the New World Columbus found, but the Old World which he carried with him in his head." The "fantasy" she tries to pinpoint could also be described as the historical mind-set, or psychology, of Columbus. She reconstructs the "mentalities" of the fifteenth century, the modes of thought and action, the tastes, assumptions, and beliefs, of the time of Columbus' contemporaries. After describing these, she tries to define Columbus' individual personality and his responses to his times, as they were revealed in his writings. Flint read everything that Columbus read, looked up all the titles in his library, and carefully analyzed his annotations of books written by others, as well as the many comments he wrote in their margins.

Mapmaking and the literature of exploration usually went hand in hand. Flint has an excellent chapter on the "mappemondes" (or *mappae mundi*) of the Middle Ages. It is interesting to follow the accumulation of information in these visual and verbal forms. The latest voyages of the Portuguese and Spanish navigators in the fourteenth century would find their way onto the maps, but so would the adventures of fictional characters such as Sinbad the Sailor, the travels of Marco Polo and John Mandeville, and the extraordinary adventures of Saint Brendan, as well as Saint Ursula with her eleven thousand virgins (Columbus named the Virgin Islands after them). The maps recorded the results of recent exploratory expeditions as well as popular, unbelievable adventure stories about cannibals and monsters, including half-human people and creatures with dogs' heads or faces in their chests. The mapmakers had a lively interest in these monsters as well as stories about gold, silver, precious stones, and spices, all of which they referred to with notations or symbols on the maps. Flint notes that in the Middle Ages, spices had great value, comparable to that of precious metals; the accounts of merchants in the spice trade who traveled by land and sea to the east were "fit to strike terror into the hearts of cooks." These accounts also found their way onto the maps. Storytelling and mapmaking shared the same imagery; the possible distinctions between them were not made in the Middle Ages.

In discussing the relation of maps to literary accounts, Flint writes:

> It is deceptive in this period, therefore (as also, of course, in many others in which a high percentage of the population cannot or will not read), to associate stories purely with the unreal or escapist world of dreams, or with a somehow inferior world of entertainment. On occasion, of course, such an association might validly be made; but so might a wholly opposing one, for stories and dramatic entertainments could be, to persons of the fifteenth century . . . [a] vital . . . means of constructing reality.

A perusal of medieval maps bears out her assertion. The book contains plates of thirteen of the most significant medieval maps, and these maps constantly refer to other maps as well as to literary texts—by brief notations or signs, by larger texts that take up significant portions of the map space, or in the geographical drawing itself. The mapmaking enterprise was collective and cumulative.

A common element uniting both maps and verbal accounts was the Bible. The cosmology of the Middle Ages was based on the Bible and its authority. Geography was rooted in Genesis. Paradise was drawn on a large number of maps, and Jerusalem was often thought to lie at the center of the world. It might come as a surprise to a contemporary general reader that these medieval maps were based on the Bible, especially in view of the significant progress that had been made by classical geographers such as Ptolemy, Eratosthenes, Aristotle, Pliny, and Avicenna. Christian cosmology, however, was radically different from Greek, Alexandrian, or Arab cosmology. It was only toward the end of the Middle Ages that the classical geographers were rediscovered. Typical medieval mapmakers attempted, for example, to assign specific locations to the gold, silver, gems and spices brought to Solomon by the Queen of Sheba mentioned in 1 Kings 10:11, or the gold, frankincense, and myrrh brought by the three Magi described in Matthew 2:1-12. It was this wealth, and that of the Great Khan, that Columbus sought. It has been said that Columbus saw the voyages as a whole as great pilgrimages to lands referred to in the Bible, and there is truth in the observation. The names he gave to the places he encountered were usually pious: Trinidad (Trinity), Isla Sancta (Holy Island), Gracia (Island of Grace), and so on.

This naming also reflected Columbus' world view. During his second voyage, when his ship was near Haiti (Hispaniola), it was reported that Columbus told his crew: "Gentlemen, I wish to bring us to a place whence departed the three Magi who came to adore Christ, the which place is called Saba." When asked the name of the place, the indigenous inhabitants replied—so it seemed—that it was *Sobo*. Columbus asserted that this was the same word, but the inhabitants did not know how to pronounce it properly.

Flint does not belittle or denigrate the contribution made by Columbus. He had faults, for example, manipulative theatricality and a lust for wealth that nevertheless tortured him. He was excessively intent on the advancement of his family and his own reputation; he could be xenophobic, anti-Semitic, aggressive, grasping, and avaricious. The author stresses what she calls his "energetic fantasy" and the persistence of his inner world. He often was divided against himself: "Columbus was a complex man, possessed of great personal piety and considerable reflective powers. But his personal ambitions and his public enterprises as an explorer and adventurer took him into a region of tremendous moral danger."

A careful historian, Flint writes that "it is always perilous to level accusations backwards across time." In seeing Columbus against the background of his own time, he becomes more interesting and more alive than in the more traditional, stereotyped versions. He was not a creature of myth or a "Renaissance man," but both imaginative and conservative at the same time, manipulative and torn, a vivid, three-dimensional, living personality.

*John Carpenter*

## Sources for Further Study

*America.* CLXVII, August 29, 1992, p. 122.
*Boston Globe.* October 11, 1992, p. 14.
*Library Journal.* CXVII, August, 1992, p. 124.
*London Review of Books.* XV, January 7, 1993, p. 10.
*The New York Review of Books.* XL, January 28, 1993, p. 38.
*Publishers Weekly.* CCXXXIX, June 22, 1992, p. 52.
*Washington Times.* October 11, 1992, p. B8.

# IN MY FATHER'S HOUSE
## Africa in the Philosophy of Culture

*Author:* Kwame Anthony Appiah (1954-    )
*Publisher:* Oxford University Press (New York). 225 pp. $29.95
*Type of work:* Philosophy; current affairs

*An important challenge to contemporary ideas regarding race as an essential definer of human difference, to the philosophical underpinnings of Pan-Africanism, and to the viability of traditional religious practices in Africa*

Kwame Anthony Appiah, Ghanaian by upbringing and birth and Western by education, has produced an important challenge to many of the most dearly held pieties of Western intellectuals of a liberal stamp regarding Africa and blackness. At the same time, Appiah gives no support to the conservative tendency to denigrate other cultures and Africa in particular: This, it seems, is so patently wrong as to allow him to ignore it. Appiah's position regarding such Western notions is antiessentialist in all aspects. He believes that the concept of race is without philosophical justification in defining one group of people as separate from another. He locates the origin of the form this concept has taken with respect to blackness in African American rhetoric, developed in the nineteenth century in a predominantly white country and illegitimately applied to black Africa. At the same time, he argues that the notion of an essential quality of "Africanness" unifying all Africans is a hollow one, useful at best in achieving certain limited political aims but without any more philosophically justifiable basis.

Appiah is aware that the beliefs that black people have something fundamental in common and that "Africanness" is a fundamental link came into existence as correctives to the assumptions of white Westerners that things white were good and that the West had a monopoly on thought and culture. For him, this is an example of accepting the form imposed by Western thought in order to make minor variations of content, of a mistake countering a mistake. Two mistakes in thought, he believes, do not make a right.

The chapters that deal with literature offer, among other subjects, a consideration of W. E. B. Du Bois' notions on blackness (what Francophone thinkers later dubbed "negritude") as well as a critique of Wole Soyinka's appeal to a Pan-African essence. In each case, Appiah punctures the bubble of too-neat essentialism. In the case of Du Bois, Appiah notes that Du Bois' notion of race as a unifying element, which he shared with the Americo-Liberian Alexander Crummell, is either circular or trivial in philosophical terms. In order to speak of the "Negro race," scattered over the world, one must presuppose something these people have in common in order to pick them out of the places to which they have been scattered. Other than a list of physical qualities (including such things as skin color and hair texture), this must include some form of precisely that which is held to unify them as a race—unless race is simply to consist of qualities such as skin color and hair texture. In this case, Southern Italians, for example, might more properly be put together in a group with light-skinned black people than with blond Scandinavians.

In the case of Soyinka's Pan-Africanist sympathies, Appiah writes convincingly of the scores of wildly divergent cultures that dot sub-Saharan Africa, contrasting his own home culture of the Asante with the Buganda kingdom in what is now Uganda, the Masai in East Africa, and the !Kung in southern Africa. What, he asks, are all these so-different cultures supposed to have in common?

The urge to essentialize blackness or to see all of Africa as somehow unified is an urge that clearly comes more from the cultural left nowadays than from the cultural right, as it did in the nineteenth century. Thus, despite many indications of sympathy with the cultural left, the thrust of Appiah's attack turns out to be against it—or perhaps most accurately, to be a critique of the cultural left from a position within it. Appiah both presupposes and leaves unconsidered those numerous studies of "the invention of Africa" (the title of his first chapter) that emphasize a negatively essentializing view of Africa. The world in which Appiah is writing this book is, rather, one in which well-meaning Western liberals essentialize both blackness and Africa in order to award it positive value. This, somewhat regretfully, Appiah refuses them through his denial of any philosophical basis to such notions.

This same urge is attacked in Appiah's analysis of the way in which Westerners have attempted to valorize the appeal to spirits and ancestors characteristic of traditional African cultures—to say that these are just as rational as the explanation systems of Western science. Appiah will have none of this, pointing out that in fact traditional approaches to the world (seeing the world as populated by spirits that must be propitiated, invoking the power of ancestors, and so on) are comparable not to modern science, but rather to the folk belief that still survives to a great extent in Europe and North America. His analyses of the way Americans have come to a kind of uneasy compromise between rationalist science and their desire to believe in a higher power, relegating the first to certain specific circumstances, are among the most revealing in the book.

Appiah observes that there is no value in dying of disease that Western science could have combated. Because he is so hard-headed and pragmatic, his explanation of why it is that traditional societies continue to believe in inefficacious explanation systems is both simple and convincing. Appiah suggests that a sort of inertia of thought is operative in cultures: People tend to believe what they are told by their parents until they have very good reasons to disbelieve it. Most of what an outsider will see as disproofs are simply not of a sufficiently high level of intensity to overcome this natural inertia.

Appiah takes on as well the attempt by contemporary Western cultural pundits to draw analogies between the postcolonial situation and the postmodern one, pointing out that the two are fundamentally dissimilar. He sees Western postmodernism, as do many other commentators, as a denial of the categories offered in modernist thought and literature. He offers a succinct summary of what he takes postmodernism to be: namely, following Jean-François Lyotard and Fredric Jameson, an end of any overarching narrative in the way history is constructed, and the commodification of virtually all facts of life. He then points out that this is found in Africa only in the tiny Western-educated upper classes and so cannot be confused with a general condition in Africa. Finally, he notes that although the African elite are attempting to overthrow the essentialized political categories they inherited at independence (the nation, usually), they do so not by claiming, as their Western counterparts do, that there is no such thing as essential categories. Instead, they do quite the opposite, appealing to Africa as a definer. This brings Appiah back to his central position regarding the inherent philosophical unjustifiability of any conception of Africa as a whole.

Appiah quotes approvingly the author Sara Suleri, who expresses her unwillingness to be used as an "Otherness-machine." By this she means she refuses to stand in as the representative of a world unlike the Western one that intellectuals in the West have such a need nowadays to believe in. In contrast to the somehow solid world of this conception, Appiah paints a picture of a world that refuses to sit still or be neatly carved up by the principles of continent or race, or to meekly enter the cage in which Westerners would like it to be, safely categorized in the multicultural zoo.

Despite Appiah's sympathy with certain aspects of postmodern philosophy (most strikingly its insistence that commodification has all but taken over cultural categories), he seems most fundamentally a man of the eighteenth century Enlightenment. He clearly demands that people not be judged by their status as members of groups, whether these are racial, national, or continental. He notes that false unities do more harm than good and insists that ultimately it is the individual who must be primary.

Appiah's point is that Western notions about Africa are exactly this: Western notions about Africa. From the transference of racial notions from the New World (the absolute black-white dualities of a Du Bois) to the attempt by the Western-educated elite in modern Africa to replace the conceptual primacy of their Western-imposed nation-states with an indefensible Pan-African ideal, Appiah sees examples of the imposition, or acceptance, of Western matrices in an understanding of Africa. He insists that the reality of this world outside the West is more complex than Western views have recognized.

Appiah wishes to celebrate precisely this variety. In the introduction to his book, he writes movingly of his various relatives of many nationalities scattered over the face of the earth. Appiah is in favor of the fructifying interpenetration of cultures. He sees the advantages of some aspects of Western culture and has so completely appropriated others that he cannot even distance himself from them. At the same time, he insists that this interpenetration will by definition not result in a smooth homogeneity and should not be based on invalid concepts that buy a false sense of comprehensibility at the price of papering over differences. Instead, the effects of cross-cultural pollination will be highly irregular, highly unpredictable, and highly individual—much like his own analyses in this book.

*Bruce E. Fleming*

## Sources for Further Study

*Choice.* XXX, December, 1992, p. 629.

*The Christian Science Monitor.* September 18, 1992, p. 13.

*The Chronicle of Higher Education.* XXXVIII, May 6, 1992, p. A7.

*New Statesman and Society.* V, March 13, 1992, p. 45.

*The New York Times Book Review.* XCVII, June 21, 1992, p. 8.

*The Observer.* March 8, 1992, p. 62.

*The Village Voice.* September 22, 1992, p. 68.

*The Washington Post Book World.* XXII, June 14, 1992, p. 3.

# IN THE HEART OF THE VALLEY OF LOVE

*Author:* Cynthia Kadohata (1956-      )
*Publisher:* Viking (New York). 224 pp. $20.00
*Type of work:* Novel
*Time:* 2052
*Locale:* Los Angeles and the Southern California desert

*A nineteen-year-old California woman comes of age in 2052, during a bleak age appropriately dubbed the Dark Century*

> *Principal characters:*
> FRANCIE, a nineteen-year-old orphan, the narrator
> AUNTIE ANNIE, Francie's aunt and guardian
> ROHN JEFFERSON, Annie's lover
> MARK TRANG, Francie's lover and a fellow student
> JEWEL, Francie's friend, the managing editor of *Campus News*
> CARL, a tattoo artist
> JAMES GOODMAN, a college administrator who solicits student prostitutes

Five-foot, three-inch Francie is dwarfed by the huge bird of paradise plant in her front yard. A miniature version is the official flower of Los Angeles, but Francie prefers the more monstrous bird of paradise: "I did not find these plants paradisical, but to me they would have made a more fitting choice for an official flower than the smaller, prettier variety, because they looked the way I saw Los Angeles—surprising and violent, full of hidden savage beauties." In her second novel, Cynthia Kadohata sees Southern California of the future in just such brilliantly brutal terms. Her vision of Los Angeles in 2052 is a nightmare of urban decay, a city whose physical and social structures have disintegrated. For those who, like Francie, know where and how to look, it is also a savagely beautiful valley of love.

Like Kadohata's 1989 literary debut, *The Floating World, In the Heart of the Valley of Love* is a coming-of-age story, though Francie, its nineteen-year-old narrator, manages to mature during a barbarous age that calls itself the Dark Century. Traffic lights still gleam, but they are routinely ignored in a city where rioting is commonplace. About half of the populace is illiterate. The air is toxic, the streets are violent, and shopping malls are boarded up. While 70 percent of women under forty are afflicted with cervical cancer, almost everyone is vulnerable to some malady. Francie's parents died, of lung cancer, when she was thirteen years old, and she herself has a common, innocuous skin disease. The wonder is how exhilarating Kadohata's fiction is, for both narrator and reader. "I felt strangely enthralled with the brutality of the world I had to face," says Francie.

Kadohata's futuristic vision of urban decay and social dysfunction has more in common with sinister cinematic fantasies such as *Alien Nation* (1988), *Blade Runner* (1982), *Escape from New York* (1981), and *Mad Max* (1979) than with more literary models. In her 2052, the fortunate few barricade themselves in "richtowns," and everyone totes either guns or mace. The police are corrupt and capricious, and people are daily disappearing into secret gulags spread across the California desert. In setting her novel beyond the lifetime of many current readers, Kadohata is interpreting the present, dramatizing it through extrapolation. In her rendition of the United States, nonwhites constitute more than half of the population, 8 percent of eligible voters go to the polls, and an ambitious chain of freeways remains unfinished, for want of funds. It takes the mail as long to arrive in twenty-first century California as in twentieth century Italy.

Much of this is plausible, though not inspired, prophecy. In contrast to futurologists who plot inexorable progress through the blessings of technology, Kadohata posits a future in which things have ceased to work—employees as well as gadgets. It is a time of mass privation, in which unremitting drought has made "water creds" more precious than official currency. Although men have walked on Mars, back in 2000, Neiman Marcus could not stay in business. Despite current confidence that faxes, modems, and bullet trains will soon link and transmute us all, Kadohata projects a retro-tech world in which people still drive internal combustion automobiles and pound out sentences on primitive typewriters. Under such circumstances, the reader shares Francie's scorn for "chirps"—those who feign a sanguine fervor incommensurate with the dismal truth. She reports that Thanksgiving has become more important than Christmas, "because the fact that there was less and less to be thankful for made one all the more thankful for what there was."

The future is another country, but not to Francie, who has lived there all her life. As narrator and a native of that grave new world, she rightly does not dwell on what makes 2052 remarkable; to do so would be as incongruous as if William Shakespeare's Julius Caesar delivered a soliloquy on ancient Roman housing. Francie incidentally notes that McDonald's has ceased serving real burgers and that the tallest building in Los Angeles is the Natsumi Hotel, but for the most part Kadohata avoids explicit disquisition on the differences between 1992 and 2052. She places her characters in a particularly bleak setting in order to test them and to dramatize the power of love.

The daughter of a Japanese mother and a black-Chinese father, Francie, who was conceived beside the rice pots of Chu's Chinese Soul Food Restaurant, typifies the increasingly hybrid and non-European population of the Untied States. Eclipse of the ethnic stock that founded and dominated the country has even begotten a kind of inverted Ku Klux Klan, the Anti-Aryan Association, or AAA. Born in Chicago, Francie moved in with her Auntie Annie in seedy Hollywood when both her parents died five years ago. Also sharing their dilapidated wooden bungalow is Rohn Jefferson, Annie's lover and Francie's surrogate father. When Rohn, a resourceful entrepreneur in the elaborate black market, disappears, Annie is devastated. It is assumed that Rohn has vanished into the chain of secret prisons that stretches across the California desert, but the mystery that taxes Francie most is not where Rohn is and why, but rather: What is the inscrutable power that transformed two middle-aged, overweight people into a vibrant, joyous couple? Love redeems the hardships of 2052 and inspires Francie's story.

After Rohn disappears, Francie moves out on her own, supporting herself by working as a messenger. Following hospitalization for injuries in an automobile accident, she enrolls in a local junior college. Much as she enjoys her classes in geology and botany, Francie is most intrigued by journalism. She joins the staff of the weekly campus newspaper, weakly named *Campus News*, and it is there that she makes the first true friends that she has had in California. She becomes close to its managing editor, Jewel, an older woman hopelessly yoked to a man who abuses her, and even closer to Mark, a reporter who becomes her lover. He brazenly pilfers napkins and mints from the restaurant on their first date, but he eventually helps to teach Francie values more fundamental than the sanctity of property. Their relationship blossoms while they spy on a college administrator suspected of soliciting sex from his male students; Mark's compassion prevents him from publishing the incriminating evidence.

The fact that Francie is an aspiring journalist accounts for the lucidity and coherence of her account, one that ascribes magical powers to writing. The child of an underclass not much drawn to reading or writing, she might not otherwise be expected to record her thoughts on paper or at least express herself in the engaging, supple prose that Kadohata fashions for her. Unlike George Orwell in *Nineteen Eighty-four* (1948), the author makes no effort to imagine a Newspeak appropriate to the society she envisions. Nor, unlike Anthony Burgess in *A Clockwork Orange* (1962), does she contrive a slang distinctive to the time, place, and class in which she situates her characters. Francie, instead, speaks and writes in standard American English, a language that seems to have evolved very little in the sixty years that separate the narrator from her first readers. She does note a 2052 neologism: "Because of the prolonged drought, people had started using 'dry' to indicate something bad or undesirable." The fluent style of Kadohata's novel poses no problem to educated, middle-class readers of 1992, unless they are bothered by the fact that a poor and poorly educated nineteen-year-old in the middle of the twenty-first century would write like a professional author in 1992.

The economics of the book are as nebulous as its linguistics. Francie hints at a national depression that put an end to a period of sustained growth that had stimulated continuing technological progress. Readers never learn, however, exactly why financial resources suddenly evaporated at the turn of the century. Neither are there enough details about current market forces to explain what went wrong and whether it is reversible. Francie makes no effort to understand why space exploration and freeway construction abruptly halted. Readers learn nothing about whether overpopulation is responsible for the scarcity of water, fuel, and courtesy in Francie's world. In fact, reversing current trends of urban sprawl, much of the area east of Los Angeles unaccountably has been abandoned. Except for a reference to local resentment over the fact that the largest building in the city was built by a Japanese tycoon, the novel is mum on foreign trade and, in general, on relations between the United States and other nations.

*In the Heart of the Valley of Love* is eloquent in its heartfelt demonstration of the claims of love. It is a novel that dramatizes the tiny truths its characters acquire through forays into a dismal landscape. Carl, a tattoo artist who etches his handiwork on both Francie and Mark, reflects on the lessons of his profession: "I've learned to know how I feel about most things. I've learned how hard to press, I've learned what I think about various types of flattery and lies and illusions. I've learned to accept and reject." The wisdom transcends tattoos and 2052. So, too, does Francie's spunk, her refusal to lose heart in the valley of love that could easily pass for a vale of tears. Though she lacks the privileges that encourage expectations, Francie cultivates hope, youthful faith in a more favorable future than Kadohata has projected for her readers. The tender image of her aunt and Rohn fox-trotting across their living room floor inspires Francie with thoughts of human promise: "The dancing made me secretly optimistic about the world, because I knew they'd both been unhappy previously, for most of their lives, in fact—deceived by friends, neighbors, lovers, or co-workers, deceived by their own hopes, goals, and ability. And then they became happy. So I believed anything was possible. Everything always worked out."

*In the Heart of the Valley of Love* makes no claim that its harsh environment is the best of all possible worlds. Everything does not work out quite the way Francie might have preferred, but the novel concludes on a note of affirmation. In a private ritual of affection and assertion, she writes down the names of those she loves and buries the inscriptions in an urban arroyo. The novel's concluding act of graphomancy, of proclaiming power through penmanship, echoes its opening one, in which Francie, Annie, and Rohn drive past a traffic accident. Concerned about a driver trapped in the rig of his truck and hanging from an elevated roadway, Francie writes on a piece of paper: "The man is going to fall and die." She then proceeds to burn the paper, confident of the ability of language to inoculate against misfortune: "I was superstitious and thought I could prevent bad things from happening by writing them down and burning the paper." Kadohata has written down an account of a raw, lawless future. Without burning her book, the reader can yet hope to avert her version of 2052.

*Steven G. Kellman*

### Sources for Further Study

*Booklist*. LXXXVIII, June 15, 1992, p. 1807.
*Boston Globe*. August 2, 1992, p. 39.
*Chicago Tribune*. August 30, 1992, XIV, p. 7.
*Kirkus Reviews*. LX, May 15, 1992, p. 629.
*Library Journal*. CXVII, June 15, 1992, p. 102.
*Los Angeles Times Book Review*. August 23, 1992, p. 1.
*The New York Times Book Review*. XCVII, August 30, 1992, p. 14.
*Publishers Weekly*. CCXXXIX, June 1, 1992, p. 51.
*San Francisco Chronicle*. September 27, 1992, p. REV4.
*The Washington Post Book World*. XXII, August 16, 1992, p. 5.

# INDIAN AFFAIRS

*Author:* Larry Woiwode (1941-    )
*Publisher:* Atheneum (New York). 290 pp. $20.00
*Type of work:* Novel
*Time:* The 1970's
*Locale:* Michigan's Upper Peninsula

*A young man, Christofer Van Eeananam, looks to make sense of his own Indian heritage while working at keeping his marriage afloat*

Principal characters:
>    CHRISTOFER "CHRIS" VAN EEANANAM, a thirty-year-old graduate student in English
>    ELLEN VAN EEANANAM, Chris's wife
>    BEAUCHAMP NAGOOSA, an American Indian and Chris's good friend
>    GAYLIN PERRIN, a young and troubled Chippewa
>    JOHNNY JONES, an old Chippewa
>    A.J. AND GRANDMA STROHE, grandparents and legal guardians of Ellen Van Eeananam

In 1969, Larry Woiwode published his first novel, *What I'm Going to Do, I Think*, wherein he introduced Chris and Ellen Van Eeananam. In that novel, Woiwode explored the problems of marriage and belief, as his characters strove to resolve the confusions of a disturbing present: their youth, Ellen's pregnancy, their troubled and uncertain love. By the novel's end, Ellen loses the child after a premature birth and Chris, rifle in hand, strides to a Michigan lakeshore to take a potshot at the fate or force that dealt out such catastrophe.

In *Indian Affairs*, Woiwode takes up the lives of these two characters again, some seven years later and in the same northern Michigan woods. However, where the dominant force in *What I'm Going to Do, I Think* was the present, in *Indian Affairs* the controlling element is the past; where the story in the earlier novel was primarily Chris's, the story in *Indian Affairs* belongs to both Chris and Ellen (though the narrative focus remains upon Chris). Both characters are attempting to find themselves, sorting through and ordering as best they can the detritus of the past, looking for sense amid their personal chaos.

The central fact of that chaos is the death of their infant son seven years previous. That particular tragedy rendered an already tenuous marriage even more fragile, and still rattles their psyches with guilt. The image of the "lost son" becomes a central figure in this novel, as Chris and Ellen try both to measure their degrees of responsibility for the death of that child and to measure the degree to which their marriage was defined by that child's presence.

And so they come again to the wilderness of Michigan's Upper Peninsula and to the same cabin (owned by Ellen's grandparents, her guardians following her parents' death) they inhabited during their honeymoon, looking to recover something of what has been lost in the intervening years. Ellen starts there the composition of a book based upon a year's journal; that book's initial page begins: "On the night I was brought the news that my first child was dead. . . ."

Ellen also comes, in related fashion, to better understand herself as woman, one of the novel's subtexts being the problem of woman-as-wife and woman-as-mother. While staying at the cabin, Ellen is drawn into a local consciousness-raising group by an odd, bearish woman named Peggy, who comes to take both a personal and a political interest in Ellen. The group seems to confuse Ellen more than enlighten her, but the protracted effect is a clearer notion of what she must be to herself and to Chris.

At the same time, too, Chris struggles for self-definition. Like his wife, Chris carries the burden of his son's death, and seeks to comprehend that death in several ways. As a son, Chris looks to his own parentage, grasping for the meaning of what might be called "sonhood." What he finds is the even more troubling question of his heritage: One of the familial threads of his ancestry runs to the Native American tradition, and Chris quickly wraps himself in the matter of accepting that ancestry.

Chris works toward that acceptance in various ways. One of his ostensible reasons for coming to the cabin is to complete his dissertation on the American poet, Theodore Roethke, and in the course of that effort he involves himself in the intellectual reconciliation of the two dominant American spiritual traditions: the Indian and the Christian (or Puritan, essentially). As these forces exerted their influences upon Roethke, so they are felt by Chris; like Roethke, who sought an empathetic connection with the native tradition, so Chris seeks a direct spiritual and blood connection. Chris must act—he must *know* what he is going to do—this time. He must acknowledge his past and claim his birthright.

While Chris puzzles out the Indian question in the realm of theory, he also lives out the very real and immediate problems of his nature. With increasingly mixed feelings, he buys liquor for some underaged Indian boys, a practice that entangles him in a web of responsibility for their actions. He acts, at first, paternally, reading to them from Vine Deloria and *Black Elk Speaks*; but as he gradually backs off from that relationship, seeing the anger and violence in their world and the ways in which he has contributed to that condition, Chris becomes the object of that same anger and violence.

What draws him safely away from this involvement—what allows him to abandon these "lost sons"—is his more complex and challenging relationship with Beauchamp Nagoosa, a college-educated Indian to whom Chris is drawn (at times, against his will) spiritually and intellectually. Beau is one of the "real ones," an Indian who has reclaimed the native tradition even after having experienced the white world. He becomes a sort of father to Chris-the-lost-son, instructing him in the ways of spirit. It is Beau, too, who serves as a sounding board, off of whom Chris bounces his ideas on Roethke and the American spiritual tradition; their discourses provide Woiwode's novel with historical and metaphysical substance, the dialectic of their arguments gradually shaping itself into Chris's own recognition.

A key stage in the process of that recognition comes when Chris and Ellen, under the influence of peyote provided by Beau, drive to nearby Sleeping Bear Dunes. There, in a scene which collects to itself a number of significant images—bear, dance, wind, scream—Chris passes through a sort of vision quest of his own; standing on the edge of an immense dune, a veritable sandcliff overlooking Lake Michigan, Chris attempts to defy nature ("Nobody's done it. Not once in the history of this place," the driver of their dune buggy tells him) and hurl a stone into waters that lie deceptively near:

> He started forward in a run that became the beginning of a dance, and the weaving cells through his body, joining the rhythm, gave off sound. This rose in volume like a rushing wind—voices mingling in at the edges—and then the wind hit him head-on, picking the air clear for his last step, and he was at the edge with blue below, gigantic, one of the original ones back to free his people. . . . He saw Ellen shade her eyes to follow the rock, and her focus brought his eyes to it, spinning out past a gull rising in angles on stiff wings, and then its momentum gave out. They all gathered at the edge as it started down, a speeded-up plummet, then flinched at the socketing hole where a wisp of whitened spray of lake water rose—a plume above its burying contact.

For this moment, at least, Chris enjoys the intensity of connection he has craved, body and spirit flowing into the being of the natural world, the self dissolving into essence. For this moment, Chris discovers visionary peace.

This peace, to be sure, is only temporary. The world-in-the-woods remains fraught with menace. A prowler stalks their cabin, and someone paints the exterior walls with mud brought up by well-diggers. Houses burn and an old Indian dies. Someone stakes a fox in a horrible, fetishistic curse upon Chris. At the same time, Chris is drawn into the political aspect of the native culture, attending a pow-wow orchestrated by outside, non-native elements. Events are manipulated, and Chris's life spins more and more out of control. Meaning proves elusive and obscure.

Which is just as Woiwode insists it must be. Over and over again in his fiction, Woiwode proves himself a writer of mystery and of the mystical. In *Indian Affairs*, he pulls together elements of both these strains, as he concurrently unravels the mystery of events and the mystical nature of spiritual meaning. Certain matters are explicable: The fires are set by Beau's protégé, Gaylin Perrin; the prowler turns out to be Peggy, a woman from Chris's past who, obsessed with avenging her ill-usage at his hands, has tracked Chris over the years and who has set her sights on "rescuing" Ellen from a similar circumstance (this particular portion of the narrative is one of the novel's weak points—the reader is asked to believe a bit too much, to indulge Woiwode's imagination a bit too generously).

Yet the more authentic rescue comes literally from within, as Ellen suspects herself once again pregnant (though she keeps that intuition to herself until her body confirms it as fact). At least one small part of the past has been clarified, the emphasis shifted to the present and the future. Woiwode is careful not to suggest that the child-to-come will redeem the marriage; as he has demonstrated in his other fiction, Woiwode considers marriage incessantly problematic, and the reader has no reason to expect significant improvement at so little cost. Nor will it heal the recollected pain of Ellen's parents' death, and the subsequent taking over of Ellen's life by her grandparents—and the special darkness wielded by her grandmother:

"A man can hurt or humiliate a woman, but not the way a woman can. A woman can take another apart from the inside—a mother can. Nana was my mother the years I grew up. She did such a job I didn't have any identity. I wasn't dumb, I was fairly sure, but she dismantled me so much I *knew* I was inept. Has all my life been spent to prove her wrong? Women want power, dammit! If not over a man, then another woman, or there's no peace."

Ellen's identity sharpens into focus as her awareness and understanding of the past deepens.

For Chris, awakening comes with the observance of death's ritual and the affirmation of his kinship to the participants in that ritual. At the funeral for Jimmy Jones, the victim of one of Gaylin's fires, Chris feels himself drawn into the circle of his racial family. Later, buying orange soda for the children surrounding old Johnny Jones, he reimagines elements of the past—the vision of a native dancer, the vision of a shotgun cast carelessly toward his heart—and moves toward acceptance:

... and then his eyes fixed on the bubbly orange liquid, struck by sunlight, simmering in the neck of the bottle as somebody tossed a handful of change across the table, and he heard the chirr of Sugar Bear's bells in celebration, his dance over the ground opening under his feet, and then an answering chorus of bells seemed to rise from the faces aswim in Chris's vision, and he experienced again the sensation of that midnight gunshot wound deep in his chest and in a rush of breathlessness felt Ellen's shoulder under his hand and thought, *I'll be an Indian.*

In a direct echo of Roethke (and in an indirect echo of Mark Twain's Huck Finn), Chris declares his heritage and claims his legacy, though one wonders if his action does not come too simplistically and with too little consciousness of its consequences.

Ultimately, as much as anything else, this novel is about possession and relinquishment and accommodation: possession of self, relinquishment of anything other than self (spouse, land, spirit), accommodation to the inherently mystical nature of the world itself. For Woiwode, a writer steeped in orthodox spirituality, that accommodation is essentially a Christian one; but creation, in its vastness and amplitude, grants space to multiple mysteries. That is part of the magic of our existence. That, too, is part of the magic of the fiction of Larry Woiwode.

*Gregory L. Morris*

## Sources for Further Study

*Boston Globe.* July 16, 1992, p. 79.
*Chicago Tribune.* July 12, 1992, XIV, p. 7.
*Christianity Today.* XXXVI, October 26, 1992, p. 86.
*Los Angeles Times Book Review.* July 26, 1992, p. 2.
*The New York Times Book Review.* XCVII, July 26, 1992, p. 15.
*The Washington Post Book World.* XXII, June 28, 1992, p. 3.

# INEQUALITY REEXAMINED

*Author:* Amartya Sen (1933-    )
*Publisher:* Harvard University Press (Cambridge, Massachusetts). 207 pp. $29.95
*Type of work:* Current affairs; ethics
*Time:* The late 1980's and 1990's
*Locale:* Worldwide, focusing on poverty in many countries

*Concentrating on matters of worldwide deprivation, Sen examines some root causes of social and economic inequalities, often bypassing the question of whether people can experience equality in favor of asking the more disturbing question, "Equality of what?"*

Amartya Sen, Lamont University Professor and Professor of Economics and Philosophy at Harvard University, has devoted his substantial professional career to examining questions that relate to the ethical implications of economic realities and inequalities. He has long been centrally concerned with questions of famine and starvation, largely in Third World countries. Such questions have been major and consistent foci in his *Poverty and Famine* (1981)), *Choice, Welfare, and Management* (1982), *Resources, Values and Development* (1984), *Commodities and Capabilities* (1985), *The Standard of Living* (1987), and *Hunger and Public Action* (1989), all influential studies that draw from expertise in Sen's two fields of crucial interest, economics and philosophy, notably ethics.

In *Inequality Reexamined,* Sen shows how social and political institutions, as they move toward democracy, characteristically call for an equality to be bestowed upon the populaces they encompass, but the equality they tout often assumes the stature of little more than a slogan meant to gain the support of—and ultimately to hoodwink—the masses. Suppressed people who are told, "All people deserve (and will be granted) equality," gain hope—until someone asks, as Sen does throughout his book, "Equality of what?" This recurrent question pricks the balloon on which the enticing slogan has been etched and plunges the notion of equalities—as well as obvious inequalities—sharply into a new, more detached context, although a less lofty one.

For Sen, then, the promise of equality is a given in any society or institution that strives toward a democratic orientation. It is not always the given, however, that the masses are led to believe it is and that they are bamboozled into expecting. Sen, taking into account the vast diversity of human abilities and potentials, suggests that the concept that all people are created equal serves only to divert attention from differences that result in vastly divergent outcomes for every individual within a society that ostensibly proclaims and promotes notions of equality for those within its compass.

In the whole question of equality versus inequality, Sen contends that equality in one sphere of human existence is nearly always linked to inequality in other spheres: prizefighters are unlikely to be concert violinists, Clifford Odets' golden boy notwithstanding; poets are unlikely to be first-rate accountants, and vice versa. The only equality among people of such divergent interests and capabilities is an equality of opportunity to do what they do best and to be valued within their social contexts for their contributions.

This treatise considers the question of "Why equality?," but it views it consistently in the light of "Equality of What?," the title of Sen's first chapter. Sen posits that one cannot address the first question without first addressing the second. But having answered the second, he suggests, the need to address the first evaporates. Sen's heavy—at times exasperating—dependence on the conventions of formal, Aristotelian logic is obvious within the first few pages of this book, as the argument cited above demonstrates. This mode persists throughout his labored discourse.

Most of Sen's chapters are set up so that two related questions are posed. Sen proceeds to play these related questions against each other according to the conventions of formal logic. Often the fundamental ideas presented are quite simple and obvious ones obfuscated by the combination of Sen's turgid, tortuous writing and his stolidly dogged adherence to a highly theoretical logical presentation unrelieved by the examples and illustrations that might help readers to follow more comprehendingly what he is struggling to communicate and to understand it within a social or human context. This caveat is not intended to denigrate the content of what Sen has to communicate. The author clearly has unique and important insights that merit— indeed, demand—serious consideration. Much of what he writes about has direct and compelling relevance to some of the most crucial social and economic issues of the early 1990's. Such matters as world hunger and its implications, as exemplified by the Somalian situation that captured the attention of the world in 1992 or the Serbo-Croatian situation that has been a burr in the public conscience during the same year, are directly related to Sen's concerns.

The rise of Adolf Hitler's dictatorship in Germany or of Joseph Stalin's in the Soviet Union might be viewed profitably in terms of Sen's theories. Somehow, however, the valuable connections Sen might make are generally missing from the pages of this study, which functions essentially at a purely theoretical level.

In writing about human achievement, Sen sets up his dichotomy by asserting that within social arrangements, achievement can be assessed in the light of actual achievement or in light of one's freedom to achieve. He develops this argument similarly in chapter 3, where he begins to articulate his "capability" theory with a consideration of well-being and the freedom to pursue well-being. Here the parallels to many existing world situations (again Somalia, Serbo-Croatia, Iraq) scream to be established, but Sen elects to discuss the compelling question of the freedom to pursue well-being within a strictly theoretical context that bears little direct relation to the immediate problems that impose themselves on his readers' minds.

One cannot fail to be impressed by the thoroughness of Sen's documentation in this instance—footnote eleven in chapter 3 lists sixty-four sources—but skimpier documentation and more relevant examples would have communicated his argument more effectively. Even Sen's attempt to provide an example in chapter 5, "Justice and Capability," where he discusses starvation in Ethiopia and Haile Selassie's attitude, biblically sanctioned in Selassie's eyes, that those who do not produce starve, departs quickly from the valuable illustrative material in favor of presenting more theoretical considerations.

Many of the chapters in this book are concerned with freedom, which is related more directly to equality of opportunity than to the overall concept of equality for all people. Obviously, within this context, as Sen presents it, some people will succeed extravagantly, some will succeed moderately, some will barely succeed, and some will fail utterly. None, however, will be deprived of the opportunity to contend. Matters of age, gender, health, native ability, and background will necessarily determine some aspects of what individuals are able to achieve. Within Sen's purview, the free and egalitarian society, democratically oriented, merely opens the door to opportunity. It clearly cannot guarantee equal attainment among its subjects.

As Sen continues to develop his capability theory, he moves into territory that will strike many American readers as insensitive and shockingly myopic. This material will appeal to the basest instincts of political reactionaries. Sen clearly takes jabs at the practice of making provisions for the economically, socially, physically, or racially oppressed to be given special considerations as they strive to become equal members of mainstream society.

In Chapter 9, "The Demands of Equality," the author writes about "attainment equality" versus "shortfall equality." He would not deny those whose circumstances have resulted in substantive shortfalls from being given the opportunity to achieve equality, but he would, in the name of protecting what he terms the "aggregative" interests of society, base attainment solely upon achievement. In other words, affirmative action and other such devices created to move the oppressed toward achieving greater social equality have no place in Sen's social scheme.

In taking this stand, Sen clearly fails to acknowledge that equality of opportunity is a hollow promise if absolute standards of achievement and performance are enforced. Indeed, his stand seems to represent simplistic social thinking. He fails to direct sufficient attention to such questions as "What can society do to help the oppressed overcome the problems that limit their achievement?" Within the enclaves of the impoverished, poor nutrition limits severely both mental and physical development. The chronically poor and oppressed are often victims of seemingly inescapable cycles of poverty that leave them feeling hopeless.

Sen's solutions do nothing to break these persistent cycles. They offer few long-term ways of moving toward a more perfect society within a democratic context. In view of the excessive documentation of this book, one might hope to find in its sixty-four-page list of references one title that clearly belongs there: Paolo Freire's *The Pedagogy of the Oppressed* (1970). If there is a major gap in Sen's understanding of inequalities, it falls precisely in the areas in which Freire is strongest: the human dimension. Cycles of social and economic oppression can be broken on a broad front only if the oppressed are given both opportunity and the helping hand that affirmative action has attempted to extend. The short-term cost may seem high both in dollars and in the compromises that it sometimes involves. Those who directly benefit from it, however, often constitute a first generation of productive citizens whose children and grandchildren will participate in a cycle of success rather than joining the cycle of poverty that may have defined their progenitors for countless generations in the past.

Sen presents compelling and counterintuitive statistics that relate world poverty to well-being. He examines the per capita gross national products (GNP) of six societies—South Africa ($2,470), Brazil ($2,540), Gabon ($2,960), Oman ($5,220), the People's Republic of China ($350), and Sri Lanka ($430)—and then presents statistics about life expectancy in the same places. While life expectancy in the four richest countries ranges from fifty-three to sixty-six years, both China and Sri Lanka have average life expectancies exceeding seventy years.

More startling is the disparity between the per capita GNP of the United States ($20,910) and that of Costa Rica ($1,780). Despite this sharp disparity in wealth, the life expectancy in Costa Rica, seventy-five years, is just one year less than the life expectancy in the United States and compares favorably to life expectancies of the most progressive and economically favored countries of Western Europe. Sen attributes these anomalies to differences not only in commodities and income but also to differences in functionings and capabilities.

It is with functionings and capabilities that Sen is largely concerned in this treatise. Some of the inequalities he examines are material inequalities, but to some extent, such inequalities are overcome in countries such as China, Sri Lanka, and Costa Rica by capitalizing on operational and/or attitudinal strengths that counterbalance the inequalities of commodities and income. Material deficiencies have threatened the very existence of such countries as Ethiopia and Somalia because of problems in functionings and capabilities, as Sen terms them.

*Inequality Reexamined* is not an easy book to read. The problems with which its author deals are often extremely complex, although many of them will be quite obvious to intelligent readers and, certainly, to readers of Sen's other books. Sen does not always seem aware of the full complexity of the social problems with which he grapples. His convoluted style of presentation creates an additional burden for readers. Those who persist, however, will find considerable stimulation in this book. Its author, although significantly biased in many ways, is well-grounded in his field. In disagreeing with some of his most crucial positions—notably for many in his American audience, his stand on affirmative action—readers will find themselves thinking through in fresh and productive ways the problems Sen presents.

This reconsideration of some of the central concepts with which Sen deals may lead readers to take positions diametrically opposed to Sen's. In arriving at these opposing positions, however, they will have been forced to reexamine many of their own most cherished social tenets.

*R. Baird Shuman*

### Sources for Further Study

*The Times Higher Education Supplement.* October 30, 1992, p. 26.
*The Times Literary Supplement.* March 12, 1993, p. 23.

# THE INTERIOR CASTLE
## The Art and Life of Jean Stafford

*Author:* Ann Hulbert
*Publisher:* Alfred A. Knopf (New York). 430 pp. $25.00
*Type of work:* Literary biography
*Time:* 1915-1979
*Locale:* Boulder, Colorado; Germany; and New York City

*Rigorously focused on Stafford's literary work and on the development of her ambivalent literary sensibility, this superbly written biography nevertheless scants a depiction of the full range of her life*

*Principal personages:*
> JEAN STAFFORD, an author best known for her short stories and a novel-writing career that was sadly aborted twenty years before her death
> JOHN STAFFORD, Jean's father, a failed writer
> ROBERT HIGHTOWER, Stafford's first male confidant, with whom she exchanged considerable correspondence
> ROBERT LOWELL, Stafford's first husband, a great poet whose uncontrollable temper led to his physical and mental abuse of her
> OLIVER JENSON, Stafford's second husband, who tried to be supportive but who lacked a profound interest in her career
> A. J. LIEBLING, Stafford's third husband, a journalist with *The New Yorker* who adored her work and gave her much pleasure

Jean Stafford is best known as a writer of short stories. *The Collected Stories of Jean Stafford* (1969) won a Pulitzer Prize, several of her stories received O. Henry awards, and her short fiction is frequently anthologized. Yet she struggled to become a great novelist, writing several unpublished novels before her twenty-sixth year and completing three that were published: *Boston Adventure* (1944), *The Mountain Lion* (1947), and *The Catherine Wheel* (1952). In the last twenty years of her life, Stafford published little fiction and some journalism, promising to deliver to publishers the great novel she seemed incapable of completing even as her health deteriorated.

Ann Hulbert relates no more of Stafford's personal life and her day-to-day existence than is necessary in order to understand the bases of her work and to evaluate the nature of her achievement. This biography has received high praise for its evocation of Stafford's literary personality, and for Hulbert's refusal to engage in what Joyce Carol Oates called "pathography" in her review of David Roberts' biography, *Jean Stafford* (1988). Oates accused Roberts of dwelling on Stafford's debilitating illnesses and indulging in a demeaning dissection of the writer's private life and final years of sickness. Roberts opened himself up to this charge by not putting enough emphasis on Stafford's work, even though in his introduction he claimed to have been drawn to her by the strength of her writing. Yet what he had to say about Stafford's illnesses was not irrelevant and not out of proportion to the way she spent her life; it was merely offensive to literary sensibilities that object to biographers who insist that all aspects of their subjects' lives should be covered.

Certainly the balance between the life and the work is managed much more skillfully in Hulbert's biography. Even readers who do not know Stafford's work should be able to follow the biographer's sophisticated sense of the way in which literature and life inform each other. Hulbert has disciplined her material, retelling Stafford's stories and novels not as plot summaries but as examples of how the writer struggles to objectify life in fiction, sometimes drawing directly on personal experience, sometimes inverting it, sometimes using it only as inspiration, a jumping-off point for the creation of a world that shakes itself free from the clutches of biography. Hulbert finds various interesting ways of showing that there is never a simple one-to-one relationship between what Stafford experienced and what she wrote about. Indeed, the biographer conclusively demonstrates that the main reason why Stafford could not complete her last novel and why she wrote so little in her last twenty years is that she could not maintain the distance necessary for her to put her experience of life into aesthetic shape.

Stafford's most important stories—such as "The Interior Castle" and "An Influx of Poets"—are discussed several times, for they represent the basic themes of Stafford's literary and extraliterary life. Never repetitious, Hulbert is ingenious in finding ways of using these stories and others to unify her approach to Stafford, revealing that Stafford had ambivalent feelings about literature itself—about the extent to which it could free her from her neuroses. Would going to a psychiatrist ruin her imagination, giving her too much insight into the sources of her stories? Stafford wondered even as she engaged in years of therapy. Similarly, was it a good idea to surround herself with a circle of writers—as she and her first husband, Robert Lowell, did in accepting the help of Allen Tate, Caroline Gordon, John Crowe Ransom, Philip Rahv, and others? Stafford found support but also back-stabbing and harsh competitiveness in literary circles. When she and Lowell separated, she rejected his encouraging letters reminding her what a good writer she was. In her view, a literary reputation was not a life, it would not help her to overcome her frailties, and it was often a way of avoiding recognition of personal failings.

Hulbert narrates with great economy and sensitivity the story of Stafford's progress from fledgling writer—working as a typist and in the shadow of her New England husband whom everyone thought was destined to be great—to best-seller (for her first novel, *Boston Adventure*), to the mature achievement of her short stories, to her final days of decline. Stafford's father looms over and over again in the narrative as her inspiration and nemesis. Apparently rejecting her domestic and complacent mother, Stafford was drawn to her flamboyant father, with his pipe dreams of becoming a great writer and provider for his family. In fact, he wrote much and sold little, never giving up on his meager talent but presenting his daughter with the example of (in her estimation) a fool—a man who lived off his family and who rarely acknowledged the utter failure of his life. Even though she was much more successful than her father, Stafford could not abolish the link established before her college years between the literary life and isolation, between writing and a certain inhumanity in the writer's sensibility. On one hand, it was grand to set oneself up as an autonomous creator; on the other hand, the position of autonomy, especially when the writer failed, looked silly and self-destructive. Stafford wavered between success and failure in her own work, between marriage to three husbands and living an isolated existence—at one time spending a year in the Payne Whitney Clinic trying to cure the alcoholism that plagued her adult life, and living out her last years in a house on Long Island turning her bedrooms into unused studies so that she would not have to deal with visitors.

Hulbert makes no explicit comment on the contrast between the patient, mild-mannered Robert Hightower—who got to know Stafford well during her year (1936) in Germany, before she had definitely settled on a literary career and had notions of becoming a philologist—and Robert Lowell, unstable, fanatically literary, and deter-mined like his contemporaries John Berryman, Delmore Schwartz, and Randall Jarrell to become a famous poet. But Hightower and Lowell represent in an almost schematic fashion the poles of Stafford's character. Although Hightower was attracted to the literary life, he did not have the drive or the talent to pursue it. In love with Stafford, he suffered through endless disappointments as she failed to make good on her promises to make a life with him. Lowell took Stafford by storm and pursued her in a thuggish manner, thrusting her into the politics of literary life. She realized that Lowell and his friends were a stimulant and probably helped to account for her growth and achievement as a writer, but their vicious competitiveness disarmed her and assaulted her fragile identity.

At least this is how the story of Stafford's life must be taken from Hulbert's biography. There might well be other interpretations. Because Hulbert concentrates memorably on Stafford's writing, the characters of others in her life are sketched but never explored. To some extent, of course, this is inevitable. A biography cannot give equal weight to every important figure in a subject's life. To do so is to risk producing a shapeless narrative; and after all a large part of the biographer's task is to understand how the subject saw her life, though there should be some room in a biography for a sense of how others saw the subject.

Lowell, Oliver Jenson (Stafford's second husband), and A. J. Liebling (her third husband), are given less than their due. Lowell appears mainly as a monster—as he did in Roberts' biography as well. Perhaps Hulbert assumes that readers of Ian Hamilton's biography of Lowell (*Robert Lowell: A Biography*, 1983) can fill in the blanks, can look to Hamilton for explanation of Lowell's behavior. It is not that Hulbert makes no effort to explain the poet's character; rather, the interaction between Lowell and Stafford is seen largely through her letters and her fiction, which means there is no Lowell apart from Stafford's vision of him. Oliver Jenson is more of a ghost than anyone else in this biography—probably because he does not figure in Stafford's writing. Liebling's significance to Stafford is deftly portrayed in remarkably few pages, but what is missing is the drama, the sense of Stafford living with him.

To point out these limitations in Hulbert's biography is not to say these are faults she should somehow have corrected; rather it is to raise questions about literary biography. If a biographer takes Hulbert's approach, then aspects of the life will surely be diminished. If a biographer takes Roberts' tack, the life becomes vivid but the work is obscured or even devalued. Biographers who have attempted to combine full treatments of life and work often serve up thousand-page narratives that divide the subjects' lives into halves that are not joined together into aesthetic wholes.

In a curious way, biographies sometimes complete each other (a fact reviewers rarely notice) or at least demonstrate that there are different ways of writing the same life based on the biographical method selected. Biography is life-writing in a very literal sense in that biographers, like their subjects, are constantly trying to find the balance between the work and the life. Hulbert represents a fine example of purely literary biography. W. A. Swanberg's biography of Theodore Dreiser (*Dreiser*, 1965) presents a vivid portrait of the man and his literary personality without coming close to the kind of analysis of texts Hulbert prefers, and Ann Waldron's biography (*Close Connections: Caroline Gordon and the Southern Renaissance*, 1987) of Caroline Gordon and her literary circle (which includes vivid glimpses of Stafford) is a remarkable depiction of literary life that does not dissect Gordon's fiction but merges it into the drama of a writer's community.

Biographers are most often accused of including extraneous details and too many anecdotes, and in general producing data because it can be retrieved rather than because it is necessary to complete a portrait. Hulbert's biography has no excess: It is austerely literary and careful never to be vulgar, even though her subject was capable of vulgarity. There is no way of knowing, of course, how Stafford would have reacted to Hulbert's style. Would she have felt honored by so much attention to her work, or would she have reacted—as she did to the very literary Lowell—with the objection that there was more to her life than literature, and that by subordinating as many events as possible to what she represented in literature, the biographer has ironically resolved the dilemma that bedeviled Stafford and that Yeats memorably put in his musings on his poetic vocation: Which was it to be, perfection of the life or of the work? Stafford could not choose. Has this biographer, in a strange way, chosen for her?

*Carl Rollyson*

## Sources for Further Study

*The Atlantic.* CCLXIX, June, 1992, p. 123.
*Chicago Tribune.* May 24, 1992, XIV, p. 1.
*The Christian Science Monitor.* June 2, 1992, p. 13.
*Commonweal.* CXIX, August 14, 1992, p. 31.
*Library Journal.* CXVII, May 15, 1992, p. 94.
*The Nation.* CCLIV, April 27, 1992, p. 563.
*The New York Times Book Review.* XCVII, June 21, 1992, p. 11.
*The Times Literary Supplement.* July 3, 1992, p. 40.
*The Washington Post Book World.* XXII, May 17, 1992, p. 3.

# INTERPRETATION AND OVERINTERPRETATION

*Author:* Umberto Eco (1932-      ), with Richard Rorty, Jonathan Culler, and Christine Brooke-Rose

Edited, with an introduction, by Stefan Collini

*Publisher:* Cambridge University Press (New York). 151 pp. $39.95; paperback $11.95

*Type of work:* Literary criticism

*A lively discussion among two novelist-critics, a deconstructionist, and a pragmatist philosopher about an author's intent and the limits of textual meaning*

*Interpretation and Overinterpretation* is based on the 1990 Tanner Lectures delivered by novelist and literary theorist Umberto Eco at Clare Hall, Cambridge. Eco was joined by respondents Christine Brooke-Rose, a novelist-critic; deconstructionist Jonathan Culler; and pragmatist philosopher Richard Rorty. Eco is professor of semiotics at the University of Bologna and the best-selling author of *Il nome della rosa* (1980; *The Name of the Rose*, 1983) and *Il pendolo di Foucault* (1988; *Foucault's Pendulum*, 1989). *Interpretation and Overinterpretation* presents revised versions of Eco's three lectures, the papers delivered by each of the three seminar participants, and Eco's response. Stefan Collini, University Lecturer in English and Fellow of Clare Hall, introduces the proceedings with a helpful twenty-one-page overview.

In the course of his three lectures, Eco expounds on his contention that

> between the intention of the author (very difficult to find out and frequently irrelevant for the interpretation of a text) and the intention of the interpreter who (to quote Richard Rorty) simply "beats the text into a shape which will serve for his purpose," there is a third possibility. There is an *intention of the text.*

In his introduction, Collini observes that Eco has grown increasingly ill at ease "at the way some of the leading strands of contemporary critical thought . . . appear to him to license the reader to produce a limitless, uncheckable flow of 'readings.'" What provides a limit, says Eco, is neither the author nor the interpreter, but the text itself. Eco's lectures are attempts to show the reasonableness of his proposal without at the same time opening himself to a charge of authoritarianism by telling an interpreter that he or she has gone too far.

Eco's first lecture charts the tortuous course of the history of ancient gnosticism and hermeticism, and the belief that certain texts contain secret meanings hidden to all those who lack the interpretive key. The similarity to contemporary reader-oriented criticism is, in Eco's mind, disquieting. If the number of possible meanings is endless, and endlessly acceptable (Eco's definition of "overinterpretation"), the notion of communal norms on which to base reasonable interpretations and reject absurd interpretations collapses. For the modern reader under the sway of deconstruction, says Eco, every line of text is under suspicion; "the glory of the reader is to discover that texts can say everything, except what their author wanted them to mean. . . ."

In his second lecture, Eco argues that overinterpretation of a text can be recognized even if one does not believe there is only one correct understanding of that text. The intent of a given text, he says, is to produce what he calls the "model reader." This model reader takes the appropriate cues from the text so that, even if multiple interpretations are produced, certain overinterpretations are discarded as preposterous. Just how the text and reader are related involves reference to the so-called "herme-neutic circle," in which one's understanding of the parts of a text can come only as one understands the whole; but the understanding of the whole is modified simulta-neously by one's understanding of the parts. As Eco writes, "the text is an object that the interpretation builds up in the course of the circular effort of validating itself on the basis of what it makes up as its result." That is, the model reader asks the ap-propriate questions about the parts and the whole of a text based on what the model reader determines is the intention (or intentions) of the text. A text may begin as a standard fairy tale, says Eco, but the model reader may discover later on that the intent of the text is for the fairy tale to be read ironically. Nevertheless, the first impression, later modified, is part of the reader's understanding of what the text intended.

This appears to leave out the intention of the "empirical author," the human writer. In his third lecture, Eco takes up the question of what or how much authority the empirical author has over the created text; and the answer, he believes, is "very little." Sometimes readers of Eco's works will find a connection that "makes sense" in the overall textual strategy, but a connection Eco the empirical author never "intended." A character named Casaubon in *Foucault's Pendulum* was not, asserts Eco, named after the Casaubon who appears in *Middlemarch: A Study of Provincial Life* (1871-1872) by George Eliot, and there are words to that effect in Eco's novel; yet in response to a reader who pointed out that Eliot's Casaubon was writing a book called *A Key to All Mythologies*, which is precisely the context of *Foucault's Pendulum*, Eco says it is "too bad for the empirical author who was not as smart as his reader." The empirical author can provide an insight into the creative process, but Eco maintains the priority of the text and the irrelevance of the empirical author in the matter of interpretation. It is the intention of the text, he says, that is a guard against overinterpretation.

Here Eco draws a distinction between the "use" and the "interpretation" of a text, one Rorty will reject. Passages of *Foucault's Pendulum*, for example, a novel replete with occultic references, might be *used* to "prove" the existence of a vast conspiracy among secret societies to rule the world. But if one is *interpreting* the same passages, one must take into account the author's textual strategies, which are expressed out of a particular culture and language. Eco calls this textual strategy the "Model Author," and there is evidence in *Foucault's Pendulum* that in part the novel is an ironic commentary on, not an argument for, the view that every text has a secret meaning.

The three respondents are variously engaged with Eco's project. Novelist and critic Christine Brooke-Rose offers an encomium for the novels of magic realism, such as *The Satanic Verses* (1988) by Salman Rushdie and *Gravity's Rainbow* (1973) by Thomas Pynchon. Brooke-Rose prefers to call magic realism "palimpsest history," an imagining of alternative histories, and says such fictions help "to stretch our intellectual, spiritual, and imaginative horizons to breaking-point."

Deconstructionist Jonathan Culler offers a defense of "overinterpretation," making much the same point as Brooke-Rose. Deconstruction, he says, is useful in framing questions about how communication occurs, and what assumptions or biases are at work to make it possible. "Many of the most interesting forms of modern criticism ask not what the work has in mind but what it forgets, not what it says but what it takes for granted." Culler's definition of "overinterpretation" does not seem to match Eco's; his point is that texts can provide scholars with more information than what the text "intended" to communicate. Such a claim would find few who would dispute it; in fact, Eco virtually ignores Brooke-Rose and Culler in his "Reply," saving most of his rhetorical energy for Richard Rorty.

Culler's ire as well is directed toward Rorty, who dismisses the significance of Culler's work and who, according to Culler, wants to change the rules of the academic "game" that brought Rorty to prominence in the first place. "To tell people they should give up attempting to identify underlying structures and systems but just use texts for their own purposes is to attempt to block other people from doing work like that for which he [Rorty] gained recognition."

Rorty responds less to Eco's three lectures than to an earlier essay, "*Intentio Lectoris*: The State of the Art," published in a collection of essays by Eco entitled *The Limits of Interpretation* (1990). In that essay Eco explicitly defends "the rights of interpretation against the mere use of a text." On the contrary, says Rorty, "This . . . is a distinction we pragmatists do not wish to make. On our view, all anybody ever does with anything is use it."

Rorty takes Eco's characterization of the hermeneutic circle and suggests that if it is valid (as Eco stipulates), a text does not come preformed with internal coherence discoverable by the model reader. Rather,

> I should prefer to say that the coherence of the text is not something it has before it is described. . . .
> Its coherence is no more than the fact that somebody has found something interesting to say about
> a group of marks or noises—some way of describing those marks and noises which relates them to
> some of the other things we are interested in talking about.

For Rorty, the distinction between the interpretation and the use of texts—as if one could tell what a text was *really* about through the application of this or that method (such as the method of deconstruction Culler favors)—is simply obscurantist. A text cannot tell a reader what it wants; all it can do is provide certain "stimuli which make it relatively hard or relatively easy to convince yourself or others of what you were initially inclined to say about it." Neither Eco's distinction nor the method of deconstruction can reveal the nature of a text, because texts do not have natures.

A distinction Rorty does allow is that between what he calls "methodical" and "inspired" readings of texts. What is in view here is not a text's internal coherence or nature, notions that Rorty rejects, but rather the fact that a given text just happens to affect a given reader in a particular contingent situation. Methodical readings apply a given literary theory to grind out standard textual interpretations; an inspired reading comes from an encounter with a text that moves the reader, "an encounter which has rearranged her priorities and purposes."

Eco replies by suggesting that Rorty's way of reading a text is merely one of a number of valid approaches, not the only approach. Rorty, too, has methodological glasses through which he reads a text. Eco insists that for a reader to think about how a text "works" means he or she must "decide which one of its various aspects is or can become relevant or pertinent for a coherent interpretation of it, and which ones remain marginal and unable to support a coherent reading." That is, the text does indeed contain certain features that readers (including the model reader) may decide to use for interpretive purposes.

These features, and how they bear meaning, are matters of what Eco calls "the consensus of a community." A reader who announces that he has found Plato to be a great relativist must do so more or less by fiat; it is unlikely that he could provide adequate engagement with the community consensus that Plato was far from being a relativist. Where Rorty would see unlimited possibilities for the use of a text, Eco would see possibilities limited more or less by the text itself if interpretation were the purpose at hand.

Here Eco fails to connect with Rorty when he accuses the philosopher of suggesting that every interpretation is as "right" as every other. Rorty would say that some interpretations are less useful than others (so that interpretations are not endlessly acceptable), and Eco has already said much the same thing. Eco pokes fun at silly or absurd interpretations but does not answer Rorty's claim that it is hopeless to search for the "correct" interpretation or group of interpretations. Both agree that their interpretations are produced against the background of some community consensus, but where Eco sees something in the text as in part determining the fruitfulness of interpretations, Rorty sees only smoke and mirrors. Yet, as Collini points out, if texts have no natures, and one can "redescribe" texts using any vocabulary one pleases, how is it that some texts offer a kind of resistance to one's project, or even end up changing that project altogether? That, as Eco might suggest, is no mere happenstance.

*Dan Barnett*

## Sources for Further Study

*Choice.* XXX, November, 1992, p. 459.
*Library Journal.* CXVII, January, 1992, p. 129.
*Philosophy and Literature.* XVI, October, 1992, p. 432.
*San Francisco Chronicle.* August 2, 1992, p. REV5.
*The Times Literary Supplement.* January 17, 1992, p. 7.
*The Virginia Quarterly Review.* LXVIII, Autumn, 1992, p. S118.

# INVENTING THE MIDDLE AGES
## The Lives, Works, and Ideas of the Great Medievalists
## of the Twentieth Century

*Author:* Norman F. Cantor (1929-    )
*Publisher:* William Morrow (New York). 477 pp. $28.00
*Type of work:* History
*Time:* 1895-1965
*Locale:* Western Europe and the United States

*Twentieth century scholars "invented" the Middle Ages in a variety of ways that reflect their*
*temperaments, training, and interaction with the social and political forces of their own time*

Principal personages:
MARC BLOCH, a French Jewish professor of economic history
ERNST ROBERT CURTIUS, a German expert on medieval Latin literature
CARL ERDMANN, a German historian of the Crusades
ETIENNE GILSON, a French expert of medieval philosophy
LOUIS HALPHEN, a French historian of the Carolingian Empire
CHARLES HOMER HASKINS, an American historian of Norman England
JOHAN HUIZINGA, the Dutch author of *The Waning of the Middle Ages*
ERNST HARTWIG KANTOROWICZ, a German historian and biographer
DAVID KNOWLES, an English monk and historian of religious orders
C. S. LEWIS, an English medieval scholar and popular author
FREDERIC WILLIAM MAITLAND, an English legal historian
THEODOR ERNST MOMMSEN, a German-born American medievalist
ERWIN PANOFSKY, a German Jewish professor of art history
MICHAEL MOISSEY POSTAN, an expert on British economic history
FREDERICK MAURICE POWICKE, an English medieval historian
EILEEN POWER, the English author of *Medieval People*
PERCY ERNST SCHRAMM, a German historian and biographer
R. W. SOUTHERN, an English medieval historian
JOSEPH REESE STRAYER, an American economic historian
J. R. R. TOLKIEN, an Oxford medievalist and author of *The Lord of the Rings*

The concept of the Middle Ages, or, as in some European languages, "the Middle Age," originated in the eighteenth century, but according to Norman Cantor, modern understanding of the millennium between the decline of the Greco-Roman world and the era commonly termed "the Renaissance" derives primarily from twenty scholars who worked between about 1895 and 1965. Some medievalists are sure to challenge Cantor's list of leading lights as well as many of the judgments he makes in this provocative study, but they will recognize that they are challenging a man of great erudition and sophistication who has been accumulating the material of this volume for four decades through wide reading and, often, through personal knowledge of his subjects.

*Inventing the Middle Ages* is an unusual book. Its title suggests a thesis along the lines that the Middle Ages are merely a later academic "invention," but Cantor's purpose is more complex than that. Its subtitle, *The Lives, Works, and Ideas of the Great Medievalists of the Twentieth Century*, seems to portend some sort of unwieldy combination of biography, literary criticism, and intellectual history, but the book is more purposeful and coherent than one might suppose. It is also a book with a personality of its own.

In the first chapter, "The Quest for the Middle Ages," Cantor asserts two main justifications for studying the medieval world: its importance as a cultural heritage and its attraction as "the conjunctive other" of the modern age, an era tantalizingly like the modern world but different enough to challenge current values and provoke thought about possible alternatives. Although Cantor sees his core of eminent medievalists as valuable from both perspectives, he emphasizes the second and less common validation of the quest.

His notable medievalists' work is not one invention but a series of them, diverse and sometimes contradictory, but not factitious—or fictitious—inventions. It appears likely, though he does not make the point overtly, that he has in mind the Latin root of "invention" as the coming upon or discovering of something. The modern "inventors" of the Middle Ages have not been makers so much as discoverers, and the diversity of their discoveries follows from the variety of their backgrounds. Thus Cantor's interest in their biographies.

Most of the principals in Cantor's book were young men during the rise of Hitler, and since the majority of them are European, their lives and outlooks were strongly influenced by political developments of the 1920's and 1930's. Two German medievalists—Percy Ernst Schramm and Ernst Hartwig Kantorowicz—concentrated their researches on two medieval emperors, the late tenth century Otto III and the thirteenth century Frederick II, respectively, by way of focusing their need for a renewal of German imperial glory in their humiliated post-World War I nation, but becoming in the process, in varying degrees, tools of the Hitler regime, as Cantor's designation for them—"the Nazi twins"—makes clear. Neither of these men can be called a mere propagandist, but their work (like the earlier philosophy of Friedrich Nietzsche and music of Richard Wagner) became useful in Nazi hands. In sharp contrast, the Nazi threat drove another German, Ernst Robert Curtius, back to a medieval field of study he had abandoned years before. Curtius had been teaching modern French literature at the University of Bonn, but when this subject became a precarious one to deal with honestly in the late 1930's, Curtius turned to medieval Latin literature and wrote the enormously influential book known in its English translation as *European Literature and the Latin Middle Ages* (1953). If Schramm and Kantorowicz yearned for Germanic glory, Curtius expressed the need for cultural stability in a world coming apart.

Another medieval scholar, the French Jew Marc Bloch, became an ardent member of the French Resistance and died before a Nazi firing squad, but not before he had time to write compellingly on the history of feudalism and set forth a theory of history informed by neo-Marxist and anthropological considerations. Erwin Panofsky, a German Jew in the process of becoming the leading art historian of his time, escaped to the United States and enjoyed a brilliant career as a teacher, lecturer, and author of highly acclaimed books such as *Renaissance and Renascences in Western Art* (1960).

Two American medievalists, Charles Homer Haskins and Joseph Reese Strayer, produced work that projected the ideals of another twentieth century leader, Woodrow Wilson, himself a history professor, onto the medieval world. A contemporary of Wilson, Haskins had established himself as a reigning authority on the political effects of the Norman Conquest on England and as the graduate dean at Harvard University before Wilson invited him to the Paris Peace Conference as one of his advisers. Having studied the benefits of the confluence of Anglo-Saxon and Norman French cultures in England after 1066, Haskins become one of the forces behind the creation of Czechoslovakia and Yugoslavia, each assembled from erstwhile hostile ethnic groups. Thus did medieval researches contribute to a design for eastern Europe that persisted until the 1990's. Haskins went on to found what has become the most important American association of medievalists, the Medieval Academy of America, and its influential journal, *Speculum*. In Cantor's opinion, Haskins' most famous book, *The Renaissance of the Twelfth Century* (1928), is flawed by an interpretation of twelfth century culture that relies inappropriately on a modern expansionist theory of history.

Most of Strayer's academic career was spent at Princeton University, where Wilson had taught jurisprudence and political economy before becoming president of the university and, ultimately, president of the United States. After obtaining the chairmanship of Princeton's history department in 1938, Strayer built the department into an academic powerhouse. The title of his best-known book, *On the Medieval Origins of the Modern State* (1970), indicates an important avenue of his thought. The fact of Cantor's having completed his own dissertation under Strayer allows him to spice his account of this eminent medievalist with respectful but not always fond recollections.

Not all of Cantor's medievalists were political. There is a chapter on the "Oxford Fantasists," as Cantor terms C. S. Lewis, J. R. R. Tolkien, and Sir Frederick Maurice Powicke, in acknowledgment of their medieval bent, perhaps most brilliantly illustrated by Tolkien's celebrated *The Lord of the Rings* (1954-1955). Despite his admission that he is not a Tolkien fan, Cantor discusses that book respectfully in no fewer than ten pages, much more than he allows Tolkien's pioneer edition of *Sir Gawain and the Green Knight* (1925) or Lewis' important *The Allegory of Love: A Study in Medieval Tradition* (1936). Cantor does not allow the enormous popularity of Lewis and Tolkien to color his judgment either positively or—as more likely with a scholar— negatively. He credits the "fantasists" with capturing features of medieval civilization often missed in scholarly work. *The Lord of the Rings*, for instance, re-creates the effects of endemic war and the perils of long journeys on ordinary people. Like many writers who lived through the horror of two world wars (both served as officers in World War I), Lewis and Tolkien came to be much at odds with the modern world, and their prodigious medieval reading contributed strongly to this aversion. Able to project themselves imaginatively into the medieval past that they loved much more, they had the facility to communicate an unusually vivid and authentic sense of that past to an unusually wide audience.

Cantor gives a fascinating account of another Englishman, David Knowles, who parlayed his research on monasticism and his own tempestuous conflicts as a Benedictine monk into a classic study of the English religious orders. Another of Cantor's English scholars, Eileen Power, the one woman in his select group, emerges as the medieval scholar produced by the first wave of feminism in the twentieth century. She called attention to the mistreatment of women in *Medieval English Nunneries, c. 1275 to 1535* (1922) and portrayed everyday life in her *Medieval People* (1924), one of the most widely read books ever written on the Middle Ages. Partly because of the example set by Eileen Power, any subsequent accounting of premier medieval scholars of the present, will, Cantor acknowledges, include a considerably larger proportion of women.

Cantor not only succeeds in bringing each of his scholars to life in the necessarily brief biographical sketches but also shows how their awareness of their own milieu both enhanced and colored their understanding of medieval people and events. Although *Inventing the Middle Ages* does not unduly glorify or glamorize its subject, the book certainly shatters the stereotype of the medieval scholar as an innocuously remote and only marginally relevant academic. No one who reads this book will be able to pick up such imposing surveys as Curtius' *European Literature and the Latin Middle Ages* or Knowles's *The Religious Orders in England* (1948-1959) without a livelier appreciation of its contents as the expression of a personality who interacted not just with books but with his contemporary world.

Cantor's style is decidedly mixed. He can deploy long formal sentences and marshal layers of academic abstractions, and he can drop into informal and even slangy diction. He refers to medieval pilgrimages to the Holy Land as "love boats of saints and prostitutes," to the followers of St. Francis as "freaked-out," to Jane Fonda (and who would expect to find her in such a book?) as "the Vietcong queen," to Ealing Priory as "the monastic bush league." He mingles academic diction and slang in the same paragraph. Thus, the learned Dante was able to "summon up any topos," but in the next sentence, the reader learns, this "traditional jazz" was not the secret of his poetic success. Interestingly, Cantor's lightheartedness invades even his endnotes, where he can be found speculating about the possibility of making C. S. Lewis' life into a television sitcom ("It's got everything").

Are Cantor's recollections to be trusted? He is inaccurate in some incidentals. For instance, he tells of visiting one of his scholars in Ithaca several times a year via a Lackawanna train from "Newark" that he would have had to board in Hoboken, and he places Virginia Woolf's death a year too early. Could he have been similarly careless in other, more germane details that most readers would have no way of verifying?

Such discordances aside, Cantor's *Inventing the Middle Ages* is an erudite, witty, and stimulating book, and his seven-page "core bibliography" in medieval studies, like his designation of greatest scholars, will stimulate veteran medievalists to test his "core" against theirs and will furnish incipient medievalists a chart for further explorations.

*Robert P. Ellis*

**Sources for Further Study**

*Choice.* XXIX, June, 1992, p. 1590.
*Journal of the History of Ideas.* LIII, April, 1992, p. 341.
*Kirkus Reviews.* LIX, October 15, 1992, p. 1318.
*Library Journal.* CXVI, December, 1991, p. 164.
*The New York Review of Books.* XXXIX, May 14, 1992, p. 12.
*Publishers Weekly.* CCXXXVIII, November 15, 1991, p. 56.
*The Times Literary Supplement.* January 31, 1992, p. 5.
*The Virginia Quarterly Review.* LXVIII, Spring, 1992, p. S52.
*The Washington Post Book World.* XXI, December 8, 1991, p. 1.
*The Wilson Quarterly.* XVI, Spring, 1992, p. 91.

# ISABEL THE QUEEN
## Life and Times

*Author:* Peggy K. Liss (1927-    )
*Publisher:* Oxford University Press (New York). Illustrated. 398 pp. $30.00
*Type of work:* Biography
*Time:* 1451-1504
*Locale:* Spain and its colonies

*A study of the life and accomplishments of Queen Isabel of Spain during a crucial era in the history of Western civilization*

> *Principal personages:*
> ISABEL, the queen of Castile, wife of Fernando of Aragon
> FERNANDO II, the king of Aragon, married to Isabel
> JUAN II, the king of Castile, father of Isabel
> CHRISTOPHER COLUMBUS, an explorer who sailed to the New World from Spain
> ENRIQUE IV (THE IMPOTENT), the half-brother of Isabel
> CARDINAL PEDRO GONZALEZ DE MENDOZA, an adviser to Isabel
> JUAN, the son of Isabel, married to Margaret of Burgundy
> CATHERINE OF ARAGON, the daughter of Isabel, married to Henry VIII of England
> JUANA, the daughter of Isabel, married to Philip of Austria
> HERNANDO DE TALAVERA, the archbishop of Granada, Isabel's confessor

Queen Isabel of Castile and Spain—traditionally known in the English-speaking world as Queen Isabella—was an extraordinarily influential woman in her own time. Her impact and decisions continued to influence both the Old and New Worlds long after her death. Too often portrayed as merely a loyal spouse to her husband, Fernando of Aragon, in reality she was a strong, independent, and ambitious figure in her own right. She survived numerous challenges to become queen of Castile in 1474. Her marriage to Fernando, then heir to the neighboring kingdom of Aragon, eventually resulted in a unified Spain. Isabel took the lead in the conquest of Moorish Granada, the kingdom of the Spanish Muslims. A product of her times, she also forced Spanish Jews to either convert to Christianity or be expelled from Spain. Her support of Christopher Columbus and his voyages saw Spain develop the largest empire in the Western Hemisphere. Her grandson, Charles V, became the greatest monarch in Europe in the sixteenth century, and his son, Philip II, ruled Spain and challenged England with a naval armada.

Attempting to rectify the relative neglect of Isabel, whose previous portrayals in Spanish historiography often have been excessively romantic and pious, Peggy K. Liss has written one of the first historical assessments in English of Queen Isabel since William Prescott's work in the mid-nineteenth century. Based upon many years of travel and study, Liss's work largely succeeds in bringing to life the world of Isabel and her Spain, a confusing, violent, and difficult world.

Born in 1451, Isabel was not expected to become Castile's queen. Her father, King

Juan II, had been married previously, and the son of the first marriage, Enrique, inherited Castile's throne. Isabel also had a younger full brother, Alfonso, who, because he was male, also had precedence over her claim. Alfonso died at the age of fifteen in 1468 and Enrique, nicknamed "the Impotent," died in 1474. Although Enrique had a daughter, his rule had been unpopular, and rumors circulated that he was not the father of his supposed daughter. When he died, Isabel, his half-sister, became queen of Castile.

Five years earlier, at the age of eighteen, she had married Fernando, heir to the throne of Aragon, a smaller and less populated kingdom than was Castile. Several months younger than Isabel, Fernando already was a figure of considerable fame at the time of their wedding. He had served his father, another Juan II, in the latter's wars. By the second half of the fifteenth century, the Iberian Peninsula contained five separate states. In addition to the kingdoms of Aragon and Castile, there were also the kingdom of Portugal, the Muslim state of Granada, and the small principality of Navarre in the far north. The medieval history of Spain, and thus Isabel's heritage, was a history of war, often motivated by religious rivalries. Myth and fact were mixed in that heritage. One of the supposed founders of Spain's earliest civilization was Hercules, whose "pillars"—later named the Straits of Gibraltar—connected Europe and Africa. Spanish royalty also traced its heritage to the German Goths who conquered Spain during the collapse of the Roman Empire. In the eighth century, the Moors had invaded and established their control over most of the peninsula. In an intolerant age, the Moorish conquest set off a long series of wars and battles known as the *reconquista*. By the time of Isabel and Fernando, the process of reconquering Spain from the Muslims had gone on for centuries, and the Muslim presence had been reduced to Granada in southeastern Spain.

The political and religious divisions in Spain were not only between Muslims and Christians; there also was a large Jewish community. Jews had been there since the Roman era, and Spain's Jewish community was perhaps the largest in Europe. Until the late fourteenth century, Jews were looked down upon but generally tolerated and protected by the rulers because of the financial and other services they rendered the monarchs. In the aftermath of the Black Death and economic depression, the Jewish community became a scapegoat, a victim of the fears and prejudices of the times. Many Jews died, some fled, and others converted to Christianity. There were numerous *conversos* among the leading advisers to the various rulers; they were a significant element in intellectual circles, and many were members of the Catholic clergy.

Other divisions had long existed in Castile and in the rest of Spain. There were regional rivalries, cities fighting for freedom from local aristocrats, and great lords who often were so powerful as to be almost entirely independent from royal control. These divisions were centuries old and common throughout Western civilization during the Middle Ages. By the fifteenth century, centralized and powerful monarchies were becoming the norm at the expense of regional and aristocratic independence. Although Liss does not compare or comment upon the similar developments in France, England, and elsewhere, the same centralizing and autocratic events in Isabel's Castile were taking place in much of Europe.

In Spain, with its medieval history of the *reconquista* and the more recent evolution of centralized monarchies, it was perhaps inevitable that a Castile and Aragon united by marriage would wage a war of conquest against neighboring Granada, with its predominantly Muslim population. Isabel's motives were mixed, but religion seemingly was of primary importance. Although relatively little remains of Isabel's own thoughts, as revealed in private correspondence—there are some letters between Isabel and Fernando that Liss quotes to good effect—the author is successful in quoting widely from Isabel's contemporaries, many of them her own advisers, in giving a secondary insight into Isabel herself.

Religious orthodoxy was of paramount concern to her and her court. Religious issues had dominated medieval life, in politics and war as much as in purely spiritual matters, but by the end of the fifteenth century the means were more readily available to enforce orthodoxy than in an earlier age. Greater financial resources at the crown's disposal, as a result of increased trade and commerce, gave the monarchs added leverage within and without their kingdoms. Gunpowder, of relatively recent use in Europe, added to the power available to rulers and their generals. Leadership could also make a difference, and here, Liss argues, Isabel played a crucial role. Although Granada's days as an independent Muslim state already were numbered, the successful ten-year campaign against Granada that ended in 1492 was in large part the result of Isabel's endeavors, not on the battlefield—that was left to Fernando—but by giving focus to religious and nationalistic feelings and in keeping the Castilian and Aragonese armies well-supplied with the necessities of war.

In another example of what a later generation would call "ethnic cleansing," in the spring of 1492, Spain's practicing Jews were ordered to leave the country within three months. Liss suggests that the decision was as much Isabel's as anyone else's. The Spanish Jewish community numbered approximately 175,000 out of a total population of five million. Like the Muslims, Jews had been in Spain for many centuries, and in the past—even during Isabel's own reign—the crown generally had taken the Jewish community under its protection. By 1492, that had changed. Many Jews previously had converted to Christianity, but in the heightened climate of the times even *conversos* became suspect. Many claimed that Jews were tainted by blood, which could not be wiped away. As many as fifty thousand Jews converted to Christianity in 1492 and shortly thereafter, but they remained suspect. Moors and Jews, converted or not, were likely candidates for one of the most notorious institutions associated with the reign of Isabel: the Spanish Inquisition.

Also in 1492, Christopher Columbus discovered, or encountered, the New World. After years of negotiation and procrastination, and three months after the decree to expel the unconverted Jews, Isabel and Fernando made the final decision to support Columbus' expedition. Like those of his sponsor Isabel, Columbus' motives were a combination of religious idealism, political and military power, economic wealth, and personal ambition, a diverse and contradictory combination that was representative of the times. For Isabel, Columbus' proposal was a furtherance of her long-stated intent to colonize and control the Canary Islands and the Atlantic and Mediterranean coasts of Africa. The author's discussion of the background to the various voyages of discovery, by both Portugal and Spain, is illuminating, and her narrative and interpretation of Columbus' own travels is more than adequate in a biography of the life of Isabel of Castile. Liss accepts the story that Isabel might well have pawned her jewels to finance Columbus' first voyage, but she points out that royal jewels were held to be pawned—their function was more as business collateral than personal adornment— and her investment in Columbus, through her jewels or otherwise, was minimal.

Columbus' four voyages were brilliantly successful for Spain and for Europe but a personal failure for the Admiral of the Ocean Sea, the title granted him by Isabel and Fernando. He was brought back in chains after his third trip and returned to Spain after his final voyage only three weeks before Isabel's death in late November, 1504. Isabel's public accomplishments were, according to the standards of the times, greatly admired. The unification of Spain, the expulsion of the Muslims and the Jews, the beginning of the conquest and colonization of the New World, and the establishment of possibly the strongest monarchy in Europe were considered marvelous accomplishments. Her personal life was not as fulfilling. According to Liss, her relationship with Fernando was successful both publicly and privately; however, the failures of their children left a void in Isabel's life. Their only son, Juan, died at the age of nineteen. Catalina, or Catherine of Aragon, first married Arthur, the son and heir of the English king Henry VII; then, after Arthur's early death, she married Henry's second son, who became Henry VIII. The failure of the marriage to produce any male heirs led to a divorce and the sundering of the Christian church in England from Rome. Queen Isabel's personal favorite, another Isabel, died in childbirth. Juana, still another daughter, married the Habsburg prince, Philip. Their son became Charles V, the powerful Holy Roman Emperor, but Juana herself proved to be a difficult daughter, perhaps as a result of mental instability.

Like many biographies, Liss's study of Isabel of Spain raises the question of to what degree Isabel was a product of her times. Her influence was profound—on Fernando, on Spain, on the New World, and on Europe generally. It seems readily apparent that her religious prejudices, her political ambitions, and her personal attitudes reflected many of the virtues and vices found in Western civilization in the late fifteenth and early sixteenth centuries.

*Eugene S. Larson*

### Sources for Further Study

*History Today.* XLII, October, 1992, p. 59.
*Kirkus Reviews.* LX, August 15, 1992, p. 1041.
*Library Journal.* CXVII, September 1, 1992, p. 184.
*The New York Review of Books.* XL, January 28, 1993, p. 38.
*The Washington Post Book World.* XXIII, January 31, 1993, p. 13.

# JAZZ

*Author:* Toni Morrison (1931-    )
*Publisher:* Alfred A. Knopf (New York). 229 pp. $21.00
*Type of work:* Novel
*Time:* 1873-1926
*Locale:* Harlem, rural Virginia, and East St. Louis

*This lyrical, multifaceted novel dramatizes the Harlem lives and the backcountry roots of a number of African American characters in the years 1873-1926*

> *Principal characters:*
> JOE TRACE, an amiable salesman of beauty products
> VIOLET TRACE, Joe's wife, a hairdresser subject to spells of emotional derangement
> DORCAS, Joe's mistress, an impressionable orphan
> ALICE MANFRED, Dorcas' aunt and Violet's confidante, a dignified widow
> ROSE DEAR, Violet's mother, a suicide
> HENRY LESTORY, also known as "Hunter's Hunter," hunting mentor of Joe Trace
> WILD, Joe's mother, a feral woman who lives in the woods
> FELICE, Dorcas' closest friend, a teenage girl

In 1987, Toni Morrison achieved a decisive plateau in her career with her fifth novel, *Beloved*, a Pulitzer Prize-winning best-seller that solidified her position as the leading African American novelist of her generation. With *Jazz*, on the other hand, Morrison has dared to risk her established position by writing a novel that is less masterful and confident, more exploratory and tentative. She begins *Jazz* not in the rural and small-town settings that are her recognized forte, but in Harlem in the 1920's; and she uses the novel to explore her mixed feelings about that legendary time and place. Also, Morrison creates quite an unconventional narrator, one who is not the authoritative master of her characters' lives and fates, but rather a character in her own right who is at times as uncertain and fallible as the other people in the book. *Jazz* thus seems at times less in control than Morrison's other novels, but its inventiveness is exhilarating, and its many stories, characters, and perspectives are richly imagined and frequently moving.

The Harlem Renaissance of the 1920's is a legendary period of African American creativity in fiction and poetry, but Morrison curiously makes no reference to the rich literary culture of that era. Rather, her emphasis is on jazz—the distinctively urban African American music that reached an early peak in the 1920's. Thus *Jazz* begins with an anecdote that seems the novelistic equivalent to a blues ballad such as "Frankie and Johnny." Joe Trace, a married man in his fifties, has a "deepdown, spooky" love for eighteen-year-old Dorcas, but he shoots her when their three-month-old affair goes awry. Joe's wife, Violet, then takes a strange revenge by bursting in on Dorcas' funeral and trying to slash the dead girl's face.

Playing off this sensational opening story, Morrison's narrative ranges in many directions, much as a jazz musician might improvise on the opening statement of a melody. In a vividly sensuous style, the author brings to life both the excitement of Jazz Age Harlem, to which many African Americans migrated in the years after World War I, and the racism, violence, and unresolved mysteries of the places they left behind—the rural South and the cities of the Midwest.

Curiously, Morrison almost never uses the word "Harlem"; instead, throughout the novel she refers to this section of New York as "the City." This nomenclature conveys the legendary power that this specific locale had in the 1920's, as well as suggesting the mythic dimensions that large cities in general had for African Americans at that time. In Morrison's hands, the City virtually becomes a character in its own right. The main narrator—an unnamed observer with a distinctly subjective personality—sounds a keynote theme of the novel when she declares early on, "I'm crazy about this City." Joe's decision to take a mistress seems as much an aspect of his love for the City as an attraction to a particular woman. The narrator notes that generally, when a man in the City sees a woman who excites him, "he'd think it was the woman he wanted, and not some combination of curved stone, and a swinging, high-heeled shoe moving in and out of sunlight." The narrator implies that Joe takes a mistress largely because he wants to feel once again the excitement that he and Violet experienced when they "train-danced" into the City in 1906, when "the ground was a dance-hall floor."

Another way that Morrison brings the City's personality into play is to connect its moods to the moods and actions of the characters. For example, Joe begins his affair with Dorcas in October—an autumnal time of his life, as well as a special time of year when he begins to notice how the color of the city sky "move[s] from a thin ice blue to purple with a heart of gold." The main action of the novel moves from this golden October, through the cold January of Dorcas' murder and Joe and Violet's despair, to the "sweetheart weather" of early spring when life begins to blossom for Joe and Violet once again.

For Morrison, the City and its music are initially a metaphor for the exhilarating liberation felt by African Americans who moved to northern cities. Her narrator says, "I like the way the City makes people think they can do what they want and get away with it." In the decade after the end of World War I, it seemed that "all the wars are over and there will never be another one. . . . There goes the sad stuff. The bad stuff. . . . The way everybody was then and there. Forget that. History is over, you all, and everything's ahead at last." With her colloquial voice and exuberant clusters of vivid images, Morrison's narrator celebrates the vitality and promise of the City in a manner that is often reminiscent of the first great New York City poet, Walt Whitman.

The characters in *Jazz*, however, hold divergent visions of the City's promise. Even more than Joe and Violet (who came to the City in 1906 as a married couple in their thirties), teenage Dorcas feels the sensual power of the City. Transformed from the sorrowful nine-year-old orphan who arrived in New York City in 1917, Dorcas becomes obsessed with Harlem's flashy styles and "lowdown" jazz, its abundant nightlife and uninhibited attitudes: "Dorcas thought of that life-below-the-sash as all the life there was." In contrast, her aunt, Alice Manfred, gains an inspiring vision of the political potential that New York City holds for African Americans. Arriving in the City in July, 1917, soon after the East St. Louis riots that killed her sister and brother-in-law (Dorcas' parents), Alice witnesses a solemn march down Fifth Avenue in protest over the two hundred people killed in the riots. For Alice, this silent march, accompanied only by drumbeats, suggests the "fellowship, discipline and transcendence" possible in a unified black community. Although this vision of black solidarity is subsumed in *Jazz* (as it has been in American society) by the sensual, individualistic energies of urban life, Alice's experience of it remains a resonant moment in the novel.

Enraptured by the City and its jazz as Morrison's narrator is, she also acknowledges that its mood of incessant liberation and excitement has a darker side of emotional volatility, despair, and violence. "Word was that underneath the good times and easy money something evil ran the streets and nothing was safe—not even the dead." How could someone as avuncular and trustworthy as Joe Trace, "a nice, neighborly, everybody-knows-him man," be capable of seducing a teenage girl and then shooting her? How could someone as good looking and industrious as Violet become so emotionally unstable as to try to steal a baby from one of her hairdressing clients, or to try to slash the face of a girl who was already dead? According to the narrator, part of the answer to these questions can be found in the nature of the City itself. She claims that the City enables people to become "their stronger, riskier selves," but after a while "they love that part of themselves so much they forget what loving other people was like." Also, the narrator maintains, "Little of [the sensual delight of the City] makes for love, but it does pump desire."

Morrison is not satisfied with such general explanations for her characters' eccentricities and sorrows, however, and she explores the more specific sources of their feelings and behavior in two important ways. Morrison frequently shifts the novel's point of view, so that the reader gets to know a character from many angles: by considering the unnamed narrator's omniscient view, by hearing the character's own voice in first-person passages, and by gaining the perspectives of other characters who hold their own distinctive views. For example, the reader's view of Dorcas becomes considerably more complex as one moves through the novel. She is seen by Alice as the defenseless victim of an older man's seduction; by Violet as the beautiful daughter she wishes she could have had; and by the narrator as a thrill-seeking adolescent who partially wished to die. Even toward the end of the novel, the two people who presumably remember Dorcas best see her in diametrically different ways. To her best friend Felice, Dorcas was a "cold," hard, less-than-attractive young woman who consistently "used people" in unscrupulous ways. To Joe, she was a "soft," beautiful girl; he claims, "I never saw a needier creature."

Morrison also complicates our understanding of her characters by exploring their roots in the rural South and the midwestern cities from which they came. All her principal characters are scarred or haunted by their pasts—often by the racism and violence that are the heritage of slavery. As mentioned above, Dorcas and Alice lost their closest relatives in the East St. Louis race riots of 1917. Also, the ancestors of Violet and Joe are presented in an intricately interwoven series of flashbacks set in fictional Vesper County, Virginia. Violet is left to endure the memories of her father abandoning his family when she was a young girl, of her family being evicted from their home by whites when she was twelve, and of her mother, Rose Dear, committing suicide by throwing herself down a well when Violet was sixteen. Joe, also an orphan, is haunted by the memory of his search for his mother, Wild, a feral woman who lived in the woods of Vesper County. Although he learned how to stalk from tracking expert Hunter's Hunter, Joe was never able to catch a glimpse of his mother.

Joe, Violet, and several other major characters are thus involved in a search for self that involves working out the family patterns that haunt them. They feel compelled to discover who their true ancestors were, to meet or understand them, and ultimately to find other people who will fill the gaps left by the relatives they have, in one way or another, lost. Morrison thus provides yet another way of understanding her characters by showing how they fit into the others' patterns of need. For example, through her mother's suicide Violet lost both her mother and her desire to be a mother, yet she comes to find in Alice and Dorcas the images of the caring maternal figure and the beautiful young daughter that she longs to have in her life. Similar patterns can be discerned in the actions of most of the major characters.

Since Morrison begins *Jazz* by celebrating the excitement and permissiveness of the City, it is ironic that those of her characters who eventually find themselves do so by rejecting such City values. Early in the novel, Alice Manfred is a spokesperson for old-fashioned values whose censorious perspective on the City's "lowdown" ways seems slightly prudish. Her critical perspective gains power as she generously takes Violet (the violator of her niece Dorcas' funeral) under her wing and helps Violet regain an old-fashioned but stabilizing sense of herself. Thus when Violet is asked late in the novel why she disrupted Dorcas' funeral, she replies, "Lost the lady"—she had lost the civilized side of herself. Also toward the end of the novel, Joe and Violet move closer to each other by embracing a quiet domestic existence that owes little of its bliss to the City's blandishments. Even Felice, the teenage best friend of Dorcas who shared her appetite for the City's frenzied nightlife, seems to be finding the "happiness" that her name denotes by gradually accepting a cozy role as Joe and Violet's surrogate daughter.

Another irony that emerges in the final chapters of *Jazz* is that as Morrison's main characters become more stable, the narrator seems to become emotionally unhinged. At the beginning of the last chapter, she declares that her love for the City has obscured her understanding of her characters: "I missed the people altogether." In the narrator's view, the characters have seized their lives so powerfully that they have taken over the novel: "They knew how little I could be counted on; how poorly, how shabbily my know-it-all self covered helplessness. . . . Sometimes they even felt sorry for me and just thinking about their pity I want to die."

The narrator's strange outburst is Morrison's way of dramatizing her realization that the fateful ending she had foreshadowed at the beginning of the novel no longer fits the way that her characters have evolved. Early in the novel, the narrator had indicated that the arrival of Felice at the home of Joe and Violet would lead to a reprise of the shooting of Dorcas, though "what turned out different was who shot whom." By the end of the novel, however, the characters have outgrown the need for such violence. Curiously, rather than excising the earlier foreshadowing passage, Morrison chooses to leave it in and to dramatize the feelings of anxious inadequacy that this narrative dissonance brings up in the narrator. To some readers, these choices might seem to display an irritatingly self-conscious emphasis on the writing process. Seen in another way, however, Morrison is providing the narrator with the same opportunity that the characters have enjoyed: the chance to realize her mistakes and to renew and reinvent herself on a stronger footing.

Toni Morrison has stated that the overarching purpose of her novels is to show readers "how to survive whole in a world where we are all of us, in some measure, victims of something." In *Jazz*, her characters are the victims of fragmented families, racism, violence, and their own appetites and illusions, while the narrator is the victim of her own arrogance and longing for certainty. The great strength of the novel lies in the many ways that Morrison dramatizes her characters moving out of their victimization, and rarely settling for mere survival. When Violet is in the depths of her despair, Alice advises her, "You got anything left to you to love, anything at all, do it." In their various ways, Joe, Violet, the narrator, and many other characters in *Jazz* all eventually absorb this all-important lesson: They learn to give and to receive a mature kind of love.

*Terry L. Andrews*

### Sources for Further Study

*Belles Lettres*. VII, Summer, 1992, p. 2.
*Chicago Tribune*. April 19, 1992, XIV, p. 1.
*The Christian Science Monitor*. April 17, 1992, p. 13.
*Ebony*. XLVII, May, 1992, p. 16.
*Library Journal*. CXVII, April 15, 1992, p. 122.
*Los Angeles Times Book Review*. April 19, 1992, p. 3.
*The Nation*. CCLIV, May 25, 1992, p. 706.
*The New York Times Book Review*. XCVII, April 5, 1992, p. 1.
*Newsweek*. CXIX, April 27, 1992, p. 66.
*Time*. CXXXIX, April 27, 1992, p. 70.
*The Times Literary Supplement*. May 8, 1992, p. 21.
*The Wall Street Journal*. April 23, 1992, p. A12(W), p. A10(E).
*The Washington Post Book World*. XXII, April 19, 1992, p. 1.

# JFK
# Reckless Youth

*Author:* Nigel Hamilton (1944-     )
*Publisher:* Random House (New York). Illustrated. 898 pp. $30.00
*Type of work:* Biography
*Time:* 1917-1946
*Locale:* United States, Great Britain, and the Pacific theater

> *An intimate biography of young Jack Kennedy during the first twenty-nine years of his life, with emphasis on his dysfunctional family, his chronically poor health, his obsession with sexual conquest, his war record as a patrol boat commander, and his early political aspirations, culminating in his election to the U.S. House of Representatives*

> *Principal personages:*
> JOHN FITZGERALD KENNEDY, the thirty-fifth president of the United States
> JOSEPH PATRICK KENNEDY, his father
> ROSE ELIZABETH FITZGERALD KENNEDY, his mother
> JOSEPH PATRICK KENNEDY, JR., his older brother
> KATHLEEN "KICK" KENNEDY, his older sister
> K. LEMOYNE "LEM" BILLINGS, his close friend
> INGA MARIE ARVAD, his wartime lover

The deliciously nasty tone and absorbingly readable yet erudite style of *JFK: Reckless Youth* is apparent from the opening lines of the prologue, ironically but fittingly entitled "The Birth of Camelot." It is 9:30 A.M., November 25, 1963. The doors to the Capitol rotunda slam shut as the body of the slain president lies in state, like Abraham Lincoln's a century before. Emulating the ceremonies held in honor of the Great Emancipator had been Jackie Kennedy's idea, and she made sure her children knew the script when it came time for Caroline to kiss the casket and John to salute, actions a generation of grieving Americans would never forget. The widow with the "whim of iron" (McGeorge Bundy's words), unable to control her husband's carousing while he lived, was determined to lay him to rest royally. Author Nigel Hamilton contrasts the snobbery of Jackie Kennedy with the frumpery of her predecessor, First Lady Mamie Eisenhower. Although the real villain in this saga, Papa Joseph Patrick Kennedy, is not on the scene, having suffered an incapacitating stroke, Hamilton skewers almost all the notable mourners, from the "hangers-on, bodyguards, pimps and court jesters" known collectively as the Irish Mafia to the matriarch Rose Kennedy, allegedly concerned only with what to wear. Columnist Joseph Alsop is introduced as the man in whose house JFK committed adultery on the night of his inauguration. President Lyndon B. Johnson, in Jackie's eyes a usurper, has been shunted temporarily to the sidelines by the woman whose houseguest on her last night in the White House was Aristotle Onassis.

Should it be judged an exercise in sleaze for this John F. Kennedy biography to dwell incessantly on salacious matters? Not so if the word "sleaze" is understood to mean flimsy or unsubstantial. Given the thirty-fifth president's lifelong obsession with sexual conquest, it would have been negligent not to have examined JFK's treatment of women in the context of his upbringing within what Hamilton depicts as a dysfunctional family headed by an overbearing, philandering father and a cold, withdrawn mother.

In this meticulously researched first volume of a planned trilogy, the Cambridge-educated Hamilton, whose previous effort was a much-praised three-volume biography of Field Marshall Bernard Montgomery, incorporates scatological letters from young Jack to Choate classmate Lem Billings, with whom he lost his virginity to the same Harlem prostitute. Hamilton makes extensive use of FBI confidential files, including excerpts from bugged hotel room conversations Kennedy had with wartime lover and suspected Nazi spy (in J. Edgar Hoover's warped mind, at least) Inga Marie Arvad, who, with an earth-mother beauty, allure, and sexual sophistication, was possibly the only woman JFK ever loved aside from his sister Kathleen.

Since the book contains few revelations not covered more gracefully in Joan and Clay Blair's *The Search for JFK* (1976), Herbert S. Parmet's *Jack: The Struggles of John F. Kennedy* (1980), or Doris Kearns Goodwin's *The Fitzgeralds and the Kennedys* (1987), what scholarly purpose does it serve? Hamilton admits that library bookshelves are virtually groaning under the weight of Kennedy biographies, but he maintains that none is "a *complete* life, in the English tradition." Whatever he means by "English tradition," his book is more intimate and irreverent than profound, more amateur psychohistory than "life and times." One learns less about the United States between the wars than of Kennedys between the sheets. Hamilton expresses the hope that his work will be reviewed in a serious, scholarly vein; but in the circus atmosphere surrounding its arrival on best-seller lists, it has been characterized, somewhat unfairly, as a hatchet job on a family that once was considered close to royalty. The book sullies the reputations of parents Joe and Rose so badly that the family went to the extraordinary length of publicly criticizing it. As for young Lancelot himself, however, *JFK: Reckless Youth* is an oddly flattering portrait of a terribly sickly, intellectually curious, legitimate war hero who had developed an ambition for high office even prior to what Hamilton tastelessly refers to as the suicidally competitive death mission of his oldest brother. As early as his maiden 1946 election to Congress, upon which volume 1 comes to an end, JFK's charisma and shrewd political instincts were on display.

The dapper son of a deracinated Irish Catholic robber baron, JFK cavorted with debutantes, chorus girls, and starlets. He was the product less of Boston's ethnic neighborhoods than the fleshpots of New York, London, Hollywood, and Palm Beach. His life represented an aristocracy of wealth and style, if not pedigree. In between bouts with venereal disease, a bad back, and mysterious fevers and changes in skin pigmentation later diagnosed as having to do with Addison's disease, young Jack Kennedy satisfied a compulsive need to lie with women—"obsessively, manically, to the point of sexual addiction." Hamilton continues: "Jack's pals were men; women, for him, were denizens from a foreign tribe, to be hunted in the dark hours and whenever possible branded." JFK's sex life is chronicled in such voyeuristically suggestive subsections as "Hot Screw," "Stripped for Action," "Slam, Bam, Thank You, Ma'am," and "All the Way."

For those titillated by the image of JFK as Lothario, alas, he was, by virtually all accounts, a lousy lover, primarily interested in the sport of the conquest. Inga Arvad described his technique as adolescent, intent as he was "upon ejaculation and not a woman's pleasure." Another woman claimed: "Our lovemaking was so disastrous that for years later I was convinced I was frigid." Narcissistic but uncomfortable with intimacy, he acted, the author concludes, out of revenge for the "oedipal loss" of motherly affection. Hamilton adds: "Born into a family with parents who largely despised each other, he had early on created his own, alternative world, one in which he tirelessly sought affirmation, attention, affection and admiration."

Blaming the parents for the sins of their second son, Hamilton portrays JFK as merely roguish, a chip off the old block. As for Rose, he quotes Jack as having once exclaimed, "My mother is a nobody." Rose was reared by a doting but overprotective father who sequestered her in convent schools, where she was taught that sex was sinful unless for procreation. Rose refused to sleep with her husband for any other purpose and, in Hamilton's opinion, was pathetically preoccupied with her sons' manners and her daughters' chastity. Jack ridiculed the lifeless group letters she sent to her offspring. The victim of a sexist age, she found her sanity in withdrawing into a routine of shopping sprees, daily Mass, and extended trips away from her family.

If Rose's character flaws were not wholly of her own making, her husband is portrayed as truly monstrous. Joe hired detectives to spy on his daughters but made advances on their girlfriends. Hamilton claims that he raped actress Gloria Swanson the first time he got her alone and then mismanaged her screen career. The author even speculates that Joe may have molested his retarded daughter Rosemary and then cruelly had her lobotomized when she became sexually precocious. His competitive demands on his sons became such a fetish that it led to their embarking on destructive behavior patterns. In prep school, for example, Jack was a mischievous prankster whose careless study habits and carefree life-style almost got him expelled. In acts of rebellion, the author concludes, he sought attention and acceptance from his father.

As for Joe Kennedy's public life, Hamilton portrays him as a boorish influence-peddler whose bungling caused a major shipbuilding strike during World War I. A cowardly appeaser in the face of Nazi aggression, he left wartime London before dark each afternoon while ambassador to the Court of St. James and issued defeatist statements embarrassing to the Roosevelt Administration. Writes Hamilton with some hyperbole: "As he had once contributed to the downfall of the New York stock market in the Great Crash of 1929, so now he was contributing to the downfall of the democracies in Europe." When Roosevelt wisely denied him a role in wartime mobilization, he became petulant and crazed with anger.

Even prior to Pearl Harbor, JFK had parted ways with the isolationism of his father (and older brother). His most significant achievement at Harvard, besides winning a football letter and acceptance into the exclusive Spee Club (honors which Joe, Jr., had failed to obtain), was a senior thesis, subsequently made into a book entitled *Why*

*England Slept.* Although its analysis of British foreign policy in the 1930's was pedestrian and probably did not merit publication, even after it was revised by others on Papa Joe's payroll, it brought JFK intellectual credentials and some notoriety, especially after appearing on best-seller lists (his father, it seems, bought up prodigious quantities of the book, even though he did not agree with its thesis).

Of JFK's naval service in the Pacific, J. Edgar Hoover later claimed that he never would have become a hero (and hence president of the United States) had it not been for the FBI hounding him out of his stateside duties because of his relationship with Inga Arvad. Hamilton, in contrast, treats Kennedy's wartime combat at the age of twenty-five as exemplifying "a son seeking to emerge from his father's shadow." He writes: "Behind the mask of happy-go-lucky, skirt-chasing, directionless youth a complicated, precocious, and serious young man sought to come to terms with conflicting realities—domestic, romantic, and overtly political."

Much has been written about JFK as commander of PT 109, including assertions that his negligence allowed a Japanese destroyer to slice his patrol boat in half (the only such case of its kind in the war). Hamilton exonerates Kennedy and credits his heroic behavior with resulting in the survival and rescue of his crew. Even if his father pulled strings to get him decorated, he deserved the medals.

If JFK's early life was a preparation for public service, as Hamilton asserts, his 1946 congressional campaign was the launching pad for his high ambitions. His father suggested that he run for lieutenant governor, incorrectly calculating that it would be a safer course (the Republican ticket actually won the gubernatorial contest). Jack preferred a seat in the U.S. House of Representatives, where he would be able to deal with global issues. Accordingly, Joe Kennedy persuaded incumbent Congressman James Michael Curley (who had ended his father-in-law's political career years earlier) to run for mayor by bankrolling his "last hurrah" campaign, then employed bribery and blackmail in an effort to buy his son the seat. The strategy might have backfired had the candidate not projected a winsome image and considerable savvy in building a devoted following.

By 1946, JFK had grown up in the sense that his personality was pretty well molded, even if his political philosophy—which did not extend much beyond paying lip service to such pieties as individual liberties and idealism tempered by realism—was still being formed. Somewhat of an enigma to friends, he detested moody introspection and assumed a fatalistic, devil-may-care attitude toward life. Tempered by political caution, his reckless streak would nevertheless remain a significant part of his personality, especially in matters of sex.

Kennedy's youth had certainly been reckless in the sense that he courted, in Hamilton's words, "medical, sexual, marital, and political disaster." (One wonders if Hamilton intended "martial" rather than "marital," since, in the face of his father's implacable opposition, JFK never came close to marriage with Inga, disastrous as that would have been to a future political career). Certainly his sexual escapades were risky to the point of folly, as were his wartime exploits in the Pacific, which weakened his already debilitated health. By 1946 he had survived life-threatening situations and reinvented what it meant to be a Kennedy. Like the test pilots who, in Tom Wolfe's words, had the "right stuff" and went on to become astronauts, he appeared to have tempted fate and won. In the future it would take a remarkable stroke of good fortune for him to overcome his father's pariah status within the Democratic Party and satisfy presidential ambitions already forming in both their minds. Nevertheless, writes Hamilton, "By his self-deprecating wit, his love of history, curiosity about others, and reckless spirit of adventure, Jack Kennedy had escaped his father's and his elder brother's narrow, selfish Boston-Irish bigotry and found a pluralistic, idealistic . . . liberal spirit that would, one day, define a whole generation of Americans."

*James B. Lane*

## Sources for Further Study

*American Heritage*. XLIII, December, 1992, p. 12.
*Boston Globe*. October 7, 1992, p. 73.
*Chicago Tribune*. November 29, 1992, XIV, p. 6.
*The Christian Science Monitor*. December 15, 1992, p. 15.
*Los Angeles Times Book Review*. November 22, 1992, p. 1.
*The Nation*. CCLV, December 28, 1992, p. 813.
*The New York Times Book Review*. XCVII, November 22, 1992, p. 1.
*Publishers Weekly*. CCXXXIX, October 5, 1992, p. 58.
*Time*. CXL, November 30, 1992, p. 74.
*The Washington Post Book World*. XXII, November 15, 1992, p. 5.

# JOHN ADAMS
## A Life

*Author:* John Ferling (1940-     )
*Publisher:* University of Tennessee Press (Knoxville). Illustrated. 535 pp. $37.95
*Type of work:* Biography
*Time:* 1735-1826
*Locale:* Massachusetts, Philadelphia, Paris, Holland, London, and Washington, D.C.

*A founding father of the United States and its second president, John Adams was a great statesman but did not consider himself a great man*

> Principal personages:
> JOHN ADAMS, the second president of the United States
> ABIGAIL ADAMS, his wife
> JOHN QUINCY ADAMS, his oldest son, the sixth president of the United States
> SAMUEL ADAMS, his cousin, a revolutionary politician
> THOMAS JEFFERSON, Adams' vice president

As portrayed by John Ferling, author of a biography of George Washington and of numerous works on the American Revolution, John Adams was a tissue of contradictions—a reluctant revolutionary who feared the "excesses" of democracy, a radical who was so conservative that at times he advocated a hereditary monarchy, a Puritan who became a Unitarian, a man who at times celebrated the basic decency of humanity and at other times viewed human nature as depraved, a politician who feared that too much democracy would enable the "poor and vicious" to plunder "the rich and virtuous" yet whose greatest fear was of the accumulation of wealth by the few, a war hawk whose greatest accomplishment as president was the preservation of peace, a family man who spent much of his married life away from his family, a workaholic whose happiest years were those of his retirement, and a vain and ambitious man of the utmost integrity.

The son of a deacon, farmer, and cordwainer, Adams realized from boyhood on that his greatest goal was recognition and esteem, the attainment of historical immortality. Thus, he took up the study of law because it seemed the readiest road to advancement. He had trouble getting his law practice established and succeeded more through hard work than through brilliance. At this time, Adams believed himself to be dull, confused, and lacking bright ideas. Often awkward as a public speaker, he was not a good actor, but he became a keen observer of successful people and tried to emulate their style. This was not easy, for Adams too often showed a prickly personality; he could be irritable and quick-tempered, and he too often hid kindness and gentleness behind a severe exterior that made people think him haughty and aloof. He faulted himself for pride and confessed that he was driven by a "Passion for superiority" while wishing to "subdue every unworthy Passion and treat all men as I wish to be treated by all." Superiority did not come easily to him; despite his acute intelligence, he lacked the glibness of Benjamin Franklin and the eloquence of Thomas Jefferson; instead,

Adams succeeded through determination and discipline.

In 1764, he married Abigail Smith, a woman of remarkable intelligence and ability, but for too long he sacrificed his marriage and family to his work and the ambition that drove it. The year after his marriage Adams called "the most remarkable" of his life, for it was then that his cousin Samuel Adams, opposing the Stamp Act, began the American resistance movement against Great Britain. John Adams began publishing essays in support of the protest movement, formulating ideas about "universal liberty." Had the American Revolution not taken place, Adams might have languished in obscurity, but when the moment came, he was the man to match it. Cautious by nature, he became an activist only gradually and discreetly, writing at first anonymously. When John Hancock's ship was seized for violating Britain's Acts of Trade, Adams became Hancock's counsel. Putting the law above popular passions, he also consented to be counsel for the defense of the British soldiers on trial for the Boston Massacre, six of whom were acquitted and two found guilty of manslaughter.

By now one of the leading lawyers in the colony, Adams was elected to the Massachusetts legislature and then was chosen as a delegate to the Continental Congress, where he was a key player through his legal skills and intellectual grasp. Ferling calls Adams "sober, learned, reflective, and meditative" and observes that he was an incredibly hard worker who carried a vastly heavier load than any other congressman, serving on ninety committees and chairing twenty-five of them. It was Adams who nominated George Washington to command the Continental army. When John Dickinson spoke opposing independence, it was Adams who rose to answer him, extemporaneously. Holding forth for two hours, Adams gave the greatest speech of his life. Jefferson called him "our Colossus on the floor," who spoke "with a power of thought and expression, that moved us from our seats."

Ferling makes it clear that the American Revolution was a civil war, one that alienated Adams and many others from some of their friends. Taking issue with previous Adams scholars, Ferling sees Adams fluctuating toward the popular resistance movement, not becoming a revolutionary until 1773, but unwavering once he was fully committed. Ferling finds that Adams developed a national rather than a provincial outlook much earlier than most of the founding fathers. Although he foresaw that war would be long and hard, Adams realized the need for independence and helped crystallize sentiment for it.

Adams, the first choice to draft the Declaration of Independence, declined because he had too heavy a work load, but he was on the committee that revised the declaration before its approval. What sort of independent nation did Adams want? He argued that the second stage of revolution, the "most difficult and dangerous Part," was the creation of independent American institutions. Consequently, in 1776, Adams wrote *Thoughts on Government*, perhaps his most influential writing. Believing that a "ravenous beast of prey" lurked in the heart of each man, Adams created the concept of checks and balances. As a conservative, he thought the essential revolution had occurred before the fighting began, and loathing the "Rage for Innovation," he did not wish further sweeping changes. Ferling maintains that Adams wanted to conserve the basic American system that existed before the war except for the royalist and imperialist elements. Adams was not an egalitarian but believed in hierarchy; he therefore wanted to restrict voting to property owners and wanted to let them elect only the members of the lower house, which would in turn elect the upper house. Over them all he wanted a strong executive.

As the war continued, Adams was made president of the Board of War and Ordnance (in effect, secretary of war) to oversee the army and the conduct of the war. As first man in a national assembly, he showed an enormous capacity for work, usually rising at four in the morning and working until ten or later in the evening. His friends admired his intellect and his integrity, but Ferling also portrays his limitations and serious defects. Adams' scholarly and intellectual interests were basically limited to law and politics; he had no interest in science and little in the arts. Although one-dimensional, he was intense in that dimension. Adams was not charismatic and saw himself as having no particular distinction. His stiff and ceremonious bearing caused him to be thought vain, but he was in fact very self-critical and knew that he had to be constantly on guard against insensitivity and explosions of temper. Unlike Washington, he was ill at ease in the company of women and disregarded his wife's plea that he should have Congress protect the ladies from the "unlimited power" of "Naturally Tyrannical" men.

Abigail Adams was one of the most able and intelligent women of her age, and the correspondence between her and her husband is famous. Ferling points out that for years, John Adams neglected his wife in favor of his political activities. For a quarter of a century, he was away from her as much as he was present. At the end of his term in Congress, Adams said he was home to stay, but he stayed only two weeks and then accepted an assignment as emissary to France, refusing to let his wife accompany him. For the next seven years, he was away 90 percent of the time.

In France, Adams was the chief administrator in negotiating a treaty of alliance. Besides considering his fellow emissary Benjamin Franklin a loathsome old libertine, Adams was jealous of Franklin's popularity at home and abroad and continued to attack him for almost twenty years after Franklin's death. Back home briefly after his successful negotiations, Adams drafted the Massachusetts Constitution of 1780, after which he was reassigned to France as minister plenipotentiary to negotiate a peace treaty. This time he was away from home for four years and did not write home for nearly half a year, not even to announce his safe arrival, so that his wife, in despair at the recurring loss of her husband, complained that for him "Honour and Fame" were more important than domestic happiness. Although he took his eldest son, John Quincy, with him this time, Adams did not allow his wife to join him in Europe until 1784.

Besides negotiating the Treaty of Paris, Adams succeeded in obtaining aid from the Dutch. He was then made American minister to London. In part to counteract radical French ideas that he considered dangerous, Adams wrote *A Defence of the Constitutions of Government of the United States of America* in 1787. The next year, the Adamses returned to America for good, becoming reacquainted with their two youngest sons, whom Adams had not seen for eight years. Because of John Quincy Adams, who became as great a statesman as his father and became president two years before his father died, the Adams family has become noted as a distinguished dynasty; John Quincy's son Charles Francis became minister to Britain during the Civil War, and Charles Francis' son Henry became one of the most eminent American historians. Ferling notes that Adams' daughter had a disastrous marriage and his youngest sons were both failures. Charles became an alcoholic whom his father denounced and vowed never to see or speak to again, a vow that he kept, even when Charles was dying of cirrhosis of the liver in his late twenties. Thomas Boylston also became an alcoholic, though his disease did not kill him, and was an underachiever. Ferling speculates that neglect by their father during their childhood may have contributed to their failures.

Adams himself went from one success to another, though he considered his role as the first vice president of the United States to be a frustratingly impotent one. During his years under Washington, he wrote *Discourses on Davila*, which contradicted much of his *Defence of the Constitutions* and in which he seemed to be backtracking somewhat from democracy. His reactionary trend at the time was partly in response to Shays's Rebellion and even more so to the excesses of the French Revolution. Adams proposed absurdly adulatory titles for the president, such as "His Most Benign Highness," and argued for a hereditary monarchy and an aristocratic house in Congress comparable to the House of Lords. Even though he believed in "the traditional deference of the many to the few," Adams, often inconsistent, feared the concentration of wealth, thought the rich a greater menace than the poor, and opposed a plutocratic oligarchy. In this, he opposed his fellow Federalist Alexander Hamilton, who hated him and whom he hated in turn. At the same time, he developed a rift with Jefferson, with whom he was close friends in Paris but who now seemed far too radical to him.

By the inefficient election rules of the time, Jefferson became vice president when Adams succeeded Washington to the presidency. The High Federalists, far more conservative than Adams, were concerned about Jefferson and his party and feared that if they took over, they would guillotine Adams and his cabinet. The High Federalists were responsible for the greatest blemish on Adams' administration—the Alien and Sedition Acts, which grossly violated civil rights. The Alien Acts allowed the president to deport any alien he considered dangerous; the Sedition Act made it a crime to criticize the president and his administration. Adams did not propose or promote the acts, but neither did he oppose them.

During his presidential years, Adams was less the workaholic; partly to escape the yellow fever that recurred each summer in Philadelphia, he spent practically half of his four years as president back home in Quincy. His main accomplishment was the prevention of war with France. In response to the French seizure of American ships during its war with England and to the XYZ affair, Adams was under great pressure to declare war, but despite some bellicose statements, he steadfastly refused to do so, fearing a war might endanger the survival of the young republic. Adams' option for peace provoked such a wildly hostile reaction from within his own party that some questioned his sanity.

Defeated for reelection, Adams thought that the growth of democracy had ruined him; he believed the "giddy, thoughtless multitude" lacked restraint and that the president should provide that restraint, lest greed destroy the government. Depressed at first in retirement, Adams stayed home waiting to die. He lived for twenty-six more years, most of which turned out to be among his happiest. For the first time, he had leisure for himself and time for his family. He not only resumed his friendship with Jefferson via a warm correspondence but also drifted away from the Federalists to a position closer to Jefferson's, and at the same time turned from Puritanism to Jefferson's Unitarianism. One of the great and symbolically appropriate coincidences in American history is the fact that on July 4, 1826, the fiftieth anniversary of the Declaration of Independence, both John Adams and Thomas Jefferson died, within a few hours of each other.

John Ferling, professor of history at West Georgia College, retells Adams' life with both a lively narrative and a judicious historical appraisal, occasionally comparing his interpretation with those of his predecessors. Ferling confesses that at first he disliked Adams but that he developed a grudging admiration for him. Adams did not think himself a great man, but Ferling notes that a survey of historians ranked Adams as a "near great president," though probably his greatest achievements came before and during the revolutionary war. Adams was the first great American nationalist, who more than any of the other founding fathers maintained the nation's position as equal to that of European powers. Despite his human shortcomings, Adams was always a person of integrity, justified in thinking that he worked for the national interest and not for partisan ones. In this sense, he could be a role model for our times.

*Robert E. Morsberger*

## Sources for Further Study

*Choice.* XXX, December, 1992, p. 684.
*Library Journal.* CXVII, March 15, 1992, p. 96.

# KATERINA

*Author:* Aharon Appelfeld (1932-    )
*First published: Katerinah,* 1989, in Israel
Translated from the Hebrew by Jeffrey M. Green
*Publisher:* Random House (New York). 212 pp. $18.00
*Type of work:* Novel
*Time:* The 1920's to the 1990's
*Locale:* Ruthenia

*A seventy-nine-year-old gentile peasant who identifies with Jews looks back at her experiences during the years in which anti-Semitism ravaged Europe*

> *Principal characters:*
> KATERINA, a Ruthenian peasant
> ROSA AND BENJAMIN, a Jewish couple who are Katerina's first domestic
>   employers
> ABRAHAM AND MEIR, their sons
> MARIA, Katerina's older cousin
> HENNI TRAUER, a wealthy, free-thinking Jewish pianist
> SAMMY, fifty-year-old Jewish sot with whom Katerina lives for a brief time
> BENJAMIN, Katerina's son whom she raises, alone, as a Jew
> KARIL, a lecherous thug who murders Benjamin
> SIGI, Katerina's anti-Semitic fellow prisoner who also worked for Jews
> KATERINA'S LAWYER, her only visitor in prison until he disappears

"Now there are no Jews in the world, and I'm the only one, in secret, evoking the memory of their holidays in my notebook," writes aged Katerina, after emerging from decades of prison isolation into a Europe very nearly purged of Jews. The last Jew in the world, as imagined by Israeli novelist Aharon Appelfeld, is a Ruthenian peasant with delusions of belonging to the breed that her fellow Gentiles are intent on eradicating. Katerina is set in a rural area claimed at various times by Romania, Moldavia, and Ukraine and tarnished by violent anti-Semitism. While Katerina is sequestered in a cell as punishment for carving up Karil, the thug who murdered her baby Benjamin, into twenty-four pieces, the Jews of Europe are transported to the Nazi death camps. "I only feel at peace among Jews," says Katerina, whose anguish, after the atrocities of Adolf Hitler, can never be abated. Katerina is the luminously spare account of a simple woman's picaresque, often sordid experiences as recalled after returning, at the end of her eighth decade, to the family farm where she began. The pilgrim's progress of a holy fool, it is also a parable of identification with the Other, of empathy with the victim, and of redemption through degradation, suffering, and reconciliation.

"Nothing Jewish is strange to me," replies Katerina when asked how she came to speak fluent Yiddish, a language scorned by the Eastern European Christians among whom she grew up. The phrase echoes Roman playwright Terence's *"humani nihil a me alienum puto"*—the humanist credo of universal compassion; "Nothing that is human is alien to me." The Jew as representative modern human is a familiar conceit in James Joyce, Franz Kafka, Bernard Malamud, and others. But in the treacherous Carpathian mountains after World War I, to elect an affinity with the Jewish Other is to test the limits of humanism.

In his ninth book published in English, Appelfeld performs a triple leap of emotional empathy. The narrator of *Katerina* is a woman and a Christian, and not only does Appelfeld—a man ineradicably Jewish to the rulers of the Third Reich, who sought to exterminate him—do a credible job of conveying her voice, he also imagines her imagining herself a Jew. "Imperceptibly, I had become bound up with the Jews," confesses Katerina, who in that regard is also speaking for Christian Europe, obsessed with the race it tried to annihilate.

After years of living with them as a servant, Katerina, who flees her own abusive father, becomes more Jewish than the Jews. While working for one, a young pianist named Henni Trauer who is more dedicated to her career than to the customs of her ancestors, Katerina is covertly paid by Henni's mother to keep a kosher kitchen. She observes the Jewish holy days and learns to read the Hebrew Scriptures. When her first employers, Benjamin and Rosa, are murdered, during separate pogroms, on Passover and Hanukkah, she runs off with their two surviving children and tries to raise them as Jews. When, after an affair with a boozy, lazy Jew named Sammy, she gives birth to a son of her own, she names him Benjamin and, though physical evidence of Jewishness is increasingly dangerous, insists on having his foreskin removed in accordance with Mosaic law. She wanders the narrow alpine roads searching for a *mohel*, a ritual circumciser.

Almost eighty as she tells her story, Katerina has returned to her native village after an absence of sixty-three years. She takes up residence, just after Easter, in a bare hut on her small ancestral farmstead. "It has one single window, open wide," she explains, "and it allows in the breadth of the world." *Katerina* is a short, simple tale of such extraordinary lucidity that it, too, seems to allow in the breadth of the world. Its world is one whose breath reeks of sots, bigots, and bullies. It is the genocidal territory that, more compellingly than any other Hebrew novelist, Appelfeld has staked out as his own. Yes, he is a "Holocaust author," and *Badenheim, 'ir nofesh* (1975; *Badenheim, 1939*, 1980), *Tor-ha-pela'ot* (1978; *The Age of Wonders*, 1981), *Kutonet veha-pasim* (1983; *Tzili: The Story of a Life*, 1983), *Nesiga mislat* (1984; *The Retreat*, 1985), *To the Land of the Cattails* (1986), and *Be-'et uve-'onah ahat* (1990; *The Healer*, 1990) have established him as one of its most moving chroniclers. But in *Katerina*, as in those novels and as in Greek tragedy, the horror happens offstage.

When, on Erev Pesach, the evening of the first Passover seder, a lecherous anti-Semite named Karil murders Benjamin, the son she conceived with the Jew Sammy, Katerina avenges herself on the brutal lout with a jackknife. It is during the next forty years, which Katerina spends in prison, that Europe's Jews are liquidated. Appelfeld registers the Holocaust not through lurid images of ovens and pyres but through the crowded railroad cars that pass in front of the prison window and the confiscated Jewish garments that end up clothing Katerina's fellow inmates. With each of his visits,

Katerina's court-appointed Jewish lawyer seems more and more wretched, until he ceases to appear at all. When, old and frail, Katerina finally emerges into the verdant countryside, it is a world devoid of Jews. She takes up pencil and paper and attempts to restore the lost tribes by writing out their words, one by one. Appelfeld's elliptical prose is kaddish reduced to a haiku. His novelistic elegy is like the memorial services that impress Katerina with their emotional economy: "In their burial arrangements, as in other ritual matters, the Jews are frightfully practical. All their pain and mourning are without a melody, without a flag, and without a flower. They lay the body in the grave and rapidly cover it, without delay."

Born in Czernovitz, Bukovina, Appelfeld was eight years old when he was mustered to the labor camp at Transnistria. After escaping, he hid in the woods for three years. It was not until the age of fourteen that he made his way to Palestine, and it was then that Appelfeld, whose family had spoken German, began to learn Hebrew. Like Jerzy Kosinski, Jorge Semprun, and Elie Wiesel, he is a translingual author, a novelist who memorializes the six million victims of the Holocaust in a language that he chose as an adult. To T. W. Adorno's pronouncement that there can be no poetry after Auschwitz, Appelfeld responds with an elemental style in which every syllable defies the void, every letter is a victory over oblivion, as well as something strange and new. Native speakers take their medium for granted, but a translingual survivor reinvents the world with every word he chooses.

Jeffrey M. Green's translation cannot duplicate the allusiveness of Appelfeld's Hebrew. The first paragraph concludes with a description of the river Prut, "whose water is blue this season, vibrant with splendor." "Splendor" is a rendering of *ha-zohar*, which to Hebrew readers also evokes the Kabala. Nor can a translator capture the strangeness of hearing an old Ruthenian peasant's voice telling her tale in the ancient language of the Jews. Green, Appelfeld's longtime translator, otherwise captures the starkness of the Israeli author's studied prose.

"Too bad the dead are forbidden to speak," muses Katerina, who learns to speak for the Hebrew dead. What struck her most about the living Jews she served was their reticence. In contrast to her fellow Ruthenians, who cherish chatter, Katerina notes that "The Jews don't indulge in idle talk." Katerina is nowhere more faithful to her memory of the Jews than in her own economy of expression. "Don't talk too much. That's a general rule that the Jews are very strict about." It is as if every Jew were, like translingual Appelfeld and his character Katerina, wary of wordiness in an adopted medium.

"There's no greater pleasure than reading," declares Katerina of the skill she acquired from Abraham and Meir, her two young Jewish charges, who taught her to decipher Hebrew Scripture. "I open a book and gates of light are open before me." Despite the obscurity of the prison cell and the rural hut from which Katerina serves as witness to the darkness of twentieth century history, Appelfeld's lucid prose illuminates the basis for endurance after the ravages of human savagery. Reading it is perverse pleasure, a triumph over the forces of the barbarians.

"All accounts are settled in the end," contends Katerina about rumors that her stepmother poisoned her father. After a wayward youth polluted by drink and promiscuity, the narrator, though spurned as a sort of local crone, has purged herself of spiritual *treyf*, or impure nourishment. Observing *kashrut* and the Jewish holy days, she laments the disappearance of her adopted people while affirming personal godly gain. Katerina's record of eighty years in this world that, echoing Talmudic wisdom, she realizes "is merely a corridor," is luminous with loss. Thus does Appelfeld refute Adorno; poetry can come only after Auschwitz.

*Steven G. Kellman*

## Sources for Further Study

*Booklist*. LXXXVIII, May 15, 1992, p. 1642.
*Boston Globe*. September 27, 1992, p. 40.
*Chicago Tribune*. September 2, 1992, V, p. 3.
*The Christian Science Monitor*. September 23, 1992, p. 13.
*Kirkus Reviews*. LX, June 1, 1992, p. 683.
*Library Journal*. CXVII, June 1, 1992, p. 172.
*Los Angeles Times Book Review*. September 27, 1992, p. 2.
*The New York Review of Books*. XXXIX, November 5, 1992, p. 18.
*The New York Times Book Review*. XCVII, September 27, 1992, p. 9.
*Publishers Weekly*. CCXXXIX, May 18, 1992, p. 59.

# KENTUCKY STRAIGHT

*Author*: Chris Offutt (1958-     )
*Publisher*: Vintage Books (New York). 167 pp. $10.00
*Type of work*: Short stories
*Time*: 1950-1990
*Locale*: Eastern Kentucky

*Nine stories provide intimate and moving portraits of Kentucky hill people as their region is absorbed into the American cultural mainstream*

The nine stories in Chris Offutt's first collection, *Kentucky Straight*, capture the imagination with their authority and speak to the heart with their humanity. They come from a writer who knows and loves the landscapes and characters of his native eastern Kentucky.

The setting for the stories is the hill country of eastern Kentucky after 1950, a time when a rich culture that had been comparatively isolated merged uncomfortably into the modern technological United States. In the previous generation, coal companies stripped the area without markedly enriching its people. Now roads, electricity, indoor plumbing, and other technologies are slowly making their ways into the area. Passing is an old way of life: subsistence farming and hunting, a clan organization, a uniquely local culture. Roads and modern communications draw people away to now-reachable towns to earn enough money to shift from subsistence living to consumerism. Although most people welcome their new freedoms and powers, they are not happy to see their cultural traditions disintegrate. The younger people often come to see their homeland as a place to get out of, and the older people are bewildered and angry but proud, simultaneously embracing and fighting change.

"The Leaving One" reflects several of these themes. Young Vaughn Boatman lives with his mother, his father apparently having abandoned them. He meets in the woods a strange old man who seems to have magical powers that connect him with the wild forest. The stranger says that he is Elijah Boatman, Vaughn's grandfather on his mother's side. Vaughn's mother had told him that the old man was dead because she felt guilty about having allowed him to be placed in a care facility. Now Elijah has returned home to find his grandson.

Elijah fought in World War I and returned with a strangeness in his character. When all of his sons were killed in World War II, he took to the woods and became even stranger. Now, at the end of a long life, Elijah wants to pass on to his only grandson the legacy of his spiritual connection with this landscape. He takes the boy on a mystical journey that leads them to "the going over place." There Elijah gives his grandson tokens and words that unite Vaughn with his deepest heritage, so that he and the landscape become intimately related.

"The Leaving One" repeatedly contrasts the irrational truths that Elijah believes with the rational facts that Vaughn knows. Elijah's knowledge seems to include both the materiality and the spirituality of the cosmos, while Vaughn has learned so far only the materiality, viewing with skepticism even his mother's superstitious belief that a bird flying into the house presages a death in the family. Elijah makes a point of living through the strangeness of the coming of modernity to pass to his male heir his most-valued old truth.

"House Raising" offers a quite different perspective on the disjunctions that result from the passing of the old culture. Newly married Aaron has leveled the top of a ridge so he can park the used house trailer he has bought. On the day the dealer tries to deliver the trailer, heavy rains make the roads impassable, and the truck towing the trailer becomes stuck on a dangerous hillside. Aaron's brother, Mercer, waits with the black truck driver, Coe, for another local man to bring his bulldozer to the rescue. Mercer and Coe become friends during their brief visit, as Mercer sees that he and Coe have much in common even though Coe is doubly the stranger, as an African American and an outsider. Mercer later amazes his friends by drinking from the same liquor bottle Coe has drunk from. When a wild joker, Old Bob, accidentally knocks his crippled but talented son, Bobby, off their bulldozer and severs one of the boy's useless legs, Old Bob refuses to let Coe, because he is black, touch his son, even though the boy is bleeding to death and Coe knows what to do. Largely on the authority of Mercer's trust, the other men let Coe tie off the artery, possibly saving Bobby's life.

Tension between the old ways of this community and the new invading ways is everywhere in the story, from the image of the used house trailer mired in the rain-soaked road to Old Bob's resistance to allowing a black outlander to help his dying son. Mercer's refusal to be governed by racial prejudice comes from an older tradition of intermarriage among races that is shown in another story, "Old of the Moon." Intervening between the times when whites and Native Americans intermarried and formed the old culture of this region and the present of racism and distrust of the outsider is American history from the revolution through the Civil War and into the twentieth century. This region has been isolated enough to preserve some of the old egalitarianism but has been invaded and exploited enough to cultivate prejudice.

Perhaps the most moving stories are "Sawdust" and "Blue Lick," two first-person narratives by young men who find themselves lost in the community. In "Sawdust," Junior sees himself as imprisoned in the hills. His main problem is that he is an intellectual in a region where a man is judged by how he acts, "not how smart he's supposed to be." Someone who continues education after the eighth grade is claiming to be above his or her neighbors. Junior wants to know about the outside world, and he is curious about ideas as well. He subscribed to several magazines, accepting all the issues publishers would send him until they realized he would not pay, reading each issue from cover to cover. He decides to earn his high school diploma through an equivalency test, arranges to take the test, prepares for it, and passes. This choice outrages his community, subjecting him to violence from his acquaintances and strong moral resistance from his family. When he is beaten by some neighbors at the post office, however, his older brother, Warren, whose ideas of advancement are essentially material, fights for the family honor, beating those who attacked Junior. When Warren says he is going to buy a new battery-powered television set simply to have it, Junior says his intentions regarding his diploma are the same. He is getting it simply to have it. The practical value of Junior's reading becomes apparent, however, when he points out that Warren was swindled when he bought a pair of alligator boots; they cannot be genuine because it is illegal to sell alligator skin.

Junior inherited his intellectual tendencies from his father, who committed suicide because he was unable to find a satisfactory outlet for his mental energy. That Junior is like his father is held over him as a threat, but he turns it into a blessing. Although he does nothing special in the short run, he feels more at home in the world after getting his diploma. He now realizes that he can go to town whenever he wants; he is not imprisoned in the hills, but is living there by choice.

In "Blue Lick," a much younger boy is caught between the old and the new, though he is unable to see that this is the case. His fiercely proud father, while fighting in the old ways to sustain the family honor, becomes enmeshed in the new laws and so loses his honor and his family. The boy narrator of "Blue Lick" is precocious but naïve, with a wonderful gift for metaphor. When a welfare worker places her hand on his, he reflects, "it was the smoothest thing, smoother than a horse's nose hole, which is pure soft. She held my hand like you do a frog when you're fixing to cut its legs off and eat them. I let my fingers lay real still so they wouldn't wiggle and give her no big ideas." His story is in some ways the funniest in a volume that has humor as a regular feature, and in other ways the saddest in a collection that generally mourns and puzzles over vital losses.

As the boy tells his story, it becomes apparent that he is the last free member of his immediate family. His father went to prison after a car accident, the owner of the car having decided to say it was stolen rather than borrowed. During his absence, the boy's mother carried on an affair with the car's owner and eventually ran away with him. The narrator blames himself for this because he caught the couple having intercourse. His father was then released from prison to help his elderly mother care for the boy and his mentally handicapped brother, nicknamed Little Elvis because he loves to make up songs. The boy's father is returned to prison as a result of an affair of honor. The boy goes into the woods at night to defecate and is treed by hunting dogs in a wildly comic scene that turns serious when one of the hunters insults the boy's father, takes a blow, and then kills his dog in reprisal. Later, the father steals and dismantles the offending hunter's car. For this he is imprisoned again, and for this the boy blames himself again. Then Little Elvis is taken to an asylum, and a welfare worker must decide where to place the narrator. At the end of the story, the boy sits by the Blue Lick River, alone, believing that he has destroyed his family. In reality, his father has failed to live his version of traditional hill-country values, thus sacrificing his family to his too-rigid ideas of personal identity and honor.

Each story in this collection draws the reader into intense relationships with interesting characters. "Horseweed" tells about a young father struggling to give his wife and three daughters a comfortable material life by the new standards while trying to hold to the old values. "Smokehouse" shows a middle-aged man trying to locate the right moral stance toward the ancient customs of male contest and feud. "Nine-

Ball" is about a young man who is sickened by the ways in which his family and his people are exploited by those who have gained money and power in the towns; he cultivates an ability to play pool that seems to provide him the means to leave.

Especially interesting are the stories that develop material about the old culture, such as "The Leaving One." "Old of the Moon" and "Aunt Granny Lith" are both framed narratives, in which a story from the past reveals old powers of the land that persist into and haunt the present. "Aunt Granny Lith" reverses the traditional story of the wife who must have sex with a powerful man in order to protect her husband; the husband's encounter with the supernatural colors the rest of his marriage. In "Old of the Moon," Cody travels out to a place of power, Shawnee Rock, to try to persuade Tar Cutler to attend his revival meeting. Cody converted to his own brand of evangelical Christianity, having been persuaded that his old pagan way of living was wrong when lightning killed the horse he was riding. For Cody, religion is a way to power. He finds Cutler dead, with a battery-powered tape recorder by his side. On the tape is a tale from the old times, when whites and Shawnees intermarried. Among the tale's many elements is a demonstration that those who mock the old beliefs are punished by spirits. Cody destroys the tape and then is destroyed himself by a storm as he tries to return home. His last thoughts are of the old way.

Offutt's stories have received wide recognition and important publications. Tightly crafted, brief, yet dense with material, these stories compare favorably with the best of Mark Twain's and William Faulkner's short fiction, with which they share humor and depth of characterization. Offutt promises to be a powerful and important voice in American writing.

*Terry Heller*

### Sources for Further Study

*The Christian Science Monitor*. February 16, 1993, p. 11.
*The New York Times Book Review*. XCVIII, January 31, 1993, p. 10.
*Publishers Weekly*. CCXXXIX, September 14, 1992, p. 115.

# KISSINGER
## A Biography

*Author:* Walter Isaacson (1952-     )
*Publisher:* Simon & Schuster (New York). Illustrated. 893 pp. $30.00
*Type of work:* Biography
*Time:* 1923-1991
*Locale:* Principally the United States

*An illuminating critical biography of the most celebrated American diplomat of the postwar era*

> *Principal personages:*
> HENRY KISSINGER, a U.S. national security adviser and secretary of state
> NELSON ROCKEFELLER, the vice president of the United States from 1974 to 1977
> ALEXANDER HAIG, an aide to Henry Kissinger, and White House chief of staff in 1973 and 1974
> RICHARD NIXON, the president of the United States from 1969 to 1974
> GERALD FORD, the president of the United States from 1974 to 1977

Henry Kissinger captured the imagination of an era and became the most renowned and controversial diplomat of his age. A brilliant scholarly student of the diplomacy of Klemens von Metternich and Viscount Robert Castlereagh, as a statesman his reputation rivaled that of his subjects. During the presidency of Richard Nixon, he shared in some of the most dramatic foreign policy initiatives in American history. He also cultivated the persona of a bon vivant, and by mixing socially with moguls and movie stars attained a degree of celebrity unprecedented for a government official. Years after leaving office, Henry Kissinger still was regarded as a leading authority on foreign relations and had become a permanent fixture as a commentator on radio and television. Walter Isaacson has written a penetrating biography of this fascinating man. Although Isaacson presents a balanced and scrupulously fair assessment of his subject, *Kissinger: A Biography* becomes a frightening indictment of the irresponsible exercise of executive power and an elegant argument for a more democratic foreign policy.

Kissinger's early years were shadowed by tragedy. He was born May 27, 1923, in the town of Fürth in Germany. History denied Kissinger a normal boyhood. As Jews, he and his family became increasingly isolated as Germany surrendered itself to Nazism. Young Kissinger grew used to the indignities meted out to Jews in his homeland. He endured discrimination in public places and in his schooling, and beatings on the street by other boys. In 1938, the Kissingers emigrated to the United States, just ahead of a new wave of terror launched against the Jews. During World War II, thirteen of Kissinger's relatives died in the Nazi death camps, a fact he rarely referred to but never forgot. Kissinger discovered in America a security and acceptance he had never known. For this he would always be grateful, and his later policies, no matter how calculated, would always rest on a firm bedrock of patriotism.

He began to Americanize himself with enthusiasm, learning the rules of baseball and how to drive. He became an honor student in high school and demonstrated a precocious intellectual brilliance. Service in the United States Army during World War II completed Kissinger's assimilation to American ways. He mixed with young men from all over the country and with very different backgrounds, and he found the experience bracing. In the Army, Kissinger also met the first of a string of mentors who would help him in his ascent. Fritz Kraemer was an anti-Nazi German serving in the American army. A bluff, brilliant man, he recognized Kissinger's talent and had him transferred from the infantry into military intelligence. Under Kraemer's tutelage, Kissinger would help root out Nazis in American-occupied Germany. Though only a sergeant, he was placed in charge of entire towns. Kissinger, despite his background, proved himself a mild and considerate governor. His Army experience gave Kissinger a self-confidence he would never lose. Kraemer encouraged him to get a first-rate education, so upon leaving the Army in 1947 Kissinger applied for and received admission to Harvard University.

Kissinger made a brilliant record at Harvard. Quickly gravitating to the government department, he won the patronage of Professor William Yandell Elliott, who became a major influence on the budding political scientist. Elliott encouraged Kissinger to pursue public service. He also inculcated in him an appreciation for philosophy, especially that of Immanuel Kant. Kissinger's philosophical concerns would color all of his later academic and political writings. After producing a 383-page undergraduate thesis on the meaning of history, the longest such thesis in the history of the university, Kissinger was accepted into the government department's graduate program. As a graduate student, Kissinger began developing the political and diplomatic skills that would make him famous later in life. He took charge of the Harvard International Seminar, which brought rising young world leaders to spend the summer at the university. Kissinger used the seminar to build an international network of contacts. Decades later he would still be in touch with seminar participants, many of whom had risen to high positions in their native lands. He edited a short-lived journal named *Confluences*, soliciting submissions from a distinguished list of contributors and further extending his world of contacts. Conscious of his own mental prowess, Kissinger was openly contemptuous of individuals he considered his intellectual inferiors, and there were few he considered either his equal or his superior. At the same time, he displayed a born courtier's gifts in flattering people he respected or needed. As a result, Kissinger made a few friends but many enemies at Harvard.

Kissinger surprised his fellow graduate students with his topic for a doctoral thesis. Instead of treating the implications of the atomic bomb or the Cold War, Kissinger turned to the seeming irrelevancies of nineteenth century diplomacy. It would be Kissinger's genius to demonstrate the enduring lessons of Metternichian diplomacy, both in print and practice. Kissinger believed that statesmen such as Prince Klemens von Metternich and Viscount Robert Castlereagh deserved study because they contained the revolutionary forces of Napoleonic France and created an enduring peace, precisely the challenge facing the United States in containing the ambitions of the

Soviet Union. Metternich and Castlereagh were successful because they created a favorable balance of power, rather than a countervailing ideological response to the French Revolution. Like his exemplars, Kissinger would be an unabashed practitioner of power politics. He firmly believed that the verities of military and economic power decided diplomacy. The infusion of idealistic or moralistic concerns into diplomacy only clouded the judgment of diplomats and confused national policy. International stability lay in achieving a worldwide equilibrium of power, and the task of a diplomat in promoting this balance. As he made clear in his life, if compelled to choose between justice and order, Kissinger emphatically preferred order.

Isaacson traces Kissinger's profoundly stark and conservative vision of the world to his origins as a refugee from the revolutionary horrors of Nazi Germany. Kissinger's experience left him with lasting doubts about human altruism and an inclination to distrust human motives. For him the international arena was a dark and forbidding place. The Holocaust served as a metaphor for the tragic drift of human history. Having seen a society fly apart, Kissinger became an instinctive conservative and scorned the glamour of remaking the world for the patient process of maintaining previous achievements. As a witness in his youth of the fruits of weakness, he became a convinced advocate of military strength and the use of force to buttress diplomacy. On a more personal level, Kissinger abandoned the faith of his youth, turning to secular means of ordering his life. The traumas of his youth encouraged in him a tendency toward paranoia regarding the people around him, and, simultaneously, a need to seek others' approval. Thus in many ways Kissinger's background differentiated him from other postwar American statesmen. It helped him become one of the architects of détente and a new direction in American foreign policy. It would also make him incapable of reaching out to the American people and building informed and solid support for his policies.

Upon receiving his doctorate, Kissinger's academic career flourished. His thesis was published as *A World Restored: Metternich, Castlereagh, and the Problems of Peace, 1812-22* in 1957. In 1955, Kissinger accepted a position with the Council on Foreign Relations, leading a group analyzing the impact of nuclear weapons on foreign policy. The fruit of this study was a book, *Nuclear Weapons and Foreign Policy* (1957), which became a surprise best-seller and established Kissinger's reputation as one of the nation's leading nuclear strategists. In this work he argued against the doctrine of massive retaliation, which limited the United States to either fighting a conventional war or launching a full nuclear strike. Kissinger believed that this precluded creative diplomacy and urged the development of a capacity to wage limited nuclear war. Although this book gave Kissinger a sinister reputation in certain circles, it brought him to the attention of important policymakers. Nelson Rockefeller, the governor of New York with presidential ambitions, took on Kissinger as a paid consultant on foreign relations. Rockefeller proved to be a generous patron and did not object as Kissinger attempted to ingratiate himself first with the John F. Kennedy and then with the Lyndon Johnson administration. Receiving tenure at Harvard, Kissinger continued to expand his network of contacts around the world. Kissinger yearned to leave his study for a position in government that would enable him to make policy.

Kissinger showed little scruple in his pursuit of office. He hovered on the fringes of power during the Kennedy and Johnson years, occasionally consulted but never extensively employed. He did figure in a back-channel negotiation with the North Vietnamese in 1967, through the good offices of two French friends. These talks came to nothing, but they did earn him access to information from the Johnson Administration on the status of the Paris peace talks. Kissinger used this privilege to curry favor with Richard Nixon's presidential campaign in 1968, passing along tidbits of news to keep the nervous Republican candidate abreast of developments in Paris. Nixon was as impressed by Kissinger's deviousness as by his academic credentials, and chose him as his national security adviser.

Nixon and Kissinger enjoyed a highly successful, though troubled, partnership. Their legacy would be mixed. Nixon was convinced that he could not trust the bureaucracies in place in Washington, especially that at the State Department. He intended to run foreign policy out of the White House, bypassing the secretary of state and normal diplomatic channels. Because of his ambition and his own paranoid tendencies, Kissinger would abet his president in this conspiracy against the American government. Indeed, Kissinger contributed a great deal to the atmosphere of secrecy and suspicion that pervaded the Nixon White House. Worried about leaks to the press concerning his various covert initiatives, Kissinger authorized wiretaps on members of his staff. His outrage over Daniel Ellsberg's leaking of the Pentagon Papers to *The New York Times* helped inspire the secret program of political espionage that led to Watergate. Ironically, despite their joint hostility to the bureaucratic establishment, Nixon and his national security adviser did not fully trust each other, and the president eventually turned to Kissinger's deputy, Alexander Haig, to keep an eye on him. Kissinger's promotion to secretary of state in 1973 largely reflected Nixon's political weakness in the wake of the Watergate scandal.

In his book, Isaacson tends to downplay Nixon's role in the foreign policy initiatives of his administration. This is a mistake. Nixon always remained in charge and provided a vision of the world order he hoped to create. For all his vaunted strategic ability, Kissinger's greatest strength would always lie in his negotiating skills. Nixon and Kissinger saw themselves as attempting to restore the power and prestige of the United States in the face of the disastrous war in Vietnam. They recognized that the war could not be won, but they were convinced that the position of the United States in the world would suffer if they decided to cut American losses and withdraw from Vietnam. Nixon and Kissinger sought instead a face-saving peace that would allow the United States to bring its troops home and give the South Vietnamese regime a few years of life before the Communists overwhelmed it. They pursued this by inaugurating a triangular diplomacy with the Soviet Union and China, playing on these powers' fears of each other to extract concessions and encourage them to pressure the North Vietnamese to make peace. At the same time, even as they rapidly reduced American troop levels in Southeast Asia, Nixon and his national security adviser signaled their resolve to the North Vietnamese by stepping up the American bombing campaign and widening the war with an invasion of Cambodia.

This reorientation of American policy produced ambiguous results. The dramatic opening to China and improved relations with the Soviet Union seemed to usher in a new era of international stability. Détente with the Soviet Union led to a Strategic Arms Limitation Treaty in May, 1972. The strategy of exploiting Chinese and Soviet goodwill to bring the North Vietnamese to terms failed. Nixon and Kissinger ultimately fell back upon a series of violent gestures in Vietnam before signing an agreement in January, 1973, only marginally different from what they could have had four years earlier.

Kissinger escaped the collapse of the Nixon Administration. His widely publicized diplomatic ventures and glamorous life-style had made him a public hero. He became seen as the indispensable man, holding together American foreign policy as Nixon's presidency fell apart. Nixon's successor, Gerald Ford, a hero to Isaacson because of his decency and democratic instincts, decided to keep Kissinger as secretary of state, though he gradually reduced his power. Kissinger would continue to enjoy triumphs, most notably his ongoing Middle Eastern shuttle diplomacy in the wake of the Yom Kippur War of 1973. Nevertheless, his glory days were over. Embarrassments in Cyprus, Angola, and elsewhere dimmed his diplomatic luster. The policy of détente came under increasing attack from figures such as Ronald Reagan, who resented what seemed like unnecessary moral compromise with a totalitarian regime. Revelations about his activities in the Nixon White House tainted Kissinger's reputation. Kissinger left office in 1977 still celebrated but already a man of the past.

Isaacson's measured biography of Kissinger will be the standard work on his subject until scholars get access to all of Kissinger's papers and the complete records of the Nixon Administration. Although Isaacson admires Kissinger's great abilities, he deplores his willingness to join with Nixon in circumventing traditional governmental practice and even the will of the people. Had Kissinger been willing to follow a more open and democratic course, Isaacson believes his successes might have been less spectacular but more enduring.

*Daniel P. Murphy*

### Sources for Further Study

*The Christian Science Monitor.* September 21, 1992, p. 13.
*European Economic Review.* XXXVI, May, 1992, p. 143.
*Los Angeles Times Book Review.* October 4, 1992, p. 1.
*The Nation.* CCLV, November 16, 1992, p. 584.
*The New Republic.* CCVII, November 16, 1992, pp. 32.
*The New York Times Book Review.* XCVII, September 6, 1992, p. 1.
*The Times Literary Supplement.* October 9, 1992, p. 4.
*The Washington Post Book World.* XXII, September 6, 1992, p. 1.

# A LANDING ON THE SUN

*Author:* Michael Frayn (1933-    )
*Publisher:* Viking (New York). 249 pp. $21.00
*Type of work:* Novel
*Time:* The 1970's and 1980's
*Locale:* London, England

*A novel describing the investigation by a young British civil servant of the mysterious death-by-falling of another government employee fifteen years earlier*

> *Principal characters:*
> BRIAN JESSEL, the civil servant charged with investigating the death-by-falling of Stephen Summerchild
> STEPHEN SUMMERCHILD, the government employee whose death was under investigation
> ELIZABETH SERAFIN, a philosophy professor who had a love affair with Summerchild

Michael Frayn was born on September 8, 1933, in London, England. He attended Kingston Grammar School until 1952. In 1952, he was conscripted into the Royal Army and sent to a Russian interpretership course at the University of Cambridge. He also studied in Moscow for several weeks. He was subsequently commissioned as an officer in the Intelligence Corps. His second novel, *The Russian Interpreter* (1966), was influenced by his experiences during this time. The familiarity of Frayn with Russia and the Russian language and people might have been a factor in his having Elizabeth Serafin, the heroine of *A Landing on the Sun*, come from Russia.

Discharged from the army in 1954, Frayn returned to Cambridge to study philosophy at Emmanuel College. The philosopher who dominated the way philosophy was taught at Cambridge was Ludwig Wittgenstein, a person having the greatest influence on Frayn and everything Frayn wrote. The work of this philosopher dealt with the nature and limits of language as a means of interpersonal communication and as a means of representing reality. The subject of the Frayn's writing is often the way people impose their own ideas on the world around them. His characters generally see what they want to see or imagine they see rather than what actually exists.

While at Cambridge, Frayn wrote humorous articles for the school newspaper. After graduation from Cambridge in 1957, Frayn worked for *The Manchester Guardian*, as a reporter from 1957 to 1959 and as a columnist from 1959 to 1962. His columns of social satire became very popular. He was a columnist for *The Observer* from 1962 to 1968. The articles written for these newspapers are collected in his books *The Day of the Dog* (1962), *The Book of Fub* (1963), *On the Outskirts* (1964), and *At Bay in Gear Street* (1967). In his newspaper columns, Frayn poked fun at human foibles, middle-class conventions, liberal-minded hypocrisy, class snobbery, and the distortion of reality through advertising, public relations, the press, and television. The dislike Frayn has for public relations and advertising is evident in the way he makes subtle fun of well-known brand names in *A Landing on the Sun*, when Jessel discovers that some missing records had been stored in as unlikely a place as an empty Quaker Oats container. Frayn refers also to Heinz tomato ketchup and other popular products.

Frayn has published six novels as well as a number of translations, a volume of philosophy, and nine plays. In the 1960's, Frayn began to write novels showing the same concerns as his newspapers editorials. Frayn's characters are obsessed by order and control and are disturbed by confusion and change. They are embarrassed by any show of emotion. In the 1970's, Frayn began to write plays that also commented on social and political issues of the times. One of his funniest plays was the hit drama *Noises Off* (1982). *Noises Off* centers on a production by an inept theater company and shows Frayn's concern with illusion and reality, and with the relationship between language, reality, and personal perception. The antics of the company contribute to the overall pandemonium and chaotic humor of the play. Frayn's dramas are usually fast-paced and full of satire and outrageous situations.

Frayn turned his hand to novels because he wanted to enter more fully and sympathetically into characters. *A Landing on the Sun* was published in England in 1991 and in the United States in 1992. The main character of the novel is a British civil servant named Brian Jessel who was called upon by his superiors to investigate the death fifteen years earlier of another civil servant, Stephen Summerchild. Summerchild had fallen to his death from a British government building. His death is somewhat mysterious, since it is unclear whether Summerchild committed suicide by jumping or had been pushed from the building. The mystery is further complicated by rumors of espionage and traded state secrets. A television news crew had become once again interested in the mystery, and it was feared that some secrets would be uncovered that would prove embarrassing to officials of the British government.

Frayn's satiric attitude toward the British civil service is evident in his portrayal of Brian Jessel. Young Jessel was content with his boring civil service job because it gave him an escape from the problems of the real world. Although he refused to admit it, his life was empty and his job was as meaningless and depressing as the job of Bartleby the Scrivener, in the Herman Melville short story. Jessel liked the office in which he worked because there was nothing personal about the place. He even hoped that he looked like a government building himself. He saw himself as having a quiet façade, with a touch of distinction. In his job, he dealt with such unexciting subjects as the Annual Assessment of Departmental Efficiency and the Treasury Overview Meeting. When he received his new assignment of investigating the death of Stephen Summerchild, he was unhappy at the prospect of his involvement in problems of the outside world, a world "of muddle and incoherence, . . . of unidentified feelings, of unresolved questions." As Jessel reluctantly continues his investigation of Summerchild's apparent suicide, he (and the reader) become more and more intrigued with the events. Jessel sees similarities between his own situation and that of Summerchild. As was Summerchild, Jessel is unhappily married and leads a lonely life. Lynn, Jessel's wife, is confined to a mental institution. The wife of Summerchild is described by Jessel as "unknowable," "self-contained," "precise," "guarded," and "watchful."

Jessel began his investigation of the Summerchild death in the slow, careful, deliberate manner typical of a civil servant. He combined all the sorts of information he could find, everything from old files, memos, photographs, tape recordings, and records of all sorts on file in the ministry office to material he found in an old, empty biscuit tin in a garret. All the information he found, however, made him and his superiors often come to the wrong conclusions. On the basis of what Jessel found, Summerchild seemed to be involved in a project with a Dr. Serafin, a philosophy professor originally from Russia. The Russian ancestry of the professor led British government officials to fear that espionage might be involved.

As the novel unfolds, just as the narrator Jessel begins to discover more about Summerchild, so does the reader learn new facts about Jessel himself. Past and present begin to blend; Jessel's regular civil service job and his new investigation, his relationship with his wife and with Summerchild's daughter are considered in view of the relationship between Summerchild and Serafin.

Summerchild's work on the Strategy Unit involved researching the philosophical question of "the quality of life." The partner of Summerchild in this research, Professor Elizabeth Serafin, turned the research into an investigation of happiness, love, and the meaning of life. Both Serafin and Summerchild had unhappy home lives and, partly because of this unhappiness, their working together led to an intimate, passionate love relationship. Jessel discovers his own desires through the story of Serafin and Summerchild. The passionate love he hears through the tapes brings him back to thoughts of his feelings for Millie, Summerchild's daughter, and his relationship with Millie that ended shortly before the apparent suicide of her father.

The narrator Jessel becomes emotionally involved in the poignant relationship between Serafin and Summerchild and begins to lose some of his own stodgy ways. The more Jessel investigates the Summerchild case, the more similarities he finds between himself and Stephen Summerchild. Jessel now realizes that he is about the age of Summerchild when Summerchild died. Both men originally had led boring, uneventful, passionless lives. In the course of his investigating the relationship of Serafin and Summerchild, Jessel begins to acknowledge and regret his own lonely solitary life, a regret shown by his involuntary sighs. Early in the novel, Jessel sighs and then, at the very end of the novel, Jessel sighs again. His sighs indicate that his life has not changed for the better. He envies Summerchild for the brief time of happiness Summerchild and Serafin were able to experience. Even though Jessel's life stays basically the same, he at least has begun to reassess and reevaluate his own emotionally starved existence.

The sympathy of Jessel for Summerchild and Serafin, a pair whose unrequited love and abortive love affair turns them into a middle-aged Romeo and Juliet, leads the investigator to hide the information that he has discovered. The report Jessel files states that the death of Summerchild was not a suicide but rather "a simple accident in the course of a rather foolish feat of bravado." The investigator suggests that the files on the Summerchild case should now be destroyed.

As readers finish this enjoyable and poignant novel by Michael Frayn, they will see in it similarities to other works that Frayn has written previously. Frayn's philosophical preoccupation with the subjectivity of truth, the contrast between objective and subjective truth, is found in *A Landing on the Sun* as well as in other works by the author. Hilarious elements result from the inability of Jessel to see what is occurring when he listens to the tapes. Jessel (and the reader) misinterpret at first what is happening when the lovers are finally alone together in their "love nest" high in a garret in a British ministry building. The sounds can all be misunderstood, until the unenlightened reader and investigator learn the reasons for the sounds—the efforts of Serafin and Summerchild to open an old, unused skylight. To get finally to a new world of love in a British ministry building in downtown London, the lovers open this skylight, place an air mattress on the rooftop close to the sun (a location particularly suitable for a "summer child"), and have as much privacy as would have been found in a retreat in the Swiss Alps.

Frayn spoofs academic discourse in this novel, as Professor Serafin changes the charge assigned to the Strategy Unit researching "the quality of life" into a philosophical investigation of love and the meaning of happiness. He spoofs the British civil service, with its bureaucracy, repetitiousness, and boring unnecessary projects. He does not use only satire. The reader also sees the sympathy of the author for lonely people trying to find objects for their affection, people who need love and are willing to love in return.

Frayn builds up to the rapid and surprising conclusion of the novel by creating the atmosphere of downtown London with locations ranging from the Parade to Scotland Yard to the government buildings at Whitehall. The further irony of the situation is that the garret that contains the Summerchild-Serafin love nest looks down on the garden in back of Number Ten Downing Street. The couple are embarrassed when their hideaway is discovered and locked and closed to them. The lovers can no longer meet, and the death of Summerchild occurs soon after.

This amusing but sad novel is an award-winning masterpiece. Frayn deserved to win the Sunday Express Book of the Year Award for *A Landing on the Sun*.

*Linda Silverstein Gordon*

## Sources for Further Study

*Chicago Tribune*. February 2, 1992, XIV, p. 6.
*London Review of Books*. XIII, September 12, 1991, p. 15.
*Los Angeles Times Book Review*. February 16, 1992, p. 3.
*New Statesman and Society*. IV, September 13, 1991, p. 39.
*The New York Review of Books*. XXXIX, May 14, 1992, p. 41.
*The New York Times Book Review*. XCVII, February 16, 1992, p. 10.
*The Times Literary Supplement*. September 13, 1991, p. 21.
*The Wall Street Journal*. January 20, 1992, p. A12.
*The Washington Post Book World*. XXII, February 2, 1992, p. 1.

# LEMPRIÈRE'S DICTIONARY

*Author:* Lawrence Norfolk (1963-    )
*First published:* 1991, in Great Britain
*Publisher:* Harmony Books (New York). 422 pp. $22.00
*Type of work:* Novel
*Time:* The seventeenth and eighteenth centuries
*Locale:* England and France

*An innovative and experimental novel that loosely brings together history, myth, and social observations of eighteenth century London*

*Principal characters:*
> JOHN LEMPRIÈRE, the hero, who is engaged on a quest dealing with the East India Company while searching for his true love
> JULIETTE CASTERLEIGH, the young girl loved by John Lemprière; the true identity of her father is one of the central mysteries of the book
> JACQUES, a member of the East India Company cabala
> CAPTAIN GUARDIAN, a merchant sea captain who befriends John Lemprière and aids his quest
> SEPTIMUS, the friend of John Lemprière who also has ties to the East India Company
> LORD CASTERLEIGH, the supposed father of Juliette and a member of the East India Company cabala

*Lemprière's Dictionary* is an unusual novel; it is an intellectual tour de force that uses the styles and structures of a number of different narrative types. There is, for example, the quest plot which is an intellectual mystery in the manner of Umberto Eco; there is the Dickensian style (and world) of many of the middle sections of the novel; there are the interrelationships between classical myth and modern life; there is a pirate chase; and, finally, there is a love story. The central element of this farrago is the quest of the main character, John Lemprière, for the documents and information that will make clear the nature of his father's death and redeem his life. That quest involves a search into the history of the East India Company and into the bowels of its mysterious and expansive archive. Norfolk intertwines this and other plot strands with a good deal of success, in a mixture of styles that are, on the whole, rather overwrought. Furthermore, there is often no clear demarcation between one plot strand and another, as the narrative quickly shifts from one to another, straining point of view and structure. The overall effect is like that of reading Charles Dickens with a lens provided by Thomas Pynchon.

The novel begins with the early life of John Lemprière on the island of Jersey. Norfolk emphasizes his prodigious classical learning and his love for Juliette, the apparent daughter of Lord Casterleigh, a part owner of the East India Company. John sorts out Lord Casterleigh's library and is given an edition of Ovid's *Metamorphoses* with a striking plate representing Diana and Acteon. At the close of this section, the classical myth comes to life as John's father, Charles Lemprière, is torn apart by Lord

Casterleigh's hounds after viewing his Diana, Juliette, bathing naked in a stream. The conversion of classical myths to real events continues to follow John Lemprière. There is, for example, an evocation of the Danaë myth when John discovers a woman who literally is filled by a shower of gold, a mineral that takes her life. These recurrences make him doubt his sanity. Later it is revealed that this was another plot by the East India Company.

John then goes to London to seek information about his father's role in the East India Company. This section imitates Dickens' *Great Expectations* (1860-1861), as the young man comes to London in search of his fortune, finds a friend, Septimus, and participates in London life. There is, for example, an extended description of a hilarious dinner at the "Pork Club," complete with games and the gorging of pork. In addition to these Dickensian events, John discovers a document that suggests that he is the owner of one-ninth of the fabled East India Company.

Septimus appears to be a friend and guide to John but, like many others, he is in the pay of the East India Company. Despite this apparent betrayal, Septimus does help John in a number of ways, and he is the one who will reveal the true parentage of Juliette Casterleigh at the end of the novel.

While searching for more evidence to support his claim, John discovers a worthwhile activity, writing a dictionary of classical mythology. This is one of the more amusing allusions of the book, since there was a historical John Lemprière and he did write a book on classical mythology. John labors on his dictionary as Samuel Johnson labored on his, and readers follow him through the alphabet, mastering entry after entry. Norfolk includes a number of entries from the real John Lemprière's work, completing this curious interaction of texts.

During this scholarly work, John finds out more about the East India Company. The company originally had a charter from the English monarch, but early reverses forced it to seek financial help from a group of French traders from the city of La Rochelle. John consults Lady de Vere about the history of the company and his right to a part of the profits. Her father, the fourth Earl of de Vere, was an original shareholder of the company, but when he fell into financial difficulties, he asked François Lemprière to aid him. François did so and thereby became entitled to one-ninth of the company's profits. Currently, the company is ruled by a cabala of nine men who are plotting to aid the revolution that is coming in France. Most members of the group have their origins in La Rochelle, on the east coast of France. They were Huguenots and were caught in the persecution and siege of the city by Louis XIV and Cardinal de Richelieu. They escaped the mass slaughter or suicide of the city's inhabitants, but the seeds of the conflict between the group and the Lemprières were sown. While François Lemprière was in London urging the ministry to rescue La Rochelle, his wife and children were killed in the mass suicide by the people. There was little hope for them, and death was preferred to subjugation under the hated French government of Richelieu. The cabala of the East India Company now plans to destroy that royal government and reestablish itself in its native land.

One of the more interesting strands of the plot, the incest barrier, now appears. It appears that Charles Lemprière—not Lord Casterleigh—was the father of Juliette and that therefore John and she are brother and sister. The answers reside in a mysterious figure called Jacques, who is a friend of Charles Lemprière and a member of the cabala. On a trip to Paris, an exhausted and drunk Charles apparently slept with one of the women in a bawdy house; the current Juliette might be the result of that encounter. The question of her paternity is not resolved until the very end of the novel.

An amusing character and plot strand is found in the section dealing with John Fielding, a magistrate. He is the brother of the famous eighteenth century novelist and author of *Tom Jones* (1749), Henry Fielding. John Fielding watches the social disruption in London. Signs on the walls suggest an uprising by "Farina," who will lead the mob in a revolution similar to the French Revolution of 1798. The plot is frustrated and Fielding becomes a benign redeemer of John Lemprière and others.

There is a mysterious Indian assassin who runs through the plot. Nazim has been sent to London by the Nawab of Carnetic, who has been having difficulties with the East India Company. Nazim intends to avenge the murder of his uncle, who had been sent some years before to deal with problems associated with the East India Company. Nazim follows John Lemprière, since he knows that one of the Lemprières is an owner of the East India company. He threatens John but never harms him. At the end of the novel, Nazim kills an assassin hired by the East India Company and perishes himself.

John Lemprière does have some allies in his quest. One of the more interesting ones is Captain Guardian, who lives in a house near the docks. The captain notices a ship called the *Vendragon* that is fully loaded but remains at a berth. This is the ship that is to carry gold to the French insurgents to begin the French Revolution. The captain watches the ship for John Lemprière and informs him of the loading of this mysterious craft. The captain is an amusing Dickensian type, and his normality in the midst of so much strangeness is welcome.

The climax of the novel, an unusually extended one, begins as John Lemprière penetrates the archive of the East India Company. He is in search of documents that will justify his claim to a share of the company and redeem his father's death and unfinished quest. He finds the necessary documents, clarifying the secrets of the company and its relationship with the earlier Lemprières.

The central scene is when John appears before the cabala and is invited to join it in a restored position in France. As it turns out, the cabala has been guiding and aiding his progress all through the novel. John never makes a response. Suddenly, one of the group attempts to kill Jacques. The meeting, however, continues, and John is asked to light a candle as a sign of his acceptance. Instead, after some body language by Juliette, he blows out the cabal's candles, and a chase ensues.

The chase includes the collapse of secret tunnels of the company as the Thames River begins to leak in. John and Juliette flee, followed by Casterleigh and Jacques. As the river inundates the tunnels, a pirate ship, *The Heart of Light*, is brought into the whirlpool and joins the fleeing leaders of the East India Company. John and Juliette manage to escape, but Casterleigh is killed. John and Juliette refuse to aid him despite his pleas, and he, along with many of the others, drowns. A mystery, however, remains.

Is he Juliette's father? Is Charles Lemprière? Or Jacques?

The book ends with the reunion and restored love of John and Juliette. Septimus, the apparent betrayer of John, is the agency of redemption as he reveals Juliette's true parentage. Many of the plot strands are left dangling, and this lone resolution is unsatisfactory. For example, the gold does reach the French and, of course, the revolution begins. The leaders of the cabala, including Jacques, all perish. Norfolk, however, does not say much about the future of the East India Company. Presumably, its power is destroyed with the death of the members of the cabala, but the institution loomed so large that more needs to be said about its fate, especially since there was a historical East India Company during the period and beyond.

*Lemprière's Dictionary* is fascinating in its density and its mixing of diverse elements. It can be confusing and it is not easy reading, but it is an ambitious and challenging novel that often succeeds. The central tale of John Lemprière's search for answers within the East India Company is wonderfully done, as is the section with John coming to London.

The final impression, after reading the novel, is of a journey through a dozen or more earlier literary texts. This intertextuality may appeal to those who are quite familiar with English literature, but it may frustrate some less learned readers.

*James Sullivan*

## Sources for Further Study

*Chicago Tribune.* November 1, 1992, XIV, p. 5.
*Contemporary Review.* CCLIX, October, 1991, p. 213.
*Kirkus Reviews.* LX, June 15, 1992, p. 743.
*Library Journal.* CXVII, June 15, 1992, p. 103.
*London Review of Books.* XIII, August 29, 1991, p. 18.
*Los Angeles Times Book Review.* October 4, 1992, p. 11.
*The New York Times Book Review.* XCVII, December 20, 1992, p. 6.
*Publishers Weekly.* CCXXXIX, August 3, 1992, p. 62.
*The Times Literary Supplement.* August 23, 1991, p. 21.
*The Washington Post Book World.* XXII, September 20, 1992, p. 1.

# LET THE DEAD BURY THEIR DEAD

*Author:* Randall Kenan (1963-    )
*Publisher:* Harcourt Brace Jovanovich (New York). 334 pp. $19.95
*Type of work:* Short stories
*Time:* Primarily the twentieth century
*Locale:* Tims Creek, North Carolina

*A series of twelve linked short stories explores the history and folklore of Tims Creek, a fictional town in rural North Carolina*

In *Let the Dead Bury Their Dead*, Randall Kenan returns to Tims Creek, North Carolina, the imaginary small, mostly poor, and mostly black town he first visited in his novel *A Visitation of Spirits* (1989). The new stories explore the sometimes disturbing and sometimes enchanting strangeness of life, even life that appears ordinary. The stories in this collection are thoughtful and passionate, and the collection as a whole is fiercely successful.

Kenan is an explicitly intellectual and at times self-consciously literary writer. Such trademarks do not always enhance good storytelling, but in Kenan's stories they do. His short stories embed themselves knowingly and successfully in a number of crisscrossing literary traditions. In a quote on the back dust jacket, novelist Terry McMillan identifies Kenan as "our 'black' Márquez." Even a cursory glance at Kenan's stories—of the folk history of a town, of the workings of strange, sometimes fabulous forces within people's lives, and of the extraordinary passions of ordinary people—reveals Kenan's similarity to Gabriel García Márquez, as well as to Toni Morrison and Charles Johnson, African American writers who also have been compared to Márquez. Similarly, the loosely linked short stories that tell of the unspoken passions of people in a small town may remind readers of Sherwood Anderson's *Winesburg, Ohio: A Group of Tales of Ohio Small Town Life* (1919), part one of Jean Toomer's *Cane* (1923) (though Kenan's stories are much fuller), or Sarah Orne Jewett's *The Country of the Pointed Firs* (1896). With his focus on the bizarre in a small southern town, comparisons of Kenan to Flannery O'Connor and William Faulkner are almost inevitable.

All of this may seem to be cumbersome baggage to bring to the writing of short stories. Kenan, however, can handle his art with ease and aplomb, as he demonstrates clearly in the first short story in the collection, "Clarence and the Dead." In this story, the narrator, speaking as the first-person plural voice of the town's memory, tells the story of Clarence Pickett, who at three years of age began to pass on advice from dead members of the town to living members, usually concerning people and details the young boy could have no way of knowing. The first paragraph of the story tells us that Wilma Jones's hog, Francis, began to talk (according to his owner) at about the same time Clarence was born and stopped talking at about the same time Clarence died at the age of five. The rest of the story dips into the well of the town's collective memory to recall things Clarence said and what people said about Clarence to one another, but especially about the "unnatural" attachment Ellsworth Bates began to have toward Clarence when Clarence started relaying messages from Ellsworth's dead wife, Mildred. Kenan is careful to use statements such as "folks said at the time" to suggest the possibility that this story has grown over the years since Clarence's death, even while making it clear that the narrator believes that he knows the unvarnished truth. Thus, this story introduces two of Kenan's favorite topics in this collection: illicit desire, especially homosexuality between men, and the histories, both personal and public, that grow around the unexplained, especially around unexplained desires. More important, it does so with a charm and a clarity of voice that make it irresistible.

Not all the stories in *Let the Dead Bury Their Dead* succeed quite so remarkably as "Clarence and the Dead," but each has its own highlights. "Things of This World; or Angels Unawares" continues the supernatural motif of the first story to tell of John Edgar Stokes's encounter with his *chi*—a term that African novelist Chinua Achebe defines in the novel *Things Fall Apart* (1958) as "a personal god," and which has some of the same connotations as "fate"—in the form of a Chinese-looking man named Chi who seems to have fallen out of the sky.

"The Foundations of the Earth," on the other hand, backs away from explicitly supernatural events to consider the result of a belief in a supernatural God on everyday life. Maggie Williams has invited Gabriel, the white, male lover of her dead grandson, Edward, to Tims Creek for a conciliatory visit. As she comes to terms with her dead grandson's homosexuality, she also rethinks her understanding of God's love for humankind, coming to the conclusion that it may be broader than she previously had thought. In this piece, Kenan lays aside some of the irresistible forward thrust that marks many of his stories to create a more contemplative mood. The story is most notable for its sharp characterizations of Maggie, Gabriel, and Edward.

"Cornsilk," "What Are Days?," and "Ragnarök! The Day the Gods Die" all focus on sexual relations that could be called socially scandalous. "Cornsilk" is written in a series of numbered epigrams that takes us inside the mind of Aaron Streeter. The fact that his father, the only doctor in Tims Creek, and his grandfather both were called Dr. Streeter may remind some readers of "Doctor Street" from Toni Morrison's *Song of Solomon* (1977), named after the only black doctor in town. The comparison is appropriate: like Macon "Milkman" Dead, the grandson of the doctor in that novel, Aaron Streeter had an incestuous affair, with his half-sister Jamonica, who was raised by their grandfather in Harlem. Also like Milkman Dead, he is a self-absorbed young man with much growing to do. "What Are Days?" tells the story of a middle-aged widow, Lena Walker, who has a brief, passionate affair with a teenager called "Shang" who suddenly disappears. The hangover from the affair forces her to encounter both her anger and her grief over her late husband. In an ending that is both touching and convincing, she accepts the fact that she is truly alone. "Ragnarök! The Day the Gods Die" takes readers inside the mind of the Reverend Barden, who is delivering a eulogy over the body of Louise Tate, a young woman with whom he had an adulterous affair. His own sermon sends his mind flying, as he retraces the course of his marriage to his wife Sarah, his affair with Louise, and the sense of heavenly grace he felt in Louise's presence. He wonders how a belief in God's grace could be so important to him without his being able to accept it as sufficient. "I was a fool who lived by grace and I abused grace, I used grace like a whore," he thinks as he preaches. "*Grace is sufficient. But why doesn't grace comfort me?*" This story is an intense study of a dilemma; although it is complete, its ending does not so much conclude as forecast the wrestling and hoping that the Reverend Barden will surely continue.

Kenan's writing style is marked by a fulsomeness of detail, which proves to be a surprisingly apt tool in some cases to convey a sense of emptiness in someone's life, particularly in the lives of some of his female characters. This is certainly true of "What Are Days?," in which adapting to loneliness is a key theme; it is also true of "The Strange and Tragic Ballad Of Mabel Pearsall," which takes readers into the tired and mixed-up world of Mabel Pearsall, a schoolteacher obsessed with the idea that her husband is having an affair with the mother of a child for whom she sometimes babysits. In the words of her principal, she has been "behaving so . . . so peculiar" that she is "beginning to frighten the children." Everything about Mabel Pearsall suggests a woman whose sense of equanimity is slowly, tiredly slipping away. Her thoughts come in fragments and one-word sentences; she scolds her daughter for not starting dinner, then wearily makes it herself rather than continue to confront her television-watching son and daughter. Her breakdown, when it comes, remains true to the overwhelming sense of loss and near despair that pervades this story.

"This Far" also tells the story of a tired person nearing an end who looks for renewal. In this case, the person is a fictionalized version of Booker T. Washington near the end of his life. The story tells of his visit to Tims Creek to see a woman, Tabitha McElwaine, on whom he had had a crush in college, and her brother, Elihu. Interspersed with quotes from Washington's speeches and writings, the story is told in the second person from the point of view of a man who knows he has done much damage over the years but believes he may have done more good than ill with his Tuskegee "Machine" and its shadow government. This visit to companions of his youth is a search for, among other things, their blessing. Instead of their blessing, however, he encounters once again the consequences of his own power and reach.

Two stories, "Run, Mourner, Run," and "Tell Me, Tell Me," deal with the moral laziness of white members of the community. "Run, Mourner, Run," returns to the theme of exploring the marginalization of male homosexuality, as it tells of Dean Williams, a white, gay man who is hired to seduce and help blackmail Ray Brown, the town's richest black man, who also is gay. Predictably, Dean falls in love with Ray. Nevertheless, when Ray is blackmailed, Dean holds on to the hope of reward to defray a sense of guilt, and the rest of the story focuses on the morally lazy Dean's struggle over responsibility for his actions. "Tell Me, Tell Me" deals with the haunting of Ida Perry by a young black boy her late husband killed years earlier. For years, Ida has lived with the knowledge that her husband, a judge, was a crude, brutal, murderous man, but has hidden that knowledge behind the material comfort of her home and her position in white society. Although Ida's complicitous guilt is presented clearly as her own, it also is representative of more than that, and the story is very much an allegory for the tolerance of racism by middle-class whites who, like Ida, should and do know better.

The longest, most ambitious story is the title piece, an intellectual, chimeric romp. Purportedly an oral history of Tims Creek by the Right Reverend James Malachi Greene, "edited" by Reginald Kain (who shares initials with Randall Kenan) and published in the year 2000, it tells the story of the founding of Tims Creek as a town named Tearshirt by an escaped slave named Pharaoh. Most of the story is told by Ezekial Thomas Cross, James Malachi Greene's great-uncle, with corrections and contradictions by Ezekial's wife, Ruth Davis Cross. A reader should not try to get all the details straight; it is not that kind of story. Complete with introductory quotes by Thomas Hobbes, Mikhail Bakhtin, and Zora Neale Hurston, it is a bravura performance in which characters met in earlier stories, such as Elihu McElwaine from "This Far" and Percy Terrell, the blackmailer behind Dean Williams' seduction of Ray Brown in "Run, Mourner, Run," make cameo appearances. At least one reading devoted especially to the footnotes probably will be required. A reader who speeds through these footnotes risks missing such delights as reference to a book of short stories by Randall Kenan himself (possibly the one that will follow *Let the Dead Bury Their Dead*) called *Go Curse Your God, Boy, and Die: Stories*, with a publication date listed as 1996. A later footnote hints that the story told by Ezekial Cross dips into a well of stories relating to Kenan's own family history.

The story also manages to serve as a sort of compression chamber, squeezing together elements of all of Kenan's favorite themes from his earlier stories. Homosexuality between men and the search for redemption are once again presented as linked forces, and the emptiness of heterosexual women's lives as they face the hypocrisy of the values they once accepted is again put on display. The supernatural is here, too, in the form of a mass rebellion by the dead, who take their revenge on the living. In the bickering between Ezekial and Ruth, it is Ruth who tells the more plausible tale, but it is Ezekial who ends the story. At the story's beginning, Hurston is quoted as saying, "Now you are going to hear lies above suspicion," and at the end, Ezekial, talking of his own tale, echoes her, saying, "All I know is what my granddaddy told me, and boy, that was like I told you, word for word, near bout. Near bout."

The title story of *Let the Dead Bury Their Dead* is more of a novella than a short story, deliberately eschewing, as it does, the seamless unity often associated with short stories. Instead, it achieves a sense of carefully stitched-together unity, helping to bind the collection of stories together as a whole. In some ways, it is a guide for reading the earlier stories. Stories, it seems to say, are fundamentally about rebirth and redemption; further, rebirth and redemption can be frightening, even horrifying, but can make for darned good stories. A reader of these dozen memorable and startlingly original tales cannot help but agree.

*Thomas J. Cassidy*

## Sources for Further Study

*Booklist.* LXXXVIII, March 15, 1992, p. 1336.
*Boston Globe.* April 17, 1992, p. 57.
*Chicago Tribune.* May 3, 1992, XIV, p. 6.
*Essence.* XXII, August, 1992, p. 44.
*Kirkus Reviews.* LX, January 15, 1992, p. 67.
*Library Journal.* CXVII, February 15, 1992, p. 199.
*The Nation.* CCLV, July 6, 1992, p. 28.
*The New York Times Book Review.* XCVII, June 14, 1992, p. 12.
*Publishers Weekly.* CCXXXIX, January 13, 1992, p. 45.
*The Washington Post Book World.* XXII, August 2, 1992, p. 1.

# THE LETTERS OF SAMUEL JOHNSON

*Author:* Samuel Johnson (1709-1784)
Edited, with an introduction, by Bruce Redford
*Publisher:* Princeton University Press (Princeton, New Jersey). Illustrated. 3 volumes. Volume
I: 1731-1772, 431 pp. $29.95; Volume II: 1773-1776, 385 pp. $29.95; Volume III: 1777-1781,
399 pp. $29.95
*Type of work:* Letters
*Time:* 1731-1781

*This new, definitive edition adds more than fifty letters or parts of letters to the Johnson canon
and corrects earlier misreadings; Redford's annotations, which incorporate the scholarship of
the forty years that have elapsed since R. W. Chapman's 1952 Oxford University Press edition,
make these volumes still more valuable to students of Johnson and his age*

> *Principal personages:*
> SAMUEL JOHNSON, a critic, lexicographer, biographer, poet, novelist, essay-
> ist, and man of letters
> JAMES BOSWELL, a Scottish lawyer, Johnson's biographer
> BENNET LANGTON, Johnson's friend
> LUCY PORTER, Johnson's stepdaughter
> FRANCES REYNOLDS, an artist, sister of painter Sir Joshua Reynolds
> JOHN TAYLOR, an Anglican divine deeply concerned with matters agricul-
> tural
> HESTER THRALE, one of Johnson's closest friends, wife of the rich brewer
> Henry Thrale

Thomas Mann defined an author as a person for whom writing is more difficult than
it is for other people. Despite his prodigious output, Samuel Johnson fits Mann's
description. On May 1, 1783, he remarked to James Boswell, "It has been said, there
is pleasure in writing. . . . I allow you may have pleasure from writing, after it is over,
if you have written well; but you don't go willingly to it again." He had expressed
similar sentiments in *Adventurer* 138: "Composition is, for the most part, an effort of
slow diligence and steady perseverance, to which the mind is dragged by necessity or
resolution, and from which the attention is every moment starting to more delightful
amusements." When Boswell pressed him on this point, expressing surprise that
Johnson did not enjoy writing, Johnson replied testily, "Sir, you *may* wonder."

Letters proved especially irksome for most of Johnson's life. If he had died in 1772,
the Hyde edition of his letters, projected to run to five volumes, would have been
complete in one. The goad of poverty that drove his pen until he received his pension
of £300 a year in 1763 provoked poems, essays, a dictionary, a play, a novel, and an
edition of Shakespeare (though published in 1765, it was at its appearance long
overdue), but no such stimulus, or indeed any other, prompted the converse of the pen.
As Johnson wrote to John Taylor on July 31, 1756, "I know not how it happens, but I
fancy that I write letters with more difficulty than some other people, who write
nothing but letters, . . . and indeed I never did exchange letters regularly but with dear

Miss Boothby." The regularity of even that correspondence is suspect, since only eight of Johnson's letters to her survive. Some seven years later, Johnson wrote to James Boswell, "I love to see my friends to hear from them to talk to them and to talk of them, but it is not without a considerable effort of resolution that I prevail upon myself to write. . . . Whether I shall easily arrive at an exact punctuality of correspondence I cannot tell." In the first decade of their acquaintance, Johnson did not. Although he would eventually write more than a hundred letters to his future biographer, only nine are dated between 1763 and 1772.

Johnson's epistolary silence resulted from a combination of factors, of which his oft-confessed laziness was but one. Money-making projects necessary to his very survival demanded much of his time; ill health and depression drained his energy. His was not a life filled with incident; in his dictionary he defined a lexicographer (that is, himself) as "a harmless drudge." When Giuseppe Baretti accused Johnson "with parsimony of writing," Johnson reminded his Italian friend that "he who continues the same course of life in the same place, will have little to tell." Not least among the reasons for Johnson's reluctance to write was his fear of failure and consequent pursuit of perfection. His *Rambler* 152 surveys the requirements of the successful letter, and he concludes that while apparent artlessness, simplicity, and ease are required, "the pebble must be polished with care, which hopes to be valued as a diamond, and words ought surely to be laboured when they are intended to stand for things."

Johnson wanted to please his correspondents; his own early doubts about his ability to do so explain to some extent the existence of fewer than fifty letters between 1731, the date of the first extant, and 1752. His correspondents may not have saved all that he wrote during this period, since he was then a Grub Street hack, not the Great Cham of literature, but Redford believes "that the distribution of the recovered letters reflects in its general shape the number of letters Johnson actually wrote." Johnson's natural propensity to procrastination was also encouraged by his knowledge that personal letters in the eighteenth century often became public. Under the date of May 8, 1781, Boswell records in his *Life of Samuel Johnson* (1791), "We talked of Letter-writing." Johnson commented, "It is now become so much the fashion to publish letters, that in order to avoid it, I put as little into mine as I can." Boswell replied, "Do what you will, Sir, you cannot avoid it."

Boswell was right. He had already angered his friend by publishing one of his letters in 1768, and by 1781 he probably knew that he intended to include hundreds in his biography. Despite his disclaimer, Johnson was not indifferent to the fate of his correspondence. He urged Hester Thrale to save his letters, and he discussed their publication with her. Arthur Murphy thus erred when he commented in his review of Hester Thrale's *Letters to and from Samuel Johnson* (1788) that "We here see Dr. Johnson, as it were, behind the curtains, and not preparing to figure on the stage; retired from the eye of the world, and not knowing that what he was then doing would ever be brought to light."

As the multiplicity of letters in the last decade of Johnson's life demonstrates, he finally reconciled himself to the form. Boswell, who had more than once felt slighted by his friend's epistolary taciturnity, recorded in his *Tour of the Hebrides* (1786) under the date August 25, 1773, "Dr. Johnson wrote a long letter to Mrs. Thrale. I wondered to see him write so much so easily." On September 20, 1777, Johnson wrote to Hester Thrale that he regarded writing to her as a duty, but one that he diligently discharged. By the end of 1779, writing letters, at least to her, had become a pleasure: "I have nothing to tell you, yet I am eager to write because I am eager for your answer." This friendship with, indeed love for, Hester Thrale would inspire nearly a third of all his surviving letters; his attachment to Boswell in the 1770's and 1780's yielded a hundred more. Even old friends heard more frequently from him. Of the 102 letters to John Taylor, only 7 belong to the period before 1761; before 1770 Bennet Langton received 7 letters from Johnson, but in the 1770's he received 13, and another 11 between 1781 and Johnson's death in 1784.

As a group, Johnson's letters conform to the requirements that he laid down for good conversation: "There must, in the first place, be knowledge, there must be materials;—in the second place, there must be command of words;—in the third place, there must be imagination . . . ;—and in the fourth place, there must be presence of mind, and a resolution that is not to be overcome by failures." Many could stand by themselves as literary masterpieces. His response to Philip Dormer Stanhope, Fourth Earl of Chesterfield's praise in *The World* of Johnson's forthcoming dictionary reveals him at his most powerful and independent. Thomas Carlyle called the letter the death knell of patronage. "Is not a Patron, My Lord, one who looks with unconcern on a Man struggling for Life in the water and when he has reached ground encumbers him with help. The notice which you have been pleased to take of my Labours, had it been early, had it been kind; but it has been delayed till I am indifferent and cannot enjoy it, till I am solitary and cannot impart it, till I am known and do not want it." Chesterfield supposedly was so impressed with the dignity of the piece that he kept it in his front hall to show to visitors. Threatened by James Macpherson for challenging the authenticity of the Ossian poems (which were, as Johnson suspected, Macpherson's forgeries), Johnson wrote, "I received your foolish and impudent note. Whatever insult is offered me I will do my best to repel, and what I cannot do for myself the law will do for me. I will not desist from detecting what I think a cheat, from any fear of the menaces of a Ruffian." Even Hester Thrale felt the force of his indignation when he learned of her marriage to Gabriel Mario Piozzi; his letter of July 2, 1784, so offended her that she wrote back "to desire the conclusion of a Correspondence which I can bear to continue no longer."

Yet as Oliver Goldsmith observed, "Johnson, to be sure, has a roughness in his manner; but no man alive has a more tender heart. *He has nothing of the bear but his skin.*" Quickly repenting of his harsh letter to his longtime friend, Johnson wrote to her again in a gentler vein, "I wish that God may grant you every blessing, that you may be happy in this world for its short continuance, and eternally happy in a better state. and whatever I can contribute to your happiness, I am very ready to repay for that kindness which soothed twenty years of a life radically wretched."

This concern for making others easy pervades the letters. Johnson secured admission to the Charterhouse Hospital for the eighty-three-year-old Isaac De Groot, great-grandson of Hugo Grotius. He repeatedly sent barrels of oysters to his step-daughter, Lucy Porter. From Elizabeth Montagu he sought help for the bankrupt bookseller Tom Davies; for the impoverished artist Maritius Lowe he wrote to William Hunter to secure a medical consultation with William's brother John. In 1779, when war threatened the pension of some women living next door, he solicited funds from the Thrales, Sir Joshua Reynolds, and the printer William Strahan. Hester Thrale sent half a guinea; Johnson gave them two in the Thrales's name. He tried unsuccessfully to save the life of William Dodd, an Anglican divine who forged Lord Chesterfield's signature to a note for £4,200. He urged his Oxford friends to help Charles Burney with his research into the history of music and secured a publisher for Thomas Percy's *Reliques of Ancient English Poetry* (1765). Redford has found a dozen letters from Johnson to Charlotte Lennox that highlight his efforts on her behalf. This list of benefits conferred might be greatly extended.

Equally characteristic of Johnson is the fund of common sense in the letters. Many, especially the early ones, resemble essays in *The Rambler*, but they are no less valuable for their impersonal tone. In response to Baretti's question about marriage, Johnson soberly responded, "if all would happen that a lover fancies, I know not what other terrestrial happiness would deserve pursuit. But love and marriage are different states." As illness or death afflicted his friends, he urged them not to succumb to sorrow, to occupy their minds with other matters and so avoid despair. He also reminded them, in words similar to those he sent to Lucy Porter after her aunt's death, "All union with the inhabitants of earth must in time be broken; and all the hopes that terminate here, must on one part or other end in disappointment." He advised Boswell and Langton not to magnify their distresses or to create imaginary ones: "Let us endeavour to see things as they are, and then enquire whether we ought to complain." Langton thought enough of these observations, which Johnson sent to him on the death of Langton's uncle, that he passed them on to the man's widow.

The lessons of Johnson's *The Vanity of Human Wishes* (1749) repeatedly surface in the letters. "Fate wings with every wish the afflictive dart," Johnson declared in the poem. To Elizabeth Carter he expressed a similar sentiment seven years later: "To every Joy is appended a Sorrow." He wrote similarly to Hill Boothby: "Of the fallaciousness of hope, and the uncertainty of Schemes every day gives some new proof."

Despite its somber realism, *The Vanity of Human Wishes* concludes that people can make the happiness they do not find. As his college friend Oliver Edwards remarked, "I have tried too in my time to be a philosopher; but I don't know how, cheerfulness was always breaking in." The letters to Hester Thrale and her oldest daughter frequently contain humorous sallies, self-deprecation, and mock moralizing. In 1770, when the Thrales's house was burglarized, Johnson assured Hester that his gang of thieves was not responsible. John Taylor's fascination with his great bull provided repeated jokes in Johnson's letters to her. Describing a dinner with Mrs. Cholmondely, he reports that the lady called him the best of critics, and he in turn told her that she was the best judge of critics. He also joked with his Oxford friends. For instance, to Thomas Warton he wrote on June 21, 1757, "You might write to me now and then, if you were good for any thing. But honores mutant mores. Professors forget their friends."

For providing an accurate, well-annotated edition (to be completed in 1994), Redford deserves the thanks of all Johnsonians, as does Princeton University Press for its attractive printing and reasonable price. One wishes that Redford had followed Chapman's practice of numbering the letters, if only to allow easier comparisons between the editions. A more serious omission is the absence of Hester Thrale's letters to Johnson, which Chapman included. In fact, the inclusion of all the surviving letters to Johnson as well as from him would have enriched this edition. Yet considering all that Redford has accomplished in presenting Johnson in his own voice, any complaint must finally appear captious and should not detract from the praise he deserves for his substantial scholarly achievement.

*Joseph Rosenblum*

## Sources for Further Study

*Choice*. XXIX, July, 1992, p. 1677.
*The Christian Science Monitor*. April 1, 1992, p. 17.
*The Economist*. CCCXXIII, May 9, 1992, p. 112.
*Library Journal*. CXVI, November 1, 1991, p. 99.
*London Review of Books*. XIV, November 5, 1992, p. 10.
*The New Republic*. CCVII, November 2, 1992, p. 36.
*The Observer*. March 1, 1992, p. 62.
*The Spectator*. CCLXVIII, May 16, 1992, p. 30.
*The Times Literary Supplement*. May 15, 1992, p. 24.
*Washington Times*. February 16, 1992, p. B8.

# LETTERS TO SARTRE

*Author:* Simone de Beauvoir (1908-1986)
*First published: Lettres à Sartre,* 1990
Translated from the French and edited by Quintin Hoare
Preface by Sylvie Le Bon de Beauvoir
*Publisher:* Arcade Publishing (New York). 531 pp. $24.95
*Type of work:* Letters
*Time:* 1930-1963
*Locale:* France, the United States, Mexico, Italy, Algeria, Tunisia, and Spain

*These letters chronicle from 1930 to 1963 the private life of Simone de Beauvoir, centered around her lifelong relationship with Jean-Paul Sartre, whom she met in 1929*

Simone de Beauvoir is one of France's most important female writers of the twentieth century. As a novelist, essayist in the realm of politics as well as philosophy, feminist, and social activist, she has come to represent the socially engaged woman who, with other French intellectuals such as Hélène Cixous and Julia Kristeva, succeeded in penetrating the male-dominated intelligentsia of France. That this was achieved is testimony to her intellectual acumen, perseverance, and strong commitment not just to feminist activity but, generally speaking, to the pursuit of her own ideals. Simone de Beauvoir, the longtime companion of the writer, philosopher, and social activist Jean-Paul Sartre (1905-1980), lived, some might argue, in his shadow. Although not possessing as powerful a literary talent as he, nor as inventive a mind, she did make an important contribution to the social fabric of modern-day France through her efforts on behalf of women, the elderly, and underprivileged social groups. Her writings, especially *Pour une morale de l'ambiguïté* (1947; *The Ethics of Ambiguity,* 1948), *Le Deuxième sexe* (1949; *The Second Sex,* 1953), and *Les Mandarins* (1954; *The Mandarins,* 1956), for which she was awarded the prestigious Prix Goncourt, reveal her to be a sensitive and prolific commentator on topics such as relationships between men and women, the Algerian question, French colonialism, and women's issues.

Beauvoir first met Sartre in Paris in the summer of 1929. At that time, both were preparing at the Ecole Normale Supériere and the Sorbonne for the very arduous exams for the *agrégation* in philosophy, which, when successfully passed the same year, saw Sartre classed first and Beauvoir second. After that summer, Sartre and Beauvoir developed a relationship that is both admirable and perplexing, including what some would see as infidelities as well as unshakable commitment to each other, to shared social values, and to what has been described as a morganatic union. Sartre referred to Beauvoir as *le Castor* (the Beaver), a nickname given to Beauvoir by a school friend, René Maheu (who appears in *Letters to Sartre* as "the Llama"), because of the phonetic similarity between "beaver" and "Beauvoir," and especially since both are constructive and enjoy the company of others. In 1983, when Beauvoir published the letters Sartre had written to her in *Lettres au Castor,* many hoped that Beauvoir would publish those she had written to him in order to complete the mosaic of their life, but Beauvoir believed them to have been destroyed, and moreover, even if they still existed, that they should not be published during her lifetime. Months after the death of Beauvoir in April, 1986, a voluminous collection of this correspondence, spanning three decades from 1930 to 1963, was found by Beauvoir's adopted and only child, Sylvie Le Bon de Beauvoir. She painstakingly deciphered often almost illegible handwriting, criticized even by Sartre in his letters to the Beaver, and made almost no cuts from the mass of letters. The original work, *Lettres à Sartre*, was published in two volumes in 1990. The translated version contains approximately two-thirds of the original edition, shortened by translator Quintin Hoare by cutting out letters that overlapped with material previously published in Beauvoir's autobiographical works.

Any translation of these letters is problematic for various reasons. First, the use of the formal *vous* throughout the letters would seem perhaps inappropriate as the mode of communication for the lovers, who used it not only in written form but also in speech. Although somewhat idiosyncratic, this form of address is not untypical of a couple of their generation. Second, Beauvoir's incessant usage of the adjective *petit* (little), while a very common element in many colloquial expressions in French, is most noticeable when referring to Sartre as her "dear little being" or her "dear little husband." *Letters to Sartre* are, fundamentally, love letters written to a man to whom Beauvoir was not wed, but who was an unwavering source of inspiration and profound love, a confidant but, in some ways, also a rival.

*Letters to Sartre* is divided into six periods: January, 1930, to July, 1939, "Before the War"; September, 1939, to March, 1940, "The Phoney War"; July, 1940, to March, 1941, "Sartre Prisoner"; July, 1943, to February, 1946, "Before Liberation and After"; January, 1947, to October, 1951, "America"; and June, 1953, to July, 1963, "Later Interludes." What is most striking at first glance is the intimate tone with which Beauvoir wrote Sartre, her attention to the minutest details concerning her daily life, from the meals she consumed to her maladies and financial situation. These elements remain constant throughout her correspondence. What is perhaps surprising to some readers is the nature of these letters, for they are not philosophical in orientation, nor sociological. They do not discuss in the abstract, but, rather, chronicle the activities of the couple's many friends as well as Beauvoir's travels within France and to the United States, Mexico, Tunisia, and Algeria. They are, quite simply, written communications between a woman and her lover during absences from each other, the most poignant of which is clearly Sartre's internment as a prisoner of war from June, 1940, to March, 1941.

The initial period of written communication between Beauvoir and Sartre (January, 1930, to July, 1939) reveals that, despite having known Sartre for only a few months, she already had developed an unparalleled passion for him, as she states in the closing of the work's first letter, dated January 6, 1930: "How are you, little man? I'm really longing for a letter from you tomorrow. We'll be seeing each other soon, won't we, my love? You promised, so I'm taking good care of myself. I love you, I love you. I am, most tenderly, your own Beaver."

Beauvoir wrote daily to Sartre during their separations. An intriguing aspect of the entire correspondence, first evident in this early period, is the sometimes surreptitious nature of their relationship, maintained that way in order not to offend their other lovers, many of whom knew each other. The frankness with which Beauvoir requests Sartre to participate in this sort of deception, from the beginning months of their relationship, is noteworthy given their philosophical quest for truth and justice. Moreover, that Beauvoir had sexual relations with Sartre's lovers, such as Bianca Bienenfeld, is perplexing, especially since these relations were discussed openly between Beauvoir and Sartre. It is precisely this sort of revelation that is one of the most unexpected, since it portrays Beauvoir as supremely manipulative. After reading countless directives to Sartre, such as: "I'm telling Kos. that I'll be staying at La Pouèze till Monday. No point in saying I'm at St Fargeau, etc. I won't come back on Friday, as I'm only leaving tomorrow. I'm telling Bienenfeld too that I'm at La Pouèze." One realizes Beauvoir's insecurities in her friendships. While wishing to cultivate friends, she seems also to have wanted to keep them at a distance when necessary, and such times inevitably were linked to her desire to spend time with Sartre. The complex web of names and alibis in *Letters to Sartre* reveals, ultimately, the capital importance Sartre held in Beauvoir's affective and intellectual life. Footnotes offer summary explanations of references to people, to literary works mentioned by Beauvoir, and to her plots to maintain friends in ignorance of some of her activities. The correspondence written in this section was composed in France, in the provinces as well as in Paris, in cafés, brasseries, and hotels. What is of note during this period is the worldly attitude that Beauvoir exhibits, traveling extensively in France and developing friendships among the Paris circle of young writers and intellectuals such as the novelist Paul Nizan and the actor and producer Charles Dullin.

The second period of the letters, from September, 1939, to March, 1940, represents approximately one-half of the entire work. One of the more fascinating letters of this period, dated September 17, 1939, the day of the Soviet invasion of Poland, was written from Crécy-en-Brie while Beauvoir was visiting the actress and playwright Simone Jollivet (Camille in Beauvoir's autobiography), nicknamed Toulouse, and Charles Dullin, with whom she lived and worked. In this letter, Beauvoir speaks of Jollivet's eccentric mother, of Louis Jouvet, an important actor, of Jean Giraudoux, a novelist and playwright, and of the necessity of supporting the production of French film. Beauvoir also recounts stories told to her during that visit by Dullin, regaling Sartre with a spicy anecdote concerning André Gide and Henri Ghéon, author of religious dramas, both of whom had a predilection for young men. Beauvoir refers to books she is currently reading, from *The Hound of the Baskervilles* to *Taras Bulba*. Through all her writing, the strongest impression the reader receives is the tenderness with which Beauvoir cherishes the private moments shared with her lover, for example, in this letter.

The third section, from July, 1940, to March, 1941, contains correspondence written during Sartre's internment in France and Germany by the Germans. From the time Sartre was taken prisoner in mid-June, 1940, following the collapse of the French armies, Beauvoir received virtually no answers to her correspondence, written on official forms until December of 1940. It is unclear whether Sartre was unable to undertake correspondence or whether such letters might have gone astray. During this time, Beauvoir speaks to Sartre about changes to Paris since the occupation, of areas in the Latin Quarter they frequented together. On January 20, 1941, Beauvoir writes: "I have constant nightmares about you: you come back (since I think it's impossible directly to dream an absence), but you don't love me any more and I'm filled with despair. At times, not knowing when I'll see you again has me literally fighting for breath." The poignancy of these comments underlines Beauvoir's helplessness in knowing that she may never see her lover again, her vulnerability when absent from him.

In the fourth section, from July, 1943, to February, 1946, Beauvoir recounts to Sartre, who is visiting the United States, meetings and conversations with the Paris literary elite of the time: dinner with the novelist and philosopher Albert Camus, lunch with the philosopher Maurice Merleau-Ponty and with the eccentric playwright Jean Genet. These were exciting times for Beauvoir, who published *The Blood of Others* in 1945. It had been written between 1941 and 1943 and was set during the Resistance, but its publication had been delayed by wartime censorship. Invited by the Alliance française to lecture in Tunis and Algiers in 1946, Beauvoir writes of the great success enjoyed by her talks on existentialism, which had received sustained public attention after the publication of Sartre's *Being and Nothingness*, begun during his captivity and published in 1943.

Beauvoir's travels took her to the United States in 1947. There she met the American writer Nelson Algren, with whom she had a romantic liaison until 1951. The penultimate section of *Letters to Sartre*, from January, 1947, to October, 1951, contains remarks on people Beauvoir met during her American tour as well as direct comments regarding the nature of her relationship with Algren. This sort of frankness is characteristic of the Beauvoir/Sartre dialogue. Nothing was left unsaid or considered inappropriate.

The final period represented in the work, June, 1953, to July, 1963, has letters composed during trips to Italy, Algeria, Tunisia, and Spain, as well as within France. Beauvoir's love for Sartre has matured; its manifestations are assuredly less effusive. Since 1929, the dynamics of their relationship have stabilized, for the couple has over the past decades established a singular life, founded paradoxically on dependence and independence. At this stage in her life, Beauvoir was an accomplished writer, having been awarded in 1954 the Prix Goncourt for *The Mandarins*. This final section of her letters has the same focus as the preceding ones: observations made during trips, such as the objectionable patriarchal atmosphere in Algeria and comments on the political situation in France. One letter from 1958 exhorts Sartre to write an article in protest of the authoritarian tendencies in the new Gaullist administration. The latter is indicative of Beauvoir's continuing activity in the sociopolitical arena. For many people, this is the legacy left by Beauvoir.

*Letters to Sartre* offers an intimate portrait of Simone de Beauvoir, of her insecurities and of her strengths. Because of her social activism, Beauvoir clearly is considered to be one of France's most important contemporary authors. The physical portrait often seen in pictures—simply dressed, neatly coiffed, often in a turban—belies personal intricacies manifested in her relationships, manipulated to her best advantage. This characteristic would seem appropriate, however, to an individual whose self-absorption was extreme, and the focus of much of her writing. What is perhaps most intriguing in her letters is the nontraditional nature of her relationship with Sartre. His confidante and lover, Beauvoir was also a supporter whose passion for this man withstood all obstacles. *Letters to Sartre* presents one voice of this renowned couple and joins, fortunately, the private voice of Sartre made public in 1983 in his *Lettres au Castor*. The mosaic now complete, *Letters to Sartre* offers an in-depth personal portrait not only of Beauvoir but also of the literary and social elite of contemporary France.

*Kenneth Meadwell*

## Sources for Further Study

*Belles Lettres.* VIII, Fall, 1992, p. 44.
*Boston Globe.* February 28, 1992, p. 33.
*Chicago Tribune.* February 16, 1992, XIV, p. 3.
*The Christian Science Monitor.* April 1, 1992, p. 17.
*Kirkus Reviews.* LIX, December 15, 1991, p. 1563.
*Library Journal.* CXVII, February 15, 1992, p. 176.
*Los Angeles Times Book Review.* May 24, 1992, p. 2.
*New Statesman and Society.* IV, Decmeber 13, 1991, p. 38.
*The New York Times Book Review.* XCVII, July 19, 1992, p. 13.
*Publishers Weekly.* CCXXXIX, January 6, 1992, p. 60.

# LIBERALISM AND REPUBLICANISM IN THE HISTORICAL IMAGINATION

*Author:* Joyce Appleby (1929-    )
*Publisher:* Harvard University Press (Cambridge, Massachusetts). 342 pp. $39.95; paperback $17.95
*Type of work:* Intellectual history
*Time:* The seventeenth through early nineteenth century, and late twentieth century
*Locale:* England, colonial and early national America, and the United States after World War II

*A collection of essays examining the ways American historians and their subjects have used the constructs of "liberalism" and "republicanism" to make sense of the American national project*

Made up of an introduction and thirteen previously published essays, *Liberalism and Republicanism in the Historical Imagination* constitutes both an intellectual biography of the author, Joyce Appleby, and a coming to terms with the "republican" point of view—first identified by Robert E. Shalhope in "Toward a Republican Synthesis: The Emergence of an Understanding of Republicanism in American Historiography," *William and Mary Quarterly* 29 (1972)—that has dominated interpretations of the American Revolution since the late 1960's.

Framed first by Bernard Bailyn, this point of view challenged that of an earlier school of "consensus" historians—best represented by Louis Hartz's *The Liberal Tradition in America: An Interpretation of American Political Thought Since the Revolution* (1955)—that saw liberalism as the American national ideology by default; original, inevitable, and enduring. Younger scholars discovered that the ideological sponsors of the American Revolution were not John Locke and Adam Smith. Colonial resistance was indebted instead to the dissenting republicanism of radical Whigs in early eighteenth century England.

Redundancy is inevitable in such a collection, but it enriches rather than blurs Appleby's discussion. With one exception, all the essays fall squarely under the book's conceptual umbrella. Only "The American Model for the French Revolutionaries," published in 1971 and reprinted here as chapter 9, seems beside the point. The other essays address intersecting subsets of her extended family of themes.

Chapter 1, "Political and Economic Liberalism in Seventeenth-Century England," and chapter 2, "Locke, Liberalism, and the Natural Law of Money," supply essential historical background. These essays speak to Appleby's original scholarly stock-in-trade, the recovery of an early tradition of liberal thinking that emerged in the seventeenth century in response to the commercialization of the English economy. They reprise the arguments in her first book, *Economic Thought and Ideology in Seventeenth Century England* (1978).

Chapter 5, "Liberalism and the American Revolution," chapter 6, "The Social Origins of American Revolutionary Ideology," and chapter 7, "John Adams and the New Republican Synthesis," present an early critique of Bernard Bailyn's *The Ideological Origins of the American Revolution* (1967), Gordon Wood's *The Creation of the American Republic, 1776-1787* (1969), and J. G. A. Pocock's *The Machiavellian Moment: Florentine Political Thought and the Atlantic Republican Tradition* (1975), the canonical texts of the republican synthesis. The availability of a protocapitalist liberal alternative to republican discourse broadened the social basis of dissatisfaction in colonial America, Appleby argues, and hastened the movement from resistance to revolution.

Chapter 3, "Modernization Theory and Anglo-American Social Theories," chapter 4, "Ideology and the History of Political Thought," and chapter 11, "Republicanism and Ideology," raise important theoretical, methodological, and historiographical issues. Chapter 3 discusses the failings of modernization theory as applied to less developed societies and its obfuscation of differences in the early English and colonial responses to economic development—a blurring resulting from neglect of the intervening variable of ideology in shaping cultural reactions to change. Chapter 4 discusses, among other things, the priority of the "Cambridge school" of Quentin Skinner, J. G. A. Pocock, and others in using social linguistics to rethink intellectual history as "ideological history"; that is, the history of the socially constructed meaning systems that shape political discourse. By challenging the importance ascribed to John Locke in the eighteenth century in liberal historiography, their work opened space for a republican rereading of Anglo-American political thought. Chapter 11, discusses what that point of view has meant in practice to historians of early America.

"The American Heritage—The Heirs and the Disinherited," chapter 8, deals with the alternative visions of community debated in the late colonial and early national eras and implicit still in different schools of constitutional jurisprudence. Stimulated by discussions of the Supreme Court and the judicial philosophies of Court appointees in the Reagan era, this essay is Appleby's most topical and pointed contribution. By subverting the legitimacy of group-based interests, a liberal discourse on rights that serves to disaggregate communities can work, she suggests, to disadvantage further those who are already outside the political nation.

"The 'Agrarian Myth' in the Early Republic," "What Is Still American in Jefferson's Political Philosophy?," and "Republicanism in Old and New Contexts," chapters 10, 12, and 13, do two kinds of work at once. The essays discuss the colonization of the early nineteenth century through a hybrid ideology of liberal-republicanism—at the levels of lived history and historical interpretation alike—on one hand, and explore the contradictions of selfishness and civic-mindedness at the heart of the American self-image, on the other. Just as classical republicanism—positing the conflict between virtue and commerce—could not acknowledge the capitalist as citizen, liberalism—rationalizing a possessive individualism—subverted the concept of citizenship itself.

To a large extent, Appleby's position is the dialectical product of engagements with other scholars. Schematically, it incorporates substantive disagreements with J. G. A. Pocock and others of the Cambridge school over the genealogy of English liberalism as well as incorporating theoretical-methodological disagreements with scholars from both camps over how the concept of ideology should be understood and exploited in mapping public discourse.

The central contention of chapter 6, "The Social Origins of American Revolutionary Ideology," is that "liberal and classical republican thought presented ideological options to the Americans, [and that] it is important to examine them as intellectual responses to the modern restructuring of England and her North American colonies." To unpack this statement is to understand much of her argument.

Bailyn's work drastically reoriented scholarship on the colonial period by uncovering an unsuspected intellectual world. The pamphlet literature Bailyn examined revealed a conceptual universe—indebted to radical Whigs and English Commonwealthmen of the early eighteenth century—in which political discourse was tailored to classical republican models. Far from being forward-looking and pragmatic, this point of view stressed the dangers of historical change. Opposing the administrative initiatives of a "court" party charged with governing a growing empire, "country" writers in England stressed the aggressive nature of power, the incompatibility of liberty and centralized authority, the conflict between virtue and commerce, and the dependence of the state upon a constitutional order that balances the claims of all estates in the body politic. Colonial elites were constrained by their adopted republicanism to see Parliamentary reforms of the 1760's—which sought to rationalize the British empire, but instead triggered the American Revolution—as conspiratorial designs on their traditional liberties. Bailyn's student, Gordon Wood, made the intellectual indebtedness of the colonists clearer still by extending discussion of the American engagement with republicanism into the postrevolutionary era and the writing of the Constitution.

The other source of Bailyn's influence was his introduction of the concept of ideology to ground his argument. Informed by a sophisticated social psychology and an anthropological understanding of culture, the concept yielded to a more plausible model of human nature. Liberalism's fetishized and timeless strawman, the rational, autonomous, self-improving individual, gave way to a historically situated "social creature given to passion, responsive to symbols, animated by moral imperatives, and bonded to others by shared worldviews." Helping historians reconstruct the mental worlds of those they studied, the concept of ideology enabled them to avoid anachronism and to investigate the thinking of the revolutionary generation on its own terms. In explaining how ideology organized experience and shaped behavior, Bailyn could explain why administrative initiatives that were reasonable and overdue from an imperial point of view triggered such a disproportionate response in the American colonies.

Although acknowledging the merits of this analysis, Appleby chides Bailyn and Wood for minor sins of omission and commission. In the former instance, she suggests, they left unexamined the classical origins of the republicanism that shaped political consciousness in the Colonies. In the instance of sins committed, their reading of ideology as culturally exclusive led them to make two questionable assumptions. The first, she suggests, was that republicanism was the only political language available to the colonists. This assumption invited an obvious question. If republicanism so dominated colonial thinking at the time of the revolution, whence came the liberal-

ism—disguised as liberal-republicanism—that flowered so quickly after independence? The second assumption—implicit in their reading of ideology as culturally
coercive—was that what human beings are able to see and say is always overdeter-
mined, that ways of interpreting the world are received and imposed rather than
sometimes somehow—whether purposefully or serendipitously—invented.

The investigation of England's century of revolution by Quentin Skinner and others
raised questions about the origins of liberalism; questions, that is, about the circumstances, timing, and language of responses to economic change. This subject was
Appleby's original scholarly preoccupation. Unlike republicanism, she argues, liberal
social thought was not distilled from political practice or classical theories of government. Instead, it derived from writings on the free-market economy dating from the
early seventeenth century. To understand these writings as protopolitical is to recover
the revolutionary significance of liberalism: its substitution of the economy for the
state as a model of the polity, and its conceptualization of the market as a natural and
sufficient mechanism of social cohesion.

Summarizing her differences with Pocock in this connection, Appleby indicates that
exploring the ideological purport of Anglo-American reactions to economic development from within the republican framework alone overlooks earlier and more radical
intellectual responses to English capitalism. In chapter 2, for example, she argues that
John Locke's discussions of money "were not simply parts of a scientific analysis of
economics; they contained important ideological assertions about power, property, and
political norms." To assume that political discourse was conducted only in an obviously political language is to misrepresent the complexity of liberalism.

In "Ideology and the History of Political Thought," Appleby indicates that the
concept of ideology deployed by the Cambridge school is that of linguists, philosophers, and anthropologists. Explaining the social construction of reality as part of the
human quest for meaning, this concept of ideology has little to say about the interplay
of the intellectual and social contexts of public discourse. The assumption that a
particular worldview will monopolize cultural authority—an assumption derived from
the study of simpler societies—both minimizes the extent to which conflict rather than
consensus exists in pluralistic modern societies and obscures the need to account for
how particular ideologies come to be socially privileged.

Instead of reading ideologies in a deterministic culture-constituting way, Appleby
urges that they should be read as decentered and partisan constructions of reality. This
has important methodological consequences. The historian must account for the
circumstances, social and intellectual, that nourish alternative worldviews. Her own
argument is a case in point. As different responses to the modern restructuring of
England and her colonies, liberalism and classical republicanism were ideological
options, she suggests, for different groups of colonists with changing concerns at
different times in the movement from resistance to revolution.

The discovery of classical republican modes of thought in the Colonies, Appleby
concedes, has forever changed the understanding of early America, displacing liberal
shibboleths about a nation born free. Ironically, the ideological approach of the

republican school has at the same time inspired a closer look at the liberal dimension of American heritage. The liberalism in question is understood now to be a historically contingent intellectual artifact, not a cultural given.

The usefulness of Appleby's work derives from her multiply articulated point of view. She brings changing interpretations of the American Revolution and its aftermath, contested prescriptions for the practice of intellectual history, and differing assumptions about the relation of thought and action within a single frame of reference. In doing so, she shows how the history of political and social thought has been transformed by borrowings from neighboring social sciences. Reflecting a career-long interest in the many dimensions of her craft, this book consolidates her status as a penetrating critic of writings on the colonial and early national periods and an important historian of ideas in her own right.

*Paul Jefferson*

## Source for Further Study

*Choice.* XXX, October, 1992, p. 367.

# THE LIFE OF GEOFFREY CHAUCER
## A Critical Biography

*Author:* Derek Pearsall (1931-    )
*Publisher:* Basil Blackwell (Cambridge, Massachusetts). Illustrated. 365 pp. $29.95
*Type of work:* Literary biography
*Time:* Approximately 1340-1400
*Locale:* England, France, Italy, and Spain

*An account of the life of England's major medieval poet, Geoffrey Chaucer, setting him in political, literary, and cultural contexts*

> *Principal personages:*
> GEOFFREY CHAUCER, poet and official of the King of England
> RICHARD II, King of England from 1377 to 1399
> HENRY IV, Richard's deposer and successor
> JOHN OF GAUNT, Duke of Lancaster, Henry's father, Richard's uncle, Chaucer's brother-in-law

Geoffrey Chaucer is universally accepted as the major English poet of the Middle Ages, author of *The Canterbury Tales* (1387-1400), the long and ambitious romance *Troilus and Criseyde* (1382), and a string of other surviving works in verse and prose. His importance was recognized soon after his death, as is shown by the careful preservation of his works and the large number of manuscripts in which they survive. His collected works were first printed in 1539 and have remained available to readers ever since. For centuries he has been one of the most influential authors ever to have written in English.

Since the start of professional study of historical records in the nineteenth century, moreover, it has become clear that Chaucer is one of the best-documented of early writers. No less than 493 documentary records of Chaucer's life survive, a number far in excess of those relating to any of Chaucer's English poetic contemporaries (of whom frequently nothing at all is known), and considerably more than those surviving for many authors working centuries later in the age of print. These records show us Chaucer captured by the French and ransomed for sixteen pounds by King Edward III on March 1, 1360; Chaucer giving evidence to a court of heraldry on the issue of who had best right to a coat of arms; Chaucer acting as member of Parliament for his county; Chaucer robbed by highwaymen or accused of rape; and above all Chaucer acting in several relatively prominent roles as a king's servant, for example as a Controller of the Customs, and later in life as Clerk of the King's Works, charged with the building and upkeep of royal castles and dwellings.

It would be possible even so to present a picture of Chaucer as simply a middle-ranking bureaucrat with a spare-time taste for poetry. Yet it has also been noticed that Chaucer had at the very least connections with the great, and perhaps a role to play in the bitter faction fighting of fourteenth century England, fighting which ended with the deposition (and almost certainly murder) of King Richard II (1367-1400) just before the end of Chaucer's own life, and which took in the execution of several people connected with Chaucer, such as his direct superior in the customs business, Nicholas Brembre, Mayor of London (hanged in 1388), and one of Chaucer's immediate poetic disciples Thomas Usk (executed by torture the same year).

Chaucer was married to Philippa de Roet, whose sister was Katherine Swynford, at first the acknowledged mistress of John of Gaunt, Duke of Lancaster (1340-1399)—King Richard's uncle and for long periods the most powerful magnate in the country—but toward the end of his life his third wife. One of Chaucer's earliest poems is *The Book of the Duchess* (c. 1370), a lament on the death of Gaunt's first wife, but a lament which also seems gently to urge Gaunt not to mourn forever—as clearly he did not. Among the historical quirks which this throws up is the fact that the man most strongly suspected of the murder in captivity of Richard II was Sir Thomas Swynford, the son of Gaunt and Chaucer's sister-in-law, Katherine, and so Chaucer's nephew. Henry IV (1366-1413), who overthrew and succeeded Richard, was the son of Gaunt and the lady about whom Chaucer wrote *The Book of the Duchess*. Quite how much Chaucer's connections through his wife brought him in touch with major figures and affairs of state is unknown. It is fair to say, though, that Chaucer was closer to centers of power than any other major English poet.

Chaucer was moreover clearly a useful servant in his own right. Repeatedly he was sent abroad on the secret business of the king. The business is described as secret in the surviving records, but since the records consist mostly of Chaucer's expense payments it is naturally impossible to say what he was doing. Chaucer was an accomplished linguist, fluent in French (like many upper-class English people at the time), but also able to read Latin better than most laymen, and with the relatively rare ability to speak Italian. It seems likely that Chaucer's trips to Italy in 1372-1373 and 1378 were connected with trade negotiations and attempts at diplomatic alliance, while in 1366 he was also sent to Spain (a country whose crown was claimed by Gaunt through the rights of his second wife). In 1377 Chaucer was one of the three principal delegates on the English side at the Anglo-French peace negotiations at Montreuil-sur-Mer. After these rather prominent appearances on the international stage, it has seemed to many that Chaucer was "stepping down" when he accepted such posts as a Controllership of Customs (held 1374-1386). There also remains the intriguing question of what (if anything) Chaucer's poetic activity had to do with his public service career and his familiarity with the great.

Derek Pearsall's biography seeks on the whole to "deglamorize" Chaucer and to play down the suggestiveness of facts such as those cited above. There is little question about the facts or about the documentary records, but naturally they can be interpreted in different ways. Pearsall sees Chaucer above all as a man disinclined to take risks and anxious rather to remove himself from the center of power than to approach it. One of Chaucer's minor poems, for instance, *Lak of Stedfastnesse*, appears to be written to urge the king to take stern action against malefactors. It has accordingly often been ascribed to one date or another in the 1380's, when Richard was locked in an increasingly bitter struggle against a group of opposing lords. In this view, Chaucer by writing the poem was taking a side and giving the teenage king good advice, which (if he had taken it) might have prevented his later deposition and death. Pearsall, however, sees the poem as largely composed of generalities, and remarks that in his view "the more point [the poem] might have, the less likely Chaucer is to make any." In similar style, Chaucer's late poem, the "Complaint to his Purse," quite clearly addressed to Henry IV after his seizure of the crown, asks Henry to renew Chaucer's pension, and in doing so carefully accepts and restates all Henry's arguments to say that he was a legitimate king: that he had been given the throne by "free election" (which was extremely debatable), that he deserved it by descent (a flat lie), and that he had gained it by conquest (which was true, but hardly legitimating). Again, several scholars have argued that Henry, whether he knew Chaucer personally or not, would have welcomed the poem as a statement by a major poet; he certainly paid Chaucer's pension, as the records show. Pearsall, however, argues that Henry probably did not even know the poem had been written, while the reinstatement of the pension was pure routine.

In putting forward this unromantic view of Chaucer, Pearsall is clearly writing in reaction to such biographies as Donald Howard's *Chaucer: His Life, His Works, His World* (1987; see *Magill's Literary Annual*, 1988), in which Chaucer figures almost as a tutor to King Richard, writing his most serious works—Howard suggests—for the young king's personal instruction, and in which Chaucer's poems are regularly related closely to events at court. The dominating image behind Howard's book is the famous frontispiece to a manuscript of *Troilus and Criseyde*, known to scholars as "Chaucer Reading to the Court of Richard II," from which it is inferred that Chaucer regularly "published" his poems by reading them aloud to audiences of the great. Pearsall points out that in this famous picture Chaucer is not holding a book. The frontispiece should be seen rather as a piece of advertising, done twenty years after Chaucer's death. The real audience for Chaucer's poems, Pearsall argues, was not the court, or at least not the "inner" or royal court, but the large body of administrators, public servants, and lawyers, increasingly concentrated in London during the later Middle Ages and beginning to provide for the first time a relatively large group of laymen familiar with books and interested in literature for its own sake.

It is a corollary of Pearsall's argument that this audience was all male, a view which runs completely counter to the common opinion of the present day that Chaucer was a writer with special sympathy for women and special understanding of their plight. One issue which Pearsall faces directly—though it is also considered with very different results by Howard—is the accusation that Chaucer was a rapist. To be strictly accurate, Chaucer was never accused of rape, or not in a document we possess. There is, however, a document in which one Cecily Champain releases Chaucer from any action arising *de raptu meo*, probably in return for an out-of-court settlement. Quite what the Latin words mean has been a subject of controversy. Some have wanted to translate *raptus* as "abduction," pointing out that the seizure of heirs and heiresses was not an uncommon medieval legal move. Pearsall, however, shows that in the legal conventions of Chaucer's time such an action would normally be indicated by two words; when the single word is used, *raptus* means "rape." Chaucer then (while never convicted or indeed accused as far as it is known) was at least liable to an action against him for rape, and seems to have thought it worthwhile to buy off Cecily, for what looks like a substantial sum—ten pounds or more, at least half a year's pay. What lies behind this shall probably never be known, Pearsall concedes, yet he concludes that some "violence of passion" appears to be hidden away behind the legal documents. It may or may not be significant that Chaucer's own marriage seems to have endured long periods of separation, while Pearsall again rejects the relatively "cozy" modern view of Chaucer as a celebrant of love and marriage in his poems, saying instead that his images are often "unblinkingly hostile," and even that there are signs of the poet trying to work out through his poems some "psychosexual problem."

All this is very far removed from the image of the great poet which modern readers would like to have, but one of Pearsall's repeated themes is dislike of finding in the Chaucer "life records" only what is currently fashionable. Pearsall notes for example a very strong urge in British scholars to push Chaucer up the ladder of class, by arguing that he must have gone to a university, or at least to the Inns of Court where lawyers were trained. Meanwhile American scholars have tried in an opposite way to make Chaucer an honorary American, rejecting suggestions that he got on by marrying well or by flattering the great, and insisting that he owed his advancement to hard work and moral virtue. Neither of these images seems to be plausible. Chaucer came from an undistinguished family, which nevertheless worked its way up: A point to which Pearsall devotes little time is the very considerable success of Chaucer's son Thomas, who became Speaker of the House of Commons and whose daughter married the Earl (later Duke) of Suffolk. Chaucer shows very little in the way of democratic sentiment. A major instance of his reluctance to comment on public affairs is his attitude toward the Peasants' Revolt of 1381. The insurgents marched into London actually under Chaucer's own house (he had an apartment over one of the city gates); they massacred foreign tradesmen very close to Chaucer's childhood home. Nevertheless, Chaucer openly mentions the events of 1381 only once, and that is to make a rather unfeeling joke (which may suggest that Chaucer was actually present at, or within earshot of the xenophobe massacre already mentioned). As Pearsall says, the more controversial a subject was, the less likely it was to find a place in Chaucer's poetry. Attempts to give Chaucer "politically correct" opinions, however one defines correctness, are doomed to failure, though continually tried.

The Chaucer which Pearsall presents is in some ways an unattractive figure—cautious, venal, possibly sexually disturbed, writing for an audience of literary bureaucrats of his own stamp. Just because it is unattractive, one cannot assert that it is untrue. Indeed, the glamorous figure presented by Howard seems implausible, precisely because it is so much what a modern scholar would like to find. One should also note that it is a strong point of Pearsall's case to see exactly what disturbed and dangerous times Chaucer lived in. During the 1380's, in Chaucer's middle age, people of his kind were briefly in danger of being lynched in the street by rebellious peasants; and then, for a much longer period, under continuing threat of legal proceedings and judicial execution by the enemies of the king. When Chaucer attended Parliament in 1386, one of its items of business was a petition to dismiss people exactly like himself, on suspicion (probably justified) of financial corruption. Whether by coincidence or not, Chaucer resigned his Controllerships shortly afterward. In view of the painful deaths which came upon several members of his circle it is hard to say that he did wrong. Caution, silence, and care not to offend were evidently necessary qualities for survival to an extent which modern people can hardly appreciate. Only those sure of their own courage have any right to condemn.

It is possible that the Pearsall view of the poet is to some extent an overreaction against previous excesses. Within the poetry there are at least some indications that Chaucer knew and traded on his familiarity, if not relationship, with the great. He seems at the very least to have been able to give his son a flying start in life. Meanwhile, the repeated assertions of critics over the decades that Chaucer was a poet distinguished for his wide sympathies with women as well as men, with poor as well as rich, cannot all be ascribed to modernistic wishful thinking. It is valuable to see Chaucer within a real political context, and salutary to be prepared to accept the unfashionable or discreditable aspects of his life. It is, however, hard to believe that a mere "time-server" would have exercised the continuing influence over generations of later writers which Chaucer has so successfully done.

*T. A. Shippey*

## Sources for Further Study

*Library Journal.* CXVII, November 15, 1992, p. 76.
*London Review of Books.* XV, January 7, 1993, p. 14.

# LINCOLN AT GETTYSBURG
## The Words That Remade America

*Author*: Garry Wills (1934-    )
*Publisher*: Simon & Schuster (New York). Illustrated. 317 pp. $23.00
*Type of work:* Intellectual history
*Time:* 1863
*Locale*: Gettysburg, Pennsylvania

*Garry Wills places the* Gettysburg Address *within a multiplicity of contexts in order to demonstrate that the oration fundamentally altered the American national political order*

> *Principal personages:*
> ABRAHAM LINCOLN, the sixteenth president of the United States
> EDWARD EVERETT, an American orator
> JOHN HAY, Lincoln's secretary
> GEORGE BANCROFT, an American historian
> THEODORE PARKER, an American transcendentalist

Although Garry Wills labels himself a conservative, he espouses positions that make some conservatives consider him a maverick, if not an outright liberal. He once supported unilateral reductions of nuclear weapons, saying that nothing is more conservative than conserving the world. Fond of quoting St. Augustine, Walter Bagehot, and John Henry Newman, he reminds one of what the nineteenth century called a political philosopher, though his academic training centered on the classics and for a number of years he taught Greek. Like a philosopher, he has a fondness for coining terms, derived from common expressions but endowed with special and sometimes arcane meanings. Often his learned approach operates at a level at which distinctions between conservatism and liberalism become blurred, having been subtly filtered through elegant intellectual constructs. During a long career in journalism and in academe, Wills has produced numerous books. In what is perhaps the clearest articulation of his political views, *Confessions of a Conservative* (1979), he expresses his admiration for the coherence and continuity of the American political system. At the same time, he admires proponents of moral progress and difficult change and finds them indispensable for institutions such as the church and the state.

In viewing a nation as a complex association of numerous interrelated and overlapping groups—from the family to entire states—Wills resembles Edmund Burke. Burke's vision comprehends the complexity and intricacy of the political and social system, and as a result he places a premium on those conventions that remain unwritten. When he wrote that he knew of no law whereby a whole people could be condemned, Burke reflected his view that law originates from the people. Being the source of laws, they could not be condemned as a whole by legislative law, no matter how rational and expedient it might be.

According to Wills, this appeal to a broad constituency and to philosophical principles undergirding the law is what Abraham Lincoln reflected when he spoke of government of the people and for the people. In 1863, it enabled him to return to the roots of democracy in the United States, to the Declaration of Independence issued four score and seven years before, as the document that founded the nation. It also enabled him to regard Southerners not as enemies but as misguided and misled rebels. As Wills points out, Lincoln never recognized secession as legal, in part because of his firm conviction that sovereignty, having been derived from the people, cannot reside within the states as units.

In *Lincoln at Gettysburg*, winner of the 1992 National Book Critics Circle Award for criticism, Wills sets himself the challenging task of producing a book-length study of a document 272 words long, a speech that required only three minutes to deliver. Scholarship boasts a long history of books about other books: Each Shakespearean play is the subject of book-length studies, and hundreds of books have been published on John Milton's *Paradise Lost* (1667, 1674). Book-length studies of single orations, however, are rare. Even so, Wills approaches the task with at least a modicum of experience, for among his sixteen previous volumes, *Inventing America: Jefferson's Declaration of Independence* (1978) elucidates the Declaration of Independence and *Explaining America: The Federalist* (1981) analyzes *The Federalist Papers* (1788).

The book reflects Wills's mastery of an interdisciplinary approach. At times he is writing history; at others, reportage, literary criticism, rhetorical analysis, philosophy, or political science. Drawing upon a generous sprinkling of disciplines, he places Lincoln's oration within a multiplicity of contexts, both obvious and subtle.

The historical account begins with the conclusion of the Battle of Gettysburg in July, 1863, and narrates events leading to the occasion of Lincoln's speech, the program dedicating the National Cemetery on the site atop Cemetery Hill on November 19, 1863. Details of the three-day battle are absent, except for the rather full narrative found in Edward Everett's florid oration, which Wills reprints in an appendix. After narrating the movements of the two armies in the battle's confused aftermath, so disappointing to the respective leaders of the Union and the Confederacy that each commander offered his resignation, Wills turns to the burial details involving temporary interment for thousands, the selection of the cemetery site, and preparations for the dedication ceremony. Wills reproduces the printed program for November 19, highlighted by Everett's two-hour oration and listing Lincoln's subsequent address as "Dedicatory Remarks."

Concerning the event, no details are too obscure for the experienced reportorial eye. Wills carefully explores the latest findings regarding the placement of the speaker's platform, which until recently had been assumed to be located near the cemetery flagpole. Wills explains that careful examination of early photographs has now placed it just outside the cemetery boundary on the town side. Frequently, Wills finds significance in details that others might overlook. Lincoln, he tells us, had a tenor voice, not the baritone of modern actors who portray him, and as a result his speech carried effectively to the audience of twenty thousand assembled for the occasion.

In analyzing the speech for its style, Wills identifies its debt to the rhetoric of other classical funeral orations. In the appendices he reprints funeral orations by Pericles and Gorgias to demonstrate thematic and stylistic similarities. By sifting early testimonial evidence and clarifying Lincoln's normal modes of speech preparation, he handily dispels the legend that Lincoln composed the address on the spur of the moment en route to the site. He examines all early versions of the text, exploring their variants, and prints the one he considers authentic. The content is remarkable for how little Lincoln has to say about the battle and those who waged it, and for how much he says about his vision of the nation and its future.

Beyond the oration and its occasion, Wills explores more subtle contexts that illuminate the developing intellect of Abraham Lincoln and clarify his purposes. Over a period going back to the Webster-Hayne debates, he traces Lincoln's evolving understanding of the Union and the slavery controversy. Clearly, Lincoln had to transcend his training as a lawyer in order to develop the views he eloquently promoted. Fundamental to his view of the nation was Daniel Webster's vision of the nation as a product of peoples, not of states, a concept that Webster articulated during the controversy over nullification with Senator Robert Y. Hayne of South Carolina. Buoyed by the rising tide of nationalism, Webster handily won the 1830 debate against his Southern opponent. On his central proposition, Webster had been influenced by his friend Justice Joseph Story, who first proclaimed the Declaration of Independence a founding document of the nation. Lincoln embraced Webster's visionary concept that the Constitution affirmed a union which was by no means satisfactorily explained as an association of states. This concept accorded well with the early analogies of the American republic to Rome, the source of republican symbols of the late eighteenth and early nineteenth centuries. To the nationalism of the nineteenth century, dissolution of the Union seemed no more acceptable than dissolution of the Roman Empire.

Although political reality forced Lincoln to keep his distance from the abolitionist movement throughout most of his career, Wills shows that he was sympathetic to the goals of the abolitionists. On the issue of slavery, Lincoln was more guarded and more pragmatic because the Constitution clearly permitted it. Once the Civil War had begun, he had no qualms about exploiting a situation that slavery advocates had created by claiming slaves as property. Since armies were legally empowered to seize property whenever it was needed, the Union armies seized thousands of slaves in conquered territories and gave them liberty. Returning them to slavery with or without a constitutional amendment became unthinkable. Lincoln's recognition of slavery as legal, however, often exasperated the abolitionists. At the same time, though preserving the Union became his primary objective, he was in agreement with their fundamental position.

Beyond American political controversy and moral conflicts, Wills places Lincoln's emerging political views within the contexts of the Greek Revival in the United States and the American Transcendental movement. On an obvious level, Wills explains that the Gettysburg National Cemetery itself was a product of the Greek Revival. The nineteenth century movement toward cemeteries, cities of the dead, located outside towns in a peaceful rural setting, was a product of the American fascination with classical Greece. To the American mind, rural cemeteries represented places of meditation and communion with nature. In oratory, the second area of influence, Greek funeral orations included a defense of society and a vision of its future, two striking elements of Lincoln's address.

Transcendentalism, the most prominent American intellectual movement of the period, conceived of government both as an ideal concept and as a dynamic growing institution. From German post-Kantian thought, the Transcendentalists borrowed the perspective that alongside the real state exists an ideal one toward which it is tending. Theodore Parker, a Boston minister, found in the Declaration of Independence an undisputed expression of the equality of man, which he believed was a transcendent ideal too long delayed. From a transcendental perspective, governmental power rightly becomes a dynamic, progressive concept moving states toward the ideal, even while political leaders who direct the movement understand that the ideal will never be fully achieved. Transcendentalism enabled Lincoln to combine progress toward the ideal with Webster's concept of the Union. By conceiving of the state as a union of diverse groups of people, historically established long before the Constitution, Lincoln could reach back to the Declaration of Independence and champion·its unrealized ideal of human equality.

Although Wills is sometimes controversial, he carefully avoids shrill or strident rhetoric. He is a conservative who seems on the side of the dispossessed and understands the need for unhurried change and reform. His solid grounding in the classics and in philosophy has contributed to a rational tone and a logical texture not easily challenged by critics. Although his oratorical analysis approaches levels of the classical specialist in its use of arcane terminology, his exposition of Lincoln's text is sufficiently clear to nonspecialists. His analysis of Lincoln will add stature to one of America's most revered political figures, but the book will surely spark some controversy. Wills clearly has no sympathy with the South and its heroes, and his treatment of states' rights too easily dismisses the legal questions that once surrounded questions of sovereignty. One can hardly dismiss Wills's interpretation of what Lincoln intended by his address or his account of Lincoln's development toward his positions, however, for the analysis is systematic, carefully reasoned, and lavishly documented. Gettysburg afforded Lincoln a platform, and he seized the opportunity to articulate his nationalism clearly, eloquently, and magnanimously.

It appears that the germ of the book's idea originated with one of Wills's mentors, the archconservative states' rights advocate Willmoore Kendall, who was on the Yale faculty during Wills's student days. While Kendall considered Lincoln's influence pernicious, Wills finds it laudatory, cleansing the Constitution by affirming a commitment to equality of all human beings and thereby removing a defect of the original document. The question that remains for historians to ponder is whether both Kendall and Wills have overestimated the influence of a single oration.

*Stanley Archer*

## Sources for Further Study

*America.* CLXVII, August 1, 1992, p. 50.
*Chicago Tribune.* May 31, 1992, XIV, p. 1.
*The Christian Science Monitor.* August 31, 1992, p. 13.
*Commentary.* XCIV, November, 1992, p. 54.
*The New Republic.* CCVII, July 13, 1992, p. 37.
*The New York Review of Books.* XXXIX, July 16, 1992, p. 3.
*The New York Times Book Review.* XCVII, June 7, 1992, p. 1.
*Newsweek.* CXIX, June 15, 1992, p. 54.
*Publishers Weekly.* CCXXXIX, April 13, 1992, p. 48.
*The Washington Post Book World.* XXII, June 14, 1992, p. 3.